The Forager Handbook

The Forager Handbook

A Guide to the Edible Plants of Britain

Miles Irving

EBURY PRESS

To my wife Ali, to the small person
who is presently wriggling around in her womb,
and to my much larger grown-up offspring,
Ezra and Rebekah.

7 9 10 8 6

Published in 2009 by Ebury Press, an imprint of Ebury Publishing
A Random House Group Company

The Random House Group Limited Reg. No. 954009
Addresses for companies within the Random House Group can be found at
www.randomhouse.co.uk
A CIP catalogue record for this book is available from the British Library

Penguin Random House is committed to a sustainable future for our business, our readers and
our planet. This book is made from Forest Stewardship Council® certified paper.

FSC
www.fsc.org
MIX
Paper from
responsible sources
FSC® C018179

To buy books by your favourite authors and register for offers visit www.randomhouse.co.uk

Printed and bound in China by C & C Offset Printing Co. Ltd

ISBN 978-0-09-191363-2

DISCLAIMER: The author and publishers disclaim, as far as the law allows, any liability arising directly or indirectly
from the use, or misuse, of the information contained in this book. The information in this book has been compiled by
way of general guidance in relation to the specific subjects addressed, but is not a substitute and not to be relied on for
medical, healthcare, pharmaceutical or other professional advice on specific circumstances and in specific locations.
So far as the author is aware the information given is correct and up to date as at February 2009.
Practice, laws and regulations all change, and the reader should obtain up to date professional advice on any such issues.

Contents

FOREWORD

BY MARK HIX

Foraging for wild food should be a way of life for all serious foodies, whether you live in the country or in the city. Kids should also be encouraged to get out there and forage – even if it's only for blackberries. I remember my Gran, when making a pie or crumble with the apples from the garden, used to send me out to pick blackberries and when it came time to pour over her thick, lumpy custard I felt that enormous sense of achievement and satisfaction that only comes from actually having been involved in the creation of something.

Through his company, Forager, Miles Irving has inspired me, as well as a number of other chefs around the country, to include foraged ingredients on our menus. He's also encouraged those of us who have the time to get out into the woods and hedgerows to gather for ourselves tasty additions to our everyday fruits and vegetables. Ten years or so ago, restaurant menus were in danger of becoming repetitive and many of the more unusual ingredients were imported. These days, because of people like Miles, we rely far more on home-grown, farmed and foraged foods.

I used to be cautious about how many foraged items I used, but I have since come to realize that these foods give my menus authenticity, rather like, say, cavalo nero, wild rocket and pourpier did some years ago. All the year round we can learn from my forager friend Miles. In fact, every month he appears with something new to taste, experiment and cook with. There are very few books on wild food that can be used with confidence, but *The Forager Handbook* will most certainly be one that I keep at close hand.

HOW TO USE THIS BOOK

How the plants are categorized

The book is divided into different subdivisions of the plant kingdom, and then into different families. I have found it much easier to identify a plant once familiar with the characteristics of the major families; I also find that it is a great aid to memory knowing which other plants a particular plant is related to. Although they don't provide the main framework for the book, habitats and seasons are also covered in depth. For information on what to find where, consult the **Places** chapter; for information on what to find when, consult the **Times** chapter; this information is also contained within the individual plant entries.

The recipes

Throughout the book there are recipes or serving suggestions, followed by initials in brackets that refer to the chef who authored these. For more information on the individual chefs, consult the **Chef Directory** (p.382).

The photographs

The photographs do not cover every possible growth stage but generally capture plants at their most useful stages, which are often not illustrated in wild flower books (for which flowering stages of plants are the main focus). The Forager website will be updated periodically with additional photographs; see also the bibliography for recommended wild flower books. Unless otherwise stated, all the photographs in the book are the same size as the actual plant or plant part.

1
Basics

AN INTRODUCTION TO FORAGING

Compared to most western lifestyles, foraging is a bit out of the ordinary. In terms of our genetic make-up and our history, though, it is as normal as breathing. I received a poignant reminder of this while collecting samphire on a vast Kent salt marsh, one of the wildest places in the south of England. Over several hours I had gradually tuned in to the drama of the place: the gulls crying mournfully, swooping above me and occasionally landing to peck at something; wading birds in small flocks flying off briskly when I disturbed them, then settling on the marsh and darting about, probing the mud with their beaks, and an occasional marsh-harrier flying over, disturbing the bustling peace. Absorbed in the simple, precise task of collecting, I realized that all of us were about the same primeval business: foraging for food.

My earliest experiences of foraging occurred near my grandparents' home in Suffolk when I was six. They lived in an old mill house with a stream, full of wild watercress, next to a wood and a meadow that between them produced several species of wild mushroom and supported numerous hazel trees – too many for the squirrels to strip bare – as well as elder trees and an area overgrown with blackberries. Both my grandparents would gather from this outdoor larder: my grandmother mostly used the bountiful berry crop, but my grandfather was a bit more adventurous. His interest in wild food may have stemmed from working for the Ministry of Food during the Second World War; he had taught himself to identify a few species of wild mushroom as well as other potential wild ingredients. Unfortunately, his dishes weren't always greeted with enthusiasm. His nettle soup was viewed with suspicion by a family wearied by his quest for alternatives that were often much harder work and less satisfactory than the conventional approach he was seeking to replace. As a small boy, though, I had no such reservations; I was fascinated and thrilled at the prospect of all these earthly delights waiting to be discovered and eaten.

Despite these rural beginnings, I gravitated to the city; for most of my twenties I was an urban forager, making only occasional trips to the countryside. However, in 2002, I moved to Petham, a Kent village surrounded by woods, fields and country lanes that was nowhere near any shops. I had just finished an undergraduate degree and had not yet found a job; with time on my hands, nowhere to buy anything and miles of unexplored countryside, my daily wild-food repertoire expanded rapidly. I was able to go outside and just wander about for a bit and come back with several different wild greens, salads and herbs. My wife, Ali, and I spent much of our courtship exploring the country-side in search of new wild edibles. It seemed a shame not to gather plentiful amounts of the good things we discovered. So we invited peo-ple round to help us cook and eat the abun-dance we brought home with us. There was something magical about the whole experience, as if we had just re-entered a sacred grove where no one had been for a thousand years.

In 2003, a stray comment in a local restau-rant sparked a conversation with the chef about wild food that led to us supplying him with a few wild ingredients. We called our fledgling wild-food business Forager. In the following months, we were introduced to several chefs with a similar approach to wild food; before I knew it I was foraging for a living. A few years prior to this, while studying for my degree, I would often be out foraging, thinking to myself, I really should be writing an essay or something. It was a great feeling to be foraging all day without the nagging sense that I should be doing something else. Since then, Forager has expanded considerably, so that we now deal with many more restaurants over a much wider area that includes London. It has been a delight to chronicle the discoveries made by so many gifted chefs, who use their experience, skill and creativity to find ways of using the wild ingredients we find for them. Many of the articles and books written about edible wild plants allude to their use in times of war, pover-ty or when crops fail. For some people, eating wild food has become almost shameful – a reminder of hard times they would prefer to forget. It amuses me to witness this attitude turned on its head; to see these humble wild plants given pride of place in some of the most prestigious restaurants in the world. In my mind's eye, I imagine them as little outcasts being dressed up in velvet and silk.

Despite the abandonment of foraging as a way of life in many cultures, we are still, by nature, by biology, foragers. Present-day indus-trialized consumer humans are a recent aberra-tion: foraging is in our blood; even farming is a fairly recent innovation and not necessarily a step forward. Over millions of years of evolu-tion, our bodies developed to require suste-nance from an optimum diet consisting of a wide variety of plant materials plus wild meat, eggs, honey, insects and fish/shellfish. This pre-agricultural diet provided superior nutri-tion. Studies of mean height of population show that people were up to 15cm taller before the onset of agriculture, around 10,000 years ago. Fluctuations in height within the same gene pool are a function of childhood nutri-tion, which indicates that people's diets were better before farming began. Hunter–gatherers would use as many as 100 plant foods in the course of a year; modern humans generally use less than 20, with a much greater emphasis on plant products containing starch. Wild plants generally have higher nutrient contents, so a diet that includes many of them is superior to one with only a few cultivars. Feeding animals mostly on wheat or soya also decreases the usefulness of meat as food; whereas the diverse, nutrient-rich diet of wild animals produces meat with a much higher unsaturated-fat content.

The human nervous system and physique is also carefully tailored for foraging. Evolutionary theory hinges on the principle of the survival of the fittest, meaning the best fit, as a key fits a lock, rather than physical fitness. Fitness as a forager means successfully unlocking resources from your surroundings. The woodpecker's body is a biological jack-hammer that agitates wood grubs from their holes. Grazing animals use their sensitive muzzles and heightened olfactory sense to feel and smell the difference between plants: the part of a pig's brain devoted to smell is several times larger than our own.

The human body and brain is no less specialized, enabling us to forage in highly complex, varied and ingenious ways, including making and using tools from foraged resources. We are physically framed and neurologically hardwired to unlock resources from our surroundings, perhaps more effectively than any other species. Walking upright, our hands are free to gather, carry and do other useful things, and we can see further to survey the land. Thumbs, which are unique to primates, enable us to grasp things in a way not possible for many animals (although crabs might be better equipped on this score alone). Using our advanced mammalian brains we plan, anticipate harvests, process wild plants for later use and coordinate our activities in highly sophisticated ways. We might wear manufactured clothes, drive around in prefabricated metal boxes and live inside concrete or stone structures, but beneath the layers are the same muscle frame and brain: the pristine purpose-built hunter–gatherer tool kit that our ancestors of 100,000 years ago possessed and used.

Gathering wild food in our own locality creates a rich and ongoing relationship with the land. When we start digging around for this forgotten knowledge, we are getting into the ground of our heritage. Our ancestors knew the places where they lived: every inch of land, every kind of plant, every sign of life. They made use of everything. They were intimately involved with their surroundings, immersed in the ebb and flow of the seasons. Their attention was anchored to the here and now as they watched with anticipation the gradual emergence of shoots and stems, flowers and fruit, waiting patiently for the time to gather and make use of them. Signs indicating the presence of plants, animals, birds and fish consumed their consciousness. With senses sharpened to the immediacy of instinct they discerned the presence of every animate or inanimate object. In doing so they were themselves powerfully present. Poet Laureate Ted Hughes was acclaimed for the intense images he evoked of the English countryside. He spoke of how his experiences while out hunting made him feel more alive than at any other time because it necessitated a heightened alertness to and consciousness of his surroundings. For me, foraging has a similar effect, but more cumulative: I become more aware of the presence of plants and the seasonal changes in the landscape with every year that passes.

What I hope most to communicate through this book is how integral foraging is to our make-up. Anyone who spends a little time learning to find and use wild food will soon understand what I mean: this is not an aspirational lifestyle choice, but a return to an ancient way of life that is part of who we are. That is not only an inspiring thought but an encouraging one: it is not hard to do something when doing it is encoded in our genes and hardwired into our nervous system. What we have lost is the culture that gives a framework to these old ways and a vehicle for passing on knowledge of local

plants and their uses. We are a bit like the dingoes in Australia; so used to scavenging human rubbish that the adults no longer teach their pups to hunt. In writing this book, I hope to play a part in restoring that cultural process. It is not that we have to rediscover the exact uses our ancestors made of certain plants, as interesting and evocative as such discoveries might be. Equally, although the wild-food traditions of other countries are frequently cited throughout the following pages, I don't see them as the primary source for a new foraging culture in the British Isles; nor do I consider it an irreparable loss where these traditions have faltered or even died out. The plants are still here, and we are still here. Put people back in touch with the plants, and the old relationship will revive. This ancient connection now has contemporary cultural tools with which to express itself: modern culinary techniques, the insights given by scientific ecology and an unprecedented respect for the culture of hunter–gatherer societies. We shall soon find new ways of harvesting, stewarding and using these plants, and, in so doing, create a brand-new foraging culture in our time and in our land.

1

HOW TO FORAGE

Acquiring plant knowledge

Edible plants are all around us, an unregistered presence, like people on our street we have yet to meet. Learning to forage awakens us to their presence. Using them for food makes us more vitally present in the places in which we live because by doing so we become part of our local food chain. Similarly, the plants you eat become part of your body and part of your life, with memories, associations and a sense of recognition when you find them again. Plants are not just resources, but nor are they like art objects or museum pieces, things to be preserved, viewed from a distance and never touched or used. The significance and meaning of the plants is enriched, rather than demeaned by gathering and using them, just as people's relationships are enriched through practical involvement.

How do we know a plant?

There are two kinds of 'knowing'. One is analytical, looking at the fine detail of shape, colour, size and so on: you could think of this as knowing about a plant. This is crucial to your initial approach, as without it you may end up poisoning yourself. A quite different kind of knowing results from involvement: actually finding, gathering and cooking a plant or a mushroom. Knowing in this sense is much more like the way we know other people; it has less to do with information and more to do with interaction. This kind of knowledge comes when my senses have been arrested, perhaps by a smell, or a glimpse of colour or form that has led to the discovery of some plant, which, once I have found it, I gather, prepare and eat. The following year, I may track this plant as it progresses through its stages, some providing food and some not, but all the time I will feel involved; I might gather the seed and scatter it near by (or elsewhere); clear other plants to give it more room, or throw a branch over the area if it happens to be a shade-loving plant. By the way, many hunter–gatherer societies are known to have engaged with wild plants in these kinds of ways for thousands of years, without ever becoming farmers.

I am now familiar enough with many plants to recognize them instantly from a distance and also to be able to distinguish them from similar species. Although I can analyse how this is done, I don't recognize any of them by an analytical process any more than I recognize a person by consciously analysing the shape of their nose, their jawline and so on. It is the face as a whole that we recognize; *Gestalt* is the German word that describes this best; the English phrase 'the whole is greater than the sum of its parts' communicates the same idea. With experience, instantaneous recognition of the *Gestalt* of a plant occurs, making it possible to spy out the land for plants from considerable distances. The first step is to identify a plant by its individual characteristics, but the plants whose *Gestalt* I recognize are usually the ones I have actually gathered and used.

First steps

The first step is to familiarize yourself with a few plants in the analytic sense, then quickly follow this up by cooking and eating them. Before the day is out, go outside, into your garden, a local park or a nearby country lane and try and locate a familiar edible plant. You will almost certainly be able to recognize one of the following: nettle, dandelion, blackberry, rose or rose hip. Other likely candidates are elderflower (or elderberry), chickweed and crab apple. Take a pair of scissors with you – and gloves for the nettles – and cut a good section of the plant or plants then gather a good quantity of the leaf, flower or fruit with which to cook. In the case of the dandelion, cut it just below all the leaves so they stay together.

Once you get home, refer to the description of the plant you have gathered and look at each detail: the shape of the leaf, the length of the leaf stalk, whether the leaf has toothed edges or is divided into leaflets. By starting with a plant whose identity you already know you have a distinct advantage; rather than using the description to identify the plant, you can use it to familiarize yourself with various common characteristics of plants. For example, you can notice perhaps for the first time that nettle leaves are cordate or oval, have toothed edges and are arranged in opposite pairs (they also have stalks, the presence or absence of which identifies many plants). If you collected a section of a bramble or rose stem, you can note that what you thought were leaves are actually leaflets, which form a compound leaf. You might also note whether the stem is rounded or angular. Common dandelion leaves are arranged in a circular pattern, growing out of a central root; this is called a rosette, a common leaf arrangement, especially for plants in their earlier growth stages. You should also notice that they are hairless, something that distinguishes them from several similar species. If the dandelion is in flower, notice that its stem is hollow and smooth, without leaves or branches (lots of similar plants have leaves or branches and no similar plant has a hollow stem) and that the 'flower' is in fact a composite of many tiny florets (see **daisy** family, p.136). As you read through the descriptions, look up any unfamiliar terms in the glossary; although it takes a bit of effort they are not hard to learn. Seeing actual examples of the characteristics to which these terms refer will make descriptions of plants you don't know less intimidating.

With a plant you know, it is easy to match the description to the characteristics that are in front of you. This kind of attention to detail will help you to look more perceptively at unfamiliar plants. Many of the plants in this book are useful at their younger, leafy stages, when there are no identifying flowers or fruits, making them harder to identify. It is possible to be sure of the identity of some plants by a distinctive detail of leaf form, texture or colour. But the fail-safe method is to get to know the plants by watching them through the seasons and noticing their various growth stages. If there is any possibility of confusion with similar poisonous species, as is the case with many carrot-family species, it is essential that you do this before you even think about eating them. However, for the task in hand I have deliberately chosen four plants with no similar poisonous species, so if you find one of them, you can, without fear, cook something straight away based on the plant entry's recipe suggestions. Perhaps a nettle soup, or dandelion with bacon and poached egg, a blackberry fool, rose-hip syrup or rose-petal jam. Whatever you end up making and eating, by the end of this process you will feel that you have actually made the acquaintance of the plant that you have used.

Learning to read the landscape

Foraging means taking your place in the landscape in a way that has been only recently forgotten as a normal human way of life. For most of our time on earth (which may be as long as 200,000 years), we humans, like most other species, spent our days foraging, becoming intimately acquainted with the land and the life forms it supports. Such intimacy has been disrupted by our modern culture of consumption and convenience, but in my optimistic moments, I feel sure that normal service will shortly be resumed. We certainly can't go on as we have been. We must reacquaint ourselves with the land; reintegrate ourselves with the other living things that surround us. This is a great objective in itself, but it happens as we go about the small and ordinary business of finding edible plants in our surroundings. To do this we have to learn to read the landscape for signs of their presence.

Reading the landscape involves most of your senses in what, in time, becomes an automatic survey of your surroundings as you move through them. You are looking for signs, cues and the definite marks of various species. For example the perception of dampness in the air on your cheek as you move from one part of a woodland to another that indicates increased humidity and a greater likelihood of finding mushrooms; recognizing the *Gestalt* of a likely place for chickweed; identifying stands of dead edible umbellifers, indicating the likelihood of fresh green material either now or later in the year; noticing the unmistakable smell of ramsons or signature plants like foxglove or broom, which signal a change in soil pH (these plants only grow on acid soils).

Forms and colours

Throughout the plant entries I point out the usefulness of noting the skeletal remains of edible plants; the same is true of the flowering stages. Some skeletal remains have seeds on them, and many flowers are edible, but these stages are often not the most productive part of the plant's growth cycle. The point is to mark the presence of the plant in a given place, especially with perennials and biennials; these marks foretell the harvests at other growth stages. A little notebook and pencil is a useful part of the foragers' toolkit; even a map on which to note down the places where these observations have been made (grid references do the same job without marking the map).

Beckoning flowers and berries

I have found many patches of lady's smock, wild marjoram, wild thyme, wood sorrel and chicory, to list just a few, that I had repeatedly overlooked, as a result of brightly coloured flowers catching my eye from a distance. The same is true of brightly coloured berries. This is pure seduction and is about reproduction; the colours are designed to attract physical attention from fertilizers (mostly insects) and seed dispersers. The only barberry tree I know in my area remained hidden in a copse on the edge of a field near my home until, one October, I happened to walk close enough to catch a glimpse of its scarlet berries. It was so intermingled with the other trees I doubt I would have given it a second look otherwise, although the bright yellow flowers would have caught my attention had I walked near it in June. Similarly, large patches of a distinctive shade of green in a certain position or with a particular form, can lead you to an abundance of leaves, for example of chickweed, garlic mustard, wild chervil or dittander. This takes a bit more work, however; the best approach is to work backwards: walk away from a good patch already found and look at it from different vantage points to get a feel for how it appears from a distance.

Geology, soil pH and altitude

Geology influences the ph as well as the moisture content of soil: for example clay has poor and chalk excellent drainage. These and other factors, such as altitude, determine what will or won't grow in any given place, so being able to read such cues will in time guide your foraging efforts either to certain places, if you are looking for a particular plant, or to particular plants if you are looking in a certain place. Once you know the kind of place you are in, you can expect to find certain plants there. For example, grassy areas on sandy soil, which are usually acidic, support very different plants to grassy areas on alkaline chalk. Many plants will only grow above or below a certain altitude, but determining whether you are at a high altitude is not always just a matter of noticing that you've been walking uphill for the last two hours – some places are flat but high above sea-level. If you are any distance inland you may have to start by finding out the altitude from a map; information about maximum altitude of plants is included in the plant entries.

Water sources

The presence of rivers, streams, ponds and the sea provide obvious cues as to which plant species are likely to be found in an area. Some plants are only found in salt- or freshwater habitats; other plants grow near the sea but not necessarily on the shore, as is the case with fennel and alexanders.

Foraging and the law

Foraging is covered by two pieces of legislation: the Wildlife and Countryside Act 1981 and the Theft Act 1978. The Wildlife and Countryside Act makes it illegal to collect wild plants or fungi on a national nature reserve (NNR) or a site of special scientific interest (SSSI), without the express permission of Natural England. Before they will even consider granting this, you would first need the permission of the owner of the land, although, in some cases, this would be Natural England themselves. Secondly, a number of plants are protected under Schedule 8 of the Act, making it illegal to collect them without a special license. Licenses are not granted to collect for human culinary use, so these plants are simply off the menu! Two of them – meadow clary and pennyroyal – are covered in this book because they have a history of use. Both are available from garden centres and can be found in plenty in other European countries. Thirdly, the Act makes it illegal to dig or uproot any plant without the landowner's permission.

The Theft Act makes it illegal to collect any wild plant or fungi *for commercial purposes* without the landowner's permission. It is not an offence to collect for personal use.

Sustainable foraging
Leaves and stems

By far the greatest part of my time foraging is spent collecting leaves, mainly because they are available all year round. They are also the least controversial part of a plant to pick as they generally grow back with no loss to the plant. However, plants vary in the degree to which they can tolerate being regularly stripped of leaves. Grass, for example, is relentless in its growth, no matter how often it is cut back, and many plants of lawns and other managed turf are the same, e.g. plantains, dandelions, self-heal and mallow. However, some plants simply won't tolerate this treatment and will eventually die if all their leaves are cut back repeatedly. Plants in the rose family fall into this category, as does sea-purslane. Sea beet, on the other hand, along with most plants in the cabbage and daisy families, can tolerate quite regular and thorough harvesting, although they must be allowed eventually to flower and set seed.

Seeds and flowers

Seeds and flowers are the future of a plant population, so they can't be harvested exhaustively, although trees, shrubs and perennials are obviously affected less drastically by over-harvesting than annuals, which will simply not grow back the following year if all their flower or seed is harvested. For annuals, take no more than a fifth of what is to be found in any given place.

Gathering roots

In most cases, if you gather the roots of a plant, you kill it, although for plants with especially deep roots it might be possible to take only part of the root and leave the plant to grow, as when taking a root cutting of a garden plant. For this reason, harvesting roots requires more thought and restraint than harvesting other plant parts, as harvesting just one root immediately depletes the plant population, at least in the short term. Assuming you have fulfilled the legal require-ment of obtaining the landowner's permission before digging up a plant, in most cases you should only collect roots where there are plenty of plants. Even then, only take a very small fraction of what is there.

However, in some cases, digging up roots promotes the growth of new plants. For example, burdock seems to thrive after the roots are harvested, as the process of digging them up also works seeds into the soil. Likewise, horse-radish is virtually impossible to eradicate by digging its roots, as the smallest fragment will produce a new plant. Certain *Campanulaceae* species may well have declined precisely because no one digs them up for food any more. (See also Gott [1982] and Hillman [1989] in Further Reading for more examples of plants benefiting from root harvesting.) On the other hand, some plants can be invasive and need digging out, which provides a good opportunity to have a wild-root feast. Alexanders is one such plant, which parks and nature reserves in our area of Kent employ people to dig out. Other roots become available when the ground is disturbed for other reasons, such as the freak waves on the Kent coast in 2008 and the field near my parents' house with masses of burdock round the edges. Every year, burdock roots are ploughed out of the ground and burdock seeds ploughed in.

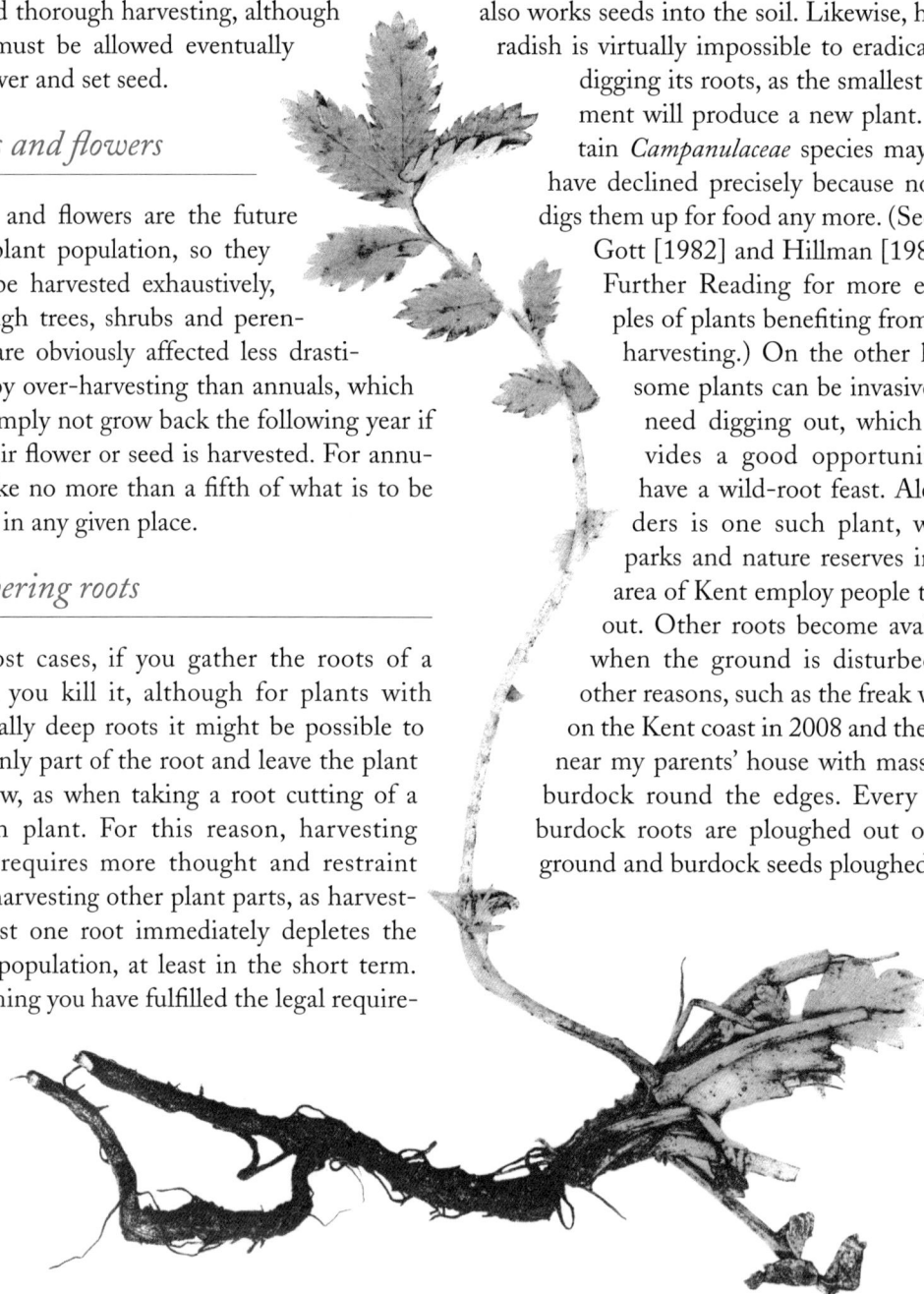

2
HOW TO USE WILD PLANTS

Recipes or serving ideas for wild plants feature throughout the book. The idea is to inspire people with the breadth and extent of what can be done with wild ingredients – and what has been done with them in some of the restaurants we supply. I have tried to include basic instructions, in some cases with cooking times and temperatures and quantities of ingredients, but sometimes there is space for no more than a description of the constituent parts of the dish; if I were to provide full details, this would be a four-volume encyclopaedia.

But space is not the only reason for this limited approach: the best results I have had with many of the recipe ideas in this book have been through having a feel for the ingredients and a working knowledge of techniques. With this in mind, I would recommend anyone who is learning about wild foods and isn't already an accomplished chef to learn to cook in this way. Invest in some really good books on cooking and food, such as Michael Booth's excellent *Sacré Cordon Bleu: What the French Know about Cooking* or Harold McGee's *On Food and Cooking: The Science and Lore of the Kitchen*. What follows is a number of general ideas for what to do with wild ingredients, which, coupled with trying out the recipe and serving suggestions throughout the book, should enable you to develop your own wild-food repertoire.

Green leaves, stems and shoots

Green leaves

Wild greens generally have much stronger flavours than cultivated varieties; there are also many more varieties from which to choose. Most greens, but especially wild greens, are high in beta-carotene, vitamin C, folic acid, calcium, iron and magnesium. In many rural communities in the Mediterranean and in other parts of the world cooking wild greens is traditional. In Greece, '*horta*', or the edible greens that flourish in the wild, comprise a salad dish of the same name that can include a wide variety of both cultivated and wild greens, which are boiled then served warm or at room temperature with olive oil and lemon juice; often bitter and non-bitter species are used together to dilute the flavour of the bitter ones. In the south of Italy lots of greens, including poppy, sow-thistle, hawkbits, oxtongues, hawk's-beards and chicory are boiled and then fried in olive oil, garlic, chilli powder and, sometimes, a tomato sauce. In Lebanon and elsewhere in the Middle East, many greens are cooked in '*fatayer*' or small triangular pies made with yeast-leavened flatbread dough, filled with wild greens and baked (for recipe, see p.154). In Turkey, thoroughly boiled greens are served with yogurt and crushed garlic or fresh lemon juice as appetizers or mezza. More robust leaves, such as plantain or mallow, are stuffed with rice or bulghar wheat then boiled. In Spain, mixtures of wild greens are often used in stews and also in pies. Many of the stronger-flavoured greens, daisy family species in particular, benefit from boiling, which dilutes the flavour; frying also coats the leaves with fat and slightly masks the remaining bitterness. In Japanese cuisine wild herbs known as '*sansai*' are eaten cooked in tempura batter (see François Couplan's recipe, p.165) or cooked in rice porridge. Often the plants are quite bitter, which in both recipes is tempered by the other ingredients. Other less bitter greens can simply be steamed, wilted or fried, either dry or in a little oil. Intense heat caramelizes the sugars in cabbage-family leaves, giving a deliciously rich flavour.

Another traditional preparation method used for greens is lacto-fermentation. Sauerkraut is probably the best-known example of this. 'Kimchee', the Korean method, uses a lot of spices and other flavourings. Lacto-fermentation is facilitated by starting a culture of lactobacillus bacterium by simply leaving plant material submerged in water, until it becomes pickled in lactic acid produced by the bacterium. The Polish *barscz* (for recipe, see p.125) made with hogweed leaves and stems, is essentially a lacto-fermented soup, but a similar method can be applied to any wild green. François Couplan has experimented extensively with lacto-fermenting wild plants and gives the following general advice:

- Make sure that plants are thoroughly covered with brine to avoid rotting. If necessary, weigh them down with some non-calcareous stones.
- The alternative is to add a lot of salt, so as to prevent the growth of rot bacteria – but the result is very salty.
- Letting the plants ferment for 3 days will yield a mild product, which must be eaten within a few days. I let it ferment for 3 weeks, after which it can be kept for over a year. The end-product will be sour, for sure. But this is no problem *per se*. The taste is not unpleasant.
- Lacto-fermentation enhances the nutritional properties of plants, especially for vitamins B and C, and it boosts the useful bacteria of our intestinal flora. Be sure to drink the juice as well.
- If the process has not worked, you'll know it: if when you open the jar the smell is 'off', discard it. Very likely, it will smell strongly, like unclean toilets, and you wouldn't eat it anyway.

For a more thorough treatment of the subject see François Couplan's book *La cuisine sauvage*.

Stems and Shoots

Several plants are used in a similar way to asparagus, with the young spring shoots being harvested, boiled lightly and served simply, like asparagus, with butter and lemon juice or hollandaise sauce. These plants include hop, bath asparagus, rosebay willowherb and marsh samphire.

Flowers

Flowers no longer form part of the mainstream British diet, but they certainly have done in the past. According to food historian Colin Spencer (in *British Food*, 2002), our enthusiasm for eating them was part of the considerable Persian influence on our cuisine in Norman times. All plants mentioned as edible in this book have flowers that are edible in principle, although some are unpalatable or too small to be worthwhile. Why would you eat a flower? Surprisingly, in many cases because they are delicious. Most are mildly flavoured or sweet, but several have savoury flavours you would really not expect from such delicate and pretty things; such as the garlic punch packed by the many kinds of wild garlic flowers, the pea flavour of pea flowers and the knock-out horseradish and mustard flavours of lady's smock and black mustard flowers, respectively. Cherry, plum and sloe blossoms all taste of almonds. Sweet violet flowers have a flavour all their own and have been used to make jam and liqueur; they have also been candied, a technique that conserves their colour and form as well as their flavour, and is also applied to primroses. Almost any flower with flavour (and most have some, however delicate) can be used to make jams, sugars and syrups, which can themselves be used to enhance desserts, poured over fruit or ice cream, for example, or used as a base for sorbet. Some flowers are robust or big enough to be more substantial ingredients, for example day-lily flowers can be stuffed, and both they and cape pondweed are used to give bulk to soups and stews. Flowers, then, are not just a pretty face. But if you have it, why not flaunt it? A major part of the appeal of flowers is their appearance, and many are used as garnishes and decoration. However, it is always fun to see people's reactions on discovering that, once past their lips, certain delicate and innocent-looking flowers launch such an assault on the taste-buds with their intense flavours. The best-known edible flower is probably elderflower, used to make the increasingly popular elderflower cordial and sorbet – in the past it was extensively used in British recipes for white meat.

Seeds

Many plant seeds (although, in strict botanical terms, most of these are actually fruits) are used as spices; these are listed under Sauces (see p.16). In addition to these, poppy and angelica seeds are excellent for baking. Seeds known as grains or nuts are familiar dietary staples, since they contain stores of carbohydrate and proteins, which left alone would provide energy for the growth of a new plant. Many carbohydrate and protein-rich wild seeds, such as those of grass, goosefoot, amaranth, pea and dock families can be used as they are or ground to make flour. The trick is to find plenty growing in a small area and to develop fast and efficient ways of processing them. Nuts are also an excellent source of energy, and they too can be ground into flour, although one of our most plentiful, the acorn, needs to be leached in order to remove its tannins first. An essential piece of kit for flour-making is either a small kitchen mill (see Brow Farm in the Wild Food Directory, p.387) if you want to do it by hand (these are better suited to larger seeds) or a high-quality blender, such as a Thermomix. Other seeds can be just sprinkled over food to add texture, flavour and plentiful nutrients. Daisy or *Asteraceae* species with their helpful pappuses are easy to gather, and the pappuses can be ground and winnowed or else parched off; evening primrose and borage seeds are both high in gamma-linolenic acid (GLA). Wild seeds can also be sprouted to make delicious micro salads: surprisingly nettles and thistles produce innocuous and delicious seedlings; cleavers seedlings are also without the textural problems of older plants. The smart move with all three (and others besides) is to find bare ground where the seeds have shed and sprouted themselves. The strongly flavoured alexanders is quite easy to find like this. The seedlings have a flavour mellow enough to use as salad. The most obvious candidates for sprouting are cress seeds (see cabbage family introduction for an explanation of this term): penny-cress, mustard and garlic mustard seeds produce something very similar to the cress sold in the shops; smaller pea-family seeds, such as lucerne (otherwise known as alfalfa) and its near relatives, the medics and trefoils produce sprouts similar to commercially produced alfafa sprouts. Crow garlic bulbils (which are not strictly seeds) produce long, thin garlicky shoots.

Roots

Several roots are mentioned under other headings in this section, either as salads or spices. The following can be used pretty much as conventional root vegetables: burdock, sea beet, sweet cicely, fennel, wild carrot, wild parsnip, alexanders, wild radish, wild turnip, salsify, goat's beard, tuberous pea and thistles. Young tender burdock roots are my all-time-favourite roasted root vegetable. Those with cultivated equivalents are generally slightly smaller, tougher and with stronger flavours than their domesticated relatives. Some roots are unlike anything cultivated, for example sow-thistle, chicory and dandelion are all quite bitter but have their place if balanced with other ingredients (for more on bitterness, see pp.136–7). They can also be roasted and used as flavouring; roasting reduces the bitterness and gives them a rich coffee-like flavour – dandelion and chicory are both sold in this form as coffee substitutes.

I have had very pleasing results candying the roots of sea holly (the main traditional use of this plant), burdock and sweet cicely. Another root use for those with a sweet tooth is in the making of fizzy drinks (see beverages, p.18).

Yet another use for roots, often those that can not be used for anything else, is for the extraction of starch. Black bryony and cuckoo pint (lords-and-ladies) tubers are both filled with toxic calcium-oxalate crystals; however, it is possible to extract starch from them for use in place of cornflour. The same use can also be made of reedmace rhizomes.

Soups

Most wild leaves can be used to make soup; the basic idea is to produce a base of sweated white vegetables, then boil these perhaps with the addition of some diced potato, if you want a slightly thicker soup, and add and blend the leaves right at the end, so that they remain fresh, colourful and flavoursome when the soup is served a few moments later. The white vegetable base can include leeks, celery, onions or shallots, garlic and turnip, which should be chopped as finely as possible and sweated for as long as possible. There are more detailed soup recipes throughout the book, which can generally be adapted for other plants.

Another kind of soup that can have many variations is gazpacho. This cold vegetable soup is now mostly made using peppers, cucumber and tomatoes (for a variation, see lettuce gazpacho, p.370), but the original Andalusian recipe was based around stale bread, garlic, vinegar and herbs/seasoning. A version closer to the origins of the dish can be made using wild leaves as herbs and seasoning. Wild rocket, sea-purslane and wild garlic are obvious examples, but you could use virtually any wild leaf. Simply blend the leaves with garlic (assuming you are not using wild garlic leaves), vinegar and water (or chicken or vegetable stock, if you prefer), add breadcrumbs and leave them to swell, then blend again. Season, chill and serve.

Salads

Through the seasons a constantly changing selection of wild salad ingredients is available, giving an extraordinary range of colours, textures and flavours. Leaves are the main component of most salads, but there are also flowers, mushrooms, roots, fruits and immature seeds. Judicious combinations often require no additional dressing or seasoning. Tartness in place of vinegar or fresh lemon juice is provided by fruit, sorrel, wood sorrel or sumach drupe hulls; salt is provided by ready salted sea-purslane, sea-blite or by other coastal plants and seaweeds salted in seawater. Many cabbage-family plants provide spicy, mustardy flavours in leaf, flower and seed-pod form; garlic mustard roots are also mildly spicy and can be shaved into salads. Fennel leaves, flowers and green seeds provide a delightful aniseed kick, which is especially interesting in a salad of many ingredients, where it crops up as a surprise only every few mouthfuls. A similar effect is created by sweet cicely leaves, flowers, green fruits and finely sliced roots. Sea beet roots bring beetroot-like sweetness, whereas alexanders roots have a unique, spicy pungency, used in fine shavings like garlic mustard; thistle and burdock roots bring a delicate, earthy, almost liquorice flavour. Finally, used sparingly, garlic leaves, flowers and seeds/bulbils bring the potency of the alliums to a wild salad for much of the year.

Wild salads can be approached in various ways. A fun approach, already mentioned, is to use masses of ingredients, resulting in a kaleidoscope of flavours that changes with every mouthful. Especially strong flavours can be balanced with other, milder ones, leaves such as chickweed, lesser celandine and self-heal, or with other stronger ones (the latter is more interesting). Another approach is to use just one leaf, where there is a chance really to explore its flavour and texture, as well as how these work in relation to other ingredients. A small salad of bitter-cress is excellent served with smoked meat or strong cheese, lady's smock with beef or smoked fish, dandelion with beetroot or gammon, blinks with a poached duck egg. I sometimes fold a particular leaf in with cooked food, so that it wilts only slightly and gives colour, texture and flavour to each mouthful, for example, of pasta or roasted vegetables. Several kinds of leaves are rather bitter and on their own quite unpalatable; however, combined with other ingredients these leaves can really shine.

Pasta dishes

One of the guiding principles of Italian cooking, which of course features a lot of pasta dishes, is to use only a few good-quality ingredients and to cook them simply. This principle has given rise to hundreds of simple pasta-based meals in my household, using two or three wild plants or maybe some wild mushrooms and nothing else, except perhaps garlic, onion and some cheese, seasoning and possibly balsamic or another vinegar. Just to give you the general idea, here is a basic method, followed by some twosomes and threesomes of wild ingredients that could be used together to complete the dish.

Basic pasta

(Serves 4) Chop 3 garlic cloves and ½ large/ 1 small onion finely, and sweat in oil or butter until soft. Add mushrooms (optional) and cook at a high heat for 2 minutes. Meanwhile, cook your pasta according to the packet instructions. Drain and stir in garlic and onions (and mushrooms, if using) plus chopped leaves. Keep pan over a low heat for a moment and grate in some Parmesan, mature Gouda, pecorino or a really mature Cheddar. Moisten with a little veg or chicken stock; if needs be, sharpen with vinegar or mustard.

The following combinations show that it is possible to base a meal around wild ingredients, but you could make up infinite combinations using tomatoes, bacon, anchovies, peppers and so on.

Sample threesome and twosome variations

Fennel, samphire and wild pea shoots • Wild garlic and sea beet • Wild chervil & ceps • Alexanders stems (first boiled for a few minutes, then chopped), black mustard leaf and alexanders leaf • Dried wild marjoram and winter chanterelles • Sea-purslane and wild rocket

Sauces and Dressings

Classic green sauces such as pesto, salsa verde or sauce vièrge are easily adapted to include some wild leaves. Here vegetarian chef Joe Tyrrell describes his basic salsa verde recipe, which can be adapted to include pretty much any wild leaf.

Other sauces, such as béarnaise, butter, hollandaise, mayonnaise, velouté, and tartare, can be enhanced at the end of their preparation with one or more wild leaves. A gravy or jus can be based around or enhanced by wild ingredients, not only particularly tart fruits such as sloes, sea-buckthorn and Oregon grape but also herbs such as bur chervil or dittander stirred in at the last minute.

The basic formula for these sauces includes cooking juices from the meat, good stock and red wine, reduced and the sticky bits in the roasting or frying pan, deglazed using either liquid. Many fish sauces, which can really shine with the addition of a few wild herbs such as fennel or bur chervil, follow a similar formula but use white wine. The classic Cumberland sauce, based around red currants, can just as well be made using cranberries, stone bramble, barberries or guelder-rose berries. Bread sauce recipes can be adapted to use wild ingredients such as conifer needles or juniper berries in place of cloves. Sauces can also be constructed from scratch with the extracted juice of leaves, using either a blender and sieve or a juicer, adding other ingredients to add texture or balance the flavours; the raw leaves can also be blended with oil and then filtered to form an emulsion (see watercress emulsion recipe, p.295). Raw leaves can be used to flavour dressings; vinegar or fresh lemon juice are particularly useful with cabbage-family leaves since the acid fixes the flavoursome but volatile mustard

Salsa Verde

INGREDIENTS A mix of leaves chopped with 1 garlic clove, a dozen capers, a few anchovies, 1 teaspoon Dijon mustard (optional), olive oil and a squeeze of lemon juice.
METHOD On a chopping board, chop up the leaves with the garlic, capers and anchovies

until quite fine, then add the mustard, olive oil and lemon juice, and mix it up with your knife. Or you could use a food processor, but it's always too fine for my liking. I often make this in the woods with whatever leaves I can find and either the root of wild garlic or the leaves.

oils found in these plants. Infusions of leaves/stems into stocks/broths can form the basis of sauces, such as the wild celery-based sauce for poached chicken (see pp.114–15). Wild spices are also invaluable in creating flavoursome sauces. Some are well known from cultivated varieties, as is the case with wild mustard, wild celery and wild fennel seeds. Sweet cicely, alexanders and hogweed also have many interesting uses. Note that most of these are carrot-family species. The coumarin-containing plants (melilot, sweet woodruff, sweet vernal-grass, bastard balm) provide a sweet, vanilla-like flavour and aroma that adds a unique element to savoury dishes (it works particularly well with rabbit).

Sweet sauces, sorbets and ices

Many sweet sauces can be made from foraged ingredients. Stock syrups are used to make sorbet or granita, for pouring on fruit, ice cream and other desserts, or as the basis for jellies or thicker fruit sauces or coulis. Stock syrups, made by dissolving quantities of sugar in an equal weight of water, can be flavoured with fruit, coumarin-containing plants (melilot, sweet woodruff, sweet vernal-grass, bastard balm), fennel (leaves, flowers or fruits), sweet cicely (root, leaves or green fruits), cherry, damson, blackthorn, elderflower, meadowsweet, pineappleweed or chamomile flowers, hogweed seeds, wild mint leaves, burdock root, bittervetch tubers, restharrow root, sorrel or wood sorrel leaves, sweet flag leaves, stems and roots and conifer needles. Fruit coulis made from fruit purée and stock syrup can be prepared with all kinds of fruit, but they are best when the fruit is pulped raw, retaining more of the flavour and nutrients; harder fruit must, of course, be cooked, but soft fruit is easy to pulp and pass through a sieve. Coulis can be served

with cooked or raw fruit, ice cream and other desserts. All the flavourings used for stock syrups can also be used to flavour custard, either infused into the milk at the beginning or, with more delicate flavours such as elderflower, infused for a minute or so just before serving. In turn, the custard can be used to make ice cream, but stronger flavours can be used for this purpose, such as horseradish, lady's smock, alexanders seeds and celery.

Fools

These gorgeous desserts can be made using pretty much any wild fruit. Gently cook 1kg fruit with 100–300g caster sugar (less for sweeter fruit), purée, cool, then fold into 600ml whipped double cream.

Vinegars

White wine vinegar is used to infuse flavour from seeds, leaves, roots, fruits or even nuts, an excellent way of extracting and preserving flavours. Often just a little sugar is used to take the edge off the acidity of the vinegar. The basic method is to bring a small quantity of water to the boil with some sugar then infuse the flavouring plant material, before adding everything to the vinegar and leaving in a sunny place to infuse further for several days. Then strain the vinegar and bottle it. For a more detailed method for fruit vinegars see page 203.

Candying

Flavoursome roots such as sweet cicely and stems such as angelica lend themselves to candying, a process that draws out the moisture from the plant cells, replacing it with sugar. Sugar acts as a preservative and the process

Beverages

Fizzy drinks were originally devised as a health tonic, using many different wild-plant extracts. They were an important part of the DIY culture of early American settlers but later mass marketed for their health benefits: even the ubiquitous and nasty cola was originally devised as a health tonic. The basic method is simple: it involves making a sugar solution, infusing the flavouring plant material in it, then making it fizzy by priming it with yeast and allowing it to ferment. Add 400g sugar per 5 litres to near-boiling water and stir until dissolved. Then infuse whatever flavouring ingredients you are using for 30 minutes or so, strain and allow the mixture to cool, then while it is still tepid, add 1 teaspoon cream of tartar and a small amount of brewer's yeast: ¼ teaspoon per 5 litres is usually sufficient. The brew is then bottled and left in a warm place for a few hours to get the yeast culture going. After this, the bottles need to be well sealed and strong, and should not be kept too long before the liquid is drunk, or sooner or later they will explode. The old brown cider bottles with the internal screw top are the strongest I know, but they are hard to come by. Corked bottles should have their corks tied down with string; I have a stock of champagne-cork wire ties, which do a good job and are easier to apply. American root beer was once made from several different wild roots; ginger beer is another root drink, and the British Isles has its indigenous dandelion and burdock. Any of the ingredients mentioned under **stock syrups** (p.17) could be used to make fizzy drinks; there is a detailed recipe for nettle beer (see p.225).

ensures none of the flavour is wasted. Many candies or sweetmeats were originally made and taken as medicines, just as fizzy drinks were consumed as tonics.

Chop the roots into short lengths and boil them until tender. Drain and reserve the liquid. Weigh the roots then place the same weight of sugar in 30ml water (including the reserved liquid) per 100g sugar, then heat and stir until fully dissolved. Pour the syrup over the root pieces and leave overnight. The following day, strain off the syrup and heat gently to reduce any water absorbed from the roots. Repeat daily four times, leaving to cool overnight each time; the last time, heat the roots and syrup together; all the water in the roots will then have been replaced by sugar.

3
FORAGING HAZARDS

Poisonous plants

The best way to forage safely is to start by learning about the really poisonous plants, so that you know what to avoid. However, don't let this deter you from foraging. Although poisonous plants do pose a real danger, there are only a few really dangerous ones. This book covers over 350 species of edible plants and less than 20 poisonous ones, of which only a handful are potentially deadly. There are other poisonous plants not described in this book, because they do not resemble any edible species, though they are listed in the Places chapter. Once you have made yourself aware of the poisonous species (which appear at the start of each plant family's entry), the next step is to build your confidence by foraging for easy-to-identify species that don't look anything like any poisonous ones. It is a good idea to begin by limiting yourself to a small but reliable repertoire. For example, you can't go far wrong with elderflower and elderberries, blackberries, young nettles, reedmace, sea kale and dandelion, to mention just a small selection. There are also a number of plant families that have no poisonous wild species, such as cabbage, mint, dock, goosefoot and rose.

Potentially deadly

Of the handful of potentially deadly plants, only foxglove, hemlock and hemlock water-dropwort, and evergreen yew leaves are likely to be confused with edible species recommended in this book. The last three can be distinguished not only by easily learnt structural characteristics but also by smell: the first two have an offensive smell quite distinct from their look-alike edible relatives; yew is odourless, in contrast to the aromatic, resinous edible conifer that it resembles. Young foxglove and borage leaves are a little harder to tell apart; the answer is only to eat borage when in flower. Apart from these four, the rare umbellifer cowbane could be mistaken for fool's water-cress by a beginner, and deadly nightshade has large, black poisonous berries, which have been eaten by mistake in the past, but neither it nor its berries closely resemble any edible species. If you stick to the principle of eating only plants you are sure you know, this kind of mistake is unlikely to happen.

There are only a few other deadly poisonous plants, including monk's-hood from the buttercup family and thornapple and henbane from the nightshade family. These are all rare plants, and none of them is similar to any of the edible species covered in this book. Green berries of black nightshade are also toxic enough to kill a child if eaten in quantities. Aside from this there are several other plants that can cause less serious poisoning if eaten by mistake, and several containing chemicals that will cause serious damage if eaten in large quantities on a regular basis.

Special cases

Certain plants have particular effects on certain people, such as pregnant women (who should avoid eating large amounts of sage or mugwort and should avoid altogether juniper, penny-royal, colt's-foot and most *Boriginaceae* species); anyone with kidney stones (who should avoid anything containing oxalic acid, such as wood sorrel, sorrel, sea beet or fat hen), and anyone allergic to a particular plant (see **Plant poisons**).

Edible vs poisonous

The boundaries between edible and poisonous plants are not always absolute; the following is a précis of some of the kinds of problems facing the novice forager. Some plants have both toxic and edible parts (e.g. black bryony); others are toxic only at certain growth stages – mature nettles, for example, have gritty particles that irritate the kidneys. Some plants are toxic raw but edible when cooked (e.g. marsh marigold); others accumulate toxins from the soil where these are present (e.g. nettles, winter-cress). These are the exceptions rather than the rule, and most do not pose a serious risk, but be sure to read any note marked **Hazards** in the individual plant entries.

Root rules

Never collect roots from a plant that you have not identified with certainty. There are two cases on record of fatal poisonings after consuming monk's-hood roots (see p.70), both of which occurred because the roots were thought to belong to other plants. Incredibly, given the lack of similarity, in one case the person thought they were eating horseradish. Thornapple (see pp.226–7) roots dug up by mistake from a patch of horseradish have also caused poisoning. Henbane roots have been mistakenly gathered instead of both wild parsnip and salsify.

Never gather roots from aquatic umbellifers: most of the plant poisonings on record in the British Isles, some fatal, are due to eating hemlock water-dropwort roots; the roots of another aquatic umbellifer, cowbane, are equally deadly and have caused numerous deaths in North America.

Plant poisons

It is difficult to make a clear distinction between poisonous and non-poisonous plant substances, since many that are essential to life can become toxic under certain conditions. Vitamins A and C can both cause adverse effects when taken in excess in the form of supplements, and many medical drugs are lethal if the dose is not strictly controlled. Another example of variable toxicity are allergic reactions to usually benign substances, which affect a minority of people; with this in mind only eat small amounts of any wild plant when trying it for the first time. Other toxic substances are neither harmful nor beneficial when ingested in small quantities, and some plants listed as poisonous in advice to livestock farmers are completely harmless in the quantities likely to be eaten by humans. For example, we eat chickweed at most by the handful, but cattle or sheep may eat several kilos at a time; consumed in this quantity, the small levels of saponins in chickweed can cause quite serious symptoms. Inferences from animal poisonings can generally be tempered by the knowledge that grazing animals usually eat huge quantities of a particular plant before showing signs of poisoning.

Two other sources of information regarding plant toxicity can also give rise to unnecessary fear. Firstly, poisoning as a result of ingesting plant essential oils have limited bearing on the edibility of plants from which they are extracted, since any potentially toxic substances are present in much greater concentrations in the pure oil than in the plant material. Secondly, recommendations are often given for limiting the use of certain medicinal plants, but these should be understood in context. As medicines these plants are consumed in concentrated daily doses, in some cases for months at a time; their use as foods is a different matter, usually involving much less regular use of much smaller quantities. Colt's-foot, for example, is harmless as an occasional food or flavouring (although pregnant women should probably avoid it) but could be harmful if consumed as a medicine on a prolonged, daily basis.

Different plant poisons affect the human metabolism in various ways. The least dangerous are irritants that affect soft tissue – these generally have immediate effect, preventing them from being swallowed – and furanocoumarins, which cause blistering following light exposure. The most worrying are those known to have caused death, but perhaps the most insidious are those with cumulative effects, such as plants containing pyrrolizidine alkaloids (see p.66). Details of most specific poisons are given in the species entries, but a few that occur across families are dealt with below.

Specific poisons that occur in more than one family

Coumarin is found in **sweet woodruff, meadowsweet, melilot, sweet vernal-grass, bastard balm.** It causes headaches if consumed in a large quantity but is a strong flavouring and for this reason is usually only present in small amounts. Coumarin-containing plants dried or stored in damp conditions can become infected by the *Aspergillus* mould, which turns coumarin into dicoumarin. *Dicoumarin* is an anticoagulant and is used to treat high blood pressure, which it alleviates by thinning the blood. However, in larger doses, it prevents blood clotting and leads to uncontrolled bleeding. Livestock eating hay or dried melilot affected by the mould have died from internal bleeding, and the chemically similar warfarin used as rat poison kills rats in the same manner. However, livestock eat massive amounts of hay, whereas only a small amount of these plants is ever used as flavouring. It may be that eating food that has merely been flavoured by affected plants would probably cause blood thinning rather than haemorrhaging. However, this is not a risk worth taking; I threw away my entire harvest of melilot one year after it got damp and mouldy. The solution is to ensure that drying takes place fairly quickly in well-ventilated conditions and that the dried plant material is stored in a dry place, in a sealed container.

Thujone is found in plants of the daisy, mint and cypress families. It is a constituent in wormwood, used to make absinthe, which was banned due to its narcotic and other damaging effects. However, the effects attributed to thujone were at least partly due to the additives, such as copper sulphate, used to colour the drink. Oil of thujone, a highly concentrated extract, is a convulsant and produces some quite drastic symptoms when taken orally. Small children have been poisoned after eating leaves of conifers of the *Thuja* genus. There are very old records of the deaths of pregnant women who consumed tansy in great quantity in order to induce abortion; whether these records are accurate is hard to say (in many cases older records prove inaccurate where further investigation is possible). Despite the reputation of thujone as an abortifacient, there are no records of miscarriage, even after consuming thuja oil. There are no recent records of poisoning from eating sage, wild clary, mugwort, yarrow or tansy; all the same, as a precaution these plants should not be eaten in any quantity when pregnant.

Pyrrolizidine alkaloids are discussed in the borage family or *Boraginaceae* introduction (p.66) but also occur in the daisy family. These poisons damage the tubules in the liver, which can easily be repaired if only small amounts are consumed on an occasional basis. However, permanent liver damage could result if plants containing high levels of these alkaloids were eaten on a regular basis. Worse still, because it happens so gradually, such damage could in theory happen without the cause being diagnosed. Plants to avoid altogether are ragwort, groundsel and hound's tongue. A plant that I choose to avoid but that some people eat in small amounts is comfrey. Plants that contain only small quantities of pyrrolizidine alkaloids and are therefore safe for moderate and occasional consumption are borage and colt's-foot.

Oxalic acid is found in the leaves of fat hen and other goosefoots, and to a greater extent in wood sorrel and other *Oxalis* species as well as all members of the dock family. In a fairly minor way, oxalic acid limits the amount of calcium that the body absorbs from food. This happens because it binds to calcium and forms calcium salts. On the other hand, fat hen is also high in calcium so it balances things out nicely. A slightly more serious matter is that eating lots of plants containing oxalic acid may aggravate the build-up of the calcium salts that cause kidney stones, bladder stones and gout. Anyone predisposed to these conditions should probably go easy on the above-mentioned species.

Hazards from thorns

Puncture wounds from thorns, in particular those of blackthorn and sea-buckthorn, can become infected, especially if tiny pieces of thorn are left embedded in the skin. Antibiotics are a swift remedy to this problem, but thick gardening gloves and protective clothing can help prevent it.

Chemical contaminants

Toxic chemical residues can accumulate in soil from a number of sources, such as car exhausts, lead and other mining activities, as well as petrol stations, old gasworks and other industrial sites. Plants are known to accumulate chemicals from contaminated soil, although the extent to which they do so varies greatly; as already mentioned, nettles and goosefoots accumulate more than most. Unfortunately, there are often no clear signs that land is contaminated, so the key lies in good local knowledge of former (or present) land use.

Places to avoid

Present or former industrial sites, gasworks in particular, unless they have been very thoroughly cleaned up, as well as former tin or lead mines (and water courses down stream from them); former sites of petrol stations; old sawmills, where soil may be contaminated by chemicals used in tanalizing. Soil by the side of roads will obviously be contaminated by residues from car exhausts, which, apart from roads built since unleaded petrol was introduced, will include lead from petrol. If you were occasionally to eat small amounts of plant material from these kind of sites you would probably not injest hazardous levels of toxic chemicals (for specific example, see **Brambles/ Blackberries** *Rubus fruticosus*). However, before harvesting in quantity from a particular site on a regular basis, make sure you are well informed about the history of that site.

Pesticides (herbicides and insecticides)

This is a subject on which it is difficult to give detailed advice. People who look at the risks posed by pesticide residues, such as the Food Standards Agency, focus their efforts on cultivated plants; they don't tend to analyse any of the wild plants growing near by that might be foraged and eaten. Avoid collecting in or around arable fields that are sprayed (even organic farms are allowed to use sprays, the residues of which you might not want to eat). On the other hand, you could get to know local farmers so that they can tell you where, when and with what they have sprayed. Unfortunately, even in some woodland areas you cannot guarantee that plants are spray-free, as many conservation organizations and foresters use pesticides as part of their management schemes. Again, the best approach is to get to know the owners or the people managing the site and ask them whether chemicals have been applied.

Specific aquatic hazards

Malign E. coli (there are also benign strains that are essential to good health) and other bacteria from sewage can contaminate seaweed in areas near a sewage outlet. In areas where shellfish is harvested, the local council food-hygiene department will produce a weekly rating for the sea water, which will enable you to judge whether it is safe. Otherwise, avoid gathering from such areas. The Environment Agency also tests the water and can provide information about bacterial as well as chemical contamination (by heavy metals for example) of the sea and of freshwater rivers and streams.

Weil's disease is carried by rats and occasionally contracted by humans. The disease organism is present in rats' urine, and it is found in river water if rats live on the banks. It produces flu-like symptoms at first, including vomiting and fever, but the patient's condition deteriorates, with symptoms such as nose bleeds, bruising and anaemia. In roughly 10 per cent of cases it leads to death. It cannot be transmitted via plant material; however, it can enter the bloodstream if even small cuts, blisters or grazes are exposed to contaminated water. If collecting plants next to rivers, be careful not to expose such seemingly insignificant wounds to the river water.

Liver fluke is a microscopic parasite that infects sheep and cattle (also rabbits) that have eaten plants with fluke cysts on them. It can cause serious liver damage and even death in animals, who sometimes consume tens of thousands of fluke cysts during several weeks' grazing. Human infections are much less serious and rarely fatal. This is partly due to the small amounts of infected plant material likely to be eaten but also due to the fluke being adapted to infect animals rather than humans. About 50 per cent of cases show no symptoms during the infection, but those who do commonly exhibit abdominal pain, fever and weight loss.

Liver fluke has several stages to its life cycle. Plants such as water-cress will only be contaminated if they are growing somewhere in which every stage can be accomplished. The first stage involves the cattle, sheep or rabbits eating vegetation bearing fluke cysts. The cyst then develops into an adult in the animal's gut, finds its way into the liver then produces eggs, which exit the animal in its faeces. Eggs can survive for up to 10 months before hatching, though they will die at temperatures of below 5°C or if they dry out. If faeces are not near water, or damp habitats favoured by snail *Lymnaea truncatula*, the life cycle will stop here. Larvae or miracidia can only live for about 3 hours after hatching, outside of the host snail. The snails are more common in areas with mildly acid soils. If they are present, larvae enter the snails and develop to the next larval stage, known as cercariae. The cercariae leave the snails then swim around before attaching themselves to submerged vegetation, or move within a film of water on wet vegetation such as grass, where they form cysts, thus completing the cycle.

Harvesting notes: aquatic greens

In fast-flowing areas, cercariae will be washed down stream and are unlikely to attach to vegetation; even in slow-flowing ones, the presence of snails need not be a concern, if banks are steep and animals never have access to the water's edge. With no faeces anywhere near the snails, no fluke eggs will be present (although rain could, in theory, wash eggs from near by). Liver fluke is more prevalent in areas of high rainfall and poor drainage, such as the north and west of England, Wales and Scotland.

Avoid collecting watercress, fool's watercress, water mint, water pepper or other plants you intend to eat raw (even heavily encysted plants are safe once thoroughly cooked) from water-logged meadows or marshy areas at the edges of ponds, streams or rivers. These are the places where the host snails are likely to occur and are most likely to be contaminated by fluke when livestock have access to them. Both livestock and snails must be present at about the same time, at some point in the year; if either one is missing the fluke cannot complete its life cycle. How-

ever, you will only know this if you visit the site often, and, unfortunately, as rabbits can also carry the fluke, it is best to assume that a suitable habitat is a contaminated one. Plants can still be harvested from this kind of site, but they must be cooked before eating.

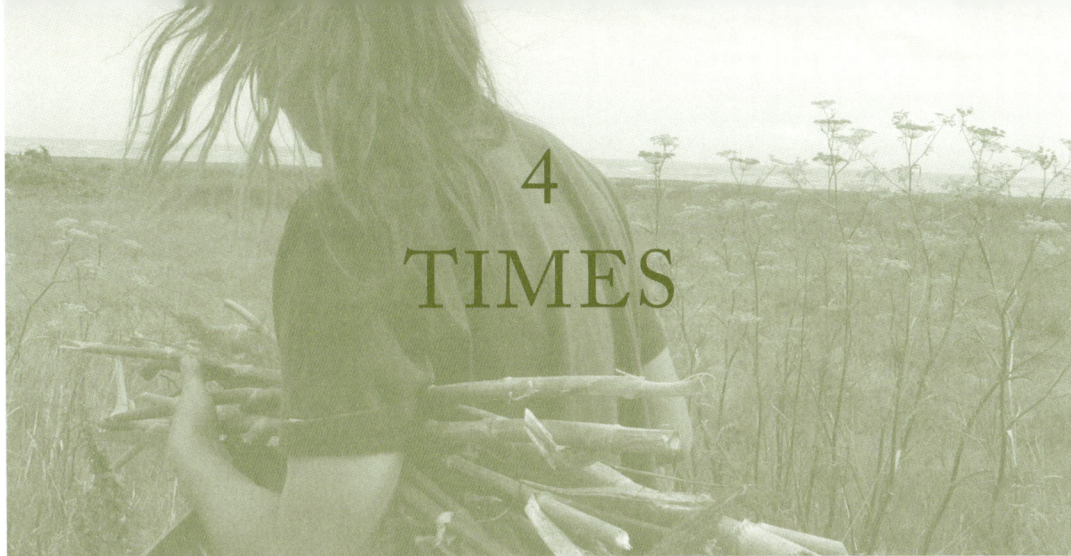

4
TIMES

Foraging is essentially tied to the seasons. I have several favourite metaphors for seasonal foraging. Firstly, it is like being on a merry-go-round with different things within reach at each moment: if you don't reach out when they are there you have to go all the way round again before you get another chance. Learning to do this is like discovering the steps to a new kind of dance, with the plants and the landscape as your partner. It is about responding in the moment but also anticipating the next move.

To begin with you do everything either too early or too late, but it soon becomes second nature. Foraging is also like a big carnival or parade going by silently and largely unnoticed; for those who tune into it, a pageant of flavours, scents and textures is happening. In fact, paying attention is only the beginning: to know what is really going on you have to participate, by gathering and eating some of the goodies on offer.

Spring

Spring is a time of flourishing growth, of edible greenery and the first edible flowers, a time when plants reassert their presence in earnest after winter dormancy. I have found some of my best patches in spring, when, several metres off any kind of beaten track, various pretty flowers announced the presence of plants. You can spot many plants in flower from a hundred or more metres away, which you would barely notice in their winter state, even just a metre away. Blossom emerges early from cherry plum and blackthorn branches, an emphatic burst of pink and white cheerfulness to mark the end of winter gloom, all the more poignant against the dark bark of their leafless branches. Even if you don't harvest the flowers, make a note of where you see them, and also of the cherry blossom, which follows a few weeks later. You can come back later in the year to collect the fruit.

Mustards and other cabbage species such as lady's smock also flower, as do three-cornered garlic, violets, primroses and cowslips. The former are variably spicy; three-cornered garlic flowers are mildly garlicky; violets taste as they smell and look very pretty, as do the last two, which have more delicate but distinctive flavours. Spring is also characterized by the absence of fruits, nuts and seeds, which fell to the ground months ago and were buried in autumnal debris. Now they are resurrected as brand-new plants. As seedlings and new growth are reaching upwards, so is the sap of the trees. When broken birch twigs produce drops of sap they are ready to be tapped. This can happen at any time from late February until as late as the first week in April.

As for edible greenery, we are spoilt for choice at this time of year. There is an abundance of wild greens such as nettles, mallow, sea beet, sow thistle, bistort and charlock. Mild salads such as spring beauty, pennywort and chickweed are also at their best. There are plenty of more intensely flavoured leaves for salads or flavouring Wood sorrel re-emerges after winter dormancy, spicy leaves such as black mustard and scurvy-grass are at their best before flowering and various aromatic wild fennel plants begin to produce their frondy leaves. By this time, however, other carrot family species such as wild chervil and alexanders, which have been producing leafy growth throughout the winter, are nearing the completion of their life cycles.

Beneath the ground, the edible roots of second-year burdock plants are good to harvest now, if you catch them before they put up a stem, as are those of goat's beard, wild salsify and wild parsnip; at the same time the many tender, young shoots of hogweed, hops, traveller's joy, wild asparagus, wild peas, vetches and rosebay willowherb are ripe for picking. Edible woodland plants such as ramsons and lesser celandine start and finish their growth cycle in spring, before the tree canopy gets so dense as to restrict the light on the woodland floor. They photosynthesize like mad, put forth their flowers, set seed, then die back as quickly as they came, having fortified their underground storage organs ready for next

year's re-emergence. This is the ideal time for digging up the tubers of lesser celandine. In late spring, the flavoursome leaves of sweet woodruff are at their best, just as the plant flowers.

Summer

By early summer, the edible leaves and stems of many plants harvested in spring are past the point of greatest usefulness as the plants reach their flowering and fruiting stages. Others have already completed their growth cycles and died back without a trace. On the other hand, several members of the goosefoot family do not even start to produce growth until late May; summer is the time for fat hen, various wild oraches and marsh samphire. It is also the time for the cactus-like rock samphire, which is especially suited to enduring desert-like conditions on rocky cliffs in the full blast of the summer sun. Some wild salads are prolific in the summer months, in particular water-cress, wild rocket and swine-cress.

Summer is also peak time for flowers. Again, you can map out the land for its edible goods with these helpful flags of edible plant presence. Bulrush flowers produce a unique wild food for just a few days in June; you can easily miss this short window of time when bulrush pollen can be collected. This is also the time to reap the benefits of your earlier observations, as wild cherries present ripe fruit in July, closely followed by cherry plums and wild damsons. However, it is worth casting an eye up into the trees for more than cherries and plums. In May and June, conifers such as Norway and Sitka spruce produce their tender pale green shoots, which are excellent flavourings, and green walnuts are ready for pickling in July. Closer to the ground, the succulent hips of Japanese rose become available in late July; then from early August soft fruit such as blackberries, raspberries, blueberries and cowberries are ripe for picking. Grass seeds also ripen from early summer onwards; it is important to watch them closely as they soon fall to the ground once they are ripe.

Many of the strongest flavours develop in the summer. Aromatic **mint** family members have their main period of growth, their leaves most flavoursome at the point of flowering. Several unrelated plants that produce the flavouring coumarin in both leaves and flowers are also at their peak season, as are the wild chamomiles. Many aromatic members of the carrot family are also in full swing; several of them, including hogweed, alexanders and fennel, producing aromatic leaves, flowers and seeds in the course of the summer months. This is also a good time to collect horseradish roots, as the large, leathery leaves make the plants easy to find. The rich flavours of all our wild fruits are also developing now – this is the main period during which fruit ripens, including those that are not fully ripe until autumn.

Seaweeds are an obvious food choice for island dwellers, and in Scotland, Ireland and Wales, more so than in England, one that has been enthusiastically taken up in the past. Certain species, most notably the green seaweeds, are summer annuals and complete their entire life cycle between spring and autumn. Seaweeds in general are abundant in summer, making the most of the more intense sunlight and longer daylight hours to photosynthesize and grow. This is a gift to foragers as it becomes a pleasure to gather them on a hot day, when you don't even mind slipping on the rocks and falling into the water: winter seaweed foraging is more of a trial.

Autumn

The abundance of fungi, fruits and nuts in autumn barely needs pointing out: this season registers for most of us more than any other as a time of harvest. Autumnal foragable fare of the fruit and nut variety includes crab apples, elderberries, guelder-rose berries, hawthorn berries, rose hips, rowan berries, wild service berries, whitebeam berries, sea-buckthorn berries, sloes, wild damsons, acorns, chestnuts, hazel-nuts, beechnuts and walnuts. There is stiff competition from other life forms, however: many nut trees are stripped bare by grey squirrels before less agile and lightfooted *Homo sapiens* gets a look in. Starlings or jays can strip a tree of its berries in a matter of hours. If you are awake to the possibilities, this time of great fecundity provokes a slightly mad scramble to gather at least some of the bounty and then to find ways of storing and preserving it. Freezing, pickling, making jams and drying the last of the summer seaweeds can fill the forager's home with sights and smells of sea-shore, forest, field and hedgerow produce, in order that we can continue to fill our bellies with these things until the same time next year.

As with flowers, many fruits draw attention to plants you might not otherwise have found. This happens for a reason: the life cycle of these plants requires them to have their fruits noticed by roaming herbivores, who make a beeline towards these colourful displays after spotting them from a distance, then, having eaten their fill, transport the seeds in their gut in the course of further wanderings and later deposit them in their droppings at a convenient distance from the parent plant. However, I often discover fruit trees not by scanning the landscape from a distance but by walking directly beneath them, looking on the ground. One of the things I like most about autumn is walking along country tracks and roads lined with mature trees and seeing the fallen fruits, nuts and berries. You start by looking down but straight away look up to see whitebeam, oak, wild damson or beech trees that had escaped your notice before.

However, autumn is not all fruit, nuts and fungi. Many edible perennial plants that die back after flowering and producing seed begin to put forth leafy growth again, and several biennials (such as garlic mustard) and winter annuals (such as bitter-cress) begin their life cycle. There are also many edible seeds available, both spices, such as fennel, alexanders and hogweed, and protein- and carbohydrate-rich grains of dock family species, such as black bindweed and knotgrass.

Winter

Winter is not as barren as might be supposed, although there is some variation across the counties of the British Isles – in especially cold parts there is less green material to be found. But in many areas, perennials, biennials and winter annuals continue to grow, producing leafy growth even beneath snow. Several wild salad plants, including winter annuals bitter-cress and nipplewort, and perennials chickweed and dandelion, seem positively to thrive during winter, as do the wild mustards. Carrot family plants alexanders and wild chervil, which started producing new leafy growth in autumn, provide a steady supply of flavoursome leaves and stalks throughout the winter months, although extreme cold will slow their regrowth. Heavy frost will damage water-cress and water-celery, especially if gathered when the frost has not yet thawed; sometimes plants left for a day or two after can make a good recovery. Certain plants continue no matter how cold it gets: cabbage-family members are especially hardy. Some plants' appearance in winter is strictly subject to a favourable climate: for example, the Mediterranean garden escape, three-cornered garlic, especially favoured by the mild winters of Cornwall, grows there profusely from December onwards.

Rose hips are often passed over by wildlife, due to variation in the seeds, making some strains too difficult to crack open for seed-eating birds like green finches. For this reason, in my area of Kent, dog-rose hips persist well into the winter months, giving a rare element of colour on the otherwise mostly brown and green landscape. They are actually at their best after the first frost, when their flesh becomes a rich, sticky pulp. Sea-buckthorn berries persist on the bushes or trees deep into the winter, although once they turn pale and yellow, they are past their best. Also remaining until finally shaken down by wind and rain are the seeds of alexanders, poignantly black on their skeletal sticks against the sparse winter landscape. In winter, spying out the land for signs of edible plant life is primarily by means of such skeletons of the past year's growth. Plants that grow in colonies are particularly easy to locate with collections of dead canes showing where they are from a considerable distance.

Some of these canes, such as burdock, parsnip and the aforementioned alexanders, mark the location of edible roots. Winter is an ideal time for harvesting roots, as the summer growth will have laid up a good store of nutrients for the winter months. First-year plants, which won't have produced flowers over the summer, are best; second-year plants will by now have woody roots. Some plants, such as burdock, die back without a trace by midwinter, so it is important to get to them before they do. First-year growth of others, such as goat's beard, wild salsify and wild parsnip, persists through the winter and so becomes easier to find as other plants die back and the grass stops growing. Dandelion roots, which in principle can be harvested at any time, are especially good at this time of year.

There is less cause to spend time on the beach in winter – most plants are dormant in such places – but sea-purslane and sea beet can still be found.

5
PLACES

Plants have some fairly stable characteristics, other than their basic form and growth patterns, among which is a preference for a particular kind of place. For some more than others, the pH level of the soil, concerned with its acidity or alkalinity, can be a major factor. Generally speaking, acid environments tend to have fewer species than alkaline, with chalk grassland being probably the most species-rich habitat of all.

Altitude is another important factor; many plants will not grow either above or below a certain altitude range. Proximity to freshwater or salt also encourages or discourages certain species from growing. All these factors give rise to particular plant communities, groups of plants that grow together in certain kinds of places. Of course, particular places are all unique in some sense, but they can be broadly classified into habitat types. Each habitat type has plants that are generally found there, but several of the more flexible species are found in more than habitat type.

Spending time in the different habitats, getting to know the various plant communities, you are certain to discover some edible species pretty much straight away. If you have somewhere you visit often, try to determine what kind of habitat it is and consult the list of edible species for that habitat. In the first place, it is a

good idea to think about where in your area examples of the different habitats occur. Getting to know the particular kinds of places where particular kinds of plants grow makes the process of identifying edible wild plants much easier. Whereas there are in total more than 350 edible plants to be found in the British Isles, there are far fewer species in any particular habitat, even the most species rich of them. Starting with the species list for a given habitat, narrow it down to a more specific list for your area, by consulting the distribution data (for which see individual plant entries); as you learn more about your area you could narrow the list down further for a particular place, for example in my area of Kent much of the soil is chalky, but there are places with acidic soil where I would not expect to find chalk-loving plants. Even after this, the list will still be extensive for certain habitats such as hedges; others such as coastal and aquatic habitats have a much narrower range of species. Before actually going out, it is worth spending some time carefully reading the plant descriptions and studying the pictures of two or three of the plants you expect to find. I own several well-illustrated field guides to British flora, but when I am on a quest for a new plant I also print off many images of the plant from the internet. To avoid any confusion I search using the Latin name of the plant, for example sea sandwort *Honckenya peploides* is known as sea purslane in North America, the name we give to a completely different plant, *Halimione portulacoides*.

Woodlands

Woodlands have been the main habitat on our islands for most of the time since the last ice-age. However, a trip back in time would reveal a very different kind of woodland from those familiar to most of us. The original wild wood was unmanaged, and much of it probably consisted of impenetrable thickets. Our familiar woodlands are either ancient woodland, which means they have been intensively managed since at least 1600, or secondary woodland, where cultivated or other non-woodland has reverted to woodland, or commercial-forestry plantations, which are generally monocultures, most often of conifers. Of these, the most rich in plants, fungi and pretty much every other kind of woodland species are the ancient woodlands. These are complex ecosystems, which have developed over long periods of time; some may even date back to the original wild wood. Their complexity and species diversity have developed as a consequence of human management; in many cases the decline of their use has led to a corresponding decline in species diversity.

General woodlands

Trees and shrubs: Silver birch *Betula pendula*, downy birch *B. pubescens*, hazel *Corylus avellana*, beech *Fagus sylvatica*, Scots pine *Pinus sylvestris*, Norway spruce *Picea abies*, Sitka spruce *P. sitchenis*, Douglas fir *Pseudotsuga menziesii*, sessile oak *Quercus petraea*, pendunculate oak *Q. robur*, chestnut *Castanea sativa*, small-leaved lime *Tilia cordata*, large-leaved lime *T. platyphyllos*, common lime *T. × europaea*, elder *Sambucus nigra*, guelder-rose *Viburnum opulus*, Darwin's barberry *Berberis darwinii*, Oregon grape *Mehonia aquifolium*, cherry plum *Prunus cerasifera*, blackthorn *P. spinosa*, wild cherry *P. avium*, whitebeam *Sorbus aria*, rowan *S. aucuparia*, wild service-tree *S. domestica*, true service-tree *S. torminalis*, Midland hawthorn *Crataegus laevigata*, hawthorn *C. monogyna*, stone bramble *Rubus saxatilis*, raspberry *R. idaeus*, bramble *R. fruticosus*, crab apple *Malus sylvestris*, dog-rose *Rosa canina*, walnut *Juglans regia*, strawberry tree *Arbutus unedo*, blaeberry *Vaccinium myrtillus*, cowberry *V. vitis-idaea*, red currant *Ribes rubrum*, downy currant *R. spicatum*, mountain currant *R. alpinum*, raspberry *Rubus idaeus*, brambles *R. fruticosus* agg. **Poisonous:** Yew *Taxus baccata*. **Herbs:** Sweet violet *Viola odorata*, hop *Humulus lupulus*, common nettle *Urtica dioica*, wood sorrel *Oxalis acetosella*, primrose *Primula vulgaris*, sweet woodruff *Geum odoratum*, wavy bitter-cress *Cardamine flexuosa*, hairy bitter-cress *C. hirsuta*, rosebay willowherb *Chamerion angustifolium*, common lungwort *Pulmonaria officinalis*, lesser celandine *Ranunculus ficaria*, honeysuckle *Lonicera periclymenum*, creeping thistle *Cirsium arvense*, nipplewort *Lapsana communis*, pignut *Conopodium majus*, ground-elder *Aegopodium podagraria*, bath asparagus *Ornithogalum pyrenaicum*, ramsons *Allium ursinum*, wood dock *Rumex sanguineus*, nettle-leaved bellflower *Campanula trachelium*, great burdock *Arctium lappa*, lesser burdock

A. minus, common wintergreen *Pyrola minor*, stone bramble *Rubus saxatilis*, strawberry *Fragaria vesca*, wood avens *Geum urbanum*. **Ferns:** Bracken *Pteridium aquilinum*, lady fern *Athyrium filix-femina*. **Poisonous:** Cuckoo-pint *Arum maculatum*, dog's mercury *Mercurialis perennis*.

Woodland rides, open woodland and woodland edges

These are plants that need slightly more light in order to flourish and include species that thrive immediately following coppicing. Both coppicing and maintenance of woodland rides encourage these species, which might otherwise not find a place in much of our woodland. In the wild wood, grazed glades would have supported such species.

Herbs: Wood dock *Rumex sanguineus*, cowslip *Primula veris*, wild angelica *Angelica sylvestris*, hogweed *Heracleum sphondylium*, dog-rose *Rosa canina*, wild plum *Prunus domestica*, dwarf cherry *P. cerasus*, ground-ivy *Glechoma hederacea*, orpine *Sedum telephium*, tall melilot *Melilotus officinalis*, corn mint *Mentha arvensis*, bastard balm *Melittis melissophyllum*, parsley piert *Aphanes arvensis*, field-rose *Rosa arvensis*, hawthorn *Crataegus monogyna*. **Poisonous:** Creeping buttercup *Ranunculus repens*, stinking hellebore *Helleborus foetidus*, green hellebore *H. viridis*.

Damp areas of woodland

Herbs: Lady's smock *Cardamine pratensis*, large bitter-cress *C. amara*, wavy bitter-cress *C. flexuosa*, bird cherry *Prunus padus*, brooklime *Veronica beccabunga*, water-pepper *Persicaria hydropiper*, pink purslane *Claytonia sibirica*, blinks *Montia fontana*, common wintergreen *Pyrola minor*, giant bellflower *Campanula latifolia*, common valerian *Valeriana officinalis*, opposite-leaved golden-saxifrage *Chrysosplenium oppositifolium*, alternate-leaved golden-saxifrage *C. alternifolium*, meadowsweet *Filipendula ulmaria*, water avens *Geum rivale*, water purslane *Lythrum portula*. **Grasses:** Floating sweet-grass *Glyceria fluitans*, tufted hair-grass *Deschampsia cespitosa*. **Poisonous:** Monk's-hood *Aconitum napellus*, yellow pimpernel *Lysimachia nemorum*.

Grasslands

Grasslands provide habitats for a broad range of species, yet they are in the main the product of human activity of one kind or another. Before people began farming, there was little grassland in the British landscape; grassland species that colonized the large areas that were subsequently cleared for farming must have done so from relatively small pockets of grassland. A very few areas in Scotland at altitudes where trees are not able to grow would have been grassland, as well as small areas on coastal cliffs where salt spray and harsh weather conditions would have discouraged the growth of trees. Most pre-agricultural grassland, however, would have been woodland glades, in most cases quite small, but in areas such as the Yorkshire Dales and the North and South Downs, large herbivores like boar, wild ox and deer may have grazed intensively enough to prevent woodland from ever developing over more extended areas. Nevertheless, the vast extent of grassland and grassland plants is a fairly recent development, having occurred only in the last 6000 years, as more and more woodland was cleared to make way for farming.

It is important to note that the various grassland categories that follow differ primarily in their different usage. Acid and chalk grasslands, on the other hand, are habitats that support specific communities of plants due to the kinds of soil on which they grow. Examples of both types occur in the aforementioned categories. Edible acid-grassland species include harebell, sheep's sorrel, stork's-bill, blaeberry and lousewort, most of which are listed under Heaths (see p.37); acid grasslands are essentially heavily grazed heaths, where shrubs such as gorse have not become dominant. Grasslands over alkaline rocks such as chalk or limestone are very rich in species. The alkaline soils in which they grow are poor in nutrients but provide a niche for specialized plants, which compete poorly in more nutrient-rich soils. Edible species typical of these kinds of habitat include wild basil, hoary plantain, salad burnet, restharrow, marjoram, large thyme, burnet-saxifrage, wild parsnip, cowslip, rough hawkbit, lady's bedstraw and wild carrot.

Lastly, churchyards often contain rich pickings for foragers as they have usually been maintained over long periods. They are essentially grassland areas and usually have a good selection of edible plants similar to those found on other grassland in the same locality.

Meadows

Meadows are grasslands that are harvested for their hay, which is fed to livestock mostly during the winter. They may also be grazed at other times of the year, but their main purpose is to produce hay.

Herbs: Common sorrel *Rumex acetosa*, lesser celandine *Ranunculus ficaria*, early purple orchid *Orchis mascula*, stork's-bill *Erodium cicutarium*, cowslip *Primula veris*, bitter-vetch *Lathyrus linifolius*, meadow vetchling *L. pratensis*, common vetch *Vicia sativa*, tall melilot *Melilotus officinalis*, ribbed melilot *M. altissimus*, red clover *Trifolium pratensis*, white clover *T. repens*, wild mignonette *Reseda lutea*, ox-eye daisy *Leucanthemum vulgare*, dandelions *Taraxacum* agg., bristly oxtongue *Picris echioides*, goat's beard *Tragopogon pratensis*, common chamomile *Chamaemelum nobile*, creeping thistle *Cirsium arvense*, cat's-ear *Hypochaeris radicata*, rough hawkbit *Leontodon*

hispidus, hogweed *Heracleum sphondylium*, wild chervil *Anthriscus sylvestris*, alexanders *Smyrnium olustrum*, pignut *Conopodium majus*, burnet-saxifrage *Pimpinella major*, keeled garlic *Allium carinatum*, field garlic *A. oleraceum*, crow garlic *A. vineale*, bath asparagus *Ornithogalum pyrenaicum*, self-heal *Prunella vulgaris*, wild clary *Salvia verbenaca*, meadow clary *S. pratensis*, ground-ivy *Glechoma hederacea*, wild basil *Clinopodium vulgare*, large thyme *Thymus pulegioides*, lady's bedstraw *Galium verum*, dewberry *Rubus caesius*, salad burnet *Sanguisorba minor*, lady's mantle *Alchemilla glabra*. **Grasses:** Sweet vernal-grass *Anthoxanthum odoratum*, couch grass *Elytrigia repens*, tall fescue *Festuca arundinacea*. **Poisonous:** Bulbous buttercup *Ranunculus bulbosus*.

Pastures

Pastures are grasslands on which livestock are grazed and in most cases would never be mown.

Shrubs: Common juniper *Juniperus communis*. **Herbs:** Stork's-bill *Erodium cicutarium*, lady's mantle *Alchemilla glabra*, red clover *Trifolium pratensis*, white clover *T. repens*, Good-King-Henry *Chenopodium bonus-henricus*, sheep's sorrel *Rumex acetosella*, common sorrel *R. acetosa*, daisy *Bellis perennis*, common chamomile *Chamaemelum nobile*, pineappleweed *Matricaria discoidea*, ox-eye daisy *Leucanthemum vulgare*, dandelions *Taraxacum* agg., spear thistle *Cirsium vulgare*, creeping thistle *C. arvense*, cat's-ear *Hypochaeris radicata*, rough hawkbit *Leontodon hispidus*, beaked hawk's-beard *Crepis vesicaria*, smooth sow-thistle *Sonchus oleraceus*, pignut *Conopodium majus*, burnet-saxifrage *Pimpinella major*, self-heal *Prunella vulgaris*, ground-ivy *Glechoma hederacea*, wild basil *Clinopodium vulgare*, large thyme *Thymus pulegioides*, common nettle *Urtica dioica*, swine-cress *Coronopus squamatus*, lesser swine-cress *C. didymus didymus*, lady's bedstraw *Galium* *verum*, spear thistle *Cirsium vulgare*, dropwort *Filipendula vulgaris*, dewberry *Rubus caesius*, salad burnet *Sanguisorba minor*, lady's mantle *Alchemilla glabra*. **Grasses:** Sweet vernal-grass *Anthoxanthum odoratum*, couch grass *Elytrigia repens*, upright brome *Bromopsis erecta*. **Ferns:** Bracken *Pteridium aquilinum*. **Poisonous:** Ragwort *Senecio jacobaea*, bulbous buttercup *Ranunculus bulbosus*.

Damp grasslands/marshes

Damp grasslands or marshes differ from bogs and fens in that they are often dry for part of the year. They are also generally part of managed farmland and are characterized by the presence of grass as well as rushes and sedges. They are usually situated in flood plains, near rivers or streams, and the underlying soil has a high mineral content from the sediment carried by these water sources.

Herbs: Curled dock *Rumex crispus*, hoary willowherb *Epilobium parviflorum*, water mint *Mentha aquatica*, sweet-flag *Acorus calamus*, purple-loosestrife *Lythrum salicaria*, alternate-leaved golden-saxifrage *Chrysosplenium alternifolium*, opposite-leaved golden-saxifrage *C. oppositifolium*, water chickweed *Myoston aquaticum*, fool's water-cress *Apium nodiflorum*, angelica *Angelica sylvestris*, wild fennel *Foeniculum vulgare*, common valerian *Valeriana officinalis*, brooklime *Veronica beccabunga*, lousewort *Pedicularis sylvatica*, monkey flower *Mimulus guttatus*, marsh marigold *Caltha palustris*, bistort *Persicaria bistorta*, water-pepper *P. hydropiper*, blinks *Montia fontana*, large bitter-cress *Cardamine amara*, wavy bitter-cress *C. flexuosa*, lady's smock *C. pratensis*, marsh woundwort *Stachys palustris*, pennyroyal *Mentha puligeum*, peppermint *M. piperita*, wild basil *Clinopodium vulgare*, common valerian *Valeriana officinalis*, marsh thistle *Cirsium palustre*, meadowsweet *Filipendula ulmaria*, silverweed *Potentilla anserina*, water avens *Geum rivale*, great burnet *San-*

guisorba officinalis, marsh sow-thistle *Sonchus palustris*, sneezewort *Alchemilla ptarmica*. **Grasses:** Tufted hair-grass *Deschampsia cespitosa*. **Sedges:** Sweet galingale *Cyperus longus*, sea club-rush *Bolboschoenus maritimus* (on brackish marshes). **Poisonous:** Meadow buttercup *Ranunculus acris*, hemlock water-dropwort *Oenanthe crocata*, tabular water-dropwort *O. fistulosa*, yellow pimpernel *Lysimachia nemorum*.

Lawns and managed turf

Like chalk grassland, these challenging environments, with all leafy growth regularly cut down to a height of just a few millimetres, provide a niche for certain species adapted to tolerate such harsh treatment. No doubt many of these plants originally adapted to tolerate constant and intense grazing, and this makes them ideal candidates for foraging.

Herbs: Common sorrel *Rumex acetosa*, dandelions *Taraxacum* agg., cat's-ear *Hypochaeris radicata*, common chamomile *Chamaemelum nobile*, rough hawkbit *Leontodon hispidus*, lesser hawkbit *L. saxatilis*, beaked hawk's-beard *Crepis vesicaria*, yarrow *Achillea millefolium*, daisy *Bellis perennis*, white clover *Trifolium repens*, red clover *T. pratense*, ribwort plantain *Plantago lanceolata*, self-heal *Prunella vulgaris*, wild clary *Salvia verbenaca*.

Hedge and hedgebanks

These entirely man-made habitats are often very rich in species, with older hedges in most cases containing the greatest variety.

Trees and shrubs: Sessile oak *Quercus petraea*, pendunculate oak *Q. robur*, elder *Sambucus nigra*, guelder-rose *Viburnum opulus*, Darwin's barberry *Berberis darwinii*, barberry *B. vulgaris*, Oregon grape *Mehonia aquifolium*, red currant *Ribes rubrum*, mountain currant *R. alpinum*, hawthorn *Crataegus monogyna*, wild

cherry *Prunus avium*, dwarf cherry *P. cerasus*, cherry plum *P. cerasifera*, blackthorn/sloe *P. spinosa*, wild plum *P. domestica*, wild cherry *P. avium*, dwarf cherry *P. cerasus*, crab apple *Malus sylvestris*, Plymouth pear *Pyrus cordata*, wild pear *Pyrus pyraster*, wild service-tree *Sorbus torminalis*, whitebeam *S. aria*, juneberry *Amelanchier lamarckii*, dog-rose *Rosa canina*, field-rose *R. arvensis*, Japanese rose *R. rugosa*, brambles/blackberries *Rubus fruticosus* agg., dewberry *R. caesius*, walnut *Juglans regia*. **Climbing plants and vines:** Traveller's oy *Clematis vitalba*, Duke of Argyll's tea-plant *Lycium barbarum/Chinese*, honeysuckle *Lonicera periclymenum*, hop *Humulus lupulus*, black bryony *Tammus comunis*. **Herbs:** Sweet violet *Viola odorata*, wood dock *Rumex sanguineus*, lesser celandine *Ranunculus ficaria*, bladder campion *Silene vulgaris*, spring beauty *Claytonia perfoliata*, primrose *Primula vulgaris*, tuberous pea/earthnut *Lathyrus tuberosus*, narrow-leaved everlasting-pea *Lathyrus sylvestris*, tall melilot *Melilotus officinalis*, wood avens *Geum urbanum*, wild strawberry *Fragaria vesca*, bath asparagus *Ornithogalum pyrenaicum*, three-cornered garlic *Allium triquetrum*, wild/ Babington's leek *A. ampeloprasum*, hedge mustard *Sisymbrium officianale*, common scurvy-grass *Cochlearia officinalis*, garlic mustard *Alliaria petiolata*, cow parsley/wild chervil *Anthriscus sylvestris*, bur chervil *A. caucalis*, sweet cicely *Myrrhis odorata*, pignut *Conopodium majus*, ground-elder *Aegopodium podagraria*, hogweed *Heracleum sphondylium*, square-stalked willowherb *Epilobium tetragonum*, broad-leaved willowherb *E. montanum*, common/stinging nettle *Urtica dioica*, early purple orchid *Orchis mascula*, orpine/ midsummer men *Sedum telephium*, pale pink-sorrel *Oxalis incarnate*, sweet violet *Viola odorata*, cleavers/goose grass *Galium aparine*, sweet woodruff *G. odoratum*, giant bellflower *Campanula latifolia*, nettle-leaved bellflower *C. trachelium*, spiked rampion *Phyteuma spicatum*,

common lungwort *Pulmonaria officinalis*, ground-ivy *Glechoma hederacea*, white dead-nettle *Lamium album*, common calamint *Clinopodium ascendens*, lesser calamint *Clinopodium calamintha*, bastard balm *Melittis melissophyllum*, wall pennywort *Umbilicus rupestris* (on stony hedgebanks), wild strawberry *Fragaria vesca*, wood avens *Geum urbanum*, wormwood *Artemisa absinthium*, greater burdock *Arctium lappa*, lesser burdock *A. minus*, nipplewort *Lapsana communis*, yarrow *Achillea millefolium*. **Grasses:** Couch grass *Elytrigia repens*, tall fescue *Festuca arundinacea*. **Ferns:** Lady fern *Athyrium filix-femina*. **Poisonous:** Fool's parsley *Aethusa cynapium*, dog's mercury *Mercurialis perennis*, stinking hellebore *Helleborus foetidus*, green hellebore *H. viridis*, greater celandine *Chelidonium majus*, white bryony *Bryonia dioica*, foxglove *Digitalis purpurea*.

Roadsides

This habitat category includes many of the same species listed under hedges and hedgerows but also covers places where there is no hedge. Due to the presence of heavy metals and other contaminants from car exhausts, plants growing on busy roadsides are not fit for human consumption. In my view, however, foraging on quiet country lanes is fine, provided that you do not base your entire diet around food gathered from such locations (see Foraging Hazards, p.22). Eating plenty of brown seaweeds would be an added precaution, as the alginic acid that they contain binds to these heavy metals and removes them from the body. **Trees and shrubs:** Darwin's barberry *Berberis darwinii*, elder *Sambucus nigra*, brambles *Rubus fruticosus* agg., dog-rose *Rosa canina*, cherry plum *Prunus cerasifera*, stag's-horn sumach *Rhus typhina*. **Herbs:** Sweet violet *Viola odorata*, Japanese knotweed *Fallopia japonica*, black bindweed *F. convolvulus*, monk's rhubarb *Rumex psuedoalpinus*, curled dock *R. crispus*, lesser celandine *Ranunculus ficaria*, long-headed poppy *Papaver rhoeas dubium*, spear-leaved orache, *Atriplex prostrata*, garden orache *A. hortensis*, common orache *A. patula*, common mallow *Malva sylvestris*, spring beauty *Claytonia perfoliata*, white melilot *Melilotus albus*, corn spurrey *Spergula arvensis*, bladder campion *Silene vulgaris*, common nettle *Urtica dioica*, redshank *Persicaria maculosa*, tall rocket *Sisymbrium altissimum*, hedge mustard *S. officinale*, perennial wall-rocket *Diplotaxis teunuifolia*, warty cabbage *Bunias orientalis*, horseradish *Armoracia rusticana*, Danish scurvy grass *Cochlearia danica*, dittander *Lepidium latifolium*, hoary cress *L. draba*, annual wall-rocket *Diplotaxis muralis*, rape *Brassica napus*, black mustard *Brassica nigra*, wild turnip *Brassica rapa*, charlock *Sinapis arvensis*, white mustard *Sinapis alba*, wild radish *Raphanus raphanistrum*, wild mignonette *Reseda lutea*, reflexed stonecrop *Sedum rupestre*, orpine *S. telephium*, great burdock *Arctium lappa*, lesser burdock *A. minus*, prickly lettuce *Lactuca serriola*, wormwood *Artemisa absinthium*, salad burnet *Sanguisorba minor*, lady's mantle *Alchemilla glabra*, silverweed *Potentilla anserine*, round-leaved mint *Mentha suaveolens*, spearmint *M. spicata*, sand leek *Allium scorodoprasum*. **Poisonous:** Monk's-hood *Aconitum napellus*.

Walls (including base of walls)

This man-made environment provides a niche for several species that would otherwise grow on dry, rocky or, in the case of walls with lime mortar, alkaline environments.

Shrubs and vines: Darwin's barberry *Berberis darwinii*, traveller's joy *Clematis vitalba*, polypody *Polypodium vulgare*, Duke of Argyll's teaplant *Lycium barbarum/Chinese*. **Herbs:** Ivy-leaved toadflax *Cymbalaria muralis*,

love-in-a-mist *Nigella damascene*, Hottentot fig *Carpobrotus edulis*, bladder campion *Silene vulgaris*, eastern rocket *S. orientale*, perennial wall-rocket *Diplotaxis teunuifolia*, annual wall-rocket *D. muralis*, wall pennywort *Umbilicus rupestris*, reflexed stonecrop *Sedum rupestre*, white stonecrop *S. album*, trailing bellflower *Campanula poscharskyana*, adria bellflower *C. portenschlagiana*, lamb's lettuce *Valeriana locusta*, red valerian *Centranthus ruber*. **Ferns:** Maidenhair fern *Adiantum capillus-veneris*. **Poisonous:** Greater celandine *Chelidonium majus*.

Waste ground

Non-managed areas such as old bomb sites, neglected pasture and vacant building plots often provide rich pickings for foragers, especially where prolific perennials such as wild rocket, Japanese knotweed or nettles have found a foothold. Some of these areas are short lived, however. They are often the same places classed in this chapter as earthworks and disturbed ground, only a year or two on; often the purpose for which they were disturbed, such as clearing the ground for building, is put on hold but later resumed. Forage from them while you can!

Shrubs: Brambles *Rubus fruticosus* agg., dog-rose *Rosa canina*, wild plum *Prunus domestica*, barberry *Berberis vulgaris*. **Herbs:** Knotgrass *Polygonum aviculare*, Japanese knotweed *Fallopia japonica*, black bindweed *F. convolvulus*, wood dock *Rumex sanguineus*, curled dock *R. crispus*, redshank *Persicaria maculosa*, patience dock *Rumex patientia*, lesser celandine *Ranunculus ficaria*, Good-King-Henry *Chenopodium bonus-henricus*, fat hen *C. album*, many-seeded goosefoot *C. polyspermum*, common orache *Atriplex patula*, common amaranth *Amaranthus retroflexus*, green amaranth *A. hybridus*, common mallow *Malva sylvestris*, white melilot *Melilotus albus*, ribbed melilot *M. altissimus*, small melilot *M. indicus*, corn spurrey *Spergula* *arvensis*, common nettle *Urtica dioica*, tall rocket *Sisymbrium altissimum*, eastern rocket *S. orientale*, hedge mustard *S. officinale*, perennial wall-rocket *Diplotaxis teunuifolia*, horseradish *Armoracia rusticana*, shepherd's purse *Capsella bursa-pastoris*, hoary cress *Lepidium draba*, swine-cress *Coronopus squamatus*, lesser swine-cress *C. didymus didymus*, rape *Brassica napus*, black mustard *Brassica nigra*, white mustard *Sinapis alba*, hoary mustard *Hirschfeldia incana*, wild radish *Raphanus raphanistrum*, wild mignonette *Reseda lutea*, reflexed stonecrop *Sedum rupestre*, adria bellflower *Campanula portenschlagiana*, trailing bellflower *C. poscharskyana*, cleavers *Galium aparine*, red valerian *Centranthus ruber*, round-leaved mint *Mentha suaveolens*, spearmint *M. spicata*, peppermint *M. piperita*, wormwood *Artemisa absinthium*, great burdock *Arctium lappa*, lesser burdock *A. minus*, spear thistle *Cirsium vulgare*, beaked hawk's-beard *Crepis vesicaria*, prickly lettuce *Lactuca serriola*. **Grasses:** Couch grass *Elytrigia repens*. **Poisonous:** Greater celandine *Chelidonium majus*, white bryony *Bryonia dioica* (berries), foxglove *Digitalis purpurea*.

Arable land and gardens

These habitats provide ideal conditions for many annual plants that thrive on disturbed ground (see also earthworks and disturbed ground, below) as well as for perennials such as nettles or horseradish, which reproduce from root fragments; these persist despite repeated attempts to remove them.

Herbs: Lamb's lettuce *Valerianella locusta*, knotgrass *Polygonum aviculare*, black bindweed *Fallopia convolvulus*, fat hen *Chenopodium album*, common orache *Atriplex patula*, common amaranth *Amaranthus retroflexus*, green amaranth *A. hybridus*, corn spurrey *Spergula arvensis*, bladder campion *Silene vulgaris*, common poppy *Papaver rhoeas*, long-headed poppy *P. rhoeas dubium*, hedge mustard *Sinapis officinale*, shepherd's purse *Capsella bursa-pastoris*, hoary cress *Lepidium draba*, rape *Brassica napus*, wild turnip *Brassica rapa*, white mustard *Sinapis alba*, charlock *S. arvensis*, hoary mustard *Hirschfeldia incana*, wild radish *Raphanus raphanistrum*, cleavers *Galium aparine*, spear thistle *Cirsium vulgare*, perennial sow-thistle *Sonchus arvensis*, parsley piert *Aphanes arvensis*.

Earthworks and disturbed ground

Building sites, civil-engineering sites, forestry plantations following tree felling and sites of excavations all fall into this category. These kinds of habitats allow dormant seeds to germinate and give rise to often short-lived populations of plants known as pioneer species. These plants are often crowded out after the first year or so of growth by secondary colonizers, such as grasses or stinging nettles. Many of these species also appear in the list for arable land and gardens (see above), which is of course regularly disturbed, but for different reasons.

Herbs: Pale persicaria *Persicaria lapathifolia*, common poppy *Papaver rhoeas*, hedge mustard *Sinapis officinale*, shepherd's purse *Capsella bursa-pastoris*, hoary cress *Lepidium draba*, white mustard *Sinapis alba*, black mustard *Brassica nigra*, charlock *Brassica arvensis*, wild radish *Raphanus raphanistrum*, wild turnip *Brassica rapa*, field penny-cress *Thlaspi arvense*, hairy bitter-cress *Cardamine hirsuta*, annual wall-rocket *Diplotaxis muralis*, wild mignonette *Reseda lutea*, chickweed *Stellaria media*, perennial sow-thistle *Sonchus arvensis*, smooth sow-thistle *S. oleraceus*, prickly sow-thistle *S. asper*, nipplewort *Lapsana communis*, wall lettuce *Mycelis muralis*, spear thistle *Cirsium vulgare*, scented mayweed *Matricaria recutita*, pineappleweed *M. discoidea*, corn chamomile

Anthemis cotula, colt's foot *Tussilago farfara*, silverweed *Potentilla anserina*, parsley piert *Aphanes arvensis*, cleavers *Galium aparine*, corn spurrey *Spergula arvensis*, curled dock *Rumex crispus*, many-seeded goosefoot *Chenopodium polyspermum*, spear-leaved orache *Atriplex prostrata*, garden orache *A. hortensis*, common amaranth *Amaranthus retroflexus*, green amaranth *A. hybridus*, red dead-nettle *Lamium purpureum*, henbit *L. amplexicaule*, corn mint *Mentha arvensis*, crow garlic *Allium vineale*, black nightshade *Solanum nigra*, great pignut *Bunium bulbocastanum*, ground-elder *Aegopodium podagraria*, square-stalked willowherb *Epilobium tetragonum*, common evening primrose *Oenothera biennis*, procumbent yellow-sorrel *Oxalis corniculata*, upright yellow-sorrel *O. stricta*, ribwort plantain *Plantago lanceolata*, small nettle *Urtica urens*, stork's bill *Erodium cicutarium*. **Poisonous:** Thornapple *Datura stramonium*, green nightshade *Solanum physalifolium*, groundsel *Senecio vulgaris*, scarlet pimpernel *Anagalis arvensis*, creeping buttercup *Ranunculus repens*.

Cliffs

These are places that are exposed to extremes of weather and salt spray, so that plants that manage to gain and maintain a foothold tend to be quite hardy. With the exception of a few plants, such as sea campion and sea plantain, plant communities on grassland at the tops of cliffs tend to be similar to other grassland in the same locality.

Trees and shrubs: Hazel *Corylus avellana*, barberry *Berberis vulgaris*, dog-rose *Rosa canina*, blackthorn *Prunus spinosa*, rowan *Sorbus aucuparia*, sea buckthorn *Hippophae rhamnoides*.
Herbs: Wild cabbage *Brassica oleracea*, sea radish *Raphanus maritimus*, Danish scurvy grass *Cochlearia danica*, black mustard *Brassica nigra*, sea plantain *Plantago maritima*, buck's-horn plantain *P. coronopus*, sea beet *Beta vulgaris*, common orache *Atriplex patula* (on seabird colonies), biting stonecrop *Sedum acre*, spear thistle *Cirsium vulgare*, colt's-foot *Tussilago farfara*.

Rocky cliffs

Rock samphire *Crithmum maritimum*, common scurvy-grass *Cochlearia officinalis*, Roseroot *Sedum rosa*.

Heaths

Heaths are rather species-poor habitats, characterized by gorse, heather and dry, acidic soil, usually on sand or gravel. Heavily grazed heaths become more grassy and are often called moors, but this term is also used to describe wetter, upland heaths. Heaths are similar to bogs and contain some of the same species; the main difference lies in their low moisture content and the absence of peat.

Trees and shrubs: Silver birch *Betula pendula*, downy birch *B. pubescens*, dwarf birch *B. nana*, Scots pine *Pinus sylvestris*, common juniper *Juniperus communis*, broom *Cytisus scoparius*, gorse *Ulex europaeus*, cranberry *Vaccinium oxycoccos*, cowberry *V. vitis-idaea*, bog-bilberry *V. uliginosum*, bilberry *V. myrtillus*, dewberry *Rubus caesius*, raspberry *Rubus idaeus*, brambles *R. fruticosus* agg., juneberry *Amelanchier lamarkii*. **Herbs:** Sheep's sorrel *Rumex acetosella*, sneezewort *Alchemilla ptarmica*, garden asparagus *Asparagus officinalis*, common wintergreen *Pyrola minor*, large thyme *Thymus pulegioides*, wood sage *Teucrium scorodonia*, Breckland thyme *Thymus serpyllum*, bittervetch *Lathyrus linifolius*, lousewort *Pedicularis sylvatica*, sea plantain *Plantago maritima*. **Ferns:** Bracken *Pteridium aquilinum*. **Poisonous:** Scarlet pimpernel *Anagalis arvensis*, foxglove *Digitalis purpurea*.

Fens and bogs

These two damp habitats differ mostly in the kind of soil found beneath the vegetation, which in turn depends on from where they derive their moisture. Fens are mostly fed by underground water sources and contain mineral deposits from underground rocks. Because most rocks are alkaline, the soil beneath fens tends to be alkaline, but it can be more acid if the local rocks are sandstone or gritstone, for example. Bogs are generally watered solely by rainfall, which if anything tends to be slightly acidic.

Fens

Much more species-rich than bogs, due to the generally alkaline character of underlying soils. This is not really reflected in the number of edible species, however. They tend to occur at lower altitudes than bogs in the British Isles, but sometimes, where underground water sources are present, upland fens known as flushes occur in the middle of bogs or heaths. **Trees and shrubs:** Bird cherry *Prunus padus* (in wooded fens). **Herbs:** Common nettle *Urtica dioica,* hoary willowherb *Epilobium parviflorum,* lady's smock *Cardamine pratensis,* sneezewort *Alchemilla ptarmica,* red currant *Ribes rubrum,* common valerian *Valeriana officinalis,* marsh thistle *Cirsium palustre,* rough hawkbit *Leontodon hispidus,* alternate-leaved golden-saxifrage *Chrysoplenium alternifolium,* meadowsweet *Filipendula ulmaria,* great burnet *Sanguisorba officinalis.* **Grasses:** common reed *Phragmites communis australis.* **Poisonous:** Yellow pimpernel *Lysimachia nemorum.*

Bogs

Similar to heath but more species diverse. The soil of bogs is comprised of acid peat made from partially decomposed plant remains, which tend to be acidic. In most of the British Isles, they generally occur at higher altitudes, where there is higher rainfall and lower temperatures, both of which help maintain moisture levels. The exceptions to this are the lowland blanket bogs of western Ireland, where there is much higher rainfall.
Shrubs: Crowberry *Empetrum nigra,* small cranberry *Vaccinium microcarpum,* cranberry *V. oxycoccos,* cowberry *V. vitis-idaea,* bog-bilberry *V. uliginosum,* bilberry *V. myrtillus,* cloudberry *Rubus chamaemorus.* **Herbs:** Sneezewort *Alchemilla ptarmica,* sheep's sorrel *Rumex acetosella,* lousewort *Pedicularis sylvatica,* opposite-leaved golden-saxifrage *Chrysoplenium oppositifolium.* **Grasses:** Common reed *Phragmites communis.*

Ponds, lakes, rivers and other freshwater habitats

Like woodland, these kinds of habitats are particularly easy to locate if you are planning your foraging outings by perusing an Ordnance Survey map. They are also quite intensively managed, with species such as water-cress, reedmace and yellow water-lily regularly being pulled out and discarded to keep them clear. It is a shame that these plants are not managed and, more to the point, eaten by local people.

In the water

More than half of these species are monocotyledons.
Herbs: Water-cress *Rorippa nasturtium-aquaticum,* water celery *Apium nodiflorum,* yellow water-lily *Nuphar lutea,* reedmace/bulrush *Typha latifolia,* arrowhead *Sagittaria sagitifolia,* cape pondweed *Aponogeton distachyos,* sweet flag *Acorus calamus,* flowering-rush *Butomus umbellatus.* **Grasses:** Floating sweet-grass *Glyceria fluitans.*

At the water's edge

Be sure to read the entry on liver fluke (see Foraging Hazards, p.23) before harvesting any of these plants.

Herbs: Marsh marigold *Caltha palustris*, mountain sorrel *Oxyria digyna*, redshank *Persicaria maculosa*, pale persicaria *P. lapathifolia*, water-pepper *P. hydropiper*, large bitter-cress *Cardamine amara*, monkey flower *Mimulus guttatus*, blue-flowered water-speedwell *Veronica anagallis-aquatica*, brooklime *Veronica beccabunga*, water mint *Mentha aquatica*. **Grasses and sedges:** Sweet galingale *Cyperus longus*, sea club-rush *Bolboschoenus maritimus*, common reed *Phragmites communis*. **Poisonous:** Hemlock water-dropwort *Oenanthe crocata*, fine-leaved water dropwort *O. aquatica*, tubular water dropwort *O. fistulosa*, cowbane *Cicuta virosa*.

On the banks

Trees and shrubs: Hazel *Corylus avellana*, walnut *Juglans regia*, red currant *Ribes rubrum*, downy currant *R. spicatum*, mountain currant *R. alpinum*, guelder-rose *Viburnum opulus*, field-rose *Rosa arvensis*, dog-rose *R. canina*, bird cherry *Prunus padus*, rowan *Sorbus aucuparia*. **Herbs:** Japanese knotweed *Fallopia japonica*, monk's rhubarb *Rumex psuedoalpinus*, lesser celandine *Ranunculus ficaria*, black mustard *Brassica nigra*, wild turnip *Brassica rapa*, pink purslane *Claytonia sibirica*, blinks *Montia fontana*, ramsons *Allium ursinum*, few-flowered garlic *A. paradoxum*, chives *A. schoenprasum*, bistort *Persicaria bistorta*, purple-loosestrife *Lythrum salicaria*, wavy bitter-cress *Cardamine flexuosa*, horseradish *Armoracia rusticana*, winter-cress *Barbarea vulgaris*, water chickweed *Myoston aquaticum*, common mallow *Malva sylvestris*, spearmint *Mentha spicata*, marsh woundwort *Stachys pulustris*, square-stalked willowherb *E. tetragonum*, hoary willowherb *E. parviflorum*, sweet cicely *Myrrhis odorata*, silverweed *Potentilla anserina*, sneezewort *Alchemilla ptarmica*, hogweed *Heracleum sphondylium*, common nettle *Urtica dioica*, wild chervil *Anthriscus sylvestris*, white horehound *Marrubium vulgare*, great burdock *Arctium lappa*, opposite-leaved golden-saxifrage *Chrysoplenium oppositifolium*, alternate-leaved golden-saxifrage *C. alternifolium*, meadowsweet *Filipendula ulmaria*, water avens *Geum rivale*, lady's mantle *Alchemilla glabra*. **Ferns:** Lady fern *Athyrium filix-femina* (in woods). **Poisonous:** Monk's-hood *Aconitum napellus*, columbine *Aquilegia vulgaris*, foxglove *Digitalis purpurea*.

Coastal habitats

Salt water

Marine algae: Dulse *Palmaria palmate*, laver *Porphyra* agg., sea lettuce *Ulva lactuca*, gutweed *U. intestinalis*, dead men's fingers *Codium fragile*, oarweed *Laminaria digitata*, sugar kelp *L. saccharina*, pepper dulse *Osmundea pinnatifida*, Irish moss *Chondrus crispus*, false Irish moss/grapestone *Mastocarpus stellatus*, bladderwrack *Fucus vesiculosus*, toothed wrack *F. serratus*, thongweed *Himanthalia elongata*, dabberlocks *Alaria esculenta*.

Salt marsh

Salt marsh occurs either on the coast or, more often, on tidal inlets and estuaries. It is subdivided into various zones that spend more or less time submerged. Some plants only occur in one or other of them. The sub-species of marsh samphire, for example, all tend to prefer different zones. This is a helpful tool for telling them apart, although I have not gone to the lengths of describing them all since all of them are delicious. Plants growing in or near salt water

are halophytes, meaning they can tolerate exposure to salt. They are also often succulent.
Herbs: *Lower salt marsh:* Marsh samphire *Salicornia* agg., annual sea-blite *Suada maritima*, sea-purslane *Halimione portulacoides*, golden samphire *Inula crithmoides*, spear-leaved orache *Atriplex prostrata*, sea aster *Aster tripolium*, perennial sow-thistle *Sonchus arvensis*, sea plantain *Plantago maritima*, English scurvy-grass *Cochlearia anglica*, sea club-rush *Bolboschoenus maritimus*. **Upper salt marsh:** Marsh samphire *Salicornia* agg., Common scurvy-grass *Cochlearia officinalis*, dittander *Lepidium latifolium*, curled dock *Rumex crispus,* wild celery *Apium graveolans*, silverweed *Potentilla anserina*, shrubby sea-blite *Suada vera,* annual sea-blite *S. maritima*, spear-leaved orache *Atriplex prostrata*.

Brackish dykes and tidal-river edges

Brackish dykes contain water that is salty, but much less so than sea or estuary water.
Herbs: Marsh mallow *Althea officinalis,* wild celery *Apium graveolans*, lesser reedmace *Typha angustifolia*, sea aster *Aster tripolium*, dittander *Lepidium latifolium*, sea beet *Beta vulgaris*, wild carrot *Dacus carota*, alexanders *Smyrnium olustrum*, spear-leaved orache *Atriplex prostrata*.
Grasses and sedges: Common reed *Phragmites communis australis*, sea club-rush *Bolboschoenus maritimus*. **Marine algae:** Sea lettuce *Ulva lactuca*, gutweed *U. intestinalis*. **Poisonous:** Hemlock water-dropwort *Oenanthe crocata*.

Shingle beaches

Shingle beaches are a type of foreshore – the other being sandy beaches (see coastal sand stretches, p.41) – which is the area above the high tidemark during spring tides. Nutrients are fed into the soil from rotting seaweed and other organic matter deposited by the tides, and plants often have very deep roots systems that enable them to tap into underground freshwater sources. Shingle beaches are unique and, internationally, rare habitats formed by the accumulation of pebbles on the foreshore. Britain has something like 75 per cent of Europe's vegetated shingle habitat. Some species, such as sea kale and sea pea, are almost exclusively found on shingle and therefore have a fairly small international distribution, despite their abundance in particular localities. According to Chris Gibson of Natural England: 'Shingle, especially vegetated shingle, forms a very thin layer over the substrate, which is inherently vulnerable to mechanical disturbance, trampling etc. At Dungeness [on the south coast of Kent], one can still see the track (as twin lines of open, non-vegetated ground) used in the erection of a fence more than 40 years ago! Vegetated shingle also often lies close to areas much frequented by recreational humans, increasing the risk of exposure of the habitat to the threat of trampling.' See **sea kale** and **sea pea** for more detail.
Shrubs: Japanese rose *Rosa rugosa*, burnet rose *R. pimpinellifolia*. **Herbs:** Knotgrass *Polygonum aviculare*, sheep's sorrel *Rumex acetosella*, common sorrel *R. acetosa*, curled dock *R. crispus,* sea holly *Eryngium maritimum*, rock samphire *Crithmum maritimum*, Danish scurvygrass *Cochlearia danica*, common scurvy-grass *C. officinalis*, dittander *Lepidium latifolium*, swinecress *Coronopus squamatus*, lesser swine-cress *C. didymus*, black mustard *Brassica nigra*, sea kale *Crambe maritima*, wild cabbage *Brassica oleracea*, sea radish *Raphanus maritimus*, sea beet *Beta vulgaris*, prickly saltwort *Salsola kali*, shrubby sea-blite *Suada vera*, spear-leaved orache *Atriplex prostrata*, sea campion *Silene uniflora*, sea sandwort *Honckenya peploides*, oysterplant *Mertensia maritima*, bristly oxtongue *Picris echioides*, colt's-foot *Tussilago farfara*, yarrow *Achillea millefolium*, biting stonecrop *Sedum acre*, white stonecrop *S. album*, cleavers *Galium aparine*, lamb's lettuce *Valeriana locusta*.

Poisonous: Ragwort *Senecio jacobaea*, yellow-horned poppy *Glaucium flavum*.

Coastal sand stretches and dunes

Parts of sand dunes are dominated by grass and so constitute a kind of grassland. In fact, it is grasses such as marram grass *Ammophila arenaria* and sand couch *Elytrigia juncea* that bind together the sand in order that the sand dune becomes a stable habitat in which many of the later colonizers are able to grow.

Shrubs: Duke of Argyll's teaplant *Lycium barbarum/Chinese*, sea buckthorn *Hippophae rhamnoides*, Japanese rose *Rosa rugosa*, burnet rose *Rosa pimpinellifolia*. **Herbs:** Knotgrass *Polygonum aviculare*, sheep's sorrel *Rumex acetosella*, curled dock *Rumex crispus*, traveller's joy *Clematis vitalba*, Hottentot fig *Carpobrotus edulis*, hoary mustard *Hirschfeldia incana*, common scurvy-grass *Cochlearia officinalis*, Danish scurvy grass *C. danica*, hoary cress *Lepidium draba*, horseradish *Armoracia rusticana*, perennial wall-rocket *Diplotaxis teunuifolia*, sea radish *Raphanus maritimus*, bur chervil *Anthriscus caucalis*, wild clary *Salvia verbenaca*, white horehound *Marrubium vulgare*, sea holly *Eryngium maritimum*, wild carrot *Dacus carota*, white melilot *Melilotus albus*, ribbed melilot *M. altissimus*, sea plantain *Plantago maritima*, buck's-horn plantain *P. coronopus*, sea beet *Beta vulgaris*, prickly saltwort *Salsola kali*, spear-leaved orache *Atriplex prostrata*, sea campion *Silene uniflora*, sea sandwort *Honckenya peploides*, corn spurrey *Spergula arvensis*, biting stonecrop *Sedum acre*, white stonecrop *Sedum album*, crow garlic *Allium vineale*, oyster plant *Mertensia maritima*, cleavers *Galium aparine*, lesser celandine *Ranunculus ficaria*, lamb's lettuce *Valeriana locusta*, bristly oxtongue *Picris echioides*, colt's-foot *Tussilago farfara*, yarrow *Achillea millefolium*, great burdock *Arctium lappa*, lesser burdock *A. minus*, spear thistle *Cirsium vulgare*, salsify *Tragopogon porrifolius*, dewberry *Rubus caesius*, silverweed *Potentilla anserine*, sand leek *Allium scorodoprasum*. **Poisonous:** Ragwort *Senecio jacobaea*, yellow-horned poppy *Glaucium flavum*, bulbous buttercup *Ranunculus bulbosus*.

Sea kale in flower

41

2
Plants

Flowering plants
Dicotyledons

AMARANTH FAMILY
Amaranthaceae

Amaranths are quite tall plants, similar to fat hen and other *Chenopodiaceae* species, but with longer, untoothed leaves. Garden plant love-lies-bleeding is a species of amaranth; if you know it you will be familiar with the general form of amaranth leaves and flower spikes. Amaranths in flower are unmistakable; the plants are upwards of 1m high at this stage; the flowers form long, fuzzy spikes at the top.

Cultivated amaranth seed was the staple food of the Aztecs and was destroyed by the Spanish invaders; growing or even possessing amaranth was outlawed. By destroying their food traditions, the Spanish general Cortés took away part of the soul of the Aztecs, a calculated aspect of their subjugation. It makes me wonder what we have lost by becoming disconnected from our own food heritage, but my wondering turns to optimism when I consider the present renaissance of British food. In India, amaranth has two names, which reflect the esteem in which it is held: *Rajgira* or 'king's seed' and *Ramdana* or 'seed sent by God'. Recent nutritional analysis vindicates such respect: amaranth has more protein than any other grain; it also contains the amino acid lysine, making it as good a source of protein as meat or fish. The leaves are also high in vitamins C and beta-carotene. Since the 1970s there has been a revival of interest in amaranth as an alternative food crop in North America, where it has become popular as a health-food grain; it is also widespread as a wild plant. Sadly, it is not so widespread in the British Isles, but where it does occur, nearly always as an agricultural weed, it is often quite persistent. Two species of amaranth occur most often, though others occasionally grow from seed from birdcages or contaminated grain.

Amaranthus hybridus

Green Amaranth

DISTRIBUTION Native of South and Central America. Up to 300m. In England, mostly southeast and east, while sporadic elsewhere and mostly absent Yorkshire, Cumbria, Cheviot Hills, County Durham and Cornwall; in Wales, found only in single locality in

Pembrokeshire; in Scotland, found only in single locality in Renfrewshire; in Ireland, in three localities in Wexford, Limerick and Clare; present Isle of Man and Isles of Scilly.

HABITAT Cultivated land and waste ground, often alongside fat hen and other *Chenopodiaceae*.

DESCRIPTION Yellowish-green, hairless annual, upright and long-branched. Leaves oval and wavy edged. Flowers in a dense spike.

Amaranthus retroflexus

Common Amaranth

DISTRIBUTION Up to 300m. Native of North America but widely introduced in Europe, including the British Isles: in England, mostly found south of line Spurn Head–Southport and especially Home Counties, Somerset and Dorset, more sparse north of line; in Wales, isolated areas in most counties; in Scotland, only in small areas of Kirkcudbrightshire, Lanarkshire, Dunbartonshire, Midlothian and Moray; in Ireland, scarce, mostly in Limerick and Tipperary, absent north except two 10sq km in west Mayo; present on Isle of Man, Isles of Scilly and Channel Islands.

HABITAT Cultivated land and waste ground.

DESCRIPTION Hairy, greyish-green annual, upright and branched, up to 80cm high. Leaves oval and wavy edged. Flowers green, July–October, in a dense spike with a few leaves.

USES/RECIPES *(for amaranth generally)* Grain can be used in bread, cooked like rice, or to thicken other dishes. Again, it is mucilaginous, so you may prefer to use it with other grains. Leaves are good as a green vegetable. In Greece, amaranths (*vlita*) are a commonly used green vegetable of the summer months. In Lebanon, the leaves are chopped and boiled then fried with an almost equal weight of onions. For Native American Tarahumara peoples in the Mexican sierras, the seedlings of wild amaranths (as well as goosefoots and brassicas), known as Quelites, are a vital food source in spring–early summer before the

Nathan Outlaw's Amaranth Soup With Smoked Oil

(this recipe works just as well with **mallow**)
Serves 4

For soup: Finely chop 1 small onion, and 2 garlic cloves, and fry for 1 minute. Add 1 large potato, peeled and thinly sliced; cover with 1 litre vegetable stock. Simmer until the potato is cooked. Fry 300g amaranth briefly until wilted. Blend with other ingredients for 3 minutes or until smooth. Season, then chill the soup over ice to retain the green colour. Chill until required.

For oil: Put 200ml sunflower oil in a metal bowl that will fit into an old pan. Heat the old pan and add 100g oak chippings; when they start to smoke put the bowl in the pan and cover with a cold, damp tea towel. Cool the tea towel in cold water four times over a 40-minute period then remove the pan from the heat. Leave covered until cold.
To serve: Reheat soup, decant into bowls and add a soup spoon of oil to each bowl.

cultivated crops mature. Quelties (for example, young amaranth, fat hen, spear-leaved orache or charlock) are cooked by frying some onion and garlic until soft and slightly brown then adding the lightly steamed or boiled greens and seasoning with chilli; pinto beans or bacon can also be added. As with **mallow**, the cooked leaves are quite mucilaginous or slimy; this characteristic can be used to good effect as a thickener or to counteract coarseness in other ingredients, for example brown rice.

Harvesting/processing notes To harvest the grain, you need to keep an eye on the plants until they reach the optimum stage. Check them regularly until a few seeds drop out when you shake them, at which point cut off the tops and take them home for processing. Rub them on a fine mesh or sieve to loosen the seeds from their husks (holes no less than 3mm wide); most of the seed should drop through straight away. Winnow (see **grasses**, processing, p.324) and allow to dry; then store in a dry place.

²⁄₃ × life size

BALSAM FAMILY
Balsaminaceae

Impatiens grandiflora

Indian Balsam

DISTRIBUTION In England, pretty much throughout but absent most Northumberland, Lincolnshire and parts of Yorkshire and Kent; in Wales, widespread, although less so in Powys; in Scotland, found mostly Argyll and on east coast, especially Fife, Tayside and Lothian, and almost entirely absent the Highlands; in Ireland, widespread in Ulster, also quite common Wicklow, Wexford, Cork and Kerry, and sporadic elsewhere; present Channel Islands and Isle of Man.

HABITAT River banks, damp waste ground and woodland.

DESCRIPTION Invasive garden escape. Up to 2m high. Reddish stem. Red, toothed leaves in whorls of 3. Flowers pink with curved spurs. Seeds in long, pointed capsules, which explode when touched.

NOTES This plant is included mostly to share the joy of touching the seed pods and seeing them unfurl like a spring. It is an added bonus that the seeds themselves are edible. The sensation experienced as the pod case propels the seeds, catapult fashion, is as if some more animate life form is hurling itself against your skin.

USES/RECIPES The seeds can be nibbled on the go, added to breads, toasted and added to salads.

HARVESTING NOTES Catch the seeds by cupping one hand in front of the pod while touching it with the other.

BARBERRY FAMILY
Berberidaceae

Berberis darwinii

Darwin's Barberry

DISTRIBUTION Up to 300m. Native to Chile and Patagonia. In England, scattered locations throughout except the northeast, Cumberland and most of East Midlands, more common in Surrey, Berkshire and the southwest; in Wales, sporadic in coastal counties with small clusters in Carmarthenshire and Caernarvonshire; few scattered sites in Ireland, the majority in Ulster; in Scotland, few locations in Central Lowlands, Moray, Caithness, Westerness, Main Argyll, Wigtownshire and Kircudbrightshire; present on Channel Islands and Isle of Man.

HABITAT Woods, roadsides, hedges, walls, gardens; becoming more popular as a landscaping plant in public amenities but also occurs naturalized from bird-sown seed. In New Zealand, a national eradication pro-

⅕ × life size

gramme is under way to prevent it taking over the forest under-storey, as rhododendron has in Wales and Scotland.

DESCRIPTION Small evergreen shrub with tiny, dark green spiny leaves, somewhat like miniature holly. Peachy-orange flowers in winter take a long time to mature into dark blue berries with a whitish bloom that look a bit like blueberries, and are finally ready to eat in July.

NOTES A widely planted garden shrub, Darwin's barberry is naturalized in some parts of the UK. Naturalized or otherwise, the fruits are delicious and mostly overlooked. The *Gardeners' Chronicle* of 1882 recorded how cottagers in Devon preserved the ripe berries, and their children ate them from the bushes with great enthusiasm. Cottagers or commoners lived by exercising rights of common on the common land of their villages. This mostly consisted of grazing their animals and gathering timber, but the essence of their way of life was to utilize local resources of all kinds for their everyday needs. The absence of this mindset

explains the uneaten berries on modern bushes; eating them from landscaped areas of supermarket premises seems a fitting way to reverse the trend!

USES/RECIPES Berries contain several quite chewy and slightly bitter seeds; remove them by pushing raw or cooked fruit through a sieve with the back of a ladle. Or just eat the berries off the bush and spit the seeds out. Use to make jam, sorbet, pies, summer puddings, fools, etc.

HARVESTING NOTES Drag your thumb and forefinger down the bunches, allowing the berries to drop into your container.

Berberis vulgaris

Barberry

DISTRIBUTION Up to 395m. In England, scattered throughout but less scarce in southeast Yorkshire, Fens, east Kent, Devon and Cornwall; in Wales, found most counties except much of Pembrokeshire, Glamorgan, Merioneth, Caernarvonshire, Anglesey and Flintshire; in Scotland, mostly Central Lowlands and southeast in Forth and Borders with scattered sites in eastern Coastal Lowlands north to Caithness, plus scattering in West and East Highland and Grampian Mountains; in Ireland, few sites in Kerry, Clare and Fermanagh; present Channel Islands and Isle of Man.

HABITAT Old hedgerows, scrub, wasteland, copses.

DESCRIPTION Deciduous shrub. Twigs yellowish and grooved, with spines mostly in groups of three. Leaves oval with a tapering base, with tiny spines around the edges.

Summer clusters of bright yellow flowers hang from the branches, making it very conspicuous, as do the small sausage-shaped berries that ripen September onwards, pink at first then bright red.

SIMILAR SPECIES The garden shrub Thunberg's barberry *B. thunbergii* is similar in overall form; looking it up at a garden centre will put you on the right track for finding barberry. It has smaller, often purple leaves and smaller (mildly poisonous) berries.

NOTES Barberry occasionally occurs as a garden escape and was widely planted as an ornamental and for its fruit from medieval times; in later centuries it was frequently planted in hedgerows. Remains found at the site of the neolithic flint mine at Grimes Graves in Norfolk suggest it is either native or was brought here by neolithic settlers. Barberry is host to the rust fungus *Puccinia grammis,* which causes blight on wheat crops. It was grubbed out and burnt in wheat-growing areas during the nineteenth century but persists in many lowland areas where wheat is not grown. It is also presently part of a species-recovery plan for the barberry carpet moth *Pareulype berberata,* the caterpillars of which feed on its leaves. This may help revive the fortunes of barberry, especially as there is no longer a conflict of interest with wheat farmers: most contemporary strains of wheat are

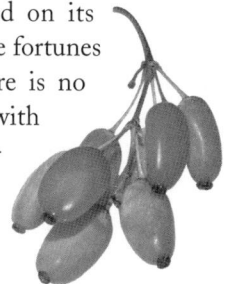

resistant to the rust that caused so much trouble in the past.

USES/RECIPES Leaves are good to season meat or raw as a substitute for **sorrel**. Dried berries can be ground and used in a similar way to sumach: this is another lemon substitute; also another berry to made into a jelly for serving with meat. But they look too interesting to be used in these ways – candied berries as a garnish for meat are more fitting. Crème brûlée or custard tart with barberries, whose sharpness cuts through the sweet, fatty richness and silky luxuriance [PW].

BENEFITS Contains isoquinoline alkaloids, berberine and berbamine, all of which are thought to be cancer inhibiting. Berberine is also strongly antibacterial and amebicidal and stimulates bile secretion, which helps with gallbladder pain, gallstones and jaundice.

Mahonia aquifolium

Oregon Grape

DISTRIBUTION Up to 300m. Found throughout England, more abundant in Midlands and further south, except Fens, east Kent and Sussex, Devon and Cornwall, where more scattered; in Wales, scattered localities but less in Glamorgan and Gwynedd; in Scotland, mostly south of Highland Boundary Fault , Stonehaven–Helensburgh, except few sites in eastern Coastal Lowlands between the Fault and Moray Firth; very few sites in Ireland, all southeast of Ulster; present on Channel Islands and Isle of Man.

HABITAT Hedges, woods, gardens, parks and other public amenities.

DESCRIPTION Small, evergreen shrub with dark green, spiny holly-like leaves and bright yellow flowers in dense clusters, which later produce blue fruit in clusters resembling bunches of small grapes. Flowers January–May; fruit ripe June onwards.

USES/RECIPES Berries for jams and jellies, or sauce for serving with lamb. Follow Elderberry game sauce recipe (see p.203), substituting 50g oregon grapes or 1 tablespoon juice for elderberries. Duck gravy: make stock from duck bones, then add plenty of port and finally a few oregon grapes to finish. Serve slices of pink, roasted wild mallard breast with sea beet or wild cabbage, some little, boiled new potatoes, rolled in butter and chopped sweet cicely or wild chervil and the grapey/porty duck gravy on top [JDW].

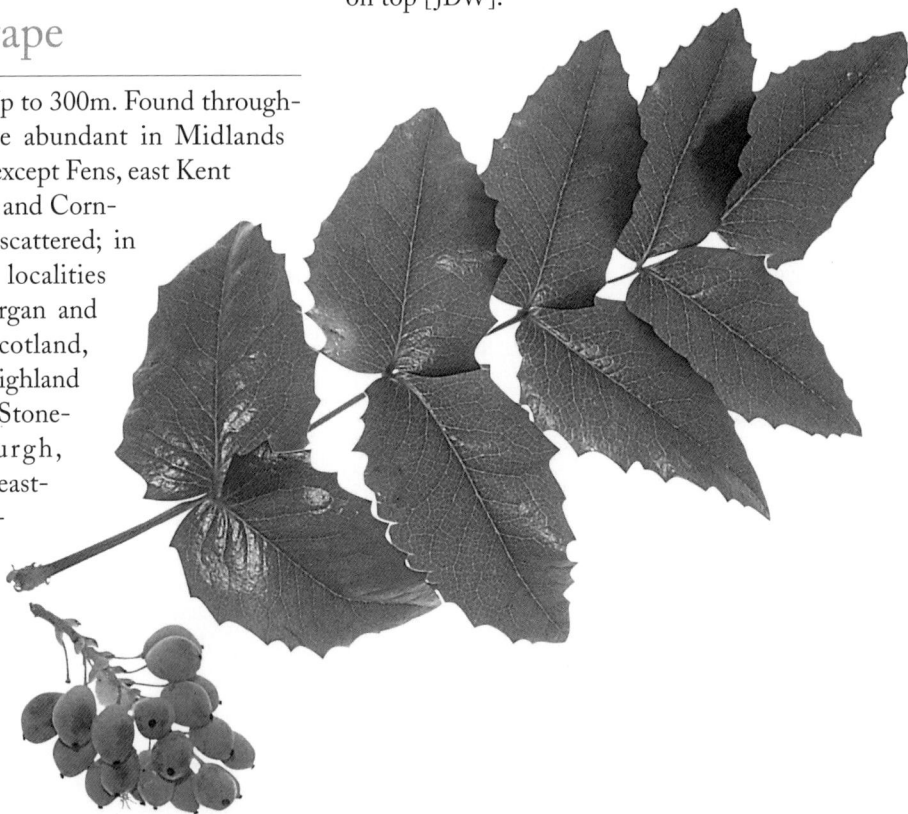

BEDSTRAW FAMILY
Rubiaceae

This family is easily identified by its distinctive whorled-leaf arrangement and scrambling growth. A few other plants have similar whorls, but none produces the spreading masses characteristic of plants like cleavers, sweet woodruff and lady's bedstraw. Most people have encountered cleavers, the commonest bedstraw species, if only through its little round burs, or bits of sticky leaf and stalk that stick to clothes after a walk.

These plants are familiar features of the British and Irish countryside: the fuzzy summer haze of flowers produced by hedge and lady's bedstraw on banks and roadsides; ancient woodlands marked by the presence of magical dark green carpets of starlike sweet woodruff leaves, which sparkle in May with little white flowers. Bedstraws also contribute a ubiquitous element of city life: coffee. Don't bother looking for wild coffee plants though – coffee doesn't grow in the British Isles. But if you want a passable native substitute, pick some of those burs off your socks and roast them.

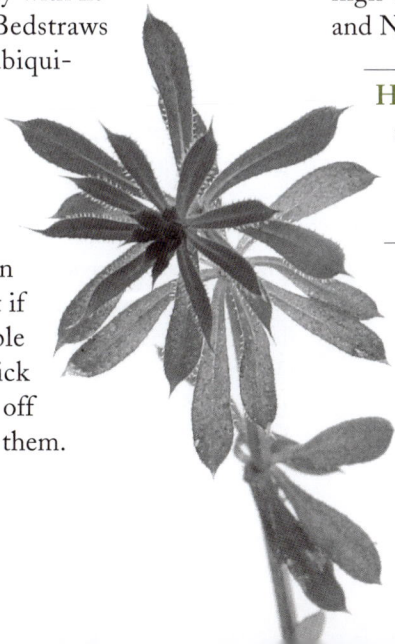

Galium aparine

Cleavers/Goose Grass

DISTRIBUTION Up to 440m. Widespread throughout British Isles except in Scotland, high-altitude areas of Grampian Mountains and North West Highlands.

HABITAT Gardens, roadsides, hedges, arable fields – mostly close to human activity of some sort – but also scree and shingle.

DESCRIPTION Very common native annual. Stems are made sticky by downwardly curved prickles. Leaves, in whorls of 6–8, are up to 50mm long, pale green and thin, with sticky, prickly edges. Young shoots grow upright; the layers of whorls quite geometric and ordered but they sprawl out as they grow, eventually forming a thick, tangled mass. Tiny greenish-white flowers grow in loose clusters from the axil of the upper leaves; the fruits are the familiar sticky burs.

SIMILAR SPECIES Sweet woodruff has smooth stems and leaves and white flowers.

USES/RECIPES Leaves and stems can be steamed and used as a vegetable in their own right, or added to soups and other dishes. They have a mild, fresh pealike flavour. Don't be put off by their coarse stickiness, which disappears once cooked. Gather burs just as they have turned brown, dry them thoroughly then rub them inside a pillow-case to remove the burry coating. Finally, toast them in a hot skillet or other cast-iron pan, shaking or stirring constantly to prevent burning, to make a mild coffee substitute.

HARVESTING NOTES Only gather young tops: older growth tends to be more stringy and bitter. Harvesting burs can be effortless: just walk through an area thick with cleavers and comb them off your clothes when you get home.

Galium odoratum

Sweet Woodruff

DISTRIBUTION Up to 640m. Widespread in England, except Bodmin Moor, Sussex, Kent, Essex, Suffolk, Fens, Leicestershire and northeast Yorkshire; in Wales, except highest areas of Cambrian Mountains and parts of Glamorgan; in Scotland, except Southern Uplands and northeast above Central Lowlands (except Glen Mor); in Ireland, present all counties but more widespread in east, central and north;

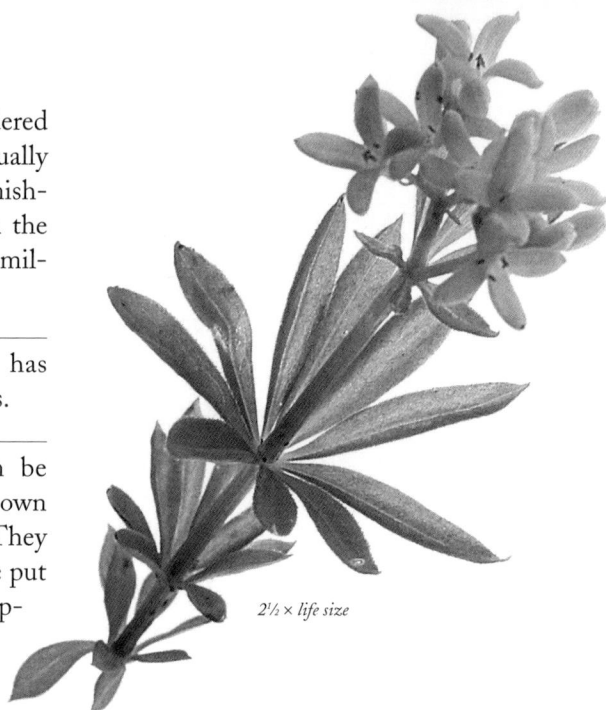

2½ × life size

also found in Channel Islands, on Jersey; introduced to Isle of Man.

HABITAT Shaded places, mostly deciduous woodland and on hedgebanks.

DESCRIPTION Native perennial, forming mats on woodland floors. Stems are hairless, as are the leaves that occur in whorls of 6–9. Flowers are white, 4–7mm wide, in several loose clusters at the top of the stalks, above the final whorl.

SIMILAR SPECIES Cleavers sometimes grows alongside sweet woodruff, which has larger flowers and wider, glossier leaves; both its leaves and stalks lack the sticky bristles of cleavers.

NOTES Sweet woodruff is a ground-cover plant of ancient woodland and can be prolific, forming gorgeous carpets of green geometric leaves peppered with starlike white flowers. The petals are covered with spherical structures, which, viewed under a microscope, have the appearance of tiny pearls.

USES/RECIPES The flavour of the leaves, somewhere between almond and vanilla, derives from the chemical coumarin, which also gives the familiar scent to hay; the coumarin content increases with drying. The leaves were traditionally used for flavouring drinks: add whole dried leaves to apple juice, cider, elderflower cordial or other cold drinks and leave to infuse for at least an hour. Fresh or dried leaves can be used as flavouring for cooked apple, milk-based puddings, such as ice cream, custard, panna cotta, etc., cooked beetroot and beetroot stocks and dressings [RR], in rabbit and chicken dishes or stuffing. The raw leaves have less flavour; fresh leaves become more flavourful as they cook.

HARVESTING NOTES Leaves prior to and during flowering are more tender and flavourful.

HAZARDS The conversion of coumarin to dicoumarin when plants are dried under damp conditions (see p.21) may explain why this plant has not been exploited commercially in recent years. However, the plant is quite safe if dried quickly and stored in a dry, sealed container.

Galium verum

Lady's Bedstraw

DISTRIBUTION Up to 780m. Widespread throughout British Isles: in England, except Exmoor, Dartmoor, Bodmin Moor, parts of Weald and Cheshire and Lancashire plains; in Wales, except parts of Carmarthenshire, Pembrokeshire and Montgomeryshire; in Scotland, except Caithness, east Sutherland, East and West Ross, Westerness, Main Argyll and Isle of Lewis; in Ireland, only

absent from highland areas and parts of Leitrim, Cavan, Monaghan and Fermanagh.

HABITAT Roadside verges, meadows and hedgebanks.

DESCRIPTION Native perennial with creeping stems and whorls of 8–10 thin leaves, which have fine points on otherwise blunt ends and downward-turned edges. Flowers form rounded, hazy clusters at the tops of the stems.

SIMILAR SPECIES The only other yellow-flowered bedstraw found in the British Isles is crosswort *Cruciata laevipes*, which has a cross-shaped whorl of only 4 leaves.

NOTES Lady's bedstraw roots were once in demand for the red dye that they contain. The plant is also said to have been used as vegetable rennet, but I doubt this is true. Carl Linnaeus, the botanist who devised the present taxonomic system for classifying plants, describes lady's bedstraw being used to strain milk and makes no mention of rennet-like effects; in fact, there are many accounts of people finding it quite useless for this purpose. It is more likely to have been used to flavour the cheese.

USES/RECIPES Flowers make a pleasant herbal tea or can be infused in chicken stock to flavour light summer sauces.

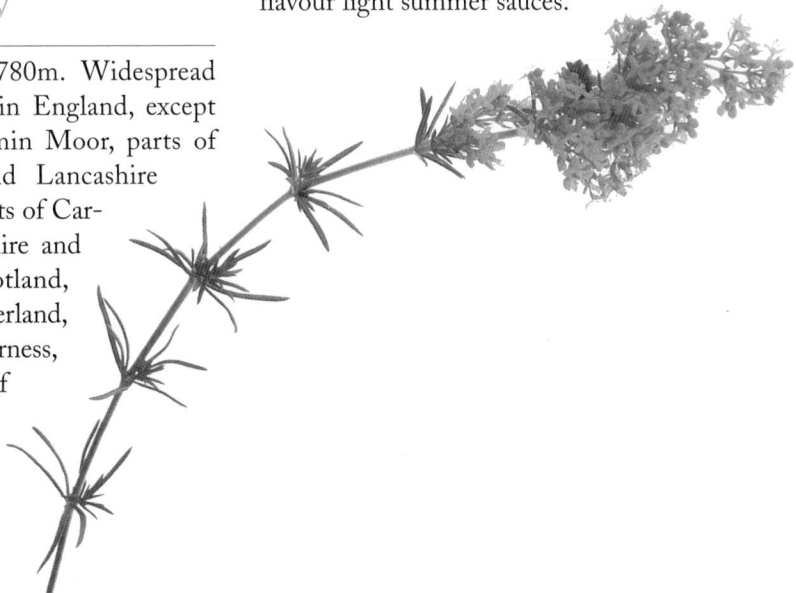

BEECH FAMILY
Fagaceae

Castanea sativa

Sweet Chestnut

DISTRIBUTION Up to 410m. In England, widespread south of line Southport–Spurn Head except large area of Fens, north of line absent most higher-altitude areas; in Wales, widespread in lowland areas; in Scotland, mostly Central Lowlands and eastern Coastal Lowlands north to Moray Firth, scattered localities Dumfries and Galloway, Argyll and Stirling, mostly absent elsewhere; in Ireland, scarce, scattered localities Ulster and coastal counties except Clare, west Galway, Mayo, Donegal and Dublin, also present northeast Galway, Longford, Carlow and Kilkenny; present Channel Islands and Isle of Man.

HABITAT Mostly a planted tree, but occasionally mature trees result from self seeding. Prefers sandy soils but can be planted in a wide variety of soil types, often forming extensive areas of coppiced woodland; also planted in gardens, parks and hedgerows.

DESCRIPTION Large, deciduous tree with broad crown, up to 30m high. Leaves up to 25cm long, lanceolate with quite large, sharp teeth. Bark smooth and greyish brown with upright cracks or splits forming a spiral up the trunk. Nuts develop in spiky cases; the first few to fall contain empty nut shells. Mature nuts begin to fall in October. Nutshells are chestnut brown, surprisingly, with a bristly tail, 1–3 in each case.

NOTES Chestnuts are one of the few wild foods that most people living in the British Isles have collected at some time or other, but most of this abundant food source still goes to waste. Every year a Chinese family congregates beneath a tree on a housing estate near me and fills carrier bags with chestnuts. They have it to themselves, yet there are enough people on that estate to harvest the crop many times over. In mountainous areas of the Mediterranean,

⅓ × life size

where grain cannot be cultivated, chestnuts have remained a staple and an important part of the culture. They are used in place of wheat to make flour for bread, pasta, polenta, cake, sweets and desserts.

Although there is evidence that the chestnut was already growing in the British Isles, chestnut trees were certainly planted in Britain by the Romans. Opinions vary as to whether the variety they brought yielded small nuts or whether this is a product of our climate: Italian chestnuts at any rate are much bigger. Many of our woodlands contain chestnut coppice; the fence posts they produce stay in the ground indefinitely without rotting. But coppiced chestnut produces few nuts. Good nut trees are generally larger and positioned where they can obtain more light. Chestnuts are traditional Christmas fare, but if you just keep them in a cupboard they will be dry and shrivelled by then. An old gipsy named Elijah taught me how to keep them fresh for longer by burying them in a big onion bag (or anything similar with plenty of holes). The dampness of the soil prevents the nuts from drying out so that they remain fresh and moist, although they will not last beyond Christmas without starting to sprout.

USES/RECIPES To roast chestnuts, split them with a sharp knife or prick with a fork to prevent them exploding, but leave one intact. When this one explodes, the rest are ready. Allow them to cool for a few minutes then crack the brittle shells to start the peeling process. The other way to cook them is by boiling: slit or prick as above then boil for 15–20 minutes; however, peeling boiled chestnuts is tiresome work. Use the cooked flesh in stuffings or cakes. Dried chestnuts are good in soups and casseroles throughout the year.
CHESTNUT FLOUR: Shell, chop and dry the nuts in the sun, on a low heat in the oven or in a food dryer, then grind them to powder in a food mill to produce a fine flour; a blender will do for a coarser result.

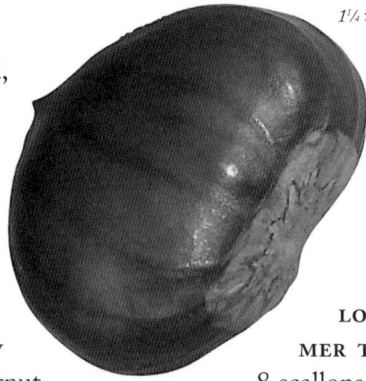

CHESTNUTS WITH RAW SCALLOPS, CHANTERELLES AND SUMMER TRUFFLES: Marinate overnight 8 scallops with a pinch of salt and sugar each, then slice each into three discs. Roast 500g peeled chestnuts, deglaze pan with 300ml milk, then purée with 100g butter. Put into a siphon while still warm and discharge two gas cartridges; keep bottle warm. Slice 12 chanterelles and 1 summer truffle finely and slice 4 raw chestnuts with a mandolin. Serve scallops with a little film of oil, then add mushrooms and finally squeeze out the warm chestnut siphon in a neat mound [RR].

BENEFITS The flour contains neither gluten nor cholesterol and is low in fat since chestnuts also contain no oil. Chestnuts are also unique among nuts in that they contain high levels of vitamin C, but, on the other hand, they contain much less protein than other nuts.

Fagus sylvatica

Beech

DISTRIBUTION Up to 650m. Native to southeast England and southeast Wales, but planted in most of rest of British Isles: in England and Wales, widespread throughout, only less so small part of Fens; in Scotland, mostly found except higher-altitude areas of Grampian Mountains and North West Highlands, absent much of North Highlands, Isle of Skye, Western Isles, Orkney and Shetland; in Ireland present in most areas; present Channel Islands, Isle of Man and Lundy.

young beech as it has similar bark and leaf shape. However, the bark has furrows or folds in its surface, so that the trunks appear twisted; beech trunks generally have a quite even surface. Hornbeam leaves are distinguished by their fine-toothed edges. Exotic species of beech produce similar nuts but no other native nut resembles beech mast.

NOTES High-quality oil produced by pressing beech mast was once widely used in parts of Europe, including the British Isles, most of it imported from France and Germany, although in the beech-rich Chilterns, locals made it for themselves. The many beech plantations of the British Isles produce an abundance of mast and could support a fairly large-scale production of oil, which is regarded as a decent substitute for olive oil and is said to improve with age. The problem is gathering enough nuts, which are small and fiddly once they have fallen to the ground, but industrial quantities were being harvested for oil in France in the 1800s, so presumably they had a method for doing so.

2 × life size

HABITAT Woods, often solely of beech, many but not all of which are commercial plantations for timber; individual trees may stand alone in fields (wood pasture) or planted avenues. Usually well-drained soils; in its native range it grows on chalk, limestone and sand.

DESCRIPTION One of our biggest deciduous trees, up to 30m high and more. Bark smooth and metallic grey. Leaves are oval, ending in a point, with slightly wavy edges; young leaves pale green and soft; upper surfaces of mature leaves smooth, dark green and slightly glossy – both the underside veins and edges are silky–hairy. The beech mast (nut) husks or cases are shaggy and egg shaped when ripening. From September onwards they are mature, and their four sides, more bristly now than shaggy, open to reveal leathery, chestnut-brown triangular nuts: each husk contains 1–3 nuts. The quantity of beech mast varies considerably from year to year.

SIMILAR SPECIES Hornbeam *Carpinus betulus* is smaller but could be mistaken for

USES/RECIPES As well as being fiddly to gather, beech mast is also very time consuming and fiddly to shell. Shelling roasted mast is much easier, but still takes ages. After doing this you might as well use the nuts whole, so you can see them as well as taste them. For example, add them to crumbles or use to decorate cakes or trifles and other desserts topped with whipped cream. The young leaves, before they have unfolded completely, can be eaten raw, for example with asparagus, asparagus mousse, butter-toasted hazel nuts and asparagus juice [RR].

HARVESTING NOTES Timing is essential for collecting beech mast: early kernels blown down by high winds are not fully developed and mostly still encased in their husks; on the other hand, ripe nuts are soon devoured by squirrels and other rodents. Keep your eyes on the ground every day from the beginning of September and harvest straight away once ripe nuts appear on the ground.

With a bit of practice you can tell the good ones at a glance: they are usually darker, with quite flat sides; the duds are hollow and tend to curve inwards.

Quercus robur

Pedunculate Oak

DISTRIBUTION Up to 450m. In England, widespread throughout, only less so Cumbria or Durham; in Wales, widespread throughout; in Scotland, mostly throughout except higher-altitude areas of Southern Uplands, Grampian Mountains and North West Highlands, absent much North Highlands, Isle of Skye and Western Isles, not found Northern Isles; in Ireland, absent much west Donegal, Mayo, west Galway, Clare and Kerry, elsewhere quite widespread; present Channel Islands, Isle of Man, Isles of Scilly and Lundy.

HABITAT Woods, as either large trees (standards) or trees with many smaller trunks in oak coppice; pollarded trees in wood pasture; hedges and fields. On a variety of soils but preferring heavy, fertile soil, tolerant of waterlogging; it does not thrive on poor-quality soils that are either thin or lacking in nutrients.

DESCRIPTION Very large deciduous tree, up to 45m high, with a broad crown. Distinguished by its short-stalked leaves and long-stalked (pedunculate) acorns; leaves are irregular in shape although always longer than wide, with deeply lobed wavy margins and small lobes at the base. Acorns and the cups that hold them are green at first but become brown before they begin to fall in the autumn. The bark is greyish brown, smooth on young trees, but with cracks and splits on older trees.

SIMILAR SPECIES Sessile oak *Q. petraea* has short-stalked acorns and long-stalked leaves, less deeply lobed, with a tapering (unlobed) base. The trees have a narrower crown (the main part of the tree, which spreads out above the trunk) preferring well-drained soil and more tolerant of strongly acidic soils. It is generally the more upland tree of the two.

NOTES Also charmingly known as the truffle oak, this is one of the trees with which all three species of European truffle form a mycorrhizal partnership. In Kurdistan, the trunk of this tree is reported to produce an exudation said to be like manna. E. Lewis Sturtevant (*Sturtevant's Edible Plants of the World*) reports what may be the same substance being found on the leaves of dwarf oaks in Smyrna: it was sweet and was used in place of butter for cooking. Look out for oak trees in your neighbourhood with manna-like exudations. Acorns are nearly always quite bitter in their raw state, but it is worth sampling the output of local trees as the occasional one consistently produces nuts with no trace of

bitterness. Perhaps their easiest edible use is meat made from acorn-fed pigs (in the 'Domesday Book' some woods were measured by how many pigs they could support by pannage, that is by feeding on the acorns or beech mast of the wood. One Italian salami recipe, though, adds the acorns of Turkey oak *Q. cerris* to the meat after the pig has been slaughtered (Guarrera, *Food Medicine*).

USES/RECIPES *(for either oak)* Roast acorns for 20 minutes; this makes shelling them much easier. Roast acorns have an unusual, slightly sweet, smoky flavour, still with a bit of bitterness from the tannins. Use them finely chopped as flavouring for cake, bread, rice pudding, with pasta and in winter stews and casseroles. To make flour for baking or thickening, chop roasted and shelled acorns and boil in several changes of water until no longer bitter. Dry the pulp thoroughly on a low heat in the oven, grind in a kitchen mill and store.

BELLFLOWER FAMILY
Campanulaceae

The name campanula means 'little bell', and the bluish-purple bell-shaped flowers that adorn many of these plants could be mistaken for little else, with the possible exception of bluebells. The similarity is expressed by the alternative name of Scottish bluebell for harebell *Campanula rotundiflora*. When not in flower, the milky sap that campanula bleed when cut can help with identification. The leaves of these plants are nearly always alternate.

GENERAL USES/RECIPES Flowers, tops and leaves of all *Campanula* species can all be used in salads or as greens. Leaves have a mild and refreshing flavour, although some are a little hairy; this is countered either by cooking or by using an oily or thick dressing. Young shoots of creeping bellflower *C. rapunculoides* and nettle-leaved bellflower *C. trachelium* are eaten cooked in Bosnia and Herzegovina. Flowers are sweet and make a pretty addition to salads, or candied as a garnish for desserts, although more often than not I simply nibble them while out walking. Roots have a sweet and delicately earthy flavour: eat them boiled, use them in soup or sliced finely into salad, either raw or cooked. The thick, fleshy roots of cultivated spiked rampion *Phyteuma spicatum* used to be quite commonly eaten; in the British Isles, the wild plant is too rare to be on anyone's menu, although on the Continent it is commonly found in hedgebanks and roadside verges. Rampion bellflower *Campanula rapunculus*, which was formerly cultivated for food, is also now a rare plant. Once commonly grown for its roots, called rampions, its use and, consequently, its cultivation, was in decline by the early eighteenth century. The wild population, derived from cultivated plants, has since dwindled, partly because it no longer has a seed bank from garden plants but also possibly because no one digs them up any more! The plant used to be grown from rhizome fragments, inevitably created when the plant is dug up (for more on this, see p.10). Of the more common bellflower species, the roots of creeping bellflower *Campanula rapunculoides*, usually found in quite large colonies, are probably the

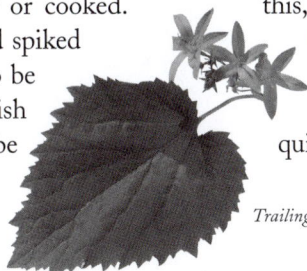

Trailing bellflower

most worthwhile, being larger and fleshier than those of other species.

CANDIED BELLFLOWERS: Mix an egg white (at room temperature) with a few drops of water, paint this all over the flower then drop it in a plate of caster sugar, and make sure that it is well covered. Leave in a warm place on a sheet of greaseproof paper; the egg white will dry and the sugar will form a crust, they will be delicately scented and beautiful to look at. Serve, for example, with a buttermilk panna cotta, perhaps with some candied foraged angelica and a bowl of wild cherry compote [JDW].

PROSECCO JELLY WITH BELLFLOWERS AND WILD STRAWBERRIES: Warm up 150g stock syrup (see p.17), dissolve into it 5 soaked gelatine leaves and mix with 750ml prosecco. Put 1cm jelly mixture in the bottom of your jelly mould or moulds (several small or one big one) and allow to set (in the fridge). Pour in another trickle of the jelly and sprinkle with flowers – the jelly will act like glue to keep the flowers in place. Allow to set, pour in another 1cm jelly mixture (if it starts to set, warm until soft again), sprinkle more flowers – and so on until you have reached the top of the mould. If you pour all the jelly and flowers in together they will all float to the top; this rather annoying process means they can be evenly distributed throughout the jelly. (The same can be done with elderflowers and elderflower jelly or champagne and rose petals, and it looks fantastic.) Serve with lots of wild strawberries. [JDW]

Campanula portenschlagiana

Adria Bellflower

DISTRIBUTION Up to 300m. In England, mostly south, particularly Vale of Gloucester and the southwest, except Wiltshire and Cornwall, Surrey, Greater London and

Berkshire, and otherwise widely scattered south of line Morecambe Bay–Tees Bay, in Wales, most abundant Lleyn Peninsula and lowland areas east to Llandudno, also Dyfed and Glamorgan; in Scotland, scarce, only Firth of Clyde, Firth of Forth and Spey Bay in Moray; in Ireland, few scattered localities Wexford, Waterford, Cork and Kerry; present on Isle of Man and Channel Islands.

HABITAT Walls, rocky banks, pavements and waste ground.

DESCRIPTION Spreading perennial; a garden escape. Leaves cordate or rounded and roughly toothed, green and shiny. Flowers are long (much longer than wide), funnel shaped and bluish purple.

SIMILAR SPECIES Trailing bellflower *C. poscharskyana* grows in similar habitats but is more grey and hairy with dual leaves with cordate bases and bell-shaped flowers, as wide as long, with long, spreading petals.

Campanula rapunculoides

Creeping Bellflower

DISTRIBUTION Up to 365m. In England, scattered throughout, but most common in east and absent much southwest; in Wales, only Radnorshire and Montgomeryshire; in Scotland, scattered localities Central Lowlands, Kirkcudbrightshire and eastern Coastal Lowlands north to Dornoch Firth, plus single locality on Eigg; in Ireland, only Wicklow and Tyrone.

HABITAT Walls, rocky banks, pavements and waste ground.

Campanula trachelium

Nettle-leaved Bellflower

DISTRIBUTION Up to 320m. In England, most frequent in west, from border counties with Wales–south to Dorset–east to Sussex and Kent excluding the Weald, and still common but less abundant in the east and East Midlands; in Wales, only eastern counties and Glamorgan; in Scotland, mostly Central Lowlands and Solway Firth; in Ireland, only native in Offaly, Laois, Carlow, Kilkenny and Wexford but introduced Galway Bay, Londonderry and Westmeath.

HABITAT Dry, alkaline soil, on banks, woodland rides and edges, scrub.

DESCRIPTION Hairy, upright perennial, up to 1m high, with nettle-like leaves. The flowers are violet–pale blue, 30–50mm long, pointing upwards.

SIMILAR SPECIES Giant bellflower *C. latifolia* has similar leaves, but narrowing, not rounded at base and larger flowers; it is found on damp soil in woods, river and stream banks and hedgerows.

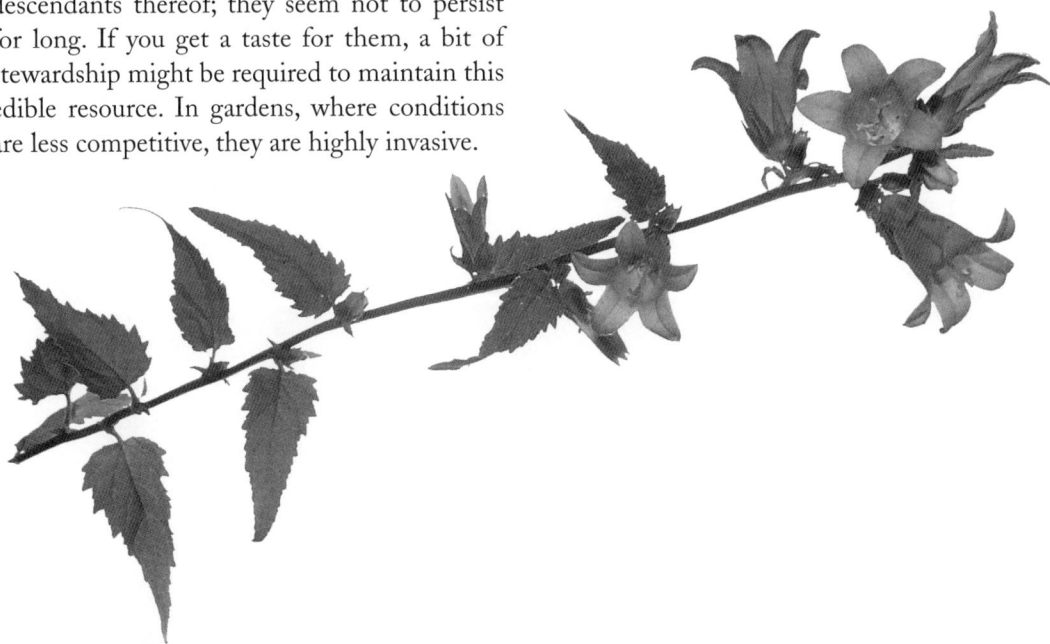

DESCRIPTION Upright perennial, a garden escape, with few small, nettle-shaped upper leaves and cordate basal leaves. Flowers are nodding and funnel shaped, ending in 5 lobes equal in length to the rest of the flower. The calyx teeth are distinctly bent back.

NOTES Formerly grown for its edible roots. Wild plants are usually garden throw-outs or descendants thereof; they seem not to persist for long. If you get a taste for them, a bit of stewardship might be required to maintain this edible resource. In gardens, where conditions are less competitive, they are highly invasive.

BIRCH FAMILY
Betulaceae

Betula pendula

Silver Birch

DISTRIBUTION In England, widespread throughout, only less so Lake District; in Wales, widespread throughout; in Scotland, widespread, except areas of Southern Uplands, Wigtownshire, Ayrshire, northeast Grampian, Grampian Mountains and much of west and east Ross, west Sutherland and Caithness, scarce on Western Isles, not recorded Northern Isles; in Ireland, scattered localities, slightly more common in northeast, central and southeast but absent much of Clare, Limerick, north Kerry and mid- and East Cork; present Isle of Man and introduced to Channel Islands.

HABITAT Mostly well-drained and acidic soils, in woodland; early colonizer of open, especially burnt, ground.

DESCRIPTION Small-to-medium deciduous tree, up to 25m high. Unmistakable by virtue of its silvery bark, with irregular, dark, horizontal lines. The bark is papery; the outer layers easily peel off. Twigs are hairless with little warts on them. Leaves are also hairless, oval–triangular and double toothed; that is, the teeth themselves are toothed. Male catkins are floppy; female ones firm.

SIMILAR SPECIES Downy birch *B. pubescens* is distinguished primarily by its brown bark; also the twigs are downy, in contrast to the warty twigs of silver birch. Leaves are single toothed and have flat bases, giving them a more triangular shape; their undersides are downy. Dwarf birch *B. nana* is a tiny shrub.

NOTES Pollen records show that silver birch was the first tree to colonize the British Isles after the last ice-age. Silver birch bark was used to make canoes by ancient Britons; Numa Pompilius, second king of Rome around 700 BC, used it as parchment on

½ × life size

which to write; the parchments survived in his tomb for 400 years: the bark contains a fungicide that prevents rotting. We own a pair of shoes made in nineteenth-century Finland of silver-birch bark, in the style of an ornate leather sandal at a time when poverty led people to make use of an ancient resource in contemporary styles. These are most useful trees, providing outer bark for utensils, shoes, shelter coverings and boat linings as well as fire-lighters; twigs for teas, chewing sticks and besom brooms; inner bark for bread and sap for drinks and sugar. It is easy to imagine how highly birches must have been regarded when people relied solely on resources available in their immediate locality.

USES/RECIPES Twigs can be used for their wintergreen flavouring, not something with which we are well acquainted in the British Isles perhaps, but in North America wintergreen flavouring is used in sweets, ice cream and root beer. Pour on hot, but not boiling water for birch twig tea. I find the flavour rather bitter, as tannin is also extracted by steeping. To separate the wintergreen flavour from the tannin, boil twigs in a pan with the ingredients to be flavoured in a sieve above the pan, with a lid covering; the steam will infuse them with wintergreen oil. Steaming peas in this way results in an interesting variation on minted peas (the flavour is somewhat similar to mint) – see p.307 for more uses of this flavour. Serve unconcentrated birch sap as a refreshing spring drink [RR]. The concentrated sap is rich and flavoursome and can be used in similar ways to maple syrup. Pour hot syrup over finely chopped rhubarb then leave to marinate for several hours; serve chilled, with rhubarb sorbet and woodruff ice cream [RR]. Birch sap syrup can also be used to flavour carrots confited in butter – it really adds depth and dimension to carrot flavour; also simply drizzled over meadowsweet icecream [ST].

HARVESTING NOTES Tap the trees in spring to get the sugary sap rising up through the xylem layer. To do this, you will need a length of plastic tube, a drill or auger and 30mm of dowelling (to stop up the hole when you have finished), both of the same diameter as the tube, and a bucket, demijohn or other container, in which to catch the sap. Bore a hole into the trunk at a slightly upward angle, deep enough – about 7cm – to reach the xylem layer. Insert one end of the tube into the trunk; direct the other end into your container. Leave for 24 hours or so, after which, remove the tube and plug up the hole. The sap is watery and has to be reduced to roughly one-tenth of its volume to obtain syrup. Commercial syrup producers mostly achieve this by reverse osmosis; in a home kitchen it will take hours of boiling. An easier and less energy-intensive way is to freeze and then thaw it; as the sugar thaws before the water, it can be drained off. The process needs repeating two or three times to obtain a more concentrated syrup.

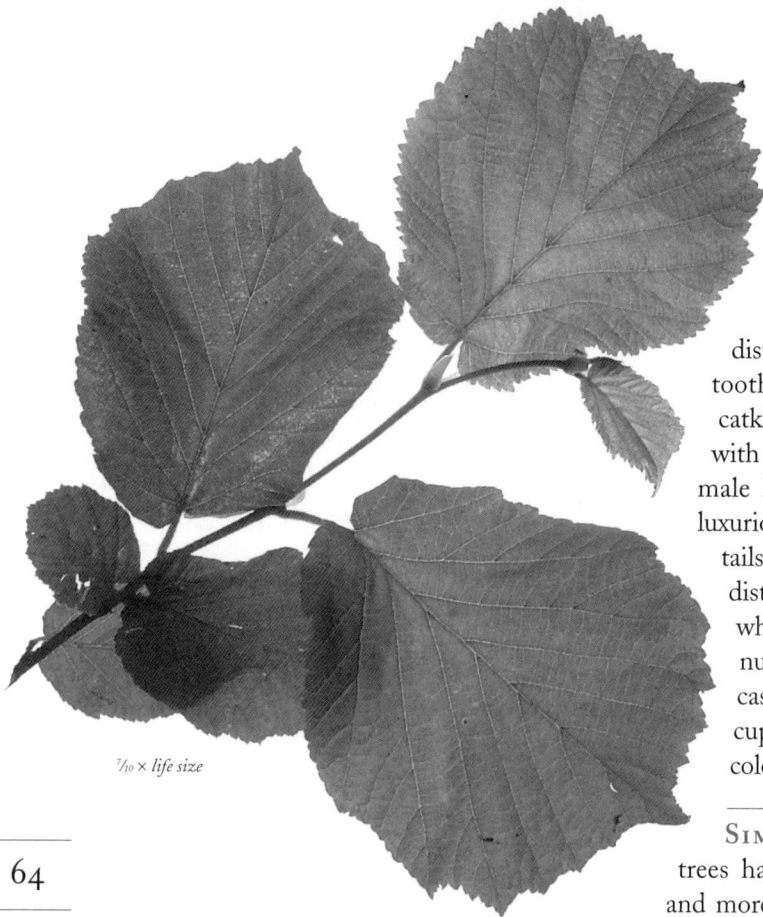

⁷/₁₀ × life size

Corylus avellana

Hazel

DISTRIBUTION Up to 640m. In England and Wales, mostly widespread throughout; in Scotland, only absent parts eastern Coastal Lowlands in Grampian, North Highlands and higher-altitude areas of Grampian Mountains and North West Highlands, introduced to Central Lowlands and Orkney; in Ireland, widespread throughout, only less so west Mayo or Clare; present Isle of Man and Lundy, and introduced to Guernsey and Jersey.

HABITAT Under-storey tree of deciduous woodland, that is, forming the lower shrub layer below larger trees such as oak; river banks, hedgerows, cliffs and scrub; mostly on damp, alkaline soils but tolerant of mild acidity.

DESCRIPTION Short, deciduous tree or shrub, rarely over 6m high. Bark smooth and pale–dark brown. Pale green leaves, rounded but with a distinct point; rough/ downy and coarsely toothed. Each tree has male and female catkins: the female tiny, resembling a bud, with red, tufty protrusions (the styles); the male long, 2–8cm, golden, hanging down luxuriously – these have been called lambs'-tails and are all the more noticeable and distinctive because they appear in winter, when there are no leaves on the trees. The nuts are green at first, in a leafy green case, resembling an egg in a shaggy egg-cup. Both case and nut later turn buff coloured.

SIMILAR SPECIES The various lime trees have similar-shaped leaves, but glossy and more finely toothed. Other trees produce catkins but none in winter. Kentish cobnut *Corylus maxima* are cultivated, mostly in Kent and Essex, with much larger nuts.

NOTES Hazelnuts were a staple food of mesolithic settlers, as evidenced by the great quantity of shells found at their settlement sites. Lucky for them that the grey squirrel was not around then, or this abundant and storable source of winter protein and carbohydrate would have been off the menu. Grey squirrels strip hazelnuts from the trees before they are ripe. If they have got there first, you will be unlikely to find any nuts at all: you may think you have found one they missed but it will probably be a dud they have rejected. Although the squirrels bury a lot of nuts for winter, green hazelnuts are not viable seed; so where grey squirrels have a heavy presence, wild hazel trees are simply not setting seed any more. Add this to the damage done to young trees and the annual slaughter of nestling songbirds by squirrels, and the case for putting squirrel on the menu becomes compelling. Squirrel with hazelnut stuffing seems like poetic justice to me.

USES/RECIPES The nuts need to be brown before harvesting. Nice enough raw, they are much better toasted – either in their shells in the oven or shelled and chopped, in an open pan with no oil (they have plenty of their own). Toasted chopped nuts make a delicious finish to salad: their sweetness and oil serves to balance any bitter leaves that might be present. To crack the nuts, try using the base of a large, flat-based bottle, ideally still with its contents, to make it heavier. If you want to do something spectacular with them, here is a dish in the inimitable style of Danish chef and wild-food pioneer René Redzepi (for more detailed recipe see Redzepi's *Noma: Nordic Cuisine*). The elaborate part is the hazelnut mayonnaise, which is made with 2 boiled eggs (4 minutes), 1 tablespoon hazelnut butter (made by roasting the nuts at 160°C and blending with a little rapeseed oil), 100ml rapeseed oil, 100ml browned butter and 75ml stock syrup flavoured with vanilla ($\frac{1}{2}$ pod per litre of syrup). Blend the eggs, then slowly add the oil, browned butter, nut butter and syrup. Place 5 dollops on each plate and put one hazelnut (previously roasted in butter) in the centre of each; serve with ice cream flavoured with aquavit-soaked raisins and apple pieces glazed in honey flavoured with caraway seeds.

Mark Hix's Roast Plums with Hazel Nuts and Clotted Cream

SERVES 4

30 wild plums
6 tbsp caster sugar
4 tbsp clotted cream, to serve

FOR THE TOPPING
2 tbsp flour
2 tbsp brown sugar

40g hard butter, chopped into small pieces
4 tbsp oats
36–40 hazel nuts, shelled and roughly
    chopped

TO SERVE
4 tbsp clotted cream

Pre-heat the oven to 200°C/Gas mark 6.

First make the topping: put the flour, brown sugar and butter into a bowl and rub together with your fingers to a breadcrumb like consistency. Mix in the oats and hazel nuts and spread out on a baking tray. Place the plums on another baking tray and sprinkle with the caster sugar. Place the plums and topping in the oven for 15–20 minutes until the plums have softened and are lightly coloured, and the topping is golden. You may need to remove the topping before the plums.

Leave the plums to cool a little, then transfer them either to one large or four individual serving plates and spoon over the cooking juices. Scatter over the hazel nut topping and serve the cream on top or separately.

BORAGE FAMILY
Boraginaceae

Several *Boraginaceae* species, including borage, hound's tongue, comfrey and gromwell, have been traditionally used as medicine; a few of them as food. However, the discovery that most contain pyrrolizidine alkaloids, which are known to cause severe liver damage, including cancers, forces the conclusion that these supposed remedies may well have done more harm than good.

In the United States the Food and Drug Administration (FDA) has outlawed the sale and use of comfrey and other Boraginaceae species; the centralized health authority in Germany placed similar restrictions on the sale of the plants as medicines. Pyrrolizidine alkaloids act by destroying small blood vessels in the liver. This could be remedied if only small amounts are eaten very occasionally. However, unborn children and children generally have less liver tissue, which is therefore not so able to regenerate; pregnant women and children should not eat these plants at all. Some of these alkaloids have also been shown to be carcinogenic, at least to rats. In conclusion, these plants should not become a major part of anyone's diet. I don't eat comfrey at all; I do eat borage occasionally, and I consider lungwort entirely safe.

Borago officinalis

Borage

DISTRIBUTION Up to 425m. In England, widespread south of line Wash–Severn Estuary but less abundant Devon, Cornwall, south Wiltshire, Kent and Northamptonshire, north of line very common in Severn river basin, distribution declines northwards; in Wales, mostly Dyfed, elsewhere sparsely present except Merioneth and Radnorshire; in Scotland, scarce, mainly Central Lowlands and eastern Coastal Lowlands; in Ireland, rare, limited to Clare, Kerry, Wexford, Wicklow,

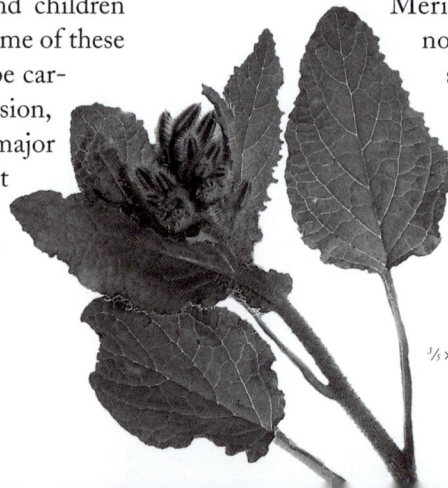

³/₅ × life size

Dublin, Tipperary, Tyrone and around Belfast; present Isle of Man, Isles of Scilly, Channel Islands and Lundy.

HABITAT Roadside verges, waste ground.

DESCRIPTION Whole plant is covered in bristly hairs: a key element of the plant's *Gestalt*; it grows upright, to maximum 60cm high. Lower leaves oval–lanceolate, stalked; upper leaves thinner and stalkless; all wavy edged. Clusters of bristly heads heavy with brown flower buds droop, appearing dirty grey, fuzzy and indistinct from a distance. Flowers have crisp, bright blue, star-shaped corollas and protruding black stamens.

SIMILAR SPECIES The young leaves have been confused with foxglove *Digitalis purpurea,* with fatal consequences, on a number of occasions. Foxglove leaves are intensely bitter; whereas borage leaves have a delicate cucumber-like flavour. Also, borage is furry to the touch; foxglove is not. If in doubt, only collect leaves from flowering plants.

NOTES Although it is not so unusual to find borage growing wild, it occurs mostly as a garden escape: feral populations on the whole do not persist but it recurs due to wide cultivation. In England, the leaves were traditionally plucked from the herb garden and added to Pimm's and other summer drinks, giving a mild cucumber flavour. In Mediterranean countries such as Italy, Greece and Lebanon, where the plant is native, it is commonly gathered and used as a vegetable.

USES/RECIPES Leaves and stems can be used with ricotta and potato to stuff pasta: they taste a little like oysters. In Lebanon, for example, the leaves and stalks are cooked in tempura, or boiled then fried with onion rings. The flowers make a stunning finishing touch to summer

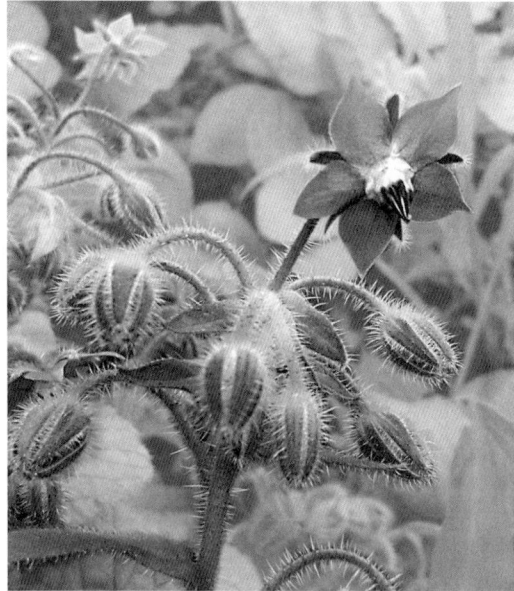

soup, salad or dessert. Finish a bowl of wild damson soup (see p.273) with two or three flowers [EC]. The seeds contain only negligible amounts of pyrrolizidine alkaloids and are used to produce starflower oil, which is higher in essential fatty acid (EFA) gamma-linolenic acid (GLA) than evening-primrose oil; they can be scattered on food as a simple way of obtaining this nutrient.

HAZARDS Although leaves and stems contain pyrrolizidine alkaloids, these are present in relatively small quantities (0.001 per cent of dry weight, compared with 0.02–0.18 per cent for comfrey), so occasional consumption is probably harmless.

Mertensia maritima

Oyster Plant

DISTRIBUTION Up to 300m. Very limited coastal distribution: in England, restricted to Cumbria; in Wales, to Denbighshire; in Scotland, localities Kincardineshire north–Caithness in east with single location East Lothian, widely separated sites in west that extend length of the country, very scarce in Western Isles, widespread in Northern Isles; in Ireland, rare, confined to the Ulster coast with a single site in west Mayo; present Isle of Man.

HABITAT Shingle, gravel and, to a lesser extent, sandy beaches.

DESCRIPTION Native perennial, short, growing along the ground (prostrate) to form bushy mats. Unique in its family for being smooth leaved and hairless, although the oyster plant's thick, fleshy leaves are characteristic of many coastal plants (e.g. **sea-purslane**, **sea sandwort** or **sea kale**). Otherwise, leaves are bluey grey and roughly spoon shaped, although some are more elongated. Flowers are only 6mm wide, starting pink, later increasingly blue.

NOTES This scarce plant suffers a great deal from being trampled by livestock with access to its coastal habitats; sadly, it also suffers from human trampling. No self-respecting forager would want to make its decline worse by trampling or eating the few plants that remain, but a careful foray and discrete nibble of the leaves will do no harm – just enough to become acquainted with this strange plant that tastes like oyster. The seeds can survive being sea borne;

Oyster plant

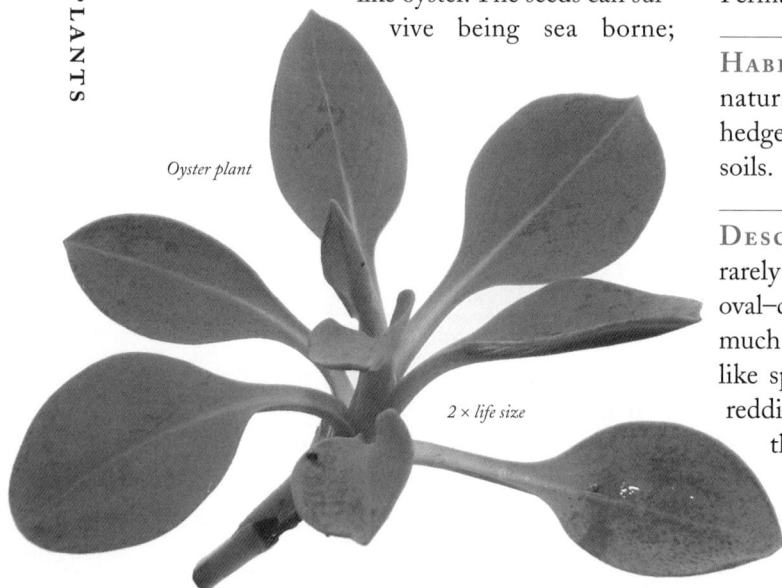

2 × life size

young plants spring up in the tangle of seaweed and debris at the drift line of the shore, but this makes them vulnerable to trampling, as they are hardly noticeable.

USES/RECIPES The possibility of pyrrolizidine alkaloids and the vulnerable status of the plant preclude any harvesting or consumption at above nibbling scale.

HAZARDS There is presently no data regarding the presence or otherwise of pyrrolizidine alkaloids in this plant, but caution should be exercised anyway.

Pulmonaria officinalis

Common Lungwort

DISTRIBUTION Up to 385m. In England, sparse, but more abundant in the southeast, except east Kent, and the southwest, except Devon and Cornwall; in Wales, present one or two 10 sq km in each county except Merioneth, where absent; in Scotland, scarce, mostly Central Lowlands and southern counties, plus scattered localities north Grampian, East Ross, east Sutherland and Shetland; in Ireland, rare, found only in Meath, Down, Tyrone and Fermanagh; present Isle of Man.

HABITAT Commonly grown in gardens but naturalized in woods, rough/waste ground, hedgebanks, scrub, mostly on chalk and clay soils.

DESCRIPTION Naturalized perennial, short, rarely more than 30cm high. Lower leaves are oval–cordate with long stalks; upper leaves are much thinner; all have distinctive white splash-like spots. The whole plant is hairy. Flowers, reddish pink–purple–blue, in loose clusters at the top of the plant.

½ × life size

FLOWERING PLANTS: DICOTYLEDONS

SIMILAR SPECIES Suffolk lungwort *P. obscura* is less hairy, unspotted or with less pronounced pale green spots.

NOTES This is the only *Boraginaceae* species that has been tested and found to be free of pyrrolizidine alkaloids.

USES/RECIPES Leaves can be boiled, steamed, fried or deep-fried in batter. They are also good as a stuffing for pasta or eaten raw, chopped finely in salads. Use flowers in salads or as decoration, for both savoury dishes and desserts.

Symphytum officinale

Comfrey

DISTRIBUTION Up to 320m. In England, widespread, only less so in few places south of line Morecambe Bay–Hull, including Cheshire Plain, Leicestershire, Norfolk, south Essex, east Kent and Devon, north of line, concentrated mostly along eastern coastal counties from north Yorkshire to Scottish border; in Wales, found all border counties and Glamorgan; in Scotland, widespread but mostly south of Glen Mor, absent high-altitude areas of Grampian Mountains and Southern Uplands, most common Central Lowlands and Dumfries and Galloway; in Ireland, sparsely but widely scattered in lowland areas; present Isle of Man and Channel Islands.

HABITAT River, stream and ditch banks, marshes and fens and generally in damp places.

DESCRIPTION Rough and hairy perennial with oval–lanceolate leaves and winged stems, up to 1.2m high. The lower leaves can be huge, up to 30cm long, with stalks; upper leaves are smaller and stalkless. Flowers appear May–June: they are trumpet shaped in spiral clusters, cream to yellow or blue to reddish purple.

SIMILAR SPECIES Before flowering could be confused with deadly foxglove *Digitalis purpurea*.

USES/RECIPES None for food that I would recommend.

HAZARDS Comfrey has a long history of use as a medicine and to a lesser extent as food; more recently, in the 1970s, it was recommended as a kind of vegetarian superfood. However, the discovery of its high pyrrolizidine-alkaloid (PA) content, including the carcinogen symphytine, means that the wild plant (there are now cultivars with negligible PA content) can no longer be considered safe to eat or use (even externally) as medicine. It is, however, very useful as liquid manure.

⅓ × life size

69

BORAGE FAMILY

BUTTERCUP FAMILY
Ranunculaceae

Many buttercup-family members are poisonous, including Britain's most poisonous plant: monk's-hood *Aconitum napellus* contains aconitine, a drug of ancient usage that slows the heart and relieves pain but can also kill. Stinking hellebore *Helleborus foetidus* and green hellebore *H. viridis* are also highly toxic. These three plants will not be described in detail since they do not resemble any edible species.

The toxin present in most species is protoanemonin, an acrid skin irritant. If you do nibble a buttercup leaf by mistake, you are sure to spit it out as it will burn your mouth. For this reason grazing livestock tend to avoid buttercups, but the chemical breaks down when plants are dried: farmers happily make hay from buttercup-filled fields.

There are a few edible species in this family, not all of them wild. The seeds of garden plants *Nigella arvensis* and love-in-a-mist *N. damascena* are used as a spice in Iran, India, Bengal, Bangladesh, Lebanon and Turkey: you have probably eaten them in Turkish bread. Ali and I are convinced that they are the source for the flavouring in bub-

blegum! In our country, most people gather the dry seed pods and discard them. As well as those described in detail below, there are a few reputedly edible wild species that deserve a mention. Several authors describe species of water-crowfoot being eaten by Native North American peoples; Hogg and Johnson (*Wild Flowers of Great Britain*) report cottagers supporting cows and horses on common water-crowfoot *Ranunculus aquatilis*, apparently rationing each cow to no more than 25–30lb daily! In *Flora Scotica* John Lightfoot also recommends boiling the roots of bulbous buttercup *R. bulbosa*, with the afterword 'they become so mild as

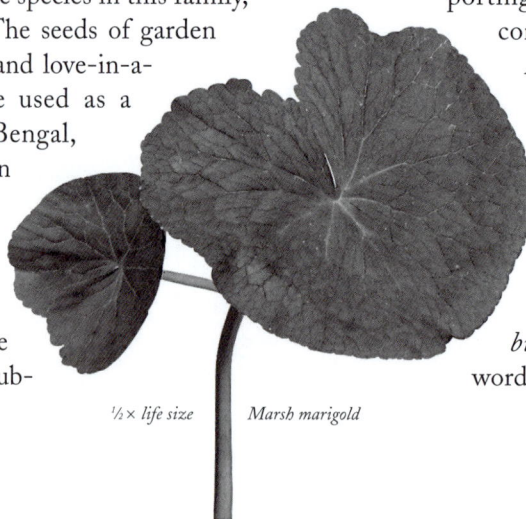

½ × life size   *Marsh marigold*

to be eatable'. I am told that buttercup leaves make passable greens after cooking, once the protoanemonin has been destroyed. Finally, there is a Persian species known promisingly as egg-yolk *R. edulis*, of which the tubers, stems and leaves are supposedly edible.

Caltha palustris
King Cup/Marsh Marigold/ Mollyblobs

DISTRIBUTION Up to 1100m. Native, found in most of the British Isles except, in England, in small parts of Cambridgeshire and Essex; in Ireland, in north Kerry, Wexford and East Cork, and generally less widespread in southern Ireland.

HABITAT Wet and often shady places, such as boggy woods, ditches, edge of ponds, rivers, lakes and canals, and wet meadows, generally on neutral or alkaline soils.

DESCRIPTION The glossy yellow flowers resemble huge buttercups, making the plant very easy to find April–July. Up to 46cm high. Hollow stems either stand upright or creep along the ground, rooting at the joints. Leaves are cordate, dark green and glossy, with toothed edges.

SIMILAR SPECIES Yellow water lily *Nuphar lutea* grows in deeper water, the whole plant submerged beside the floating lily pads and flowers.

NOTES King cup leaves and roots were eaten by Inuit in Alaska; nineteenth-century Kent botanist Matthew Henry Cowell wrote that in his day the buds were used pickled instead of capers, which is still a popular use of the plant among a remnant of wild-food enthusiasts in Europe and North America.

USES/RECIPES To pickle the flower buds, salt them overnight then heat in spiced pickling vinegar and jar. Use leaves and stems as vegetables; I find the older stems are best, with a delicious asparagus-like flavour.

HAZARDS Contains protoanemonin and helleborin, both of which are destroyed by cooking. Also said to cause skin rashes if handled for long periods.

Clematis vitalba
Traveller's Joy/ Old Man's Beard

DISTRIBUTION Up to 305m. In England, common in south, except parts of Devon and Cornwall, north of Midlands, sparser towards Scottish border; in Wales, widespread except Cambrian Mountains, Brecon Beacons and Snowdonia; in Scotland, scattered localities in Central Lowlands, Kirkcudbrightshire and Wigtownshire; in Ireland, mostly widespread but more abundant in south and east; present Channel Islands, Isle of Man and Isles of Scilly.

HABITAT Native: mostly alkaline soils, of which it is a reliable indicator. Edge of woods, climbing over hedges, trees, shrubs and thickets; walls (where lime mortar can substitute for alkaline soil), ruins, railway embankments and disused quarry faces.

DESCRIPTION Deciduous, climbing shrub – leaf stalks wrap themselves tendril-like around any available means of support. Leaves usually have oval-toothed leaflets, usually 5 when mature. Flowers are green and slightly fragrant. Most conspicuous feature is the fluffy seed heads, from which its name derives: these are good for initial identification but mostly absent in spring, when the plant is harvested.

1½ × life size

a bit of bacon and found them very good, with a rich, nutty flavour.

HAZARDS An HMSO publication (Forsythe, *British Poisonous Plants*, 1968) reports traveller's joy as having poisoned livestock and cites protoanemonin as the poison responsible. However, historical texts describe how in spring the young shoots were commonly eaten by country folk in England and were pickled in France. They are still consumed in parts of rural Italy without any apparent ill effect, which has also been my experience. It may be that the poisons are absent from the young shoots; in any case, protoanemonin breaks down during cooking.

HARVESTING NOTES Use the very first growth, when only 3–4cm long, after this the shoots become bitter.

SIMILAR SPECIES Cultivated clematis (which is poisonous) is similar. Other climbers have poisonous leaves, and all are simple (without leaflets) and untoothed: ivy (palmately lobed or unlobed), honeysuckle (simple) and white bryony (palmately lobed). Hop, which is good to eat, has toothed, palmately lobed leaves. Black bryony, with cordate leaves, has edible leaves and shoots, but poisonous berries.

USES/RECIPES In Italy, young shoots are pickled, used in omelettes, boiled and seasoned with olive oil in soups; for example, the classic Tuscan soup Acquacotta, which has a base of pork fat, onions and garlic, combined with seasonal vegetables (Guarrera, 'Food medicine', 2003). I have tried them fried with

1½ × life size

Ranunculus ficaria

Lesser Celandine

DISTRIBUTION Up to 750m. Native, found pretty much throughout the British Isles except, in Scotland, much of Lewis, parts of Grampian Mountains and much of east of North West Highlands; in Ireland, most of Mayo and some areas in central southern Ireland.

HABITAT Hedge banks, roadsides; river and stream banks and other areas that are seasonally flooded; deciduous woodlands, meadows and shady waste ground.

DESCRIPTION Hairless perennial growing close to the ground. Leaves are long, stalked and cordate, patterned with markings darker or lighter than the main leaf colour. Flowers often solitary, with lots of narrow, glossy yellow petals. Subspecies *bulbilifer* has bulbils where the leaf stalk joins the main stem and at the roots.

NOTES Lesser celandine is a late winter and spring wild salad or green vegetable. Country people in Sweden used to boil and eat the leaves. In Italy, they still do so and, in Kent, so do I! It is often quite abundant and easy to spot as it grows when there is not a great deal of other vegetation. According to the doctrine of signatures, God gave useful hints regarding the uses of plants by causing them to resemble body parts. Lesser celandine's alternative name, pilewort, refers to its role as a cure for haemorrhoids, a use suggested by the form of its tubers.

USES/RECIPES Leaves are attractive; the flavour quite mild: good bulking for wild salads containing other, stronger flavours or on their own, for example, with lamb chops, stewed lamb and purple sprouting broccoli with just a

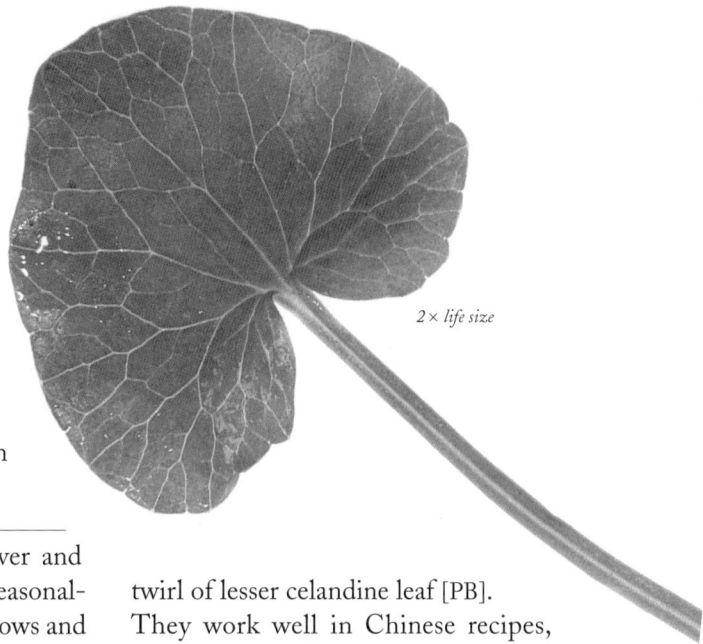

2 × life size

twirl of lesser celandine leaf [PB]. They work well in Chinese recipes, especially a stir fry, as the stems retain their succulent texture when cooked. The bulbils at the leaf bases and around the roots can be boiled or fried. The tubers have a flavour and texture quite similar to potatoes: use boiled or roasted.

HAZARDS Leaves contain protoanemonin, but in minute quantities. Levels are said to increase as the plant comes into flower, but I have eaten plenty of leaves from flowering plants and come to no harm. Protoanemonin is not a cumulative poison; any ill effects are tangible: you know you are ingesting harmful quantities if your mouth starts to burn.

HARVESTING NOTES Tubers are best when the whole plant has withered, shortly after flowering. Before this stage they are very tough; no amount of cooking would soften them. Look for bulbils at the leaf bases of subspecies *bulbilifer* just after the flowers have withered.

CABBAGE FAMILY
Brassicaceae

With the exception of the carrot family, this is probably the family with which I have spent most time working, due mostly to the abundance of good edible species that it contains but also partly to the amount of head scratching initially involved in telling the similar ones apart. Unlike the carrot family, however, the cabbage family contains no poisonous species, so these fine distinctions are a matter of purely culinary importance, rather than safety.

If I were naming it, I would probably call this the mustard family, as the spiciness of the mustard oils contained in most species is their most obvious culinary hallmark. Pretty much everything correctly called cress belongs to this family, but cress is a much misused term. True cresses are mustardy salad leaves, not seedlings in little plastic tubs. Think watercress – cress that grows in water – and you are on the right track. Garden cress *Lepidium sativum* is usually sold at its seedling stage, but mature plants resemble the closely related field penny-cress, a common agricultural weed or delicious spicy salad leaf, depending on whether you have a farmer's or a forager's perspective. Even raw cabbage leaves provide a hint of this mustardy spiciness. Various kinds of mustard, all of which grow wild in Britain, produce seeds from which the familiar condiment can be made, while the pungent

roots of fellow *Brassicaceae* horseradish were initially used as a substitute for those of the native dittander. Probably the best-known cabbage-family salad leaf is garden rocket *Eruca sativa*, which sometimes grows wild as a garden escape. It has several wild namesakes, which can be used in similar ways, some of them much milder, some a great deal hotter.

BOTANICAL CHARACTERISTICS The old name of this family, *Cruciferae*, refers to the typical Maltese-cross shape of the flowers, formed by their four evenly arranged petals. Many cabbage species have yellow flowers, and most yellow cross-shaped flowers belong to this family (but beware of greater celandine, see p.252). Rose family species tormentil and cinquefoil also have yellow flowers with four petals, but both are medicinal plants that will do you no harm and may even do you some good if eaten. Yellow flowers are often a sign of something good to eat: wild-food plants in the rose and daisy families have them, but buttercups are mildly poisonous and greater celandine deadly, so this is not a general rule. Bushy plants with yellow flowers often turn out to be cabbage species, such as wild mustards, radishes or rockets (though in rape-growing areas, feral rape plants may be most common). They are so abundant and easy to find that it is well worth the effort learning to distinguish them. The other main anatomical characteristics to note are the alternate leaves and the arrangement of flowers in racemes.

Some *Brassicaceae* species are particularly winter hardy; quite how hardy was brought home to me during the heavy snow of February 2004. Kevin Gratton, who was at the time head chef at London restaurant Le Caprice, had just placed his first order, which included a quantity of bitter-cress; I didn't feel we could let him down. Not sure what I would find, I headed to a woodland bitter-cress patch and shovelled through the half a metre of snow that was covering it. Much to my surprise the bitter-cress was pert and glossy; it almost seemed better for it. I have also gathered dandelions from beneath snow, so I am sceptical of historical accounts of winter malnutrition occurring due to lack of greens. If it happened, it was probably due more to ignorance of what was available than to a lack of edible winter plants.

Plants in this family are generally early colonizers of disturbed ground and often do not persist when other vegetation gets a foothold. For this reason they are often found as agricultural or garden weeds. Charlock, penny-cress, bitter-cress and shepherd's purse can be so prolific that without weeding or herbicides they out-compete cultivated crops. Farmers have sought to eradicate them for hundreds of years, but they still hold their own against selectively bred and deliberately sown plants. Perhaps our

combative approach to plant husbandry is ill-judged. In many countries where agriculture is less industrialized, people harvest and use so called weed crops as a matter of course.

Green vegetables in the cabbage family include wild cabbage (coastal ancestor of most of our cultivated green vegetables), sea kale, many of the spicy salad leaves, tamed somewhat by cooking, and the leaves of plants more familiar for other edible parts, notably mustard, radish and turnip greens. Stronger-flavoured leaves can also be used as purées, in pestos, dressings and cooked sauces, though with minimal heat exposure, since the mustard oils that give them flavour are volatile and evaporate when heated. These mustard oils are good digestives, because they promote secretion of digestive juices, so spicier leaves (or roots) are good ingredients to include in starters. Leaves of cabbage-family plants are also those most commonly used to make as lacto-fermented pickles, of which the German sauerkraut and Korean kimchee are well-known examples (see p.12). Finally, the roots of garlic mustard, which has a similar mild spiciness to the radish, as well as those of wild radish and wild turnip can be eaten; the latter are not nearly as

Flowering watercress

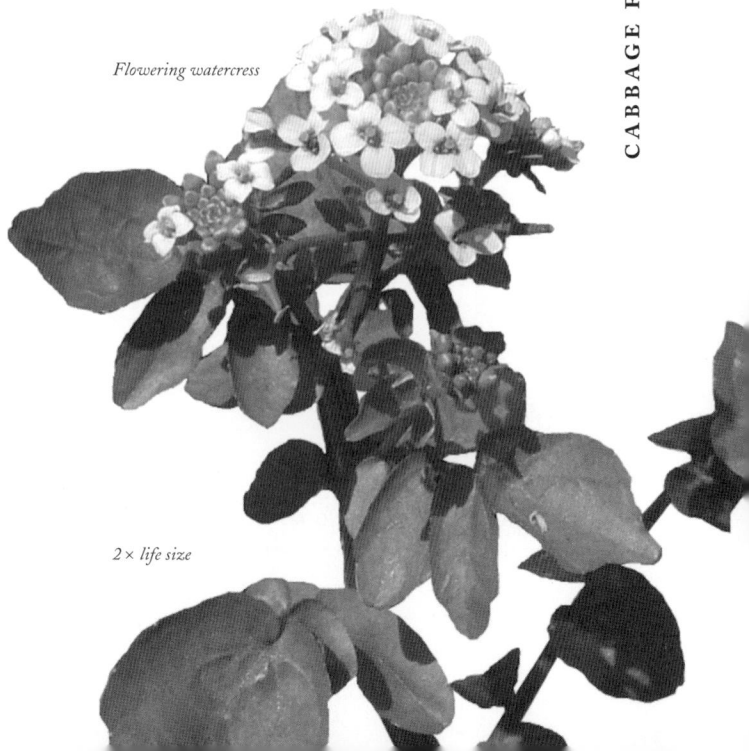

2 × life size

swollen as cultivated varieties. There are also well-documented anti-cancer effects associated with these plants, due to the presence of chemicals known as indols.

FAMILY HAZARDS Basal rosettes of mildly toxic **ragwort** could be confused with some species with quite long basal leaves, such as hedge mustard, hoary mustard *Hirschfeldia incana* and wild radish. All three have thicker, rougher leaves; ragwort has an unpleasant smell once crushed. Glucosinolates, which are present in all *Brassicaceae* species, are toxic in large amounts, but you would need to eat a wheelbarrow full of leaves to ingest that much. Finally, on agricultural land, beware of gathering plants that have been sprayed with herbicides (for further details, see pp.22–3).

Alliaria petiolata

Garlic Mustard

DISTRIBUTION Up to 535m. Widespread throughout England, apart from Northumberland, and Wales; in Scotland, found central and eastern Coastal Lowlands as far north as Moray Firth and in south in Dumfries and Galloway; in Ireland, widespread in much of Leinster, east of Munster and in Ulster south and east of Sperrin Mountains but absent Mourne Mountain area; present Channel Islands; introduced into Isle of Man and few areas in west Scotland.

HABITAT Field margins, road verges, hedge, river and stream banks, edges of woods and ditches.

DESCRIPTION Native biennial. First-year growth consists of long, stalked cordate leaves with regular, sawlike teeth and a crinkly-looking network of veins; the main stem appears in spring of the second year and has paler green nettle-like leaves. The whole plant is tall, thin and nettle-like. Leaves have a distinct smell of garlic when crushed. Small white flowers (6mm wide) appear in clusters from mid-April; seed pods are long, up to 60mm, and 2–3mm thick, curving out from the stem.

NOTES Garlic mustard is a curious plant, its name aptly describing the two elements of its flavour. Like most other members of this family, it contains mustard oils that stimulate the appetite, which explains why once I have begun nibbling garlic mustard flowers, I tend to keep on nibbling. The flavour is bitter at first, but the warm, garlicky flavour that follows wins over most people.

USES/RECIPES Slight bitterness of the leaves is tempered by their traditional combination with fatty or salty ingredients. Ethnobotanist James Duke recommends using them to spice up mutton and pork, both fatty meats, and saltfish. They finish risotto nicely: tear them and put them in with butter or Parmesan. Use in herb crust, mixed with wild chervil, garlic, rosemary, mustard, seasoning and breadcrumbs, to smear on to roast beef or pork for last 5 minutes' cooking time (see also p.338:

A plate of allium flavours). They can also be chopped and mixed into cream cheese or used sparingly with scrambled egg and in salads or sandwiches. Pre-flowering roots can be chopped and used in place of radishes, or creamed liked horseradish and served with beef. [PW] The white flowers make a delightful salad ingredient or garnish. Use green seed pods as spices, chopped finely and added to hollandaise or mayonnaise, or placed whole into pickling vinegars for other vegetables. Harvest and use the seeds as you would other mustard seeds.

BENEFITS Contains glucosinolates and apigenin flavonoids, both known to have anti-tumour effects. The leaves also contain cancer-preventing chemicals typical of both garlics (allyl sulphides) and mustards (isothiocyanates). They are also high in vitamin A. Unfortunately, the presence of anti-terpines, which inhibit the absorption of proteins in the small intestine, slightly negates these good effects.

HARVESTING NOTES The flowers are easily recognizable from a distance, as are the pale green leaves. The plants grow close together and often form a distinctive lump of colour at the edge of a field or on a hedgebank. The first-year plants produce tender leaves, which can be harvested like cress when very small; second-year growth starts with large-leaved rosettes; collect both these and the bushy tops just prior to flowering.

ECOLOGICAL CONSIDERATIONS Garlic mustard is a host to caterpillars of the orange tipped butterfly, which feed on the leaves and seed pods, so don't gather too much in any one area.

Armoracia rusticana

Horseradish

DISTRIBUTION Up to 300m. Widespread throughout much of England except higher-altitude areas such as Bodmin Moor, Dartmoor, Exmoor, Pennines, Cleveland Hills, Cumbrian Mountains and Cheviot Hills; in Wales, all counties at lower altitudes; in Scotland, confined to the lowlands south of Tayside and Clackmannanshire except scattered areas around Moray Firth in west Sutherland and on Orkney; sparse in Ireland, with small concentration around Dublin, several sites along west coast of Ulster and coastal areas of Wexford, Waterford, Cork, Kerry and Clare, absent from most of central lowland; present on Channel Islands and Isle of Man.

HABITAT Grassy areas such as roadsides, stream and river banks; waste ground, old gardens, railway embankments; sandy ground near the sea.

DESCRIPTION Naturalized, patch-forming, hairless perennial. Instantly recognizable by large, shiny, green leathery leaves with toothed edges and sometimes 1m long. Lower stem leaves are pinnately lobed and basal leaves also occasionally take this form. Flowers are white, up to 9mm

wide, in long, narrow sprays, with small, short-stemmed leaves beneath. Viable seed is rarely produced; reproduction by root fragments.

SIMILAR SPECIES Larger dock leaves are similar at first glance but untoothed, with brown sheaths at their base, generally darker. Dittander leaves are upright and can be quite large, but dull grey-green, ending in a distinct point, in contrast with the more rounded ends of horseradish leaves. You might also mistake a stray sugar beet for horseradish: if your grated horseradish lacks heat and is slightly sweeter than usual, this is the likely explanation.

NOTES Horseradish was introduced to Britain before 1500 and at first used only for its medicinal properties. In time, the roots were discovered to have similar culinary properties to dittander. Within 150 years, it had begun to replace dittander in kitchen gardens, the root being larger and easier to work. Horseradish is stubbornly persistent – just a tiny root fragment is enough for a new plant to grow. I remember as a child seeing people put tough black plastic over areas of their garden in the vain hope of eradicating it; the horseradish simply broke through and carried on invading. This persistence is good news for foragers. Most people have horseradish growing somewhere near by; you need the landowner's permission to uproot it, but many people would be only too glad to have it removed. Although you may think you have taken everything, you are bound to leave behind a small piece to ensure a new crop.

USES/RECIPES Root is well known as an accompaniment to beef and salmon; it is also excellent with beetroot. Best used freshly grated, with a little vinegar to fix the volatile oils. I was given a tub of Richard Corrigan's horseradish ice cream. I offered a spoonful to visitors; no one guessed the flavour. We contributed to the evolution of the recipe by bringing lady's smock flowers to Corrigan's restaurant Lindsay House in 2005: they taste strongly of horseradish, and Richard worked them into the recipe. Oddly, the flowers taste more like cabbage; likewise the leaves, though quite edible, taste only vaguely of horseradish. For the ultimate horseradish-flavoured dish, use horseradish root, dittander leaves and lady's smock flowers.

HAZARDS To be avoided by anyone with low thyroid function.

HARVESTING NOTES Digging up horseradish roots can be a slog. However, I found substantial

Richard Corrigan's Horseradish Ice Cream with Hot Summer Jam

FOR THE HORSERADISH ICE CREAM
355ml double cream
180ml milk
100g sugar
1 tsp grated fresh horseradish
3 egg yolks
1 tsp horseradish juice
a handful of lady's smock flowers

FOR THE SUMMER JAM
50g caster sugar
2 pieces of lemon peel
2 fresh rosemary sprigs
50g pitted cherries
50g strawberries
50ml stock syrup
50g blackberries
50g raspberries

TO SERVE
crystallized rose petals, to garnish
biscuits, to serve

PREPARE THE ICE CREAM. Pour the cream and milk into a pan and heat, being careful not to boil. Add half the sugar and the grated horse-radish, and bring to the boil. Put the remaining sugar and the egg yolks into a clean bowl, set over a pan of simmering water and whisk until thick, pale and frothy.

Fill a sink with 8–10cm cold water. Whisk the hot milk and cream mixture into the frothy egg yolks. Remove the bowl from the heat and stand in the cold water. Stir in the horseradish juice and the lady's smock. Either place into an ice-cream maker and churn until frozen or tip into a plastic container and freeze, stirring every hour until frozen. Freeze overnight.

PREPARE THE SUMMER JAM. Put the sugar in a pan and heat gently. Add the lemon peel and rosemary, and when the sugar starts to melt, add the cherries and strawberries. Pour in the stock syrup and turn up the heat slightly. Stir in the blackberries and raspberries, and when they just begin to soften, take the pan off the heat. To serve, spoon the hot summer jam into a bowl. Top with a scoop of the ice cream and finish with a scattering of crystallized rose petals and a biscuit.

plants growing on wasteland near me, where the soil had been turned over by machinery: the roots had been cut into pieces, some of which I collected; the rest produced plants in nicely loosened soil. I subsequently returned and pulled up some by hand; each fragment had developed a substantial portion of new root. In Romania, the plants are harvested regularly, by simply cutting the top 10cm or so of the root and allowing it to grow back.

Barbarea vulgaris

Wintercress/Yellow Rocket

DISTRIBUTION Up to 380m. In England, widespread throughout, except Devon, Cornwall, Cumberland, Yorkshire, Durham, Northumberland and Cheviot; in Wales, widespread except the west, south of Caernarvonshire; in Scotland, found Central Lowlands and eastern Coastal Lowlands north to Moray Firth and a few places West Highlands and Argyll and Sterling; in Ireland, all counties but more scattered from Wicklow Mountains to the west coast and in western coastal counties; present Isle of Man.

HABITAT River and stream banks, ditches, roadsides and field edges; generally, though not always, damp habitats, where ground is disturbed either by water or human activity.

DESCRIPTION Native biennial/perennial, up to 1m high. Leaves dark green and glossier than any other cabbage species, very smooth to touch; at least 10cm long; large, rounded end lobe and several pairs of smaller lobes. Plant starts as a large basal rosette that becomes quite bushy before put-ting up a main stem that produces several separate, tight bunches of small yellow flowers, 7–9mm wide, during a long flowering season May–September.

NOTES Wintercress is so called because of its availability in the depths of winter, a fact also alluded to by its Latin name *Barbarea:* St Barbara's Day is in December, at which time the leaves are at an ideal stage for eating.

USES/RECIPES A peppery salad or green vegetable, much stronger than the closely related landcress *Barbarea verna*. Its high levels of vitamin C led to its global transportation by sailors, who referred to it as scurvy cress. Use the unopened flower buds like broccoli.

BENEFITS According to ethnobotanist Paolo Guarrera ('Food medicine and minor nourishment in the folk traditions of central Italy', 2003), in parts of rural Italy a broth made from the plant is drunk for respiratory diseases.

⅓ × life size

HAZARDS Its liking for roadsides, stream banks and field edges is problematic as it is known to accumulate toxic chemicals, such as heavy metals from car exhausts, agricultural chemicals from fields and from water sources that receive their run-off.

Brassica nigra

Black Mustard

DISTRIBUTION Up to 300m. In England, mostly south of line Morecambe Bay–Flamborough Head, less abundant Exmoor and Dartmoor, Hampshire Basin, east Kent and parts of East Midlands; in Wales, confined to lowland areas; in Scotland, to Central Lowlands, except for limited areas of Moray and Shetland; in Ireland, found along south coast with other localities Longford, Sligo, around Belfast and lowland area south of Shannon Estuary; present on Channel Islands, Isle of Man and Isles of Scilly.

HABITAT Only mustard commonly found on sea cliffs, shingle beaches or river and stream banks, where often found in abundance; also by ditches, on waste ground, roadsides and arable field edges.

DESCRIPTION A tall annual, up to 3m high, but usually 1.5–2m, with branches almost at right angles to the main stem. Lower leaves are lyre shaped, pinnately lobed; upper leaves long, thin and tapered at the base: at earlier growth stages covered in rough pimples. Seed pods point upward and clasp the stem: 12–20mm long with a seedless beak. Seeds are reddish brown and oblong.

SIMILAR SPECIES Hoary mustard *Hirschfeldia incana*, the branches of which grow at a steeper angle to the stem; leaves pinnately lobed at all stages. The beaks of the seed pods contain a single seed, making the whole pod look a bit phallic. Charlock has larger seed pods, which do not clasp the stem; the younger leaves are much less rough.

NOTES Black mustard is the only wild mustard that is unequivocally native to the British Isles and has been grown in Europe since at least the thirteenth century. There are four species of wild mustard; five if you include Chinese mustard *Brassica juncea*, which is occasionally found naturalized; in Asia its stems and leaves used to make kimchee. Their flavours, textures and uses differ slightly, but what unites them is the wide, bushy form of mature plants, crowned with yellow flowers. The arrangement of seed pods along the lengths of the side branches is a useful tool for telling them apart. Black mustard, hedge mustard and hoary mustard have seed pods clinging tightly to the stem; white mustard has seed pods pointing away from the stem. Charlock is somewhere in between. The seed pods themselves are also quite individual.

USES/RECIPES Black mustard was formerly cultivated for its seeds for mustard condiment, which is now mostly made using seeds of Chinese mustard *B. juncea* and white mustard. Black mustard seeds are pungent and spicy, rather than hot. The seeds of all of our wild mustards (as well as those of perennial and annual wall-rocket, garlic mustard, field penny-cress and shepherd's purse) can be

⁷/₁₀ × life size

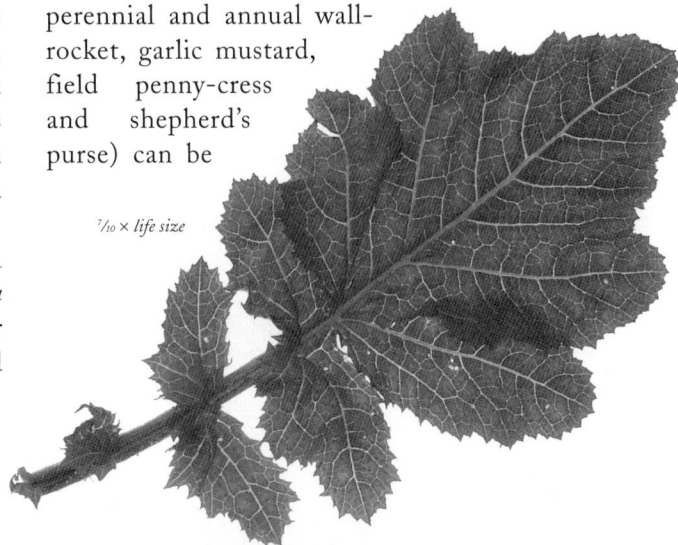

gathered (for method, see harvesting notes) and used as spices. Either add them directly as spice, ground or whole, or use them to make mustard condiment, with vinegar for continental mustard or with water for English. Only make English mustard for immediate use as it soon loses its bite (vinegar prevents the volatile mustard oils from breaking down). The seeds can also be sprouted. The leaves have a strong, warm, lingering, spicy flavour and are best used raw or slightly wilted – the oils that provide its clout dissipate when heated. Blanching them for less than a minute mellows the flavour slightly and also softens the texture. Thoroughly cooked leaves still taste very good, just not as spicy. Raw leaves have an intense flavour and coarse texture; on both counts its best to chop or tear the leaves, discarding the larger stalks. Serve with fatty or strongly flavoured meats. Wilted leaves can be served for example with roast turbot fillet, crab mash and shellfish sauce, roast partridge and wild mushrooms, braised rump of lamb with celeriac and rosemary gnocchi. Finely chopped raw leaves to vinaigrettes and white sauces, for example in a white wine velouté served with haddock fish cake. Such sauces need some acidity and a strong stock base to balance out the heat of the mustard [ST]. The flowers have a hot mustard flavour. Use to finish ham, bacon or beef dishes, or add to buttered new potatoes, wilting them for a few seconds.

MUTTON AND BLACK MUSTARD WINTER WARMER: Mutton braised in water with veg, thyme, bay leaf and peppercorns, in low oven for 4–5 hours. Remove meat and veg, pass braising liquor through sieve, thicken with butter and flour, add double cream, a little bit of English mustard and finely chopped black mustard leaf [PB].

HARVESTING NOTES (SEEDS) When the pods are brown and dry, and beginning to split, carefully cut the branches with sharp secateurs without shaking them; place a bag over the top and turn over the branches to shake out the seeds. Inevitably, some of the seed is lost this way. To avoid this, strip them off the branches when they are still green and take them home to ripen. When they are brown and beginning to open, put them in a sieve and break them up so that the seeds drop down through the sieve. Dry them a while longer before grinding; once ground you should dry them a bit more if you want to store the powder.

Brassica oleracea

Wild Cabbage

DISTRIBUTION Up to 300m. In England, sparse throughout, with slightly higher concentrations Cornwall, Dorset, Worcestershire, Leicestershire and Greater London; in Wales, sparse except Powys and Merioneth; in Scotland, few sites Central Lowlands and eastern Coastal Lowlands north to Moray Firth plus isolated sites Easterness and Clyde Isles; in Ireland, few locations, north, in Londonderry and Antrim, east in Dublin and west, in Leitrim, Sligo and Mayo; present Channel Islands, Isle of Man and Isles of Scilly.

HABITAT Coastal cliffs and beaches; on chalk, limestone and other alkaline soils.

DESCRIPTION Native, hairless perennial, with solid, woody stem up to 4cm wide and thick, dull, green fleshy leaves very similar to cultivated cabbage. Heart

1½ × life size   *Black mustard seed pods*

leaves are small, crinkly and tinged with purple. Flowers large, yellow, 20–30mm wide, in long spikes.

SIMILAR SPECIES Sea kale leaves are more bluish grey than green; sea kale also produces great domes of white flowers.

USES/RECIPES As you might expect from the source plant of cabbage, Brussels sprouts, broccoli, cauliflower and kale, these leaves are very tasty! The texture is robust and the flavour rich, stronger than any of its derivatives, but not overpowering. Older leaves are massive but still good to eat: strip the leafy part from the stem before cooking. Serve pan-fried fillet of John Dory on a bed of buttered wild cabbage, garnish with brown shrimps and finish with a light shellfish sauce [PB].

SPAGHETTI WITH WILD CABBAGE AND TOMATO SAUCE: Reduce some tomatoes and season, sauté a few shallots and a little garlic until soft, cut the cabbage into thin strips and sauté for a few minutes, combine the ingredients, return to heat for a few minutes, then stir into spaghetti (this recipe can also be used for sea kale). A classic combination: fried with bacon, game birds, pigeon, venison or mackerel. Before and after opening, boil or steam the flowers and serve like broccoli.

HARVESTING NOTES These are hardy plants, but they are nationally scarce and should be treated with respect; only take a small proportion of the leaves or racemes from any one plant.

²/₃ × life size

⅓ × life size

Brassica rapa

Wild Turnip

DISTRIBUTION Up to 300m. Possibly native, although there are three subspecies: subsp. *campestris* is probably native along river banks and abundant on stretches of the Thames above London; the other two are relics of cultivation. In England, most widespread south of a line Humber–Mersey estuaries but absent from Exmoor, Dartmoor and Hampshire Basin, and less abundant to east and in north of England, absent from Lake District, Pennines and Cheviot Hills; occurs throughout Wales except Cambrian Mountains; sparsely scattered in lowland areas of Scotland, except Caithness; widespread throughout Ireland, except western half of the Central Lowlands and parts of Donegal and Down; present on Channel Islands, Isle of Man and Isles of Scilly.

HABITAT River and canal banks, cliffs, waste places, arable fields and road verges.

DESCRIPTION Hairy annual/biennial. Basal leaves up to 40cm long, bright green and deeply indented with a large end lobe; stem leaves greyish green, stalkless with bottom lobes clasping main stem, of which lower leaves are pinnately lobed, upper ones lanceolate. Yellow flowers extend above the flower buds.

SIMILAR SPECIES Similar to rape, but rape flowers are below or at the same height as the unopened buds, and all leaves are dull grey-green.

USES/RECIPES Cultivated turnip greens have a mild, very slightly cabbagey flavour and were once a popular salad green and vegetable; in the United States, Italy and France, they still are. Pak choi and Chinese leaf are both varieties of turnip green. However, the wild leaves are quite bitter and need to be cooked with something rich, acid, fatty or salty. Add a few leaves to chitterlings chopped into small pieces, fried in duck fat in a very hot pan until nicely brown and crispy; fry for a couple more minutes then add diced roasted beetroot. Add a splash of chicken stock and warm through; when it is all nice and hot again add a few of the turnip leaves; finish with Dijon mustard, red wine vinegar and olive oil dressing. The dish combines earthy, salty, sweet and bitter flavours [JL].
LAMB STEW: Put diced braising lamb in a pot with onions, carrots and celery cut the same size as the diced lamb and add a bouquet garni. Cover with water, bring to the boil and simmer; season. For the last half an hour add turnip roots (preferably wild). Add a few of the greens 1–2 minutes before serving [JDW]. Young flower buds and their stems can be cooked as a spiced-up version of broccoli, served with butter and lemon or a rich sauce. The large, yellow flowers are sweet with a slight mustardy bite; they make a good addition to summer salads or a garnish for soups. Roots are not as swollen as cultivated turnips but can still be quite large; they should be collected from first-year plants before they produce a flowering stem. The flavour is like cultivated turnips, but much more intense. Roast duck breasts with wild turnips and apples, glazing everything with honey and spices (ginger, cinnamon, cloves, nutmeg, white pepper); serve with a bit of wilted turnip greens [JDW].

Capsella bursa-pastoris

Shepherd's Purse

DISTRIBUTION Up to 780m. Universal, grows world wide, though native in Europe and Asia. Very widespread throughout most of British Isles, only less so: in Scotland, parts of Highlands and Isle of Lewis; in Ireland, parts of Donegal, Mayo, Galway, Clare and Kerry.

HABITAT Gardens, waste ground, arable fields and other open ground.

DESCRIPTION Basal rosettes consist of simple–pinnately lobed, light green leaves, which are usually hairy. The flowering stem has smaller leaves with arrow-like points at their base, clasping the stem, and small, white flowers in

⁷⁄₁₀ × life size

The rice is cooked in chicken stock, with egg stirred in. When the rice is half done, the herbs are added. The dish is served with a plum, a piece of turnip and radish. In Korea the leaves are parboiled and served with soy sauce or used in a bean curd and shredded pork soup. The fully mature seeds have a strong mustard flavour; it is easy to collect a lot in a short space of time if you have a patch with plenty of plants on it. Just run your hand up the stem to remove the little purse-shaped seed pods; rub your hands over the seed cases to release the seeds then **winnow** (see p.324). The root is said to be a mild ginger substitute; those I have tasted were bland at first and just slightly hot after a minute or so, but not very ginger-like.

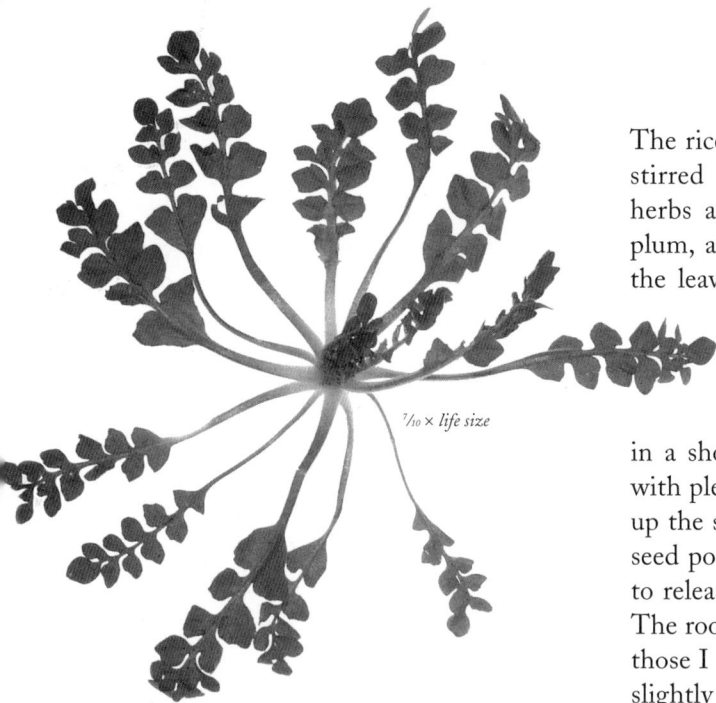

rounded clusters at the top of the plant. The flowers turn into the purse-shaped seed pods that give the older plants an easily recognizable form.

NOTES A very common annual wild plant that can germinate at any time of year if conditions are suitable, so possible to find it at all stages of its growth cycle all year round. In China there are cultivated varieties, which are used in many different recipes.

USES/RECIPES Raw leaves look very attractive with a mild flavour and a crisp texture. In Shanghai cuisine they are stir fried, for example with bamboo shoots, or included in a kind of meat dumpling; in Japan they form part of the late winter dish Haru no nanakusa gayu ('Rice porridge and seven spring herbs'), with chickweed, radish greens, turnip greens, nipplewort, Japanese water-dropwort and a form of cudweed – this dish could almost be made here! The leaves are boiled for a few seconds, refreshed and squeezed dry then chopped to 1cm lengths.

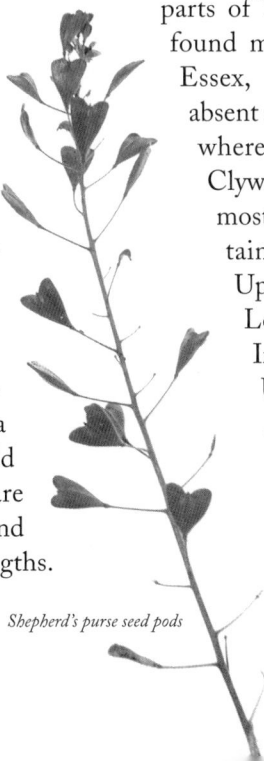

Cardamine amara

Large Bitter-cress

DISTRIBUTION Up to 640m. In England, widespread in northeast, northwest, West Midlands, Yorkshire and Humber, except parts of Yorkshire and Lincolnshire, also found much of Norfolk, Suffolk, north Essex, Kent, Sussex and Surrey, but absent southwest except Gloucestershire, where sparse; in Wales, few sites in Clywd and Powys; in Scotland, found most areas south of Grampian Mountains except parts of Southern Uplands, also found eastern Coastal Lowlands north to Moray Firth; in Ireland, only score or so sites, all in Ulster, north and east of Cavan.

HABITAT Damp/wet areas in meadows, marshes and woodlands; by or even in streams and rivers.

Shepherd's purse seed pods

DESCRIPTION

Perennial, producing much of its leaf in the winter months. Similar to hairy bitter-cress but larger and hairless, and without a basal rosette. Leaflets oval, the end one rounded. Large flowers, white or purplish, with distinctive violet anthers, April–June.

SIMILAR SPECIES On banks or edges of streams and rivers, it can be confused with watercress, but is more upright, with lighter leaves and larger flowers.

USES/RECIPES The flavour is similar to that of lady's smock and scurvy-grasses; use in similar ways.

Cardamine hirsuta

Hairy Bitter-cress

DISTRIBUTION Up to 1190m. Widespread throughout British Isles: except absent in Scotland, from Grampian Mountains and parts of east, west and north Highlands; in Ireland, less abundant in Connaught and counties west of Leinster, Tipperary, Clare and Donegal.

HABITAT Dry gardens, orchards, arable fields, rocky outcrops, especially bare and disturbed ground.

DESCRIPTION Native, over-wintering, hairy annual. Basal leaves have many pairs of small, round, angled leaflets, which are hairy on their upper surfaces; the upper leaf leaflets are much narrower. Stems are upright or wavy, branching mostly from the base. Flowers are tiny and white. When the seeds are mature, the capsules explode and catapult seeds in all directions.

SIMILAR SPECIES Wavy bitter-cress *C. flexuosa* is similar and just as good to eat; found in damp woodlands, shady marsh areas, by rivers and streams and in gardens. Its stems are always wavy and hairy, branching only above the base, and with more leaves.

NOTES Hairy bitter-cress is an ubiquitous garden weed; with its own built-in self-seeding mechanism, it only needs a little bare ground to get a foothold, as practically any gardener will tell you. In fact I first found hairy bitter-cress in my neighbour's garden, just a few small rosettes growing among the lamb's lettuce I was gathering. A few days later in a nearby conifer plantation, I came across masses of wavy bitter-cress plants, all much larger and denser than the bitter-cress in my neighbour's garden. Some had clearly been eaten by rabbits, encouraging even more vigorous growth; the same thing happened when we cut the rosette from its base with scissors, producing multiple harvests from each plant. When I returned the following year to find barely any, I worried at first that our harvesting regime had done for them. But the plants had eventually been left to go to seed so our picking could not have been the cause. It had been growing on an area of ground disturbed by forestry activities, being one of the first plants to colonize bare ground. By the time we came back the second year, secondary colonizers simply crowded out the bitter-cress. Plants such as bitter-cress, with a liking for bare soil, get on very well in tidy gardens. Sadly, gardeners who inadvertently create such an ideal environment for wild salads rarely eat the fruits of their labour! The flavour is like rocket, watercress and cabbage combined, mildly peppery in winter then quite fiery just before it flowers, when the leaves briefly take on an elegant purple tint. It is one of the most visually stunning wild foods; chef Anthony North uses smaller, younger rosettes, which he likens to spiders' webs, whole as a garnish. This queen of winter wild salads proved fit for a queen, when it was served up at Elizabeth II's seventieth-birthday banquet, courtesy of Richard Corrigan, as part of BBC TV's first *Great British Menu* series.

USES/RECIPES Like watercress, bitter-cress's fiery flavour cuts through fat and strong flavours, for example with pâtés or fatty cold meats such as ham or lamb, or balances strong-flavoured foods such as game. For something unusual, try it instead of parsley with deep-fried pig's trotters. Use in warm salads; also with sweeter salads, grated apples and shallots, for example, using apple juice, olive oil and salt as a dressing (although, ordinarily, lighter oils such as sunflower or peanut are best with this leaf) [EC]. Try with beetroot and mustard dressing (pickled beetroot vinegar, olive oil, Dijon mustard) [BW], or with smoked eel fillet with creamed horseradish and new potatoes [KG]. **FISH SAUCE:** Reduce fish stock, add confit of garlic and blend in bitter-cress at the end. It also finishes butterbean soup nicely [BV]. **BITTER-CRESS SOUP:** Make a base of sweated potato, onion and garlic, boiled with stock; the bitter-cress is blended in at the last minute, and a couple of pickled oysters added to each bowl [BW].

HARVESTING NOTES Grasp the centre of the rosette and use scissors to cut just below the lowest leaves. Once in flower, there are fewer leaves, which are rather fiddly to pick.

Cardamine pratensis

Lady's Smock

DISTRIBUTION Up to 1080m. Widespread throughout almost entire British Isles: only less so in parts of Laois in Ireland; North West Highlands of Scotland.

HABITAT Damp and seasonally wet places in woodland, meadow, fen and mossy mountain areas.

DESCRIPTION Native perennial, up to 60cm high, with basal rosette of leaves with rounded leaflets, the end leaflet being much larger than the rest. Otherwise a lot like the bitter-cresses, although without a basal rosette. Leaves are often tinged with purple or even red. Flowering

1½ × life size

them in a salad, especially with beetroot, salmon or beef. Any dish that uses horse-radish could find room for them if you want to add a bit of beauty and colour. Both roots and leaves are also eaten in cooked dishes in Bosnia and Herzegovina.

stem is upright, stem leaves with very narrow leaflets. Flowers are purplish pink, 12–18mm wide.

USES/RECIPES What happens when you eat the leaves is more than a taste sensation: the essential oils somehow affect your sinuses producing a strange, warm tingling as if you have been punched on the nose. The flavour is like horseradish but with a strange, medicinal overtone. More a spice than a salad leaf, you only need a minute amount for any dish. Add a few leaves to a little salad of horseradish and beetroot, served with smoked eel, potato pancakes and crème fraîche [EC]. With beetroot, soft-boiled egg and capers; it makes a pesto with a lovely green gloss to it, using lady's smock, parsley, garlic and tarragon [RL]. The pretty pink flowers also taste of horseradish, though not quite as intensely as the leaves. Use them to finish horseradish ice cream (see p.79). Lady's smock-flavoured chilled custard goes nicely with **Japanese knotweed**, which is in season at the same time: add a few flowers at the beginning of the cooking process and stir in the rest when you leave it to cool [AC]. Put a few of

Cochlearia danica

Danish Scurvygrass

DISTRIBUTION Up to 300m. Coastal: in England and Wales, all counties but less abundant along east coast; in Scotland, common English border–Central Lowlands but sparser further north; in Ireland, common along south coast and coast of Londonderry, Antrim and Down in northeast, and handful of sites on remainder of east coast. Inland: in England, all counties; in Wales, mostly northeastern counties; in Scotland, in a few places south of Grampian Mountains either side of Southern Lowlands; in Ireland, a few sites in eastern counties of Ulster and isolated 10 sq km Mayo, Westmeath, Kildare, Tipperary and Limerick. Present on Channel Islands, Isle of Man and Isles of Scilly.

HABITAT Very common on roadsides due to the use of salt grit, its original habitat was coastal where it is still found on sea walls, sand dunes, shingle and rocky shores as well as on walls and pavements in coastal areas.

DESCRIPTION Native perennial/biennial, prostate, with stems up to 20cm long. Leaves shiny, dark green; basal ones cordate–ivylike on long, straggly stalks; upper leaves generally stalked, oval. Flowers, Feb–June, tiny, 4–5 mm wide, lilac/white; spherical seed pods in autumn.

SIMILAR SPECIES Leaves of common scurvy-grass *C. officinalis* are more fleshy; basal leaves

often kidney shaped and stem leaves unstalked. Flowers, May–August, are larger, 10–12mm, white. Basal leaves of English scurvy grass *C. anglica* taper into stalk and flowers are 5–7mm wide.

NOTES Sailors once preserved these plants in large quantities and ate them with their daily victuals to prevent scurvy or vitamin-C deficiency. As a sailor's choice it makes sense since it is adapted to the salty soil of coastal places. The Latin genus name *Cochlearia* comes from the shape of the leaves of the smaller species, which is somewhat like the bowl of a spoon, of which *cochlear* is the Latin name.

USES/RECIPES (for all three *Cochlearia*) The leaves have a flavour like horseradish, similar to lady's smock but not quite as strong. Use in salads, blended into dressings and pesto, on their own with boiled eggs (dressed with sweet balsamic vinaigrette), cold meats or strong cheeses, or chopped finely and add to sauces.

Coronopus squamatus

Swine-cress

DISTRIBUTION Up to 300m. In England, widespread south of line Severn Estuary–Flamborough Head, except Devon and Warwickshire, also along much of northeast coastal areas, but sporadic elsewhere; in Wales, all counties except Merioneth, but mostly coastal areas; rare in Scotland; scarce in Ireland but in all coastal counties except Donegal, Londonderry and Wicklow with greatest concentrations along southeast coast; present Channel Islands, Isle of Man, Isles of Scilly and Lundy.

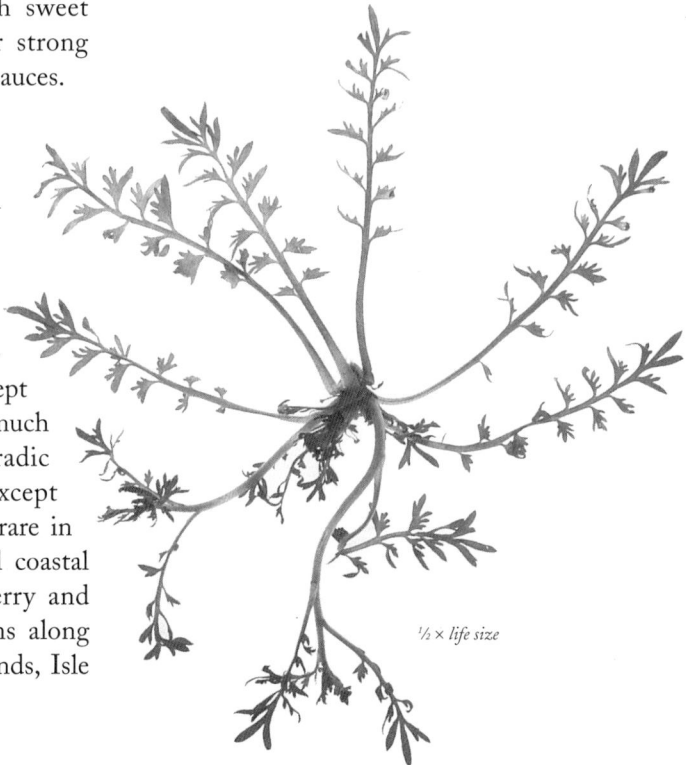

HABITAT Farmyards, gateways, waste ground, pavements, gardens and shingle beaches.

DESCRIPTION Annual/biennial, starting with a clear basal rosette, leaves 1–2 times pinnate. Flowers tiny, white, in crowded clusters at intervals on the stems.

SIMILAR SPECIES Lesser swine-cress *C. didymus didymus* is brighter green with long, branched and scrambling stems and smaller, feathery leaves, 1–2 times pinnate. It has petalless flowers and is more widespread than swine-cress in south of Ireland and northwest of England.

USES/RECIPES Swine-cress has mildly mustardy, fleshy leaves; lesser swine-cress has a more pungent, earthy smell and a hotter mustard flavour. Younger leaves can be used in their entirety, but older lesser swine-cress leaves need to be picked from their rather woody stems; the leaves themselves are quite soft and

½ × life size

Crambe maritime

Sea Kale

DISTRIBUTION Up to 300m. In England, found mostly in coastal northwest locations and much of the coast from north Devon to south Norfolk, scarce or absent elsewhere; in Wales, on coastal Gwynedd and Clwyd in north and southeast tip of Pembrokeshire; in Scotland, very scarce, mostly in the southwest; present Channel Islands, Isle of Man and Isles of Scilly.

HABITAT Shingle beaches.

DESCRIPTION Native perennial. In winter only gnarled, brown root tops with protruding reddish shoots visible, like an alien life form. The rest of the time sea kale is prominent in its open-shingle habitat: small, purplish cabbage-like leaves in spring, later bluey-green reaching up to 40cm long; in summer crowned with stunning domes of creamy-white flowers (see page 41), infusing the beach with the smell of honey. The strange spherical, translucent green fruits are also distinctly eye-catching.

SIMILAR SPECIES The only other large-leafed, cabbage-like plant that may grow on beaches is wild cabbage, which has darker and greener leaves and yellow flowers.

NOTES Sea-kale populations were damaged by the nineteenth-century trend for digging up plants for gardens. Sea kale readily reproduces from seed or root cuttings, both of which could have been achieved without damaging the wild population. More recently sea-kale colonies have been destroyed by the construction of sea defences on shingle beaches. During the foot-and-mouth crisis of 2001, beaches were closed and the population flourished, since the plants were not so frequently trampled. Traditional

delicate. The strength of the flavour makes this more of a herb or spice than a salad. Both species work in many of the combinations listed for bitter-cress, but for lesser swine-cress much less leaf is needed. Serve in a salad with rabbit terrine or cold poached salmon, roasted baby beetroot, **chickweed** and **wood sorrel**. Serve on a base of vinaigrette made from puréed beetroot, vinegar and olive oil [JDW]. A simpler combination is just with beetroot and soft-boiled duck eggs, with a few swine-cress leaves sprinkled on top.

¹/₂ × life size

use of sea kale
for food, however,
did no harm to the plants. Local people no
doubt took greater care than now not to trample the plants, heaping up shingle on top of the
emerging leaf shoots in order to blanch them
and increase their length. These spears were
harvested for sale at market, and the plant was
left to continue its growth cycle. A similar
method has been applied in the large-scale cultivation of sea kale, particularly in France.

USES/RECIPES Up to and including the flowering stage, the leaves are tender and sweet and
could even be used sparingly in salads. Cooked,
they are richly flavoured and delicious. Young
flower buds resemble purple sprouting broccoli, but have a much stronger flavour. The
greatest treats, however, are the fully opened
flower heads. They smell strongly of honey; if
you catch them before the bees they taste of
honey too. Use raw with fish or meat or in salads. Poach in a little milk for a few seconds;
serve with boiled root vegetables or pan-fried
pigeon breasts.

ECOLOGICAL CONSIDERATIONS Only grows
on shingle beaches, a form of habitat scarce not
only in Great Britain but also globally. The last
thing anyone wants is for one of its signature
plants to decline as a result of enthusiasm for

wild food. Pick only a few leaves,
buds or flowers from each plant.

Diplotaxis tenuifolia

Perennial Wall-rocket

DISTRIBUTION Up to 300m. In England, mostly London, Home Counties,
Kent, East Anglia, north Somerset and
Gloucestershire but also along south coast,
from Chesil Beach eastwards, in Derbyshire,
Merseyside, Durham and Tyne and Wear and
few areas in Cornwall; in Wales, mostly in Colwyn area, on Gower Peninsula and northeast to
Carmarthen and along south coast from Barry
eastwards; in Scotland, very scarce but found in
and around Edinburgh; in Ireland found only
in Belfast; present Channel Islands.

HABITAT Dry places on roadsides, old walls,
waste ground, docks and well above the tide-mark on beaches.

DESCRIPTION Naturalized perennial. Leaves
greyish–dark green, deeply or shallowly pinnately lobed or, occasionally, unlobed. Flowers pale
yellow, up to 20mm wide; seed pods upright, up
to 25mm long. Younger leaves are bushy, not in a
basal rosette; stems thick and woody.

SIMILAR SPECIES Annual wall-rocket *D.
muralis* occurs in similar habitats, also in cracks
on pavements. It is annual, much smaller, with
paler, smaller green leaves, mostly in a basal
rosette, pinnately lobed, with rounded lobes;
flowers are smaller and a paler yellow. Leaves of
mature **ragwort** and **groundsel** are similar but
have a strong, unpleasant smell.

NOTES Several wild species bear the name
rocket, but eastern, tall, London and false London rockets are mild and cabbagey in flavour; it

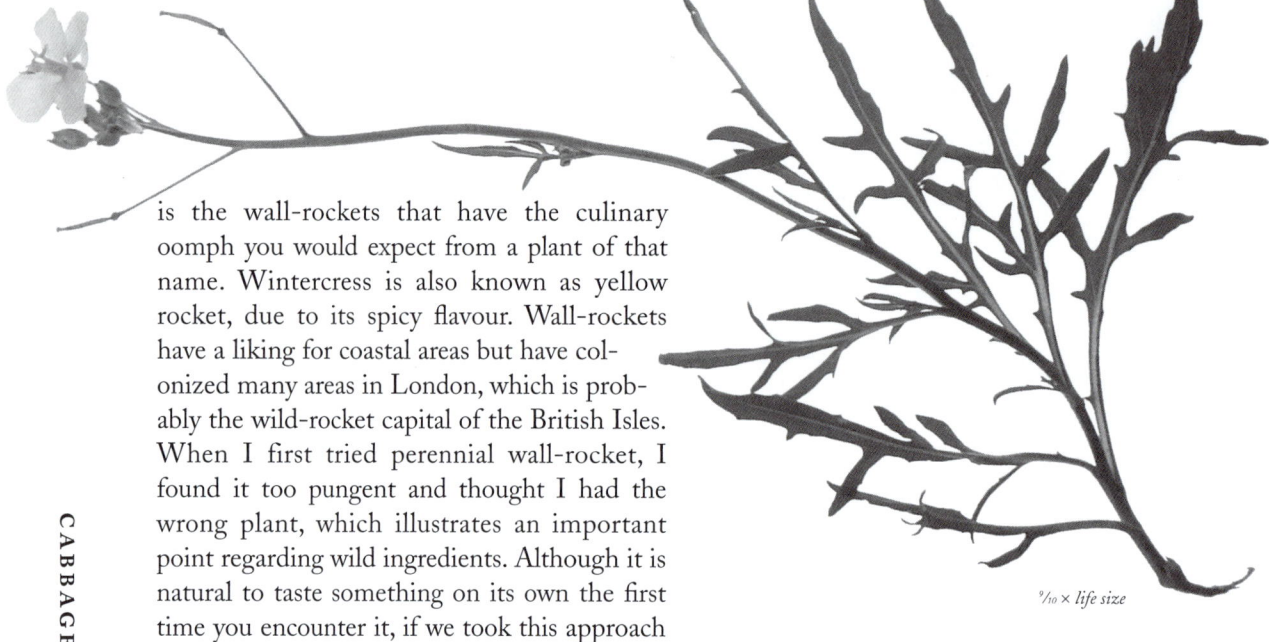

is the wall-rockets that have the culinary oomph you would expect from a plant of that name. Wintercress is also known as yellow rocket, due to its spicy flavour. Wall-rockets have a liking for coastal areas but have colonized many areas in London, which is probably the wild-rocket capital of the British Isles. When I first tried perennial wall-rocket, I found it too pungent and thought I had the wrong plant, which illustrates an important point regarding wild ingredients. Although it is natural to taste something on its own the first time you encounter it, if we took this approach

⁹⁄₁₀ × *life size*

Derek Quelch's Salad of Wild Rocket, Jerusalem Artichokes, Wild Mushrooms and Poached Duck Eggs

25g wild rocket
25g Jerusalem artichokes
1 clove of garlic, halved
olive oil
20g mixed wild mushrooms

a knob of butter
white wine vinegar
1 duck egg
red wine vinegar
salt and pepper

Pick through the salad leaves to remove any thick stalks or brown leaves, then wash thoroughly two or three times to remove any insects and allow to dry.

Preheat the oven to 180°C/350°F, Gas Mark 4. Scrub and dry the artichokes, cut them in half (and in half again if large) and place on a baking tray with the garlic, some salt, pepper, and a drizzle of olive oil. Place in the oven for 6–10 minutes or until cooked.

Wash the mushrooms two or three times and dry well. Season with salt and pepper, then cook with a knob of butter in a very hot pan. A lot of moisture will come out at first,

but this will evaporate, allowing the mushrooms to sauté.

Meanwhile, boil some water in a pan with a little white wine vinegar and salt. Crack the duck egg into the water and poach it until the white is cooked but the yolk is soft. Take out of the water and place on a plate to drain.

Make the dressing by mixing one part red wine vinegar with two parts olive oil and some salt and pepper. Place the salad leaves in a bowl with the artichokes and wild mushrooms and mix in some dressing. Place the warm duck egg on top, drizzle a little of the dressing over the egg and serve.

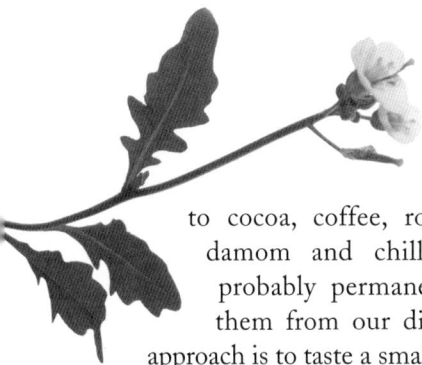

Annual wall-rocket

to cocoa, coffee, rosemary, cardamom and chilli we would probably permanently exclude them from our diets. A better approach is to taste a small amount, but reserve judgement until the ingredient has been tasted in combination with other things. With many wild foods we are only just beginning to re-discover their potential, especially considering the long, unbroken traditions associated with many better-known ingredients. Wild rocket is probably somewhere in the middle: rocket is familiar, even the commercially grown leaves bogusly sold as wild rocket, so there are conventions of use, but the powerful kick of the real thing is in a different league.

Uses/Recipes Good with meaty fish like monkfish or as a simple salad with shavings of pecorino or Parmesan [MH]. In a salad with apples, goat's cheese, tomatoes and lemon and olive oil dressing or even just with plain fresh lemon or lime juice or cider vinegar [DQ].

Lepidium draba

Hoary Cress/Whitlow Pepperwort/Thanetweed

Distribution Up to 300m. Naturalized. In England, widespread southeast of line Severn Estuary–Flamborough Head and found most counties elsewhere; in Wales, more sparsely widespread; in Scotland, mostly Central Lowlands and eastern Coastal Lowlands with few sites to west in Argyll and Sterling, and Strathclyde and Ayrshire, also Grampian and Orkney; in Ireland, few sites, mainly Antrim, Down, Dublin, Wicklow and Waterford with single site in west in Galway; present Isle of Man and Channel Islands.

Habitat Arable fields, roadsides, sand dunes and upper salt marshes, railways, disturbed ground of any sort.

Description An invasive perennial, spreading relentlessly by seed and rhizomes. Leaves are oblong, pale greyish-green, with slight teeth interspersed with concave curves and bluntly pointed lobes at the bases. Its small white flowers appear in dense clusters resembling umbels.

Similar species Smith's pepperwort *L. heterophyllum*, found mostly in the West Country in England and west of Ireland, is distinguished by its winged fruits, which somewhat resemble those of field penny-cress.

Notes During the Middle Ages, *Lepidium* species were widely used as herbs in central and northern Europe (Pieroni, 'Gathered wild food plants of the Upper Valley of the Serchio River', 1999). This particular species has been used for

food in both Europe and the United States. It has been introduced at times in several places but arrived in Kent as seed in the bedding of soldiers returning from the ill-fated 1809 Walcheren expedition. A farmer ploughed it into one Thanet field, from which it spread to become a major agricultural weed and colonizer of roadsides, earning it the local name Thanetweed. An officer for the Kent Wildlife Trust challenged me to find edible uses for it, as it is considered a nuisance by farmers and conservationists alike. I offered it to our customers, and we now have several who use it enthusiastically. We are not yet selling enough to curtail its spread, but we are working on it.

USES/RECIPES Leaves are good in salads; chop finely and add to sauces just prior to serving; fry dry, in just a little butter, until slightly crispy – don't let it go soft like spinach [PW]; chiffonade into soups. Use with simple, strong flavours, for example in smoked salmon omelette or in a salad with smoked mackerel. Whole flower heads can be used like broccoli at the bud stage. Seeds are a hot spice, best harvested when green.

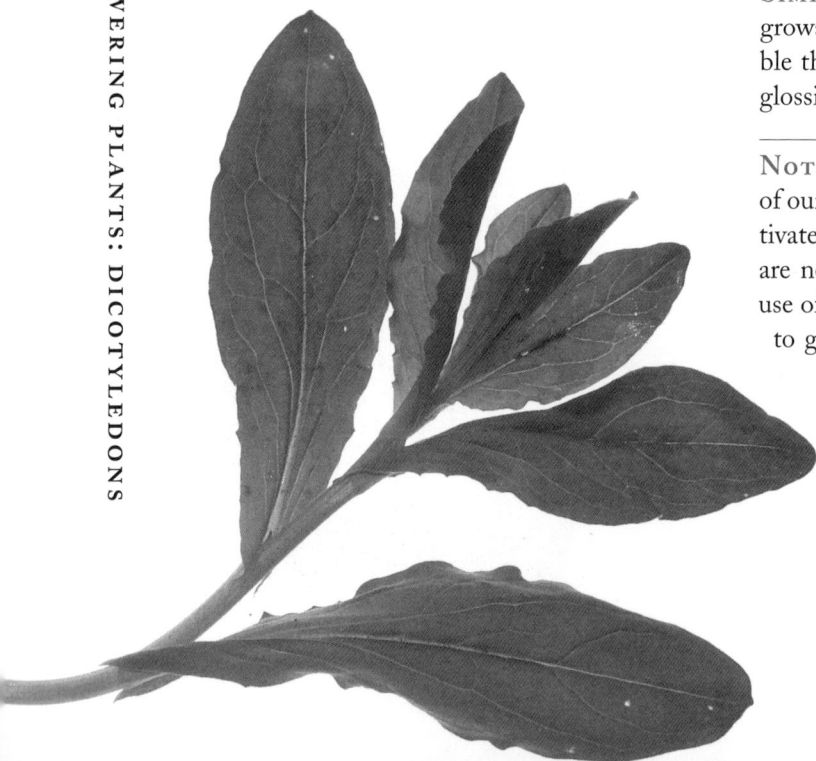

Lepidium latifolium

Dittander

DISTRIBUTION Up to 300m. Native only to England, Wales and Channel Islands: sparse naturalized inland locations throughout England and Wales. In England, found Gloucestershire, Worcestershire, inland and coastal areas of Essex, Kent, Suffolk and Norfolk, Thames Estuary and small area of West Sussex coast; in Wales, Monmouthshire; in Scotland, East Lothian; in Ireland, Dublin and Cork.

HABITAT Near both freshwater and saltwater, on river banks, sea walls, upper shores; on waste ground, roadsides and railways.

DESCRIPTION A perennial plant forming quite large colonies. Large, oval, leathery greyish-green leaves (up to 30cm long) with finely toothed edges emerge in spring beneath last year's dead stems; later stem leaves much smaller and thinner. Flowers, white and quite tiny, in large, loose clusters.

SIMILAR SPECIES Sea beet *Beta vulgaris* often grows right next to dittander; its leaves resemble those of young dittander but darker green, glossier and without serrated edges.

NOTES Dittander is another living document of our culinary past, at one time commonly cultivated; its roots once used as horseradish roots are now. Its limited distribution precludes the use of roots of wild plants but it is easy enough to grow; at least one UK seed company sells dittander seeds (if you can't gather your own). The plants suffer no ill effects from the removal of a few leaves per plant – I have seen it repeatedly mown and still grow back. It is closely related to garden cress *Lepidium sativum* and is probably the hottest cress of all.

USES/RECIPES Leaves have a robust texture and a strong flavour somewhere between mustard and horseradish, which is all but lost when heated. For this reason, pesto is an ideal use, or as a dressing (for cold meats), mix shredded dittander, capers, olive oil, fresh lemon juice and zest, salt and pepper, garlic purée. It goes well with steak or any cold meat as very fine chiffonade. Add finely chopped leaves to béarnaise sauce immediately before serving with rare beef and thick chips; also add to beef gravy. Seeds are hot when green and can be used as a spice; they rapidly lose flavour as they mature.

One winter morning I was out foraging on a beach with Paul Brown, at that time head chef of Le Caprice, and we came across masses of dittander roots that had been dislodged by waves during a storm. Paul took a few back to London to experiment, with the following result.

SALMON AND OYSTER SALAD WITH DITTANDER ROOT DRESSING: *Salad* Fool's watercress, dandelion, amaranth, hot smoked salmon and oysters dipped in flour, milk and breadcrumbs and deep fried. *Dressing* Combine mustard, olive oil, garlic, salt and pepper, white wine vinegar and the root peeled and blitzed, then olive oil added slowly to make an emulsion. Dress the salad with this, then finely grate a little more dittander root over the top.

HARVESTING NOTES Having identified dittander and got a feel for where it grows, it is easy to spot patches from a distance. In summer they are greyish green

Dittander plant just prior to flowering

½ × *life size*

with leaf, later with a cream-coloured fuzz of flowers around the top 25cm or so; in winter the straw-coloured canes, with the remnant of the seed heads, are equally conspicuous. Check the base of the canes at this final stage: there is often a second wind of very large leaves in the autumn, before winter die-back.

Raphanus raphanistrum

Wild Radish

DISTRIBUTION Up to 380m. In England, widespread south of a line Tees Bay–Mersey Estuary, except Exmoor, Dartmoor and a belt running northeast Weymouth Bay–Wash, also absent from belt running northwest coast of Suffolk–Peak District, and in north of England far less abundant with main concentration in bay area Morecambe–Liverpool; in Wales, mostly in south with scattered localities along the coast; in Scotland, limited to lowland areas particularly Central Lowlands and eastern Coastal Lowlands and widespread in the Northern Isles; in Ireland, main concentration in southwest and along

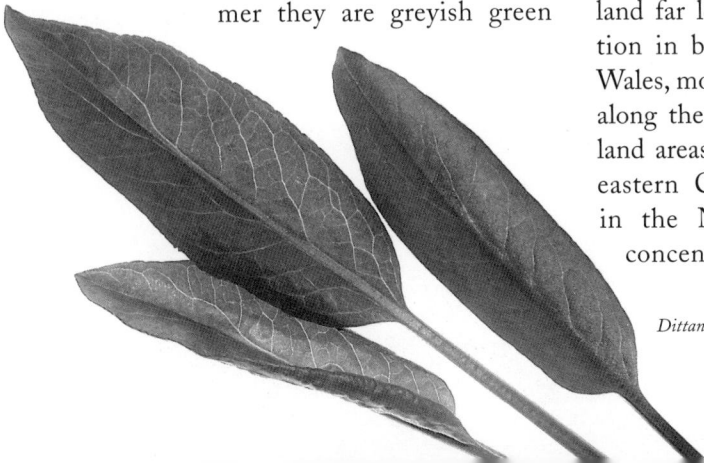

Dittander basal leaves

southeast coastal region with few scattered locations in north; present on Channel Islands, Isle of Man and Isles of Scilly.

HABITAT Arable fields, waste ground and road verges – rarely far from human activity.

DESCRIPTION Native, hairy annual. Deeply cut basal leaves have staggered lobes; upper leaves are stalked, not indented but with rough teeth. Flowers are white or yellow and often have purple veins. Seed pods are distinctive, with segments like a series of beads stacked on top of one another and a long, tapering beak at the end.

SIMILAR SPECIES Charlock flowers are a darker yellow and have neither purple veins nor upright sepals; the seed pods are not beaded. Basal leaves of wild radish are longer than those of charlock. Coastal plant

2 × life size

sea radish *R. maritimus* is biennial/perennial; older plants distinguished by thick, woody stems. Winter rosette leaves are large and dark green with leaflets crowded and overlapping; the flowers always pale yellow. Seed pods have fewer, larger 'beads' and a much shorter beak.

USES/RECIPES Lower leaves are rather coarse; all leaves cabbagey and only slightly spicy. Use in similar ways to charlock. This is a popular vegetable in Turkey: in the Bodrum area, leaves are roasted with onions and olive oil then served with yoghurt; in central Anatolia they are boiled until completely soft, then served with yoghurt mixed with crushed garlic or fresh lemon juice and served as an appetizer or *mezza* (**dandelions** are served in a similar way). The midrib of sea radish leaves is

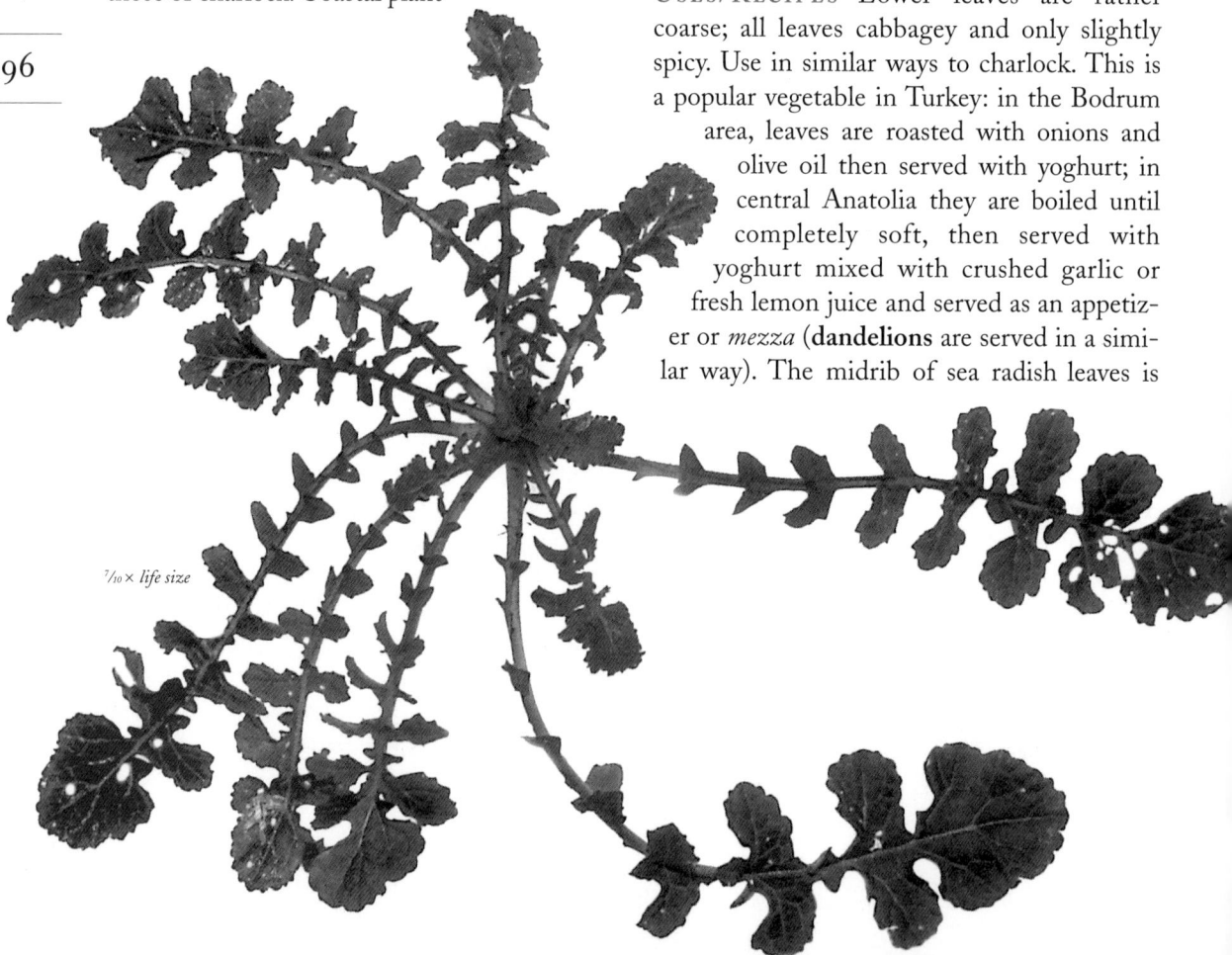

⁷/₁₀ × life size

Sea radish leaf

$^2/_3$ × *life size*

$^3/_{10}$ × *life size*

Sea radish seed pods

thick and juicy, with a lovely radish flavour. It works well in salads, once stripped of the green leaf part, and also as crudités. Young seed pods can be preserved in vinegar, cooked or chopped and used in salads.

Rorippa nasturtium-aquaticum

Watercress

DISTRIBUTION Up to 300m. Widespread throughout England south of line Morecambe Bay–Wash, except north Devon, Suffolk, Northamptonshire and south Lincolnshire. North of line less so, especially at higher altitudes; in Scotland, found in most of the lowlands including Western and Northern Isles; found in all counties of Ireland but more concentrated around Cork, Waterford, Dublin and Down; present Channel Islands, Isle of Man and Isles of Scilly.

HABITAT Edges of rivers, streams and ditches.

DESCRIPTION Native. A creeping water plant forming large mats. Leaves with many crinkly-edged, stalkless leaflets, round–oval on younger leaves, more elongated on older ones. Flowers small and white, in tight clusters at the tops of the plants.

SIMILAR SPECIES Large bitter-cress has distinctly stalked leaflets; fool's watercress *Apium nodiflorum*, often found growing among watercress, has paler, tooth-edged leaflets with pointed tips; the base of its leaf stalks surrounds the main stem with a swollen sheath.

NOTES Wild watercress is the same species as the cultivated variety but reaches a more advanced stage of growth than the delicate, round leaves that appear in shops. Cultivated on a large scale for the last hundred years or so, it has been commercially wild-harvested for centuries. Contrasting the two, chef Peter Weeden has strong views about the difference between them: 'Wild watercress has a much cleaner flavour, looks better, has a better texture. Everything about it is superior. The farmed variant is like bulk-volume wine, made from fast-growing, high-yield vineyards as opposed to low-yield old vineyard wine, which gives character and depth of flavour. Wild plants are nearly always in distress, struggling against the odds and perhaps this gives rise to their superior qualities.'

USES/RECIPES Pretty much the whole plant can be used, including the thick stems (which are best cooked – René Redzepi uses the cooked stems as a vegetable, having first removed the leaves, which are used to make wild watercress emulsion, see Turbot with herbs, p.295) as well as the older, longer-lobed leaves. The flavour is far stronger than cultivated watercress: watercress soup, for example, boasts a much gutsier flavour using the wild plants. Use it raw as a bed for whole roast fish, beef or soft-boiled duck egg peeled; for the latter, spoon homemade mayonnaise over the top and sprinkle with wild celery salt [MH].

WILD WATERCRESS SOUP: (follow basic green leaf soup recipe, p.14) is excellent served with a poached egg and a swirl of cream, with wild chervil leaf blended into it [PB]. Wilt and blend with sautéed onions to make a purée. The raw leaves are of course excellent in salads, for example combined with salsify and wild mushrooms [DQ]. The small, white and peppery flowers can be used in salads or to finish off cooked dishes.

BENEFITS An established and well-deserved status as a super food: a potent source of vitamin E, iodine, manganese and sulphur. According to ethnobotanist James Duke (*Medicinal Plants of China*, 1985), in China it is eaten with lean pork as a cure for coughs, lung complaints and sore throats.

HAZARDS There are a number of potential hazards. First, the liver fluke parasite, which may be present if there are sheep or cattle grazing with access to the water (for further detail, see p.23). Second, watercress is one of several plants that takes up large amounts of toxins from soil, including nitrate wash-off from agricultural land. Third, plants can carry bacterial contamination, for example

2 × life size

from sewage outlets. Your local Environment Agency office should be able to tell you whether a particular stretch of water is affected by such hazards.

HARVESTING NOTES Watercress gives you an excuse to wade into a river up to your armpits and get a duck's-eye view of things; at its peak this is the only way to get at it. I have a pair of waders expressly for this purpose. In our locality of Kent, watercress encroaches several feet on either side of a fast-flowing river, but once a year the Environment Agency ruthlessly cuts it back to the bank to prevent it from taking over completely, which means no more watercress for a few months.

Sinapis alba

White Mustard

DISTRIBUTION Up to 300m. In England, mostly south of a line Morecambe Bay–Flamborough Head, most widespread in the east, southeast and southwest, except Kent, Sussex, Devon and Cornwall; scattered sites in Wales plus small concentration in northern coastal counties; in Scotland, Central Lowlands and eastern Coastal Lowlands as far north as Moray and in the west on Isle of Arran, Uist in Western Isles, Isle of Skye and Orkney; in Ireland, sparse, mostly Central Lowlands; present Channel Islands.

HABITAT Arable fields, waste ground and roadsides, preferring calcareous soil.

DESCRIPTION Annual, up to 1m high but often shorter. Stems more or less hairy. Leaves pale green, smooth and soft, always pinnately lobed, always with stalks. Seed pods 20–40mm long, with long, flat beak at least as long as the rest of the pod,

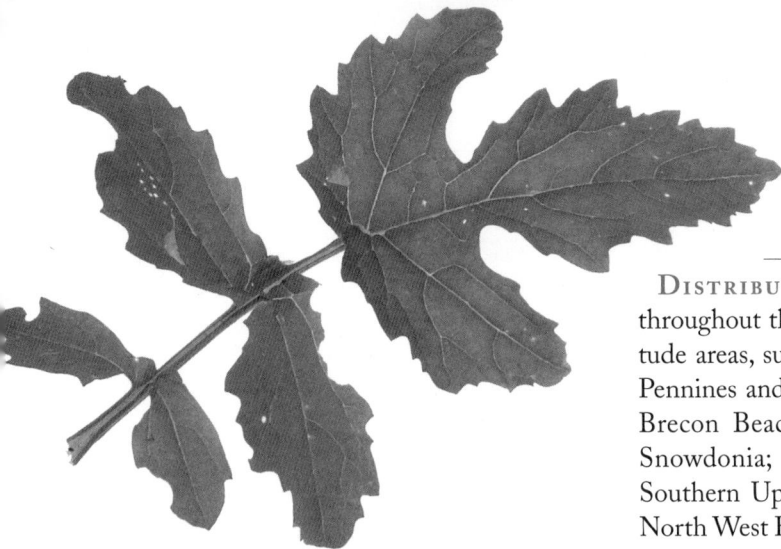

Sinapis arvensis

Charlock

DISTRIBUTION Up to 450m. Widespread throughout the British Isles except higher-altitude areas, such as, in England, Cheviot Hills, Pennines and Cumbrian Mountains; in Wales, Brecon Beacons, Cambrian Mountains and Snowdonia; in Scotland, absent much of Southern Uplands, Grampian Mountains and North West Highlands; in Ireland, absent higher-altitude areas in west as well as Wicklow and Mourne mountains in east.

HABITAT Arable fields, roadsides, especially where roadworks have recently been carried out; waste ground and railways.

DESCRIPTION Hairy annual, 20cm–1m high. Lower leaves are lyre shaped, deeply toothed and slightly or not at all pinnately lobed; upper leaves stalkless and toothed, roughly diamond shaped but sometimes with two small leaflets at the base. Seed pods are 25–40mm long, arranged loosely around the stem. Seeds are dark brown.

SIMILAR SPECIES Rape *Brassica napus* often grows in or near fields where it has been cultivated and is also naturalized in waste places, disturbed ground and docks. It has greyish-green leaves: the basal ones stalked and pinnately lobed, the stem leaves stalkless, not pinnately lobed, clasping the main stem. Seed pods are long, 50–100mm, with a long, thin beak, spreading out from the stem.

NOTES In much of northern England and Scotland, charlock is the only species of wild mustard you are likely to find, thus saving the extensive head scratching required in other localities (such as mine in Kent) where all four species grow. Charlock was eaten in the Outer

---

which is quite short and stubby. Seeds yellow, larger and more rounded than black mustard.

SIMILAR SPECIES Charlock leaves are either unlobed or shallow lobed and generally coarser, larger and darker.

NOTES White mustard has long been cultivated for its seeds and sprouted seeds, sold as 'cress' in combination with either rape or garden cress. The young leaves were also once a popular winter-salad leaf. They are hot, but the flavour doesn't exactly burn: it produces a pleasant and invigorating sensation as it infuses your nasal passages. The seeds are the hottest of all the wild mustards.

USES/RECIPES Leaves are my favourite wild mustard for salads. The texture is softer than black mustard or charlock, and the flavour, though spicy, is not overpowering. For example, a salad of wild rabbit with white mustard leaf, apple and black pudding; crab salad with white mustard leaf, lime and chilli dressing [ST]. Cooked they make a vegetable side dish of their own, especially good with garlic and cheese, or cream, butter and fresh lemon juice. Young flower buds and their stems can be cooked as a spiced-up version of broccoli, served with butter and lemon or a rich sauce.

White mustard seed pods

Sisymbrium officianale

Hedge Mustard

DISTRIBUTION Up to 315m. Found throughout British Isles except, in Wales, Cambrian Mountains; in Scotland, Southern Uplands, Grampian Mountains and North West Highlands; in Ireland, only less widespread in west.

HABITAT Nearly always close to human activity, particularly arable fields and field margins, road verges and hedgebanks.

DESCRIPTION A widely branching plant, the profile of which soon becomes familiar once you have identified it a few times, as do its small yellow flowers and small, tightly clasping seed pods. Rosette leaves are deeply lobed, the lobes opposite; later leaves small, delicate and arrow shaped, whereas the basal leaves, which form conspicuous rosettes, are long and chunky looking, dark with many deep indents.

SIMILAR SPECIES At the rosette stage, it could be confused with the coarser, hairy leaves, with irregular lobes, of wild radish.

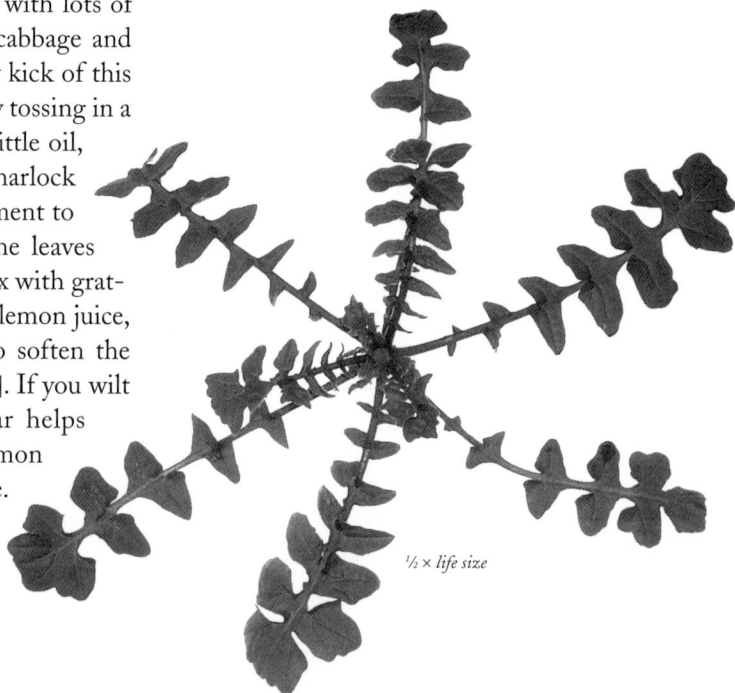

½ × life size

Hebrides until at least the eighteenth century and was at one time sold on the streets of Dublin.

USES/RECIPES Leaves are more sturdy and less hot than white or black mustard; their flavour is mildly spicy and cabbagey. Very young leaves are good in salads; older leaves are best as cooked greens. In a winter vegetable broth, with pearl barley, blanched and added just before serving [ST]. Charlock with confit of pork belly, braised red cabbage and caramelized apples. A winter dish with lots of colour, sticky greasy meat, sticky cabbage and apples, contrasted by the mustardy kick of this vibrant green veg, slightly wilted by tossing in a hot pan for a few seconds with a little oil, pepper and salt [JDW]. Creamed charlock with horseradish as an accompaniment to bream and razor clams. Blanch the leaves and squeeze out the liquid then mix with grated horseradish, sugar, cream, fresh lemon juice, salt and pepper. Cream is used to soften the flavours and sugar to sweeten [PW]. If you wilt the leaves, using a bit of vinegar helps retain the volatile oils, as the lemon juice does in the preceding recipe. Tender young green pods can be added to salads or pickled [RR].

⅓ × life size

NOTES The rosette leaves baffled me when first I found them, as they bear no resemblance to leaves of the mature plant, with which I was already familiar. My wild plant books only illustrate it at flowering stage, so I had to watch it develop before identifying it.

Known as singer's plant because of its reputed curative effects on the human voice.

USES/RECIPES Upper leaves are a good salad leaf but too small, fiddly and bothersome for cooking. Flavour range is cabbagey–horseradishy, reminiscent of lady's smock. Basal leaves are coarse and just cabbage flavoured: steam, boil, fry or chop them quite small and add to salads.

Sisymbrium orientale

Eastern Rocket

DISTRIBUTION Up to 300m. Naturalized and increasing everywhere. In England, widespread throughout, except Cheviot Hills and south Northumberland, more abundant south of line Morecambe Bay–Flamborough Head, but less so in Lincolnshire, southeast except Home Counties, Shropshire, Herefordshire and southwest; in Wales, mainly Gwynedd, Clwyd, Glamorgan and Gwent, although also Pembrokeshire and Montgomeryshire; in Scotland, only Central Lowlands and eastern Coastal Lowlands north to Kincardineshire; in Ireland, scattered localities throughout plus clusters around Belfast and Dublin; present Channel Islands and Isle of Man.

HABITAT Rough and waste ground, railways, roadsides.

DESCRIPTION Annual up to 80cm high; whole plant is hairy, including seed pods. Basal and lower stem leaves have lobes pointing squarely outward from midrib; end lobe is lanceolate. Upper stem leaves are unlobed or with only 3 lobes; all leaves are stalked. Flowers pale yellow, 5–8mm wide. Seed pods very long, 50–100mm.

SIMILAR SPECIES Tall rocket *S. altissimum* also has very long seed pods, but upper leaves have wiry thin lobes. London Rocket *S. irio* was common in London after the Great Fire of 1666 but mysteriously declined in subsequent years; it is now only regularly seen in east London and is nationally a rather scarce plant. It is smaller, up to 60cm high, less hairy, all leaves lobbed, with an especially long end lobe. Pale yellow flowers, 3–4mm wide, the young seed pods extend above them. False London rocket, *S. loeselii*, is hairier, with flowers less pale and seed pods ending below flower clusters. In Jammu and Kashmirit it is used as a herb.

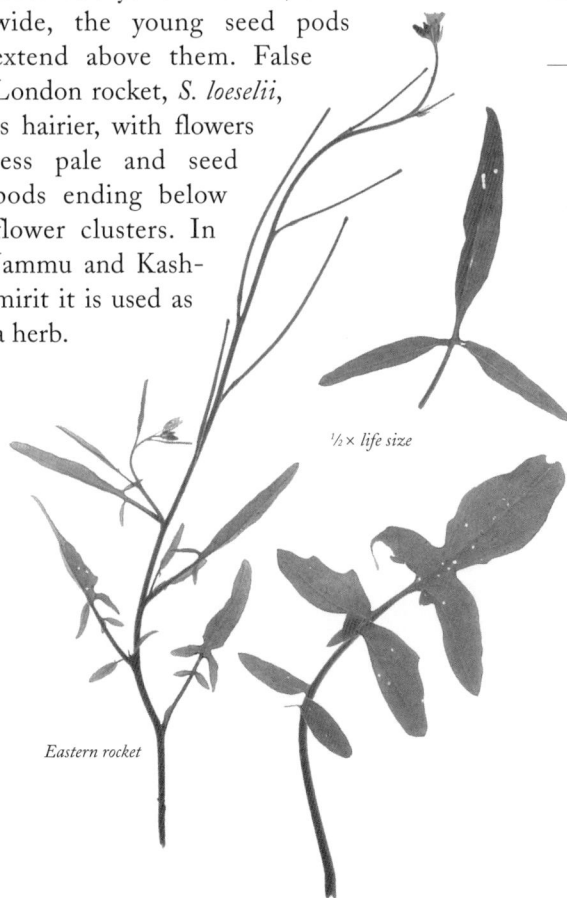

½ × life size

Eastern rocket

USES/RECIPES The four species, eastern, tall, London and false London rockets, can all be used as salads or greens.

Thlaspi arvense

Field Penny-cress

DISTRIBUTION Up to 330m. In England, widespread, except higher-altitude areas; in Wales, mostly coastal counties to the north and south, although isolated 10 sq km in most other counties; in Scotland, Central Lowlands and eastern Coastal Lowlands as far as East Sutherland in north in Northern Isles, also West Sutherland and scattered areas to south of Isle of Mull; in Ireland, concentrated in Ulster, coastal counties of Leinster and northern areas of Munster as well as isolated 10 sq km elsewhere; present Channel Islands, Isle of Man and Isles of Scilly.

HABITAT Cultivated fields, roadsides, waste ground and gardens.

DESCRIPTION Hairless annual, up to 30cm high. Leaves shiny, yellowish–dark green, toothed; stem leaves are without stalks, lanceolate, clasping the stem; lower leaves are stalked and do not form a rosette, with just 2–3 growing upright from the beginnings of a main stem. Flowers tiny and white, seed pods flat and heart shaped, very distinctive.

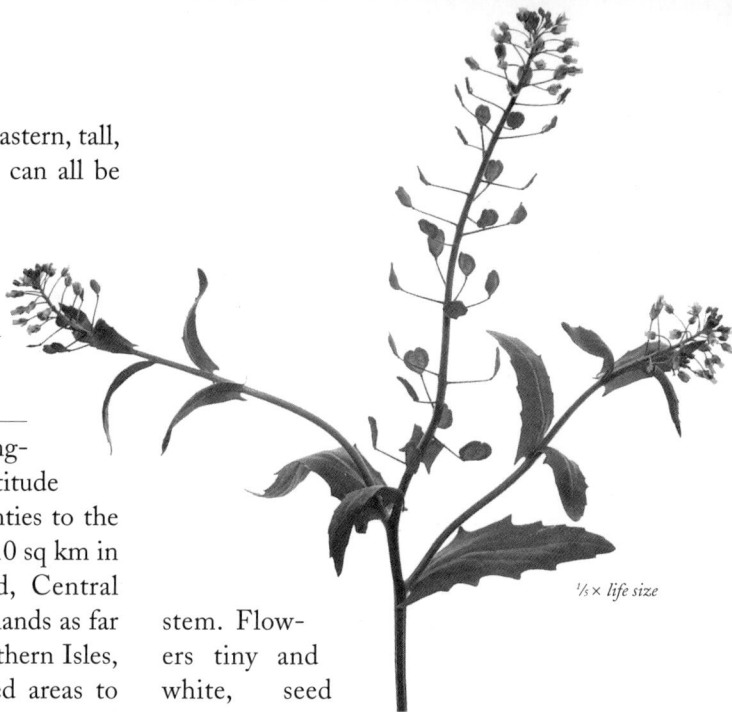

⅕ × life size

USES/RECIPES Flavour of the leaves and stem is between garlic and cauliflower. Use raw in salads or wilted slightly to add flavour to cheese sauces. An emulsion is made by wilting the leaves, refreshing then blending, then adding oil slowly to the blender. Drizzle on cauliflower or pork chops. Also makes flavoursome greens with pork or mixed with other greens such as sea beet or charlock.

BENEFITS Leaves are high in protein and vitamin C.

CARROT FAMILY
Apiaceae (Umbellifera)

EDIBLE VS. POISONOUS PLANTS

The carrot family contains many delicious plants, but, unfortunately, some very poisonous species as well. Don't let this put you off foraging for them, but do take the necessary time to learn to distinguish between them. Although there are only five really dangerous species, one of which is extremely rare and two of which do not closely resemble any of the edible ones, the remaining two are potentially deadly and are responsible for the majority of deaths from plant poisoning recorded from the British Isles. On the other hand, at least 34 of the 70 *Apiaceae* species recorded in Preston, Pearman & Dines's *New Atlas of British & Irish Flora* (which includes garden escapes dill, caraway and coriander) are good edibles. Only the lacy-leaved species and wild celery are likely to be confused with poisonous species, but if you learn the characteristics that distinguish them, as described in the tables on pp.113, 115 and 117, it is possible to collect even these edible species without fear.

My own experience with this family has certainly been tempered by a healthy degree of caution. For years I watched the hedgerows and roadsides in frustration as various *Apiaceae* species appeared and died back until only their dry stick skeletons remained, without touching any of them. I knew that some were edible but also that this basic knowledge was enough to get me killed if I ate the wrong one. Eventually, sufficiently irritated at the thought of all the good edible species I was missing, I took the time to learn which were safe and which were not.

Carrot-family plants are also called umbellifers, a reference to their umbrella-like flower clusters or umbels. These are pollinated by many species of insect, including mosquitoes – it is nice to know that even such maligned creatures have a positive role to play in our ecosystems. Insects are attracted to umbels by their semblance of giant flowers, enhanced in some species by the enlarged outer petals of peripheral flowers. All parts of the plants are usually quite aromatic, due to the presence of aromatic essential oils. Caraway seeds and fennel leaf and seeds are familiar spices or herbs, but raw carrot, parsnip and celeriac roots and the flowers and seeds of parsnip, carrot and hogweed also have spicy aromas and flavours. The leaves of plants such as ground-elder, hogweed and rock samphire are something between a herb and vegetable: whereas herbs only contribute flavour, and maybe a little colour to a dish, these leaves have unique but less intense aromatic flavours and also contribute body and texture. Across the seasons all kinds of plant part are used: roots, young shoots, leaves, stems, flower buds, flowers, mature and immature seeds. Variation in growth cycles help to distinguish species such as pignut and burnet-saxifrage that have similar leaf forms, habitat and height but different flowering times.

FORAGING SAFELY FOR CARROT-FAMILY SPECIES Learning to distinguish poisonous and edible species is not hard, but it does require attention to detail. It is important to know which edible species have poisonous look-alikes and then to study the descriptions and pictures of each in order to learn what the differences are. Because many of these plants are aromatic, several of them have a quite distinctive smell, which provides an additional tool for telling them apart. For a summary of what to look for in order to tell the different species apart, see table below. Wild celery is easily confused with the deadly hemlock water-dropwort. There are a number of other water-dropwort species, of which tubular

Distinguishing Edible Umbellifers From Poisonous Look-alikes

In order to be sure of the identity of both edible and poisonous species, watch plants through a year of their life cycle. As you follow them through the seasons, ask the following questions in order to narrow down their identity.

Leaves
Are they once, twice or three times pinnate?
Do they have a distinctive end lobe?
Are the edges toothed, and, if so, are the teeth blunt or sharp?
Is there a distinctive smell when they are crushed?
Are they dull or shiny?
Are they rough, hairy or smooth?

Main stem
Is it hollow?
Is it grooved, smooth or hairy?
Is it blotchy?
How tall is the plant?

Umbels
Do they have yellow or white flowers? No poisonous umbellifer species in the British Isles has bright yellow flowers (although

cream-flowered species could sometimes be pale yellow; white or cream flowers could also become yellow when dried.)
How many umbellules are there and how far apart are they?
Are there bracts beneath umbels/bracteoles beneath the umbellules?
Is there a peduncle, and, if so, how long is it?
Are the umbels terminal (at the top of main stem), growing from leaf axils, or both?
What month is it; in what month does the plant flower?

Seeds
Look at shape and features such as grooves, ribs and burs. Seeds are quite distinct and generally clinch the identification.

Once you are confident that what you have found is an edible species, continue to check for the similar poisonous species in that vicinity. Hemlock and wild chervil often occur together, as do hemlock water-dropwort and wild celery. Avoid collecting if both are present. Even when you are sure an area has only the edible species present, don't be complacent.

water-dropwort *O. fistulosa* and fine-leaved water-dropwort *O. aquatica* are known to be toxic; the others should also be assumed to be unsafe. Lacy-leaved edible species (wild chervil, bur chervil, sweet cicely and wild carrot) can be confused with the deadly hemlock (see Table 1, p.113). Two other lacy-leaved species – fool's parsley and rough chervil – are said to be toxic, although this has probably been exaggerated, and there are no recent records of poisoning. You should also be aware of the phototoxic effects of hogweed and parsnip, which are quite variable, as well as of giant hogweed, which are much more extreme.

POISONOUS PLANTS

Aethusa cynapium

Fool's Parsley

DISTRIBUTION Up to 300m. In England, widespread, only less so in high-altitude areas of Pennines, Cheviot Hills and Lake District; in Wales, everywhere except hilly and mountainous areas of Cambrian Mountains, Brecon Beacons and Snowdonia; in Scotland, found mostly within a few miles of firths of Tay and Forth and almost entirely absent north of Dundee and in much of borders and Central Lowlands; in Ireland, naturalized, mainly southeast, with few sites in Connaught, scattered locations elsewhere; on Channel Islands but introduced to Alderney and Isle of Man.

HABITAT Gardens, cultivated fields, hedgebanks, waste ground.

DESCRIPTION Hairless annual, usually 50cm or less high but up to 1m. Stem hollow with fine ridges, leaves shiny, 2–3 times pinnate, final subdivisions finely toothed. Leaves end in a more distinct point than similar species. Umbellules

½ × life size

have 3–4 long, beardy bracteoles and white flowers. Seeds are egg shaped and ridged.

SIMILAR SPECIES The young leafy stage could be confused with wild chervil or sweet cicely. Leaves of both species are larger and rougher and have distinctive smell. Wild carrot has long thin bracts; the whole plant is coarse and hairy. See also Table 1, p.113.

HAZARDS Contains the poison aethusin, which is similar to coniine found in hemlock. However, there are no recent, recorded cases of human poisoning; any attributed to fool's parsley in older records may in fact have been due to hemlock. The plant has caused one recent case of animal poisoning, of a goat, in 1975; it is certainly not safe to eat but may not be as dangerous as was once thought.

Cicuta virosa

Cowbane

DISTRIBUTION Up to 300m. Thankfully, now very rare: in England, strongholds Norfolk, Cheshire and Shropshire and very locally West Sussex, Worcestershire and Nottinghamshire; in Wales, extends Shropshire–Denbighshire–Flintshire; in Scotland, one 10 sq km on South Uist in Western Isles and scattered locations south of Glen Mor; in Ireland, area either side of north–south border has greatest concentration of sites anywhere in British Isles and scattered locations elsewhere, with isolated records Clare, east Mayo, northeast Galway and Offaly.

HABITAT Shallow, still or slow-flowing water, on the edge of ponds, lakes, streams, canals and ditches.

DESCRIPTION Leaves are 2–3 times pinnate, leaflets in several groups of 2–3, 2–10cm long with sharply toothed edges. The white umbels are 7–13cm wide, with widely spaced umbellules, no bracts and many bracteoles. The thick, many chambered rhizome exudes a yellow juice when cut.

SIMILAR SPECIES Greater water-parsnip *Sium latifolium* has once pinnate leaves and bracts beneath the umbels, but similar leaflets. Fool's water-cress has once pinnate leaves and leaflets are much less similar, more rounded and less sharply toothed, but you must be certain you know what cowbane looks like before gathering this plant.

HAZARDS Contains the poison cicutoxin, a deadly convulsant, that works in a manner similar to oenanthotoxin in hemlock water-dropwort.

Cowbane was at one time notorious for causing cattle deaths and has declined partly as a result of eradication attempts for this reason. Human poisonings, including deaths, have also occurred, perhaps due to the enticingly pleasant celery- or parsnip-like smell of the roots. Never eat roots from umbellifers growing in aquatic environments.

³/₁₀ × *life size*

Conium maculatum

Hemlock

DISTRIBUTION Up to 305m. In England, pretty much throughout but not recorded at higher altitudes in Pennines, Lake District and Cleveland and Cheviot hills; in Wales, found everywhere except Cambrian Mountains, Brecon Beacons; in Scotland, mostly Eastern Coastal Lowlands, extending from border north to Caithness, and sparsely scattered localities in the west, north to Mid Ebudes but including Western Isles and a single locality in Orkney; in Ireland, widespread but more common in south becoming less abundant towards the northwest; present Isle of Man, Isles of Scilly, Channel Islands and Lundy.

HABITAT Roadsides, waste ground, fields, river banks and ditches.

DESCRIPTION Tall annual or biennial, up to 2.5m high, but can be much smaller. Whole plant is hairless; stem is hollow, smooth and shiny with purple blotches. Leaf stalks are also hollow; triangular leaves 2–4 times pinnate, usually dark green and quite flat. Umbels of white flowers with bracts; seeds roughly spherical with bumpy ridges, unlike those of any other umbellifer. When bruised all parts of the plant have an unpleasant musty smell, said to be like mouse urine.

SIMILAR SPECIES Wild chervil *Anthriscus sylvestris* has leaf stalks with a U-shaped groove and roughly grooved stems, with no purple blotches. Wild chervil leaves are rougher, with a distinctive, sweet smell. The umbels have no bracts, the seeds are long and thin. The main danger of confusion is therefore before the flowering stem has appeared. Wild carrot leaves are much narrower and smell of carrot. Sweet cicely has paler leaves, often with white

Lacy-leaved umbellifer species

all ¼ × life size

Hemlock

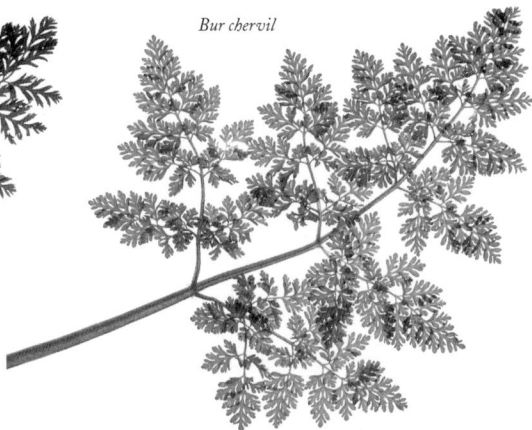

Bur chervil

Rough chervil

Wild chervil

Sweet cicely

Wild carrot

Fool's parsley

blotches and smelling distinctly of aniseed when crushed. The stem of the much smaller rough chervil *Chaerophyllum temulum* also has purple blotches but is very hairy. For summary of differences, see Table 1, p.113.

HAZARDS The young leaves and green seeds are most toxic, but the whole plant contains several toxic alkaloids, of which coniine is present in the greatest quantities. Symptoms within 1–2 hours of eating plant material include stomach pains, convulsions and vomiting, followed by depression of the central nervous system and slowing of the heart. If enough poison has been ingested, death follows when the muscles that control breathing become paralysed, causing suffocation while still conscious.

Oenanthe crocata

Hemlock Water-dropwort

DISTRIBUTION Up to 320m. In England, very common except in east, Yorkshire and Pennines to north, East Midlands, where very scarce; in Wales, widespread throughout; in Scotland, common in west, including Western Isles and along east coast to east Sutherland, with single 10 sq km in Orkney; in Ireland, abundant in northeast and south, present in chain of localities along east coast, sporadic in remainder of Leinster and Connaught; present Isle of Man, Isles of Scilly, Channel Islands and Lundy.

HABITAT Marshes, ditches and edge of ponds, lakes, brackish dykes, rivers and streams; also often on dry ground several metres from water.

DESCRIPTION Native perennial, with a strong and unpleasant smell; entirely hairless with hollow, grooved stem, up to 1.5m high. Basal leaves 3–4 times pinnate, that is stalks branched several times and with many leaflets; leaflets roughly oval/rounded with deep lobes and teeth, the latter with blunt tips. Stem leaves 2–3 times pinnate, leaflets narrower, with wedge-shaped base and 2–3 blunt teeth. Umbels of 12–40 rays, each with 5 bracts, umbellules widely spaced, each with 6 bracteoles. Leaves have an unpleasant smell, but the tuberous roots, known as dead men's fingers, smell and taste like parsnip and have been responsible for many poisonings. Flowers June–July.

SIMILAR SPECIES Basal leaves could be mistaken for wild celery *Apium graveolens*, best distinguished by its strong smell of celery, see Table 2, p.115. Fine-leaved water-dropwort *O. aquatica* has much finer leaves and a thick, swollen stem base. It is usually found in ponds and ditches. Tubular water-dropwort *O. fistulosa* is smaller, up to 60cm, with narrow stem, swollen between leaf axils; umbels with only a few rays.

HAZARDS The poison oenanthotoxin is present in all parts of the plant: a powerful convulsant, it causes vomiting, seizures, hallucinations and death. Many cases of poisoning due to this plant have been reported following

¹⁄₁₀ × life size

consumption of leaves – usually mistaken for celery – or roots – mistaken for water-parsnip or skirret *Sium sisarum*, once a popular vegetable, not to be confused with greater water-parsnip *S. latifolium*. Despite being deadly poisonous, the roots of hemlock water-dropwort are said to taste quite pleasant, but since there are no umbellifers with edible roots that grow in such damp habitats, there is no reason to make this mistake. Do not collect umbellifers from stream sides until you are sure you can identify both this and the other water-dropwort species mentioned on p.105.

EDIBLE PLANTS

Aegopodium podagraria

Ground-elder

DISTRIBUTION Up to 450m. Widespread throughout British Isles: only less so in high-altitude areas of Grampians, North West Highlands and North Highlands in Scotland; coastal counties of west Donegal, west Mayo, west Galway, Clare and Kerry in Ireland.

HABITAT Shady places on disturbed ground on roadsides, in gardens, woodland paths, hedgerows, churchyards.

½ × life size

DESCRIPTION Hairless perennial, spreading invasively by rhizomes and forming dense patches; 30–60cm high. Leaves are 1–2 times ternate; lower leaves with oval–elliptical leaflets with finely toothed edges; stalks hollow with a U-shaped groove; upper leaflets are smaller and more elongated, with short, fat stalks. Umbels of 10–20 umbellules, usually white, sometimes pink. Flowers May–July.

SIMILAR SPECIES Dog's mercury *Mercurialis perennis*, which is mildly poisonous, often grows in the same place; its simple, hairy leaves are a similar shape and size to ground-elder leaflets.

NOTES Ground-elder is another botanical relic of the Roman occupation of Britain. Like alexanders, it persisted for some time as

François Couplan's Ground-elder Brandade

SERVES 4–6

Chop up 400g ground-elder leaves finely. Boil and peel 2 medium-sized potatoes, mash them up with a fork. Boil 500g cod or pollock in water for 8 minutes. Let cool and take off all bones. Heat up 250ml olive oil in a deep pan (it must be very hot). Add fish and stir madly as if for a cheese fondue. Add mashed-up potatoes and stir well. Add 100ml milk to soften up the mix. Add chopped up ground-elder, and stir again. Add 5 small crushed garlic cloves. Stir in a further 400ml milk. Season with salt and chilli pepper to taste. Finish up with the electric hand mixer to get a smooth, green cream. Serve either with boiled potatoes or on toasts.

a standard herb or vegetable in kitchen gardens before falling into disuse. Unlike alexanders, it persists in many gardens as a pestilent weed and may even still grow where Roman gardeners planted it. Modern gardeners consider this a curse, but tasting it reveals it to be a blessing.

USES/RECIPES The flavour of the leaves is slightly lemony and aromatic. Cooked leaves have a papery texture and are unsuitable as greens. Use them instead as a herby vegetable, big handfuls of it chopped finely and added to casseroles and soups or fried in olive oil then added to crushed potatoes, pasta or white sauce for fish. Use young leaves whole in salads; use the stems of older leaves as a vegetable in their own right.

Angelica sylvestris

Wild Angelica

DISTRIBUTION Up to 855m. Widespread throughout British Isles: only less so in Caithness in Scotland and parts of Channel Islands.

HABITAT Edge of woodland rides, grassy verges and damp meadows. Angelica does not grow in such great swathes as some fellow umbellifers; instead the plants are generally dotted around – several in the same vicinity, but widely spaced.

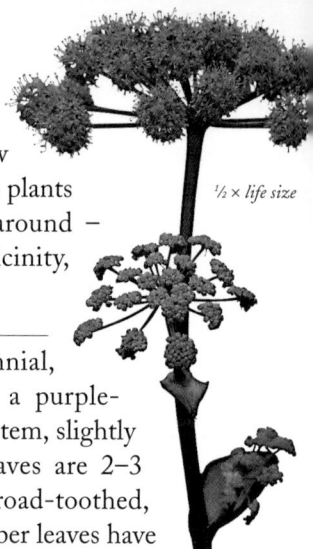

½ × life size

DESCRIPTION Perennial, 30cm–2m high, with a purple-tinged, ridged, hollow stem, slightly hairy at the base. Leaves are 2–3 times pinnate, with broad-toothed, oval-oblong leaflets; upper leaves have fat sheaths that enclose the umbels before they emerge. Umbels are dome shaped, with many compound umbels; flowers white/slightly pink, 3–15cm wide, with few or no bracts. Flowers July–October.

SIMILAR SPECIES Alexanders has more rounded, deeper green leaflets and yellow umbels. Hogweed has similar form from a distance but has once-pinnate leaves with large, irregularly shaped leaflets and flatter umbels. Cultivated angelica *A. archangelica* has larger umbels, up to 25cm wide, with greenish flowers.

USES/RECIPES Cultivated angelica is best known for its candied stems and leaf stalks; the wild plant can be used in the same way. Follow the basic candying method on p.17, but peel the stems after boiling and discard the water in which they were boiled. Use the candied stems and stalk, as you would candied citrus peel, in sweet things like cakes and cake fillings: for example, in the wonderful Italian cassata cake. Stems and stalks can also be used as vegetables, as you would celery: braised or in soups, for example. If they are bitter, cook in at least one change of water first, discarding the water. In Italy the unopened buds and their sheaths are cooked in several ways, the following recipes are based on the late Patience Gray's account in *Honey from a Weed*.

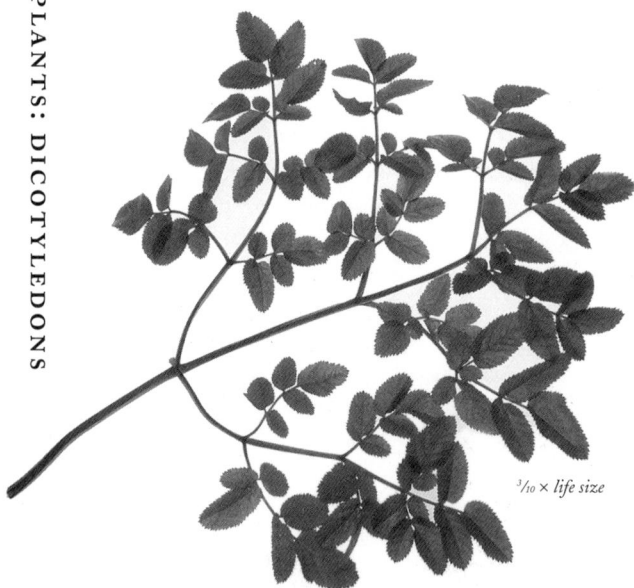

³⁄₁₀ × life size

ZAVIRNE ABBRUSTOLITE: Barbecue them, then slice lengthwise into three or so pieces and serve with olive oil, salt and wine vinegar.

ZAVIRNE FRITTE: Blanch, then leave for an hour in the cooking water. Drain. Dip first in beaten egg, then in flour and deep fry.

Use leaves in small amounts in salad or to flavour fruit and cheese sauces. Use seeds as a spice, in cakes or to flavour fruit soups, such as damson or rosehip, but don't store for long as their aromatic oil soon dissipates. They were traditionally used to flavour gin and vermouth.

½ × life size

Anthriscus caucalis

Bur Chervil

DISTRIBUTION Up to 300m. In British Isles, less widespread and less prolific than wild chervil: in England, strongholds on sandy ground in Norfolk, Suffolk and Essex, especially the Brecklands, elsewhere mostly coastal areas south and southwest; in Wales, only north coast and Anglesey plus few sites in Pembrokeshire and Gower Peninsula; in Scotland, locally common on Firth of Forth and Moray Firth; in Ireland, rare with scattered localities along east coast and around Lough Foyle, Meath, Longford, Roscommon and Kerry; present Isle of Man, Isles of Scilly and Channel Islands.

HABITAT Dry, often sandy ground, such as upper shore of beaches, hedge banks, waste ground and fields.

DESCRIPTION Annual, up to 60cm high, with hairless, hollow stems and pale green, fine, lacelike, thrice-pinnate leaves with white hairs underneath; when crushed leaves have distinctive, sweet aromatic scent. They have the most delicate leaf patterning of all the British umbellifers. The smallest subdivisions of the leaflets have noticeably rounded tips. White umbels have only 3–6 umbellules; flowers May–June. The egg-shaped seeds are 3mm long and covered in tiny hooks or burs, which attach to passing animals.

SIMILAR SPECIES See Table 1, p.113.

USES/RECIPES One of my favourite wild herbs: softer, sweeter, more flavoursome and aromatic than wild chervil. Use young leaves in salad, particularly with a sweet dressing or in sauces, such as sauce béarnaise, served with grilled steak and wild watercress [EC] or gravy, or to finish potatoes or soups, such as shellfish broth [PW] and casseroles. It has the effect of lifting the flavours of pretty much anything to which it is added.

Anthriscus sylvestris

Wild Chervil/Cow Parsley

DISTRIBUTION Up to 845m. Widespread throughout much of British Isles: everywhere in England and Wales; in Scotland, everywhere except North Highlands, Harris and Isle of Lewis in Western Isles and higher-altitude areas of Grampian Mountains and North West Highlands; in Ireland, except extreme west in Donegal, west Mayo, west Galway, Clare and Kerry; present in Isle of Man, Isles of Scilly, Channel Islands and Lundy.

HABITAT Woodland, roadside verges, hedgebanks, river banks, meadows. Often the dominant plant; in many places the commonest roadside plant.

DESCRIPTION Native perennial, 60cm–1.3m high. Stems are usually hollow, slightly hairy at base, hairless and grooved higher up. Leaves are thrice pinnate, final subdivisions coarsely serrated; leaf stalks solid or with narrow, hollow centre. Leaf stalks and stems often tinged with purple, but never with purple blotches. Umbels creamy white, with long peduncles and short, rounded bracteoles but no bracts. Seeds long, thin, smooth and black, with a groove top to bottom. Flowers April–June, much earlier than fool's parsley and rough chervil.

NOTES Lining our roadsides and hedgebanks, like crowds of parasol-waving onlookers, wild chervil is another of our superabundant wild foods. Although more commonly known as cow parsley it is closely related to garden chervil *Anthriscus cerefolium* and only distantly related to parsley. Hemlock has a nasty habit of growing in the same place: I had the spine chilling experience of finding hemlock leaves among the wild chervil I brought home one of the first times I collected it. Unless you have an experienced forager to confirm its identity, it is best to follow this plant through a year of its life cycle before you start using it.

SIMILAR SPECIES See Table 1, p.113.

USES/RECIPES Tear the leaves and add to salad or roast vegetables, especially beetroot. In general it can replace parsley, chopped and used immediately, for example with potatoes or in a sauce for mussels; add to any sauce for chicken.

WILD CHERVIL CREAM: Add finely chopped chervil to cream, or add a swirl, again finely chopped, to soups before serving; for shellfish/ lobster/crayfish bisque, add a drop of brandy as well.

WILD CHERVIL BUTTER SAUCE: For firm meaty fish, like salmon or trout: poach shallots/onion in white wine vinegar and white wine; stir in finely chopped, chilled butter but don't overheat or the sauce will split. Add chervil at the end [PW].

Wild chervil counteracts saltiness and strong flavours such as lemon and garlic, balancing and mellowing these flavours. Use to make herb butter for serving with fish or chicken or with leeks and carrots.

HARVESTING NOTES Winter and early spring leaves are the most sweet and fragrant. Once in flower the leaves are few and too coarse to bother with, but new growth can begin as early as August.

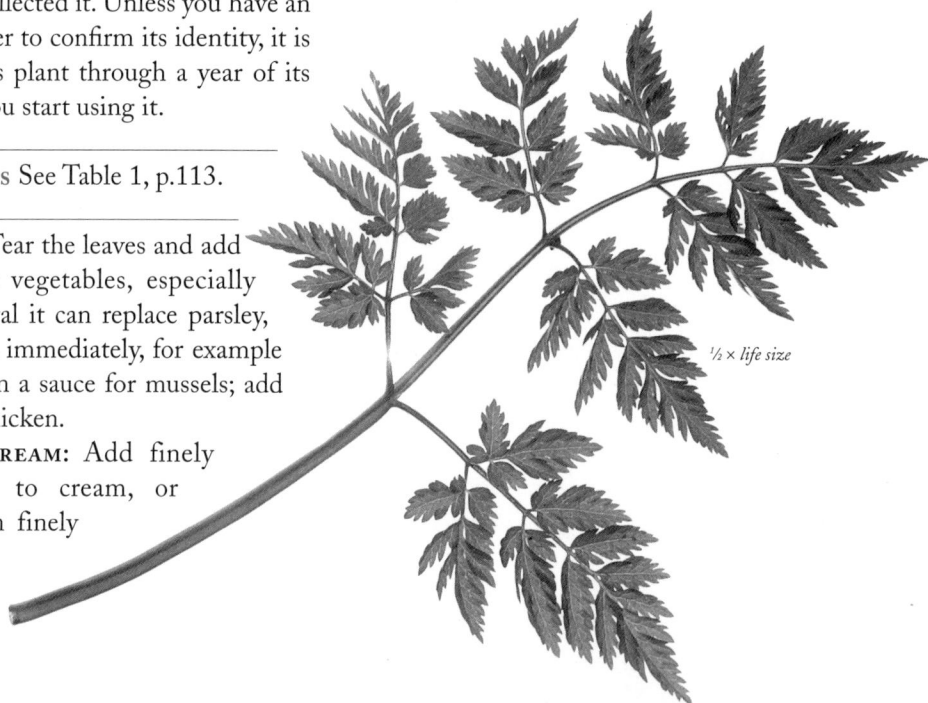

½ × life size

Table 1 Distinguishing Edible Umbellifers From Poisonous Look-alikes

	Hemlock	Fool's parsley	Rough chervil	Wild chervil	Bur chervil	Sweet cicely	Wild carrot
Edibility/ toxicity	Deadly poisonous	Poisonous, but not as dangerous as was once thought	Said to be poisonous but no recent records of poisoning	Edible	Edible	Edible	Edible
Plant	Hairless annual or biennial	Hairless annual. Usually only found from late spring onwards	Hairy biennial	Sometimes slightly hairy, leaves and stems (not leaf stalks) rough to the touch	Hairy annual	Slightly hairy perennial; such hairs as there are, are soft to the touch	Hairy annual or biennial
Height	Up to 2m	Up to 60cm	Up to 1m	Up to 1.3m	Up to 60cm	Up to 1m	Up to 1m
Stem	Hollow, hairless, smooth but with slight grooves, with purple blotches	Hollow, slightly grooved, hairless	Hairy, with purple blotches	Solid, no purple blotches, but sometimes tinged with purple, grooved	Hollow, hairless, purplish towards base	Hollow, variably hairy	Solid, ridged
Basal leaves	Up to 50cm long. Triangular, 2–4 times pinnate, usually dark green. Quite flat. Smooth to the touch	Up to 25cm long. Triangular–lanceolate, 2–3 times pinnate	Up to 30cm long. 2–3 times pinnate. Dark green, hairy above and beneath	Up to 35cm long. 3 times pinnate; rough to the touch	Up to 25cm long. 2–3 times pinnate. Hairless above, white hairs beneath	Up to 30cm long. 2–3 times pinnate. Pale beneath, often with white blotches above	Up to 25cm long. 2–3 times pinnate, narrow, feather-like
Stem leaves	Many, slightly smaller than basal leaves	Smaller than basal leaves	Dark green–purple	Few and much smaller than basal leaves	Plentiful, almost as large as basal leaves	Plentiful, almost as large as basal leaves. Often with white blotches above	More triangular in outline than basal leaves
Leaf stalks	Obviously hollow, tapered from wide base	Short, with distinct groove down the middle, smooth to touch	Very long on basal leaves, rough to touch	U-shaped groove down middle; solid or with narrow hollow centre, smooth to touch	Swollen at base	Stem leaves have broad-sheathed stalk bases	Long on basal leaves
Fragrance	Unpleasant, musty smell, resembling mouse urine	Slight, not unpleasant	Slight, not unpleasant	Sweet, aromatic	Sweet, aromatic	Strong smell of aniseed	Smells of carrot
Umbels	Bracts and bracteoles	Bracteoles long and very obvious, but no bracts	Bracteoles but not bracts	Small bracteoles but no bracts	Bracteoles but no bracts	Bracteoles but no bracts	Long, conspicuous bracts, no bracteoles. Central flower deep red
Seeds	Roughly spherical with bumpy ridges	Egg shaped with distinct ridges	Oblong, with tapered top end. Often purple	6mm long, thin, with distinct groove down middle	Egg shaped, 3mm long, covered with tiny burs	Up to 25mm long, ending in distinct point	Egg shaped, up to 4mm long, spiny
Flowering period	June and July	June–September	May–early July	April–June	May and June	May and June	June–August

Wild Celery

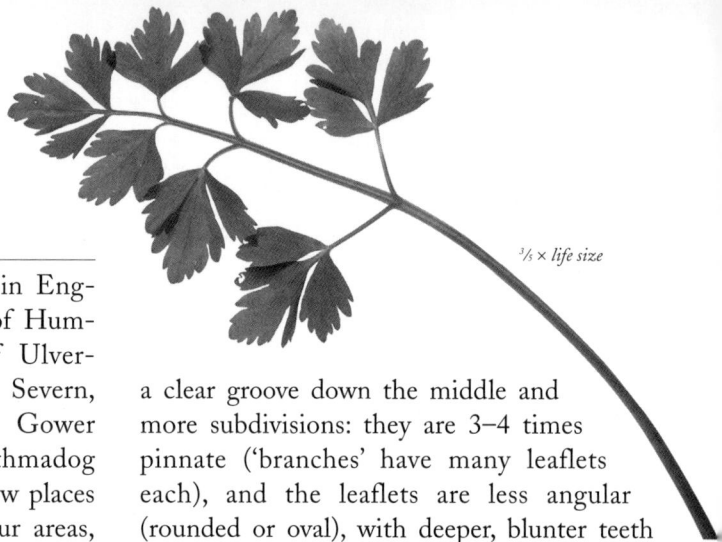

⅓ × life size

DISTRIBUTION Coastal locations: in England, widespread but absent north of Humber–Middlesbrough, and north of Ulverston–Siloth; in Wales, on the rivers Severn, Milford Haven and Dee, around Gower Peninsula and in Bangor and Porthmadog areas; in Ireland, southeast coast, a few places such as Cork and Waterford Harbour areas, also in Limerick and in Sligo Bay as well as around Belfast, Dundalk and Dublin. Inland: on aforementioned rivers and sporadically elsewhere as a garden escape.

HABITAT Often near salt water on upper salt marsh, at the high tidemark and sea walls; freshwater marshes, by rivers, ditches and brackish dykes.

DESCRIPTION Hairless biennial, thickset, smelling strongly of celery – the surest way to confirm its identity. Stems deeply ridged and branched. Usually 30cm–1m high, but can reach 1.5m and sometimes prostrate. Lower leaves once pinnate, that is with 'branches' (2–3 pairs) that carry only 1 leaflet; these are triangular or diamond-shaped, glossy, dark green and toothed, usually with 3 distinct toothed lobes. Leaf stalks have clear groove down the middle. Upper leaves 1–2 times ternate, or simple but with 3 distinct lobes. Flowers yellowish–greenish white in short-stalked umbels at the top of plant or stalkless umbels in leaf axils, both with long rays.

SIMILAR SPECIES Basal leaves can all too easily be confused with those of deadly hemlock water-dropwort, often found in similar habitats. Hemlock water-dropwort leaves are distinguished by an unpleasant smell, not at all like celery when crushed, round stalks, without a clear groove down the middle and more subdivisions: they are 3–4 times pinnate ('branches' have many leaflets each), and the leaflets are less angular (rounded or oval), with deeper, blunter teeth and irregular lobes – not always 3 distinct ones per leaflet. Mature hemlock water-dropwort plants are less easily confused, often 1.5m high with long, stalked umbels at the top of plant, no umbels in leaf axils and much larger, 2–3 times pinnate upper leaves.

NOTES Also known as smallage, this is the wild precursor of cultivated celery, which was used thousands of years before growers succeeded in producing the thick, blanched stems that are now so familiar. It is still used as a wild spice, herb and vegetable in Ireland, Turkey, Spain, Italy, Indonesia and North Africa.

USES/RECIPES Leaves and stalks are mostly used as a herb for all sorts of dishes but especially in soups, stews (such as lamb or beef), broth (chicken in particular) and sauces. Use raw leaves sparingly in salads. Wild celery gives any dish a vitality that makes you feel it must cure you of something!

POACHED CHICKEN IN WILD CELERY BROTH: Put a 1–1.5kg roasting chicken into a suitably sized pot and cover with approximately 3 litres consommé or clear chicken stock, add 12 button onions (leave whole) and (roughly cut) 3 stems or several leaf stalks wild celery, 2 peeled carrots, ½ peeled celeriac and 1 leek. Bring the pot to the boil and simmer for approximately 30–40 minutes. Remove the veg. Turn off the heat and leave the chicken to sit for 20–30 minutes in the stock. Cut the chicken into portions and place in a serving dish. Bring the stock, with the veg reinstated, to the boil. Add the chopped wild celery leaf and pour some of the stock and some veg over the chicken. Serve with a few new potatoes on the side. The remaining stock can be eaten as soup as it is or strained and used as a stock for another soup [DQ].

WILD CELERY TAPENADE: Green olives, shallots, mustard, olive oil, garlic, new potatoes, wild celery leaf [EC].

Table 2 Distinguishing Wild Celery From Hemlock Water-dropwort

	Wild celery	Hemlock water-dropwort
Edibility/ toxicity	Edible	Deadly poisonous
Plant	Thickset hairless, sometimes prostrate	Hairless, upright
Height	30cm–1m	Up to 1.5m
Stem	Solid, deeply grooved and branched	Hollow, grooved
Leaf stalks	Clear groove down middle	Rounded
Basal leaves	Only once pinnate	3–4 times pinnate
Leaflets	Distinctive triangular or diamond-shaped leaflets are glossy, dark green and toothed, and, if lobed, with 3 distinct lobes	Roughly oval or rounded with blunt lobes and teeth
Stem leaves	Upper leaves are either divided into threes, once or twice, or simple but with 3 distinct lobes	Stem leaves 2–3 times pinnate, leaflets narrower, wedge-shaped bases and 2–3 blunt teeth
Fragrance	Strong celery fragrance	Unpleasant
Umbels	Flowers are yellowish–greenish white in short-stalked umbels at the tops of plants and stalkless umbels in the leaf axils, both with only 4–12 rays. No bracts or bracteoles	Umbels of white flowers have 12–40 rays, each with 5 bracts, the umbellules widely spaced, each with 6 bracteoles. No umbels in leaf axils
Flowering period	June–August	June and July

CHRIS MCGOWAN'S WALNUT AND WILD CELERY SOUP WITH STICHELTOM CHEESE: (We had this on Christmas Day one year, and in our household it is now known as Christmas soup.) Sweat down 2 finely chopped banana shallots, 2 garlic cloves, some thyme, a handful of wild celery stalks. Cover with 500ml chicken stock. Immediately before serving, blend in 75g sticheltom cheese (an English blue, such as Stilton, can also be used), a handful each of walnuts and wild celery leaves.

CELERY SALT: Dry leaves in lowest temperature possible, in fan oven with door open overnight, or microwave; crunch it up when dry and brittle with sea salt [MH]. Use seeds as a celery-flavoured spice, in casseroles, sauces, stew and soup, sprinkled on to salads and in bread.

Apium nodiflorum

Fool's Watercress/Pie-cress

DISTRIBUTION Lowland plant, but up to 335m. In England, throughout, except Pennines, high-altitude areas in Lake District, much of Northumberland and parts of East Sussex; in Wales, most areas but absent Cambrian Mountains and parts of Snowdonia; in Scotland, mostly absent, except Kirkcudbrightshire, Wigtonshire, Outer Hebrides, Clyde Isles and a few other scattered locations; in Ireland, widespread but absent some inland areas Antrim, Donegal and Tyrone; present Isle of Man and Channel Islands.

HABITAT Shallow water of ponds, streams, rivers and ditches; ground that is covered by water at other times of the year, such as pond edges, dry ditches and streams.

DESCRIPTION Perennial. Stems hollow with shallow grooves. Main stems are prostrate, with roots developing at their nodes, but leaf

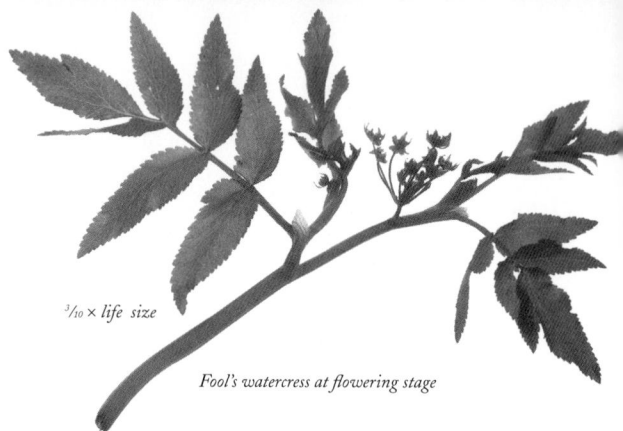

³/₁₀ × life size

Fool's watercress at flowering stage

stalks and flower stems are upright, 30cm–1m high. Leaves alternate, light green, shiny with bluntly toothed, oval–lanceolate leaflets. Flowers June–September; white, in the leaf nodes (hence *nodiflorum*); bracteoles, stalks very short or absent. Seeds egg shaped.

SIMILAR SPECIES Lesser water-parsnip *Berula erecta* has very similar basal leaves, but these are distinguished as follows: they have a dark, constricted or swollen ring towards the base of the stalk, which is often tinged with purplish red; the leaflets are dull bluish or greyish-green with more irregularly and sharper-toothed leaflets. At the flowering stage, lesser water-parsnip is easily distinguished by its much deeper-toothed leaflets and the conspicuous bracts on the umbels, which grow both in leaf axils and at the top of the plant. Greater water-parsnip *Sium latifolium* has longer, more pointed leaflets at an angle to the leaf stalk, layered like shelves. Both species are said to be poisonous, although I know of no records of human poisoning. Cattle eat large amounts of greater water-parsnip with no apparent ill effects.

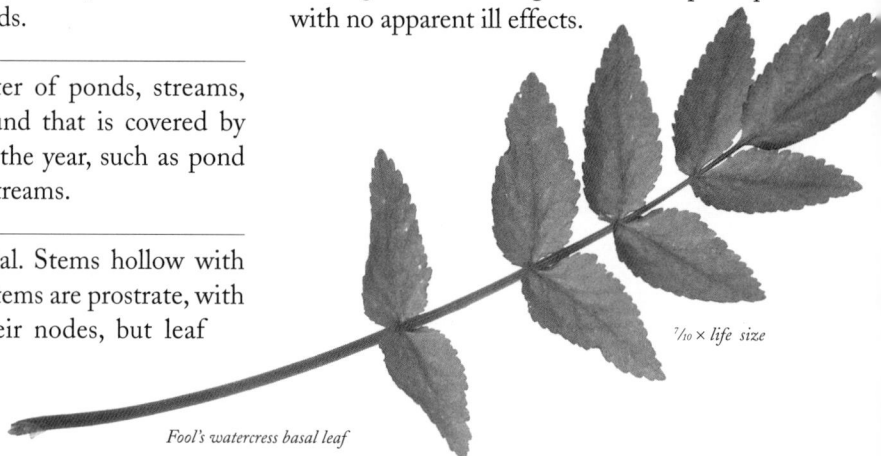

⁷/₁₀ × life size

Fool's watercress basal leaf

Table 3 Distinguishing Fool's Watercress From Poisonous Species

	Fool's watercress	Lesser water-parsnip	Greater water-parsnip (rare)	Cowbane (rare)
Edibility	Edible	Said to be toxic but no recent records of poisonings	Said to be toxic but no recent records of poisonings	Deadly poisonous
Plant	Upright or prostrate with glossy bright green, once pinnate leaves	Upright or prostrate with dull bluish or greyish-green, once pinnate leaves	Upright, with bright green, once pinnate leaves	Upright. Leaves 2–3 times pinnate
Height	Up to 1m (but often prostrate)	Up to 1m (but often prostrate)	Up to 1.5m	Up to 1.5m
Stem	Green, smooth, hollow	Green–reddish purple, smooth hollow	Hollow, grooved	Hollow, grooved
Stem leaves	Leaflets with shallow, blunt teeth	Leaflets deeply and irregularly toothed	Often have only 5 pairs of leaflets, which are regularly toothed	
Basal leaves	Leaflets with regular teeth, which are variably pointed or blunt	Very similar to fool's watercress but leaflet edges more sharply and irregularly toothed	Up to 50cm long. Leaflets regularly toothed, arranged above one another in shelflike fashion	
Leaflets	Oval. Up to 7.5 cm long, 2cm wide	Oval. Up to 6cm long, 2cm wide	Lanceolate–oval. Up to 15cm long, 3cm wide. Edges very firm to the touch	Linear–lanceolate with deep, widely spaced teeth. Up to 9cm long, 1.5cm wide
Leaf stalks	No ring on stalks	Distinct ring towards base of basal leaf stalk. Stalks often tinged with reddish purple	On basal leaves, long. On upper leaves, short and sheathing	
Fragrance	Smells of parsnip	Smells of parsnip	Smells of parsnip	Pungent unpleasant smell, not at all like parsnip
Umbels	No bracts; bracteoles same length as flowers	Long bracts and bracteoles	Short bracts and bracteoles	Bracteoles but not bracts
Flowering period	July–August	July–September	July–August	July–August

Watercress has opposite leaves (not leaflets), wavy, untoothed leaflets and leaf stalks without a sheathed base. Two deadly poisonous umbellifers grow in similar habitats: hemlock water-dropwort and cowbane. Neither is very similar to fool's water-cress, but it is a wise precaution to familiarize yourself with them.

NOTES Ivan Dumbrell at Wingham Well Watercress and Spring Water Nursery looked at me in disbelief when I turned up at his cress beds one day, asking if he'd mind if I weeded out the fool's watercress. Ivor spends a substantial part of his working year removing it and had no idea it was edible! This much overlooked, edible plant is called fool's watercress due to its similarity to mature watercress, among which it often grows. We found the name derogatory and adopted the name water celery, by which it is known in New Zealand. The name is not as apt as we thought: recent research has shown that wild celery *Apium graveolens* is not closely related. At any rate it tastes more like parsnip than celery, but unfortunately the name water-parsnip is already taken. So at present, there is no English name that we are happy to call it, with the possible exception of pie-cress – an old West Country name derived from its popular use there in meat pies and pasties.

USES/RECIPES Leaves and stems are used as a wild herb, salad and vegetable in Spain, Sicily, Lebanon, Crete, Italy, Turkey and Tunisia. Leaves/leaflets are a good salad ingredient or sole accompaniment to chicken dishes, to garnish a parsnip purée or other parsnip preparations. Flavour gravy, sauces, stock and soup, especially any with a base of chicken stock, with puréed raw leaf, added just before serving. Add chopped leaves to stuffing for chicken. Serve raw leaves with cold meats, artichoke salad, smoked feta cheese or in lobster cocktail [KG]. Finish with beetroot dressing and serve with seared fillet of mackerel, marinated in white wine, white wine vinegar, coriander seeds and olive oil [PB]. Wilted leaves make a good accompaniment to slow-baked salt lamb and roast parsnips. Serve the more tender stems and leaf stalks as a side vegetable, cooked in a little stock and butter.

HAZARDS The liver fluke parasite may be present if there are sheep or cattle grazing with access to the water (for further detail, see p.23).

Conopodium majus

Pignut

DISTRIBUTION Up to 700m. In England, absent only Cambridgeshire and parts of Kent; in Wales, found throughout; in Scotland, absent only parts of Highlands and Outer Hebrides; in Ireland, pretty much throughout Ulster and Munster but absent much of Roscommon, Sligo, Laois, Meath and parts of Mayo, Galway and Carlow.

HABITAT Acidic–neutral soil on edge of woods or in open woodland, meadow, pasture, road verges, hedgebanks.

DESCRIPTION Virtually hairless perennial, slender with few branches, usually 8–50cm high but up to 90cm. Stems slightly ridged, becoming hollow after flowering. Lower leaves triangular but blunt or

Lesser water-parsnip at flowering stage

rounded at the end, thrice pinnate, with large sheaths at base and slightly hairy round the edges. Rather sparse upper leaves are twice pinnate with thin, spindly lobes. Umbels are 3–7cm wide with 6–12 umbellules and few or no bracts. Flowers May–June. Tuber 1–4cm wide.

SIMILAR SPECIES Greater pignut *Unium bulbocastanum* prefers disturbed, chalky soil, is taller (up to 1m high) and many branched; leaves wither before flowering, and flowers have many upper and lower bracts. It is only found in Hertfordshire, Bedfordshire and Cambridgeshire, and is too scarce to harvest.

NOTES Some of my older relatives and acquaintances recall, as children, rooting around for pignuts and eating them. It is a great British foraging tradition, even mentioned by Shakespeare in *The Tempest* when Caliban says: 'I pray thee let me bring thee where the crabs [crab apples] grow and I with my long nails will dig thee pignuts.' As you will notice if you read the all the carrot family entries, this is one of three edible umbellifers mentioned by the Bard. In Sweden there was once a trade in pignuts; in the British Isles some northern meadows/pastures might support commercial harvesting if carefully managed (see Harvesting notes).

USES/RECIPES I use the tubers sliced and lightly fried, in salad as a tasty garnish or in game sauce. They can also be boiled or roasted.

HARVESTING NOTES The quaint way: follow the stalk, then the root down into the soil to the small, fat tuber at its end, by scratching at the ground with a small stick and

1½× life size

your fingers. If you snap the stalk or root, you've lost your lead and have to widen your search. You may be frustrated by many small stones masquerading as pignuts before you locate your quarry. The easy way: use a garden fork to dig a few inches below the plant and sort through the clump until you find the nut. Bigger plants generally have bigger tubers. Obviously, it is unsustainable to harvest more than a few tubers, unless you are actively stewarding your local pignut patch by planting seeds from the remaining plants.

3/10× life size

Crithmum maritimum

Rock Samphire

DISTRIBUTION Up to 300m. Only coastal locations, in England and Wales, Cumbria–Dover with few additional sites north Essex and east Suffolk; in Scotland, on Isle of Lewis and discontinuous on west coast from Kirkcudbrightshire–Kintyre; in Ireland, almost continuous distribution from Kerry in west along south coast to Meath in east; also found in north Clare and Slyne Head–Kilkieran Bay, in Donegal Bay, Tory Sound, around Belfast and Dundrum Bay.

HABITAT Coastal, on rocks and cliffs, sandy and shingle upper shore.

DESCRIPTION Bushy, hairless perennial, 15–45cm high. Stem bases often woody. Leaves fleshy, greyish-green, diamond-shaped, once or twice pinnate, looking somewhat like deer antlers. Tight umbels of yellow flowers with bracts and bracteoles. This plant is distinctive and unlikely to be confused with other species.

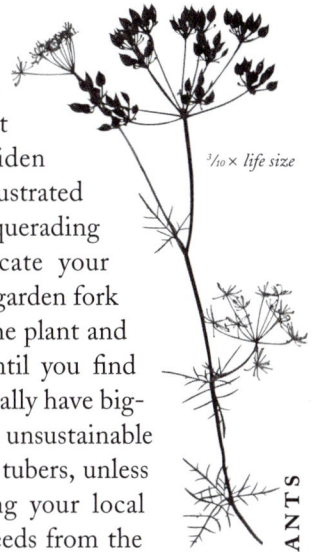

NOTES Rock samphire is well suited to life in its rather challenging niche on coastal rocks and cliffs. The succulence and aromatic oils of the leaves enable it to endure the mid-summer sun and the harsh salt-laden winds, while the roots often penetrate deep into the cracks in rocks, anchoring it against turbulent weather and high tides. In the days of its popularity, great barrels of brined rock samphire were sent up to London to be pickled. Demand was such that people are said to have abseiled down cliffs to gather the harder-to-reach plants, as is alluded to in *King Lear*: 'Half-way down, Hangs one that gathers samphire; dreadful trade!' William Salisbury, writing in *The Botanist's Companion* in the nineteenth century, reports this 'profession of great danger' as a still current practice in Kent. Even such daredevil tactics could not fulfil the demand – the seventeenth-century diarist John Evelyn complains about the pickles being adulterated with other, less tasty plants, such as the unrelated golden samphire *Inula crithmoides*. Marsh samphire also derives its name from its use as a rock-samphire substitute; such adulterations were almost certainly a factor in the decline in its use.

½ × life size

USES/RECIPES Leaves have herby, citrus-like flavour. Blanch and serve with butter or chop and use as an aromatic vegetable, with crushed potatoes, in sauces, soup, with pasta (use in place of wild cabbage for Spaghetti with wild cabbage and tomato sauce recipe, p.83).

SAUCE VIERGE WITH ROCK SAMPHIRE: Take some olive oil (not too peppery), fennel seeds, ground alexanders seeds and chopped wild herbs. To give body and texture, add blanched rock samphire, shallots and capers, finely chopped: for one cup of dressing use ½ cup chopped rock samphire, 1 shallot, a few capers and ½ cup leaves (such as bur chervil, ground-elder, burnet-saxifrage). Serve with fish [PW].

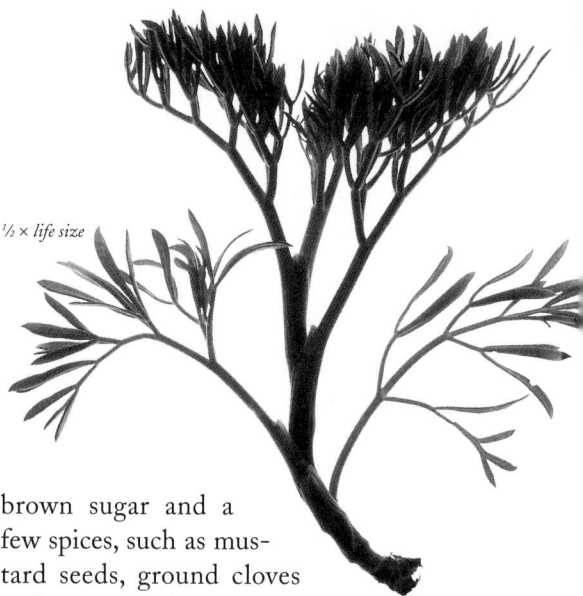

Preserve in brine or pickle: we add a little brown sugar and a few spices, such as mustard seeds, ground cloves and turmeric, but otherwise use the Farley method that follows (see below). The leaves are barely cooked in the pickling process and are quite overpowering initially, but after 2–3 months the flavour mellows greatly.

From John Farley, *The London Art of Cookery*:

Lay green Samphire into a clean pan, and throw over it two or three handfuls of salt; then cover it with spring water. Let it lie for twenty-four hours, then put it into a clean saucepan, throw in a handful of salt, and cover it with good vinegar. Cover the pan close, and set it over a low fire. Let it stand till it be just green and crisp, and then take it off at that moment; for if it should remain until it be soft, it will be spoiled. Put it in your pickling pot and cover it close. As soon as it be cold, tie it down with a bladder and leather and keep it for use. Or you may keep it all the year, in a very strong brine of salt and water, and throw it into vinegar just before you use it.

BENEFITS Rock samphire is high in omega-3 oils.

HARVESTING NOTES Harvest mostly late April–August. In harsher winters, it dies back, but if the winter is mild, the plants may continue to produce leaves.

Daucus carota

Wild Carrot

DISTRIBUTION Up to 400m. In England, widespread south of line Severn Estuary–Flamborough Head, only less so north Devon; north of line, widespread except hilly/higher altitude areas; common in Wales, except high-altitude areas; in Scotland, widespread along west coast and particularly on islands, including Western Isles, also around Moray Firth, inland in Lanarkshire and coast of East Ross; in Ireland, widespread, except higher-altitude areas; present Channel Islands, Isle of Man, Isles of Scilly and Lundy.

HABITAT Often near coast, just above the beach in grassy areas; inland on dry grassland.

DESCRIPTION Biennial, up to 1m high, with solid stems and coarse, slightly hairy, 2–3 times pinnate lacy leaves. Basal leaves (see page 107) are long, narrow with widely spaced leaflets; stem leaves are much broader. Umbels of white/pinkish-white flowers, with long, thin bracts beneath. Coastal plants often have a dark red central flower. When seeds have formed, edges of umbels curl up and form a hollow in the centre, reminiscent of birds' nests.

SIMILAR SPECIES See **hemlock** and Table 1, p.113.

NOTES Carrots were probably first cultivated by the Romans, but our present cultivars date back to Afghanistan around AD 600. From there, they were widely distributed and reached Europe by the fourteenth century. Basal leaves could also be confused with **yarrow**, which has more leaflets with fewer subdivisions. With so many *Apiaceae* species with edible roots, I wonder why wild carrot was chosen? It's a valid question for the British Isles with our 70 species, but more so in Afghanistan and the surrounding region, which includes Iran and Turkey and has the largest concentration – over 500 – of *Apiaceae* species on Earth.

The name Queen Anne's lace, by which the plant is sometimes known, relates to the dark reddish-purple flower in the centre of the umbel. Legend has it that Queen Anne pricked her finger while making lace, and a drop of blood fell on the lace – although this is hard to follow, as lace is made by winding thread around pins firmly fixed to a board. Quite apart from the folk meanings attached to this dark flower, it has a practical purpose, acting as a decoy to attract beetles.

USES/RECIPES In the Outer Hebrides, roots were once eaten raw as a snack; elsewhere, the wealth of folklore relating to them suggests that they were used extensively. They are much smaller than cultivated carrots and pale white. Roots of younger plants are tender and sweet, but older ones are like small pieces of wood. Use young leaves as salad or garnish or to add a slightly carroty herb flavour to cooked food. The seeds taste a bit like caraway and can be used in similar ways, but avoid if pregnant (see Hazards). Add to stews and sauces or use to

flavour fruit coulis and other desserts. Add flowers to summer wild herb salad; chop and sprinkle over cooked dishes; use to flavour sauces or crushed potatoes or deep fry the whole umbel or use fresh, for example to garnish the following dish from Noma in Copenhagen: crayfish cooked in beer, served with pumpkin cubes with pumpkin and crayfish bisque [RR].

BENEFITS Although cultivated carrots are rich in carotene (which derives its name from the plant and after passing through liver becomes vitamin A), wild carrot contains little or none! Carotene makes cultivated carrots orange; wild ones are white.

HAZARDS Seeds should not be eaten when pregnant, as they have been known to cause miscarriage.

Eryngium maritimum

Sea Holly

DISTRIBUTION Up to 300m. Native to Asia, Europe and Africa. In British Isles, found only on coast: in England, common, except parts of Cumbria, Bristol Channel, Devon, Cornwall, Dorset, Sussex, Kent, the Wash and east coast Spurn Head–Scottish border; in Wales, found throughout except Cardiganshire and Pem-

brokeshire; in Scotland, scarce, only scattered locations along west coast Dumfriesshire–Mid Ebudes and on Western Isles; in Ireland, found most coastal areas but absent Donegal Bay, Sligo Bay, Killala Bay, Arran Islands–Loop Head, and parts of Antrim and Down; present Isle of Man, Isles of Scilly and Channel Islands.

HABITAT Above the high tidemark of shingle and sandy shores; on sand dunes.

DESCRIPTION Hairless perennial; 15–60cm high, height and width roughly equal. Holly-like leaves are also as long as they are wide; greyish blue, very stiff, with spikes and thick white margins and veins. Flowers bluish-white in dense rather un-umbrella-like umbels, June–September.

NOTES With its bluey-grey spiky leaves and small blue umbels, sea holly looks more like a thistle than a carrot. Its sun-parched beach habitat necessitates deep roots to ensure a supply of water: a useful characteristic in a plant whose roots were once in great demand as food, in a candied preparation known as kissing comfits or eryngoes. They became popular in the Elizabethan era when the Colchester apothecary of Robert Burns supplied them to the royal family, and in *The Merry Wives of Windsor*, Shakespeare had Falstaff imploring, 'Let the sky . . . hail kissing comfits, and snow eringoes'. Other *Eryngo* species, including the rare field eryngo *E. campestre* have been used for food or medicine, but sea holly is the only coastal species.

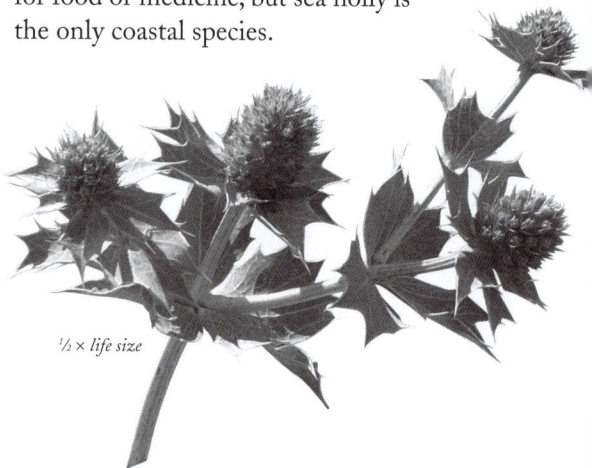

½ × life size

USES/RECIPES First spring leaves are tender enough to eat, though the flavour is quite overpowering, similar to the roots. Use to infuse flavour into puddings or sauces. Roots are candied with sugar and orange flower water. Follow candying method in 'How to use wild plants', p.18.

These candied roots were formerly used as flavouring for all sorts of pies, salads and sweet dishes. The candying process is really a way of preserving the flavour in a convenient form; the roots could equally well be used fresh as spice; uncandied the flavour is similar to the Indonesian spice galangal and can be used in similar ways. Uncandied roots were also formerly eaten roasted, boiled and pickled.

HARVESTING NOTES Digging up whole roots without some sort of stewardship scheme to nurture local populations is unthinkable. The seventeenth-century trade in eryngoes must have had something in place to ensure the sustainability of their business, or it would have been very short-lived. However, the careful removal of a small side root will do no harm. The flavour is very strong, and a little goes a long way.

Foeniculum vulgare

Wild Fennel

DISTRIBUTION Up to 300m. In England, widespread in east and southeast but absent areas of Huntingdonshire, Northamptonshire, north Hampshire, Oxfordshire and Cambridgeshire; common Somerset and Dorset but less so Cornwall and Devon; only a few coastal locations north of line Flamborough Head–Morecambe Bay; in Wales, present on or near the coast throughout; in Scotland, rare; in Ireland, scarce, mostly coastal sites south and east but also few widely scattered inland localities; present Isle of Man, Isles of Scilly and Channel Islands.

HABITAT Sea walls, coastal paths, waste ground, roadsides and marshes.

DESCRIPTION Hairless, tall perennial. Stems solid and shiny up to 2m high. Umbels bright yellow with many tiny, ring-shaped flowers. Leaf stalks short with a broad sheath. Basal leaves with many hairlike leaflets, emerging in bushy clumps from the root-stock of each plant. Stem leaves fewer with fewer leaflets. Flowers July–September.

SIMILAR SPECIES Spignel, scented mayweed, pineappleweed and yarrow all have similar leaves but lack the aniseed fragrance. They are all edible.

USES/RECIPES Leaves add a wonderful aniseed tang to wild-leaf salads but can equally well be served on their own, chopped and dressed with salt, fresh lemon juice, olive oil and garlic. Excellent with fish and seafood, for example, baked fish on a bed of wild fennel with a splash of Pernod and some spicy chorizo [AN]. Serve pan-fried scallops on a bed of wild fennel purée, and dressed with confit of fennel and toasted pine-nut dressing [PB]. Use also as a vegetable with other greens after boiling or frying; in south Italy cooked leaves are served with fava bean purée; in Spain they are cooked in stews or with rice and beans. Also use to

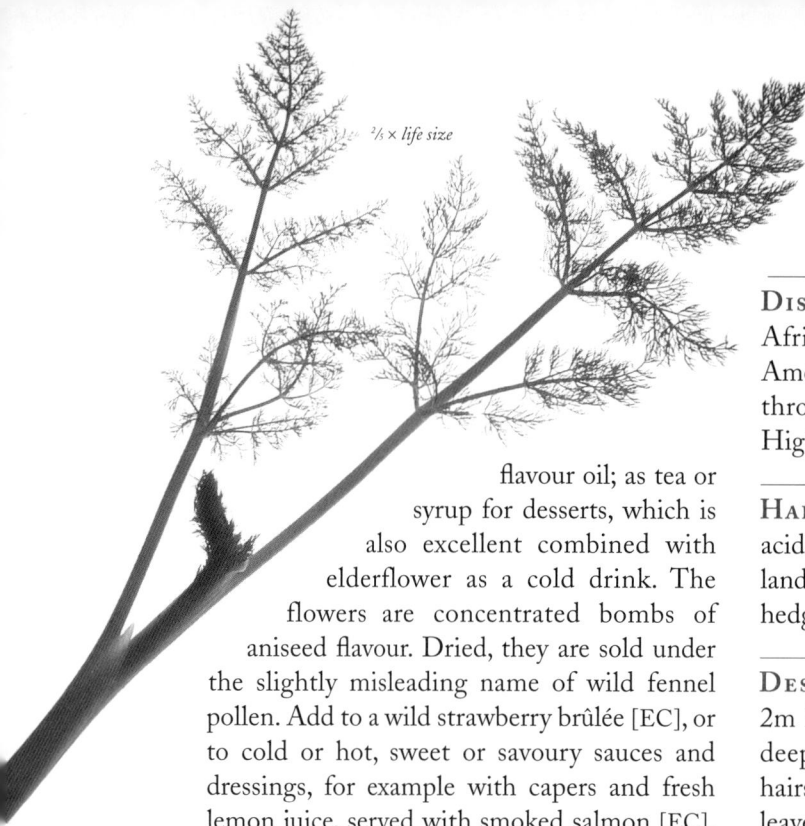

Heracleum sphondylium

Hogweed

DISTRIBUTION Up to 1005m. Native to Asia, Africa and Europe, introduced to North America. In British Isles, found pretty much throughout, except a few areas in Scottish Highlands.

HABITAT Dry/damp, neutral–alkaline but not acidic soils; in meadows, waste ground, woodland edges, roadside verges, tracks, river banks, hedgebanks.

DESCRIPTION Tall perennial, usually 50cm–2m high but can reach 3m. Stems hollow and deeply grooved. Leaves and stems produce hairs as defence against insects. Has the largest leaves of all native umbellifers (leaves of non-native giant hogweed *H. mantegazzianum* are larger still); they are once pinnate, with several (usually 5) leaflets, coarsely lobed and toothed. Umbels large, 10–15cm wide, dirty white, with flower petals on the outer edge noticeably larger. Seeds aromatic, flat and oval. Young shoots emerge in April and quickly unfold but recur throughout summer where plants are cut back by grazing, mowing or strimming.

SIMILAR SPECIES From a distance, wild angelica could be confused for hogweed, especially in woodland sites. Wild parsnip is generally much shorter but also has flat seeds and has similar leaves; these have narrower leaflets. Giant hogweed has huge, hairy stems, up to 3.5m high and 5cm wide, and with purple spots. Its leaves are also much larger and with sharper teeth.

NOTES Hogweed gets its name from its former use as pigs' fodder, yet it is one of the best of our wild vegetables. The flavour is aromatic, sweet and slightly citrus. Hogweed's old

flavour oil; as tea or syrup for desserts, which is also excellent combined with elderflower as a cold drink. The flowers are concentrated bombs of aniseed flavour. Dried, they are sold under the slightly misleading name of wild fennel pollen. Add to a wild strawberry brûlée [EC], or to cold or hot, sweet or savoury sauces and dressings, for example with capers and fresh lemon juice, served with smoked salmon [EC]. Fennel flower tempura is excellent with goats' cheese tart and rosemary sauce [SW]. Serve chopped and steamed with crayfish [SW]. Fennel flower bread is fantastic. Use seeds as a spice or tea, in bread or for flavouring oil. They are eaten in Indian restaurants after a meal to cleanse the palate and are said to relieve wind and prevent flatulence. Leaf stalks (especially the sheathing bases) and younger main stems are quite tender and can be used as a vegetable. **WILD FENNEL PURÉE:** Chop the stalk, sweat slowly for an hour with onion and garlic, blitz and serve with fish with skin [EC]. Older stems, even as the plant dies back, can flavour fish stocks or be (foil) baked or barbecued with fish – try putting a few in with the charcoal. Roots of first-year plants can be used as a vegetable. They have a sweet, mild flavour with only the slightest hint of aniseed.

HARVESTING NOTES If cut back before flowering, plants will produce a second crop of leaves and stems. Picking the flowers also promotes a second crop.

Hogweed seeds

finely and add to salads, or add to milk when poaching white fish.

HOGWEED FLOWER BUDS IN BUTTER: Cook sous-vide style (see alexanders roots, pp.131–2) at 80°C for 20 minutes, with fresh orange juice, reduced down with zest, lots of unsalted butter and coriander seeds dry fried in pan. Serve on their own with some hollandaise, with oily fish or red mullet, or cold with a terrine or potted duck [SW].

Seeds have an orangey, almost cardamom flavour, and when dry and brown are an excellent pudding spice. Use to flavour stock syrup, fruit sauces, jelly, rice pudding, panna cotta or custard. The green seeds have more flavour but are slightly bitter; use to flavour beans or bulghar [FC].

BARSCZ: (recipe courtesy of Polish ethnobotanist and forager extraordinaire, Lucasz Luczaj) Collect hogweed leaves and stalks: shiny ones are preferable, with thick leaf stalks making up 50 per cent of the bulk. Wash and chop them and pack them tightly in a pot (you can fill the pot with them). Add salt to taste then pour boiling water just to cover hogweed. Cover the pot and leave it at room temperature. Check the taste every day; it is ready to use when it becomes sour and fizzy: 2–3 days is usually ideal, after which it becomes very acidic. It is served boiled with cream or butter,

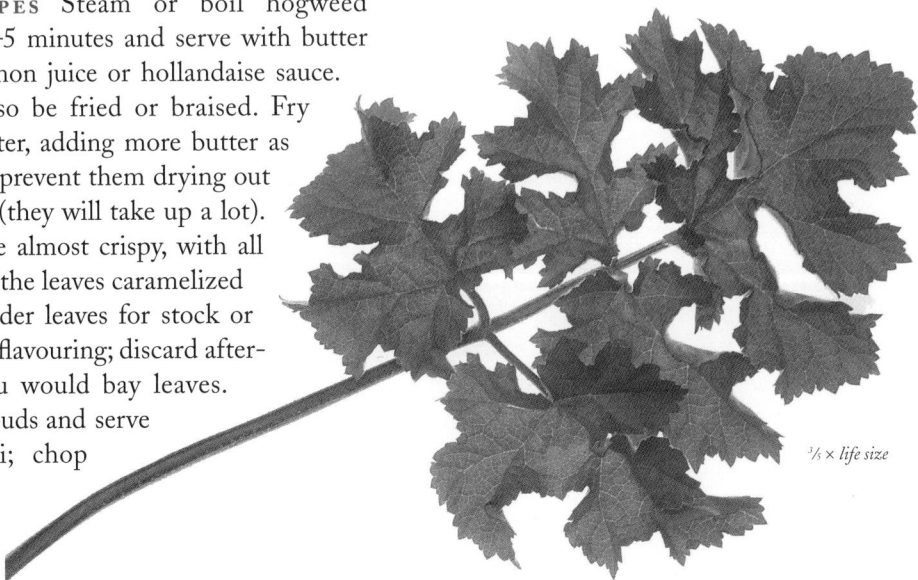

Russian name, '*borschevnic*', is similar to the name of the soup borsch; in Polish, both soup and plant are called '*barscz*' (pronounced 'bahrshch'). The soup was originally made using lacto-fermented hogweed; by the end of the nineteenth century, *barscz* had come to mean a soup with beetroot (not lacto-fermented) as the main ingredient. In Romania, sour liquid from lacto fermented plants is called borsch, and is added to soups to sharpen the flavour.

USES/RECIPES Steam or boil hogweed shoots for 3–5 minutes and serve with butter and fresh lemon juice or hollandaise sauce. They can also be fried or braised. Fry leaves in butter, adding more butter as they cook to prevent them drying out and burning (they will take up a lot). They become almost crispy, with all the sugars in the leaves caramelized [DQ]. Use older leaves for stock or generally for flavouring; discard afterwards as you would bay leaves. Boil flower buds and serve like broccoli; chop

³⁄₅ × *life size*

with eggs poached in the hot soup, with runny yolks. In spring the whole thing is eaten; later in the year the stalks and leaves are too tough and only the liquid is consumed.

HAZARDS Phototoxic furanocoumarins in leaves and stems make skin highly sensitive to ultraviolet radiation. Direct sunlight on skin following handling of these plants can lead to swelling, blistering and increased tanning. We have known this to happen after collecting large quantities of hogweed during sunny periods; we now wear gloves. Symptoms following contact with giant hogweed are similar but much more extreme.

3/10 × life size

Ligusticum scoticum

Scots Lovage

DISTRIBUTION Up to 300m. In England, absent, except Northumberland coast; in Wales, absent; in Scotland, found most of coastline but absent few areas of Kirkcudbrightshire, Wigtownshire, west Sutherland, east Sutherland and Western Isles and completely absent coastal Dumfriesshire; in Ireland, only found coast in north from west Donegal–Antrim and at single site in Down.

HABITAT Rocks on coastal cliffs and shores; shingle beaches and stable sand dunes.

DESCRIPTION Hairless perennial with stout, ridged stem, up to 90cm high but usually smaller. Compound leaves have 3–5 widely spaced leaflets, roughly egg shaped and bluntly toothed only on the upper half. The stalks of lower leaves are long, sheathing at the base, the main stalk of the upper leaves is one big sheath. Umbels of greenish white flowers, 8–14 rays with bracts and bracteoles.

USES/RECIPES Collect leaves in early summer when they are still tender. Eskimos used to store the leaves in seal oil; eventually the oil became infused with a sweet flavour. SCOTS LOVAGE SOUP: Sweat some onions, garlic, diced potatoes and bay leaf in olive oil, add water (or chicken/vegetable stock); season it up well. When the potatoes are soft, add the lovage, cook for a good 5 minutes and leave off the heat. When less hot, blend and re-season then pass through a sieve. This soup is lovely very cold from the fridge, with a blob of crème fraîche and some crusty bread [JDW]. Also lovely in tomato and lovage salads, sauces and with slow-roasted lamb, with shallots, white wine reduction and butter [PW].

Meum athamanticum

Spignel/Badmonnie

DISTRIBUTION Mostly lowland, below 300m, but up to 610m in Dumfries and East Perth. In England, only Kendal/Coniston area of Cumbria and one locality near Newcastle; in Wales, only Dolgellau area; in Scotland, found mostly Dumfries and Galloway, Tayside, Grampian, Strathclyde and Fife; in Ireland, only introduced at one site in Down.

HABITAT Dry acid or neutral soils on unimproved grassland and roadsides, often in hilly areas.

DESCRIPTION Branched, hollow-stemmed, hairless perennial with herby aroma, 7–60cm high. Leaves mostly at plant base with stiff, dry sheathing bases; 3–4 times pinnate, with very distinct primary subdivisions and densely crowded, fine, frondy final subdivisions. White/yellowish flowers have 5–15 rays and 1–2 bracts, if any. A distinctive feature is the fibrous, dead leaf matter that remains at the base of the plant, although with young plants this may be absent.

SIMILAR SPECIES Whorled caraway *Carum verticillatum*, the leaves of which are only once pinnate, with clearly separated whorls of leaflets; young fennel is also similar, but with a distinct aniseed aroma and less clearly defined primary leaflets.

NOTES The roots were harvested on a large scale to provide a scent for snuff. This trade led to a serious decline of the plant in the Pennines, an object lesson in how over-harvesting roots can adversely affect a species. Spignel is now quite scarce; its roots should only be harvested if you are actively encouraging its growth in some way. It can be purchased from quite a number of specialist growers, if you want to grow it yourself.

USES/RECIPES Roots can be grated for use as a spice. Use leaves in salad or as a herb; they taste like curry plant.

½ × life size

Myrrhis odorata

Sweet Cicely

DISTRIBUTION Up to 500m. In England, scattered locations in south but mostly upwards from Derbyshire, Cheshire and North Yorkshire, although absent high-altitude areas Cumbria and Durham; in Wales most counties but more widespread in the north; in Scotland, mostly south and east. Also on Orkney and Shetland Isles and north to Dornoch Firth. Absent Grampian Mountains and almost entirely absent Highlands; in Ireland, only Ulster, mostly in Tyrone; present Isle of Man.

HABITAT Grassy areas, field margins, roadsides, hedgebanks; by rivers and streams. A once popular garden herb, often (but not always) found near sites of past or present human dwellings.

DESCRIPTION White-flowered perennial with lacy leaves. Similar to wild chervil but plants wider, with more foliage when flowering. All foliage is a lighter green. Leaves also flatter and less shiny, softer to the touch, older or larger ones often with white marks. Flowers white, in umbels of 4–10 umbellules. Seeds are unmistakable: about 1.5–2.5cm long, pointed and upright, starting green, later blackish brown.

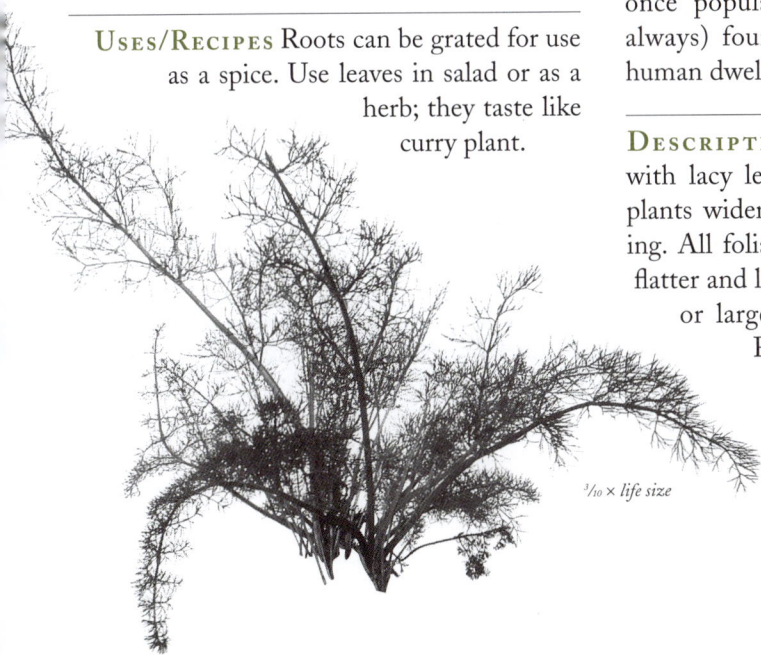

³/₁₀ × life size

The whole plant smells strongly and sweetly of aniseed when crushed.

SIMILAR SPECIES See **hemlock** and Table 1, p.113.

USES/RECIPES Aniseed-flavoured leaves in savoury and sweet cooking and salads. Serve poached salmon, with a little salad of radishes, nasturtium leaves, campanula leaves and flowers, rocket, spinach and sorrel in a simple vinaigrette, with crème fraîche whipped up with lemon zest and plenty of chopped sweet cicely. Garnish with a few torn pieces of sweet cicely leaves [JDW]. Gustav Otterberg from Sweden uses sweet cicely to flavour stock for a sauce served with pike, beetroot and oysters, finishing the dish with raw leaves. Seed pods can be dried for use in winter and spring. Cooked with fruit, the sweet aniseed flavour counters acidity in place of sugar, so less sugar is needed. Green seeds can be used similarly but have a much more intense aniseed flavour. For example, chop finely and add to rhubarb fool [SW]. Roots can be eaten cooked like carrot or parsnip, and this was once common practice. Other carrot-family roots that were at one time commonly eaten include caraway, chervil and parsley; the latter two are now regaining popularity. Roots can also be candied.

2 × life size

Pastinaca sativa
Wild Parsnip

DISTRIBUTION Up to 380m. In England, widespread much of south, but absent parts East Sussex, Cornwall and much of Devon and Somerset, more patchy in Midlands and absent most Shropshire, Staffordshire and much of Herefordshire, Leicestershire, Derbyshire and north Lincolnshire, present on Cheshire and Lancashire plains, north of Morecambe Bay and Cleveland Hills, elsewhere sparse; in Wales, mostly Carmarthenshire, Glamorgan and Monmouthshire with couple of sites in Pembrokeshire; in Scotland, scarce, mostly Central Lowlands; in Ireland, rare; present Channel Islands and Isles of Scilly.

HABITAT Roadsides, rough ground on neutral and especially on calcareous soil.

DESCRIPTION Hairy biennial, up to 1.2m high with fibrous, ridged stem, hollow or solid. Leaves once pinnate with several pairs of coarsely toothed and lobed leaflets. Flowers yellow, similar to fennel, with umbellules quite widely spaced. The whole plant smells of parsnip. Seeds flat and winged, like hogweed, but smaller and narrower.

SIMILAR SPECIES Hogweed is bigger with broader leaves and white flowers; its hollow stems are easier to snap.

NOTES Wild parsnip is undoubtedly the source plant for our cultivated variety. It is a particularly British favourite, never having been as popular elsewhere in Europe. In France, for example, the leaves have been used far more than the roots.

USES/RECIPES Leaves have a strong, herby parsnip flavour, but are quite coarse. Chop

finely or use whole to extract flavour; parsnip leaf soup will need passing through a sieve to remove the fibres. Roots are smaller than the cultivated variety, and when cooked retain a soft fibrous texture. Older plants have a woody, inedible core, but once cooked the outer flesh can be stripped off and eaten. The flavour is excellent, so retain stock when boiling them or allow it to cook back into the parsnips. Toss cooked roots in a warm pan with a few wild rocket leaves, olive oil and a little champagne vinegar, just long enough to wilt the leaves. Flowers taste strongly of parsnip, add them to salads or use to finish hot or cold sauces or soups. Use seeds as a spice; for example a white sauce for gammon: simmer crushed fruits and finely chopped onion in milk, strain and thicken with cornflower or white roux.

HAZARDS Leaves contain furanocoumarins (see **hogweed**); avoid collecting with bare hands in bright sunlight.

Pimpinella saxifraga

Burnet-saxifrage

DISTRIBUTION Up to 810m. In England, widespread, but less so parts of Fens, Leicestershire, Shropshire, Lancashire, Yorkshire and Cheviot Hills; in Wales, found throughout; in Scotland, in Tayside and Clackmannanshire, Central Lowlands south to border, elsewhere few localities in Grampian, Easterness and East Ross in east, along coast of west Sutherland in north, and Main Argyll, Westerness and the Mid Ebudes in west, with single locality on Orkney; in Ireland, throughout Leinster, also Tipperary, Waterford, east Cork and east Galway, and sparse elsewhere; present Isle of Man.

HABITAT Woodland edges, meadow and pasture, occasionally roadsides.

DESCRIPTION Leaves at plant base look like **salad burnet** leaves, with 3–9 leaflets, toothed at the edges, more rounded than greater burnet-saxifrage. Stem solid, hairy with shallow ridges. Leaves on the stem smaller and fleshier with irregular teeth and a swollen base. Flowers white, June–September. Seeds shiny, with faint ridges, in contrast to those of greater burnet-saxifrage.

129

SIMILAR SPECIES Pignut has similar leaves, but flowers much earlier. Greater burnet-saxifrage *P. major* has a hairless, hollow stem with deep ridges and a greater preference for shade; its seeds were once candied as comfits or sweets.

1½ × life size

NOTES This plant is closely related to anise *Pimpinella anisum*, the seeds of which are the source of aniseed flavouring. Burnet-saxifrage seed has an unpleasantly pungent flavour and is nothing like aniseed.

USES/RECIPES Use leaves to flavour sauces, herb butter or soft cheese, or add to salads. In green sauce (salsa verde) with boiled eggs and other chopped leaves; serve with meat or fish.

HARVESTING NOTES Collect basal leaves before emergence of flower stem.

Smyrnium olusatrum

Alexanders

DISTRIBUTION Up to 300m. In England, found mostly in southwest, along south coast, east and Thames Estuary, scattered elsewhere and almost entirely absent northwest, though range extending north; in Wales, mostly coastal counties but also few inland areas; in Scotland, scarce, mostly Central Lowlands especially around Firth of Forth plus few Ayrshire, Clyde Isles, north Aberdeen and Banffshire; in Ireland, coastal counties from west Donegal in north around east coast to Cork, elsewhere scattered but mostly absent Connaught; present Isle of Man, Isles of Scilly, Channel Islands and Lundy.

HABITAT Mostly coastal areas, which is puzzling as once established it grows well inland. Often in dense colonies on sea walls, cliffs, roadsides and path edges, occasionally wood edges and in meadows.

DESCRIPTION Biennial, growing in extensive clumps. Bushy and quite tall, 60cm–1m high, with dense, yellow umbels. Leaves twice pinnate, with dark green glossy final leaflets,

3–8cm long, with finely toothed edges. Unmistakable once in flower – other yellow-flowered umbellifers, including wild fennel and wild parsnip, have very different leaves. The large black seeds remain on the skeleton umbels well into winter and mark the spot for the following year's growth. Plants often produce leaves throughout winter until flowering stems develop in March.

SIMILAR SPECIES Wild angelica leaves are similar, but paler and less glossy. The two plants occur in very different habitats.

NOTES Alexanders is a relic of the Roman occupation, brought here by the then colonizers, along with ground-elder, good-king-henry, sweet chestnut and possibly wild fennel. It was an important medicinal herb in Greece and was mentioned by both Pliny and Collumell in the 1st century AD. The name derives from the medieval *Petroselinum Alexandrium* ['rock parsley of Alexandria'].

A widely used herb and vegetable until the sixteenth century, when celery, previously used as herb or spice, was developed into a milder, thick-stalked vegetable. Alexanders looks a bit like the improved version of celery, but the flavour is only vaguely similar. Nevertheless, as

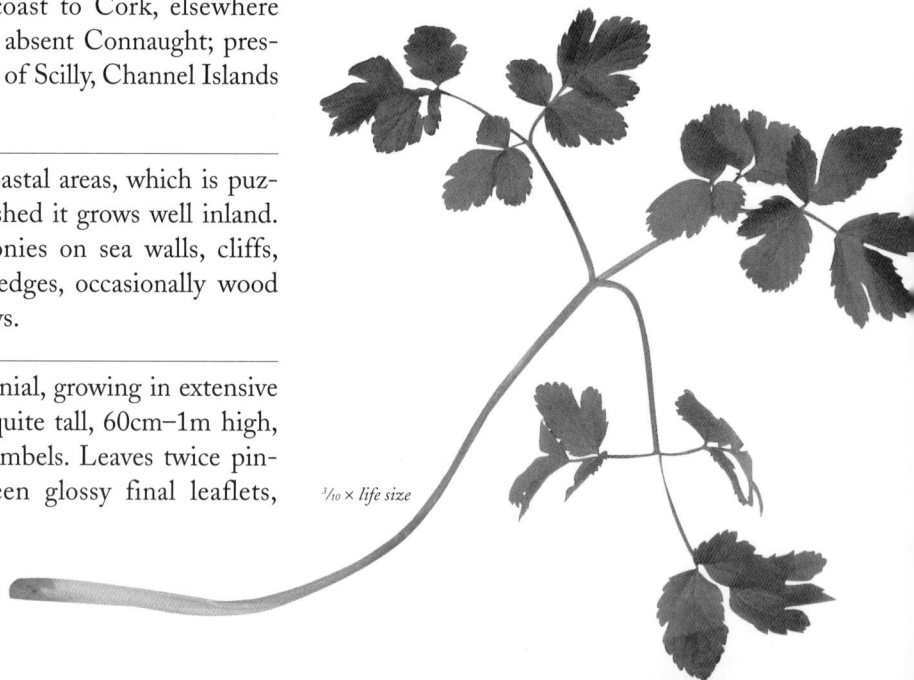

1/10 × *life size*

celery became more popular, alexanders was used less and less, although it was still grown in some kitchen gardens until the mid-eighteenth century. Since then it has persisted as a naturalized relic of cultivation. The flavour of alexanders is fragrant but sweet; food writer Jill Dupleix describes it in *The Times* as 'warm and spicy, like cumin-scented spinach'. In my opinion the flavour is unique, but the Latin name *Smyrnium* alludes to the resemblance of its scent to myrrh, so perhaps it also tastes like myrrh.

USES/RECIPES Stalks and leaves are good winter and spring vegetables, for example cooked with a little pheasant stock, butter and seasoning and served with roast pheasant, chestnuts and wild mushrooms [AN]. Make risotto (**see** p.245, for basic recipe) with blue cheese and alexanders, or a fresh apple salad with spicy walnut vinaigrette with sultanas and (warm) braised alexanders, chopped into tiny pieces [BW]. As a bed for veal: fry shallots until translucent, then fry some alexanders stalks for a bit, add white wine, then veal or chicken stock, bring to boil then simmer, add blanched **sea aster**; serve with juices [PW]. They are also good in stews or pot roasts, or used in place of celery to flavour stock. Use leaves sparingly in salads or as herbs, for example with braised whelks: dice and fry some onion or shallot, add white wine and blanch whelks, then remove and chop, add again and simmer, add chopped alexanders right at the end. Their myrrhy soapiness counterbalances the strong flavour of the whelks [PW]. Also use leaves to flavour chicken stock, dropped in right at the end [BW]. The main stems can be up to 3cm thick. These are excellent peeled and boiled or steamed, until the plants are fully in flower when they become fibrous throughout.

ALEXANDERS IN WILD BOAR STEW: Brown the off-cuts of the boar meat in a large casserole with a little flour, salt and pepper. Add the alexanders (cut like celery) and cook gently with carrots, onions and swede, a little bouquet garni and boar or chicken stock, covered in a casserole dish until a rich, raguey stew. Grill the boar loin to medium, then add chopped alexanders leaf to the stew before serving to freshen it up. Slice the loin on top, and drizzle a little whole grain mustard cream sauce with it [JDW].

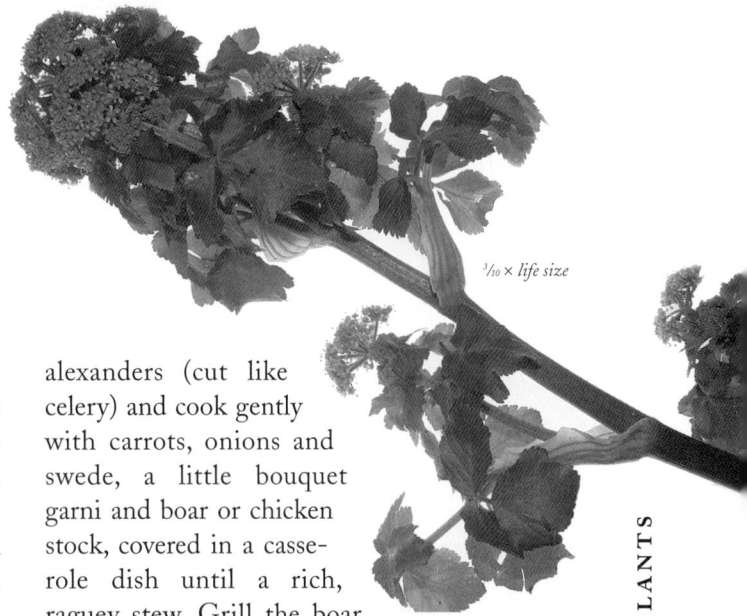

Buds and yellow flowers can be cooked like broccoli and served with hollandaise sauce, as tempura, and or fried with shallots in butter, seasoned with salt and pepper, and served with shavings of Parmesan [SW]. Grind seeds and use as a condiment. They are quite soft, so either toast them until brittle enough to be ground in a pepper grinder, or put them in a blender. They were commonly used until the introduction of pepper; they have a similar aromatic flavour but none of the heat of peppercorns. Use as seasoning for fish (but also with meat and game). Add ground seeds to softened butter with lemon, a splash of white wine, salt and chopped wild chervil. Put 1 level teaspoon per scallop (left in the deep half of the shell), top with breadcrumbs and bake in a medium oven for 5–8 minutes until the scallop is just set and the breadcrumbs crispy [PW]. Roots can be sliced finely (using a potato peeler) into salads. Cook sous-vide style in a vacuum-packed bag, sealed with no air; at home you could cook in a sauteuse pan with a little water with sugar, salt, pepper, tarragon, cinnamon, bay leaf, thyme and a tiny knob of butter, covered with a

³/₁₀ × life size

Mark Hix's Red Gurnard with Alexanders and Three-cornered Garlic

SERVES 4

Alexanders are prolific in the south of England, and you have more than likely driven through roadside avenues of these edible plants and not even realized. I must admit I was only introduced to them a few years ago by Miles and have been experimenting with them ever since. For me they are somewhere between cardoon and celery with the look and shape of angelica. I do love it when I'm introduced to a new vegetable.

250–300g young alexanders stalks, leaflets removed
2 tsp sugar
4 fillets, from a large gurnard
3 tbsp vegetable oil

120g butter
a handful of three-cornered garlic or wild garlic leaves
salt and freshly ground black pepper

Cut the alexanders into 8–9cm pieces, peel them as you would celery and cook in boiling, salted water with a couple of teaspoons of sugar for 5–6 minutes, or until tender, then drain.

Skin the gurnard then cut along the central pin bones nearest the top of the fillet. This leaves you with the thicker top part of the fillet, which is the best, meatiest bit. Heat some vegetable oil in a (preferably) non-stick frying pan and cook the fillets for 3–4 minutes on each side, adding a knob of the butter to the pan towards the end of cooking.

Melt the rest of the butter in a pan, tear the garlic leaves into small pieces and cook gently in the butter for a minute or so until they wilt. Add the alexanders and just re-heat for a minute or so and season. Spoon this over the gurnard fillets and serve.

cartouche until soft. In the sous-vide bag, add all these ingredients except for the water and cook for about 20 minutes (or until soft) in a large pot of simmering water. Surrounded by heat, none of the flavour or taste escapes. Serve cut pieces with some braised pearl onions, sautéed wild mushrooms in a beurre blanc (butter sauce) accompanying a piece of steamed halibut and a little tarragon perhaps [JDW]. Alternatively, braise alexanders root in butter and fish stock, serve alongside poached turbot served on Jerusalem artichoke purée, with Jerusalem artichoke chips [JDW].

HARVESTING NOTES Alexanders is invasive and aggressively extending its range so there is no present danger of over harvesting. Many parks and nature reserves would welcome the removal of alexanders – leaves, stems, roots and all – we are presently doing so on behalf of Thanet District Council, along the northeast Kent coast!

CASHEW FAMILY
Anacardiaceae

Rhus typhina

Stag's-horn Sumach

DISTRIBUTION Up to 300m. Native of North America. In England, sparsely present in the north and Midlands, more widespread south of line Severn Estuary–Wash with clusters in Norfolk, Home Counties, Somerset, Dorset and Devon; in Wales, sparse, most common in Cardiganshire; in Scotland, one location recorded in Strathclyde and Ayrshire; present Channel Islands and Isles of Scilly.

HABITAT Naturalized on roadsides and railway embankments; cultivated in gardens.

DESCRIPTION Small shrub, which, in the British Isles, reproduces by suckering. Leaves are divided into several pairs of long, thin opposite leaflets; these turn a dramatic orange in the autumn. Sumach flowers are small and green, growing in dense clusters at the branch ends; they mature to form velvety clusters of deep red fuzzy berries or drupes, which can remain on the tree until the emergence of the following year's flowers.

SIMILAR SPECIES Poison sumach *R. vernix* is sometimes grown in gardens. It has widely spaced oval, toothless leaflets, greenish-white flowers and drooping clusters of white drupes, arranged much less densely than stag's-horn sumach. Any skin contact causes long-lasting, painful rashes.

NOTES Numerous plants in this family are used in various parts of the world, usually for their berries, which are processed to produce a tangy spice. None is native here but stag's-horn sumach is a common, small, ornamental garden tree. Sadly, due to its tendency to sucker and spread, my father destroyed a large sumach in his garden, only weeks before I discovered its edible usefulness! Sumach is a

¹/₄ × life size

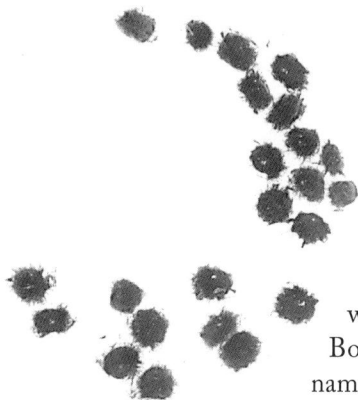

viable alternative to lemons (sea-buckthorn berries, sorrel and wood sorrel are others); good news for anyone wanting to exclude from their diet plant products with high food miles. Both French and German names for this plant translate as 'vinegar tree', because of the sharp flavour of the berries. They contain no vinegar (acetic acid) but do contain malic, citric, tartaric and ascorbic acids: all the acids normally found in fruit.

USES/RECIPES Berries or drupes are dried and rubbed across a sieve to remove the red outer coating, which is collected in a container below. The resulting coarse powder is the seasoning sumac, used in Turkey, Iran, Jordan and Lebanon to season rice (sprinkle on before serving), meat and vegetables, as well as in soups and egg dishes. Marinate meats in oil infused with the ground drupe cases and tarragon for at least 4 hours before barbecuing or grilling. Mix with salt before using in salads with red or white onions, salad leaves and fresh lemon juice. To make a drink a bit like lemonade, infuse the sumac powder (or whole berries) in cold water for several hours, then strain the liquid and add sugar to taste. Without the sugar, the same liquid can be used in place of lemon juice. The new spring growth tips are mildly sweet with a pleasant fruity flavour: strip off leaves and outer skin and use as crudités, in fruit salads and savoury salads.

BENEFITS High in vitamin C.

HAZARDS Some people are allergic to these berries so use in moderation, at least initially.

HARVESTING NOTES Gather berries as soon as they are ripe, when the colour has turned rich reddish purple. Although they remain on the trees for months, rain will gradually leach out the flavour.

CROWBERRY FAMILY
Empetraceae

Empetrum nigrum

Crowberry

DISTRIBUTION Up to 1270m. In England, few sites on Dartmoor and Exmoor, in Birmingham, Isle of Man, North York Moors, Pennines, Lake District, Cheviot Hills; in Wales, most areas but not south coast or Anglesey (that is, lowland areas); in Scotland, widespread but absent parts of Fife, Aberdeenshire, Kincardineshire and Caithness; in Ireland, mountains of Antrim, Donegal, Mullaghmore, Mourne, Slieve Bloom and Wicklow, mountains and moors in Galway, Mayo and Kerry.

HABITAT Moorland and mountains, on well-drained acid soils; often on slopes or over scree, both well-drained places.

DESCRIPTION Native evergreen shrub, forming low mats, 15–50cm high. The tiny, dark green, heather-like leaves are alternate, glossy and untoothed, on reddish stems. Flowers are minute and pink. Berries, only found on female bushes, are round and black, 4–6mm wide.

SIMILAR SPECIES Other moorland plants with black berries are bilberry (which has a bluish bloom) and arctic bearberry *Arctostaphylos alpinus*, both edible. The leaves look superficially like cross-leaved heath *Erica tetralix*, but they protrude from the stem at all angles and are alternate; leaves of cross-leaved heath are opposite and form a definite cross.

USES/RECIPES Berries are rather watery with a delicate taste that intensifies with cooking. In Finland they are harvested in great quantities for jam. Use them to make fruit pies or to garnish highland game, such as venison or grouse.

HAZARDS Said to cause nausea if eaten in quantity.

2 × life size

DAISY FAMILY
Asteraceae

A number of familiar foods are derived from the daisy family. Cultivated varieties produce lettuce, chicory, globe and Jerusalem artichokes, sunflower seed and chamomile flowers. Burdock root is hugely popular in Japan as a vegetable whilst salsify roots are perhaps better known in Europe.

Among the wild plants, the most widely used in traditional cuisines in Europe are the variably bitter rosette leaves of chicory, dandelion, thistle, sow-thistle, hawk's-beard, hawkbit and cat's-ear, all of which are eaten both raw and cooked. There are also a number of plants with aromatic leaves that are used for flavourings and teas, the best known of which are the chamomiles. Plants of this family have no characteristic culinary attribute like the mustard spiciness of the cabbage family or the aromatic flavours of the mint and carrot families. What they do have in common are their health-promoting properties; in fact the daisy family is perhaps better known for medicinal plants than food plants. Many are rich not only in antioxidants, minerals, beta-carotene and vitamin C but also in substances that can be used to treat specific ailments. To supply substantial international markets for herbal medicines, echinacea (North America) and yarrow (Europe) are wild harvested in great quantities; several other wild species are cultivated, for example, burdock, scented mayweed, common chamomile, chicory and milk thistle.

All these species can also be used for foods and/or beverages. Sometimes they straddle the boundary between food and medicine (see Pieroni & Leimar Price, *Eating and Healing*, for further discussion of the dual use of plants as food and medicine). Many popular fizzy drinks, such as root beer and cola, were originally produced as health tonics. Dandelion and burdock is no exception - the roots of both plants are effective detoxicants commonly used by herbal practitioners. Similarly, chamomile is drunk as much for its calming and stomach-settling properties as for its pleasant taste. Bitter principles are present in the leaves and stems of several plants in this family. Our sugar-gorged palates are generally quite intolerant of bitterness, but in parts of rural Italy, where wild foods have remained part of many people's diets, bitter dishes made with ingredients like wild chicory leaves are eaten with relish because bitterness is (quite rightly) believed to promote health. Many cultures have a traditional use of liquids made from bitter herbs – known as bitters – which are taken as a health tonic. Bitter substances of widely varying chemistry all stimulate bitterness receptors in our taste buds, which then trigger the release of hormones and numerous gastric secretions which improve appetite and enhance digestion, as well as regulating blood-sugar release and reducing food sensitivities.

BOTANICAL CHARACTERISTICS The composite flower head is the major botanical characteristic that unites the daisy family. Yet what we commonly call the flowers of this family are not really flowers at all: dandelions, daisies, marigolds, and so on, are in fact collections of hundreds of tiny flowers, known as florets. When I first learnt about this, even the best explanation left me unwilling to accept it; I suppose because it so blatantly contradicts our common language. Only when I broke up a few of these 'flowers' and examined their constituent parts did my mind stop rebelling (see image below). A daisy has a ring of long, flat, white florets (called ray florets) that look cunningly like petals, which surround a tight disc made of many yellow tube-shaped florets (called disc florets), which have the appearance of stamens and anthers. This deception is apparently designed to hoodwink insects into thinking they have found a big flower, so

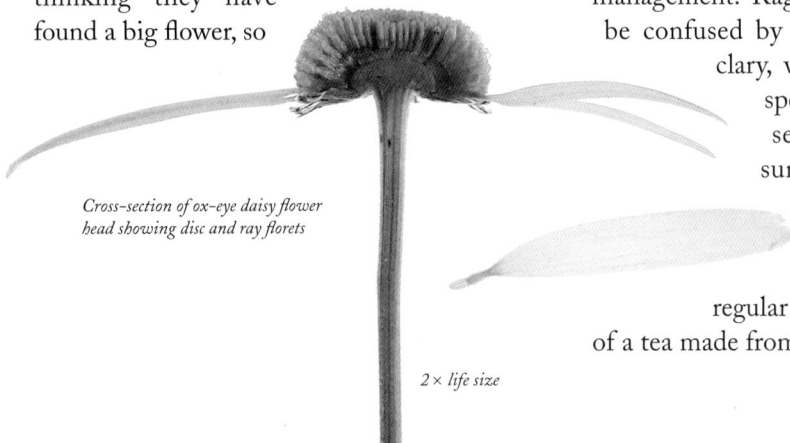

Cross-section of ox-eye daisy flower head showing disc and ray florets

2 × life size

that they walk all over it in search a big cache of nectar, collecting and depositing pollen as they go. The fact that we also fall for this disguise is incidental. Flower heads of some species consist of only one kind of floret, for example dandelions have only ray florets; thistles and burdocks have only disc florets.

Many daisy-family species possess the following, slightly less challenging botanical characteristics: basal rosettes, a white, milky latex produced when the stem or leaves are cut (also characteristic of other plant families, including poppy, campanula and the toxic euphorbia, none of which is likely to be confused with species from this family), and fluffy attachments to the seeds known as pappuses, which act like a parachute and enable them to be blown to pastures new.

POISONOUS PLANTS

In the rogues' gallery are two very common poisonous plants, ragwort and groundsel, which contain pyrrolizidine alkaloids. They are a danger to horses and cattle (but oddly not to sheep), and landowners are legally required to remove them before they go to seed. During a trip to Maramures in Romania, where every inch of grassland is used either for hay or grazing, the only place I found ragwort was on a railway track. On meadows and pasture, it has been all but eradicated by centuries of careful management. Ragwort leaves could possibly be confused by sight (but not smell) with clary, wild rocket or wild mustard species, although they are not a serious danger unless consumed regularly and/or in quantity. Human poisoning – liver cirrhosis – has been recorded following regular and prolonged consumption of a tea made from *Senecio* species.

Senecio jacobaea

Common Ragwort

DISTRIBUTION Up to 670m. In British Isles, widespread throughout, only less so in Scotland, in Easterness, Sutherland and Shetland.

HABITAT Waste ground, pasture, roadsides on nutrient-poor soils, sand dunes and shingle beaches.

DESCRIPTION Virtually hairless perennial, up to 1.5m high. Basal leaves are lanceolate and pinnately lobed, with a large end lobe; upper leaves have more spindly lobes. Many flower heads, like yellow daisies. Robust and tough with an unpleasant smell at all stages (an alternative name is stinking billy).

SIMILAR SPECIES Basal leaves could be confused with young wild clary, black mustard or hoary mustard by sight, but not by smell.

Senecio vulgaris

Groundsel

DISTRIBUTION Up to 550m. In England, Wales and Ireland, widespread throughout, only less so in Donegal, Galway and Clare; in Scotland, common, but scattered in Grampian Mountains, North West Highlands, North Highlands and Isle of Lewis; present

Channel Islands, Isle of Man, Isles of Scilly and Lundy.

HABITAT Open, disturbed or cultivated ground (in contrast to ragwort, which is a grassland plant).

DESCRIPTION Similar to ragwort, but shorter, more branched and elegant with less dissected leaves. Flower heads are usually without ray florets. However, some plants in towns and on sand dunes have small ray florets, which can be confusing.

SIMILAR SPECIES Leaves could possibly be confused with perennial or annual wall rocket, but are fleshier.

EDIBLE PLANTS

Achillea millefolium

Yarrow

DISTRIBUTION Up to 1210m. Widespread throughout the British Isles.

HABITAT Gardens, fields and other grassland, verges and hedgebanks; sand dunes, shingle beaches and mountain habitats.

DESCRIPTION Native. Small perennial, 8–40cm high, young plants produce bushy clumps of long, feathery, dark green leaves; dense clusters of flower heads, white but often tinged with pink look like umbels of carrot-family species, but are corymbs of flower heads, not flowers. Stems have smaller, stalkless leaves. All leaves aromatic when crushed.

USES/RECIPES Leaves make a refreshing tea and can be added to salads. A simple dressing of fresh lemon juice and sugar draws out their

aromatic
flavour; served
this way they make a
good accompaniment to white fish. They taste
similar to rosemary and can also be used to
flavour light sweet and savoury sauces.

BENEFITS Yarrow has many traditional uses as a healing herb, many of which are supported by modern research. In Romania, large amounts are collected and sold as a remedy for circulatory disorders. It is a useful remedy for colds and fevers, and has an anti-inflammatory and healing action through its volatile oils, including chamazulene, also present in chamomile.

HAZARDS Handling it can cause skin irritation for some people. Like tansy, it contains thujone, which is toxic if consumed in quantity. It is unlikely to pose a risk when consumed as food, although to be on the safe side, avoid if pregnant.

Achillea ptarmica

Sneezewort

DISTRIBUTION Up to 770m. In England, widespread north of line Spurn Head–Severn Estuary, only less so Lincolnshire and southeast Yorkshire, but south of line sporadic, except Devon and Cornwall, where common; in Wales, widespread; in Scotland, widespread, only less so Easterness, West and East Ross and Western Isles; in Ireland, in Ulster and Longford, but sporadic elsewhere except sparse in south-central areas; on Isle of Man and naturalized on Alderney, Channel Islands.

HABITAT Damp–wet habitats such as scrub, heath, meadows and waste ground, marshes and fens, edges of rivers and streams; occasionally woodland. Mostly on acid soil; seldom on chalk.

DESCRIPTION Native greyish perennial up to 60cm high, with long, thin leaves, the edges of which are serrated like a saw blade. Flower heads greenish, resembling a much larger yarrow flower head, 12–18mm wide, arranged in loose clusters; flowers July–September.

NOTES The Latin *ptarmica* means 'sneeze': both the English and Latin names refer to its use to induce sneezing. Marcus Harrison of the Wild Food School in Cornwall describes eating the older leaves as 'like putting your tongue on the terminal of a live battery' – raw material for practical jokes rather than for food. The young leaves on the other hand have a pleasant numbing effect like Szechuan peppercorns; Marcus recommends them chopped finely and added to soy sauce as a dip.

BURDOCKS

For a thousand years greater burdock has been a popular vegetable in Japan, where it is known as 'gobo'. In several countries in South East Asia it is cultivated in specially prepared, stone-free soil so that the roots don't fork, and most of it is exported to Japan. In the wild, burdock seems to prefer stony ground, and the roots inevitably do fork. Few other of our wild edibles are so highly prized overseas, yet it is almost totally overlooked as a vegetable in the British Isles.

The flavour of burdock roots is mild, earthy and sweet. It can be concentrated either by drying the roots or making a tincture by steeping them in alcohol. Steeping draws out every last drop of flavour; the alcohol acts as preservative, so that the flavour is as fresh as the day the root came out of the ground. I once spent an afternoon with my herbalist friends Darren Rickard and Amanda Oliver tasting all their tinctures. I wanted to explore all the flavours they were inadvertently extracting from the plants; burdock was by far the most interesting.

Arctium minus

Lesser Burdock

DISTRIBUTION Up to 390m. In England, widespread, only less so south Northumberland; in Wales, widespread; in Scotland, most areas but sparse Grampian Mountains, North West Highlands, North Highland, Isle of Lewis, Northern Isles and parts of Southern Uplands; in Ireland, all counties but less so west and southeast; present Channel Islands, Isle of Man, Isles of Scilly and Lundy.

HABITAT Roadsides, railway embankments, waste ground, open woodland and margins, and scrub.

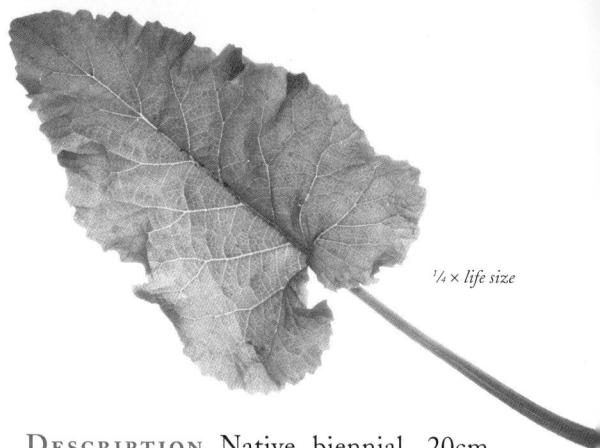

¼ × life size

DESCRIPTION Native biennial, 20cm high (first-year growth); 1.3m high (second-year growth). First-year growth solely large, cordate, hollow-stemmed leaves that are longer than wide. Tall green–purplish stem in second year with smaller leaves and purple, egg-shaped flower heads, little hooked bracts, the burrs from which the plant gets its name. Flower heads arranged in racemes and individual flower-head stems less than 2cm long.

SIMILAR SPECIES It is possible to confuse first-year growth burdock with butterbur *Petasites hybridus*. Both have very large leaves; however, butterbur leaves are rounder, with a downy underside. Butterbur contains liver-damaging pyrrolizidine alkaloids. Greater burdock *A. lappa* has solid-stemmed leaves as long as they are wide and spherical flower heads arranged in corymbs; each flower-head stem is greater than 2.5cm long. It often grows on river and stream banks.

NOTES Velcro is based on the hooks of burdock-fruiting heads: before humans were so much as chipping flint, burdock was attaching its seeds or burrs to animal fur by this means. Having hitched a ride, the seed can travel considerable distances, as you will know if you have ever found the burrs on your clothes or dog. The global distribution of burdock illustrates what an effective reproductive strategy this is.

USES/RECIPES For both species of burdock leaf stalks are eaten raw in Spain but are rather

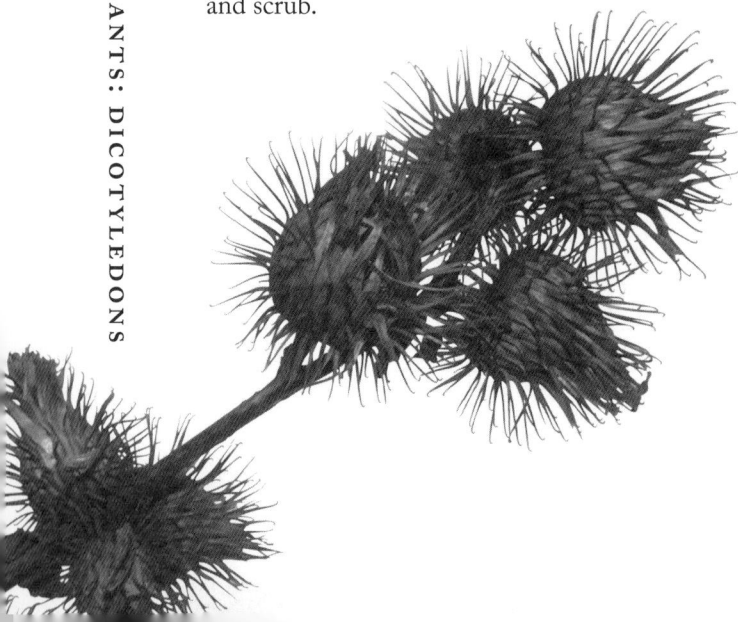

bitter and fibrous; however, blanching (see **dandelion**) makes them pleasantly crisp and much less bitter. Flower-head stems of second-year burdock can be used before the flowers buds appear, once the bitter peel has been thoroughly removed, as crudités, in salads and stir fries, or boiled until soft and served with butter or hollandaise sauce. Greater burdock roots have the better flavour; it is this plant that is cultivated in Asia. Wild roots, particularly larger ones, are more fibrous than cultivated gobo, but chopping finely or thinly, or grating, makes this less noticeable. Scrub them clean and slice finely then fry as an individual vegetable dish, or in stir fries. Grate and add to soups and stews. My favourite way to eat them is roasted after parboiling, as for roast parsnips.

ISAAC MCHALE'S GOBO PURÉE: Fry slices of burdock and onion, then add stock, soy, mirin, black sesame, sugar and veg stock and blend; to accompany roast duck breast in the Japanese style. Use dried roots or tincture made with larger, tougher roots (steep chopped roots in neat vodka, 250g/100ml, for 10–14 days) to flavour sorbet, fruit, ice cream, panna cotta and other desserts.

BENEFITS Burdock roots contain inulin, a slow-release carbohydrate that is useful for diabetics and anyone suffering from hypoglycaemia. However, it is also somewhat indigestible and can cause wind! An excellent source of potassium and a good source of calcium, phosphorus and protein, burdock roots are a good option on nutritional grounds alone. The root is also an important medicinal herb in skin and joint disease through its eliminative properties.

HARVESTING NOTES Harvest roots of first-year plants before the leaves die back in autumn; second-year plants before flowering stem is more than 10cm high, after which the

roots become woody and tasteless. Burdock's preference for stony ground necessitates a fairly heavy-duty extraction procedure, if you want to get at it reasonably quickly (although I have harvested massive roots from previously ploughed land, using just a garden fork): it's a variation on the oldest tool known to man, the digging stick. Early humans used a stick with a fire-hardened, sharpened tip, but I use a wrecking bar (a solid, round iron bar with a sharpened point) and a sledge or lump hammer. Hammer the bar into the ground to create a hole right next to the root then wiggle it around to create space for the root to move into; do the same on the other side of the root. Grip the plant firmly at the stem base or root top and move it back and forth between the two spaces. It soon becomes loose enough to pull up a substantial portion; these roots go so deep that it is unusual to get the whole thing.

Artemisia vulgaris

Mugwort

DISTRIBUTION Up to 420m. Widespread in England, only less so Northumberland and Durham; in Wales, absent only from highland areas; in Scotland, common in Central Lowlands, eastern Central Lowlands north to Angus and Western Isles, elsewhere mostly sporadic but absent from montane areas and North Highlands; in Ireland, most common in east, scattered in west and sparse in southwest; present Channel Islands, Isle of Man and Isles of Scilly.

HABITAT Waste places (especially in towns), roadsides, field and track margins; mostly lowland areas.

¹⁄₃ × life size

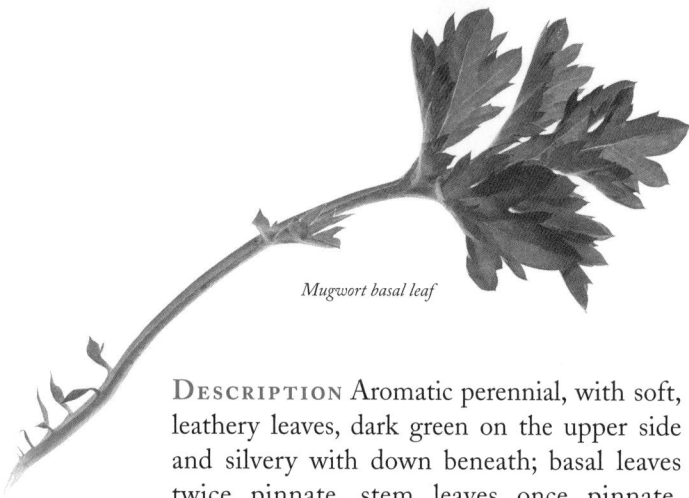
Mugwort basal leaf

DESCRIPTION Aromatic perennial, with soft, leathery leaves, dark green on the upper side and silvery with down beneath; basal leaves twice pinnate, stem leaves once pinnate. Flower heads egg-shaped and small, only 3–4 mm long, varying yellowish–reddish brown–purple and occurring in dense clusters, interspersed with the smaller leaves, which have fewer, more regularly shaped lobes.

SIMILAR SPECIES Chinese mugwort *A. verlotiorum*, naturalized in London, is more aromatic and flavoursome; flowering branches are arched and very leafy.

NOTES Mugwort is a remnant of the last ice age, originally a plant of steppes and tundras, but now adapted to our temperate climate.

USES/RECIPES Closely related to tarragon, mugwort has an aromatic menthol flavour; its leaves have traditionally been used to counter the fattiness of certain meats such as pork, mutton and especially goose, or oily fish such as mackerel and herring. In east Germany people still gather mugwort to use for stuffing goose; they even collect extra and dry it for use through the winter. Young leaves are added to sweet rice cakes called '*kusa mochi*' in Japan: ingredients are just rice flour, sugar and mugwort ('*yomogi*') leaves finely chopped, blanched and then ground. The cakes are sometimes filled with sweet bean paste. Dried or finely chopped fresh leaves are used to flavour soups, sauces, boiled rice, minced meat and batter. Mugwort has a cool, fine, furry texture that feels like kid leather. This makes them pleasant to touch but makes older leaves too dry and papery to use whole: young leaves are tender enough to add to salads. Young stems can be peeled and eaten raw. Flower heads are more aromatic than the leaves; use for flavouring soups and casseroles.

BENEFITS A medicinal herb: the leaves are used to stimulate appetite and bile flow and to induce menstruation. While milder than **wormwood** and **tansy**, it also has a worm-expelling action.

HAZARDS Contains small amounts of thujone, which is toxic if consumed in any quantity. It is unlikely to pose a risk when eaten as food, although to be on the safe side you should avoid it if pregnant. See Foraging Hazards, p.19.

Artemisia absinthium

Wormwood

DISTRIBUTION In England, widespread in Midlands, Herefordshire and London area, intermittently on remainder of coast, except

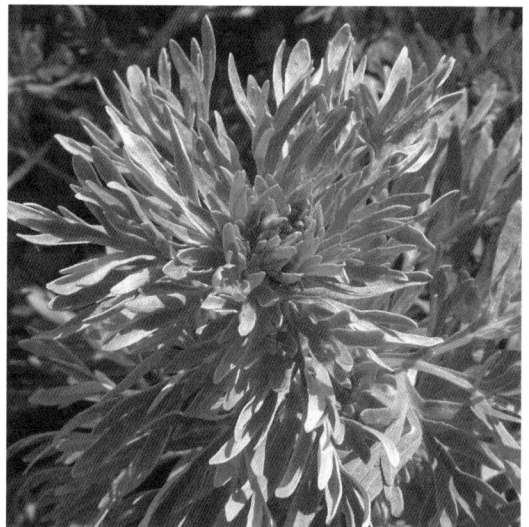

northwest; in Wales, north and south coastal areas, intermittently on remainder of coast; in Scotland and Ireland, very scarce.

HABITAT Mostly near human activity, path edges, rubbish tips, waste ground, gravel pits, quarries.

DESCRIPTION Upright, aromatic perennial, up to 90cm high. Leaves twice pinnate, greyish green, with thin, blunt leaf segments, soft to the touch. Florets dingy yellow, in half-round flower heads.

NOTES Wormwood achieved some notoriety through its use in the alcoholic drink absinthe. Absinthe has been known to cause hallucinations and convulsions, symptoms that were at one time attributed to the thujone content of wormwood. Because of these effects, absinthe has been banned in several European countries. However, it is now known that thujone does not cause these symptoms.

USES/RECIPES Leaves can be used as flavouring for savoury sauces, especially in combination with white wine: for example, French chef Edouard Loubet serves frogs' legs with a white wine and wormwood sauce. Wormwood was also an ingredient in purl, a beverage commonly drunk in the mornings by labourers in nineteenth-century London.

BENEFITS This is an important herb in modern herbal medicine, not only for its use in expelling worms. Known as an aromatic bitter, the bitter taste reflexly increases stomach acid and bile secretions, so improving the absorption of nutrients. It is also carminative, easing wind and bloating, and a useful insecticide and insect repellent.

2 × life size

Aster tripolium

Sea Aster

DISTRIBUTION Up to 300m. In England and Wales, all coastal areas, rare inland; in Scotland, abundant in west, but sparse Wigtownshire, Ayrshire and north of Skye, present most east coast, except Grampian and North Highland, and sparse Western and Northern isles; in Ireland, on much of the coast; on Alderney and Guernsey in Channel Islands, and Isle of Man.

HABITAT Coastal, mostly salt marsh, but on coastal cliffs in west.

DESCRIPTION Hairless perennial. Leaves dark green, thick and succulent, either strap shaped or lanceolate; basal leaves become quite large, up to 30cm long; upper leaves much smaller. Flower heads like large, scruffy purple daisies, mostly late summer–autumn.

USES/RECIPES Use the larger, young, fleshy leaves, or later the bushy leafy tops of plants just before flowering, in sauce vierge (see p.120), in salads or as a green vegetable, for example blanched and served with slow-braised salt-marsh lamb.

⅕ × life size

The flavour is quite strong, sharp and slightly herby, bordering on fruity.

SHELLFISH GRATIN: Steam and clean some razor clams, sweat a little crushed garlic and a shallot or two with a few sea aster leaves, toast some breadcrumbs in a dry pan; at the same time, chargrill the clams for a few seconds then chop them and mix with everything but the breadcrumbs. Top with breadcrumbs. Everything needs to be hot when assembled but don't overcook the razor clams or they become chewy [PB].

WITH STEAMED MACKEREL FILLETS: Blanch leaves for a few seconds in salted water, enough to soften so they will roll up without breaking the midrib. Roll each mackerel fillet in 2 aster leaves, wrap in cling film and steam, ideally in Chinese baskets. Serve with pickled kelp and salted cucumber (peeled, the core removed, cut in strips with peeler, salted to draw out water, then squeezed). *Dressing* 100ml rice wine vinegar, 50ml mirin, 25g sugar, a few finely chopped water-pepper leaves [EC]. As a bed for veal with **alexanders**; for recipe, see p.131.

Bellis perennis

Daisy

DISTRIBUTION Up to 915m. Widespread throughout British Isles.

HABITAT Well-maintained or heavily grazed grassy areas such as lawns, parks, playing fields and pasture.

DESCRIPTION Native perennial. Leaves in basal rosette; small, slightly hairy, short stalked, spoon shaped with blunt lobes. Flower heads throughout the year, on leafless stems, 1 per stem, a central yellow disc surrounded by many disc florets, white with pinkish tip or underside.

SIMILAR SPECIES **Ox-eye daisy** has much bigger leaves and flower heads. The daisy-like flower heads of chamomile and mayweed species appear on many branched stems with fine, fernlike leaves.

2 × life size

NOTES Alongside blackberry-picking, dandelion clocks, games of conkers and using dock leaves as a remedy for nettle stings, making daisy chains is one of our few widespread, unbroken traditions of wild-plant use. I can't prove it, but given our former fondness for eating flowers in the British Isles, I am fairly sure there is also a forgotten tradition of using daisy flower heads in salads.

USES/RECIPES Leaves can be used in salads or sandwiches; the great thing about them is that you will be able to find them on pretty much any lawn that has not been treated with herbicides. They are much nicer cooked, though; these small delicate leaves look more attractive than other larger greens, which tend to collapse when cooked; they also have a good, succulent texture and a mild but pleasant flavour. Flower heads are not the most flavoursome but look lovely in salads.

BENEFITS They have many uses medicinally, including treating coughs and colds due to their expectorant action.

Chamaemelum nobile
Common/ Roman Chamomile

DISTRIBUTION Up to 465m. In England, only common parts Cornwall, Devon, Hampshire, Sussex and Surrey, very sparse elsewhere but persists on grazed commons and lawns in southern England, including London's Kew Gardens and Buckingham Palace; in Wales, rare, only Glamorgan, Pembrokeshire and Lleyn Peninsula; in Scotland, naturalized and rare; in Ireland, common west Cork and south Kerry but very sparse elsewhere, restricted to coastal counties; present Channel Islands, Isles of Scilly and naturalized on Isle of Man.

HABITAT Sandy, mildly acidic damp grassland, especially where grazing or trampling discourages competitors.

DESCRIPTION Low, hairy, sweetly aromatic, spreading perennial with fine, feathery leaves and daisy-like flower heads, which grow one to a stem June–August.

SIMILAR SPECIES Scented, sea and scentless mayweeds grow upright rather than creeping, with many flower heads per stem. Scentless mayweed flowers later, July–October, with larger flower heads, up to 4.5cm wide. It does not smell of chamomile, nor does the aptly named stinking chamomile *Anthemis cotula*; both plants grow on arable land. The coastal sea mayweed *Ripleurospermum maritimum* is only faintly aromatic.

NOTES The name chamomile comes from the Greek *khamaimelon*, meaning 'apples on the ground'. There are several chamomiles, or chamomile-like plants, that lend themselves to edible uses, of which scented mayweed or German chamomile *Matricaria recutita* is by far the most common. Sadly, common chamomile is now quite rare in the British Isles, although it is grown commercially for essential-oil extraction. It has declined due to loss of suitable habitats; careful, small-scale foraging is unlikely to harm its fortunes. Another edible chamomile, corn chamomile *Anthemis arvensis* (see p.155) is also quite scarce but for a different reason: it has declined as a result of more effective herbicides on its arable habitats.

USES/RECIPES As for **scented mayweed**.

BENEFITS Both German and Roman chamomile have long been used medicinally as sedative, anti-inflammatory, anti-spasmodic and healing herbs. They are frequently used in creams to treat eczema and other skin conditions.

Cichorium intybus
Chicory

DISTRIBUTION Up to 300m. In England, widespread south, except Dartmoor, Exmoor, Bodmin Moor, North and South Downs and Bedford Levels; sporadic in Midlands, decreasing northward; in Wales, sporadic in coastal counties but absent Anglesey and Merioneth; in Scotland, sparse south of Glen Mor, in Central Lowlands and

⅓ × life size

eastern Coastal Lowlands; in Ireland, scarce but most localities in Ulster and around Dublin; present Channel Islands, Isle of Man and Isles of Scilly.

HABITAT Roadsides; waste ground; edge of paths and fields.

DESCRIPTION Native/ naturalized perennial. Basal leaves either lobed or deeply toothed; stem leaves either toothed or untoothed. Main stems grooved, hairy and tough (I know this from trying to snap off tops for the mature seeds; in the end I had to use a knife). Flower heads, up to 4cm across, are a delightfully eye-catching sky blue, particularly as held aloft on tall stems. July–October, when in bloom, there is little leaf, but these are perennial plants – having noted the spot you can return the following spring to gather the basal leaves.

NOTES Although chicory is widespread throughout England and Wales, opinion varies as to its status as either a native or an introduced species, since it was formerly commonly cultivated as a fodder crop. It has a liking for the verges of busy roads, where unfortunately it is too contaminated to eat, but at least the flowers get to be seen by a wider public! The white-leaved vegetable sold as chicory is endive, although chicory itself has been commercially grown to produce both salad leaves and bitter roots.

USES/RECIPES Leaves are very bitter, but improved by blanching; unblanched leaves can be used raw, pretty much like dandelion leaves. In Italy, they are boiled and dressed with olive oil, salt and vinegar. Italian ethnobotanist Andrea Pieroni tells me that the cooked leaves

¹⁄₄ × life size

were traditionally accompanied by fatty pork and chillies. In Lebanon, chopped, raw leaves are served with salt, onion, 'kichik' (a kind of flour) and olive oil. In Iran, flowers are not only used to make flower water, which is used as a skin tonic, but also in cooking, for example to make a sauce with tamarind and chilli. The flower water has a strange, earthy flavour that I find quite refreshing. In the 14th century chicory flowers were used to make a kind of confectionary to stave off thirst in hot weather. The roasted roots have a long tradition of use either combined with or as a substitute for coffee. These give an earthy flavour to cakes, ice cream, milk puddings as well as savoury sauces. To obtain the flavour from them, either make an infusion in milk or water, or roast at 120°C for 2 hours or until dry enough to grind, then chop and grind. Fresh roots can also be used as a vegetable or to flavour rich savoury sauces, especially with pigeon or veal.

HARVESTING NOTES Harvest first-year roots before the plant has flowered, after which they become woody.

THISTLES

It would be hard to confuse a thistle with any other kind of plant, except possibly sow-thistle, which is distinguished by having soft prickles or leaf edges that only resemble prickles. The thistle has several culinary applications, despite its prickly exterior; in fact, in part because of it. Bitterness is a defence mechanism used by plants to discourage grazing, but because the thorns perform this function no part of a thistle is bitter. The parts of most interest are the roots and young basal leaves of pre-flowering plants, though if you can be bothered you can also eat the nutty bases of the flower buds, which are like miniature globe artichoke hearts. The peeled stems are also edible, as are those of cardoons – cultivated thistles with much larger stems than the wild varieties. It is not possible to make a serious mistake with thistles: the basal leaves and roots of any thistle are edible in principle, although some leaves are too rough and hairy to be palatable. The flavour of the roots also varies. I have only described three of the more common thistles here, but it is worth experimenting with all the species. Thistle roots of related genera *Silybum* and *Centaurea* are used today for their action as liver tonics, though the leaves of all edible species may benefit the liver and digestion. Marsh thistle stalks were once considered equal to those of the famous milk thistle *Silybum marianum*, though today it is milk thistle seeds with their silymarin that are used as a liver-cell protector against toxins.

GENERAL THISTLE USES/RECIPES Leaves have a pleasant, mild flavour. Thistle cress is lovely: look out for it below old, dead plants in autumn and spring – it has no prickles. The very young, tender leaves can be cooked without treatment as the spines are soft, but trim spines off older leaves before using, or strip off the sides and use only the midrib, as a salad either raw or cooked. Large midribs of Scotch thistle *Onopordum acanthium* are popular in Bodrum, Turkey. The rosettes are harvested with about 3cm of their root, then stripped (wearing gloves!) to the midribs, which are boiled, then tied together with string and stuffed, a few centimetres at a time, with rice, onion and spices, then deep fried in batter. Young, pre-flowering stems of larger species can be peeled and used in salads or as crudités, or boiled and served with butter. Pull or dig up roots of first-year plants at the rosette stage, which on disturbed ground can be at any time of year. Taste is similar to **burdock**; they can be used in similar ways. Creeping thistle, being a perennial, has rather fibrous roots, which are not worth bothering with.

Cirsium arvense

Creeping Thistle

DISTRIBUTION Typically up to 700m. In British Isles, widespread throughout, only less so: in Scotland, Grampian Mountains, North West Highlands and Isle of Lewis.

HABITAT Roadsides, cultivated ground, meadows, open woodland and heavily grazed pasture; generally on fertile soil.

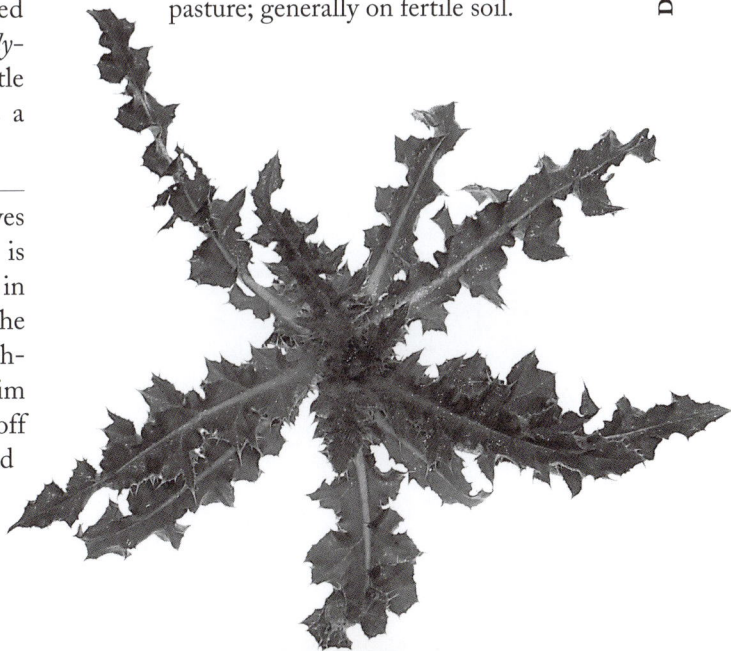

DESCRIPTION Native, branched perennial, reaching 90cm high. Leaves lobed (but much less so than marsh thistle), greyish green, glossy and hairless; only lower leaves have stalks. Stems have no spines or wings. Flower heads lilac–white, with purplish bracts, solitary or in loose clusters of 2–5.

Cirsium palustre

Marsh Thistle

DISTRIBUTION Typically up to 760m. In British Isles, widespread throughout, only less so: in Scotland, Grampian Mountains, North West Highlands and Isle of Lewis.

HABITAT Damp meadows, marshes, fens and similar damp places.

⁷/₁₀ × life size

DESCRIPTION Native biennial, up to 1.5m high. Leaves are lobed (those on the stems more deeply so), dark green with purple tints and glossy, despite being hairy (but not prickly) on their upper surface; basal leaves are stalked; leaf lobes are spiny along edges, not just at tip. Stem has continuous spiny wings. Purple flower heads are 1.5–2cm long, in dense clusters.

Cirsium vulgare

Spear Thistle

DISTRIBUTION Typically up to 685m. In British Isles, widespread throughout, only less so: in Scotland, North West Highlands.

HABITAT Disturbed ground in well-drained and fertile areas; sand dunes and beaches at drift line; heavily grazed pasture.

DESCRIPTION Tall, native perennial, 30–150cm high. Stalk has intermittent spiny wings. Leaves are dull, with prickly hairs on upper surface; they are deeply lobed with either short stalks (on basal leaves) or none and long, thick spines; stem leaves are distinguished by long end lobe. Purple flower heads are solitary or in flat-topped clusters, 20–40mm long, with yellow-tipped bracts.

¹/₅ × life size

themselves being the first), up to 2.5cm wide, yellow but underside of outer florets have orangey-red stripes.

SIMILAR SPECIES Rough hawk's-beard is much hairier and taller, up to 1.2m high; outer florets have no orange stripe and basal leaves are like rougher, hairier dandelion leaves; stem leaves stalkless but without clasping basal lobes; stems hairy and much branched, flower heads like dandelions, but many, in a loose corymb.

USES/RECIPES Use in similar ways to **cat's-ear** and **hawkbit** species.

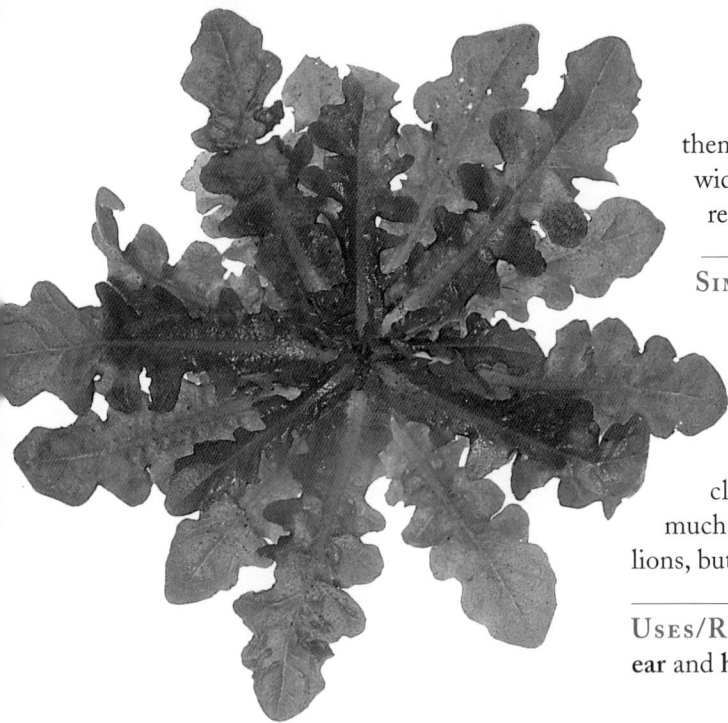

Crepis vesicaria

Beaked Hawk's-beard

DISTRIBUTION In England, widespread in south and east, becoming scarce north and west of Linconshire and Leicestershire but found in a few areas of north and south Yorkshire; in Wales, mostly found north of Porthmadog; in Scotland, almost entirely absent; in Ireland, mostly south, most widespread in Leinster, Limerick and south Cork.

HABITAT Hedgebanks, roadsides, lawns, pasture and meadows.

DESCRIPTION Naturalized biennial, up to 70cm high. Basal leaves downy, lyre shaped, thick and fleshy with wavy edges to begin with, by the flowering stage becoming deeply lobed, with a distinct diamond-shaped end lobe. Stems branched several times, with clasping leaves much less deeply lobed and flower-head buds upright. In May, the flower heads arranged in loose corymbs are the second of the dandelion-like species to appear (dandelions

Hypochaeris radicata

Cat's-ear

DISTRIBUTION Up to 610m. In British Isles, widespread throughout, only less so in Scotland, Caithness; in Ireland, northeast Galway. Naturalized on Shetland and Fair Isle.

HABITAT Lawns, meadows, pasture, waste ground, roadsides, on sandy and slightly acidic soil.

DESCRIPTION Native perennial, 20–60cm high. Stems unbranched or with one or two branches, thickening just below the flower head, hairless, with small, dark-tipped bracts in place of leaves. Basal rosette leaves are rough and hairy with wavy teeth. Flower heads are large and yellow, slightly smaller than dandelion.

SIMILAR SPECIES Basal rosettes of beaked hawk's-beard and larger specimens of rough hawkbit could be confused with cat's-ear. At the flower-

ing stage, the former has leafy stems, the latter hairy, unbranched stems. Both species are good to eat.

USES/RECIPES Leaves are chunkier and usually less bitter than dandelion; the two plants can generally be used interchangeably. Add to salads raw or blanch for warm salads, or use in cooked dishes such as fatayer pies, quiches, soups, stews, pasta, etc.. Use flower heads whole or broken up as garnish and in salads.

CAT'S-EAR PAKORAS: 60g chickpea flour, 1 teaspoon each of turmeric, paprika, ground coriander and ground cumin, a pinch of salt, 200ml cold water, 1 finely chopped garlic clove, 500g blanched, squeezed and shredded cat's-ear leaves. Make a paste out of the flour, spices and water then combine with the garlic and leaves; this mix should stand for 20 minutes and should also be quite thick. Heat vegetable oil in either a deep-fat fryer or a heavy-based pan. A good tip is to add a potato peeling to the cold oil and when it is golden the oil is ready for frying. Spoon dollops into the oil, fry for a couple of minutes until they are well coloured and crispy [JT].
(This recipe is also good with wild mushrooms, nettles and dandelion flowers.)

⅓ × life size

Lapsana communis

Nipplewort

DISTRIBUTION Up to 440m. In England, Wales and Scotland, widespread, only less so in Western and Northern Isles, Isle of Skye, North Highland and higher-altitude areas of Grampian Mountains, North West Highlands and Southern Uplands; in Ireland, widespread, only less so west Donegal and west Mayo; present Channel Islands, Isle of Man, Isles of Scilly and Lundy.

HABITAT Disturbed ground in shady places, such as open woodland and woodland edges, hedgebanks, churchyards and field edges, roadsides and gardens.

DESCRIPTION Native annual, 15cm−1.2m high. Basal leaves have soft, hairy undersides. The large, rounded end lobe has toothed edges

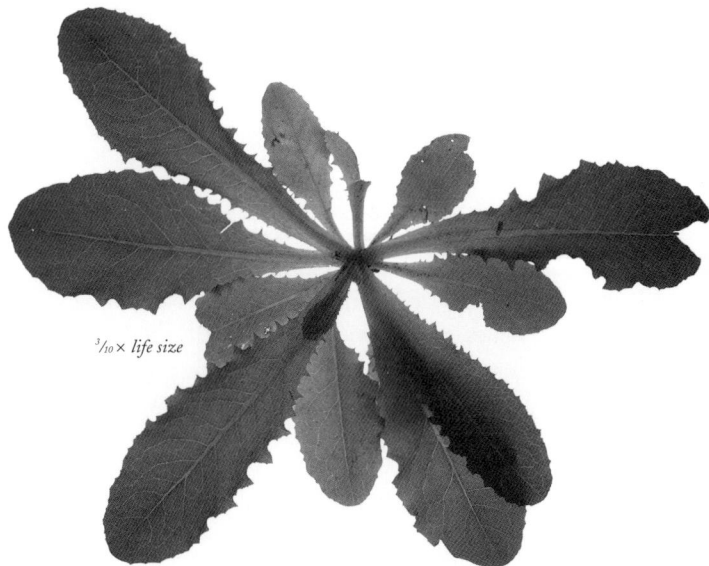

¼ × life size

and ends in a point; below it are two pairs of narrow lobes and a long, winged stalk. Upper leaves unstalked with toothed edges. Stems are stiff, leafy and usually branched. Pale, yellow flower heads like tiny dandelions, in branched clusters; on sunny days only open in the morning 5–10am. Unlike other dandelion-like plants, there is no milky latex in the stems and leaves and no pappus on the seeds.

SIMILAR SPECIES Wintercress *Barbarea vulgaris* has similar-shaped leaves but is darker, glossier and hairless. Great, least and prickly lettuce also have small, yellow flower heads but stem leaves are lobed at their base, clasping the main stem; wall lettuce has small, yellow flower heads but with only 5 florets, in petal-like formation. Check what time it is: flower heads open much after 10am on sunny days are probably not nipplewort.

NOTES Nipplewort was named by John Parkinson (botanist–apothecary and author of one of the earliest systematic works on the British flora, *Theatrum botanicum*, 1640), who recorded its use in Prussia for healing ulcers of the nipples. Similar use has been recorded in the Scottish Highlands. Nipplewort is resistant to frost and produces many pale green rosettes, which are easy to spot when little else is growing.

USES/RECIPES Use leaves in winter and spring salads, or cooked in soups, stews and casseroles, or in a mixture of wild greens. Raw leaves are sometimes slightly bitter but become sweet once cooked.

Lactuca serriola

Prickly Lettuce

DISTRIBUTION Up to 300m. In England, widespread in and to south of Midlands, mostly absent Cornwall, Devon and parts of Shropshire, Derbyshire and Lincolnshire, sporadic north of Midlands, south Lancashire and mid-west, southeast and northeast Yorkshire; in Wales, sporadic, but present all counties except Anglesey, Caernarvonshire and Merioneth; in Ireland, recorded two 10 sq km in Dublin and one 10 sq km in Tyrone; on Guernsey and Alderney.

HABITAT Sea walls, waste ground, railways, gravel pits, sand dunes and roadsides, especially the latter, which it often colonizes following road works.

DESCRIPTION Annual/biennial, hairless with reddish stems containing much latex. Plants reach up to 1.2m high. Basal rosettes like cos lettuce leaves but flatter, greyish-green, sometimes with a pinkish tint and slightly toothed edges. Stem leaves upright, sometimes slightly lobed, with spines along the back rib. Flower heads small in relation to height of plant, 11–13mm wide, in clusters of 7–12, with irregular bracts.

³/₁₀ × life size

SIMILAR SPECIES The less common great lettuce *S. virosa* is taller, growing up to 2m high; its leaves are also more purple; the rare least lettuce *S. saligna* has basal leaves with broad, white midribs.

NOTES All modern lettuce varieties are derived from this plant. The leaves are generally extremely bitter in their wild state, but leaves of young first year plants can be much milder, like miniature cos lettuce leaves.

USES/RECIPES Raw leaves are especially bitter, but ethnobotanical studies have recorded their use in several parts of Europe. For example in Lebanon they are served with parsley, fresh lemon juice and garlic, all ingredients that temper the bitterness. To eat the leaves cooked, boil for 10 minutes then discard the water before either boiling a second time, frying or braising, or using them as stuffing. They will still have a strong, earthy and bitter flavour; in order for this not to be too overpowering, use them with ingredients such as boiled eggs, cheese, cream, sugar, vinegar/lemon juice, chilli and garlic.

BENEFITS Wild lettuces have gentle sedative, antispasmodic and analgesic actions, so are useful for coughs and insomnia.

Leontodon hispidus

Rough Hawkbit

DISTRIBUTION In England, throughout, except much of Cumbria, Greater Manchester, Merseyside, Cornwall and parts of Devon; in Wales, mostly widespread but less so in northeast; in Scotland, almost entirely absent; in Ireland, mostly in Offaly, Meath, Westmeath, Galway and Clare.

HABITAT Meadows and pastures, roadsides and railway banks; often on calcareous soils.

DESCRIPTION Native, hairless or slightly hairy perennial of very variable height, 5–60cm. Stems unbranched, leafless and hairy, swollen just below flower head. Basal leaves lanceolate, hairy with wavy toothed edges. Flower heads appear June–September, 2.5–4cm wide, bright yellow but outer florets reddish beneath.

SIMILAR SPECIES Lesser hawkbit *L. saxatilis* is shorter, up to 40cm high, and flower stem is hairless above and not swollen below flower head; outer florets grey beneath.

USES/RECIPES *(for both hawbits)* Add to salads raw or blanch for warm salads, or use in cooked dishes such as quiches, soups, stews, pasta, etc. Use flower heads whole or broken up as garnish and in salads.

FATAYER PIES: *Pastry* Dissolve 1 teaspoon dried yeast, ½ teaspoon sugar and 1 teaspoon salt, in

160ml warm water. Then, bit by bit add 260g flour and knead for a few minutes on a board dusted with flour. Divide dough into 16 pieces and leave covered under a damp cloth. *Filling* Boil 300g hawkbit leaves (or other wild greens) for 3 minutes then drain and squeeze out excess water; chop and season with salt. Fry ½ finely chopped (medium-sized) onion in 20ml oil until onion is transparent then add hawkbit and fry gently for a further 10 minutes. Season with pepper and a pinch of nutmeg then leave to cool. Blend 60g feta and 90g ricotta with the juice of 1 lemon and 1 tablespoon olive oil then add to hawkbit mixture. *Making and baking the pies* Make each piece of dough into a ball, then flatten into a 8cm diameter disc and divide the filling equally. With a dollop of filling in the centre of each disc, fold up the edges in three places, making the base into a triangle. Pinch together the edges to seal the pies then bake at 220°C for about 15 minutes, until light brown.

Leucanthemum vulgare

Ox-eye Daisy

DISTRIBUTION Up to 845m. In England and Wales, widespread throughout, only less so in Cheviot; in Scotland, mostly common, but absent parts Wigtownshire, Ayrshire, Jura, Isle of Mull, Western Isles, Grampian Mountains, North West Highlands, North Highland and eastern Coastal Lowlands Angus–Banffshire; in Ireland, widespread, only less so Donegal; present Channel Islands, Isle of Man, Isles of Scilly and Lundy.

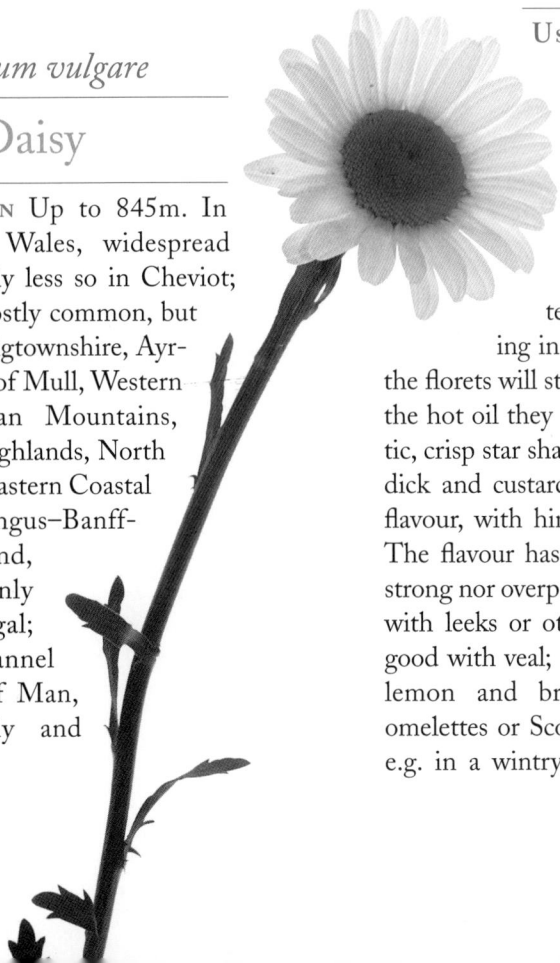

HABITAT Grassy areas, such as meadows, lightly grazed pasture, churchyards, coastal cliffs, roadside verges, on fertile, alkaline to neutral soils; widely sown in wildflower seed mixtures.

DESCRIPTION Native. Basal leaves long, stalked, spoon shaped with roundly toothed edges; stem leaves also toothed, thin, oblong and stalkless, in a spiral around the stem. Flower heads like greatly enlarged daisy *Bellis perennis*.

NOTES This plant is an almost ubiquitous feature of the British summer; its nodding white and yellow heads declare its presence brightly and cheerfully from roadside verges, meadows, gardens and waste ground.

USES/RECIPES Flower-head buds are pleasantly aromatic; used whole or finely chopped to flavour sweet and savoury dishes. Flower heads make a striking addition to summer salads.

BATTERED STARS: To cook in tempura, they need a good sloshing in the batter to cover all surfaces; the florets will stick together at first, but once in the hot oil they spread out, producing a fantastic, crisp star shape. Serve as garnish for spotted dick and custard. Leaves have a unique sweet flavour, with hints of cucumber and liquorice. The flavour has an affinity with lamb, neither strong nor overpowering. Blanch briefly and mix with leeks or other greens like **ramsons**. Also good with veal; in light meat sauces/gravy with lemon and brown butter [PW]; in herb omelettes or Scotch broth [ST]. Raw in salads, e.g. in a wintry salad with roast pumpkin or

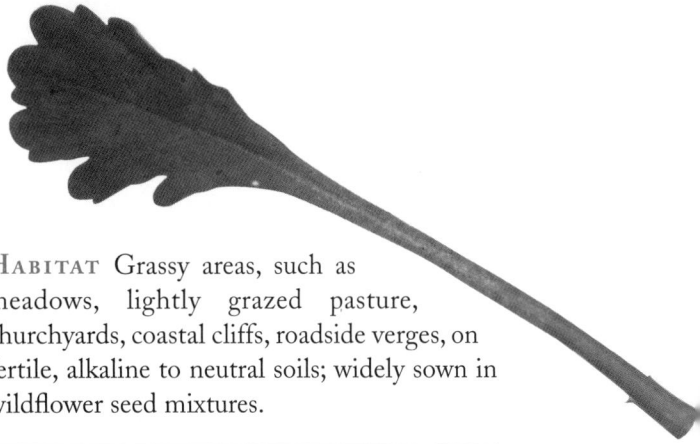

butternut squash, shavings of Parmesan, vinaigrette with roasted pumpkin seed, olive oil, fresh lemon juice: a good contrast of soft/crisp and crunchy textures, sweet/sharp and aromatic flavours [JDW].

HARVESTING NOTES Once you have seen the leaves growing on a flowering plant, you can look in the same place for similar basal leaves when they begin to grow in the autumn.

ECOLOGICAL CONSIDERATIONS Tolerant of grazing (and trampling) but needs to produce seed, as it doesn't reproduce well vegetatively.

Matricaria discoidea

Pineappleweed

DISTRIBUTION Lowland, but exceptionally at 845m. Throughout British Isles, widespread, only less so in Scotland, Grampian Mountains, North West Highlands or North Highland.

HABITAT Fertile, disturbed ground on field margins, pasture (especially gateways), path edges, waste ground and roadsides; thrives where trampled.

DESCRIPTION Introduced. Short erect hairless annual, growing to 20cm high with feathery leaves. Green flower heads lack disc florets and at first glance look like unopened chamomile buds; they smell and taste of chamomile and pineapple.

NOTES Pineappleweed arrived here as a garden plant from northeast Asia in the eighteenth century. In the late nineteenth century it escaped from Kew Gardens and spread prolifically; it is now found throughout the British Isles, which perhaps slightly

mitigates the decline of the other three wild chamomiles. The first time we received an order for this plant, we arrived at our best site just before dark to find it had been ploughed. The order was fulfilled in the dark, using car headlights to locate and collect the plant on nearby headland.

USES/RECIPES Flower heads and leaves can be used raw in salads, for example with lobster with a little pineapple, water celery, small amaranth leaves, with mamauza dressing made from fresh lemon juice and Chardonnay vinegar, soft tarragon, chervil [PB]; or cooked with fruit. **SUMMER FRUIT JELLY:** Infuse a few sprigs of pineappleweed in water warmed to just under boiling point, add 1kg sugar/litre water; use 5 leaves gelatine/litre syrup. Pour jelly into moulds and add a few blackberries to each jelly [AN]. The Flathead tribe of Montana use it to preserve meat.

HARVESTING NOTES Scent is often strong enough to enable you to detect the plant before you see it. Harvest before flower heads go to seed, at which stage they still look like flower heads but are fluffy and unpleasant to eat.

1½× life size

Matricaria recutita

Scented Mayweed/ German Chamomile

DISTRIBUTION Up to 365m. In England, widespread, but sporadic parts Devon, Cornwall, North Yorkshire and high-altitude areas north to border; in Wales, present every county but less abundant highland areas, Pembrokeshire and Anglesey; in Scotland, sporadic Central Lowlands southward, sparse in north, found mostly east, south of Glen Mor, and on Shetland; in Ireland, sparse apart from areas in Dublin, Wexford, Cork and along Shannon river; present Channel Islands and Isles of Scilly.

HABITAT Arable field edges and waste ground, usually on light or sandy soils.

DESCRIPTION Upright/spreading aromatic annual, smelling distinctly of chamomile, reaching up to 50cm high. Leaves feathery and hairless. Flower heads daisy-like, 10–25mm wide, with hollow centres and ray florets turned downwards soon after they appear July–August.

SIMILAR SPECIES Corn chamomile *Anthemis arvensis*, also aromatic, stems and leaf undersides downy. Flower heads larger, 20–30mm wide, centres solid. Leaves of scentless mayweed *M. perforata* are similar but slightly darker; they are bitter and vile. The plant is sometimes prostrate, flowering after scented mayweed and with larger flower heads.

NOTES Scented mayweed or German chamomile has a similar aromatic essential oil to common chamomile. Like corn chamomile it has declined as a weed plant among crops where herbicides are used, but can still commonly be found in abundance on the margins of cultivated fields.

¾ × life size

USES/RECIPES Flower heads can be used to flavour custard, fruit, sorbet and ice cream or made into syrup for pouring, flavouring or diluting as a drink; they combine well with elderflower. Use to flavour delicate sauces for white fish. Leaves have a refreshing, sweet chamomile taste. Delicious in salads and fruit salads, they can also be used as flavouring in similar ways to the flowers. For example, infuse in milk, blend, then use as basis for panna cotta and serve with strawberries [ST].

Mycelis muralis

Wall Lettuce

DISTRIBUTION Up to 500m. In England, widespread, but sparse Northumberland, Cheviot, southeast Yorkshire, East Midlands, Cornwall, Devon and east of England (but common in Norfolk); in Wales widespread, but absent parts Anglesey, Cardiganshire, Pembrokeshire and Glamorgan; in Scotland, locally frequent in Forth and Borders, Argyll and Sterling and East Highlands, absent Isle of Skye, Western Isles, North Highlands and Orkney, sporadic elsewhere; in Ireland, scarce, but common in parts of Galway and Clare; present on Isle of Man.

½ × life size

HABITAT Walls, roadsides, gardens, arable field margins, rocky areas, woods and wood margins; prefers chalk and limestone soils.

DESCRIPTION Similar to sow-thistle but with gorgeous purple-tinged basal leaves; stem leaves have deep, large-toothed square-ish lobes with reddish ribs. Small, yellow flower heads, 7–8mm wide, quite distinctive, with only 5 ray florets, July–September.

USES/RECIPES As a salad I slightly prefer this to sow-thistle: it looks more elegant and the flavour and texture are also a bit more delicate. Use cooked in similar ways to sow-thistle.

HARVESTING NOTES Whenever I see a mound of earth with greenery on it, I head straight there, as many of the plants that colonize earthworks are edible. Wall lettuce is one, as are **chickweed**, **fat hen** and **sow-thistle**.

Picris echioides

Bristly Oxtongue

DISTRIBUTION Up to 300m. In England, widespread south of line Severn Estuary–Flamborough Head, except Dartmoor and Exmoor, sporadic north of line, decreasing northward, absent Cumbria, Northumberland and Cheviot Hills; in Wales, concentrated in south and less so north, and sporadic elsewhere; in Scotland, rare, only Berwickshire, Midlothian, Renfrewshire, Dunbartonshire, Lanarkshire, Firth of Lorn, Western Isles and Orkney; in Ireland, restricted to coastal localities in east and south with isolated locality in Kerry; on Channel Islands, Isle of Man and Isles of Scilly.

³⁄₅ × life size

HABITAT Waste ground, farm tracks and field edges, rough grassy places.

DESCRIPTION Naturalized from contaminated crop seeds. Annual/biennial, growing year round with branched stems. Leaves with bristly pimples: basal leaves long, wavy or straight edged with stalks; stem leaves cordate and stalkless. Flower heads dandelion-like but paler, in branched clusters.

SIMILAR SPECIES Hawkweed oxtongue *P. hieraciodes* leaves are similar but bristles lack swollen white bases. Small teasel *Dipsacus pilosus* and wild teasel *D. fullonum* have similarly pimply basal rosettes but with a distinct row of prickles, not bristles, on the midrib underside.

USES/RECIPES The leaves of this bristly plant look forbidding, but once chopped and mixed into a salad with an oily dressing the bristles become unnoticeable. The young rosettes are quite pleasant cooked and are still used as greens in parts of rural Italy. Chop roughly, blanch for a minute, then fry for 2–3 minutes, alone or, for example, with mushrooms, shallots or tomatoes. Australian aboriginal people eat them after cooking in earth ovens.

BENEFITS Flower heads are rich in vitamin A.

SOW-THISTLES

Sow-thistles resemble thistles superficially but lack sharp prickles. They have dandelion-like flower heads, but unlike dandelions these grow in branched clusters from a main leafy stem. Occurring as an arable weed in most parts of the Earth, they have been used as food in the Philippines, Indonesia, Australia, New Zealand, Africa, America and Europe. In northern Italy the leaves, especially those of prickly sow-thistle, form part of the wild leaf salad *Insalata di Campo* (field salad), which, as its name suggests, is gathered from the edge of fields. Often they are combined with more bitter species such as **chicory** and **dandelion**, but also with **common sorrel** and **salad burnet**. In southern Italy, sow-thistles are generally eaten cooked, as in Spain, Greece, Turkey, Lebanon and New Zealand. Maoris use the plants at later growth stages, crushing them and then washing them in running water before cooking them in an earth oven, often with fish. The Greek hero Theseus ate a dish of sow-thistles to gain strength before fighting the Minotaur (a bit like Popeye and his tins of spinach); to this day, Maoris consider it a plant that makes a person strong.

USES/RECIPES *(for all three sow-thistles)* Rosette leaves of smooth sow-thistle are a bit dry and powdery raw, and require a sharp dressing to counter this. Cooked, they turn a deep green and have a soft but substantial texture. Cooked sow-thistle rosettes (all species) are delicious, especially leaf ribs and the succulent centre holding the leaves together. Boil for 5 minutes or fry in slightly browned butter. In New Zealand, a traditional Maori stew, Puha, is made from pork bones, stock and sow-thistle leaves, which the Maori call '*raraki*'. Raw sow-thistle works well with potted pork made from a pig's head salted to draw out moisture then poached, the flesh dragged off into strands,

potted with shallots then sealed with clarified butter – if you can't obtain a pig's head, use the meat from pork belly salted overnight then slow braised with white wine and herbs [PW]. Florets of perennial sow-thistle are best. Unlike those of the other sow-thistles, they are sweet, with a faint almond taste.

HARVESTING NOTES The leaves of basal rosettes are best; less bitter than stem leaves, which are, however, softer, although the tougher spines of older leaves of prickly sow-thistle render Use cooked in similar ways to sow-thistle.them inedible. We have found a spectrum of flavours, mild–sweet–quite bitter, even from plants harvested on the same day, in the same area. Use scissors underneath the rosette to cut it just above the root, or uproot the whole plant if you intend to use the root. Snip the yellow tips of the florets of perennial sow-thistle with scissors; the remainder is fluffy and inedible. Take care not to contaminate your harvest by getting the bitter liquid of the sticky stem hairs on your fingers.

Sonchus arvensis

Perennial Sow-thistle

DISTRIBUTION Up to 445m. In England, widespread, less so only Cumberland, Northumberland or Cheviot Hills; in Wales, widespread, less so only Merioneth; in Scotland, widespread but absent much Isle of Skye, Isle of Lewis, North Highland, Shetland, Grampian Mountains, North West Highlands and Southern Uplands; in Ireland, widespread, but absent many upland and montane areas such as Blue Stack, Derry Veagh, Sperrin and Antrim mountains in north, Wicklow and Knockmealdown in south and Maumturk Mountains and Nephin Beg range in west; present Channel Islands, Isle of Man and Isles of Scilly.

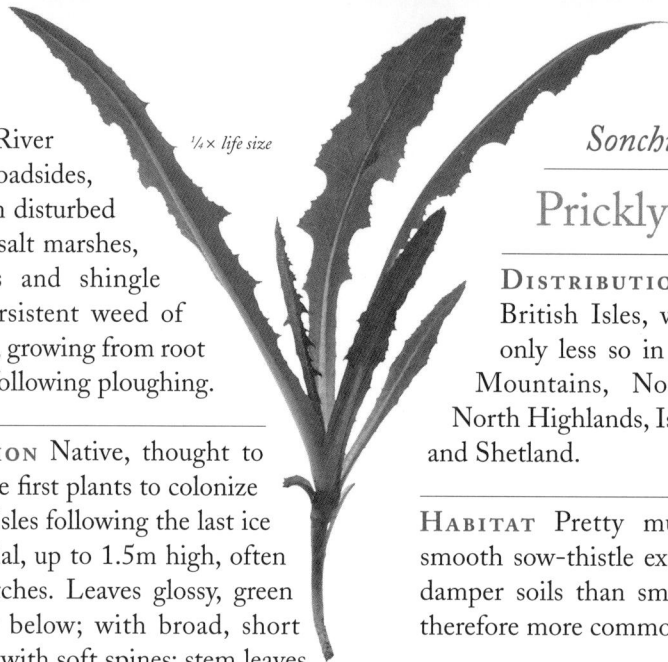

HABITAT River banks and roadsides, especially on disturbed ground; on salt marshes, sand dunes and shingle beaches; persistent weed of arable fields, growing from root fragments, following ploughing.

¼ × life size

DESCRIPTION Native, thought to be one of the first plants to colonize the British Isles following the last ice age. Perennial, up to 1.5m high, often forming patches. Leaves glossy, green above, grey below; with broad, short lobes edged with soft spines; stem leaves clasp the stem with rounded lobes. Flower heads rich golden-yellow, up to 50mm wide, quite shaggy. Stalks are covered in sticky yellow hairs (some populations are hairless).

SIMILAR SPECIES Marsh sow-thistle *S. palustris* is taller, up to 2.5m high. Basal leaves with long, thin, finely toothed lobes; upper leaves lanceolate, untoothed, with long, sharp lobes, including basal lobes that clasp the stem. Stems covered in sticky hairs. Flower heads pale yellow, up to 40mm wide. By fresh/salt-water rivers and ditches, also fens, among reeds and other tall marsh plants. Rare: should not be harvested.

USES/RECIPES

CANDIED PERENNIAL SOW-THISTLE: Cover the florets in sugar until the whole mixture becomes soggy, then dry in the sun. Tease apart the florets once dry. Sprinkle the candied (or uncandied) florets on desserts: they look spectacular on top of panna cotta. Roots can be eaten boiled or fried, or even raw, chopped into small pieces in salads.

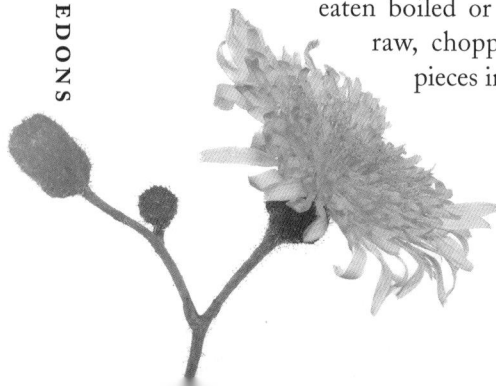

Sonchus asper

Prickly Sow-thistle

DISTRIBUTION Up to 395m. In British Isles, widespread throughout, only less so in Scotland, in Grampian Mountains, North West Highlands, North Highlands, Isle of Skye, Isle of Lewis and Shetland.

HABITAT Pretty much as perennial and smooth sow-thistle except that it will tolerate damper soils than smooth sow-thistle and is therefore more common at higher altitudes.

DESCRIPTION Native, over-wintering annual. Younger basal rosette leaves shallow toothed and not lobed, ending in soft spines; stem leaves clasp the stem with rounded lobes; otherwise not lobed or shallowly lobed, but always with deep teeth ending in spines, harder than basal leaves but softer than spines of true thistles; all leaves dark green and glossy. Flower heads rich yellow, up to 2.5cm wide.

⅓ × life size

¹⁄₂ × life size

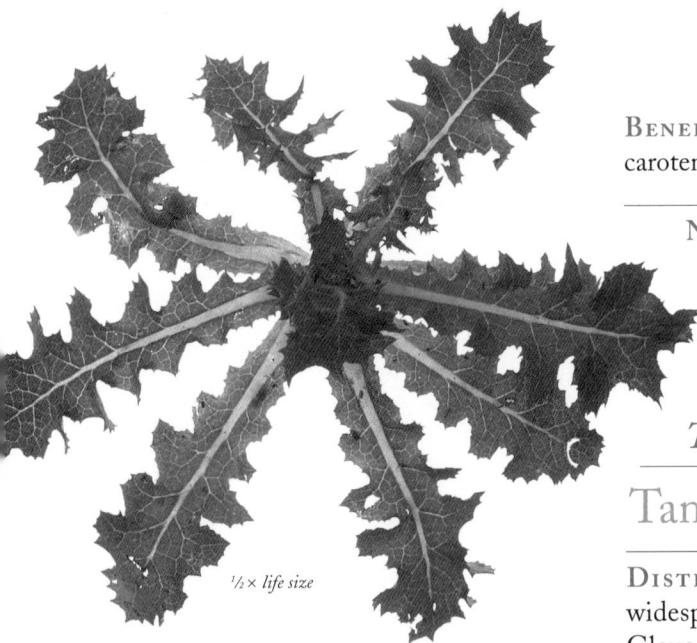

Sonchus oleraceus

Smooth Sow-thistle

DISTRIBUTION Up to 365m. In England, widespread throughout, less so Northumberland; in Wales, widespread throughout; in Scotland, mostly widespread but absent much Isle of Skye, Isle of Lewis, North Highlands, Shetland, Grampian Mountains, North West Highlands and Southern Uplands, and naturalized on Shetland; in Ireland, widespread throughout, only less so parts of west Donegal; present Channel Islands, Isle of Man and Isles of Scilly.

HABITAT Opportunistic invader of open soil in gardens, arable fields, pasture trampled by livestock, cliffs, pavements, and roadsides.

DESCRIPTION Native, over-wintering annual. Leaves distinctively dull greyish green, lobed without prickles, though at first glance they seem to have them. Flowers pale yellow and small, 10–20mm wide. Seeds germinate and produce rosettes autumn–May, but peak germination March–May. Later the plant produces a milky stem with larger, glossier leaves that clasp the stem with arrow-like lobes.

BENEFITS Leaves are high in vitamin C, beta-carotene and protein.

NOTES The Latin name *oleraceus* was evidently ascribed to the plant by someone who understood its culinary virtues: it means 'edible vegetable'.

Tanacetum vulgare

Tansy

DISTRIBUTION Up to 380m. In England, widespread, only less so Cornwall, Sussex, Gloucestershire, Staffordshire, Lancashire and Yorkshire and counties north; in Wales, absent only highland areas; in Scotland, common in parts of Central Lowlands, eastern Central Lowlands north to Moray Firth, Western Isles and Shetland, sporadic elsewhere but absent upland and montane areas; in Ireland, naturalized and sporadic in all counties; present Channel Islands, Isle of Man and Isles of Scilly.

HABITAT Grassy areas such as river banks, sea walls, roadsides and waste ground.

DESCRIPTION Native, but also a garden escape. Perennial, up to 1m high, forming large patches. Leaves and flower heads distinctive by sight and smell. Basal leaves up to 25cm long with long, thin, toothed lobes, forming widely spreading clumps. Flower heads yellow, doughnut shaped, arranged in flat-topped clusters.

NOTES Tansy was once a very widely used herb, a staple of kitchen herb gardens; it is now grown as an ornamental. It is a fairly common wild plant with a powerful aroma and an equally strong flavour. People's palates have evidently changed in

¹⁄₄ × life size

the centuries since it was last widely used, but perhaps even then it was used sparingly – and at times for its medicinal properties of expelling worms, rather than for its flavour – old English recipes rarely give quantities. In its traditional combination with eggs, I find it unlike anything else I have eaten but not at all unpleasant. It is called sweet mace in Derbyshire and was also once used to preserve fish and meat.

USES/RECIPES A sweet custard used to be made from tansy leaves with a little spinach to give the dish a green colour. Sweet omelettes flavoured with this plant were once eaten at Easter, given the name tansies. A strongly flavoured black pudding, Drisheen, is made using tansy in southwest Ireland.

TANSY DRESSING: 400ml pomace olive oil, 100ml extra virgin olive oil, 200g tansy blanched then refreshed, blitzed into oil with ½ teaspoon Dijon mustard, 1 teaspoon honey, the juice of ½ lemon and a pinch of salt. Serve with whole black bream (scaled then scored, fried 2 minutes each side, finished in hot oven for 5–6 minutes) and fennel braised in olive oil with basil and crushed potatoes [SW].

BENEFITS An old carol contains the lines: 'sonn at easter cometh alleluia, With butter cheese and a tansay'. Like Easter Ledge or Dock Pudding made (also at Easter) from **common bistort**, tansy was eaten in the belief that it purified the body after a winter diet containing few fresh vegetables.

⅓ × life size

HAZARDS Tansy contains thujone, which is toxic if consumed in any quantity. It is unlikely to pose a risk when eaten as food, although to be on the safe side you should avoid it if pregnant.

HARVESTING NOTES Tansy can often be located just by its pungent smell. Basal leaves grow in bushy patches before the plants flower; this is the best time to harvest.

Taraxacum officinalis

Dandelion

DISTRIBUTION Up to 1220m. In British Isles, widespread.

HABITAT Grassy areas of various kinds, especially lawns, parks and sports fields, but also wild mountainous areas.

DESCRIPTION Native, hairless perennial. Basal leaves shiny, usually dark green, more or less lobed, but, if so, often with large, irregular, angular lobes. Stems smooth, leafless and hollow with only one flower head, which can be up to 6cm wide.

SIMILAR SPECIES There are many micro species of dandelion with subtle distinctions too numerous to detail here. Several related plants have similar flower heads which could be mistaken for dandelions from a distance, but dandelion flower-head stems are unmistakable. Rough and lesser hawkbit and some hawk's-beard (*Crepis* species) leaves are similar, but all are either downy or hairy; leaves of smooth cat's-ear *Hypochaeris glabra* are much shorter. All of these species are edible.

NOTES On the Continent, dandelions are commonly eaten, as they were in the British Isles in former centuries. In Lebanon gathering and preparing dandelion leaves in the spring is something of a festivity, with everyone out picking, then making salads and little pasties with the leaves. Dandelion has been cultivated in North America, France and Britain since at least the mid-nineteenth century. A particular strain is now popular in restaurants; its leaves are large and white due to growing it in the dark to reduce bitterness. The technique is called blanching: you just place a bucket or pot (without a hole) over the plant when the leaves are still small and leave it for a few weeks until they become pale yellow. Dandelions were once cultivated in Russia for the white latex in the stems and roots, which was extracted to make rubber.

USES/RECIPES Either or both the roots and leaves can be used to make a tea; both for dandelion beer (for basic fizzy drink method, see 'How to Use Wild Plants', p.18). Roots, sliced thinly, can be used in salads, or boiled then fried and added to salads or stir fries. Combine with sweet, fatty or bland flavours. Roast to make a mild coffee substitute. Use this or an extract of the fresh roots for flavouring panna cotta and other desserts. Add flower heads or unopened buds to salads, pancakes and omelettes or pickle buds like capers. Break up flower heads and mix the yellow florets through salads. Serve wilted dandelion leaves with sweet root vegetables, or add them to rich meat stews and casseroles. Dandelions are also excellent fried with bacon, finished in a little white wine and served with a poached egg: an English forager's breakfast. Raw leaves go well with grated beetroot and carrot, and the combination of bright orange, purple and dark green is stunning. Combine Chardonnay and Chardonnay vinegar or fresh lemon juice, shallots, apple juice and olive oil;

serve with the leaves and nothing else except a few grapes [EC]. A simple combination with another, milder salad leaf works well.

SMOKED SALMON SALAD: Pieces of hot smoked salmon tossed in a salad of **chickweed** and dandelion dressed in a lemon and olive oil dressing, garnished with poached rhubarb, freshly grated **horseradish** and chiffonaded **black mustard leaf** [PB].

Coat a poached duck egg in breadcrumbs, deep fry, and serve with chicken livers, dandelion and chickweed dressed in vinaigrette [PB].

BENEFITS Leaves high in iron, calcium and vitamin A. Roots contain inulin.

HARVESTING NOTES When we first started harvesting dandelion commercially, we took the whole rosettes by cutting the root about 10mm below the ground. However, we soon noticed that they weren't growing back. The groundsman of the cricket ground where we were gathering them was delighted, but we

soon amended our technique. Now we cut the rosettes at the base, just before the root starts; this way the leaves still stay together, but the plant is unharmed.

Tragopogon porrifolius
Wild Salsify

DISTRIBUTION Up to 300m. In England, sporadic in Midlands and southwards, growing more frequent in southeast and east, less frequent north of Midlands in Yorkshire, Cheshire, Lancashire and Lincolnshire, absent elsewhere; in Wales, rare, found in a few coastal counties but absent Caernarvonshire and Merioneth; in Scotland, found in one 10 sq km of each of Wigtownshire, Ayrshire and Firth of Lorn; in Ireland, likewise, west Cork, Wexford and border Louth–Meath; present Channel Islands and Isle of Man.

HABITAT Rough grassland, often seaside locations on sea walls and cliffs but also roadside verges.

DESCRIPTION Very similar to goat's beard but taller, reaching up to 1.2m high, with swollen stem just below purple flower heads, which are often larger than goat's beard; flowers May–August.

NOTES If you are familiar with goat's beard you might have seen salsify and thought it was a large purple version of it – and that's pretty much what it is. Another vegetable known as salsify is presently enjoying a revival in popularity. It is more properly called scorzonera (the very rare native plant viper's-grass *Scorzonera humilis* is a closely related species); it tastes similar to salsify but differs in its yellow flowers and long, barely tapering black root – salsify root is white and tapered like a parsnip. Its acquired name, black salsify, has been shortened to salsify over time. Salsify itself is now grown as an ornamental, but was once an important part of our cuisine and grows in abundance in quite a few places as either a relic of cultivation or a more recent garden escape.

I first found salsify growing on the edge of a playing field next to a salt marsh, my attention arrested by the vivid purple flowers. I had been visiting this place for years to collect various wild plants yet had never noticed it before, perhaps because I had not approached the spot from the right angle while the plants were in flower. Good foraging sites are often like this: they keep secrets hidden from you and gradually reveal them over the years, as you keep going over the same ground; it is like finding out something unexpected about an old friend.

USES/RECIPES Wild roots often fork to get around stones, making them fiddly to prepare (cultivated roots have the advantage of being grown in loose, relatively stone-free soil, which enables them to grow straight). Once cleaned, they should be placed in a bowl of water with vinegar or fresh lemon juice to prevent discolouring. Young tender roots can be eaten raw; older ones should be cooked for 30 minutes in salted water, with fresh lemon juice and butter if you like. A film of flour on top of the cooking water will help reduce further discolouration. As with goat's beard you will need to have seen the mature plant before you can collect the grass-like leaves with confidence. They can be used as vegetables or in salads. Flowerhead buds can be eaten boiled, steamed or fried (see goat's beard).

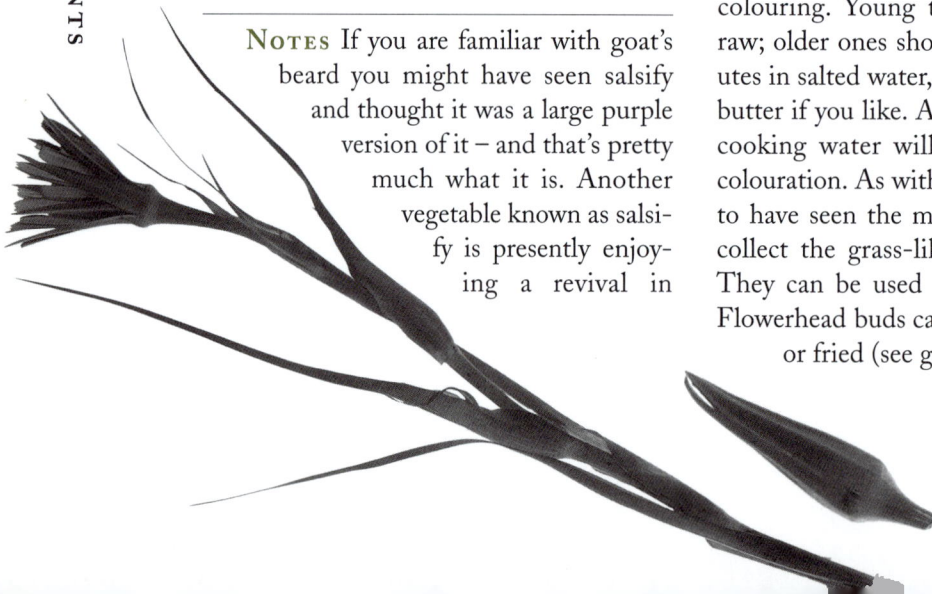

HARVESTING NOTES Harvest roots at the end of the first year's growth (plants with leaves only, no flowering stem), October onwards. Don't take more than a few roots per site in any given year and make a positive impact on the population by gathering and scattering seed, or even clearing a few 5sq cm patches near to where you harvest and sowing the seed there.

Tragopogon pratensis

Goat's Beard/ Jack-go-to-bed-at-noon

DISTRIBUTION Up to 365m. In England, widespread, only less so Cornwall, Devon, Cumberland and Northumberland; in Wales, common in coastal counties, especially north and south, scattered elsewhere; in Scotland, mostly Eastern Coastal and Central Lowlands, north to Angus, sparse southwest of Southern Uplands and coastal areas Angus–west Sutherland; in Ireland, scarce, mainly Central and east Central Lowlands, sporadic elsewhere, except absent Donegal, Londonderry, Tyrone, Mayo and west Galway; present Alderney and single naturalized site on Isle of Man.

HABITAT Among tall grass in meadows, field margins, waste ground, sand dunes, roadsides and railway embankments.

DESCRIPTION Native annual, up to 90cm high. Leaves long, thin, tapered and hairless, somewhat like grass but greyish green and fleshy. Stems bleed milk when broken (as do leaves) and branch only once or twice if at all. Yellow flower heads, only open in the morning (hence Jack-go-to-bed-at-noon); after noon they close, resembling a goat's beard (hence goat's-beard). The pointed bracts protrude beyond the ray florets to form a striking star shape in the morning; they enclose the flower heads in the afternoon. The seed heads are big balls of pappus-bearing seeds, like dandelion clocks only bigger. Flowers May–July.

NOTES When I first saw pictures of goat's beard in a wild-food book, it looked strangely familiar. The following summer, I cycled along the path that had been my daily route to primary and secondary school for ten years and found it on the majority of the route. A similar thing happened with **spring beauty**, which also grows abundantly in the village where I grew up. The great thing about learning about edible wild plants is that many of them are not hard to find; if they are hidden, it is only by our inattention. A good proportion of the plants in this book probably grow in places you walk past every day.

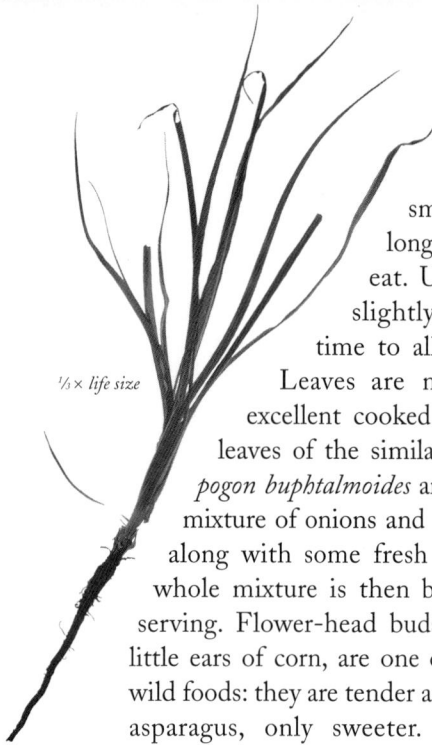

⅓ × life size

Uses/Recipes

Roots are quite small, only 8–10cm long, but still good to eat. Use as salsify, with slightly shorter cooking time to allow for their size. Leaves are nice in salad but excellent cooked. In Lebanon, the leaves of the similar bull's eye *Tragopogon buphtalmoides* are added to a fried mixture of onions and crushed chickpeas, along with some fresh lemon juice. The whole mixture is then briefly fried before serving. Flower-head buds, which look like little ears of corn, are one of the nicest of all wild foods: they are tender and taste a little like asparagus, only sweeter. Serve boiled or steamed, with butter or olive oil, for example with steamed Scottish halibut, crushed Charlotte potatoes and wild asparagus [JDW].

HARVESTING NOTES Young plants are hard to notice let alone identify, since the leaves look so much like grass. You need to find them when they are young as the edible roots are best then; at later stages they become woody, though still pleasant if you strip off the soft outer pulp with your teeth and discard the tough, woody remainder. Look out for the very distinctive flower heads and seed heads then look closely at the leaves; there should be other plants in their (leaves only) first year of growth near by.

Tussilago farfara

Colt's-foot

DISTRIBUTION Up to 1065m. In England and Wales, largely widespread throughout; in Scotland, largely widespread south of Glen Mor but north of Glen Mor absent parts of Westerness, West Ross, east and west Sutherland, Caithness and Western Isles; in Ireland, widespread but scarcer in west; present Guernsey and Isle of Man.

HABITAT Often pioneering on disturbed ground such as arable fields, crumbling cliffs, river banks and landslides; sand dunes, shingle and rough grassland.

DESCRIPTION Native perennial, spreading by rhizomes, forming large patches. Pale yellow flower heads emerge early spring before leaves. Stems 5–15cm long, thick, covered in purple bracts, with one flower head, 13–35mm wide. Flower heads only open when the sun is shining and from a distance resemble small dandelions; closer up they look more like yellow daisies, with both ray and disc florets. Initially upright, they droop as the flower fades, at which point the leaves appear, before becoming upright again once the dandelion-like head of seeds has formed. Leaves downy at first, then smooth above, woolly below, up to 20cm wide with shallow lobes and angular teeth, like the underside of a horse's hoof (hence 'colt's-foot').

SIMILAR SPECIES Leaves can be confused with winter heliotrope *Petasites fragrans*, but these are smooth on both sides and appear with the flowers or with young butterbur *P. hybridus* (later leaves are huge), which have grey down below and are smooth above. To avoid all confusion, however, only collect leaves where you have observed flower heads. The Japanese eat a form of butterbur, which they call 'fuki', in a dish called Fukinotou, but a *Petasites* species caused severe liver damage when consumed regularly as herbal tea.

NOTES I was first shown this plant by friends in Switzerland, who gathered the flower heads to make a delicious fresh tea. I was subsequently delighted to discover that it is quite abundant in most of the British Isles.

USES/RECIPES Flower heads are a flavoursome addition to salads: sweet, aromatic and slightly aniseed. Infuse in milk to make custard for ice cream.

COLT'S-FOOT FLOWERS NITUKE: 60 colt's-foot flowers with their scaly stems, 3 tablespoons olive oil, 15g butter, 3 tablespoons tamari or soy sauce, 4 slices bread. Wash the flowers well, as they might be quite dusty, and dry them thoroughly with a towel. Heat up the olive oil and butter in a pan, and add the colt's-foot flowers. Let them cook slowly for 3 minutes. Pour in the tamari or other soy sauce and stir well. Remove pan from the heat. Toast the bread slightly and spread the flowers evenly on each slice. Serve warm [FC]. Flower heads and leaves are good with elderflower and elderberries to make a winter tonic cordial for coughs, colds and flu symptoms. Leaves can be used a vegetable, after removing the wool on their under surface.

BEIGNETS DE TUSSILAGE: 1 egg, 3 tablespoons white flour, sifted, ½ tablespoon salt, 240 ml water, 240 ml beer, groundnut oil, for frying, 16 colt's-foot leaves, 1 lemon. Beat the egg yolk and add flour and salt. Add water and beer, mixing thoroughly to get a smooth, liquid batter. Beat the egg white until stiff , then fold delicately into the mixture. Let rest, covered, for half an hour. Heat up the oil in a pan – it must be as hot as possible but not smoking. Dip a colt's-foot leaf in the batter, let it drain for a few seconds and dip into the hot oil. Wait until the oil has heated up again and add another leaf. Remove when golden brown and drain on tissue paper. Sprinkle with some salt and lemon juice, and serve piping hot [FC].

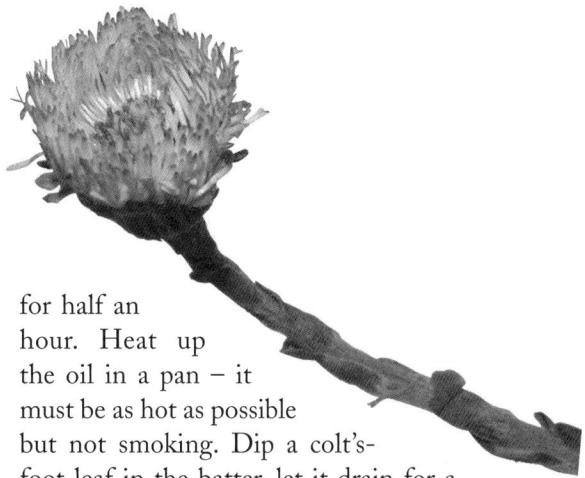

BENEFITS Colt's-foot is best known for its use as a medicinal plant: the botanical name *Tussilago* is derived from the Latin *tussis ago*, which means 'I drive out a cough'. The leaves contain pectin, which loosens mucilage; they are the main ingredient in a well-known cough sweet. It is believed to relieve a cough by thinning the phlegm in the lung, so making it easier to bring up. They also contain the anti-cancer compound beta-sitosterol.

HAZARDS Contains pyrrolizidine alkaloids senkirkine and senecionine in minute but variable amounts. Erring on the side of caution, it should only be consumed occasionally and in moderation, especially by young children or while pregnant or breastfeeding.

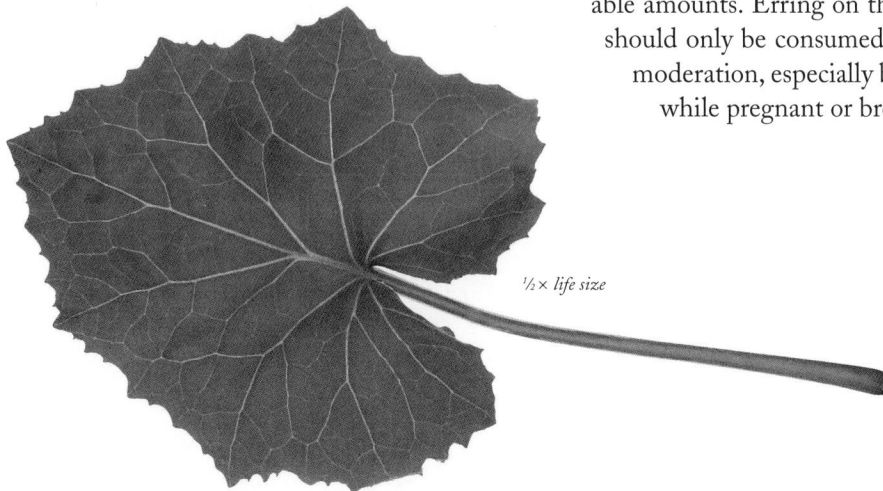

½ × life size

DEW PLANT FAMILY
Aizoaceae

Carpobrotus edulis
Hottentot Fig

DISTRIBUTION Native to South Africa. In England, found only on the coast, mostly in southwest, especially Cornwall and Devon, also in Essex, Hampshire and Isle of White; in Wales, in Anglesey, Gwynedd and Gwent; in Scotland, found Whiten Head area; in Ireland, scattered localities along east coast; present Channel Islands, Isles of Scilly and Isle of Man.

HABITAT Coastal habitats, including sea cliffs, sand dunes, walls and rocks.

DESCRIPTION Succulent, creeping, mat-forming perennial. Leaves are very fleshy, like triangular fingers, slightly curved towards the end, 7–10cm long. Flowers are deep pink or yellow, looking like daisies, but much larger, up to 10cm wide. However, they are true flowers, not composites: they have petals rather than florets. Flowers May–September. Fruits are somewhat figlike in appearance and structure, being sticky inside with many seeds; they taper from top to bottom, and the top ends in 5 pointed lobes around its edge.

USES/RECIPES The most obvious use of the fruits is to eat them as they come, ripe from the plant, by biting off the end and sucking out the pulp. They are slightly sweet but also a little bit salty. They can also be used to make jam. For cooking, it is better to get them less ripe, when they are firm and the leafy green sides of the fruit can be peeled off to get at the main part in the middle. The leaves are said to make a good pickle.

BENEFITS Juice from the leaves staunches bleeding and speeds the healing of wounds. It is also good for mouthwash and gargling for ulcers and sore throats, and is used to treat eczema as well as insect bites and stings.

DOCK FAMILY
Polygonaceae

Dock leaves are often touched and handled, because many people use them to soothe nettle stings. This is so commonplace as not to receive a second thought, but few other wild British plants are so widely known in this way. If you have ever picked a dock leaf and rubbed it on a nettle sting, you will know its robust, leathery texture, which is something of a signature: toughness is a quality possessed by dock plants in several respects.

On ground that is repeatedly driven over or walked on, broad-leaved dock leaves or knotgrass plants persist and are often the only green thing remaining. Similarly, all gardeners know first hand the doggedness of the roots, so hard to grasp firmly enough to pull up. Even if you succeed, the plant just grows back from small pieces of root left in the ground. The most powerful illustration of this tenacity is Japanese knotweed growing up through concrete and tarmac. *Itadori*, the Japanese name for the plant, aptly means 'strong plant'. Dock leaves are also robust in texture when cooked, holding up much better than most green vegetables. Several dock species communicate their strength through their nutrient content: dock leaves contain a lot of iron, buckwheat seeds yield more protein than any other grain, and knotweed roots are the most potent known plant source of the antioxidant resveratrol.

BOTANICAL CHARACTERISTICS Plants that belong to the dock family are distinguished by the presence of sheath-like stipules, unlobed and untoothed leaves and small, tightly grouped flowers with green or pink perianth segments, which are not quite petals and not quite sepals. Flower heads of docks, redshank, bistort and pale persicaria are especially dense; those of *Fallopia* species and the rest of the knotgrasses are less so. The upright inflorescences and seed heads of bistort and the docks can be distinguished from quite a distance. Flower heads of *Fallopia* species all droop somewhat, as do those of water-pepper. The flowers, especially some of the green ones, do not conform to most people's idea of a flower, since they are neither fragrant, nor colourful nor large enough to see the component parts easily. But once you get used to their general form, they become a useful indicator that a plant belongs to this family. Patches of redshank, pale persicaria and water-pepper are recognizable in this way, though the conspicuous pink flowers of redshank are also quite eye-catching and distinct in their own right. Japanese knotweed is recognizable by the sheer height and bulk of its collective growth.

GENERAL HAZARDS No member of the dock family is toxic if consumed in moderation. However, leaves and stems of most species have a fairly high oxalic-acid content – the sorrels especially. People in poor health should avoid eating large quantities of leaves of sorrels and other *Rumex* species; there are two separate cases on record of people who were already very ill dying after eating around half a kilo of dock leaves in one sitting. In both cases their deaths were attributed to effects of oxalic acid. This should, however, be considered alongside the many millions of people who eat sorrel and rhubarb – both with high oxalic content – every year with no ill effects. Also avoid cooking these species in aluminium pans as oxalic acid reacts with aluminium to produce toxic salts. Oxalic acid is discussed in more depth in 'Foraging Hazards', p.19.

Fallopia convolvulus

Black Bindweed

DISTRIBUTION Up to 450m. Widespread throughout much of British Isles, except in England, absent from higher-altitude areas of north; in Wales, absent Brecon Beacons, Black Mountains, Snowdonia and Cambrian Mountains; in Scotland, absent parts of Southern Uplands, Grampian Mountains, North West Highlands and North Highland; in Ireland, found mostly in east and southwest, scarce in western counties; present Isle of Man.

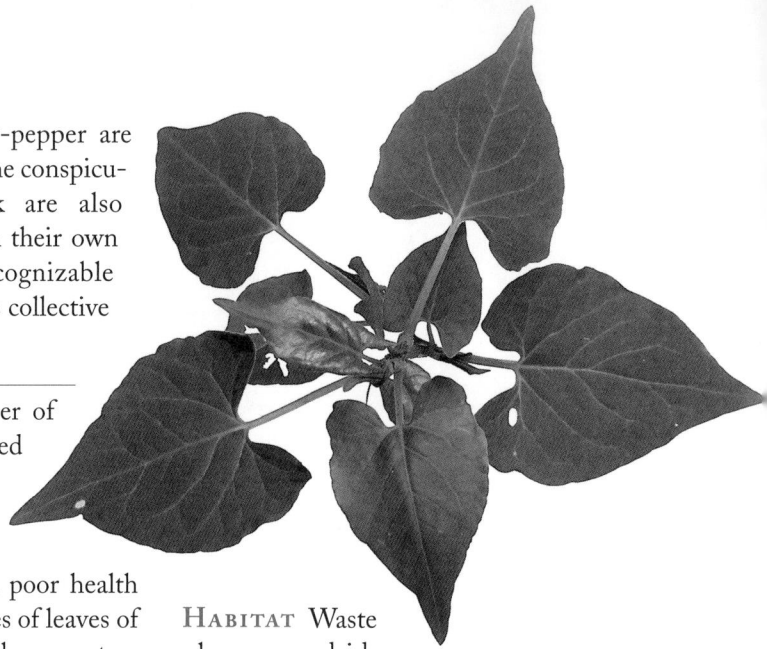

HABITAT Waste places, roadsides, rubbish tips, gardens and arable land.

DESCRIPTION With its trailing, twisting form and cordate leaves it resembles the unrelated field bindweed *Convolvulus arvensis*, but black bindweed leaves are darker with a mealy texture underneath. Black bindweed also lacks the typical trumpet-shaped flower of the bindweed family; its flowers are greenish pink/greenish white, with flat faces, 5–6mm long. Seeds black, triangular, like smaller buckwheat. A large seeded variety has been observed that is perhaps the relic of plants selectively grown for food.

SIMILAR SPECIES Buckwheat *Fagopyrum esculentum* has arrow-shaped leaves and is more upright. The seeds are larger and are available commercially, but the plant frequently occurs in the wild as a casual in scattered localities throughout England and more rarely in Ireland, Wales and Scotland. Buckwheat flour is used to make Russian blinis, Breton crêpes and Japanese soba noodles.

NOTES This annual weed of cultivation has been here since at least neolithic times

and was the worst seed contaminant before seed-cleaning procedures were improved.

USES/RECIPES The seeds have been used since at least the Bronze Age. Once the perianth segments have been removed, they can be ground and used as flour or used as other grains, especially in place of buckwheat.

BENEFITS The following is true of buckwheat seeds; it is reasonable to assume that black bindweed seeds have similar properties: high protein content (9 per cent), containing amino-acids lysine and arginine, which are not found in cereal grains. Buckwheat proteins are known to reduce cholesterol.

HARVESTING NOTES As with **knotweed** and **pale persicaria**, the flowering and fruiting stages are indistinguishable until the plants are examined closely. The perianth segments look pretty much the same at both stages and surround even the ripe seeds; however, it is easy to tell, by feeling them, whether they contain a seed.

Fallopia japonica

Japanese Knotweed

DISTRIBUTION Up to 300m. Very widespread throughout most of British Isles, but none in some places, including: in England, areas of Cleveland and Cheviot hills and Pennines; in Scotland, much of Grampian Mountains, North West Highlands and Southern Uplands; in Ireland, much of central lowlands.

HABITAT In Victorian and Edwardian times a popular garden plant, Japanese knotweed has now colonized a variety of habitats, including river banks, edges of woods and railway embankments, forming patches and often considerable thickets.

DESCRIPTION Tall, woody perennial. Left alone a knotweed patch leaves a stand of tall, reddish brown canes (up to 2m high) at the end of the year's growth, making it easy to spot, especially in winter. In mid–late April, the plants put up shoots that resemble fat, red asparagus stalks, which open out into oval–triangular leaves with pointed tips. After this the plants grow rapidly and form dense clumps with thick, hollow stems and much larger leaves.

NOTES Japanese knotweed falls into a category of plants for which *un*sustainable use is the byword: it is an invasive species that foragers could eat to extinction to the widespread applause of conservationists, gardeners and builders alike. Widespread but not universal: dissident voices point out that knotweed stands provide a welcome habitat for certain kinds of lizard as well as numerous species of insect and communities of spring-flowering plants.

The roots of knotweed are so strong and persistent that they can break up concrete foundations and grow through concrete slabs to emerge inside buildings. Removing knotweed is a lucrative trade but an annual knotweed-eating festival in Pennsylvania celebrates a culinary approach to the same problem, summed up by German knotweed-jam manufacturer Peter Becker's marketing slogan: 'My appetite, your herbicide!' Despite its unpopularity elsewhere, Japanese knotweed is highly regarded in Japan as a medicinal plant, where the name *Itadori*, variously rendered in English as 'strong one' and 'one that heals', alludes to both its destructive and curative properties.

USES/RECIPES Shoots and stems can be used for both sweet and savoury

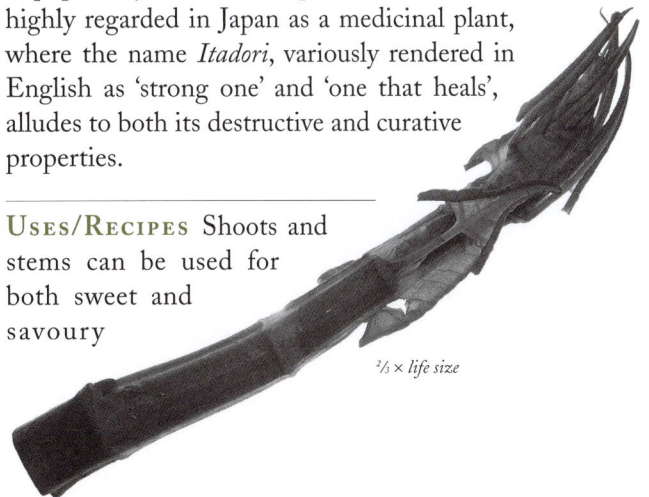

²/₃ × life size

Ali Irving's Japanese Knotweed & Blackthorn Blossom Custard Tarts

MAKES 24 SMALL TARTS

FOR THE PASTRY
130g unsalted butter
80g caster sugar
1 egg lightly beaten
250g fine grade flour
a pinch of salt, to season

FOR THE CUSTARD
4 egg yolks
100g caster sugar
25g plain flour
500ml milk
50g blackthorn/sloe (or cherry or
    wild damson) blossom

FOR THE PASTRY Cream the butter, sugar and a pinch of salt in a bowl, then stir in the egg and flour in one go. Turn out onto a work surface and knead until flour is completely absorbed. Wrap in cling film then leave to stand for 1 hour.

FOR THE CUSTARD Beat the egg yolks and sugar in a pan until pale and fluffy. Gradually stir in flour until evenly mixed. In a separate pan bring the milk to boiling point with the blossom, turn down heat and simmer for 15 minutes then strain. Gradually add hot milk to the egg-yolk mixture then cook over a low heat, stirring constantly for 3–4 minutes until thickened. Pour into a bowl then leave to cool, stirring occasionally to prevent a skin forming.

FOR THE KNOTWEED Wash 15 young knotweed shoots, roughly 10cm long. Cut into 5mm pieces. Place in a pan with 3 tablespoons of water and cook over a gentle heat until the pieces are softened but still hold their shape. Use a slotted spoon to remove pieces from the liquid. Add 2 tablespoons of golden caster sugar and the juice of a lemon to the liquid, and bring to boil, reducing to a syrup consistency and taking care for it not to burn.

ASSEMBLING AND BAKING THE TARTS Roll out the pastry and cut 16 rounds to fill a tart tin. To each tart case, add 2 rounded teaspoons of the custard mixture, flatten slightly then spoon on 1 teaspoon of the softened knotweed pieces and drizzle over just a little syrup. Bake for 8–12 minutes at 180˚C. When cool add a little more cool syrup and dust with icing sugar.

dishes; make syrups and otherwise infuse flavour from tougher stems. The flavour closely resembles rhubarb, but I prefer it to rhubarb: it is less tart and the texture less slimy and stringy. Pretty much any recipe for rhubarb can be adapted to use knotweed, for example, JAPANESE KNOTWEED SORBET: Poach 300g knotweed in 500ml syrup (500g sugar in 500ml water), cool and melt 2 sheets leaf gelatine in the same; blend with 200g raw knotweed then strain. Cool then freeze into sorbet in an ice-cream maker [RR]. As a savoury, the tart flavour recommends it for use as for sorrel, but of course it has more substance. Variations on sorrel and eggs work well – my favourite is with a poached egg and fresh crab.

KNOTWEED COMPOTE WITH MACKEREL: Slice about 500g peeled knotweed, add half a handful of sugar and plenty of water, cook until soft (about half an hour) in a pan with lid on. Sweat down finely chopped onion, garlic and horseradish, mix with crème fraîche. Roast mackerel, serve on top of a couple of spoons of knotweed compote and drizzle the crème

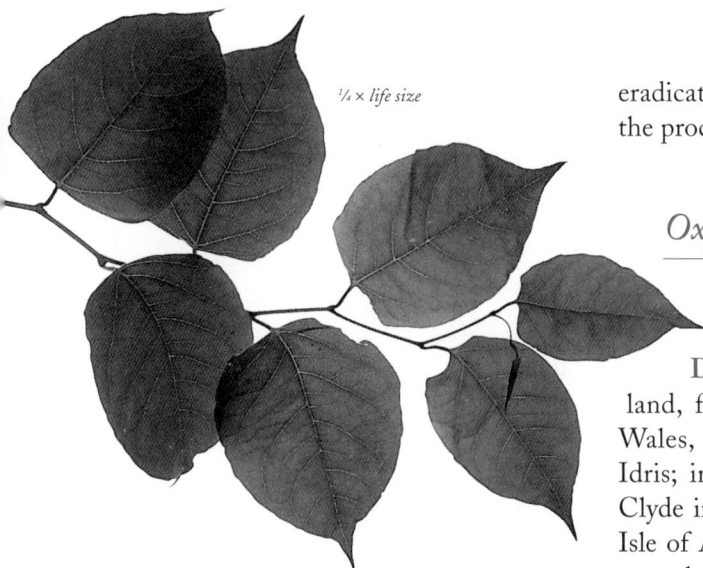

eradicate it you may as well enjoy eating it in the process.

fraiche and horseradish over the top. Serve with a few sprigs of wild watercress [EC]. The stout rhizomes can be used to make a tonic tea.

BENEFITS Recent analysis of the plant for phytochemicals has confirmed its reputation as a medicinal plant: knotweed contains high levels of the antioxidant resveratrol, also found in peanuts and red wine, which has anti-carcinogenic and anti-tumour properties; resveratrol supplements are now made from the root of Japanese knotweed. Resveratrol increases the lifespan of yeast, roundworms and fruit flies; experimental work with single human cells suggests it may also have anti-ageing effects for humans.

HARVESTING NOTES Knotweed is easiest to use at its asparagus-like stage, when it needs little or no preparation. As it gets taller, it develops a fibrous skin, which needs peeling. Once it has produced branches, the main stems are usually too tough but the top 10–13cm of the leafy branches are soft enough to use, minus the leaves, but it takes much longer to gather what you need at this stage. Cutting down the plant repeatedly throughout the summer will force it to produce new shoots and eventually kill it. If you are trying to

Oxyria digyna

Mountain Sorrel

DISTRIBUTION Up to 1190m. In England, found only Cumbrian Mountains; in Wales, found Snowdonia including Cader Idris; in Scotland, mainly north of Firth of Clyde in west and Grampian Mountains, also Isle of Arran, Western and Northern Isle and sparsely in Southern Uplands; in Ireland, higher-altitude areas of west Donegal, Sligo, west Mayo, west Galway, Kerry, Limerick and Tipperary; introduced into Isle of Man.

HABITAT Mountains, in damp, stony areas free of grazing, on cliffs and ledges, and by streams. Seeds sometimes transported by water to lower altitudes and found growing on river shingle.

DESCRIPTION Smaller than common sorrel with kidney-shaped leaves, mostly concentrated at the base of the plant.

USES/RECIPES As for **common sorrel**.

Persicaria bistorta

Common Bistort/ Passion Dock/Snake-root

½ × *life size*

DISTRIBUTION Up to 430m. In England, sparsely present in most areas, rare in Lincolnshire, the Fens, Kent and Essex; more widespread north of Humber and West Midlands; in Wales, found in most areas, but less common Gwynedd, Glamorgan and south Pembrokeshire; in Ireland, sparse in Ulster, Sligo and south Munster; present Isle of Man.

HABITAT Mostly acid or neutral soils in hilly areas; among grass in damp places, such as meadows, woodlands and river banks.

DESCRIPTION Native, mostly hairless perennial forming colonies by spreading S-shaped rhizomes; hence the name snake-root. Basal leaves resemble dock leaves but less scruffy, as flatter and less crinkled round the edges; they are oval, with blunt ends, cordate bases and long, partially winged stalks. Stem leaves more triangular; lower ones also winged. Stems unbranched, producing dramatic pink spikes of flowers July–August.

USES/RECIPES The spring leaves that appear in April can be used as greens or in salads; older leaves make good greens but are too tough for salad. They are delicious cooked in a good, strong ale and served with something rich, such as a roast vegetable and tomato quiche or steak and ale pie (an *assiette* of alliteration: beef, bistort and beer). Historical sources record the roots being used roasted, after steeping in water. However, even after steeping and roasting they are too astringent to eat under anything less than desperate circumstances; they contain a lot of starch so would make a good survival food.

A TRADITION OF PUDDINGS

Each spring in the north of England the young leaves of bistort are made into a traditional dish known as Dock Pudding in Yorkshire or Easter Ledge, Easterma Giant or Herb Pudding in Cumbria. Although the recipes no doubt have a common origin, these two regional dishes are made in slightly different ways and eaten always at breakfast in Yorkshire but often with a main meal in Cumbria. The dish is a pudding in a sense not widely used these days: food cooked within a casing (muslin) and including a binding agent to make it semi solid (barley or oatmeal). Sausages were originally described as puddings, as black pudding still is.

In the Calder Valley near Halifax, West Yorkshire, the annual World Dock Pudding Championships attracts a respectable number of entrants, but, sadly, few international participants. Ali and I went along in April 2007. It felt uncanny, witnessing this small surviving English outpost of traditional edible wild-plant use; a bit like discovering a tribal people living in Epping Forest. As we entered the venue, an elderly woman was cooking up the dock pudding and offering portions on a slice of buttered bread for 50p. It's a homely sort of dish, a basic but tasty comfort food. Shortly

afterwards everyone in the packed community centre sat down to watch the competitors cook up their recipes, then waited while the judges sampled them all and came up with a winner. After the event, we spent the afternoon with Joan Whitworth, the only person to have won the competition three times in succession. She kindly gave us a recipe but it is slightly different from the one she uses in the competition, which is a closely guarded secret!

Joan Whitworth's Dock Pudding

a carrier bagful of bistort leaves
175ml water

porridge oats and savoury oat biscuits, to
   thicken
a few bacon rashers (optional), to finish

De-stalk the leaves, by folding them in half along the stalk and tearing off the green part. Wash and pat dry, put in pressure cooker with 175ml water for approximately 4 minutes; season to taste. Mix with the oats and biscuits. Only put in what the liquid takes up; drain if too much. Fry with bacon for best result.

With first-hand experience of the Yorkshire tradition, I was curious about the traditional use of bistort in the Lake District. With no other place to start, I placed an advert in several Cumbrian newspapers, asking for recipes for Easter Ledge pudding. The following recipe is an amalgam of the many responses I received; a couple of the stories that came with them are reproduced overleaf. For the spring leaves, young bistort and nettle tops are always used, but some people also use lady's mantle, dandelion, other kinds of dock leaves, watercress, gooseberry or blackcurrant leaves (only one or two of these), leeks, sprout tops, chives and mint.

Easter Ledge/Easterma Giant/Herb Pudding

450g spring leaves
1 large onion
110g/1 cup barley
½ tsp salt
a pinch of pepper

1 raw egg or several hard-boiled eggs (see
   serving suggestions)
oatmeal (see serving suggestions)
a large knob of butter or bacon dripping (see
   serving suggestions)

Remove stalks from the bistort leaves and other leaves, if necessary. Chop the greens and the onion finely, add the washed barley, season the mixture then tie it up in muslin (pudding poke or linen bag) and boil or steam for 1½–2 hours.

SERVING SUGGESTIONS
1 Mix in the butter or bacon dripping and a raw egg, and malt vinegar, if you like.
2 As for 1, but shape into patties and fry before serving (some recipes add a little fine oatmeal at this point).
3 Add only the dripping or butter and spread the mixture over some hard-boiled eggs in an ovenproof dish and brown under the grill.

JUDIE JOHNSTON FROM CARLISLE: My mother used to get it from two sisters on the market, in Carlisle on a Saturday. There were special stalls for country people to sell their produce, eggs, flowers, chickens, dressed ready for the oven. People would hire them for the morning, pay a pound or two pounds to the market people for the use of the stall. They went round the hedgerows and collected the nettles and the dockings [bistort leaves]. Mother used to say a pound or two pounds or whatever; they had their scales on the little counter. She used to bring it home and cook it. My mother maintained it was a cleaning out, you know for all the toxins you get in the winter, colds and flu and things like that. Used to give it [herb pudding] to us, as a vegetable, with a main meal with meat and potatoes. We used to enjoy it; it was delicious.

MR GLOBE: Bill Burrel of Penrith used to swear by it [herb pudding], lived into his nineties, didn't do him any harm. He used to make it quite regular. I used to go eeling with him and gather watercress and dockings. Off the side of the river near pasture land, where there is a good water course. Watercress was a big thing that people used to gather. I'm going back to the early fifties when we used to gather it. Quite a lot of people used to collect it for their own use.

Persicaria hydropiper

Water-pepper/Arsesmart

DISTRIBUTION Up to 505m. Widespread throughout much of British Isles, except: in Scotland, absent Northern Isles, Isle of Lewis, much of east and north Highlands and Grampian.

HABITAT Damp places, such as paths or path edges in woods, pond and lake edges.

²⁄₃ × life size

DESCRIPTION An annual, 20–70cm high, that forms small, dense patches, although appearing sparse and thin, due to widely spaced, alternate leaves that are slender and lanceolate. Flowers are small, greenish white or pink, arranged on a thin, drooping inflorescence. Seeds are oval, dark brown or black, up to 2.5mm long.

NOTES Water-pepper gained its outrageous synonym through its use as a flea repellent in bedding. Leaves would occasionally find their way into sensitive places, with the result alluded to by the name. It has been widely overlooked, even dismissed, because our approach to food doesn't recognize the usefulness of ingredients with the sole attribute 'hot'. However, in Japan, several cultivated varieties are used to give pungency, without undermining or masking other flavours, in particular the subtleness of certain seaweeds and of sushi.

USES/RECIPES Young shoots and sprouted seeds can be added (sparingly) to salads or used in place of pepper or chilli powder. Raw leaves can be chiffonaded and served with steak or sushi. Leaves can also be dried for later use, in place of pepper or chilli.

BENEFITS Contains highly beneficial micro-nutrient rutin, a bioflavanoid that is good for circulation, can help reduce high blood pressure and prevents bleeding from weak capillary walls such as in varicose veins and haemorrhoids: so water-pepper is not all bad for your backside…

Persicaria lapathifolia

Pale Persicaria

DISTRIBUTION Up to 450m. In England, widespread, except parts of northeast and Yorkshire; in Wales, absent higher areas such as Brecon Beacons and Cambrian Mountains; in Scotland, absent North Highland, most of Grampian Mountains, North West Highlands and Southern Uplands but found Isle of Lewis, Orkney and introduced into Shetland; in Ireland, found in most areas but less common towards west and central area; present Channel Islands, Isle of Man and Isles of Scilly.

HABITAT Waste ground, such as development plots, occasionally a pestilent agricultural weed and often in damp places, such as by streams, ponds and ditches.

DESCRIPTION Annual, growing to 90cm but often smaller. Leaves long, thin and pointed often with distinctive black marks or chevrons, said to look like a lady's thumb print. Distinctive sheath-like stipules at the stem bases. Small, pale green flowers arranged in tight cylindrical spikes.

SIMILAR SPECIES Redshank *P. maculosa* is generally smaller, with thinner, pink flower spikes and can be used in similar ways. A major culinary herb of Vietnam, Vietnamese mint *P. odorata*, looks similar but is not found wild in the British Isles.

USES/RECIPES Leaves can be used chopped in salads (the texture is rough and needs diluting through the salad) or as a cooked green. Not the best wild green: it doesn't really stand up on its own and is best added to soups and casseroles. The Vikings are known to have used the seeds in their pottages. Rub through a sieve to remove the perianth segment then winnow and grind in a kitchen mill or pound to break the tough seed coating. Use to thicken soups and stews or in baking.

HARVESTING NOTES Look for it from early summer onwards. Flowers and seeds appear identical at first glance; you have to squeeze them to find out which is which. Harvest ripe seeds by clasping your thumb and forefinger together and dragging the seeds from the stems.

Polygonum aviculare

Common Knotgrass

DISTRIBUTION Up to 670m. In England, widespread throughout, except areas of Suffolk, Yorkshire, Durham and Cumbria; in Wales, widespread in the south, Anglesey and Caernarvonshire; in Scotland, absent much of Grampian Mountains, North West Highlands and Isle of Skye, introduced into Shetland; in Ireland, common in most areas; present Channel Islands, Isle of Man and Isles of Scilly.

HABITAT Waste ground, cultivated fields, beaches.

DESCRIPTION Knotgrasses are our smallest dock-family species. These ground-hugging, straggly, annual plants form dense patches, often on otherwise bare soil. The stems can be as long as 1m, with small oval, elliptical or lanceolate leaves, no more than 10mm long and 4mm wide; tiny green and white flower groups of 5–6. Seeds 3mm long.

SIMILAR SPECIES There are several other species of knotgrass, of which Ray's knotgrass *P. oxyspermum* is probably of most interest, since it has much larger (6mm long) seeds. A coastal plant, it is mostly found in the west of mainland Britain but also in south Cornwall, Dorset and Ireland.

USES/RECIPES Seeds were used by the Vikings and can be used in similar ways to **pale persicaria**.

HARVESTING NOTES See **pale persicaria**.

Rumex acetosa

Common Sorrel

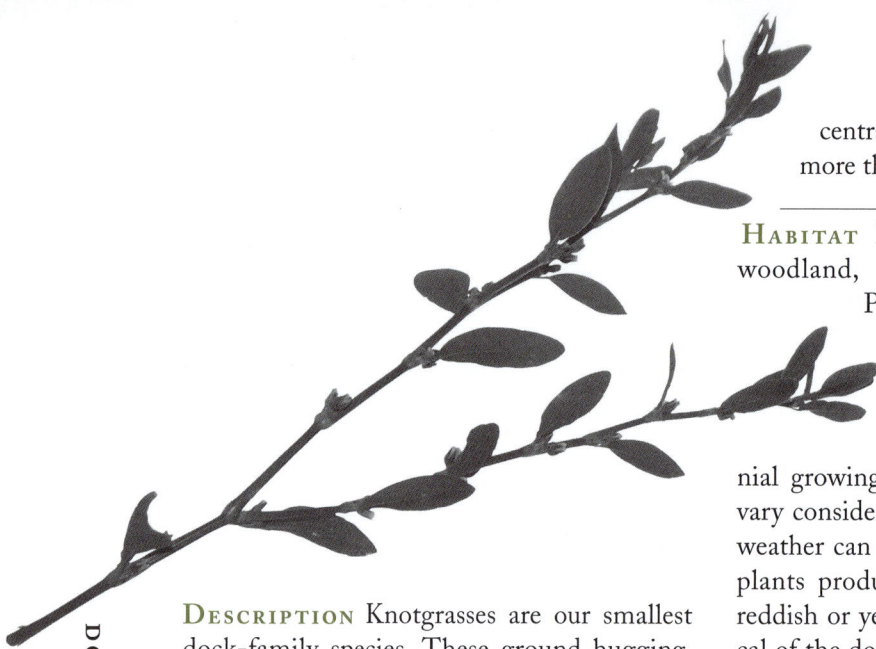

DISTRIBUTION Up to 1215m. Widespread throughout the British Isles; only in parts of central Ireland would you have to travel more than 10km to find it.

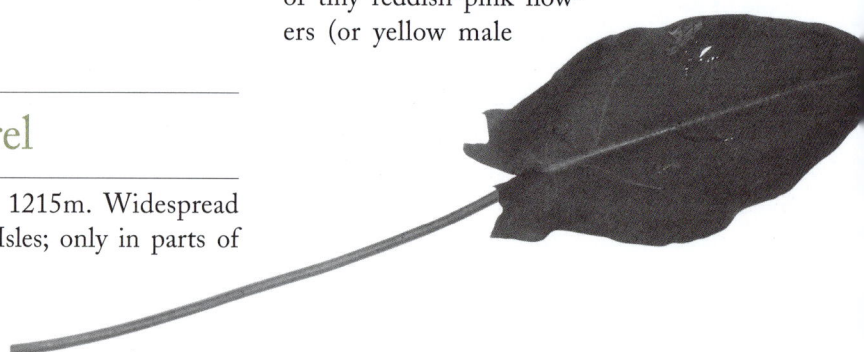

HABITAT Meadows, grassy banks, open woodland, coastal grassland and lawns. Prefers neutral–lightly acidic soil but can grow well enough on alkaline soils.

DESCRIPTION Hairless perennial growing to 30–80cm high. Basal leaves vary considerably in size but during mild wet weather can reach 12cm long. In summer the plants produce conspicuous spikes of small reddish or yellowish flowers in the form typical of the dock family. Stem leaves are smaller (not so good to eat) and more pointed, clasping the stem.

SIMILAR SPECIES The garden plant of the herb bed, subsp. *ambiguous*, which has more oval leaves and a densely branched inflorescence, occasionally turns up on waste ground. Sheep's sorrel has paler, often smaller leaves, with lobes that point outwards and forwards. Cultivated French sorrel *R. scutatus*, sometimes naturalized on walls and rough ground, has more branches and broader, shieldlike, often greyish leaves with out-turned lobes, the upper leaves stalked.

NOTES The name sorrel is a compound of the Anglo-Saxon *sur* meaning 'sour' and *el* meaning 'all'; an alternative name is sour dock. In summer the sorrels are instantly recognizable from a distance: the stems topped with masses of tiny reddish-pink flowers (or yellow male flowers) that stand out against most backgrounds. As with many edible plants, it is past its best by this point, with nothing but the stem and a few small leaves, but this is a good time to map out sorrel in your area. Having said that, chewing on the stems brings welcome thirst relief on a hot summer's day, a tradition my mother recalls from her childhood in Wales and also mentioned by poet John Clare in his song cycle *The Shepherd's Calendar:* 'the mower gladly chews it [sorrel] down, and slakes his thirst as best he may'.

USES/RECIPES *(for all the sorrels)* Sorrel has remained a key element of classic French cuisine (and is the lemon of northern and central Europe), yet professional chefs are often unfamiliar with the wild plants. Wild sorrels have a more intense flavour than cultivated varieties so that less is needed. Sorrel leaves are lovely in salads, fresh green and crisp, with a lemon flavour that is its own dressing. Cooking them sacrifices colour and texture for flavour as they inevitably become brown and sludgy. Add a few leaves to other greens for bite or wrap whole, raw sorrel leaves around sea trout fillet and cook sous-vide style. The best sorrel sauce is a simple butter emulsion, made with water, brought to the boil, then removed from the heat, into which is added some chilled, diced butter (stirred in over a very low heat), a little fresh lemon juice to stabilize the sauce and some finely shredded sorrel. Good with wild oily fish like salmon or trout; also with haddock fishcakes, made with cooked potatoes, haddock flakes, lemon zest and chopped parsley. Dip in flour, then beaten egg then breadcrumbs and shallow fry for a few minutes on each side. Serve on a bed of the sauce and courgette ribbons (made using veg peeler) blanched for 30 seconds and a few shredded leaves on top [JDW]. Sorrel is also good in desserts and other sauces (e.g. mayonnaise, hollandaise, gravy), where it is used as a milder alternative to lemon or vinegar. Use in sweet tarts, fruit pies or to flavour milk for crème brûlée. Shredded sorrel serves as a garnish for Pimm's jelly [PB]. Sweet sorrel granita is excellent served with sheep's milk mousse. A savoury sorrel granita can also be served with crab salad and beetroot [RR].

BENEFITS Sorrels are rich in vitamin C; during the early nineteenth-century Franklin expedition to the Arctic, the large quantity of wild sorrel eaten was almost certainly a factor in keeping the men free of scurvy.

HAZARDS Sorrels have a high oxalic-acid content, the source of their tangy lemony flavour, so should be eaten in moderation and avoided by people with kidney stones.

HARVESTING NOTES If you investigate patches of small docklike leaves in meadows and verges you can find common sorrel pretty much any time of year. However, in a harsh winter it can be hard work gathering a decent quantity; leaf growth is limited in summer (except where plants are mown), when the plant concentrates its vitality is on its flowering stem. Stem leaves are astringent and really not worth bothering with. The ideal time for gathering is spring, just before it flowers, when the leaves are large and plentiful.

Rumex acetosella

Sheep's Sorrel

DISTRIBUTION Up to 1050m. Widespread throughout British Isles, except few scattered 10 sq km; only in Ireland, in parts of Connaught,

Leinster and north Munster, would you have to travel more than 10km to find it.

HABITAT Generally drier areas than common sorrel, with a particular liking for grassland on sand and gravel. More common on acidic soils than common sorrel and will not grow well on alkaline soils.

DESCRIPTION Much lower growing than common sorrel and more spreading, forming bushy clumps or covering small areas of ground that are grazed or mown. Leaves are also paler, their upper two-thirds more curved and their two lobes pointing both outwards and forwards; under certain conditions leaves can be quite tiny, less than 10mm long, but they also may reach 50–60cm long; in autumn they turn reddish. Flowers similar to common sorrel.

Rumex alpinus

Monk's Rhubarb

DISTRIBUTION Up to 375m. In England, found in score or so 10 sq km in Lake District, Pennines and one area in Surrey; in Scotland, Central Lowlands and eastern Coastal Lowlands, Firth of Forth–East Sutherland, plus sites in Strathclyde and Ayrshire; elsewhere in British Isles, absent.

HABITAT Near old buildings, on grassy roadsides and on stream banks in hilly or mountain districts.

DESCRIPTION A thick-set perennial up to 1m high with dense flower spikes. Leaves are cordate, up to 40cm wide and unlike any other dock plant. It forms very thick patches.

USES/RECIPES Stems make delicious compotes and tarts [FC]. They are like rhubarb but less sharp and can be eaten raw after peeling or prepared in similar ways to **patience dock**.

³/₅ × life size

Rumex crispus

Curled/Sour Dock

DISTRIBUTION Up to 845m. Found throughout the British Isles, except in Scotland, parts of Highlands and Grampian Mountains.

HABITAT Roadsides, waste ground, pasture with disturbed ground, arable fields, coastal shingle beaches, estuarine tidal mud and upper salt marshes.

DESCRIPTION Native perennial, reaching 1m high, occasionally up to 1.5m or more. Long, thin, lanceolate, short stalked leaves with wavy edges; bases either tapered or rounded. Rather dense flowers and fruits in branched inflorescences.

USES/RECIPES Young leaves are more tender and sweet; older ones often too tough and bitter to be worthwhile. Fry with onions and garlic (older leaves may need blanching first); they hold up better when cooked than many other greens, including bistort. Serve with cooked tomatoes or hard-boiled eggs. In Greece, the young leaves are used in salads.

Rumex patientia

Patience Dock/Danser

DISTRIBUTION Up to 300m. Introduced: found mainly in and near London, Bristol and other large towns; in England, present only score or so 10 sq km, mostly Thames Valley, east of Berkshire plus other sites Gloucestershire and Somerset and several counties north of the Wash.

HABITAT A dock of docks! Also on river and canal banks and near breweries; waste ground generally.

DESCRIPTION Very tall perennial, reaching up to 2m high. Leaves very long, up to 80cm, lanceolate, tapered–rounded at base. Flowers thickly crowded on branched inflorescences; when in flower it looks a bit like rhubarb.

SIMILAR SPECIES Curled Dock *R. crispus*, which is smaller, with less dense inflorescences.

NOTES Formerly cultivated as a vegetable ('herb patience') and still sometimes eaten in Europe. Once known as winter spinach in Germany and served mixed with spinach.

USES/RECIPES The succulent leaf stalks can be eaten raw after peeling; they are refreshing and juicy. Use in salads or as crudités. The green part of the leaf should be stripped off and used separately as greens, for example, fried briefly in butter and served on toast with a dash of Worcestershire sauce or walnut ketchup. Make a warm salad with stalks blanched and peeled and cut at an angle into lozenge-shaped slices, served with the green leaf fried separately. Dress with vinaigrette and serve with red mullet [PW]. Also use stems instead of rhubarb for jams, sweet c r u m b l e s and pies.

¹/₆ × life size

Rumex sanguineus

Wood/Blood-veined Dock

DISTRIBUTION Up to 380m. In England and Wales, absent only a few 10 sq km in; in Scotland, present much of lowlands south of Grampian Mountains with scattered localities in East and West Highland and north Grampian; in Ireland, found mostly throughout, apart from scattered higher-altitude areas and parts of central lowland; present Channel Islands and Isle of Man.

HABITAT Woodland paths and edges, roadsides, hedgebanks and waste places. Prefers damp, clay soils but will grow elsewhere.

DESCRIPTION Perennial, up to 1m high. Leaves oval–lanceolate, with rounded base; the variety *sanguineus* (formerly grown for salads and occasionally found in the wild) has blood-red veins, hence the plant's alternative name. Main stem has only a few upright branches, giving the plant a sparse and narrow form; the flower stems only have leaves at their base.

SIMILAR SPECIES Clustered/Sharp dock *Rumex conglomeratus* has branches at wider angles to the stem, and its inflorescences are more leafy. The larger, more robust and spreading broad-leaved dock *Rumex obtusifolius* has larger leaves, which are much wider in proportion to their length than those of wood dock.

USES/RECIPES As for **curled dock**.

FIGWORT FAMILY
Scrophulariaceae

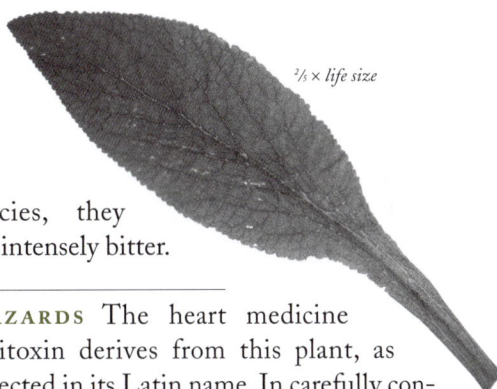

²/₅ × life size

POISONOUS PLANTS

Digitalis purpurea

Foxglove

DISTRIBUTION Pretty much throughout the British Isles, except in England, scarce in parts of the Fens and Lincolnshire; in Scotland, scare north of Lewis; absent central Ireland.

HABITAT Open woodland and scrub, nearly always on acid soil.

DESCRIPTION Hairy biennial/short-lived perennial, up to 1.5m high. Leaves greyish green, the lower large, oval–lanceolate with winged stalks; the upper smaller. The deep pink tubular flowers have dark spots within and are arranged in a tall spike.

SIMILAR SPECIES In flower you are unlikely to confuse foxgloves with anything else, but you might confuse basal leaves with **burdock**, **comfrey** or **borage**. Unlike the later two

species, they are intensely bitter.

HAZARDS The heart medicine digitoxin derives from this plant, as reflected in its Latin name. In carefully controlled doses it is used to treat heart conditions. Large doses, however, can be fatal: symptoms of poisoning include vomiting and dizziness, followed by heart disturbances, blurred vision and delirium. The plant is so bitter that it is amazing anyone has eaten it, but many fatalities have been recorded.

EDIBLE PLANTS

In addition to the edible species that follow, this family includes the many speedwell species, all of which are in theory edible, but I have yet to find one that is especially palatable. However, Ken Fern, author of *Plants for a Future*, recommends both blue water-speedwell *Veronica anagallis-aquatica* and grey field-speedwell *Veronica polita*, both of which I have yet to try. Also, in Turkey, the flowers of a species of mullein are eaten by children.

¹/₄ × life size

Cymbalaria muralis

Ivy-leaved Toadflax

DISTRIBUTION Up to 450m. Native to mountains of south-central and southeast Europe. In England, widespread throughout, only less so southeast Yorkshire and Northumberland; in Wales, widespread; in Scotland, widespread except higher-altitude areas of Southern Uplands, Grampian Mountains and north of Glen Mor; absent Western and Northern Isles; in Ireland, found in every county but more widely scattered in west; present on Channel Islands, Isle of Man, Isles of Scilly and Lundy.

HABITAT On pavements, walls and base of walls and rocks; shingle beaches.

DESCRIPTION Perennial, naturalized from gardens. Leaves are ivy-like, as is tendency to creep along the ground and attach to walls. Plants are hairless; leaves dark green. Violet (occasionally white) flowers, April–September, are two lipped with a spur and a yellow patch inside lower lip. Seeds are clasped by sepals then released by the plant into suitable places for germination.

SIMILAR SPECIES Mature **Danish scurvygrass** can be found in similar habitats; it has similar, but fleshier leaves, and simple, 4-petal flowers.

USES/RECIPES Leaves make a pretty addition to a salad, though the flavour is really nothing special. At the Ivy in London,

head chef Alan Bird likes to garnish some of his signature dishes with a single, destalked toadflax leaf as a kind of emblem – and whoever's fiddlesome job it is to prepare these leaves groans when the toadflax delivery arrives.

Mimulus guttatus

Monkey-flower

DISTRIBUTION Native of North America. In England, widespread Northumberland, Durham, Norfolk, most of southeast, West Midlands, south Somerset, Dorset and south Devon, and sporadic elsewhere; in Wales, common in north except Anglesey, Denbighshire and Flintshire, found in south in Carmarthenshire and along Severn Estuary; in Scotland, scattered localities throughout Southern Uplands, Central Lowlands, eastern Coastal Lowlands north to Glen Mor and coastal areas of west Sutherland, also Shetland and Isle of Lewis; in Ireland, scattered localities in coastal counties of north, south and east; also found on Isle of Man and Channel Islands.

HABITAT Edging streams, ponds and rivers; in marshes, open woods and damp meadows.

DESCRIPTION Naturalized, upright perennial, up to 50cm high, with creeping runners. Hairless except calyx and flower stalk. Leaves 2–7cm long, in opposite pairs, oval, ending in a point and toothed. Large yellow flowers, up to 45mm long, have two lips and red spots inside.

USES/RECIPES Leaves and stems are slightly salty and rather bitter but improved by cooking. Use in soups, stews, omelettes and warm salads.

Pedicularis sylvatica
Lousewort

DISTRIBUTION Up to 915m. In England, widespread in northwest and southwest, mostly absent East Midlands and east, and sporadic elsewhere; in Wales, widespread; in Scotland, widespread, only less so Caithness, Grampian, around Firth of Tay and in Roxburghshire; in Ireland, in every county, but most abundant Ulster and southwest; present on Isle of Man, Isles of Scilly, Channel Islands and Lundy.

HABITAT Damp heath, moor and grassland, also less waterlogged areas of bog and marsh, on acid soil.

DESCRIPTION Perennial/biennial, with many unbranched, upright stems. Leaves crinkly, dark green, oblong, pinnately lobed, with toothed lobes. Flowers, April–July, arranged sparsely at top of each stem: two lipped and pink, the top lip with two teeth, calyx broad and hairless with 5 angles.

SIMILAR SPECIES The much rarer marsh lousewort *P. palustris* has many more flowers on each stem with 4 teeth on the upper lip and hairy calyxes.

USES/RECIPES The pleasant-tasting leaf can be eaten raw or cooked. Flowering tops make a very pretty addition to spring–summer dishes; flowering tops of similar species woolly lousewort *P. lantana* were lacto-fermented by Alaskan Inuit. Roots were eaten by Inuit of north Canada.

HAZARDS This plant is parasitic and will take up toxins from the roots of its host. Before eating any part of lousewort, ensure that there are no poisonous plants growing near by.

Veronica beccabunga
Brooklime

DISTRIBUTION Up to 845m. In England, widespread throughout; in Wales, widespread throughout, only less so Merioneth; in Scotland, widespread south of Highland Boundary Fault line (Stonehaven–Helensburgh) but north of the fault absent higher-altitude areas of Grampian Mountains, North West Highlands and North Highland, and sparse in Western Isles and Shetland but widespread in Orkney; in Ireland, widespread throughout, only less so Laois, Mayo and west Donegal; present Isle of Man and Channel Islands.

HABITAT Open areas on marshes, edges of ponds, streams and rivers and in damp woods.

DESCRIPTION Hairless perennial with upright stems reaching 30cm high; stems also creep and root along the ground. Leaves in opposite pairs, fleshy, short stalked, bluntly oval with fine toothed edges, up to 6cm long. Delicate flower stalks grow out of the leaf axils bearing many small, chalky blue flowers, each with 4 slightly pointed petals, May–September.

USES/RECIPES Leaves were once popular in salads as well as in spring juices, a health drink made from fresh leaves of brooklime and watercress. I find brooklime bitter without any redeeming features; I wonder whether at least some historic references to edible uses of this plant might in fact refer to **fool's watercress** *Apium nodiflorum*, which was previously also known as brooklime.

¹/₄ × life size

GERANIUM FAMILY
Geraniaceae

There are no poisonous wild plants in this family, but stork's-bill is the only one I find good to eat. Cut-leaved crane's-bill *Geranium dissectum* roots were roasted and eaten by aboriginal Tasmanians, who call it 'native carrot', but I have, so far, found them tough and with no great flavour.

Erodium cicutarium

Stork's-bill

DISTRIBUTION Up to 420m. In England, widespread, except at higher altitudes; in Wales, all coastal counties, a few low-lying sites inland; in Scotland, south of line Montrose–Isle of Eigg widespread in coastal regions; north of line more scattered, inland only around Moray Firth; in Ireland, in coastal regions of all coastal counties.

HABITAT Field edges, paths, meadows, pasture and other grassy areas; disturbed ground.

DESCRIPTION Annual/biennial with hairy, spreading stems; leaves feathery, leaflets deeply cut, arranged irregularly along leaf stalk. Pink flowers are about 1cm wide and the fruits noticeably long and beak shaped, as the name suggests.

SIMILAR SPECIES Sometimes known as hemlock stork's-bill due to the similarity of its leaves to those of **hemlock**. Hemlock leaf stalks are not hairy, and the whole plant has an unpleasant smell. Sticky stork's-bill *E. lebelii* and musk stork's-bill *E. moschatum* are both much less common with sticky leaves; musk stork's-bill also has a distinct musky smell.

USES/RECIPES A mild and pretty leaf but with a slightly coarse texture when raw. Use in salads with thick or oily dressing, or add to omelettes, meat stews or fatayer pies.

½ life size

GOOSEBERRY FAMILY
Grossulariaceae

Well-known plants such as blackcurrant and gooseberry, which are generally thought to occur only as escapes from cultivation (although some consider them to be native), are not discussed here and are in any case easily recognized by their fruit.

Ribes rubrum

Red Currant

⅔ × life size

DISTRIBUTION Up to 455m. In England and Wales, widespread throughout; in Scotland, mostly found throughout but more sparse west of Southern Uplands and northwards to Grampian Mountains and West and North Highlands with one locality on both Orkney and Barra; in Ireland, not native, found scattered throughout but cluster of sites to north in and around Sperrin Mountains; present Channel Islands and Isle of Man.

HABITAT Woods and hedges. Smaller-berried plants growing by woodland streams and in woodland fens may be native; most, however, are escapes from cultivation.

DESCRIPTION Leaves hairy and unscented, with cordate base. Flowers pale green, tinged with purple, on drooping racemes. Berries shiny, bright red.

SIMILAR SPECIES There are two other red-berried species, both with edible berries. Mountain currant *R. alpinum* has upright racemes; bracts below its flowers are all long; leaves have only three lobes; berries are bland and mealy; in Finland, used as a hedge plant. Downy currant *R. spicatum* racemes are upright at first then slightly drooping. Both plants are found on limestone; neither has a pronounced cordate leaf base.

USES/RECIPES

RED CURRANT JELLY: (follow basic jelly recipe on p.269) is good as it is, served with meat, or can be incorporated into other sauces, such as Elderberry game sauce (p.203) or the classic Cumberland sauce. For dessert, add the berries to summer fruit pies and jellies or cook them in a little sugar and serve with chocolate and rosemary sauce (white sauce, made with rosemary-infused milk, then as much cocoa as you dare and sugar to taste).

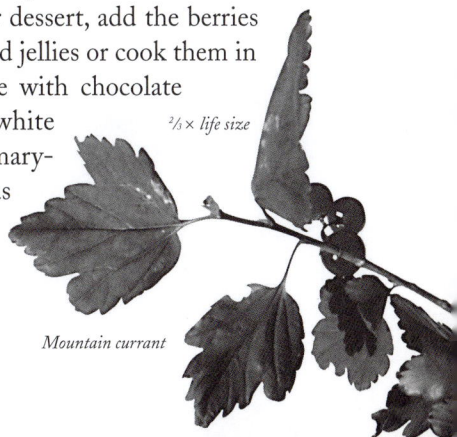

⅔ × life size

Mountain currant

GOOSEFOOT FAMILY
Chenopodiaceae

The Goosefoot family gets both its Latin and English names from the goosefoot shaped leaves of *Atriplex* and *Chenopodium* species (including fat hen, Good-King-Henry and the oraches): *Chenopodium* means 'goose foot', from the Greek *chen*, 'goose' and *podion*, 'little foot'. Aptly, some of these plants grow in fields where wild geese feed.

Seeds of fat hen and other *Chenopodium* species are similar to, but smaller than those of their cultivated South American cousin quinoa. Often grown as ground cover for pheasants, quinoa plants are almost indistinguishable from fat hen. Fat hen seeds were eaten in Europe until at least the time of the Vikings but wild species of this family are more usually gathered these days for their edible leaves; between them they provide wild greens, vegetables and salads all year round. Most of the greens can be used like a more familiar *Chenopodiaceae* species, spinach *Spinacea oleracea*. If you ever see a perennial spinach plant the resemblance is clear.

The chemistry of this family requires hot summers; these are plants of warm, temperate regions and many of them are halophytes – plants tolerant of salty soil. Growing on salt marshes, strand lines of beaches or otherwise close to salt water, they survive using an internal mechanism similar to modern desalination technology. The ideal *Chenopodiaceae* situations

are salty deserts or coasts, with lots of nitrates – a beach with lots of rotting seaweed is perfect. It's not surprising then that the majority of our coastal edible plants belong to this family.

GENERAL HAZARDS Fat hen and other **Chenopodium/Atriplex** species contain oxalic acid and should be eaten in moderation by anyone with kidney stones (the same is true of spinach). They also accumulate chemical contaminants from soil, so avoid gathering from contaminated land (see p.22). On land fertilised with nitrates these plants will have a high nitrate content. Occasional, moderate consumption as part of a balanced diet is no problem for adults but children are less able to metabolise nitrates. Goosefoots from this kind of ground should not be eaten in large quantities or too often by anyone and should never be eaten by children. Finally, young plants of the deadly **thorn-apple** *Datura stramonium* could be mistaken for **maple-leaved goosefoot** *Chenopodium hybridum*.

Atriplex hortensis

Garden Orache

DISTRIBUTION In British Isles, a casual in scattered localities: in England, in Suffolk, Norfolk, Somerset, Dorset, East Sussex, Lincolnshire, Humberside and Cheshire; present Guernsey and Isle of Man.

HABITAT Rubbish tips, waste ground and roadsides; persistent weed of gardens and allotments.

DESCRIPTION Tall, upright annual with slightly toothed leaves, most often with the purple-flushed variant. The seeds, with almost circular winged bracts, are distinctive.

NOTES Widely cultivated mid-sixteenth–eighteenth century; a red variety is still grown for ornament and increasingly as a salad vegetable. Surprisingly, it has not been successful as a naturalized, wild plant, particularly as it thrives in central and southern Europe; widely cultivated in central Europe – in Romania, for example, where it is used in soups.

USES/RECIPES As for other Chenopodium/Atriplex species. Use September leaves in autumnal game salad with hare or venison, dandelion and dressing made with walnut oil, red onion, game jus and elderberries [PB].

Atriplex prostrata

Spear-leaved Orache

DISTRIBUTION Most coastal areas of British Isles, but less widespread on the Scottish coast. Inland: in England, present throughout the south and Midlands but absent much of the north, Wales, Scotland and Ireland.

HABITAT Salt marshes, other wet or at least moist places either near sea or on neutral soil; due to salt gritting, near roads; a weed of cultivation inland.

DESCRIPTION Annual, usually upright, up to about 60cm high. Leaves with bases roughly at right angles to the stem and less mealy than common orache, frosted orache and fat hen.

SIMILAR SPECIES Common orache *A. patula* is found on cultivated ground and waste places. It is unlikely to occur on salt marsh or drift line of beach. It has mealy leaves with distinct, upwardly pointing lobes, forming a triangular base.

USES/RECIPES

WITH PORK CHOPS AND MUSTARD SAUCE: Dry fry pork chops standing up on their skin-sides on low heat for 30 minutes to render the fat and crisp up the skin, then fry on each side for 2 minutes each (for thicker chops finish in a hot oven for a further 3–5 minutes). For sauce, reduce some white wine vinegar to syrup, add white wine, reduce again by half, add a pinch of sugar, mustard powder and whipping cream. Thicken with a bit of butter. Serve chops and sauce with blanched orache leaves/tops [PW]. Larger leaves, blanched can be stuffed with well cooked rice, onion, garlic, herbs, butter or cheese. Fold leaf into little parcel, then place folded side down; serve cold or warmed in a hot oven for a minute or so [RL].

Beta vulgaris

Sea Beet

DISTRIBUTION Up to 300m. In England, coastal areas throughout, except parts East Sussex, Norfolk, Yorkshire and Tees Bay–Scottish Border; in Wales, coastal areas throughout; in Scotland, mostly Dumfries and Galloway, but few isolated localities in Clyde Isles, Ayrshire, Mid and South Ebudes, West Ross, Moray Firth and Western Isles; in Ireland, throughout, except parts Antrim, Wexford, Mayo and Sligo; present Isle of Man, Isles of Scilly, Channel Islands and Lundy.

HABITAT Upper part of beaches, sea walls and land within a few hundred yards of the coast; occasionally on roadsides inland.

DESCRIPTION Shrubby perennial with cordate lower leaves and diamond-shaped upper stem leaves. All leaves are glossy and fleshy with wavy edges. Stems are variably reddish purple; the redder plants showing their affinity to beetroot.

NOTES This widespread native coastal plant is the parent plant of root crops beetroot, sugar beet and manglewurzel. The wild plants themselves have quite substantial, sweet roots which were used as food by our ancestors; charred remains have been found at Mesolithic sites in Denmark. Plants with purple on their leaf stalks will also have purple in the roots; this trait has been concentrated by selective breeding to produce purple beetroot. The potential of the leaf and stalk have also been developed to produce the numerous varieties of chard.

USES/RECIPES This is a prince among wild greens, especially in spring when the leaves are bigger, lusher and easier to gather in quantity. It has been referred to as sea spinach and looks quite similar to some forms of spinach. However, it is superior in every way: the flavour is richer, the texture holds up much better on cooking, and it has higher nutrient levels. Bigger leaves should be stripped either side of the stalk; the stalk chopped and cooked separately; for smaller leaves remove just the part of stalk below where the leaf blade ends. Leaves can be blanched, boiled or steamed, or wilted in a little butter or oil. Serve blanched sea beet, buttered, as a base for fish or seafood, for example fillet of John Dory pan-fried, finished with cockles and chive butter sauce [PB]. In a warm salad with caramelized baby onions, caramelized apple and chestnuts, served with roast goose; wilted sea beet with confit of goose legs served with pistachio stuffing or with roast pheasant with chestnut and wild mushroom sauce [AN]. Chestnuts generally combine well with sea beet.

CREAMED SEA BEET: Shallots softened in butter with thyme and a little garlic. Add cream and reduce slightly then mix in blanched sea beet; serve with sea bass. Boil roots and use to make salads, for instance, with other ingredients such as anchovies, bacon, boiled eggs, prosciutto, pork, smoked fish, herring or walnuts [ST]. Spanish chef Rafael Lopez learnt the following recipe from his mother: flavour some olive oil with garlic by gently cooking some crushed garlic in it, then removing. Fry some bread in the oil, then break it down into crumbs, add more oil, a little paprika and a splash of vinegar. Blanch the sea beet, squeeze out liquid then toss it in this dressing before serving.

Chenopodium album

Fat Hen

DISTRIBUTION Most of British Isles, except in Scotland, the Highlands; in Ireland, patchy in west.

HABITAT Fertile, disturbed soil such as arable field margins, gardens, earthworks at civil-engineering sites, roadsides and waste ground; dung heaps. It tends to get a foothold before other colonizers of disturbed ground such as nettles; after a year or so nettles win the territory. A plant of sunny situations, I have yet to see it (or any *Chenopodiaceae* species) in a woodland location.

DESCRIPTION Upright and usually branched annual, generally 10cm–1m high but up to 2m. Leaves are quite variable, but more oval and less angular than other *Chenopodium* and *Atriplex* species; usually, but not always, toothed. They have a water-repellent white bloom that is especially obvious on young shoots and leaves. The bloom causes water to form tiny droplets, which roll off the leaves if disturbed.

NOTES Mr Figgis, a local Kent fruit farmer who grows mostly strawberries and no figs, invited me to harvest the fat hen growing on fallow land on his farm. It was a good site, as no nitrates had been applied since before the last crop of strawberries. Mr Figgis has a large seasonal workforce that stay on the farm in the summer months. Fat hen nearly always appears between his strawberry rows and needs regular weeding out, but one year the rows remained mysteriously clean for several weeks. Then at 5 a.m. one morning, he saw several of his workers, of Indian origin, scuttling around among the rows. When he asked what they were doing they sheepishly showed him the bundles of young fat hen plants they had been gathering. They recognized the plant because the similar but much larger giant goosefoot *C. giganteum* is widely grown and/or gathered for food in India. Where Mr Figgis saw a weed, they saw an abundance of free greens.

USES/RECIPES Leaves, whole young plants or tender tops of older plants are good in salads or cooked, in place of spinach or other greens: fat hen has a short cooking time, 3–4 minutes maximum; steam to retain its many nutrients, although it is tastier sautéd in foaming butter with salt, pepper and a little nutmeg. Also, as for other Chenopodium/ Atriplex species.

WARM SALAD WITH FAT HEN, CHICORY AND TOMATOES: Fry finely chopped shallots until beginning to brown then add a few ripe tomatoes. Cook for a few minutes then add some finely sliced white chicory. Just before serving stir in some fat hen leaves. As side veg, for example with roast chicken, blanche, squeeze and chop leaves; add a little butter and serve topped with lots of crispy shallot rings [PW]. The flowering tops can be harvested and used as you would broccoli. Pull the seeds with their seed cases from the plants by running your hands up the stalks. They can be used as they are, to add flavour and thicken soups. To obtain pure seed, spread them out and allow them to dry; then loosen the seed coating by rubbing them between your hands or grinding in a pestle and mortar then winnow (see **processing the grains**, p.324). Put the seeds through a kitchen mill or good-quality blender to reduce them to flour, or use them whole in breads, soups and casseroles.

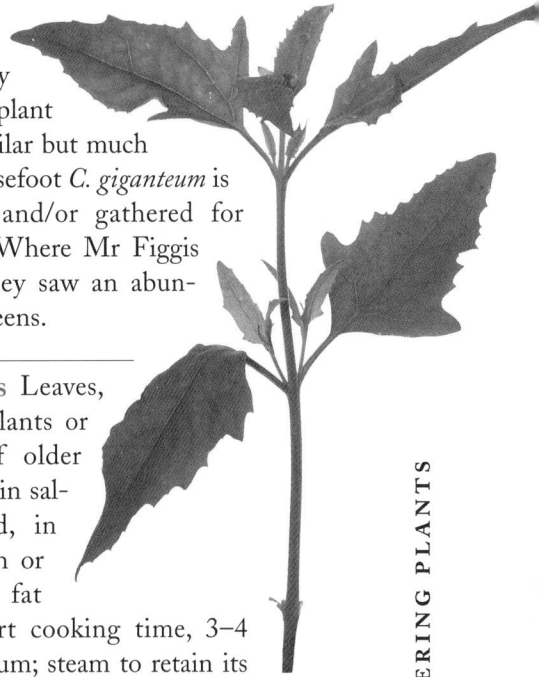

BENEFITS Leaves are high in magnesium, calcium, and sodium, as well as vitamins A and C.

HARVESTING NOTES Seedlings appear in May, and June is peak month for tender fat hen greens; the flowering and seed stages also provide good eating August–October. The growth season is probably restricted by the plant's sensitivity to frost.

Chenopodium bonus-henricus

Good-King-Henry

DISTRIBUTION Found in England, in Somerset, Gloucestershire, parts of Midlands, Norfolk, Lake District and Yorkshire, rare Newcastle–Edinburgh; found much of Welsh–English border and North Wales; mostly absent in Scotland; rare in Ireland.

HABITAT Disturbed fertile ground, usually near past or present human habitation; roadsides, waste ground and, occasionally, limestone grassland. In the Alps it tends to occur near snow patches, which, in summer, attract animals in search of water: the concentration of droppings makes the ground rich in nitrates. The same is true of ditches around historic

buildings, such as castles or Godstow Nunnery near Oxford, into which people once threw their sewage.

DESCRIPTION The only perennial goosefoot growing in the British Isles. Usually 30–50cm high but up to 80cm. The stems are often tinted red. Opposite leathery leaves are up to 10cm long and 8cm wide, larger than any other goosefoot; mealy when young, they are dark green, triangular and wavy edged.

NOTES Good-king-henry has been here since the time of the Romans, who probably introduced the plant, and was commonly cultivated at least until the beginning of the twentieth century. Native to snowy mountain areas of south and central Europe, it is strangely absent from British highlands. It persists as a wild plant but is in decline, having no cultivated population from which to seed.

USES/RECIPES As for other Chenopodium/ Atriplex species.
JAPANESE SPRING ROLLS: Blanche larger leaves to soften slightly then, midrib side up, fill with shredded spring onion, thin slivers of carrot, bean sprouts, soy sauce and pink ginger. Fold in the edges and roll leaves into little cylinders; serve with satay or chilli dipping sauce [JT].

Chenopodium polyspermum

Many-seeded Goosefoot

DISTRIBUTION In England, widespread south of Midlands; in Wales, sporadic along the coast, inland widespread only in Monmouthshire; in Scotland, only found in Fife, west of Glenrothes, and few other places in south; in Ireland, only few miles west of Newtownabbey on shores of Lough Neagh.

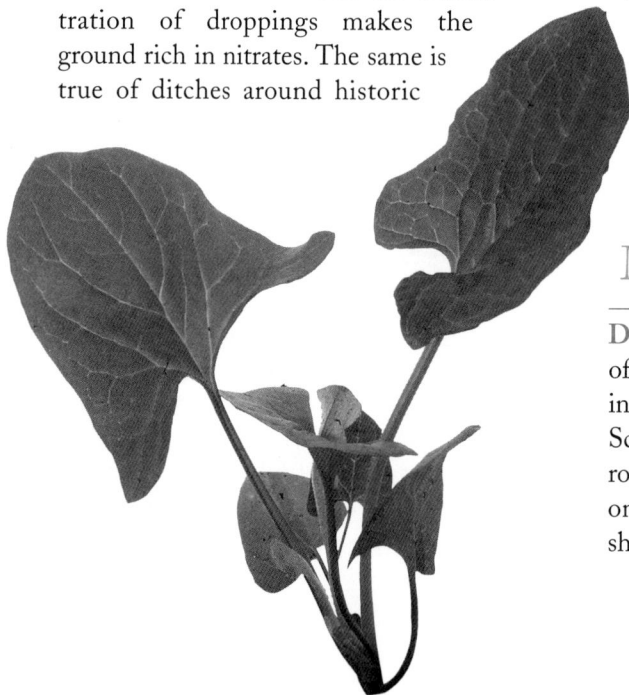

HABITAT Disturbed ground with fertile, light soils, mostly cultivated ground but also newly coppiced areas and dried-up ponds.

DESCRIPTION Annual, either upright or prostrate, stems square and often red; leaves oval and untoothed, glossy, sometimes slightly mealy on underside. Flowers yellow, July–October.

NOTES Known as 'sirken' or 'sirgen' in Turkey, where it is sold in bunches at markets and used in place of spinach.

USES/RECIPES As for other Chenopodium/Atriplex species. As a main meal, just before serving, fold leaves/tops into combination of boiled butter beans and sliced courgettes, cooked in garlic and butter; top each serving with a good tablespoon of goat's or cow's curd [JL].

SAG ALOO: roast some potatoes with tumeric and mustard seeds; blanche leaves/tender tops, squeeze dry then fold into potatoes just before serving with a little lemon juice and a grind of black pepper [JT].

Chenopodium rubrum

Red Goosefoot

DISTRIBUTION In England, widespread in most areas, except Somerset, Lake District and Durham; in Wales, rather rare South Wales, absent much North Wales; in Scotland, mostly absent; in Ireland, rather rare, absent Northern Ireland.

HABITAT Mostly farms, especially manure heaps or cattle fields; dried-up pond and reservoir margins; coastal areas flooded by spring tides.

DESCRIPTION Prostrate or upright annual, generally 10–50cm high, sometimes up to 90cm. Stems often red, especially when the plant is in flower. Diamond-shaped leaves are toothed, smooth and shiny – not at all mealy; often red tinged, particularly on underside. Red flowers appear in dense spikes.

USES/RECIPES This species can be slightly bitter so is less suited to being used on its own. Use with strong-flavoured or acid ingredients, for example in curry, sweet and sour dishes, with tomatoes, cheese or bacon.

FLOWERING PLANTS: DICOTYLEDONS

191

GOOSEFOOT FAMILY

Halimione portulacoides

Sea-purslane

DISTRIBUTION In England, along most of coast but absent much of Cornwall, Somerset and Middlesbrough–the Humber; in Wales, found on coast of North and South Wales, but not mid-Wales; in Scotland, absent; in Ireland, on east coast, south of Belfast.

HABITAT Salt marshes between high and low tidemarks, especially margins of creeks and drainage channels; sometimes on cliffs and rocks.

DESCRIPTION Bushy perennial, shrublike plant that forms extended mats, with small, elliptical, fleshy greyish-green leaves in opposite pairs on woody stems. Tiny, yellowish flowers grow on 5cm spray on branch ends. The seeds, encased in angular, fleshy bracteoles, stay on the plant well into winter.

SIMILAR SPECIES Pendunculate sea-purslane *H. pendunculata* is an annual with alternate leaves. It is extremely rare; found only in Essex.

NOTES This edible salt-marsh plant is both abundantly present and constantly available. At its flowering stage it is easy to see the family resemblance with other goosefoots. If you have ever been to a salt-marsh area you will certainly have seen it growing in colonies near the shore, along the backs of salt-water creeks and across land covered by tidal water. The name

derives from the similarity in shape and succulence of the leaves to salad plant **purslane**.

USES/RECIPES Apart from a couple of centimetres' new stem growth that occurs most prolifically in spring, most of the leaves need picking off the stem before using – a bit fiddly but worth every minute. The leaves add natural salt to any dish and make a flavoursome and colourful garnish to any kind of seafood/fish recipe: when cooked, they turn a glorious bright green. Also good complement for lamb, especially salt-marsh lamb (which may even have grazed on the leaves). Cook with roast potatoes, as you would thyme or other herbs, or mix in with crushed new potatoes. It makes great tapenade, with lemon zest, olive oil and garlic, which can be served as a snack or nibble on its own, or mixed into couscous with sun-dried tomatoes, olives and red onion, and served with chicken or fish. Marinate leaves in olive oil, fresh lemon juice, **wild fennel** fronds and capers. Quickly fry this mixture just before serving with mackerel or herring. This also works well with smoked fish and can even be used to dress other wild leaves for a fresh, zingy salad [BW].

HARVESTING NOTES Too much time under water produces thin, tough leaves; the best are found on higher ground. Bunch together the tops of a number of plants then cut the top 10cm of the bunch using a long, sharp knife – a bread knife is good. Further down, the woody stems become thicker and the leaves more sparse.

ECOLOGICAL CONSIDERATIONS The seed of sea-purslane forms an important element of the winter diet of rare finches, such as twite and corn bunting, so don't gather too much from one place during the winter months. Small-scale or intermittent harvesting does no harm; in fact the plants seem to flourish as a result, as garden shrubs do after pruning. However, they eventually die when heavily grazed by livestock. Our commercial harvesting of these plants is rotated around several sites.

Salicornia species
Marsh Samphire/ Glasswort

DISTRIBUTION Up to 300m. Coastal areas throughout British Isles: in England, except parts of Devon and Cornwall, East Sussex, east Kent, Yorkshire and Cumberland; in Wales, except Cardiganshire and Galmorgan; in Scotland, less frequent, absent much Wigtownshire, Ayrshire, West Ross, west Sutherland, Caithness in west and north, and east Sutherland, Banffshire, Aberdeen, Kincardineshire and Berwickshire to east; in Ireland, less abundant but present in every coastal county, most concentrated in Down, north Kerry and Cork; present Isle of Man and Channel Islands.

HABITAT Salt marshes, upper and lower (depending on the species).

²/₃ × life size

DESCRIPTION Samphire is largely stem for most of its growing period; stems are branched and noticeably segmented, with tiny lobes instead of leaves at the base of each segment. Tiny yellow flowers appear between lobes and stem on upper branches.

NOTES Marsh samphire can be any one of several similar edible *Salicornia* species, each with a distinct ecological niche in the salt marsh. In Norfolk it has been gathered for food for centuries. When rock samphire *Crithmum maritimum* was at the height of its popularity,

this was one of many plants used as a substitute, which is how it came to be known as marsh samphire (the name glasswort dates back to when it was used to obtain soda ash for making glass and soap). Daisy-family plant golden samphire *Inula crithmoides* was used in similar ways and derives its English and Latin names from this connection with rock samphire. The three plants are unrelated, but each has fleshy succulent leaves and/or stems.

USES/RECIPES Young marsh samphire is tender throughout, but the lower parts of the stems develop a woody heart a few weeks into the season. True seasonal eating means using things in their many phases and forms; most people only use the un-woody tips, but this a waste: older stems can be eaten by dragging the flesh off with your teeth. By the end of September the stems become gritty because of numerous tiny seeds; this is where I draw the line. Samphire is cooked by boiling in unsalted water for 30 seconds, if you like it crunchy, or 3 minutes until soft.

SERVING SUGGESTIONS With pasta with just a little wild fennel, olive oil and Parmesan. In a light butter sauce with cockles: the colours of the dish are very alluring, with the green of the samphire contrasting with the yellow sauce and orange of the cockles. A similar effect is made serving samphire with prawns [PB]. With wild salmon, sea trout or wild brown trout, lightly poached in water acidulated with a little white wine and white wine vinegar, and flavoured with onion, bay leaf and celery; add fish then bring to simmer and take off heat. Let liquid cool down, salt, remove skin and serve on a bed of crunchy buttered samphire, pouring the stock over the fish [PW].

HAZARDS Foraging is a great way of connecting to the landscape, but you could get more connected than you wish while gathering samphire; in other words, stuck in the mud. Collecting samphire barefoot might be easier; mud creates much less suction on bare skin but there is a risk of injury from submerged objects. Another solution is to wear snow-shoes, which spread your weight to stop you sinking. In places such as creeks, where the water comes in substantially higher than the mud, getting stuck as the tide comes in could be life threatening. Avoid gathering alone or standing on bare mud in such places; instead, keep to areas where there is at least some vegetation.

HARVESTING NOTES The little green shoots begin to emerge from the mud of salt marshes in May. It takes longest to gather at this stage, but the tenderness of the shoots makes it worth the effort. Samphire is best harvested using scissors. It will store well if kept cool and dry, but don't leave it in unsalted water or in a warm place as it will quickly deteriorate.

ECOLOGICAL CONSIDERATIONS Samphire, followed by sea-blite and sea-purslane, is one of the first plants to colonize salt marshes. Cutting it does no harm as the stems continue to grow and eventually flower and go to seed. On the other hand, pulling it up is destructive and also senseless, as it still needs cutting before use.

Suaeda maritima

Annual Sea-blite

DISTRIBUTION Round much of coastal British Isles except in England, Middlesbrough–Humber, north Cornwall; in Wales, Aberystwyth–Cardigan; in Scotland, the Highlands, Ayr–Luce Bay (Bay of Herbs); in Ireland, Arklow down to Rosslare.

HABITAT Middle and lower parts of salt marshes.

DESCRIPTION Annual sea-blite has soft, thin, half-round leaves that look a bit like pine needles; they grow to about 3cm, are slightly greyish green, becoming reddish/purplish from late summer. They are soft and silky to the touch, making them a pleasure to pick. Young stems are soft but soon become woody. Plants about 30cm high.

NOTES Annual sea-blite *Suaeda maritima* is common and similar to the Italian monk's beard *Salsola soda*, known in Italy as Barba di Frate and used as a serving bed for fish, or chopped finely to finish soups or in pasta sauces. Annual sea-blite can be used in similar ways, as can the perennial shrubby sea-blite *Suaeda vera*, which is restricted to East Anglia. Our only *Salsola* species is prickly saltwort *Salsola kali*, which is one of the plants known elsewhere as tumbleweed. This plant is not really edible unless you can tolerate a mouthful of prickles but has variants that grow elsewhere – and occasionally in the British Isles as a result of seed contamination – that are prickle free and reportedly good to eat.

USES/RECIPES Sea-blite is delicious with little embellishment, and generally it can be used in place of samphire. Use leaves and stems in salads or steam the young plants whole and serve with fish or meat; it is great with lamb and mutton. Chop older plants and fry with meat or add to simple pasta dishes (for recipe ideas, see pp.15–16) such as tagliatelle tossed in olive oil and garlic garnished with sea-blite and morels [PB].
SPAGHETTI VONGOLE: Sea-blite with cockles, white wine, olive oil, garlic – no need for any extra salt [MH].

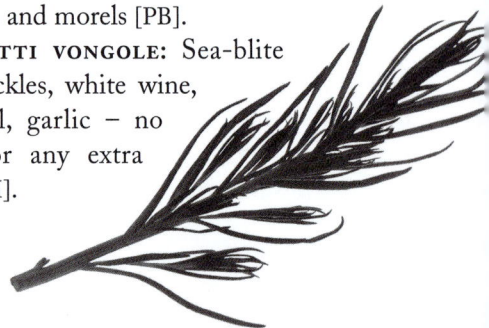

HEATHER FAMILY
Ericaceae

Heather-family species grow predominantly on acid soil, which is not typical of my east-Kent foraging ground, most of which is alkaline, chalk soil. Consequently they don't play much of a part of our local foraging repertoire: although there are blaeberries in Kent, in acid woodland around Sevenoaks for example, they generally don't fruit well. My best experiences of foraging berries of these plants have been in northern England, Scotland and Finland in the acid woodland and moorland more typical of these regions.

Often the plants carpet the ground on moors or beneath trees in woodland and forest; the abundance of wild fruit they produce rivals the output of energy-intensive commercial fruit-growing enterprises. In the British Isles, much of this bounty goes unharvested, but in Finland an estimated 50 million kg of wild berries (including non-*Ericaceae* species such as cloudberries and sea-buckthorn) is collected annually.

GENERAL HARVESTING If you live in an area plentiful with bilberries or cowberries, it is worth investing in a berry comb/rake, a device that enables you to collect quickly, by dragging all the berries of several branches at once. If you collect from bushes heavily laden with berries, it is possible to harvest large amounts very quickly; however, the quicker you pick the more likely you are to remove leaves at the same time.

REMOVING LEAVES FROM BERRIES *Method 1* At an angle of about 45 degrees, prop a screen of wire mesh at a gauge slightly larger than the diameter of the berries. Pour berries down the screen; they fall through the mesh and most of the leaves stay on top. *Method 2* Take a length of drain-pipe and make a hole about half-way down, just the right size to attach at a slight upward angle a 50cm length of pipe, of a diameter slightly smaller than the hose of your vacuum cleaner. Clamp the pipe to the edge of a table with the lower end in a bucket. Attach a vacuum-cleaner pipe to the spur and pour the berries into it through a hopper (a wide-mouthed funnel) in a steady stream. The vacuum cleaner sucks out all the leaves while the berries fall into the bucket.

Arbutus unedo

Strawberry tree

DISTRIBUTION Native in southwest Ireland, where there is a rather mild and wet climate unlike anywhere else in the British Isles. A rare tree these days, having been depleted by the use of its wood for charcoal in past centuries. In mainland Britain, it has a scattered presence as a garden escape, particularly in coastal areas of Devon, Dorset and Somerset in England and including a colony in Gt Orme, South Wales.

HABITAT Oak woods, on rocky terrain.

DESCRIPTION A small tree or shrub, up to 12m high. Leaves elliptical, shiny dark green, pointed and toothed; flowers in panicles, cream coloured and bell shaped, hanging down. The fruits are 1.5–2cm across, brownish red and covered in gritty warts. The tree is remarkable in that flowers and ripe fruit are present on the tree at the same time; the fruit is formed from the previous year's flowers.

NOTES Strawberry tree grows wild in much of Europe and is even cultivated in the south of France. The fruits, known as arbutus berries, are used to make alcoholic drinks and confectionery.

USES/RECIPES Fruit has a tough and somewhat gritty skin that taints the flavour a little, as it is slightly bitter. It is possible to scoop out the flesh, but this is fiddly. Alternatively, break up the fruit gently, then thin the pulp with a little water and pass through a fine sieve. This removes most of the gritty skin and what's left can be used to make a fruit syrup for pouring over ice cream. The berries are mostly used to make jam, however, since the addition of sugar masks the bitterness; this obscures the rather delicate flavour, something like guava or mango. Leaves and stems are used in Spain to harden and thereby preserve olives.

BENEFITS Berries are a good source of niacin, vitamin C and beta-carotene.

Vaccinium myrtillus

Bilberry/Blaeberry/ Whortleberry

DISTRIBUTION Up to 1300m. In England, almost entirely absent between line Flamborough Head–Severn Estuary and line Severn Estuary–Thames Estuary; present in Sussex, Surrey and west Kent, common in south Hampshire, Dorset, Devon and Cornwall, widespread in north except Tees Bay–Vale of York and on Cheshire and Lancashire plains;

in Wales and in Scotland, widespread throughout; in Ireland, widespread but absent in patches of Central Lowlands and other low-lying areas; present Isle of Man.

HABITAT Upland heaths and moors, peat bogs, pine, birch and oak woodland on well-drained or dry acid soil.

DESCRIPTION Native, deciduous, hairless shrub, short, reaching max. 60cm high. Stems upright, green and square; leaves alternate, oval and pointed, bright green, finely toothed. Flowers, April–June, greenish pink, bell shaped. Berries dark blue with violet bloom, 7–10mm wide; end of each one has a distinctive circle with a dot in the middle; ripe August–September.

SIMILAR SPECIES Bog bilberry *V. uliginosum* is taller, up to 1m high, with rounded, brown stems, white/pink flowers and untoothed, bluish-green leaves, with rounded ends and netted veins; berries lighter in colour, with clear juice and an irregular crown of sepals. They are also very good to eat, less sweet and sharper than ordinary bilberries.

NOTES These delicious wild berries are now largely overlooked, though in the past they were an important part of the rural economy and food culture in many areas of the British

Bog bilberry: 2 × life size

Isles. In Surrey, for example, many villages relied on an annual income from bilberries (known as whorts or hurts), gathered from the commons and sent up to London markets. In Ireland, a special day, Fraughan Sunday (the Sunday closest to 1 August), is reserved for gathering them.

USES/RECIPES (both species) **IRISH FRAUGHAN SUNDAY CAKE WITH FRAUGHAN CREAM:** *For the cake:* 170g granulated or caster sugar, 170g butter, 2 eggs, beaten, 225g self-raising flour, 3 tbsp milk, 110g bilberries, Combine sugar and butter, then gradually fold in eggs; sieve in flour a little at a time, folding it in as you do. Then fold in milk and carefully add bilberries, mixing gently until evenly distributed. Place in a buttered 18cm cake tin (a nice deep one) and cook for an hour in an oven pre-heated to 180°C. Leave to cool on a wire rack for at least an hour. *For the Fraughan cream:* Whip 175ml whipping cream and half a tablespoon of icing sugar until stiff, then add 50g pulped bilberries. Serve cake and cream together.

Mark Hix makes a spectacular Dorset bilberry trifle, incorporating a bilberry sponge, bilberry jelly and bilberry, white wine and cream topping. The only part of the trifle that doesn't have bilberries in it is the custard! Perhaps the best of all ways to eat the wild berries, though, is to gorge on them raw and in situ. As the father of my Norwegian friend Kristin Olsen used to say, 'Dessert is in the forest!'.

BENEFITS This species contains higher levels of anthocyanins than blueberries and other *Vaccinium* species. Anthocyanins are blue pigments found in the skin of various fruit. They

are powerful antioxidants, which help protect skin against harmful effects of UV light and also help rebuild capillaries walls. Anthocyanins alleviate conditions where swelling is caused by fluid retention due to weak capillary walls.

HAZARDS Symptoms of intoxication occasionally reported after eating bog bilberries may be due to the fungus *Sclerotina megalospora* that sometimes occurs on the berries.

Vaccinium oxycoccos

Cranberry

DISTRIBUTION Up to 760m. In England, scarce in south and east, with isolated locations on Exmoor, Dartmoor, Bodmin Moor, South Downs, Norfolk and Lincolnshire, widespread in higher-altitude areas from Peak District north; in Wales, common in hilly and mountainous areas; in Scotland, widespread south but decreases northwards with scattered locations in Grampian Mountains; in Ireland, scattered locations throughout, with a cluster of sites in north Cuilcagh–Antrim mountains and more common in parts of Central Lowlands; present Isle of Man.

HABITAT Blanket bogs and wet heaths, on top of deep, spongy peat, often among heather, sphagnum moss and cotton grass, with bog asphodel, round-leaved sundew or crowberry.

DESCRIPTION Low-growing evergreen shrub, reaching up to 30cm high, with thread-like creeping stems. Not a typical shrub – usually occurs intermingled and entwined with moss and would go unnoticed if not for the berries or flowers. Cranberries sit on top of the moss, as if the moss itself had produced them, often partly veiled by heather or other vegetation. Younger berries are white with masses of

red dots, as if spray painted. Fully or over ripe berries are deep red, like large drops of blood. Closer inspection reveals nearby sprigs of light green, thyme-like leaves (widely spaced, alternate, oval and pointed), poking out of the moss. Each berry can be traced back to one of these sprigs, attached by a tiny, tough, brown twiggy thread. The flowers are also eye catching, with folded-back pink petals and bunched yellow stamens protruding boldly.

SIMILAR SPECIES Small cranberry *V. microcarpum* is similar, but with slightly hairy flowering stalks and even smaller leaves. It is mostly found in the Highlands of Scotland, outside the range of cranberry. Both kinds are good to eat.

NOTES Cranberries are much less common than they once were, due to loss of the blanket-bog habitat that they prefer. However, great quantities were at one time harvested from Lincolnshire, Norfolk and Longtown in Cumbria. Like bilberries, they were sold at market, providing an important annual income to the gatherers. Many of the bogs from which they were harvested were drained and enclosed in the eighteenth and nineteenth centuries, but as a result of ongoing habitat-restoration projects, in Ireland at least, cranberries are beginning to recolonize.

USES/RECIPES Cranberries will last for a long time after harvesting and, like cowberries, will preserve other fruit that is stored

with them. They also share a common use as an accompaniment to meat. Serve crème brûlée with poached cranberries; poach the cranberries in syrup made with sugar, water and fresh lemon juice, with a little Irish whiskey added towards the end [PW]. The flavours of cranberry and rosehip combine well in a sorbet [AN].

BENEFITS High in vitamin C, also contain the preservative benzoic acid. Cranberries are also said to stimulate bile and prevent diarrhoea.

Vaccinium vitis-idaea

Cowberry

DISTRIBUTION At 30–1095m. In England, mostly in higher-altitude areas, such as Peak District, Pennines, Cleveland and Cheviot Hills and Lake District, also a few places in Somerset, Devon, Berkshire and Surrey; in Wales, high-altitude areas, such as Black Mountains, Brecon Beacons, Cambrian Mountains and Snowdonia; in Scotland, widespread, including Northern Isles and parts of Western Isles, but absent low-lying areas such as Central and eastern Coastal Lowlands; in Ireland, found mostly in upland areas in north and elsewhere only in Wicklow Mountains in the east and Partry and Maumturk mountains in west; present Isle of Man.

HABITAT Peaty heaths, moorland and drier parts of blanket bogs; in oak, birch and especially pine woods.

DESCRIPTION Native, prostrate, evergreen shrub, with dark green, shiny oval–obovate leaves, broadest in the middle, with edges rolled under and tiny black spots on the underside. Cowberries are bright red with a protruding calyx like an apple, which soon falls off.

SIMILAR SPECIES The rather dry and bland fruit of bearberry *Arctostaphylos uva-ursi* resembles cowberries but has dimples at its ends and no calyx; leaves are broadest at the ends with margins not rolled under.

USES/RECIPES Cowberries contain more sugar than blaeberries, but seem less sweet because they are also slightly bitter; once harvested they last indefinitely, since they contain their own preservative. Use for preserving other fruit, by placing both with water in sealed jars. Cowberries are mostly used to accompany meat. In Sweden, where they are called lingonberries, they are mostly used in simple sauces made with either berries or jelly and meat juices combined with butter and cream/soured cream; these are served with Swedish meat balls, salmon or venison. Innovative Swedish chef Gustav Ottoberg makes a spectacular dessert using malt and lingonberries. A caramel, made with malt, crème fraîche and buttermilk, is served with lingonberry ice cream, malt and lingonberry cake and lingonberry liquor, frozen with nitrogen. Norwegians call cowberries '*tyttebaer*' and simply heat them with sugar before serving with venison, moose or beef. In Finland they are served with liver (see recipe on p.266 for meadowsweet leaves). Cowberries also make good jam and jelly, for use in pancakes, sponge cakes, semolina and whatever else you do with jam. Because of their high pectin content, not much sugar is needed for the jelly.

HEMP FAMILY
Cannabaceae

Humulus lupulus

Hop

DISTRIBUTION In England and Wales, widespread, except high-altitude areas, such as Pennines, Cumbrian and Cambrian mountains, Snowdon and Bodmin Moor; in Scotland, scarce, but more widespread in Lothian and coastal Galloway; in Ireland, scarce and sporadic; present Channel Islands, Isle of Man and Isles of Scilly.

HABITAT Hedgerows, woodland edges, roadsides, scrambling over fences and other vegetation, including trees and shrubs.

DESCRIPTION Native scrambling vine, often also found as an escape from cultivation. Three-lobed palmate leaves, up to 15cm wide, with long stalks and toothed edges like nettles; young growth has spearhead-shaped tips, the as yet unopened buds of leaves. From July onwards, the plants may be detected by the presence of female catkins, commonly known as hops and often used to decorate pubs.

USES/RECIPES Young shoots should be cooked for no more than a minute in water. Serve with hollandaise and a wedge of lemon or dipped in balsamic reduction (balsamic vinegar boiled down to syrup-like consistency) then, like soldiers, into the yolk of a soft-boiled duck egg.

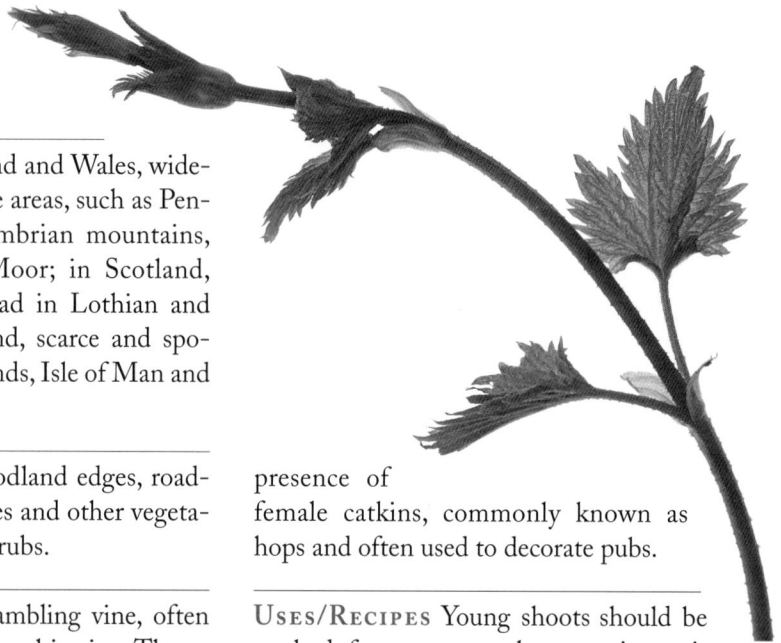

HONEYSUCKLE FAMILY
Caprifoliaceae

Lonicera periclymenum

Honeysuckle

DISTRIBUTION Up to 610m. In British Isles, widespread throughout except in England, absent parts of Fens; in Scotland, absent areas of Caithness, Isle of Lewis, Grampian Mountains and North West Highlands; in Ireland, absent areas of Mayo; present Channel Islands, Isle of Man and Isles of Scilly. Introduced into areas of Orkney.

HABITAT Woods, hedgerows and scrub.

DESCRIPTION Climbing perennial, found up to 6m high. Leaves entire, opposite, oval–elliptical, greyish green. Flowers up to 12 per head, all growing out from a central point, trumpet shaped with two lips, orangey pink with protruding stamens; with a strong, sweet fragrance. Berries bright red in a tight cluster.

NOTES The name of this plant probably refers to the nectar being sucked from the base of the flowers.

USES/RECIPES Eat flowers from the bush or use in salads or as a garnish for puddings, especially summery ones like ice cream or chilled fruit soups. Berries are edible in small quantities but are rather lacking in flavour.

BENEFITS Flowers are said to alleviate asthma and ease coughs.

½ × life size

HAZARDS Berries are poisonous if eaten in large amounts, due to the presence of saponins.

Sambucus nigra

Elder

DISTRIBUTION Up to 470m. Found pretty much throughout the British Isles but absent: in England, from few places in Lake District and Durham; in Scotland, most inland areas of Highlands and large part Outer Hebrides and Shetlands; in Ireland, parts of Galway, Mayo and Donegal.

HABITAT On fertile ground in woodland, fields, hedges, waste ground and roadsides.

DESCRIPTION Native deciduous shrub or tree.

Elder bark is greyish brown and corky but often covered with a green algae. Twigs are pithy inside. Leaves have 5–7 oval/elliptical leaflets, which are pointed and toothed; they have an unpleasant smell. Flowers, creamy-white, in flat-topped umbels, sometimes up to 24cm wide, appear May–early July; by September they have become great clusters of deep purple berries (green when unripe) 4–6mm diameter.

SIMILAR SPECIES Wayfaring tree *Viburnum lantana* and rowan *Sorbus aucuparia* also have white or cream umbels. Wayfaring tree flowers earlier and from a distance used to catch me out every year! However, the scent of elderflowers is very distinctive. Rowan leaves have 5–7 pairs of leaflets, which are longer and thinner than elder; wayfaring tree has rough, oval, greyish leaves. Rowan berries are bright orange. Wayfaring tree has black berries that are dull and waxy and in much smaller clusters than elder; elderberries are shiny with bunch stems distinctively pinkish purple.

USES/RECIPES The queen of summer drinks is elderflower cordial, the basis for elderflower sorbet or ice cream. The best cordial is made by using flowers with lots of pollen (the cream-coloured dust that shakes off when you pick them) and by not heating them too much.

ELDERFLOWER CORDIAL: Dissolve 1.5kg sugar in 1 litre hot water and cool to blood temperature (cool enough to dip a finger in), then add 20 flowers, with most of the stalks removed, 75g citric acid, the zest of two unwaxed lemons and the lemons themselves, halved, and leave for 24 hours. Strain, bottle and

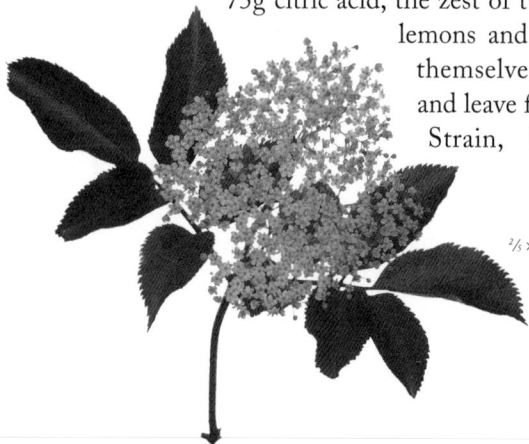

²/₃ × life size

chill in a refrigerator (or freeze if you have made a lot). Sterilizing the bottles is pointless as the flowers are full of wild yeasts. The cordial makes a refreshing summer dessert jelly (make up cordial to desired strength, warm slightly then add 5 leaves gelatine/litre liquid and then drop a few loose flowers into the jelly as it begins to cool).

¼ × life size

GOOSEBERRIES AND ELDERFLOWERS: Either cook them with cordial, or better still, shake in some flowers as you finish cooking them in sugar and honey. Serve with elderflower jelly.

ELDERFLOWER FRITTERS: Dip umbels in batter and deep fry for just a moment, serving with a dusting of icing sugar.

ELDERFLOWER CUSTARD: Dip whole umbels into egg custard for a minute just before serving.

Elderflowers were formerly used in combination with white meats, in stews or in sauces served with meat; they were dried to allow for year-round use. To do this, shake flower heads (still attached to tree) into a paper bag or a pillowcase – thus collecting only loose flowers and leaving the ovaries to mature into berries. Leave in a warm, dark place to dry. The dried flowers can also be rubbed into belly of pork before long, slow cooking or used to marinade the meat overnight before cooking. They add a delicate, aromatic flavour that beautifully complements the sweetness of the pork. You can also store apples or potatoes with the dried flowers – after a few days they begin to take up the flavour.

Extract the juice from berries, by crushing then boiling and passing through a jelly bag or, better still, use a wine press. The juice can be made into syrup, by dissolving 150g sugar per 100ml juice, and the syrup used for sorbets or dessert sauces. Juice can also be used for savoury sauces or to make what I consider the best of all fruit vinegars. The flavour of elderberries, which is unimpressive on its own, is somehow greatly enhanced by the presence of acid ingredients such as vinegar, wine or lemon juice.

ELDERBERRY GAME SAUCE: Sprinkle half a tablespoon of flour into the pan in which your meat has cooked, stir over medium heat for about a minute, add a glass of red wine, half a teaspoon of red currant jelly and 500ml chicken (or game) stock. Reduce by half then strain and add 100g elderberries or two tablespoons of elderberry juice [MH].

ELDERBERRY VINEGAR (and other fruit vinegars): Forager-herbalist Mandy Oliver allows 500ml white vinegar for 350g fruit. Add the vinegar to the fruit, leave covered for 3-5 days, stirring occasionally, then strain off the liquid. Add 350g sugar per 260ml liquid, boil for 10 minutes, then bottle. Mandy regards it as a better alternative to balsamic vinegar, and uses it in stews, tomato-based sauces and as a dip with olive oil and fresh bread. She also recommends elderberry vinegar as a winter tonic when coughs, colds and flu are around.

BENEFITS Flowers contain flavonoids, including rutin, as well as sterols, triterpenes and phenolic acids. Berries contain flavonoids, anthocyanins (see **bilberry**) and vitamins A and C.

HAZARDS Leaves and twigs contain toxic levels of cyanogenic glycosides.

HARVESTING NOTES The elder is a good tree for novice foragers. It has highly visible and quite distinctive flowers and berries (to be quite sure, see similar species, p.202). The green algae covering the bark flags up the bare tree in winter; this makes it easy to spot and leads you to another harvest: Judas ear fungus *Auricularia auricula-judae*, to which the elder plays host. This parasitic species can be found year round: either dried and shrivelled during dry weather or in full-blown jellied strangeness after rain.

Viburnum opulus

Guelder Rose

DISTRIBUTION Up to 400m. In England, found in most areas but absent west Cornwall, parts of Cambridgeshire, Humberside; in Wales, found in most areas but largely absent North Wales; in Scotland, found areas of east Dumfries and Galloway, much of Central, Fife, south Tayside, north Strathclyde, Skye, Mull and scattered Highlands areas; in Ireland, fairly widespread but absent most coastal areas except northeast.

HABITAT Scrub, woodland and hedgerows; planted in parks and gardens; on neutral and calcareous soils.

DESCRIPTION Deciduous shrub, up to 4m high. Palmate leaves. White flowers form clusters of a few larger (5–10mm wide) infertile flowers on the outside and many smaller fertile flowers (4–7mm wide) on the inside. Berries bright red.

USES/RECIPES Berries have a high pectin content and make good jams and jellies, especially useful with fruit with low pectin content. The flavour is similar to cranberry, but more rich and hearty, with a touch of bitterness. This is another tart red berry, along with cranberry, cowberry and red currant, which can be used to accompany meats. Like cranberry and cowberry it contains its own preservative; guelder-rose jam or jelly will last indefinitely. The downside is the fruit's characteristic smell of wet dog, which progresses to a blue-cheese aroma in jam that has sat for a couple of months. To prevent this, add lemon or orange zest when cooking the berries.

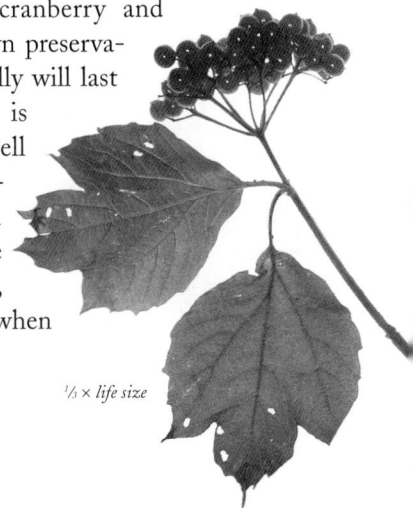

⅓ × life size

LIME FAMILY
Tiliaceae

Tilia cordata

Pry/Small-leaved Lime

¾ × life size

DISTRIBUTION Up to 600m. Present, although not common, in much of England, scarce or absent in Fens, Northamptonshire, Kent, Berkshire, north Hampshire, south Wiltshire, south Somerset, Devon and Cornwall; in Wales, common most counties except Anglesey, Caernarvonshire, Merioneth, Pembrokeshire and Carmarthenshire; in Scotland, absent north of Glen Mor, scarce elsewhere; in Ireland, mostly in the north; present on Channel Islands.

HABITAT A tree of ancient woodland, except where planted.

DESCRIPTION A tall, deciduous tree, up to 30m high. Young trees have smooth grey bark; this later develops many brown cracks. Leaves are virtually hairless, up to 8cm wide, thick and heart shaped with a pointed tip and finely toothed edges, translucent when young. The flowers are pale yellow with a long, papery bract beneath them, upright, in loose clusters. The fruits are woody, with 5 angles and hairy. In summer, the aphids that inhabit the leaves produce a sticky sap.

SIMILAR SPECIES Large lime *T. platyphyllos*, found in rocky woodland is taller, up to 40m high. Leaves up to 15cm wide, thinner with short hairs above and tufts of hairs beneath and longer than their stalks. Flower clusters hang down. Common lime *T. × europaea*, a hybrid of the other two limes, is commonly planted in parks and gardens. Leaves are smooth on top and only slightly hairy below.

USES/RECIPES (For all three limes.) The paler, young leaves have a slightly gelatinous, cooling texture and a mild flavour. Use in spring salads or fill with savoury stuffings, vine leaf style. Older, darker leaves make excellent greens. Lime or linden blossom can be dried for use as a tea that is used as herbal medicine: it is mildly sedative and a decongestant. The flavour is rather subtle but pleasant. Gather the blossoms as soon as they open. They can be used fresh or laid out on a cloth to dry in the sun and stored for later use.

MALLOW FAMILY
Malvaceae

Mallows are found on all continents; their name is given to the marshmallow sweet that was originally made using an extract from the root of marsh-mallow *Althaea officinalis*. The mucilage that was its main component is found in the roots, leaves and stems of all mallow species and easily extracted by boiling in a little water. Wild-food educator John Kallas uses it to make meringues, with a little egg white just to get them started.

A Turkish chef told me that wilted mallow leaf and scrambled egg is a favourite breakfast in Turkey. He, his mother and his brothers used to drive around Kent when he was a teenager, collecting huge bagfuls to freeze as a ready supply of breakfast ingredients for the whole year!

Malva sylvestris

Common Mallow

DISTRIBUTION Up to 300m. In England and Wales, widespread except at higher altitudes; in Scotland, scarce north of Glen Mor, but present in the south around southern area of Moray Firth and in Central and eastern Coastal Lowlands; in Ireland, in most counties but more abundant east coast and south of central lowlands, absent much of Connaught; present Channel Islands, Isle of Man, Isles of Scilly and Lundy.

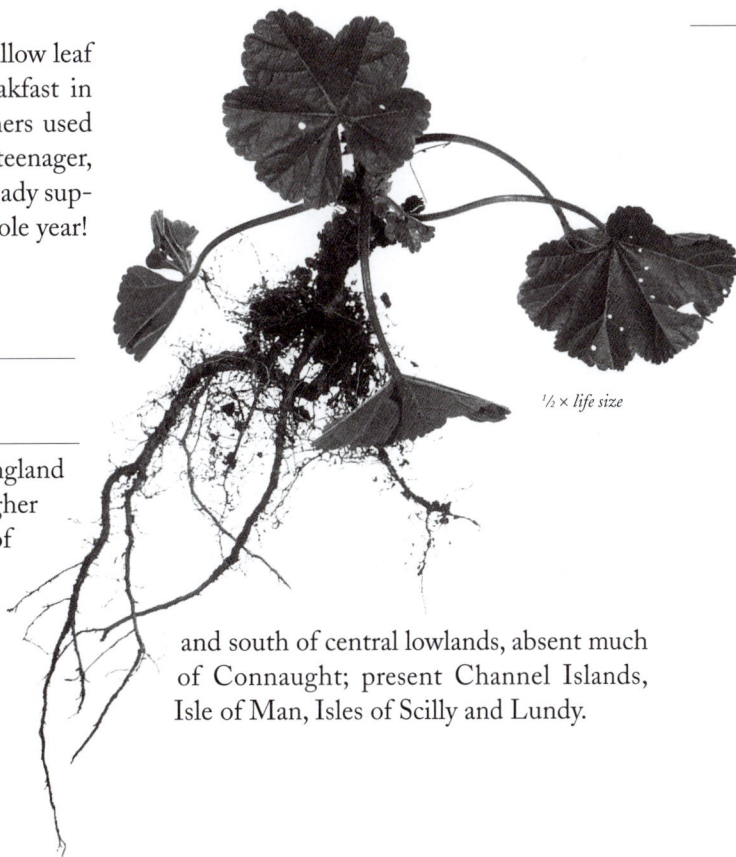

½ × life size

Habitat Dry ground on field edges, waste ground, gardens, path edges, canal banks; resilient in face of heavy grazing and mowing.

Description Slightly hairy perennial, sometimes prostrate, especially when grazed or mown. Upright plants can be 90cm high.

Sam Clark is chef–proprietor of Spanish-Moroccan restaurant Moro in London; the other Sam to whom he refers in the piece that follows is the other Sam Clark, Sam's wife, who is also chef–proprietor of Moro.

The markets or souks of Morocco are bewildering with romance and mystique. Sam and I continually try to decipher what spices and herbs might be before us; in one such instance we recognized some beautifully displayed tight glossy bunches of greens as a plant that grows freely on our allotment. 'It's mallow,' said Sam.

Every spring since we have picked mallow leaves on the canals and parklands of London. For our ancestors, mallow would have been very important, but now such goodies have been forgotten. Although it is still used widely in the eastern Mediterranean and all of North Africa, the recipes we use are mainly from Morocco. There are many different varieties – none said to be harmful. We like to use small, green glossy-leaved varieties, as they do in Morocco. We discard the stalks and use the leaves like spinach.

Sam & Sam Clark's Harira with Mallow, Tomato and Coriander

SERVES 8 AS A STARTER,
4 AS A MAIN COURSE
1 neck of lamb
2.75 litres cold water
2 large onions, finely chopped
4 garlic cloves, finely chopped
4 celery sticks, finely chopped
a pinch of saffron (roughly 40 threads)
½ tsp each of ground cinnamon, turmeric and ground ginger
2 whole cloves, ground
grated fresh nutmeg (5 grates on a fine grater)
1 large bunch fresh coriander, stalks and leaves separated, washed and chopped
110g small green lentils
120g chana dhal (small, split and skinned chickpeas)
500g small–medium ripe sweet tomatoes, quartered
2 tbsp roughly chopped parsley
150–200g mallow leaves, roughly chopped, stalks finely chopped
3 tbsp plain flour, mixed with 3 tbsp extra virgin olive oil
a squeeze of fresh lemon
sea salt and black pepper

Put the lamb and water in a large pan, bring to the boil and simmer for 5 minutes, skimming off any scum or fat. Add onions, garlic, celery, saffron, spices, some salt and pepper and the coriander stalks. Cook for 1 hour before adding the lentils and chana dhal, then cook for another half an hour. Remove lamb, and pull it off the bone and flake a little, then return it to the pot, season, and add the tomatoes and parsley. Cook for another 10 minutes, then add the chopped mallow and simmer for a further 5 minutes. Finally, add the flour mixed with the oil and stir briskly. Add the coriander leaves and lemon juice. Continue to cook the soup for another 10 minutes, or until the pulses are soft.

Leaves have long stalks and are dark green, shiny and palmately lobed. Lobes have fine teeth and reddish-purple veins, forming a red spot where they meet. Pink flowers grow singly from the leaf axils; they have 5 notched petals, purple veins and noticeable gaps between them. The seeds form in rings, with each seed a segment, green at first; later, when they turn brown, they can be separated from their bases and look like tiny doughnuts.

SIMILAR SPECIES Dwarf mallow *M. neglecta* is smaller and prostrate; its flowers are pale lilac and much smaller. Other plants with palmately lobed leaves are **lady's mantle** and **cloudberry**; the former has paler, downy leaves; the latter grows in boggy places, where mallow is unlikely to occur.

USES/RECIPES Leaves, when cooked, are quite mucilaginous, similar to okra or lady's fingers (also a mallow family species), making it good for thickening. Raw, its mild flavour makes it a good bulking salad ingredient. For mallow soup, follow recipe for amaranth soup and smoked oil (see p.46), substituting mallow for amaranth. Flowers can be used as garnish or in salads. Seeds, or cheeses as they are sometimes called, are good for on-the-spot snacking when still green. The dry, brown seeds can be ground and used in breads or as a thickener.

BENEFITS Leaves are high in protein and are also a good source of calcium, iron, vitamin C and copper. Mucilage contained in all parts of the plant soothes irritation and inflammation and relieves coughs.

2 × life size

MIGNONETTE FAMILY
Resedaceae

The mignonette family also includes the cultivated plant mignonette *Reseda odorata*, which is native to Egypt and has a gorgeous aroma, as well as weld or dyer's rocket *R. luteola*, used to obtain a yellow fabric dye. The name mignonette is French for 'little darling'.

Reseda lutea

Wild Mignonette

DISTRIBUTION Up to 440m. In England, present in most areas; in Wales, mostly in southern and northern coastal counties; in Scotland, mostly Central Lowlands, scarce and sporadic elsewhere; in Ireland, scarce, mostly Leinster and Dublin; present Channel Islands and Isles of Scilly.

HABITAT Grassy areas, waste ground and disturbed ground, especially on chalk soils.

DESCRIPTION Biennial/perennial, either upright or spreading. Stems ribbed and branched; leaves once or twice pinnate. Flowers yellow, in long racemes, later forming cylindrical seed pods with tiny black seeds.

USES/RECIPES This cabbagey, slightly peppery leaf is reminiscent of some members of the cabbage family. It is excellent in salads, like a milder version of rocket. Serve roast chicken terrine with lightly dressed mignonette. The leaves have a good crunchy texture, with a flavour not too over powering, which makes a perfect combination with the soft texture and mild flavour of the chicken [PW].

WILD MIGNONETTE COLESLAW: Cabbage, carrot, parsnip, celeriac, and mignonette with a grain mustard vinaigrette [JDW]. With couscous: cook couscous in the usual way, adding a crumbled chicken or vegetable stock cube (or half), fresh lemon juice and lemon zest, plenty of salt and pepper, olive oil, ras el-hanout, and some golden raisins; put the mignonette in at the last minute before serving to ensure crunch [JDW]. The seed pods (but not the seeds themselves) are peppery, which calls to mind the seasoning also known as mignonette which consists of coarsely ground pepper and coriander. Use as spicy capers.

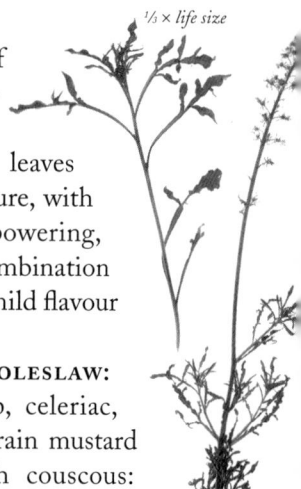

⅓ × life size

MINT FAMILY
Lamiaceae

Most of our favourite culinary herbs belong to the mint family (and most of the rest to the carrot family), which is characterized by the presence of aromatic oils in many of its species. Mints are plants of the summer months; the aromatic essential oils are at their peak just as they flower.

These enable the plants to retain moisture in the hot, dry conditions that many of them seem to prefer, and also repel insects and herbivore predators by their pungent, bitter taste. We perhaps don't think of them as bitter as we usually experience them mixed with other ingredients – when was the last time you ate a few leaves of sage, thyme or marjoram on their own? Recipes or dishes that incorporate them often include strong, meaty flavours, vinegar or sugar and cream, which mask, counter or otherwise temper the effects of bitterness.

Mint-family species are characterized by square stems and opposite leaves and tubular, two-lipped flowers. These are easy characteristics to learn, and with no really dangerous plants and no similar poisonous plants, this is a safe plant family with which to work. You should, however, be aware

of hazards associated with pennyroyal and wood sage.

Clinopodium ascendens

Common Calamint

DISTRIBUTION Up to 380m. In England, most widespread in Norfolk and in the southwest as far east as Salisbury Plain, elsewhere a disjointed distribution decreasing northwards; in Wales, mainly southwest, with smaller areas Lleyn Peninsula and Bangor–Conwy; absent from Scotland; in Ireland, found south of Central Lowlands except one locality in Sligo and another in Londonderry; present on the Isle of Man.

HABITAT Dry, grassy areas, on woodland edges or paths, hedgebanks, scrub, road verges, usually on alkaline soil.

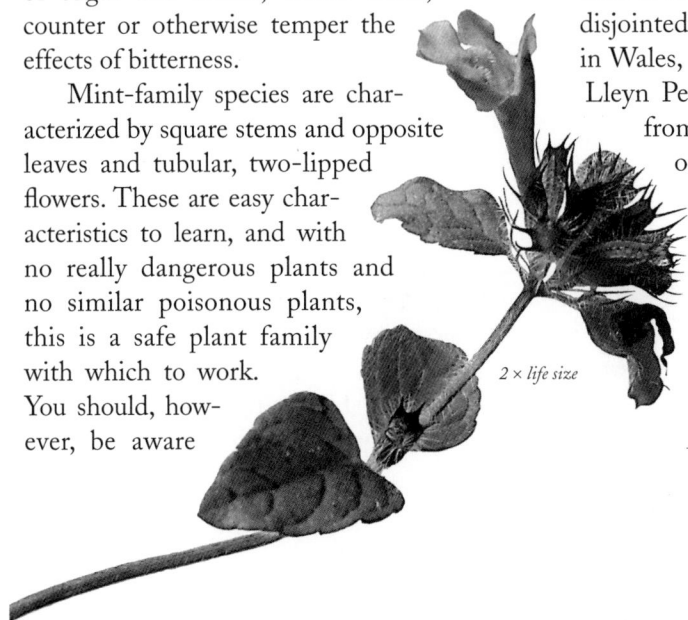

2 × life size

DESCRIPTION Plants have one main stem, with several long branches at a 45-degree angle. Leaves greyish green, long stalked, oval with blunt tips, up to 4cm long, hairy, shallow blunt teeth. Flower whorls spread out along the top third of the plant, with pale pink flowers on little branched stalks.

USES/RECIPES See **lesser calamint**.

Clinopodium calamintha

Lesser Calamint

DISTRIBUTION Up to 300m. In England, only southeast and east, and common Essex and south Suffolk, also found Cambridgeshire, Norfolk, Kent, Berkshire, Buckinghamshire and Hertfordshire; in Wales, border of west Gloucestershire and Monmouthshire; absent Scotland and Ireland; present Channel Islands.

HABITAT Roadside verges and path edges, churchyards and waste ground, on dry ground.

DESCRIPTION More aromatic than common calamint, with smaller (up to 2cm long), greyish-green leaves and a stiff, slightly downy stem. The lilac flowers seem disproportionate to the leaves, up to 1.5cm long; each flower stalk arising from the main stem can branch two or three times to support 2–3 flowers.

NOTES A small mint that is localized in its distribution, but abundant where it occurs. It grows in profusion in a small area of the Suffolk village where I grew up, with scarcely a 5m stretch of path or road to be seen without it.

USES/RECIPES *(for common and lesser calamint)* These fragrant mints lend themselves well to recipes using something equally fragrant, such as lemon. The much stronger flavours of water mint, peppermint or spearmint are almost harsh in comparison. The delicate flavour of calamint works well with elderflower sorbet, for which these other mints would be too overpowering. Infuse in warm liquids, rather than boil, so as to avoid losing the aromatic oils.

JIMMY SHAVE'S LEMON POSSET WITH CALAMINT: Simmer 280g double cream and 140g sugar, then add juice and zest of 2½ lemons. Simmer again for 10 minutes, take off heat, add 4 sprigs flowering calamint and allow to infuse for 5 minutes. Pass through a sieve, let it cool down then pour into glasses. Chill for 2–3 hours then serve.

Clinopodium vulgare

Wild Basil

DISTRIBUTION Up to 395m. In England, found all counties but less abundant Cornwall, Devon and areas north of line west from the Wash; in Wales, occurs in coastal and border counties; in Scotland, mainly in east below Grampian and in west only in Firth of Lorn; in Ireland, only where introduced to Cork coast and to Sligo.

HABITAT Hedges, banks, road verges, woodland edges, grassy banks and dry grassland, often on chalky soils.

DESCRIPTION Hairy perennial with soft leaves, pale green, oval, with blunt tips,

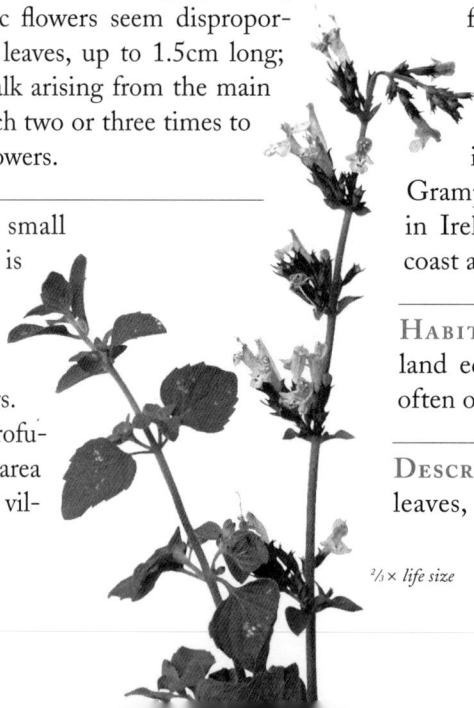

⅔ × life size

and blunt toothed, with short stalks. Purplish-pink flowers, large in proportion to the leaves, appear July–September in dense, tufty whorls, well spaced along the top half of the main stem, which is usually unbranched, though sometimes branched once or twice.

Wild basil

USES/RECIPES Wild basil doesn't really taste of basil: its flavour is mildly aromatic, somewhere between mint and marjoram. Use in salads or as flavouring, for which you will need quite large quantities to impart its rather faint presence to a dish.

Glechoma hederacea

Ground Ivy

DISTRIBUTION Up to 465m. Found throughout British Isles except in Scotland, Western Isles, North Highlands and other highland areas; in Ireland, large areas of coastal counties.

HABITAT Woods and woodland edges, grassy areas, gardens and hedgerows.

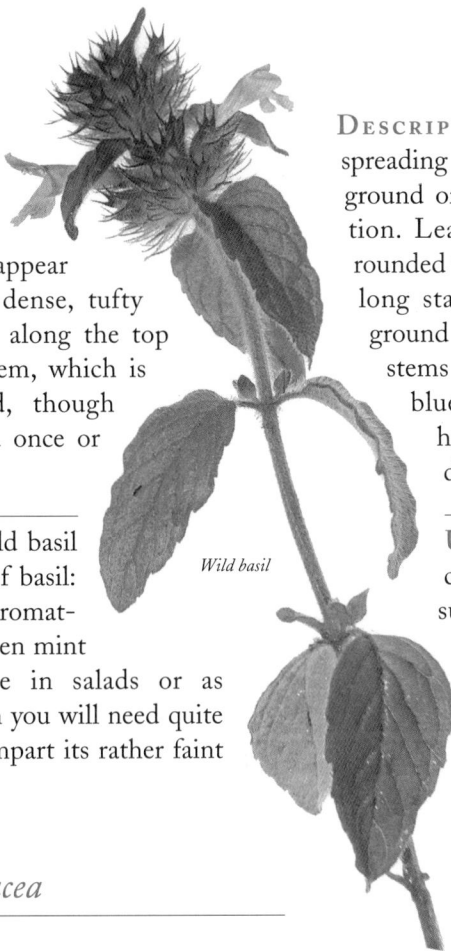

DESCRIPTION Native perennial often spreading over quite large areas, covering the ground or intermingling with other vegetation. Leaves kidney-shaped–cordate, with rounded teeth, often tinged bronze and with long stalks. Main stems creep along the ground and put down roots but flowering stems are more upright. Flowers purplish blue. The whole plant has a strong, herby aroma, similar to that of the dead-nettles.

USES/RECIPES Leaves and stems can be used instead of other herbs, such as mint or thyme, in soups, with eggs, and to flavour minced-meat preparations, such as meat-loaf, meatballs and burgers. Tea made from the leaves, known as gill tea, is very pleasant. Juiced leaves and stems can form the basis for savoury sauces. Used in sweet recipes, the flavour takes on a different aspect, for example candied with egg white and sugar [FC]. Or prepare them like mint sauce to serve with lamb [PW]. This was a key ingredient for flavouring beer before hops came into use, hence ground ivy's older name 'alehoof'.

Lamiastrum galeobdolon

Yellow Archangel

²/₃ × *life size*

DISTRIBUTION Up to 425m. In England, widespread but absent north of Yorkshire, parts of Norfolk and much of the Fens; in Wales, widespread except 20 miles or so inland for much of coastal Wales, although present Carmarthenshire and

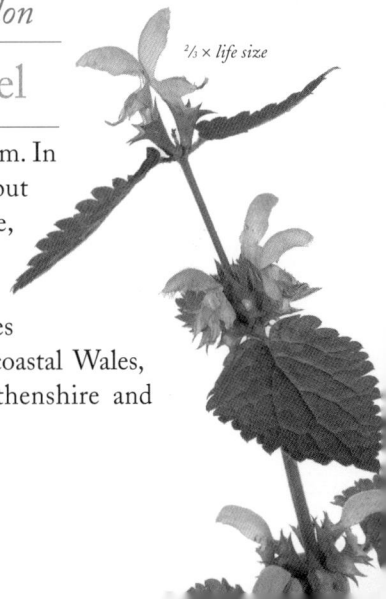

rest of southeast coast and also Conwy and rest of northeast coast; in Scotland, scarce; in Ireland, restricted to a few areas in north and southeast, notably around Dublin and Belfast.

HABITAT Damp, shady places, mostly in woods but also on hedgebanks; an indicator plant of ancient woodland.

DESCRIPTION Similar to white dead-nettle, but with darker, more slender leaves. Plants are either low and creeping when not flowering, or upright when flowering, up to 60cm high; 2 lipped flowers yellow, with darker streaks.

SIMILAR SPECIES Subspecies *argentatum* has variegated leaves and is a garden escape.

USES/RECIPES Use in similar ways to white and red dead-nettle. However, the colours might suggest different uses for raw flowering tops, with their deep green and dramatic yellow. René Redzepi uses this plant in a dish of hay-baked celariac, black pudding and brown butter sauce. The dish is embellished with the archangel leaves, a little of the burnt hay, ramsons seeds salted and pickled in vinegar and hazelnut purée.

Lamium album

White Dead-nettle

DISTRIBUTION Up to 345m. In England, widespread, only less so Lake District, Pennines and Cheviot Hills; in Wales, widespread except Black Mountains, Brecon Beacons, Cambrian Mountains and Snowdonia; in Scotland, common central and eastern Coastal Lowlands, except eastern Grampian and north of Moray Firth, sporadic in west, south of Glen Mor; in Ireland, sparse throughout except northern

Leinster and eastern Ulster; present Channel Islands, Isle of Man and Isles of Scilly.

HABITAT Hedgebanks, roadsides, gardens.

DESCRIPTION Perennial, 20–60cm high, forming dense patches. Leaves nettle shaped, but paler and without stings. Flowers white, two lipped; the corolla up to 2cm long, in crowded whorls in the leaf axils.

NOTES One of my earliest wild-food plant experiences was sucking the nectar from the back of white dead-nettle flowers. You had to get there in the morning before the bees, though, or you'd just be sucking air. Honey, which is essentially nectar from flowers, is probably one of the most universally eaten products made from wild plants.

USES/RECIPES The leaves and young stems, prior to flowering, are tender and juicy. Use them in salads or steam and eat as a side veg with butter, olive oil or a cheese sauce. You can also incorporate them in other dishes, for example with couscous or rice. When the plant is bigger, the leaves are still palatable; cook briefly and use as any other green. For white

dead-nettle soup, follow the recipe for nettle soup (p.225), using leaves or young tops in place of nettles.

Lamium amplexicaule

Henbit

DISTRIBUTION Up to 455m. In England, found throughout but most prevalent south of Humber except parts Herefordshire, Devon, Cornwall, Kent and Sussex; in Wales, found all coastal counties; in Scotland, scattered locations, more common on east side of Central Lowlands, also Western and Northern Isles; in Ireland, smattering in coastal counties, mainly east but also to north and west; present Channel Islands, Isle of Man and Isles of Scilly.

HABITAT Walls, dry arable land, waste ground.

DESCRIPTION Small, downy annual, up to 25cm high, with rounded, bluntly toothed and long-stalked lower leaves and stalkless, rounded bracts clasping the stem, forming a rough disc shape, from which the pinkish-purple flowers emerge.

USES/RECIPES Young stems and leaves in salads; cooked as **dead-nettle**, although the flavour is slightly milder.

Lamium purpureum

Red Dead-nettle

DISTRIBUTION Up to 610m. In England and Wales, found pretty much throughout; in Scotland, mostly east and south, though scarce in mid-Central Lowlands, Grampian Mountains and Highlands; in Ireland, mostly throughout, although scarce in the west.

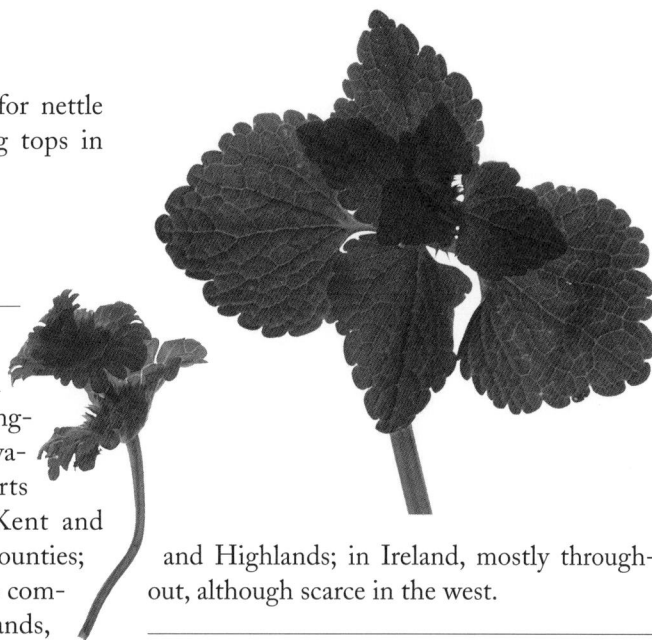

HABITAT Arable fields, gardens, pasture, hedgebanks, waste ground.

DESCRIPTION Small annual, with branches and long-stalked, purplish leaves and pinkish-purple flowers. Leaves coarsely toothed, oval–cordate.

USES/RECIPES As for **white dead-nettle**.

Marrubium vulgare

White Horehound

DISTRIBUTION Lowland plant. Very scarce and native only: in England, in south Sussex, north Somerset, the Breckland, Isle of Wight, east Devon and Dorset; in Wales, the Gower peninsula and north of Conwy. Also occurs as an alien in Berkshire, Hampshire, Forest of Dean and the Wakefield area of Yorkshire.

HABITAT Open, grassy areas, often on banks, verges and slopes, on chalk/limestone or sand.

DESCRIPTION Upright perennial, up to 60cm high. Leaves rounded–oval, wrinkled with

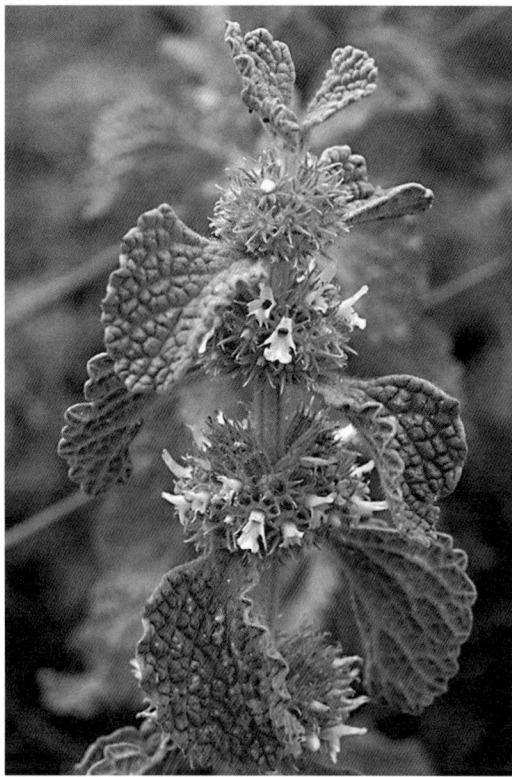

blunt teeth, lower leaves with stalks. Stem and underside of leaves covered with white down, tops of leaves with grey down. Flowers white, in dense whorls in leaf axils.

USES/RECIPES A cough sweet flavoured with white horehound was formerly manufactured on a large scale.

WHITE HOREHOUND LOZENGES: Infuse ¼ cup dried/1 cup fresh leaves and stems in 3 cups warm water for 30 minutes. Strain through a fine sieve then add 3 cups sugar, 1 teaspoon cream of tartar and 1 teaspoon fresh lemon juice. Boil until it reaches 115°C then add 1 teaspoon butter and keep boiling to 135°C then pour into a flat greased tin or, better still, a candy mould with squares. When hard, cut into squares or remove from candy mould, shake in a tin with some icing sugar and store between greaseproof paper in a dry, airtight container.

Melittis melissophyllum

Bastard Balm

DISTRIBUTION Lowland plant, confined in British Isles to in England, Cornwall, Dorset, Hampshire and Sussex (a 10 sq km); in Wales, Pembrokeshire.

HABITAT Hedgebanks, scrub, woodland edges and rides, cleared or coppice woodland, generally in damp, shaded conditions, often among brambles or bracken.

DESCRIPTION Strong-smelling, with scent a mixture of dead-nettles and melilot. Upright perennial, up to 50cm high, with hairy stems, oval leaves, 5–8cm long, with blunt teeth and long stalks. Whorls of few flowers, with two-lipped bell-shaped calyx, corolla large, up to 4cm long, cream–pink, lower lip with a deep pink blob.

USES/RECIPES The whole plant contains coumarin, the vanilla-almond flavouring also found in **melilot, sweet woodruff** and **sweet vernal-grass** and may be used to flavour sweet and savoury dishes. The leaves have a pleasant, soft texture that lends well to using them

½ × life size

whole in salads. Coumarin levels increase as the plant dries.

HAZARDS If drying, do so thoroughly and quickly and store in dry conditions, to avoid potential hazards (see p.21).

HARVESTING NOTES Listed as vulnerable in *The Vascular Plant Red Data List for Great Britain*. Only take a few leaves from each plant, as it won't tolerate being cut right back while growing; populations in the New Forest survive by growing among brambles, where wild ponies can't reach them. Don't collect flowers or seeds. The plant is widely available from garden centres if you want to use a lot of it.

WILD MINTS

Wild mints are often difficult to identify precisely, due to their tendency to crossbreed, producing many slightly different variants. Even seasoned botanists are known to avoid tackling them! This needn't be a serious concern as all the wild mints are edible, but their flavours are distinct, and it's nice to have some idea of which one you are eating.

GENERAL USES With lamb, with couscous, mint and peas; in sweets with chocolate; with blackberries and other soft fruits; made into mint syrup for pouring on desserts or for use as a soft drink.

Mentha aquatica

Water Mint

DISTRIBUTION Up to 455m. In British Isles, widespread throughout except in Scotland, Grampian Mountains and northwest High-

lands, and northern areas of the Western and Northern Isles.

HABITAT Very damp or submerged ground, on pond, river and stream edges, ditches, marshes and wet woodland.

DESCRIPTION Upright perennial, often found in great abundance. Height variable, 15–60cm. Leaves oval, edges bluntly toothed, up to 4cm long, all stalked; young leaves more rounded, often reddish purple. Flowers lilac, concentrated at top of plants in large, rounded clusters.

SIMILAR SPECIES Corn mint *M. arvensis* has smaller, thinner leaves and widely spaced whorls of flowers. It occurs in damp areas on the edges of woodland paths, arable fields, ditches and waste ground, but not in fully submerged areas.

NOTES Water mint is the most abundant of our wild mints. When it first appears in early spring it is quite red with short, almost round leaves. This threw me at first, since I had first encountered it at a later growth stage when it looks quite different.

USES/RECIPES Leaves provide a mild peppermint flavouring. In Portugal, the Café Alentejo

2 × life size

Joe Tyrrell's Water Mint and Dog-rose Chermoula

a handful of dog rose petals and water mint leaves (plus extras such as wild garlic, jack-by-the-hedge and a plain leaf such as chickweed) zest of 1 orange	1 tsp each of turmeric, ground cumin and ground coriander chilli powder, to taste salt and pepper a squeeze of fresh lemon juice a splash of olive oil

This is a sort of fragrant and spicy Middle Eastern pesto; it works as a dip or flavouring to cooked couscous. Either blend all the ingredients in a food processor, or use a pestle and mortar to make a paste, then loosen with the lemon juice and olive oil.

in Evora uses it in a fish soup with sea bass. I have experimented with water mint as an ingredient for drinks: my favourite is a combination of water mint and liquorice; for some reason, this concoction turned a dramatic greeny black. Flowers can be broken up and put through salads, scattered over blackberries and used generally as a flavoursome garnish for desserts.

Mentha piperita

Peppermint

DISTRIBUTION Up to 450m. Distribution is almost the same as spearmint, but peppermint is less abundant and does not occur in Anglesey in Wales or on the Channel Islands.

HABITAT Likes damp soil; often found on waste ground.

DESCRIPTION Hybrid of water mint and spearmint: stalked leaves like water mint and elongated flower spikes like spearmint.

USES/RECIPES Peppermint is the mint most commonly used for mint tea; the flavour is peppery, hence the name. It is used more in con-fectionery and desserts than in savoury dishes.
MINT COULIS: Made by simply infusing the chopped leaves in syrup and straining, can be used to make jelly or sorbet, both of which are excellent served with desserts made from citrus fruit or chocolate. Peppermint oil is used in mainstream medicine as an anti-spasmodic.
EGYPTIAN MINT TEA: 570ml water in about 1 full cup bruised, fresh peppermint leaves, 2 teaspoons gunpowder green tea, brown sugar to taste (in the pot). Leave to infuse for at least 3 minutes. Pour from a height to oxygenate the tea/be theatrical; drink from clear glasses.

Mentha pulegium

Pennyroyal/Pudding-grass

DISTRIBUTION Up to 300m. In England, scattered locations south of line Cleveland Hills–Forest of Bowland, native only to Devon, Cornwall, Herefordshire, Buckinghamshire, Hampshire and Sussex; in Wales, only Glamorgan and Carmarthenshire; in Scotland, only west Ross, where introduced; in Ireland, native to five areas – four in Kerry and Cork and one in Londonderry; native to Isle of Man and Channel Islands.

HABITAT Grassy areas that are periodically submerged, such as tyre ruts, animal hoof prints, edges of ponds and damp fields; usually restricted to silt and clay areas. It used to occur on village greens when they were grazed and has declined along with this practice.

DESCRIPTION Creeping perennial with long, reddish stems. Its leaves are short stalked, only 1–2cm long, with blunt teeth and blunt ends. Whorls of lilac flowers are separated along the length of the stem.

NOTES Like meadow clary, this species has declined through loss of its preferred habitat, which has become much rarer due to changes in land use. Pennyroyal is part of an on-going species-recovery plan, although non-native strains are cultivated in gardens.

²/₃ × life size

USES/RECIPES Pennyroyal was formerly a popular culinary herb in English cookery, mainly as a seasoning for meat dishes. It became known as pudding-grass because it was an ingredient in forcemeat, known as pudding, in the Middle Ages and also commonly used in black puddings. Forcemeat is meat and so on, chopped, spiced and seasoned for stuffing or garnishing various savoury dishes; many different kinds are made to accompany various dishes. *blood pudding:* (from *The Cook's and Confectioner's Dictionary* by John Nott). To make blood puddings the English way: boil a quart of whole oatmeal in a quart of milk, and let it stand till the next morning to swell; then put to it a pound and a half of beef suet, shred small, season them with salt and pepper; mince a little thyme, a handful of parsley, and a handful of pennyroyal, and put them to your other ingredients, and mix them well with three pints of hog's or sheep's blood, and a pint of cream; give

them a warm over the fire, fill the guts, tie them up and either boil or fry them.

HAZARDS Pennyroyal contains pulegone, which causes liver damage if consumed in large amounts. Ingestion of pennyroyal essential oil (see p.21 for more on poisoning due to essential-oil extracts) has caused adult poisonings. Eating the plant or drinking pennyroyal tea is not known to have poisoned adults, but a baby is recorded as having died from liver damage due to repeated doses of pennyroyal tea to treat colic. Because a baby and, especially, an embryo has much less liver tissue than an adult they are vulnerable to the effects of pulegone. For this reason, pregnant women should not consume pennyroyal.

HARVESTING NOTES/ECOLOGICAL CONSIDERATIONS Pennyroyal is protected under Schedule 8 of the Wildlife and Countryside Act 1981; it is an offence to gather it from the wild. Wild harvesting will only become possible again if the present biodiversity action plan for the plant is successful. For now those wishing to try this important element of our wild food heritage can satisfy their foraging instinct by seeking out a garden centre that stocks it.

Mentha spicata

Spearmint

DISTRIBUTION Up to 350m. Naturalized. Found throughout the British Isles: in England and Wales, throughout; in Scotland, more common in south and east but extends to Shetland; in Ireland, less abundant, only a handful of scattered localities country wide.

2 × life size

HABITAT Damp verges, by ditches and roads, river and stream banks and waste places.

DESCRIPTION Perennial, hairless or slightly hairy. Leaves longer, thinner and darker than other mints, stalkless, with roughly cut teeth. Pinkish-purple flowers form long, thin spikes, 3–8cm, at the end of the flowering stems.

NOTES This sweet-flavoured mint is the one most frequently used for cooking; it is the mint of mint sauce. It is also used as flavouring for toothpaste and chewing gum.

USES/RECIPES Add, for flavour, to hollandaise sauce and serve with fish, for example John Dory. Make into classic salsa verde with parsley, basil, capers, mustard, or create a wild herb salsa with **wild chervil** and **ramsons** [MH]. Serve with lamb, pork or vegetables such as **alexanders**, one of Britain's forgotten vegetables. Toss leaves in a Greek-style salad with feta, broad beans and cucumber.

Mentha suaveolens

Round-leaved Mint

DISTRIBUTION Up to 300m. Native only to southwest England, Isle of Wight and west Wales, but introduced to many places, most in south Wales, north of the Severn Estuary and on Salisbury Plain; in Scotland, present Firth of Forth, Angus coast, Isle of Skye and Inner Hebrides; in Ireland, handful of localities in north and south and in Dublin.

HABITAT Damp ground on roadsides and waste places.

DESCRIPTION Quite tall, up to 90cm high. Leaves unstalked, hairy, with white or grey woolly hair beneath, very wrinkled, with pointed teeth but curled down, making them appear blunt. Leaves usually rounded, but sometimes with more pointed tips. Larger leaves can be 45mm long and 40mm wide. Flowers pale lilac, concentrated in long spikes at the top of the plant.

NOTES Not a common mint, nor as intensely flavoured as some species, but worth mentioning because it is native. Hybrids of this and spearmint are quite commonly grown (often called apple mint or Bowles' mint) and frequently escape from gardens into damp ditches and hedgerows.

USES/RECIPES This pleasantly mild, sweet mint is suitable for desserts and salads. It works well with apple sorbet and makes a light mint syrup for poaching fruit, such as apples or gooseberries [PW]. Add leaves to a salad of ricotta, spinach, pistachio nuts and pomegranate seeds [JDW].

Origanum vulgare

Wild Marjoram

DISTRIBUTION Up to 540m. In England and Wales, found in most areas, but most common in North and South Downs, Chiltern Hills and Salisbury Plain; in Scotland, in Central Lowlands, eastern Coastal Lowlands and to the west in Argyll and Stirling; in Ireland, found in most areas, but most common in central-lowland areas; present Isle of Man and Channel Islands.

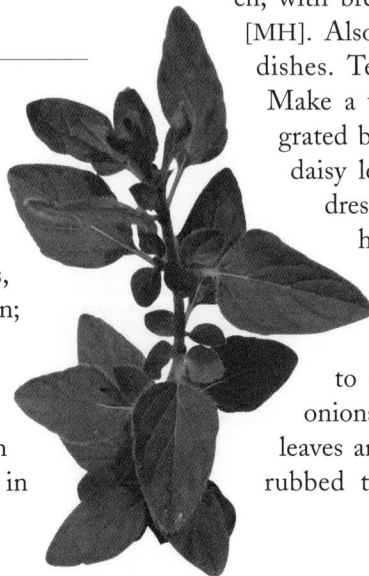

HABITAT Roadside verges, meadows, banks, old walls, churchyards, scrub, on dry, calcareous soils.

DESCRIPTION Sweet-smelling perennial with short-stalked, oval, downy leaves, usually untoothed, and several branched clusters of purple, pink or occasionally white flowers at the top of the plant. Each cluster contains many flowers. Stems become quite tough and woody, though tender in the early spring.

NOTES A very common plant in many areas, often forming large clumps – I have filled a carrier bag with it in 10 minutes on a particularly good spot. Wild marjoram does not differ greatly from cultivated varieties, although the flavour is certainly stronger. Its appeal lies in the fact it is so freely available; as is the case with so many wild plants, once you discover it, you will probably start noticing it everywhere.

USES/RECIPES The flavour is quite strong, so use it with other hearty flavours, such as leg or shoulder of lamb, inside a partridge or grouse. Use wild marjoram in stuffing for roast chicken, with bread instead of sage and onion [MH]. Also works well in tomato-based dishes. Tear a few leaves into salads. Make a warm salad with pinto beans, grated beetroot, finely chopped ox-eye daisy leaves, lots of dried marjoram, dressed with balsamic vinegar and hazelnut oil. With spaghetti and aubergine: thin, dry-fried slices of aubergine (salted for a few hours first to draw out liquid), caramelized onions, reduced white wine and dried leaves and flowering tops of marjoram rubbed through a sieve. Finish with

Parmesan. Also use in breads, herb jellies and herb vinegars. The young, fresh flower heads are excellent rubbed into a salad or for flavouring oil.

PORK BELLY WITH MARJORAM SAUCE AND HOGWEED: Sweat shallots, mushroom trimmings, marjoram stems and flowers for a few minutes, deglaze with veal stock, reduce slowly until it coats the back of a spoon, finish with double cream, then pass through a sieve. Serve with confit pork belly, cooked slowly (2–3 hours, 160°C) in goose fat then roasted. Serve with **hogweed** (or **fat hen**) and apple purée. Cut the skin from the belly into nuggets, deep fry like pork scratchings, and sprinkle over the top [DQ].

Prunella vulgaris
Self-heal

DISTRIBUTION Up to 755m. Throughout the British Isles.

HABITAT Woods, grassy areas, including damper parts of mown lawns, waste ground.

DESCRIPTION Hairless perennial, with upright flowering stems and creeping runners. Leaves stalked, oval and widest at their base. Flowers purple, in whorls at the top of the plant.

USES/RECIPES Leaves work well in salads, pretty much all year round – they are mild and provide a good background to other flavours.

Salvia pratensis
Meadow Clary

DISTRIBUTION Up to 300m. Only occurs naturally in a few areas in south England but not Devon and Cornwall, though naturalized in east and to north in Lincolnshire, Yorkshire and Staffordshire; in Wales, one locality on Severn Estuary.

¾ × life

HABITAT Dry meadows, road verges, path and lane edges on chalk or limestone soil.

DESCRIPTION Similar in form to wild clary but leaves unlobed, paler and longer, tapering to a point, with many fine, rounded teeth. The flowers are blue, much larger than calyces. The whole plant smells more distinctly of sage than wild clary.

HAZARDS Contains thujone in small amounts, as does cultivated sage.

NOTES This plant is very scarce in the British Isles, due to a reduction in suitable grazing practices; in 1999 a species recovery plan was started, administered by Plantlife International, the charity dedicated to the conservation of wild plants and fungi. Pastures where it grows are grazed through the autumn, then left during summer so that the plants can flower and set seed. On the continent it is a common plant of meadows and roadsides in many areas; I have found it growing in abundance on hillsides in Switzerland.

USES/RECIPES It tastes slightly more sagey than wild clary, and the leaves were formerly added to summer drinks.

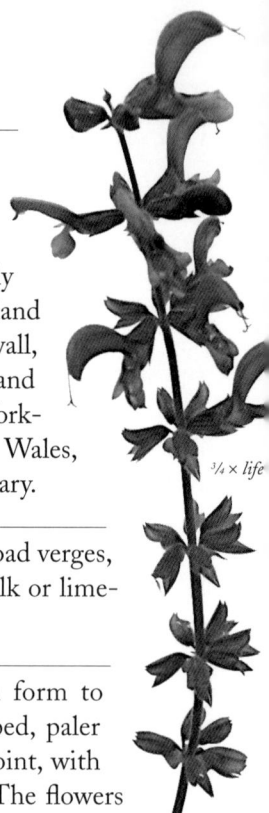

HARVESTING NOTES/ECOLOGICAL CONSIDERATIONS Protected under schedule 8 of the Wildlife and Countryside Act 1981; collecting it from the wild is a criminal offence. Of course, the object of the protection and recovery efforts is to make it more widespread, if successful it will be possible to gather it again, as in the past. In the meantime, if you are keen to try it, either find it on the continent or grow it in your garden; native seeds are available from British Wild Flower Plants in Norfolk (www.wildflowers.co.uk).

Salvia verbenaca

Wild Clary

DISTRIBUTION Up to 300m. In England, found all counties south of line Humber–Severn estuaries, with greatest occurrence in east; elsewhere widely scattered coastal localities: in Scotland, found only Firth of Forth and Ayrshire; present Channel Islands.

HABITAT Dry, grassy areas, usually on calcareous or sandy ground, often near the sea and in churchyards.

DESCRIPTION A distinctive plant, 30–80cm high. Basal leaves wrinkly, with blunt, roughly cut teeth up to 12cm long, long stalked, in rosettes. Stem leaves few, stalkless, well spaced, purplish towards the top of the plant. Flowers in whorled spikes, purple blue, protruding only slightly from long calyces; these are what catch the eye when you see the plant profile, especially when enlarged after the

flowers die back. The whole plant smells mildly of sage.

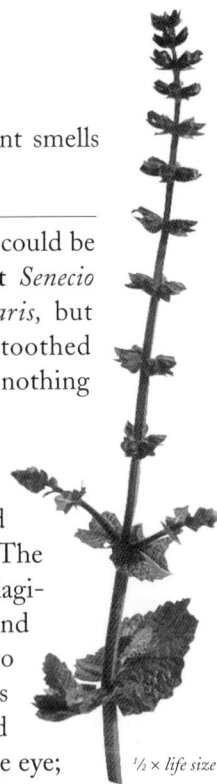

SIMILAR SPECIES Basal leaves could be confused with those of **ragwort** *Senecio jacobaea* or **groundsel** *S. vulgaris,* but both species have lobed, not toothed leaves and an unpleasant smell, nothing like sage.

NOTES Wild clary (and meadow clary) is closely related to cultivated sage *S. officinalis.* The seeds of wild clary become mucilaginous after soaking in water and were once commonly used to remove dirt or other particles from the eye: the particles would stick to the mucilage, clearing the eye; clary is a contraction of 'clear eye'.

⅓ × life size

USES/RECIPES Leaves taste faintly of sage, but can be used in salads, chopped finely and sprinkled on soups, or deep fried in tempura. Flowers are elegant, with a distinct sage flavour, use as garnish for sweet or savoury dishes or in salads. Add seeds to soups and stews as a thickener or toast and sprinkle on salads.

HAZARDS Contains thujone in small amounts.

⅓ × life size

Stachys palustris

Marsh Woundwort

DISTRIBUTION Up to 540m. Widespread throughout the British Isles except in England, parts of Lincolnshire and Yorkshire; in Scotland, Grampian Mountains and northwest Highlands.

HABITAT Damp places, usually by water, such as stream and river banks, by ditches and ponds and also marshes and fens.

DESCRIPTION Native, hairy perennial with hollow stems. Leaves lanceolate–oblong, with slightly toothed edges. Upper leaves stalkless; lower leaves short stalked. It has very a faint odour, if any. Purple flowers form a dense spike of numerous whorls at the top, more widely spaced further down.

SIMILAR SPECIES Betony *S. officinalis* has a rosette of long-stalked basal leaves and stalked upper leaves. Leaves of hedge woundwort *S. sylvatica* are more nettle shaped; stem leaves are stalked.

NOTES Described in *Flora Scotica* (1777) by John Lightfoot – the first botanist seriously to record the native plants of Scotland – as 'farinaceous', meaning good to eat, the thin, white tubers of this plant were once commonly unearthed for food in late autumn. They are known to have been used in several European countries and have even been considered for development as a cultivated crop. One obstacle to this is that mice are keen on them, collecting and storing them in huge quantities for winter. Polish forager and ethnobotanist Lukasz Luczaj is a great enthusiast for these roots, which grow in profusion in his region of Poland; he saved himself a lot of digging once he discovered

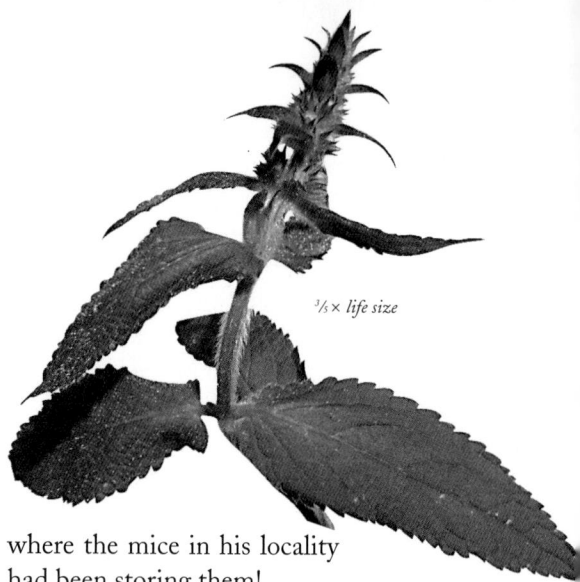

⁴/₅ × life size

³/₅ × life size

where the mice in his locality had been storing them!

USES/RECIPES Tubers have a crisp texture even when cooked but can be eaten raw. They have a slightly sweet, nutty flavour, a bit like chestnuts. Lightfoot says, in *Flora Scotica*, that they were 'boiled, or dry'd, and made into bread'.

HARVESTING NOTES This plant does not form extensive colonies in my area of southeast England, so I have harvested only a few tubers from a single plant, which seemed none the worse for it. It can, however, be abundant in marshy areas.

Teucrium scorodonia

Wood Sage

DISTRIBUTION Common most areas of British Isles, except: in England, East Midlands, Cambridgeshire, parts of Essex, Oxfordshire; in Scotland, east of central areas and Highlands; in Ireland, central areas.

DESCRIPTION Aromatic, downy perennial, with a sweet, almost sickly, sage-like smell. Leaves in well-spaced pairs are oval, with cordate base, soft and wrinkly with toothed edges. Flowers cream, in opposite pairs, on long, branched spikes.

HABITAT Dry woods, heath and grassland, particularly on low-nutrient acid or chalky soils.

HAZARDS Contains clerodane diterpenes, which can cause liver damage; this plant should not be eaten regularly or in any quantity.

Thymus pulegioides

Large Thyme

DISTRIBUTION Up to 300m. In England, main concentration south of line the Wash–Severn Estuary, excluding Devon and Cornwall and parts of Kent, Essex, Suffolk and Norfolk, and also found West Midlands, south Lincolnshire and southeast Yorkshire; in Wales, in Brecknockshire and Monmouthshire.

HABITAT Dry grassland, bare ground, banks, often in among other species.

DESCRIPTION Creeping perennial forming shrublike masses, with small oval–elliptical leaves, 6–10mm long, with sides turned up. Flower stems are distinct in their two hairy, opposite angles, the two thinner faces downy and the other two smooth; they reach maxi-mum 25cm high. The pinkish-purple flowers have two lips, the lower of which has three lobes, in spikes with gaps between the whorls, July–August. This is the most aromatic – and therefore the most useful – of the three wild thymes.

SIMILAR SPECIES Wild thyme *T. polytrichus* is less aromatic, with only one dense whorl; the flowering stem has two hairy and two smooth faces. It is also less tolerant of competition from other plants. Breckland thyme *T. serpyllum* grows on sandy heaths, grassland and inland dunes; very similar to wild thyme but with a rounded, all-round hairy stem. Restricted to the Norfolk Brecklands; even there it is scarce so foragers should beware of collecting by mistake. It is, however, common in parts of Europe and used to give flavour and aroma to cheese in the south of Italy.

NOTES Treading (or sitting!) on large thyme often releases its scent and reveals its presence. Otherwise, it can be hard to find when not in flower – I have gone to a site where I know it grows and searched in vain, only to see it all over the place when in flower a few weeks later.

USES/RECIPES As for cultivated thyme, but you may need more of it, especially if using the less aromatic species. Thyme provides a background flavour in a similar way to lemon or garlic when added at the beginning of a dish. Unlike something like rosemary, which can tend to dominate, thyme is much more subtle and can work in most recipes. If added at the end you get a more intense flavour, which works particularly well with apple or pear in puddings; for apple pies add the thyme just before you put on the pastry lid [PW]. Be sure to use it when it is in flower: the flavour is at its best at this point, and the flowers are both pretty and delicious.

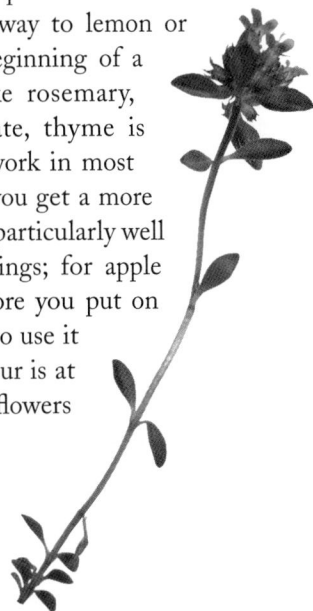

NETTLE FAMILY
Urticaceae

Nettles have been used as food, tea, medicine, fibre for cloth and rope, dyes, hair products, soil cleanser, compost activator, a source of chlorophyll, liquid manure, fly repellent, attractor of pestilent insects to protect economic crops and vegetable rennet. Even the sting is useful, alleviating symptoms of arthritis by introducing uric acid into the bloodstream.

During the First World War, when cotton was unavailable, in Germany there were 23,000 ha of land under cultivation for nettles to make army uniforms; nettles were a widely used fibre plant in Europe before cotton was introduced in the seventeenth century. Cotton is easier to harvest and spin, but nettle fibre is otherwise superior, being both softer and more hard-wearing.

Urtica dioica
Common/Stinging Nettle

DISTRIBUTION Up to 850m. Widespread throughout British Isles, only less so in Scotland, in North West Highlands.

HABITAT Waste ground, woods, pasture, gardens, river and stream banks, hedgebanks and roadsides, generally on nutrient-rich, especially phosphate-rich soils in fairly damp areas; colonizer of disturbed ground.

DESCRIPTION Unusual in that it can easily be identified by touch alone! Common nettle is perennial, forming large patches and reaching up to 1.5m high. Leaves are opposite, hairy, oval–cordate, ending in a distinct point and with toothed edges. Flowers are pale green and tiny, on drooping stems like knotted string, emerging from the leaf axils. Flowers distinguish nettles from **dead nettles** or other mint family species, which have much larger, more colourful flowers.

SIMILAR SPECIES Small nettle *U. urens*, which is not as tall, has smaller leaves and is annual.

USES/RECIPES *(for both species)* Despite their harsh exterior, nettles have a surprisingly delicate flavour and texture. The stinging hairs are reinforced by silica and act like a glass hypo-

⅓ × life size

dermic needle by injecting uric acid into the skin. Heating or crushing the leaves disarms the stings, rendering the leaves edible. Wash the leaves and pound them to eat them raw. Boiled, steamed or fried briefly (no more than 5 minutes), they make excellent greens. They also make a wonderful quiche and work well to finish risotto made with offal.

NETTLE AND HORSERADISH SAUCE: Sweat chopped onions, add the nettles, cook quickly and cool down immediately, then blend with grated horseradish, cream or crème fraîche. Serve with fish. In rural Italy, pasta verde is made with boiled, squeezed leaves. The leaves are also boiled with other herbs, fried with garlic and peppers (P. M. Guarrera, 'Food medicine and minor nourishment in the folk traditions of central Italy', 2003).

NETTLE PESTO: Simply blend the following ingredients: 500g raw nettles, 250g pine nuts or other nuts, 250g freshly grated Parmesan, 8 garlic cloves, salt, olive oil [BW].

NETTLE SOUP: Very thinly slice 2 shallots and 1 small onion. Put in a heavy-based pan with 60g butter, a sprinkle of salt and cook very slowly with a lid on for over an hour. Don't let the onions colour – you want them to be so soft that you could squeeze them in your finger and they would just fall apart; you don't want a strong onion taste, just a background flavour. Peel and very thinly slice 1 small potato, wash under cold water to get rid of surface starch and add to the onions. Cook for a further 10–15 minutes, being careful not to let the mix stick. Add 1 litre water, boil, season again with salt and add 100g nettle tops. Allow the nettles to cook for a few minutes or until it's just about to bubble again – if you undercook the nettles the soup will go brown; overcook them and the soup will end up a light green/brown. Either way, it doesn't look right and the flavour won't be right. Purée the mix in a high-speed blender, pour through a conical sieve into a metal container and place this in a sink and surround with ice to cool as fast as possible. Check for seasoning when you reheat it and garnish either with snails fried in brown butter, chopped three-cornered garlic or a bit of sorrel [JL].

NETTLE BEER: A great tonic, fizzy drink, which my mother drank as a child. Boil 1kg nettle tops in 5 litres water for 1 minute then leave to infuse for 30 minutes. Strain and add 400g brown sugar, 1 tsp cream of tartar, lemon juice and zest from 2 lemons then follow general fizzy drink method (see p.18). Once it becomes fizzy, keep in the fridge and drink within a week: for some reason this is the most explosive fizzy drink and will cause even a thick glass bottle to explode if left too long.

BENEFITS Very high in protein; also high in calcium and other minerals, vitamin C and beta-carotene.

HARVESTING NOTES Nettle tops should be gathered during their spring and autumn growth spurts. During the summer they become gritty with little particles called cystoliths made of calcium carbonate, which can cause kidney pains if eaten in quantity. Use only the top 5–8cm: below the stalk is stringy and the leaves less tender.

Small nettle

NIGHTSHADE FAMILY
Solanaceae

The nightshade family provides several familiar cultivated species and at least one wild species that defy the neat categories of 'poisonous' or 'non-poisonous'. Capsaicinoids in chilli peppers stimulate heat-detecting nerves in the mouth, creating the illusion of heat, but damage mucus membranes even in small doses, as anyone who has rubbed their eyes after chopping a chilli will know.

Deadly nightshade

Leaves and stems of tomato plants contain tomatine, a kind of saponin that causes intestinal irritation. Potato plants contain solanine in all parts, except the tubers, but even these become toxic if they turn green. Black nightshade, on the other hand, is known for its toxicity but has lesser-known edible uses. The deservedly sinister reputation of this family derives from the poisonous species such as deadly nightshade, thorn-apple and henbane. All three have caused fatalities, not all of them accidental: in 1910 the equally sinister-sounding Dr Crippen poisoned his wife using an extract of henbane. Fortunately, henbane does not resemble any wild edible species found on these islands. Deadly nightshade berries have been eaten by mistake, despite their berries being unlike those of any edible species. The deadly thorn-apple is thankfully rather scarce, but it could easily be confused with maple-leaved goosefoot *Chenopodium hybridum*, which

for this reason is not recommended as a wild food in this book. Fellow nightshade tobacco has an equally deserved reputation as a self-inflicted cause of death. Yet Duke of Argyll's teaplant, also a nightshade species, now has a global reputation (and a global market) for the life-extending properties of its berries.

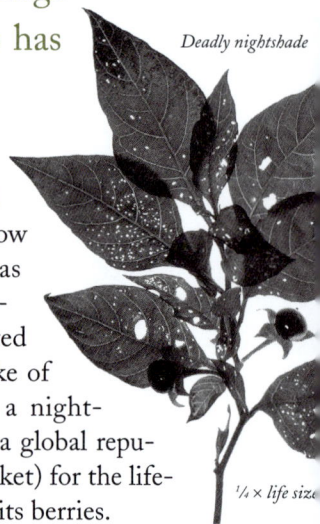

¼ × life size

POISONOUS PLANTS

Datura stramonium

Thorn-apple

DISTRIBUTION Up to 300m. Most abundant in England, particularly south of line Liverpool–

⅓ × life size

Thorn apple leaf: ⅓ × life size

Skegness, but more patchy in areas such as east Cornwall, Devon, east Kent and East Sussex, Wiltshire and northern parts of Fens; sparse north of line; in Wales, sporadic all counties; in Scotland, rare, recorded only in Berwickshire and East Lothian to east, Renfrewshire, Ayrshire and South Ebudes to west; in Ireland, single locality in Limerick; present Isle of Man, Scilly Isles, Channel Islands and Lundy.

HABITAT Among crops; on waste ground; on sea walls.

DESCRIPTION Up to 1m high, with oval, coarsely toothed, alternate leaves that curl up at the edges, quite thick and leathery with a strong nutty smell. White trumpet-shaped flowers are distinctive, as are spiny fruit capsules, from which the plant gets its name.

SIMILAR SPECIES When not in flower, could be confused with maple-leaved goosefoot *Chenopodium hybridum*, as the leaves are very similar in outline. However, maple-leaved goosefoot leaves are delicate, much flatter, with cordate base and no noticeable smell.

HAZARDS Thorn-apple contains poisons similar to deadly nightshade, but causes much more disturbing psychotropic effects. All parts of the plant are highly toxic and have led to many fatalities.

EDIBLE PLANTS

Lycium barbarum/chinese

Duke of Argyll's Teaplant

DISTRIBUTION Up to 350m. Mostly found in England, where widespread south of line Flamborough Head–Chester and absent only parts Cornwall, Devon, Sussex, Kent, north Wiltshire and Herefordshire, less abundant north of line; in Wales, throughout north coast, including Anglesey, also Lleyn Peninsula, Cardigan Bay, St Bride's Bay, Carmarthen Bay and Severn Estuary; in Scotland, on west coast only Kirkcudbrightshire, Wigtownshire and Ayrshire, on east coast, mainly around Moray Firth and Firth of Forth, and on Orkney; in Ireland, mostly coastal, mainly Waterford and Wexford, and around Dublin and Down; present Isle of Man and Channel Islands.

HABITAT Hedges, old walls and gardens, waste ground, sea walls, shingle beaches and other coastal situations. Spreads by suckering, but probably also seeded by birds.

DESCRIPTION Small shrub with long, trailing, often spiny branches, with a distinctive arching form. The leaves are greyish green, lanceolate, up to 60mm long, in clusters of 3 or more at intervals along the stem. Flowers are purple, with typical form of nightshade flowers: 5-pointed petals creating a star shape and central beaklike protrusion of the clustered stamens. Berries are bright red and egg shaped.

NOTES The fruits are sometimes called wolfberries but are now widely known by the name goji berries. In certain areas of the Himalayas, where they grow in profusion, people are said often to live to beyond 100, due to regular consumption of these berries. The plant was introduced to the British Isles in the seventeenth century as a hedge plant or ornamental garden shrub. Once familiar, the long, trailing, creeperlike branches declare its presence at some distance. They flail in the wind, above the main body as if searching for something: it is a suckering plant, so any branch finding a resting place in some crevice will put down roots. The pretty purple flowers and little red fruits are also quite eye catching and distinctive.

USES/RECIPES The fresh berries are really quite bitter; once dried (the form in which they are sold) they become sweeter. Serve with congee (Asian rice porridge): cook 100g rice with 1 litre water, adding a little salt and a knob of fresh root ginger, bring to the boil and leave the whisk in it, turn it down really low. Cook for 2 hours, stirring occasionally, and it will turn into a thick, smooth rice porridge. You can also start with leftover rice. Serve with plenty of condiments on top, such as coriander, spring onions, ginkgo nuts, beansprouts, shredded chicken, pork or duck, chopped chilli, soy sauce, sesame seeds and, of course, goji berries [JDW]. Sprinkle goji

berries, black sesame seeds and honey over sweet rice pudding or tapioca. Finish white chocolate mousse (see **sea-buckthorn**) with a layer of crisp white chocolate with the wolfberries set like raisins in the hard chocolate, acting as a bitter/sour foil to the very sweet chocolate [JDW]. The leaves can be used to make tea, hence the name teaplant.

Solanum nigrum

Black Nightshade

DISTRIBUTION Up to 300m. In England, widespread south of line Flamborough Head–Chester; in Wales, found throughout except highland areas; in Scotland, scarce, found mainly Central Lowlands, Moray and Banffshire but also South Ebudes and Dumfries and Galloway; in Ireland, scarce, restricted to central and east Central Lowlands, east of Ulster and south coast in Wexford, Waterford and Cork; native to Isle of Man, Isles of Scilly and Channel Islands.

HABITAT Waste ground, railway sidings, pasture, cultivated land.

DESCRIPTION Bushy annual plant; up to 50cm high, hairless or only slightly hairy. Stems are either spreading or upright and

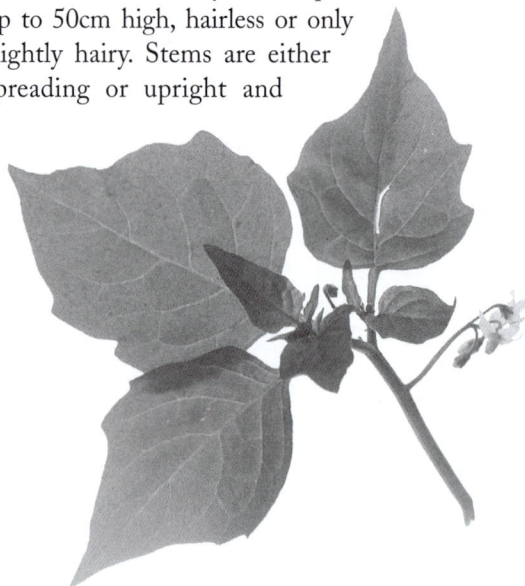

sometimes quite dark. Leaves roughly oval, ending in a point, with edges smooth–slightly lobed or even slightly toothed. Flowers white, in clusters of 5–10, star shaped with 5 petals and bold yellow anthers pointing out of the centre. Berries 6–10mm wide, green at first but shiny black when ripe – August onwards and sometimes as late as December.

²/₃ × life size

SIMILAR SPECIES Green nightshade *S. physalifolium*, common in parts of Norfolk and Suffolk, is hairier; berries are green, even when ripe. Woody nightshade *S. dulcamara* is a creeping plant with leaflets at base of its leaves, purple flowers and red berries; deadly nightshade *Atropa belladonna* is a much larger plant (up to 1.5m) with much larger (15–20mm wide) poisonous black berries, which appear singly, not in bunches like black nightshade. The brownish-purple, bell-shaped flowers distinguish it at earlier stages. It prefers alkaline soils and is found in woodland, scrub and disturbed ground near buildings. It contains the toxic alkaloid atropine, symptoms of which include accelerated pulse, pupil dilation, sweating, breathing difficulties, hallucinations and coma. Just 2–5 berries for a child, 10–20 berries for an adult could prove fatal; the leaves are also highly toxic.

NOTES Although often cited as a poisonous plant, black nightshade has been cultivated as a food crop on several continents, including Africa and North America. It was imported to Australia from Mauritius during the gold rush for use as a vegetable and is even the subject of a book on neglected crop species (Edmonds and Chweya, *Black Nightshades*, 1997). It is the leaves of the cultivated plants that are eaten; in Turkey, the leaves of wild plants are eaten like spinach. The green berries, however, have caused serious human poisonings due to the high level of the poison solanine they contain, and reports of livestock poisoning are almost certainly due to their having eaten plants with green berries.

USES/RECIPES Use leaves thoroughly cooked – boiled for at least 5 minutes – like other wild greens, in soups, as horta, in fatayer pies and quiches. They have a strong and slightly bitter flavour and a good texture. Also a good addition to rich tomato sauces. Ripe, black berries are sweet and salty, with a flavour something like tomatoes but with hints of liquorice and melon.

BENEFITS Leaves contain the amino-acid methionine, which is not usually found in plants. They are also high in calcium, iron, beta-carotene and vitamin C. The berries and seeds are also high in both beta-carotene and vitamin C.

HAZARDS Green berries contain solanine, and if eaten cause nausea, diarrhoea, dizziness and, in extreme cases, delirium, difficulties breathing and coma. The solanine content of leaves is known to vary, with some studies having found none at all, while leaves of older plants are said to contain higher levels. At any rate, solanine is destroyed by boiling, although not by baking and possibly not by frying either. Therefore, only boiled leaves should be considered absolutely safe to eat.

HARVESTING NOTES Collect only young, pre-flowering plants as greens, thus avoiding the risk of gathering plants with green berries.

PEA FAMILY
Fabaceae

The pea family contains a surprising number of edible varieties. Cultivated food crops include peas, beans and lentils as well as the spices fenugreek and liquorice. Other pea-family species are used for fodder, including lucerne (which is farmed in my locality of Kent for the elephants at Howletts wild-animal park!); many of our wild *Fabaceae* species are naturalized from fodder crops. These plants are also important for fixing nitrogen in the soil; crop rotations are planned to include pea species with this purpose in mind.

Most of the pulses sold dried do not grace our shores, even as cultivars, although lentils were formerly cultivated here. However, many native and naturalized species produce small peas, which, although a little fiddly to harvest, are worth eating. In Poland, pretty much all the vetches were formerly used to supplement grain flours for bread. Many traditions combine legumes and cereal grains, with their complementary proteins (a meal with just one of them is nutritionally incomplete). For example, peas and rice (Afro-Caribbean), dahl with naan or chapattis (India) and pottage (thick soups) made using dried peas and eaten on flat bread (which served as a plate) in Anglo-Saxon England.

Shoots, roots, buds and flowers of edible species are also used. Probably the most interesting edible flower occurs on the Judas tree *Cercis canadensis*, which does not occur wild in Britain,

although you could always forage its flowers from a garden tree. This enigmatic tree has purple-pink flowers, which grow out of the bark on the trunk and branches. The flowers have a pleasant sour taste; in Turkey they are used in salads, or fried in butter or as fritters. The tree shares with elder the ignoble legendary status as the tree upon which Judas Iscariot hung himself.

FAMILY HAZARDS Although the seeds of cultivated laburnum *Laburnum anagyroides* cause severe poisoning, this several-metres-high tree is unlikely to be confused with any of the edible species discussed here. There is a syndrome associated with this family known as lathyrism, which occurs when people on the verge of starvation have consumed pea species in large amounts. Sadly, this still happens when, as in India and Ethiopia, crops fail, but it is unlikely to occur when the plants are eaten as part of a balanced diet. The seeds of common vetch and *Vicia* species contain various toxins, including cyanogens and amino acids. Small amounts of these peas can safely be eaten raw; boiling for 2 hours or, better still, pressure cooking for 20 minutes, removes all but the smallest traces of these toxins, rendering the peas safe to eat in larger quantities, provided that the liquid in which the peas are cooked is discarded.

Cytisus scoparius

Broom

DISTRIBUTION Up to 640m. In England, widespread throughout, except parts of north-west, southeast and midwest Yorkshire, the Fens, Buckinghamshire, Oxfordshire and Gloucestershire; in Wales, widespread; in Scotland, widespread but absent North West Highlands and much of North Highland; in Ireland, widespread in coastal counties of Wicklow, Wexford, Waterford, Cork, much of Kerry and in Ulster; present Channel Islands, Isle of Man, Isles of Scilly and Lundy.

HABITAT Broom almost never grows on chalk or limestone soils, preferring sandy, acidic terrain, so it is a good indicator of soil type. Roadsides, heaths, railway embankments, river banks; generally dry and sunny places.

DESCRIPTION Upright, deciduous shrub. Thin green stems with 5 angles and no spines; lower stems have small, long-stalked leaves with 1–3 leaflets, upper leaves are simple and shorter stalked. Flowers are golden yellow, up to 20mm long; seed pods black and hairy.

SIMILAR SPECIES The deadly poisonous laburnum tree, *Laburnum anagyroides* also has

yellow flowers, but these hang down in long, pendulous racemes.

NOTES The plant is called broom because its branches were formerly tied together to make besom brooms.

USES/RECIPES Flower buds: just before they turn yellow, these were once commonly pickled in place of capers and the tops mixed with hops for brewing beer. Many restaurants now use the buds in salads and as a garnish.

Pickled broom buds: Take as many Broom buds as you please, make linen bags, and put them in, and tye them close, then take some brine with Water and Salt, and boyle it a little, let it be cold, then put some brine in a deep earthen Pot, and put the bags in it, and lay some weight upon them, let it lye there till it looks black, then shift it again, so you must doe as long as it looks black [until they turn green], you must boil them in a little cauldron, and put them in vinegar a week or two, and then they be fit to eat.
from Elizabeth Grey, Countess of Kent, *True Gentlewoman's Delight*

LATHYRUS SPECIES

These plants tend to have quite large seeds or peas, which are tender and green when young and can be used pretty much as garden peas.

Lathyrus japonicus

Sea Pea

DISTRIBUTION Up to 300m. All sites are coastal. In England, scarce, with single sites

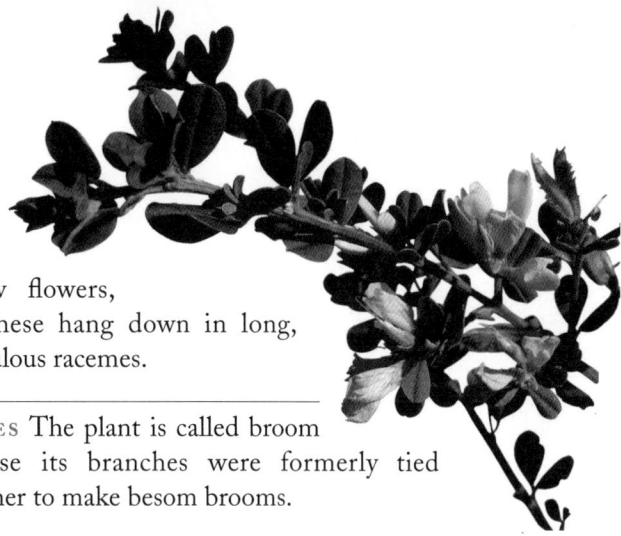

recorded for Northumberland, north Norfolk coast and Isle of Wight, plus a string of localities Suffolk–Essex, along Kent and Sussex coasts and a couple in Dorset; in Scotland, sparse in Grampian, Angus and on northern tip of Shetland; in Ireland, sparse, isolated sites Donegal, Mayo, Galway and Kerry in the west, and in Cork and Wexford in the south; found in one 10 sq km in Guernsey on Channel Islands.

2 × life size

HABITAT Mostly shingle beaches but occasionally on sandy beaches.

DESCRIPTION Greyish-green scrambling perennial, often forming large patches. If the stems are more upright then the mass of intertwined stems reaches 90cm high, however, no one stem is more than 1m long. Leaves have 2–5 pairs of elliptical leaflets, and usually, but not always, end with a tendril. Stems are angled and not winged. Flowers are large, up to 2cm long, purple at first, becoming bluer, with 5–15 flowers on each short stalk. Pods up to 50mm long.

SIMILAR SPECIES Broad- or narrow-leaved everlasting peas are similar, but with much longer leaves. They are less likely to be found on beaches, although I have seen narrow-leaved everlasting pea on the shingle at Dungeness in Kent.

NOTES In the past, dishes of very humble

origins often appeared on the table of the nobility, particularly in countries such as France and Italy, yet the upper class gentlemen who have written much of British history have often had little knowledge of the everyday diet of the rural poor. An account written by the rector of Blaxhall in Suffolk tells of the miraculous provision by which the inhabitants of nearby Orford avoided starvation when their crops failed in 1555 by eating sea peas. The bumper crop that year may have been providential, but the implication of the rector's account, repeated in the 1633 edition of *Gerard's Herbal*, is that they were eaten neither before nor since. Sea peas are too good a vegetable to have been overlooked, even though the eating of them in less troubled times may have been.

USES/RECIPES Peas: use when pods are still green like garden peas, fresh from the pod, especially if you get peckish on the beach. Or they are excellent in pasta or risotto, along with fresh wild leaves, a squeeze of fresh lemon juice and a sprinkling of Parmesan. Just add the peas and leaves towards the end of the cooking [JT]. When pods have turned brown, the peas need longer cooking, as for other dried pulses. Shoots: the young shoots are lovely in spring salads or in cooked dishes after briefly blanching or frying. Superb as a delicate garnish for fish mousse. See **narrow-leaved everlasting pea** for more pea-shoot ideas.

¼ × life size

HARVESTING NOTES This rather rare plant, although locally frequent, is very vulnerable to trampling: the leaves will die after being trodden on just once. This effect is graphically illustrated by the fact that in places like Aldeburgh the density of plants increases the further away you get from car parks.

Lathyrus latifolius
Broad-leaved Everlasting-pea

DISTRIBUTION Up to 340m. Grown in British Isles since the fifteenth century and now a well-established garden escape: in England, occurs mostly south of line Morecambe Bay–Spurn Head, particularly common Home Counties, less abundant Sussex, east Kent, Wiltshire, north Hampshire, Devon and Cornwall; in Wales, a few, mainly coastal sites; in Scotland and Ireland, very scarce; present Channel Islands, Isle of Man and Isles of Scilly.

HABITAT Railway embankments, waste ground, roadsides, cliffs.

DESCRIPTION Sprawling and bushy or else climbing where the opportunity presents itself, such as over fences, other plants or walls. Can reach up to 3m high. The leaflets, in a single pair, are rounded and broad, as the name suggests, with branched tendrils. Flowers, June–August, are quite large, 15–30cm long, bright pink (though sometimes white), in clusters of 5–15 on long stalks. Pods up to 110mm long.

SIMILAR SPECIES Narrow-leaved everlasting pea *L. sylvestris* has narrower leaves and smaller, paler flowers.

USES/RECIPES The following is a kind of pesto/houmous hybrid: 200g wild peas, blanched for a minute then smashed in a pestle and mortar with a garlic clove, 20g grated Parmesan, a few sprigs of fresh basil and mint, thinned with olive oil, fresh lemon juice and seasoned. Use a thin version as a sauce for pasta or dressing for a roasted flat fish like brill or turbot. A thick version for a stuffing for deep-fried courgette flowers or for flat fish that have had the bones removed while keeping the fish whole [JT].

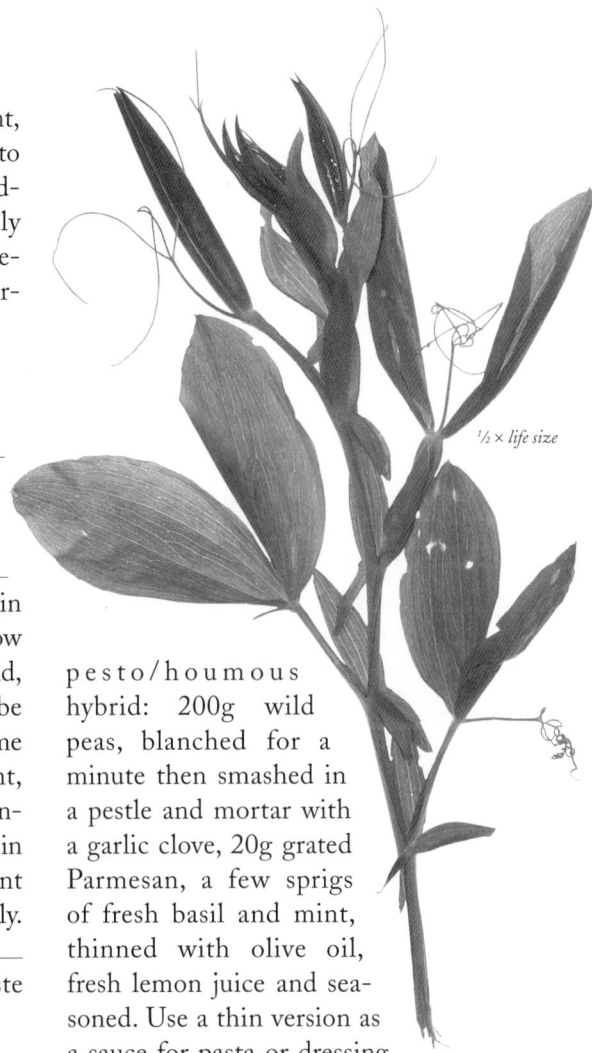

PEA SHOOTS WITH PASTA AND WILD FENNEL LEAF: Boil pasta with some broad beans and a garlic clove. Crush two more garlic cloves and fry with pea shoots for 4 minutes. Drain pasta and beans, add pea shoots, shaved pecorino cheese, wood sorrel, wild fennel leaf and black pepper. The flowers taste of peas, and their bases are sweet. Add them to crayfish or lobster bisque or summer salads with mint leaves or, better still, mint flowers, for a twist on the classic English combination of mint and peas.

½ × life size

Lathyrus linifolius

Bitter-vetch

DISTRIBUTION Up to 760m. In England, widespread except East Anglia, north Somerset, parts of Home Counties, East Midlands, Merseyside and parts of east Kent and south Yorkshire; in Scotland, widespread throughout except areas of West Highland, Argyll and Sterling, Caithness, Grampian and Western Isles, and absent Northern Isles; in Wales, widespread throughout; in Ireland, widespread to north and in coastal counties of south and southeast as well as Galway, Clare and Tipperary; present Isle of Man.

HABITAT Grows on poor soil, neutral–acid, particularly on moist, sandy banks, often on roadsides; also in meadows, heaths and open woods.

DESCRIPTION Native perennial, stems winged; leaves with 2–4 pairs linear–elliptical leaflets, up to 40mm long, with small points at their end in place of the tendrils of other *Lathyrus* species. Flowers start crimson, later becoming more blue, on long stalks with 2–6 flowers. Pods are brown, rounded in cross-section and 25–45mm long.

NOTES In Scotland the roots were at one time commonly eaten to stave off hunger and thirst, and also dried, then chewed while drinking whisky to impart extra flavour. M. H. Cowell, writing in *A Floral Guide for East Kent* in the nineteenth century, said that 'the roots have a sweet taste like liquorice, and when boiled are savoury and nutritious'; he goes on to recommend their cultivation. Over a century later the Agronomy Institute at Orkney College has taken his advice and is developing cultivars for edible use.

USES/RECIPES First-year tubers can be cooked and eaten in their entirety; older ones are tough and should be grated like horseradish or boiled and the starchy liquor used as flavouring. It works particularly well with orange segments (with all skin removed first) poached in syrup [BW]. This probably serves a similar function to chewing them while drinking whisky, taking away the harshness and rounding off the flavour, perhaps because of the starch content. Use them to impart liquorice flavouring: unlike liquorice, which becomes bitter when cooked, bitter-vetch improves with cooking. There is also a bamboo-shoot element to the flavour, and bitter-vetch works especially well in Chinese dishes. Another oriental-style use for the tubers is as flavouring for kelp or 'kombu'; Japanese pickled kombu uses liquorice as a flavouring.

Lathyrus pratensis

Meadow Vetchling

DISTRIBUTION Mostly lowland plant, but in Tyne and Wear found at 450m. In England, Wales and Ireland, pretty much throughout; in Scotland, found most areas, except parts of Grampian Mountains and inland areas of North West Highlands; present Channel Islands, Isle of Man and Isles of Scilly.

HABITAT Meadows, hedgebanks, scrub.

DESCRIPTION Native perennial, scrambling, often forming dense masses. Leaves have long stalks ending in two parallel veined grey-green lanceolate leaflets, 1–2.5cm long, with tendrils. At the leaf base are large arrow-shaped stipules. Yellow flowers (5–12) are grouped on even longer-stalked racemes. Pods are 25–35cm long, becoming black with age.

USES/RECIPES Use peas and shoots as for other *Lathyrus* species.

Lathyrus sylvestris

Narrow-leaved Everlasting-pea

DISTRIBUTION Up to 300m. In England, most abundant south of line the Wash–Lleyn Peninsula, with locations in most counties, especially in Somerset, Oxfordshire and Bedfordshire, plus string of coastal sites in south Devon and Cornwall; in Wales, scarce, found only in lower-altitude and coastal areas, and absent Brecknockshire, Anglesey and most of Pembrokeshire; in Scotland, rare; Ireland, absent.

HABITAT Woodland edges, cliffs, hedges, roadsides, railways, rough banks, waste ground.

DESCRIPTION Native perennial, but on roadsides and railways it is likely to be a garden escape. Grows in a similar manner to broad-leaved everlasting pea, but rarely reaches above 2m high. Leaflets are lanceolate, thin and ribbed, in a single pair with branched tendrils. Stems have broad wings; flowers, June–August, greenish/pinkish yellow, tinged with violet, much smaller than broad-leaved everlasting pea at 7–15mm long. Pods up to 70mm long.

SIMILAR SPECIES See broad-leaved everlasting-pea, *L. latifolius*, p.233.

USES/RECIPES Wild pea shoots nicely finish dishes such as pan-fried fillet of sea trout served with cockles, bacon laver bread and a light butter sauce or char-grilled pork chop with buttered carrots and a white wine *jus*. Serve asparagus spears and soft-boiled duck eggs with a simple salad of dandelion and wild pea shoots dressed with herb vinaigrette [all pea-shoot recipes PB].

½ × life size

Lathyrus tuberosus

Tuberous Pea/ Earthnut

DISTRIBUTION Scarce but persistent lowland plant. In England, present in one or two 10 sq km in most eastern and southern counties (although absent Kent), the Midlands and south Yorkshire; in Scotland, only in East Lothian; in Wales, near Neath and one 10 sq km south Powys; elsewhere, absent.

HABITAT Grassy banks, scrub, hedgerows.

DESCRIPTION Scrambling perennial, up to 1.2m high. Stems angled but not winged. Leaves have two elliptical leaflets. Flowers crimson, 12–20mm long, 2–7 on each side, on each long-stalked raceme. Pods are rounded, 20–60mm long.

USES/RECIPES Once cultivated for its edible tubers in Holland and France, Ken Fern of *Plants for a Future* says they are the nicest edible tubers he has eaten. They certainly are delicious, with a lovely, clean flavour, reminiscent of raw hazelnut, roasted chestnut and baked potato all the same time, and with a pleasant nutty texture. It is a shame it is not more common as a wild plant; I have resorted to growing them in my garden to ensure a supply. The green parts of wild plants are eaten cooked

in Boznia-Herzegovina, and the leaves are eaten as salad in Turkey.

BENEFITS Leaves have a very high potassium, phosphate and vitamin C content and are also high in protein. The peas have one of the highest levels of protein of any legume.

HARVESTING NOTES This is a scarce wild plant in the British Isles. If you are keen to try its edible tuber, either grow it yourself (it is available from Cotswold Garden Flowers: Sands Lane, Badsey, Evesham, Worcestershire WR11 7EZ, tel: 01386 833849, www.cgf.net), or look for it in Turkey or Poland, where it is abundant.

Medicago lupulina

Black Medick

DISTRIBUTION In England and Wales, throughout; in Scotland, widespread in lowland areas of south, also found coastal areas to north and east of Inverness; in Ireland, mostly widespread throughout although less so in north; present Isles of Scilly, Channel Islands and Isle of Man.

HABITAT Dry grassland, often on south-facing slopes, banks, walls, beaches; not on acid soils.

DESCRIPTION Prostrate or slightly upright, scrambling annual/biennial, stems up to 60cm long. Leaves trifoliate, leaflets oval–circular, sometimes toothed. Middle leaflets end in a

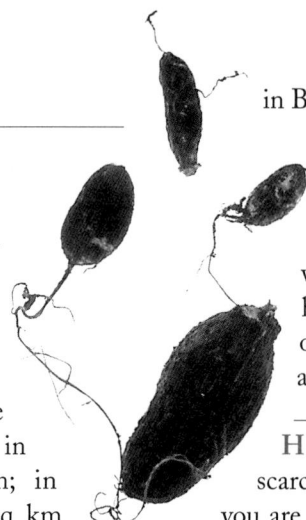

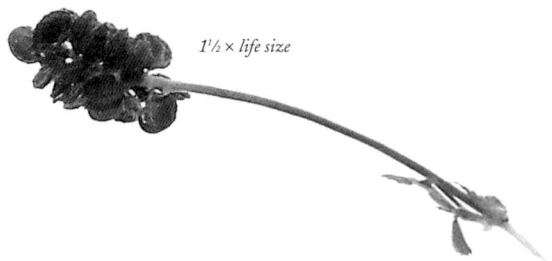

1½ × life size

small bristle-like tip. Flowers yellow, tightly bunched like clover flower heads, but smaller. Pods black, up to 3mm long, tightly coiled and arranged in bunches like miniature grapes.

USES/RECIPES As for lucerne.

Medicago sativa

Lucerne/Alfalfa

DISTRIBUTION In England, common East Anglia, Home Counties, East Midlands and Somerset, elsewhere more scattered; in Wales, confined to southwest and north coastal areas; in Scotland, most frequent Moray Firth and elsewhere scarce; in Ireland, a very few places on east coast; present Isle of Man and Channel Islands.

HABITAT Roadsides, hedgebanks, waste ground, meadows.

DESCRIPTION Hairless perennial, up to 80cm high. Leaflets trifoliate, oval–oblong, with toothed ends. Flowers bluish-purple–lilac, in racemes up to 40mm long. Pods smooth, in a hollow spiral.

SIMILAR SPECIES Subsp. *falcata* is a native species confined to Norfolk and north Suffolk; it has yellow flowers and curved pods and is more prostrate.

USES/RECIPES Seeds may be sprouted, young tops cooked or eaten raw; flowers broken up for garnish.

Melilotus altissimus

Tall Melilot

DISTRIBUTION Up to 300m. In England, widespread east of line Sunderland–Severn Estuary except Dartmoor, Exmoor, the Fens and Cleveland Hills, and west of line scattered localities on Cheshire Plain; in Wales, most concentrated in south and absent Cambrian Mountains; in Scotland, rare, found only scattered localities in Central Lowlands; in Ireland, mostly limited to area around Dublin and Belfast Lough; found on Alderney in Channel Islands and on Isle of Man.

HABITAT Roadsides, waste ground, banks, dunes, meadows; tolerant of salt.

DESCRIPTION Hairless biennial. Upright, with branched stems; sometimes reaching 1.2m high. Leaves have 3 oblong leaflets with toothed edges. Many yellow flowers, 5–7mm long, on upright racemes. Pods black, around 5mm long, oval with netlike veins.

SIMILAR SPECIES Ribbed melilot *M. officinalis* has less crowded racemes; its lower petals are shorter than the upper. Small melilot *M. indicus* has much smaller flowers.

Melilotus albus

White Melilot

DISTRIBUTION Up to 335m. Distribution similar to tall melilot, but more abundant in Scotland and less abundant elsewhere; present throughout Channel Islands and on Isle of Man.

HABITAT Roadsides, waste ground, railway sidings.

DESCRIPTION Very like the other melilots but with white flowers.

NOTES The name derives from two Greek words – *meli* 'honey' and *lotes* 'to bloom' – that together make 'honey flowered'. Melilot was cultivated as a forage plant until it became a major weed of wheat crops. All four species are now widely naturalized (although tall melilot may be a native) and easy to find due to their tall bushy form. A close relative of melilot, *Trigonella melilotus-caerulea*, is used to flavour the Swiss hard cheese Schabzieger. The plant was brought back from western Asia by Crusaders and has been used for flavouring cheese since the twelfth century. Leaves are added to the curd to give flavouring and green colour; they also stop further bacterial action.

Like **sweet woodruff,** when melilot is dried a chemical reaction occurs that produces coumarin (some of which is already present in the fresh plant material), with its sweet haylike smell. We enjoy the full benefit of this in the Forager business unit in Kent, where we dry and store melilot. The whole place becomes filled with a gorgeous aroma that greets us as soon as we open the door. The flavour is somewhere between almond and vanilla but with a delicate hay element.

USES/RECIPES *(for all species of melilot)* Dried leaves and flowers make a glorious sauce for rabbit and were used to flavour soups and stews throughout Europe in previous centuries. Flavour milk with them and use to make custard, serve with buttermilk panna cotta and milk ice cream [SW]. They also work well in sausages and stuffings.

HAZARDS Plants dried in damp, poorly ventilated conditions may contain dicoumarin (see p.21)

Scott Wade's Potted Rabbit

MAKES ABOUT 8 PORTIONS AS A STARTER

1 rabbit
10g dried melilot
1 litre semi-skimmed milk
2 gelatine leaves
juice of ½ lemon
200g unsalted butter
1 tbsp grain mustard (preferably Maldon beer mustard)
sea salt and freshly ground white pepper, to season

Joint the rabbit: take off the legs and cut the back legs in half, then cut the saddle into 8cm pieces. In a casserole dish, preferably earthenware or an enamelled-iron cocotte, infuse the melilot into the milk, bringing it slowly to a simmer, then leaving on a very gentle simmer for 35 minutes.

Season the rabbit with sea salt and white pepper, and add to milk infusion, leaving the melilot in. Simmer gently for about 2–2½ hours with the lid on. Take off the heat and allow to cool.

When cold enough to work with, take out the rabbit joints and flake the meat off the bone into a bowl. Put the bones and any melilot back into the milk. Reduce the milk down by two-thirds – don't worry if it splits out in the pan. Pass the liquid through a muslin cloth into a small bowl and let cool slightly.

Soak the gelatine in cold water until soft then squeeze out excess water. Add the gelatine to the liquid, and stir to make sure it has all melted, then add the liquid to the flaked rabbit meat. Work the meat with two forks, season again and add the fresh lemon juice. Taste and correct seasoning. Put into moulds leaving a few millimetres' space at the top.

Soften the butter until you can whisk it then add the mustard. Top the moulds with the softened mustard butter and set in the fridge. Serve with apple sauce, a wedge of lemon and toast.

Ononis repens

Common Restharrow

DISTRIBUTION Up to 365m. In England, most areas except parts Exmoor, Dartmoor, the Weald, Fens, Leicestershire, Lancashire and Lake District; in Wales, absent upland areas; in Scotland, absent upland areas plus North Highland and Northern Isles; in Ireland, mainly eastern and southern coastal counties with scattered inland, southern localities; present Channel Islands, Isle of Man and Isles of Scilly.

HABITAT Well-drained grassy areas and banks on poor, alkaline soil, dunes, sandy and shingle beaches.

DESCRIPTION Generally a creeping perennial, but can be more upright, with downy stems and sometimes spines. Leaves are small and toothed, either simple or with three leaflets. Flowers July–September, pink.

NOTES The name of the plant derives from the tough, woody roots and stems that

were able to arrest the harrows of medieval farmers. In *Theatrum botanicum*, John Parkinson wrote, 'In former times the young shoots and tender stalks were pickled up to be eaten as meate or sauce wonderfully commended against foul breath, and to take away the smell of wine in them that had drunk too much.' The roots were also once chewed for their faint liquorice flavour.

Uses/Recipes As the name suggests, the roots are far too tough to eat, but can be used, as liquorice root, to impart liquorice flavouring. The flavour is nowhere near as strong as liquorice root, however, and the root can be quite hard work to dig up. The younger leaves and tops can also be used in salads or lightly blanched as a vegetable.

Trifolium pratense

Red Clover

Distribution Up to 850m. Widespread throughout British Isles; only in West Ross and east and west Sutherland would you have to travel more than 10km to find it.

Habitat Grassland, on pretty much any kind of soil except very acidic.

Description Leaves trifoliate; leaflets have white crescents and are longer and thinner than white clover. Flower heads pinkish-purple with many flowers, growing on straight stem.

Similar species Zigzag clover *T. medium* has a zigzag stem and only grows on neutral soil; hare's-foot clover *T. arvense* has narrower flower heads with white down, which gives them a soft, furry appearance.

2 × life size

Benefits The flowers are high in isoflavones, calcium, chromium, magnesium and thiamine. Also contains salicylic acid, from which aspirin is made, and genistein, which is thought to inhibit blood flow to cancerous growths. The leaves are a good source of both protein and calcium.

Trifolium repens

White Clover

Distribution Up to 880m. Widespread throughout the British Isles.

Habitat Grassland and grassy areas on most soil types, except very damp or acidic.

Description Leaves with 3 oval leaflets with a white pattern, which would form a square if there were a fourth leaf. Flowers form a near spherical flower head of many white flowers.

Uses/Recipes *(for both clovers)* Flowers: add to breads, soups and stews; broken up into salads they look very pretty and add a delicate pealike flavour. Leaves: add to salads or cooked dishes of any kind. They are not very palatable, but the nutri-

tional content probably justifies their use. Seeds can be sprouted.

Benefits Leaves are an excellent source of protein and calcium.

Ulex europaeus

Gorse

Distribution Up to 640m. Widespread in England, though less so parts of Fens and Pennines; in Wales, widespread in most areas; in Scotland, only absent areas of Southern Uplands, Grampian Mountains, Caithness and Shetland; in Ireland, mostly widespread, except north of Clare.

Habitat Roadsides, heaths, railways, fields, waste ground, generally on acid, sandy soil.

Description Spiny, evergreen shrub, with yellow coconut-scented flowers that can be found all year round (although not on the same plant). As the old saying goes, 'Gorse stops flowering when kissing goes out of fashion'.

Uses/Recipes Use blossoms as a garnish or to make tea; this infusion can also be used to flavour ice cream or added to cooked fruit.

Vicia faba

Broad Bean

Distribution As a garden escape in areas where it is cultivated: throughout the British Isles.

Habitat Paths near cultivated fields, among crops as a weed or on land left fallow, field edges, waste ground.

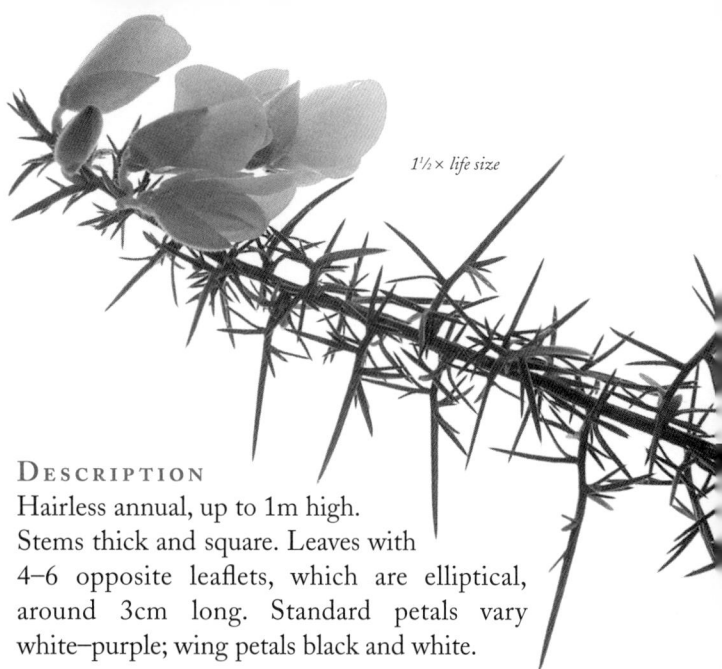

1½ × life size

Description
Hairless annual, up to 1m high. Stems thick and square. Leaves with 4–6 opposite leaflets, which are elliptical, around 3cm long. Standard petals vary white–purple; wing petals black and white.

Notes Occurs as escape from cultivation, persisting for many years, especially on arable land. Flour made from beans is the main ingredients in falafel.

Uses/Recipes Tops: greatly overlooked and just as delicious and versatile as the beans. Chop them into salads; use the leaves in sandwiches or boil, steam or fry them.

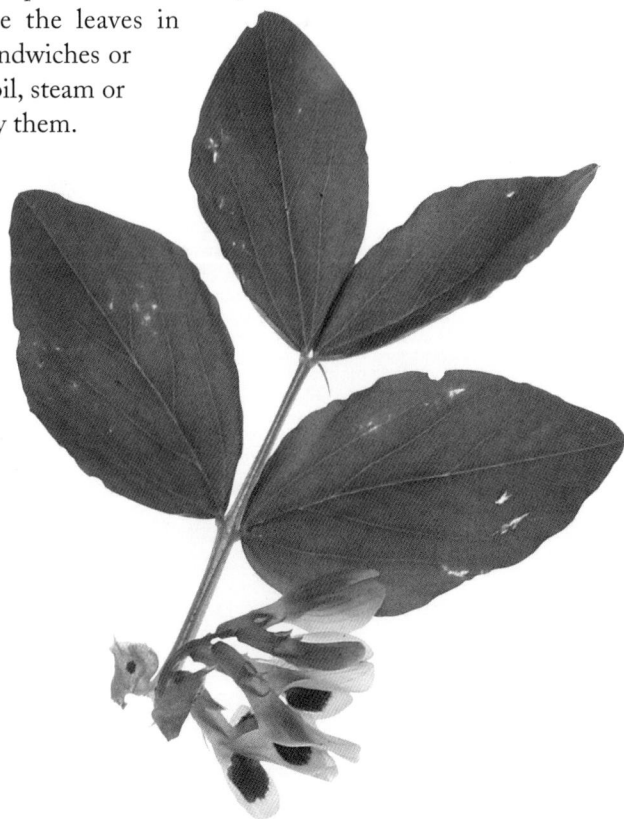

HAZARDS Ensure plants growing on arable fields have not been sprayed with herbicides.

Vicia sativa

Common Vetch

DISTRIBUTION Lowland plant. In England and Wales, found throughout up to the Midlands, mostly absent north and west Yorkshire and north Cumbria; in Scotland, mostly confined to Southern Uplands and east coast; in Ireland, found most areas in east and south west but scarce Connaught and Donegal; found on Isle of Man, Channel Islands and Isles of Scilly.

HABITAT Hedgebanks, scrub woodland rides, meadows.

DESCRIPTION Native, downy annual, upright (up to 40cm high) or scrambling. Leaves with 4–8 pairs thin leaflets, 10–20mm long, and simple or branched tendrils. Flowers, pink/purple, in twos or threes in leaf axils. Pods brown, hairy, up to 7cm long with 4–12 seeds.

USES/RECIPES Young shoots can be used in salads, as for the *Lathyrus* species; they combine well with salad burnet as a side salad with lasagne or other rich pasta dishes. The peas of this and other vetches are small but good to eat; eat as garden peas when they are tender and green, but only in small quantities. Only eat dried peas after pressure cooking for 20 minutes and discarding the liquid. Use in soups or in breads.

HAZARDS See p.231.

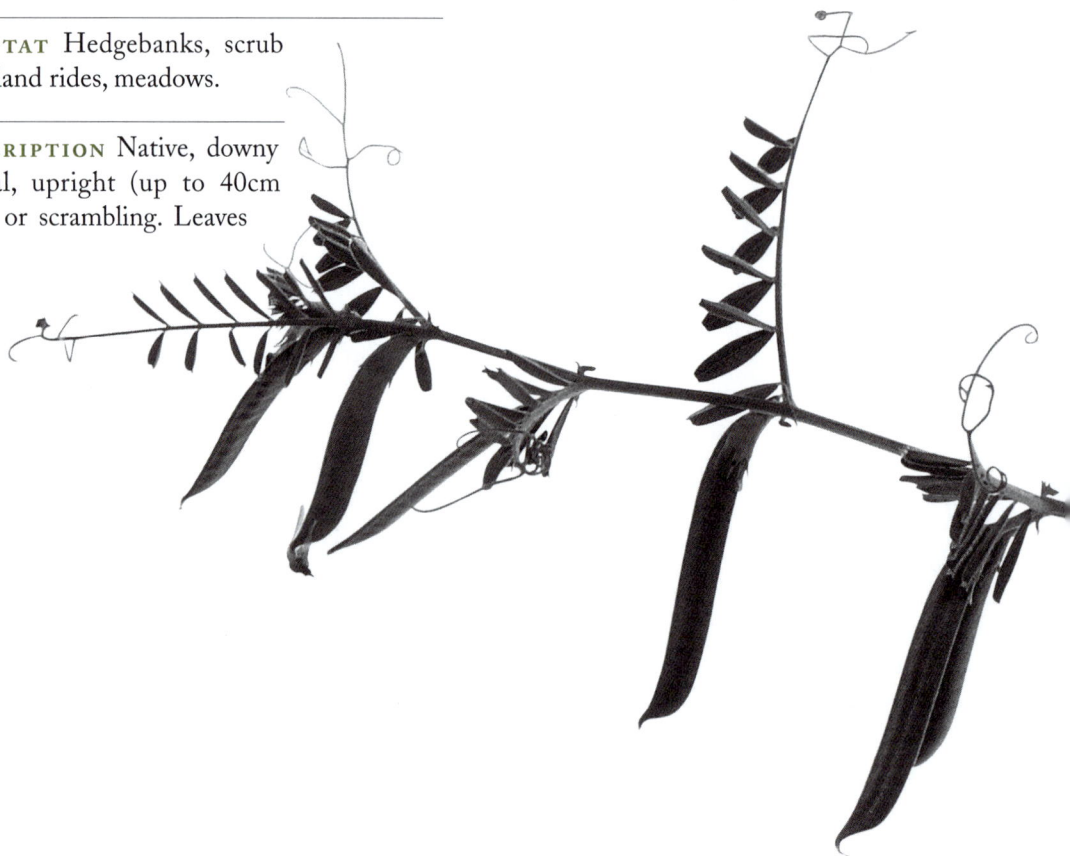

PINK FAMILY
Caryophyllaceae

Honckenya peploides

Sea Sandwort

DISTRIBUTION Up to 300m. In British Isles, widespread along coastal areas.

HABITAT Sand and shingle beaches.

DESCRIPTION Creeping annual, often forming extensive mats. Leaves are small and succulent, a deep vibrant green, oval but ending in a sharp point and stalkless. Flowers are greenish white, 5–6mm wide with 5 rounded petals.

NOTES Sea sandwort is known as sea purslane in North America. A traditional food plant of the Inupiaq Eskimos of northern Alaska, who pick young shoots and use them either fresh or lacto-fermented (after cooking), sometimes flavoured with blueberries or crowberries. It was also formerly preserved by lacto-fermentation in Iceland. It was one of the adulterants that led to the decline of the trade for rock samphire.

USES/RECIPES Leaves and stems are used in their entirety. The leaves are tender and sweet in the spring, and can be used raw, for example in a salad with orpine, sea plantain and fiddleheads, served with pea purée, lobster and black pudding sauce (made with brown chicken stock, browned butter, chopped shallots, parsley and black pudding) [RR], or blanched and served with butter. By midsummer they are a bit spiky and slightly bitter in the raw, but they soften and sweeten with cooking. Use in spring and summer vegetable broths in place of peas, broad beans, green haricot beans or leeks. Use in vegetable minestrone with shellfish (langoustines, cockles or razor clams) [ST].

HALIBUT, MUSSELS AND SEA SANDWORT SAUCE: (serves 4) *For mussels and sauce:* Finely chop 3 banana shallots, 4 garlic cloves and 2 medium chillies, briefly soften over low heat. Turn up heat, add 1kg mussels and stir; as they begin to open (discarding any that don't), add 200ml white wine and cover for 5 minutes. Remove mussels, reduce sauce, lower heat and add 30g chilled, cubed butter, seasoning and juice of quarter a lemon. *For halibut:* (1 halibut fillet per person) Season then fry each side of the halibut until golden brown; finish in oven (220°C) for 5 minutes. Squeeze a

3½ × life size

little fresh lemon juice over each fillet and leave to rest for a couple of minutes. Add lots of sea sandwort to the sauce 5 seconds before serving [Simon Wadham].

HARVESTING NOTES Look for sea sandwort in suitable habitats from late spring. By summer it forms dense carpets that can be quite extensive, so if it's there, it should be easy to find.

Silene vulgaris

Bladder Campion

DISTRIBUTION Up to 360m. In England, widespread, except much of Lake District, Pennines, Cleveland Hills, Fens, Weald, New Forest, Exmoor and Dartmoor; in Wales, mostly northern and southern counties; in Scotland, mainly Central Lowlands and eastern Coastal Lowlands north to Angus, around Moray Firth; sporadic on west coast; in Ireland, sporadic in north, in Lough Neagh and Strangford Lough areas, more widespread in Central Lowlands, and in Cork, especially along coast; present Channel Islands and Isle of Man.

HABITAT Loose soils in open/partially shaded places such as hedgebanks, open woodland, cultivated and fallow arable fields, walls, quarries and gravel pits.

DESCRIPTION Native perennial, up to 90cm high. Leaves are waxy, grey and hairless, quite rubbery to touch; oval, ending in a point with a distinct midrib; stalkless, except for the basal leaves, in opposite pairs, with each successive pair rotated at right angles to the previous one. Flowers white, 10–18mm wide, with forked petals and a ribbed and swollen calyx tube. This becomes a distinctive bladder-shaped seed pod that remains visible well into the winter.

SIMILAR SPECIES Sea campion *S. uniflora*, which is also good to eat, found mostly on beaches and coastal cliffs, has waxier leaves and upright flowers without swollen calyx tubes.

NOTES The boiled leaves are said to have sustained the inhabitants of Minorca in 1685, when locusts destroyed their corn crop. Many English cookery and kitchen-garden books refer to their use in salads – Charles Bryant, in his 1783 *Flora Diaetica*, even proposed that they should be cultivated as vegetables – and there are traditions of use in Lebanon (where it is known as maiden's tears), Italy, Spain, France, Turkey and Greece. The flowers of the closely related clove campion *Dianthus caryophyllus* were once preserved in sugar, syrup and vinegar for their clovelike flavour or used fresh, to adorn and flavour both food and beverages.

USES/RECIPES Young leaves have a sweet flavour like a combination of honey and peas. Use in salads, blanch or steam or stir fry briefly. Bar Restaurante El Imperio in Madrid uses them fried with scrambled eggs. Older leaves are rather bitter but less so when cooked.

HARVESTING NOTES Basal leaves are most worthwhile, being easier to pick in quantity and sweeter than later leaves. The easiest way to learn to identify them is to observe the plant through its growth cycle: the bladder-like flower bases/seed pods are easy to recognize, and the leaves on flowering stems are pretty much the same as the basal ones. The previous year's swollen seed pods mark places where it grows well into the winter.

Nathan Outlaw's Bladder Campion Shoots with Horseradish Sauce, Scrumpy-cured Salmon & Beetroot, Apple & Wild Fennel Risotto

SERVES 4

FOR BASIC RISOTTO:
25ml olive oil
50g unsalted butter
1 white onion, finely chopped
150g carnaroli risotto rice
500ml hot vegetable stock

TO FINISH THE RISOTTO:
200g cooked beetroot, peeled
1 shallot, finely chopped
1 garlic clove, chopped
50ml red wine vinegar
50ml olive oil
50ml vegetable stock
25g unsalted butter
1 apple, peeled and diced
50g Parmesan, grated

10g wild fennel, finely chopped
salt and pepper, to season

FOR THE HORSERADISH SAUCE:
200ml vegetable stock
50ml double cream
200ml semi-skimmed milk
50g creamed horseradish
salt and pepper, to season

FOR THE SALMON:
400g salmon fillet, trimmed and pin boned
50g salt
50g caster sugar
50ml strong scrumpy

TO FINISH:
24 bladder campion shoots, picked and washed, to garnish

FOR THE SALMON: Put salmon in a baking dish. Mix together the salt and sugar, and sprinkle over the salmon. Pour over the scrumpy; cover the dish with cling film. Chill for 2 hours. Wash the salmon, then wrap tightly in cling film. Chill overnight for best results.

Divide the salmon into four equal portions. Heat a non-stick pan and add some olive oil. Place the salmon presentation-side down and cook until golden (about 3 minutes). Turn over and cook for a further 2 minutes then serve immediately with the risotto, horseradish sauce and bladder campion shoots.

FOR THE RISOTTO: Heat a large pan and add the oil and butter. Add the onion and cook for 1 minute; do not allow to colour. Add the rice and cook for a further minute, then ladle by ladle add the hot stock, stirring continuously for approximately 15 minutes.

Remove from the heat and stir for a further 3 minutes. Put the rice in a baking dish and spread out to allow it to cool.

Square off the beetroot by trimming and retain the trimmings for purée. Cube into 5mm dice and marinate with the shallot, garlic, vinegar and olive oil. Season.

Put the cooked rice, stock and butter in a pan and bring to a simmer. Stir for 2 minutes to emulsify. Remove from the heat and add the beetroot purée, beetroot and apple dice, Parmesan, fennel herb and seasoning. Serve immediately.

FOR THE HORSERADISH SAUCE: Reduce the vegetable stock to 3 tablespoons. Add the double cream and milk, and season with salt and pepper. Bring the sauce to 80°C and froth with a stick blender or whisk. Taste, then add the horseradish sauce. Bring back to 80°C, froth and serve.

Spergula arvensis

Corn Spurrey

DISTRIBUTION Up to 450m. Only found as a native on Channel Islands but widespread as a naturalized species throughout much of British Isles. In England, present in most counties, but absent much of Cambridgeshire and the Pennines; in Scotland, absent much of Grampian Mountains, Northwest Highlands and North Highland; in Ireland, widespread in Ulster, west Mayo, Wicklow, Wexford, Waterford, Cork and Kerry.

HABITAT Formerly a common arable weed; found on sandy, lime-poor soil on waste ground and arable-field edges.

DESCRIPTION Long, thin leaves arranged in a whorl around stem somewhat like **bedstraw** species (e.g. cleavers). Both leaves and stems are sticky and hairy. Flowers arranged loosely on multiple-branched stems at top of the plant; they are similar to chickweed flowers, but with unforked petals.

USES Seeds are rather small, but if you find enough of them they could be used in breads or toasted and added to salads. They are known to have been widely used in the past to thicken gruels and potages, and a large-seeded strain persists in some areas, which may be a relic of a cultivated variety. The leaves can be used in salads.

Stellaria media

Chickweed

DISTRIBUTION Up to 950m. In British Isles, widespread throughout except in Scotland, absent parts of Grampian Mountains, North West Highlands and Caithness; in Ireland, absent areas of Donegal, Mayo, Galway, Clare, Laois and Kerry.

HABITAT Pasture, gardens, grassy areas, waste ground, arable fields.

DESCRIPTION Chickweed in abundance forms dense mounds, which can be as high as 50cm, although it can also be prostrate and straggly. The green cordate leaves have one main vein and are 8–20mm long. Stems are round, with a single row of hairs running along one side. Flowers are white and star shaped with 5 forked petals, hence the Latin name, *Stellaria*, from *stella*, meaning 'star'.

SIMILAR SPECIES The closely related woodland plant three-nerved sandwort *Moehringia*

Corn spurrey

trinervia has three distinct parallel veins on its leaves and unforked petals. It is not poisonous but has a disgusting, bitter, soapy taste. Scarlet pimpernel *Anagallis arvensis* and yellow pimpernel *Lysimachia nemorum* have similar, slightly darker leaves but scarlet/yellow flowers. Yellow pimpernel is found in woods; scarlet pimpernel in similar but drier habitats to chickweed and is also distinguished by its square stem. Both are mildly poisonous and bitter. Mouse ear *(Cerastium)* species have downy leaves with more rounded tips; water chickweed *Myosoton aquaticum* has larger, rather thin leaves, resembling a bigger version of chickweed; it is found in marshes, damp fields and river banks. These two species can be used in similar ways to chickweed.

NOTES Chickweed is one of the most abundant wild-food plants and can be gathered and eaten all year round, especially after periods of high rainfall. During dry spells it becomes flaccid but is easily revived by soaking in water. Most gardens with areas of bare soil will have some chickweed emerging and then colonizing if not kept in check. However, if you deliberately refrain from keeping it too much in check, in exchange for less effort, you will have a constant supply of a nutritious salad vegetable.

USES/RECIPES With its mild flavour and delicate texture chickweed tops are one of the best wild-salad bases, providing a background for stronger flavours and coarser textures. Works well with crab, perhaps with a few fool's watercress leaves as well; also with chicken and game birds.

GREEK-STYLE CHICKWEED AND PIGEON SALAD: Boil whole leeks until soft, slice and keep warm with vinaigrette. Marinate wild mushrooms in rapeseed oil, chopped shallots, thyme and lemon juice. Roast pigeon breast. Serve pigeon on top of leeks, then mushrooms and finally chickweed, dressed with tarragon vinaigrette [JDW]. Try

serving a whole chicken with pieces of pear sautéd briefly in oil with a bit of sugar, until lightly coloured, finished with chickweed for the last few seconds and dressed with lemon juice, sugar and olive oil [EC]. Poached duck egg salad with chickweed and deep fried capers, and lemon juice dressing [DQ]. Serve pieces of Arbroath smokie with chickweed and dandelion finished with Pommery mustard vinaigrette, parsnip crisps and soft-boiled quail's eggs [PB]. Chickweed is also good cooked more thoroughly; you need a lot, though, as it reduces down greatly. Steam for 3–4 minutes and serve with butter and/or cream/Parmesan and freshly ground black pepper. Added to other dishes, such as stews, casseroles or pasta sauces, it is advisable to chop it finely, or the result can be quite stringy, especially if cheese is involved.

BENEFITS High in magnesium, phosphorus, copper, vitamins C, B_6, B_{12}, D and A, and rutin.

HAZARDS In huge quantities, mildly toxic due to the presence of saponins, which have caused poisoning to livestock that ate several kilos at a time. For this reason, farmers periodically to spray pasture with herbicides. Before collecting it on any kind of farmland, first check with the farmer whether it has been sprayed.

HARVESTING NOTES Look out for bright green moundlike forms on pasture, slightly lighter than surrounding grass; I have found many gorgeous chickweed patches in this way. This is a good starter plant for beginners: it is very common and poisonous lookalikes are easily distinguished by the absence of a row of white hairs on one edge of the stem. Cut only the top growth, usually no more than 5–8cm as below this it gets stringy and tough. Ariel parts of very young plants can be harvested in their entirety. Plants up to and including the flowering stage produce the lushest growth; after this they tend to be a bit straggly. Chickweed is an agricultural weed that is quite a nuisance to farmers and gardeners, so you can only make friends by offering to harvest it.

Ecological considerations Give the plants a rest from harvesting when they go to seed as the seeds form an important part of the diet of a number of wild birds including grey partridge, linnet, bullfinch, chaffinch and reed bunting. Quite a few of the seeds pass undigested through the gut of these birds and are deposited in pastures new, contained in parcels of manure to get them started. Seeds are also transported by ants and can survive transportation in sea water.

PLANTAIN FAMILY
Plantaginaceae

Plantains are incredibly resilient plants, often growing in places that are repeatedly trampled by livestock or people. Greater plantain, introduced to North America by white settlers, was referred to by the indigenous peoples as 'white man's footsteps': it seemed to crop up wherever they went, probably because the tiny seeds were carried on the soles of shoes. It was not a bad plant to take travelling: plantains of one sort or another have been used as medicines on every continent.

Plantago coronopus

Buck's-horn Plantain

DISTRIBUTION Coastal areas throughout the British Isles; also inland in England, in the east, southeast and Cornwall.

HABITAT Often near the coast, on cliffs and grass; also trampled grassland inland.

DESCRIPTION Leaves downy, pinnatifid, somewhat resembling antlers, in a rosette. Flower spike short.

NOTES Buck's-horn plantain was formerly cultivated as salad in both England and France.

USES/RECIPES Leaves lend a mild, nutty flavour and crisp texture to any dish; they also look so spectacular I tend to leave them whole. Use either raw or briefly cooked.

HARVESTING NOTES The whole rosettes can easily be harvested by cutting them from beneath.

¼ × life size

Plantago lanceolata

Ribwort Plantain

DISTRIBUTION Up to 845m. Widespread throughout British Isles.

HABITAT Grassland of all kinds, sand dunes and cliff edges, roadsides, cultivated fields.

DESCRIPTION Native perennial, hairless, with long, thin parallel-ribbed leaves in a rosette and a short flower spike.

USES/RECIPES Leaves are less mushroomy than greater plantain, but can otherwise be used in similar ways. The flowerheads, on the other hand, are intensely mushroomy, but since the texture is worse this flavour is best harnessed by briefly infusing them in stock or cream (too long and they become bitter) before discarding them.

RIBWORT PLANTAIN GREEN DIPPING SAUCE: Put a few rosettes in a blender, blend with 1 egg yolk then season. Fold in 2 egg whites that have been beaten until stiff, a little lemon zest and a few gratings of Parmesan. Flowers and seeds can be used as for greater plantain but are also small enough to be used whole in salads or blanched and served with butter or a warm vinaigrette. However, spikes have a distinct mushroom flavour and can be used as a flavouring substitute for mushrooms.

Plantago major

Greater Plantain

DISTRIBUTION Up to 845m. Widespread throughout British Isles, only less so in Scotland, in Grampian Mountains and Caithness.

HABITAT Open and disturbed ground, such as paths and tracks, field edges and roadsides.

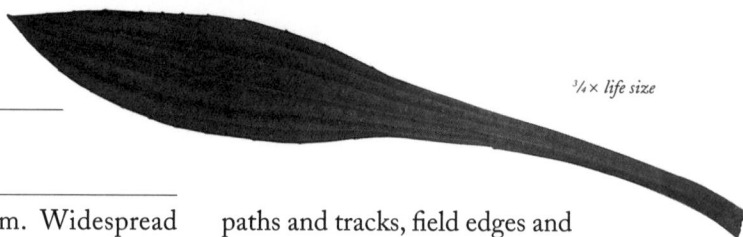

DESCRIPTION Native perennial. Hairless, leaves in a rosette, oval–elliptical with pronounced parallel ribs and short stalks. Flowers on a tall spike, up to 15cm long, tiny and cream coloured; only part of the spike has open flowers at any time.

SIMILAR SPECIES Hoary plantain *P. media* has shorter leaf stalks and narrower leaves, and is downy; its flowers have pinkish-purple tips to their stamens.

USES/RECIPES Leaves of greater and hoary plantain can be quite tough, so only use paler, younger ones; for older leaves, you may need to remove the rather stringy veins or else chop the whole leaf finely. Really young leaves can be used in salads; older leaves cooked as spinach. All leaves have a distinctly mushroom flavour and are slightly bitter; boiled for a few minutes and served with just a little butter, I find them quite delicious. Flowers can be scraped from

the stem and used to thicken soups and stews. Seeds can be winnowed and used in breads and soups, but it is a fiddlesome process.

BENEFITS High in phosphorus and calcium.

Plantago maritima

Sea Plantain

DISTRIBUTION Up to 790m. In coastal areas throughout the British Isles; also found further inland in Cornwall, the Pennines, the West of Scotlandm the Western Isles and the Scottish Highlands. In Ireland, found in much of Sligo, Mayo, Galway and areas of waterways, inlets or loughs; present Channel Islands, Isle of Man, Isles of Scilly and Lundy.

HABITAT Upper and middle zones of salt marshes, coastal grassy areas, rocks and cliffs, coastal heaths; inland on scree, stream banks and species-rich pasture.

DESCRIPTION Native perennial. Long, thin somewhat grasslike fleshy leaves, with only faint ribs. Flower spikes green, flowers with yellow-tipped stamens.

USES/RECIPES Leaves are succulent and delicious. Before flowering, they are floppy, soft, succulent but afterwards become a bit tough and stringy. Raw they are salty and succulent, with a slightly bitter, almost chivey flavour. Use chopped in salads; fried, steamed or boiled; in soups and sauces (e.g. sauce vièrge, see p.120), and as a main garnish with fish. If serving whole, blanch briefly and refresh immediately: they become slippery like spaghetti when cooked any more than this.

WITH BEETROOT AND LAMB: Blanch leaves – no need for salt in the water as they are salty enough. Peel beetroots, cook whole in water with vinegar, sugar and salt: for a litre of water, 100ml vinegar, 100g sugar, 15g salt. Bring to the boil, then cook for 10 minutes if big, or simply take off heat and leave to cool if small. After roasting lamb, add a glass or so of red wine to roasting juices and deglaze pan. Add warm sliced beetroot to this, warm back to boiling then add Dijon mustard vinaigrette and finely diced shallots. Make a nest out of the sea plantain on each plate, put beetroot and gravy in the middle and place the carved lamb (served pink) on top [PW].

BENEFITS Plantains are a very good source of calcium and phosphate. They are also used medicinally for skin irritations such as insect bites and rashes, as well as for sore throats, diarrhoea and cystitis.

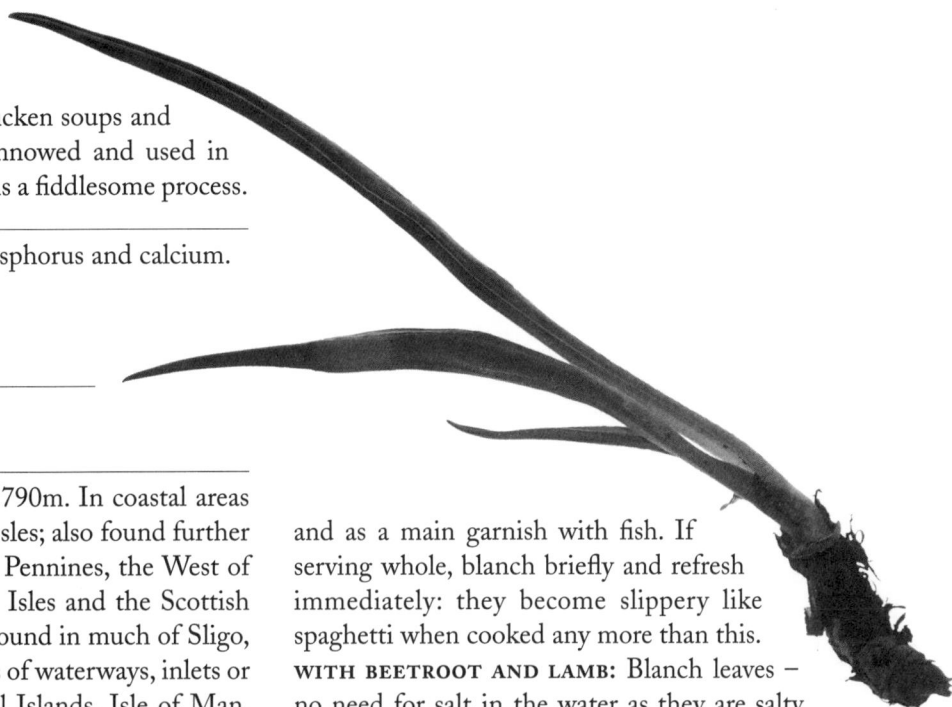

POPPY FAMILY
Papaveraceae

POISONOUS PLANTS

Chelidonium majus

Greater Celandine

DISTRIBUTION Lowland plant. In England and Wales, found throughout except Pennines and Cambrian Mountains; in Scotland, very scarce; in Ireland, most frequent inland parts of Ulster, less frequent in Leinster and almost entirely absent elsewhere.

HABITAT Old walls, ruins, banks and path edges near old buildings, probably due to its former cultivation for 'medicinal' use.

DESCRIPTION Hairy perennial, branched, reaching up to 90cm high. Leaves broad, with rounded pinnate lobes, like misshapen oak leaves, but dull greyish green. Stems and leaf stalks bleed orangey-yellow sap when broken. Flowers, May–August, small, up to 2.5cm wide, with 4 petals, bright yellow in clusters of 2–6.

HAZARDS Has caused poisoning through the use of extracts for various dubious medicinal purposes. Symptoms include kidney failure and vomiting. A small boy suffered acute intestinal inflammation and subsequently died from circulatory failure after eating it. How he came to swallow any of it is a mystery, as it is foul smelling and extremely acrid, although cattle have been known to eat seedling plants, so it may be less acrid at this stage of growth.

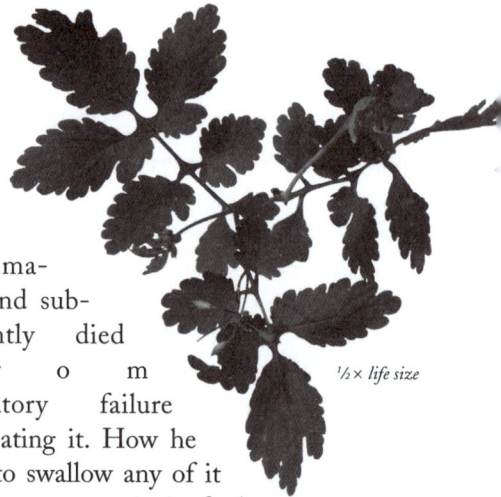

¹⁄₂ × life size

Glaucium flavum

Yellow Horned-poppy

DISTRIBUTION In England, Wales and Scotland: found much of coast Galloway's Luce Bay–the Humber (but not north Pembrokeshire, north Cornwall and east Norfolk coasts) and on coast of Firth and Alland Isles; in Ireland, found only east and south coasts; present Channel Islands, Isle of Man and Isles of Scilly.

HABITAT Shingle beaches and waste ground.

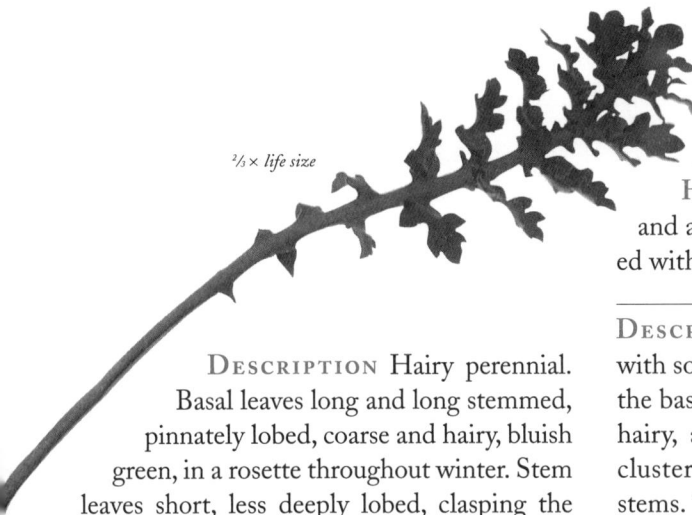

²⁄₃ × life size

DESCRIPTION Hairy perennial. Basal leaves long and long stemmed, pinnately lobed, coarse and hairy, bluish green, in a rosette throughout winter. Stem leaves short, less deeply lobed, clasping the stem. Plants are branched and reach 60–90cm high. Flowers large and yellow, similar to other poppies but seed pod is quite unique, very long, thin and curved, hence the name. Flowers June–September.

HAZARDS Contains the same alkaloids as **greater celandine**, but there are no contemporary records of poisoning by this species. Edible oil has been obtained from the seeds.

EDIBLE PLANTS

Papaver rhoeas

Common Poppy

DISTRIBUTION Up to 300m. In England, widespread, except higher-altitude areas; in Wales, absent hilly and mountainous areas; in Scotland, most common in Central Lowlands and lower-lying areas south to the border plus a few sites Grampian and East Highland around Moray Firth and to the west in Argyll and Stirling, as well as Northern Isles; in Ireland, mostly concentrated in counties in Leinster and Tipperary, Waterford and Cork in Munster, sparse elsewhere; present

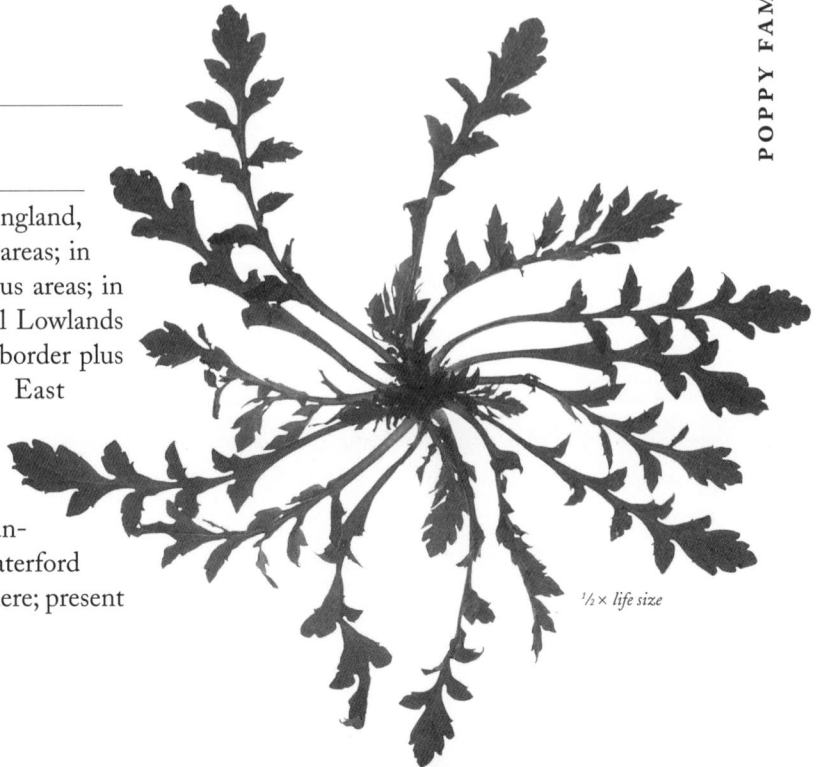

Channel Islands, Isle of Man and Isles of Scilly.

HABITAT Annual of disturbed ground and arable fields, especially on edges untreated with herbicides.

DESCRIPTION Well known for its red flowers with soft, tissue-paper-like petals, often dark at the base. Leaves are pinnate, greyish green and hairy, a flat basal rosette at first, then dense cluster before the emergence of the flower stems. These are also hairy, branched and with few leaves. Seed capsules are egg shaped with a conical top with spoke-like ribs and gaps underneath to allow the seeds to escape when the plant is shaken.

SIMILAR SPECIES The equally edible long-headed poppy _P. dubium_ is mainly distinguished by the longer seed capsules that give this poppy its name. It also has paler petals, usually without dark bases, and is more frequent in Scotland than common poppy.

¹⁄₂ × life size

NOTES Poppy leaves were commonly used throughout southern Europe until quite recently, usually boiled and served with olive oil. Common poppy flowers were traditionally used to produce red syrup, coloured by the alkaloid rhoeadine, which was first isolated from this plant.

USES/RECIPES Leaves are tender and juicy with a mild flavour and make a pleasant addition to salads. They are slightly hairy, but this isn't noticeable once they are in a mixed salad or a sandwich. They can also be used in soups and as a cooked green. Flower buds can be added to salads; for example, in Morocco, they are blanched then sautéed with **mallow, bladder campion** and **common purslane**, and eaten with olives and perserved lemons (*Gathered Mediterranean Food Plants*, Rivera et al, 2006). Petals make a colourful addition to summer salads. In Italy the seeds are used, with those of rape *Brassica napus* to make a bitter vegetable dish called broa. They can also be used in bread and cakes or toasted for use in salads. In Germany and Poland a paste, made using the ground seeds (they can be ground using a good blender or electric coffee grinder), is used as a filling for cakes and pastries, such as the following:

POLISH POPPY SEED BREAD: *For the filling:* Mix 50g dried fruit and peel, 2 tbsp rum, 125g ground poppy seeds and 4 tbsp honey and allow to soak overnight. *For the bread:* To make the dough, rub together 250g strong bread flour, $1/4$ tsp salt, 2 tsp sugar, 50g unsalted butter, $1/2$ tsp instant yeast and, lastly, 100ml warm milk. Knead for 5 minutes. Cover and allow to rise for $1 1/2$ hours. Roll out the dough so it is 1cm thick, spread the filling across it and roll up like a Swiss roll. Transfer to a baking sheet, brush with beaten egg yolk and again allow to rise for 1 hour. Bake in a pre-heated oven (180°C) for 35 minutes. [JT].

HAZARDS Cattle have been known to show signs similar to opium poisoning after consuming large quantities of these plants, although they contain no opiates. There is no risk of poisoning to humans (unless you plan to eat 2kg or so of leaf and flower in one sitting).

HARVESTING NOTES Collect seeds once the seed pods have turned brown. Cut several stems at once with large scissors or, preferably, secateurs, and place them in a bag or bucket upside down to shake out the seeds. If you move quickly you can collect quite a bit of seed. My daughter Becki and I once found a whole bank colonized with a larger garden species; we filled two big jars with seed in 10 minutes.

PRIMROSE FAMILY
Primulaceae

POISONOUS PLANTS

Anagallis arvensis

Scarlet Pimpernel

DISTRIBUTION In England, throughout south and east, Midlands and much of north, but absent Pennines, much of Northumbria and Cumbria; in Wales, throughout, except parts Cambrian Mountains; in Scotland, scarce, found only some coastal areas and absent Highlands; in Ireland, mostly found but not most inland parts Connaught and Ulster; present Channel Islands, Isle of Man and Isles of Scilly.

HABITAT Open ground in gardens and on cultivated fields; by rabbit warrens, on heaths, sand dunes and chalk downlands.

DESCRIPTION Winter annual that starts its growth cycle in winter and is most in evidence then. The whole plant is hairless. Leaves oval, ending in a point; stems square, up to 30cm long in a mostly creeping, though sometimes more upright, fashion. Flowers tiny and scarlet, with 5 petals, appearing June–August.

SIMILAR SPECIES Chickweed *Stellaria media* has a round stem with a single line of hairs, slightly paler leaves and white flowers. Yellow pimpernel *Lysimachia vulgaris* is always prostrate, with slightly wider leaves up to 4cm long, a round stem and yellow flowers.

HAZARDS Due to the presence of cell-damaging saponins, it is reported to have killed sheep that ate large amounts; human poisonings have also been recorded, resulting in headaches, nausea and body pains. Poisoning by yellow pimpernel produces similar symptoms.

3 × life size

Primula obconica

Poison Primrose

DISTRIBUTION Not recorded in the wild but a widely grown house plant.

HABITAT Houses and conservatories.

DESCRIPTION Leaves are stalked (primrose *P. vulgaris* leaves unstalked) and more rounded than primrose; several flowers on each long stem, of various colours including red, pink, blue and yellow.

HAZARDS Causes allergic reaction to skin on handling leaves and the green calyxes of flowers.

Edible plants

Primula veris

Cowslip

DISTRIBUTION Up to 845m. In England, found in most areas except parts of Devon, Cornwall, Kent, Essex, Cambridgeshire, south Lancashire, southwest Yorkshire, Lake District, Northumberland and Cheviot; in Wales, absent higher-altitude areas; in Scotland, concentrated in Forth and Borders, Tayside and Clackmannanshire. In Ireland, widespread in central and east Central Lowlands but more sparse to west into Connaught and southwest into Munster. Present Isle of Man.

HABITAT Dry, grassy places, mostly on chalk or other alkaline soil, in open woodland, banks, meadows and churchyards.

DESCRIPTION Native perennial. Leaves taper into stalk further up than primrose leaves and are broadest near their base. Flowers, cup shaped, a rich yellow, with orange streaks radiating from centre, in drooping umbels of 10–30 with flowers facing various directions.

SIMILAR SPECIES Oxlip *P. elatior* has paler, less crinkled leaves, paler and larger flowers without orange streaks, which all face the same way. It is almost exclusively a plant of ancient woodlands.

USES/RECIPES Young spring leaves and flowers raw in salads or, for example, with celery, turbot, and watercress vinaigrette [RR]. Young leaves as greens. Use flowers in general as for **primrose**. The cowslip pudding that follows is a great example of an old English recipe, in which there is a tendency to give quantities for only some of the ingredients and no cooking times, all of which is left to the cook's judgement:

Cowslip pudding Cut and pound small the flowers of a peck of cowslips, with half a pound of Naples biscuits grated, and three pints of cream. Boil them a little, then take them off the fire, and beat up sixteen eggs, with a little cream and rose water. Sweeten to your palate. Mix it all well together, butter a dish, and pour it in. Bake it, and when it be enough, throw fine sugar over it, and serve it up. When you cannot get cream, new milk will do well enough for these sorts of puddings. from John Farley's *The London Art of Cookery*

ECOLOGICAL CONSIDERATIONS The Duke of Burgundy fritillary caterpillar feeds on the leaves.

1½ × life size

Primula vulgaris

Primrose

DISTRIBUTION Up to 850m. Widespread throughout British Isles, only less so in England, the Fens, south Lancashire and southwest Yorkshire; in Scotland, the Highlands; in Ireland, Mayo.

HABITAT Moist and shady in deciduous woods, hedgebanks and field edges.

DESCRIPTION Native perennial, with rosettes of unstalked, obovate–spoon-shaped crinkly leaves. Flowers, saucer shaped, a pale yellow corolla, with 5 notched lobes; each sits on a long woolly stalk growing out of the centre of the leaf rosette.

2 × life size

USES/RECIPES Flowers: in spring and summer salads or, either candied or fresh, to garnish puddings. Leaves: cooked or in salads; they have slightly honey-like flavour that takes a while to register and lingers for some time after eating.

PURSLANE FAMILY
Portulacaceae

A small family of mild, succulent leaves, all but one of which are present in the British Isles as garden escapes. In other countries, the seeds and roots of many purslane species have been used in the past, but my experience with them has been primarily as salad plants. The plant that gives its name to this family, common purslane *Portulaca oleracea*, was until quite recently a popular winter salad, cultivated in the British Isles from the thirteenth century using hot beds.

Common purslane is scarce as a wild plant on our frost-prone islands, but it may become more widespread as global warming sets in. I asked the Botanical Society's county recorder for Kent, Mr Philp, if he knew of a Kent location for it. He showed me the only recently recorded site: his back garden, where it grows as a weed and, due to the location and design, seems to escape frost. In Mediterranean countries, the wild plants are an important part of people's diet in many rural areas, not least because they are rich in beta-carotene (4700 ppm) and an excellent source of omega-3 oil alpha linolenic acid, known to lower cholesterol and blood pressure.

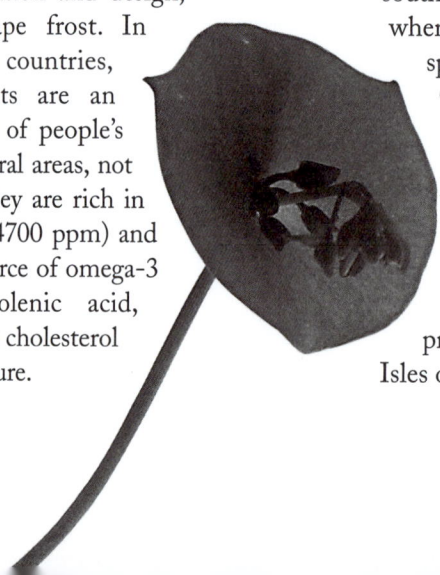

Claytonia perfoliata

Spring Beauty

DISTRIBUTION Up to 300m. In England, widespread Home Counties, Norfolk, Suffolk and much of Midlands, southwest Yorkshire, south Lancashire and Cheshire, sporadic elsewhere, absent much of the Fens; in Scotland, sporadic in Central Lowlands and eastern Coastal Lowlands, widespread around Firth of Forth and Moray Firth, sporadic North Highland and Shetland, absent Orkney and Western Isles; in Wales, sporadic on north and west coasts; in Ireland, sporadic Cork, Wexford, west Donegal and Belfast area; present Channel Islands, Isle of Man and Isles of Scilly.

⅓ × life size

HABITAT Sandy, open ground; on banks and field edges and in gardens. Flourishes best in light shade.

DESCRIPTION Appears in late winter with a rosette of oval leaves: long stalked, pale matt green and fleshy. As the plant matures it takes on a distinctive form with two fused leaves perched saucer-like on top of the stem, with tiny white flowers, up to 5mm wide, emerging from their centre. At this stage they are almost unmistakable (but see similar species).

SIMILAR SPECIES Be careful not to collect poisonous spurge (*Euphorbia*) species, which have tiny yellow flowers emerging from fused bracts. Yellow centaury *Cicendia filiformis* and the rare thorow-wax *Bupleurum falcatum* also have fused leaves; as does yellow-wort *Blackstonia perfoliata*. None of them has white flowers; nor are they poisonous.

NOTES Spring beauty looks great twice: both at the early rosette stage and the later fused-leaf flowering stage it is unique and elegant. It originates from western North America, where it is eaten as a salad and known as miner's lettuce. It was generally cultivated in the British Isles, and the wild European population also arose from garden escapes. In France it is still quite commonly used, known as *pourpier d'hiver* or 'winter purslane'. This is a good plant to give to anyone new to wild food, as there is nothing challenging about its appearance, texture or flavour.

USES/RECIPES Leaves are versatile, mildly flavoured, with a succulent texture. They work well not only with fish dishes, white meat and other delicately flavoured ingredients but also as a neutral accompaniment to stronger flavours. Try in a simple salad with goats' cheese and toasted walnuts [MH] or with **bur chervil** (which often grows in the same place as spring beauty) and capers to accompany a shellfish salad [ST]. Older, tougher plants can be cooked.

Claytonia sibirica

Pink Purslane

DISTRIBUTION Up to 950m. In England, widespread Devon, Cornwall, west from Cumbria south to Staffordshire and parts of northeast Yorkshire and Norfolk, sporadic elsewhere; in Wales, around borders of Caernarvonshire, Merioneth and Denbighshire as well as parts Carmarthenshire, Brecknockshire and Radnorshire; in Scotland, common in eastern Coastal Lowlands north to Moray, south of Grampian Mountains, sporadic in Highlands, Northern Isles and Western Isles; in Ireland, sparsely found Londonderry, Antrim, Down and Tyrone in northeast and Tipperary, Cork and Wexford in south; present Channel Islands and Isle of Man.

HABITAT Damp and shady places on acid and sandy soils, often in woodland and on stream banks.

DESCRIPTION Spreading perennial, often covering wide areas of ground. Leaves are oval, like young spring beauty, but darker green and glossy with clearly visible veins. At the rosette stage they are also fewer, with slightly shorter stalks; later in opposite pairs, without stalks, just below the flower stem, which produces several pink flowers, each with 5 notched petals. The flowers are about 10mm wide, much larger than spring beauty.

NOTES Pink purslane is a garden plant that has become widely naturalized and is considered a pest in some areas. The corms of a similar species, *Claytonia caroliniana*, are used by Canadian tribal peoples, known to them as wild potatoes; the Chilcotin people have a mountain range in British Columbia called the Potato Mountains, after the plant. None of our species has tubers that can be used in this way.

USES/RECIPES Leaves are slightly bitter when eaten alone and without dressing, but this becomes unnoticeable when combined with other ingredients. They taste somewhat like raw beetroot and work well in combination with cooked beetroot. A good, succulent and very attractive salad leaf. Older, tougher plants can be cooked. Flowers are not strongly flavoured but are also very attractive; serve a single stem with leaves and flowers for a spectacular finish to a dish.

Montia fontana

Blinks

DISTRIBUTION Up to 945m. In England, in north mostly absent East Midlands and east of Yorkshire, except North York Moors, but widespread West Midlands and throughout remainder of north, in east found only Norfolk and Colchester–Tendring area of Essex, in southeast absent much of Kent, Sussex and Home Counties but widespread Surrey, London and Berkshire, in southwest absent most of Wiltshire and Gloucestershire but elsewhere mostly widespread throughout; in Wales and Scotland, found throughout; in Ireland, concentrated in the north, Kerry, Cork, Waterford and Wexford, but also in a few areas in the west of both Galway and Mayo.

HABITAT Damp, bare ground, in woods, fields or by non-chalky springs.

DESCRIPTION A low, straggling plant with round stem and thin spoon-shaped opposite leaves, up to 2cm long, but usually much smaller. Flowers, tiny, white, growing from leaf axils in twos/threes or singly at the top of the plant.

NOTES The only native species belonging to this family, blinks is traditionally used as salad in Portugal and Spain, and appears on menus in restaurants in Madrid.

SIMILAR SPECIES Bog stitchwort *Stellaria uliginosa* has square stems.

USES/RECIPES Add leaves and stems to salads. Like other members of this family, the flavour is mild and the texture pleasantly succulent.

2 × life size

ROSE FAMILY
Rosaceae

The name of the rose family immediately evokes images and sweet scents of one of our best-loved flowers. In our culinary past and in many different cultures, the name would also bring flavour to mind. Our wild roses have particularly delicate flavours that the chefs with whom we work are beginning to introduce in contemporary dishes. Trees in the rose family have stronger, almond-flavoured flowers, but their best offerings are their fruit.

The rose family is a fecund fruit-bearing plant tribe, providing rich colours, scents and aromas, as well as cancer-fighting and other beneficial phytochemicals. The silky texture of rose petals, the promise of sweetness in the plump tenderness of ripe plums and the yielding firmness of raspberries as they are picked also make these plants a pleasure to handle (although many also have sharp thorns). I got embroiled in an hilarious cherry-blossom fight one spring, when the petals had fallen. We were all sweeping up great handfuls and hurling them in one another's faces, but no matter how hard we hurled, their impact was as delicate as a finger massage.

More than any other family these plants are part of our lives, worked into our culture and landscape and our own hands-on experience – much of which involves putting them into our mouths. In Kent, where large areas of countryside were once devoted to growing various fruits of this family, people feel the disappearance of orchards, now replaced by more fields of wheat and rape. Yet wild ancestors of these fruits remain, and most have their own exquisite and peculiar qualities, not least their wild forms on the landscape. Bramble bushes thick with blackberries sprawl over banks, hedgerows and anywhere else they can; rowan trees with clusters of bright orange berries are a modern feature of gardens and municipal plantings but an ancient element of Scottish and Welsh landscapes; white-blossomed, bare, black branches of sloe or blackthorn bushes line the hedgerows in spring and are peppered with sloes in autumn. We still feast our eyes on all these, but, with the exception of blackberries, we no longer bring them to our feasts.

FAMILY HAZARDS Seeds of several fruits contain cyanogenic glycosides, which, given the right conditions, synthesize into cyanide, but in the human digestive tract this happens slowly and inefficiently. However, the particularly toxic kernels of *Prunus* species peach, bitter almond and wild apricot (none of which occurs as wild species in this country) have all caused severe poisonings. The flesh of the fruit of some naturalized *Cotoneaster* contains levels high enough to produce mild poisoning. The kernels of wild *Prunus*, bird cherry in particular, should not be eaten, although the leaching out of almond flavouring during cooking or pickling of unpitted fruits is not hazardous, and it is very tasty. Apple seeds contain moderate levels, but you would need to chew thoroughly and swallow upwards of 5000 seeds in order to ingest a fatal dose.

Alchemilla glabra

Lady's Mantle

DISTRIBUTION Up to 1215m. In England, widespread in Peak District and northward, but mostly absent south of the Wash, though similar *Alchemilla* found in Midlands and southwest; in Wales, widespread, except south and southwestern coastal areas, and Anglesey; in Scotland, widespread, also Orkney, but less so north Highlands and Western Isles; in Ireland, widespread in north, above Sligo and Cavan, but almost entirely absent from south.

HABITAT Pasture and meadows, by streams, on roadsides and banks, especially where the soil is damp. Often found in areas that become temporarily waterlogged.

DESCRIPTION Leaves palmate, with 9 coarsely toothed lobes. The flowers small and greenish, in tight clusters.

NOTES The appearance of lady's mantle leaves can be quite magical after dew or rain; the leaf surface is water repellent and water balanced on the surface or caught in the centre of the leaf becomes separated into mercury-like globules that glisten like jewels.

USES/RECIPES Leaves can be used as greens, in combination with a few other spring leaves. They are mentioned as ingredients in some versions of Easter Ledge pudding.

Amelanchier lamarckii

Juneberry

DISTRIBUTION Up to 300m. In England, sparse but widely distributed, more common in parts of Hampshire, Dorset, Sussex and Surrey; elsewhere in British Isles, mostly absent. Naturalized trees are from bird-sown seed of American trees, planted in gardens.

HABITAT Open woods and woodland edges, roadsides, scrub and heaths on acidic, sandy soil; also planted in parks and gardens.

DESCRIPTION Small tree or shrub, up to 10m high. The finely toothed leaves are oblong–oval, purple and hairy first but later grey-green and hairless. In April–May, flowers with long white petals make the tree distinctive. Juneberries ripen in July: black and round, 7–10mm wide.

NOTES Also known as service or sarvis berry because early American settlers thought it was similar to wild service-tree. There are no *Amelanchier* species native to Britain, but

1½ × life size

A. ovalis is native to south and central Europe. Saskatoon *A. alnifolia* is now grown on a large scale in Canada for its berries.

USES/RECIPES The berries have a deliciously sweet and penetrating flavour, something between an apple and a pear; the soft seeds add a nutty, almond-like flavour. A tangy syrup can be made to complement meringues and panna cotta; also use berries in pies, cakes, jams and jellies. Blend the whole berries and freeze for a delicious fruit granita, enhanced by the almond flavour of the seeds.

BENEFITS Juneberries are a rich source of iron and copper.

Aphanes arvensis

Parsley Piert

DISTRIBUTION Up to 610m. In England, found in most areas, but less so north Devon, south Lincolnshire, south Lancashire, southwest Yorkshire and Durham; in Wales, mostly absent Merionethshire, Montgomeryshire and Glamorgan; in Scotland, common in west and south, in Dumfries and Galloway, but mostly absent north of Grampian Mountains except Loch Ness and Moray Firth; in Ireland, frequent in south, especially Limerick, Cork and Waterford, and in northeast, in Down and Londonderry, mostly absent west and central Ireland.

HABITAT Arable fields, bare patches of summer-drought land, such as open woodland tracks (the first kind of place in which I found it).

DESCRIPTION Very low growing, at the most forming a small mound of leaves and often sprawling completely flat on the ground. The tiny fan-shaped leaves rarely reach 1.5cm long; they have three lobes with almost square teeth; the flowers are tinier still and appear in small clusters opposite a leaf.

NOTES Parsley piert eluded me because my wildflower books all showed it larger than life. I knew it grew in my area of Kent, but despite concerted efforts I could find none of it. I kept stooping for leaves of buttercup and crane's-bill, both round and deeply toothed, like the photographs at which I had looked repeatedly until parsley piert's leaf form became branded on my brain. I had an eureka moment one afternoon when I spotted a little clump of tiny leaves on a woodland path: the leaves looked uncannily familiar though strangely out of context. I picked a sprig; it was indeed parsley piert, but a quarter of the leaf size in the wildflower-book photos. Other than a lesson learnt – to read plant descriptions thoroughly (I went back to the books and found the size of the leaves described quite precisely) – this was not a major foraging breakthrough. Parsley piert is unnoteworthy as a salad ingredient, its main selling point probably its pretty, tiny leaves. In the past it was thought to heal kidney stones because of its ability to break through hard ground. An earlier name for parsley piert was parsley break-stone; the parsley connection probably due to the fact that garden parsley was also thought to heal kidney stones. Nutritional-supplement companies market parsley piert in tablet form for this purpose, though the company I approached was vague about its active constituents.

USES/RECIPES Leaves are good in salads with other wild leaves or, better still, on their own so you can show off the leaf shape. Pickle in slightly sweetened white wine vinegar, with a few spices such as mace, peppercorns and mustard seeds.

Crataegus monogyna

Hawthorn

DISTRIBUTION Up to 610m. Widespread throughout the British Isles except in Scotland, higher-altitude areas of Grampian Mountains and northwest Highlands, and introduced to Northern Isles.

HABITAT Hedgerows, woodland edges or open woodland and scrub.

DESCRIPTION Native shrub or small tree, 2–10m high. Smaller branches are very thorny; larger branches have two distinctively flattened sides. Glossy leaves longer than they are wide, deeply lobed with 3–5 deeply toothed or untoothed lobes. White or very occasionally pink blossom with rounded petals appears from May in large clusters. Hawberries, also known as haws, are dark red with one large seed; they are fully ripe in September.

SIMILAR SPECIES Midland hawthorn *C. laevigata*, a plant of ancient woodland, old hedges and boundary banks, has shallower leaf lobes with more rounded ends, leaves wider than they are long and berries with 2–3 seeds. The other major hedging plant is blackthorn or sloe; it flowers when its branches are still bare and has longer, unlobed leaves.

NOTES In May the eponymous blossom of hawthorns thickly cover the branches and great corridors of the landscape. Hawthorn means 'hedge thorn'; it is one of our most widespread hedging plants, planted extensively in the eighteenth and nineteenth centuries to enclose and privatize areas formerly open and held in common. But hawthorn can be forgiven for this: its use as a hedging plant is much older, and the plant has its place in our common heritage. In his book *Wild Fruits and Nuts*, Dr Geoffrey Eley recalls, 'Four or five generations of a cottager's family at Wymeswold' enjoying 'an annual spring dinner of hawthorn buds' in the form of a hawthorn suet roll.

USES/RECIPES My mother and paternal grandmother both remember eating young hawthorn leaves and buds in spring and calling them Bread and Cheese. Use them raw in salads or nibbled off the tree as they did, or add them to your cooked meals. Flavour wise, they are nothing special, but their heart-tonic properties are an incentive for eating them. Use flowers in salads, or cooked with rabbit. In Anglo–Norman cuisine, they were used in red meat stews. The texture of the berries is like avocado, but with so little pulp on each berry it can be a bit tiresome spitting out the pips. Haws are high in pectin and make a thick jelly (see **crab apple**) used to accompany meats; for a lighter jelly add apples, pears or lemon juice. For **Hawthorn Turkish delight:** Make a jelly

with less water, lots of sugar and flavour with dried rose petals; cut into squares and dust with icing sugar. Pure berry pulp is made by pressing berries through a sieve. It makes a really firm jelly, which Okanogan–Colville and Lillooet first peoples in Canada used for dipping in soups. Fresh pulp thickens and flavours savoury dishes or other fruit. Add it to dough for sweet breads and flat breads. Mix pulp with vinegar, spices and sugar for haw ketchup.

BENEFITS Hawthorn leaves, flowers and especially berries are reputed to improve heart function, lower cholesterol and indirectly help reduce high blood pressure. Among the active constituents are flavonoids, including rutin, and tannins. Berries are also high in vitamin C and several B vitamins.

HARVESTING NOTES Pick flowers when they have just opened, at which point they smell sweetly of aniseed; afterwards they develop an unpleasant smell that attracts dung flies and midges to pollinate.

Filipendula ulmaria

Meadowsweet

DISTRIBUTION Up to 880m. Pretty much the whole of the British Isles; only less so in Guernsey or parts of the Isle of Lewis.

HABITAT Mostly damp places, on the edge of rivers and streams, on marshes and in ditches.

DESCRIPTION Perennial, with bushy leaf growth in winter and spring, and later a woody stem (up to 1.5m high), topped by flowers from midsummer onwards. Leaves in several pairs of oval, finely toothed, pleated leaflets (30–80mm

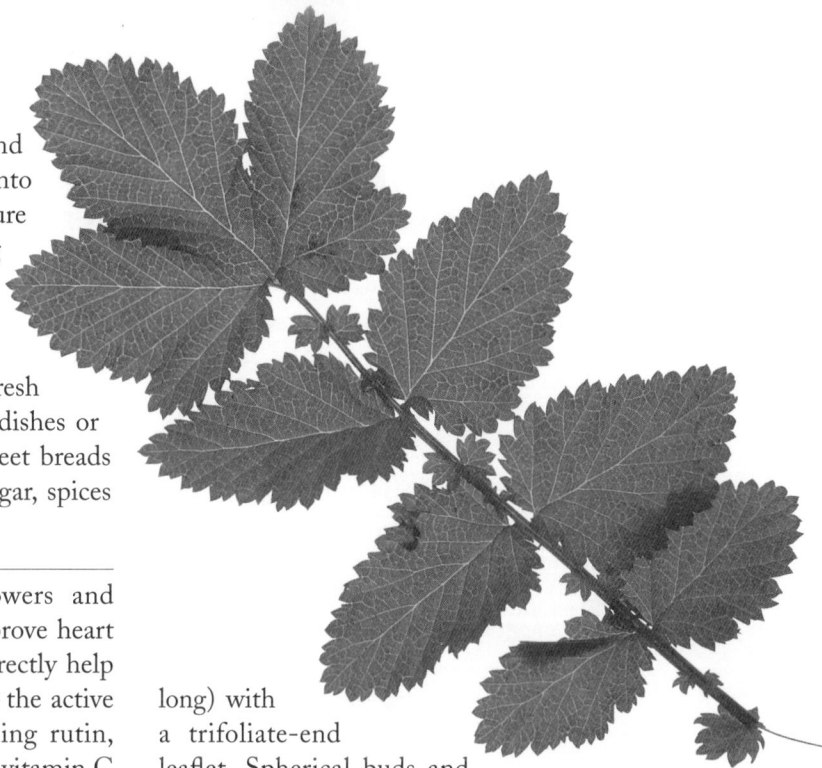

long) with a trifoliate-end leaflet. Spherical buds and small creamy white flowers are crowded together in messy clusters.

SIMILAR SPECIES Dropwort *F. vulgaris* grows on much drier soil; it is shorter, has larger and fewer non-fragrant flowers and smaller leaflets; its leaves, though less flavoursome than meadowsweet, can be used in salads.

NOTES How meadowsweet got its name has nothing to do with meadows and everything to do with mead, the fermented honey drink once flavoured with meadowsweet flowers. The flowers have an extraordinary honeyed almond scent, a lure for pollen-seeking insects and foragers, but they produce no nectar. When foraging for flowers, we inevitably collect some of the tiny black beetles that feed on the pollen. We once had beetles flying and crawling around the inside of our van; now we keep bags full of meadowsweet sealed until we get home then leave them outside until all the beetles have escaped.

Eating meadowsweet is a good way to 'let medicine be your food', as Hippocrates instructed.

ROSE FAMILY

Salicylic acid, from which aspirin is synthesized, was first isolated from meadowsweet. Whereas aspirin attacks the lining of the stomach, meadowsweet tea soothes both heartburn and nausea at the same time as it relieves pain. Importantly, it is also pleasant to drink.

USES/RECIPES Leaves have a refreshing wintergreen flavour and are excellent in salads, with the leaflets stripped from the stalks. Sauté pigeon breasts; set aside to rest then sauté slices of pears in the same pan. Serve breasts on a bed of meadowsweet and violet leaves – a good contrast of soft-textured (violet) and coarse-textured (meadowsweet) leaves.

REINDEER LIVER PÂTÉ WITH MEADOWSWEET: Grind the following in a blender: 500g reindeer (or venison) liver, 250g minced beef, 100ml duck fat, 50g bacon, 100ml double cream, 20ml cognac, 50ml finely chopped fresh meadowsweet leaves, 1/2 teaspoon chilli powder, 1/2 teaspoon ground black pepper, fine sea salt. Place the resulting mixture in a buttered ovenproof dish and cook at 160°C with a thermometer until the inner temperature is 54°C. Let the pâté cool down and serve it with **cowberry** syrup or jam [AH].

Both dried and fresh meadowsweet leaves have been used for flavouring drinks, and meadowsweet tea can be made from leaves, flowers or both, either fresh or dried. Jekka McVicar infuses the flowers in vinegar, which makes a delightful salad dressing. A syrup or cordial can also be made from the flowers, which are also wonderful for flavouring custards: hold the stem and stir them slowly through the custard for a minute or two before serving. Also use to flavour jellies, crème brûlée, sorbets and stewed apple.

MEADOWSWEET CRÈME CARAMEL: (6 portions) *For the sugar syrup:* Toast 75ml caster sugar in a frying pan until slightly brown. Add 125ml water and 1/2 teaspoon fresh lemon juice; cook until it forms a thin syrup. Set aside. *For the crème:* Heat 150ml double cream cream, 150ml organic milk, 2 meadowsweet flower heads (fresh or dried) and 125ml caster sugar until the sugar has melted. Whisk 1 egg and 2 egg yolks in a large bowl. Add the warm cream mixture. Put about 5mm sugar syrup on the bottom of each ramekin. Pour the crème gently over the syrup. Cover each ramekin well with cling film. Cook them in a water bath in an oven preheated to 100°C for 30 minutes. Cool well. To remove the crème caramels use a little knife. Serve with the remaining sugar syrup and fresh strawberries [AH].

BENEFITS Contains flavonoids, including rutin.

HARVESTING NOTES You will probably first positively identify meadowsweet in flower, the clusters like clots of cream catching the eye against the green, even among the dense growth of other plants. Once familiar, meadowsweet is easy to recognize by its leaves at any time of the year. Pick flowers into a damp cloth bag to prevent them wilting.

ECOLOGICAL CONSIDERATIONS Meadowsweet is one of a number of British plants, the seeds of which need cold weather in order to germinate; with global warming its range may decrease. Because it is intolerant of grazing, stripping plants of leaves will eventually kill them, but meadowsweet often grows in colonies and you can usually get what you need by gathering just a few leaves from each plant. Be sure to leave some flowers as food for beetles.

1/2 × life size

Fragaria vesca

Wild Strawberry

DISTRIBUTION Up to 640m. In British Isles, mostly widespread throughout, except: in Scotland, entirely absent Western Isles, Orkney and Shetland, and higher-altitude areas of Grampian Mountains and North West Highlands; in Ireland, absent parts of west coast.

HABITAT Dry ground in woodland, roadsides, railway embankments, hedge banks and scrub; rocky areas and scree. Usually on alkaline soil or rock.

DESCRIPTION Creeping native perennial with long runners, 5–30cm high. The leaves have the familiar trifoliate-toothed form of cultivated strawberries. Flowers white. Strawberries small, 1–2cm.

SIMILAR SPECIES Barren strawberry *Potentilla sterilis* has similar leaves and flowers, but no fruit and short runners. The two plants are distinguished by the way the leaflets end: the end tooth of wild strawberry protrudes beyond the two on either side of it, whereas the end tooth of barren strawberry leaflets is shorter than the two on either side. Mock strawberry *Duchesnea indica* is found in shady places in gardens and churchyards but rarely as a wild plant; its berries are similar to wild strawberries, but quite bland.

1½ × life size

Barren strawberry leaf

NOTES Wild strawberries bring back memories of childhood holidays in Wales, where we used to pick these sweet and delicious red berries from lane verges. Their flavour is superior to that of any cultivated variety and makes up for the fiddliness of picking them: they are much, much smaller than any cultivated variety. They also have a gorgeous fragrance; in fact their Latin name *fragaria* is derived from this word.

I have equally sweet memories of wild strawberry ice cream made by friends who cultivated wild strawberries on their allotment: they had a bumper harvest, which makes me wonder why so few people grow them.

USES/RECIPES Leaves can be used in salads, but not when Grizzled Skippers are present. This butterfly has such an intriguing name, I had to mention it! The caterpillars feed on wild strawberry leaves, but if you tread carefully, your foraging activities are unlikely to interfere with them – or they with you. You can mix the berries, say about 80g, with 1 teaspoon caster sugar and a dash of balsamic vinegar; marinate for 5 minutes then sprinkle over a dessert such as crème brûlée, vanilla pudding or home-made ice cream.

HARVESTING NOTES Plan future excursions by noting the presence of the leaf and flower earlier in the year. It can be difficult to see the bright red berries concealed among the leaves as you walk through a wild-strawberry patch, but they come unexpectedly into view as you change position: there may be more there than you think.

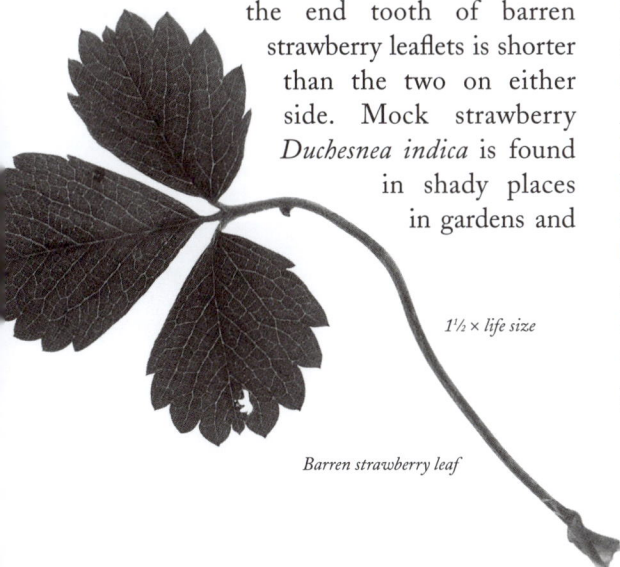

Geum urbanum

Herb Bennet/Wood Avens

DISTRIBUTION Up to 450m. In England and Wales, widespread; in Scotland, widespread in south, but mostly absent northwest Highlands and Grampian Mountains, and entirely absent Western Isles and Shetlands; in Ireland, found in most areas, except higher, coastal areas of Donegal, Mayo, Galway and Kerry.

HABITAT Dry, shady places such as woodland paths and edges, hedge banks and roadside verges.

DESCRIPTION The leaves are highly visible in winter and early spring when little else is around; they have several uneven pairs of small hairy leaflets and a large 3-lobed end leaflet. Upper leaves are stalkless with 3 toothed, pointed lobes. The yellow flowers look a lot like buttercups and are easily overlooked, but the seeds in their purple spiky ball of burrs are eye-catching; they also catch fur and clothes, enabling the plant to disperse its seeds.

SIMILAR SPECIES Water avens *G. rivale* has a large, rounded, unlobed end leaflet that has sharp teeth and is sometimes as wide as 10cm. Its bell-shaped flowers range cream–peachy pink. To confuse matters, the two plants hybridize when they both occur in the same area, but this doesn't really matter as they have similar uses.

NOTES The name herb bennet is a shortened version of the Latin *herba benedicta*, 'blessed herb'; the Latin *geum* comes from *geuo*, 'taste'. Both names testify to the traditional usage of this plant. The leaves were formerly much used in soups and stews and the roots as flavouring for ale; both leaves and roots also have a multitude of uses in traditions of folk medicine.

USES/RECIPES Leaves are pleasant, chopped and added to soups and stews, or boiled in a mixture of wild greens. The roots have a clove-like scent and taste. Use them in place of cloves, either dried (at a low temperature so as not to destroy the active principle) or fresh. Tie them in bundles so they can be easily removed, and allow the flavour to infuse into whatever you are cooking, for example stewed apple, pickling vinegar or white sauce.

ECOLOGICAL CONSIDERATIONS Using the roots need not be controversial. Herb bennet is a common and persistent garden weed, so it should be fairly easy to find plants that someone wants removed.

APPLES

Malus domestica, our cultivated apple, is easily recognizable and needs no introduction. It is distinguishable from the crab apple by larger fruit and no thorns, although there is a continuum of variants between the two.

Malus sylvestris

Crab Apple

DISTRIBUTION Common in ancient woodland and hedgerows across the British Isles.

HABITAT Hedges and woodland, especially oak, sometimes deep within the wood.

DESCRIPTION Native small tree or shrub, usually solitary, up to 10m high. Branches are thorny; flowers white, flushed with pink, growing in clusters. The apples are small, about 2cm diameter, yellow–green, sometimes flushed red.

USES/RECIPES Crab apples are good cored and roasted with pork or goose. Baked crab apples, with plenty of sugar, are also exquisite served with crème fraîche.

CRAB APPLE JELLY AND CHEESE: Jellies have such a low yield, the perfect way to make them viable is to be less greedy for jelly and to use the remaining pulp for cheese (like the Spanish membrillo or quince cheese). Gather as many crab apples as time will allow, minimum 2kg. Cook whole with a little water to help them to pulp without burning. Liquidize (add a little more water if the pulp is stiff), pass through a fine strainer, then hang in muslin overnight over a bowl. Take the resultant liquid (for the jelly) and pulp (for the cheese), boil each with an equal volume of sugar, skimming off any scum and saving it for a crab apple drink

(mixed with water, lemon and ice). Test for setting point: put a few drops on a cold plate, put it in the fridge for a minute; if it looks like skin and wrinkles when you push your finger into it, it is time to stop cooking. Pour into sterilized jars and keep until you can't resist eating with cooked meat and cheese. This recipe works just as well for other wild fruit; some with less pectin may need a few crab apples to help them set [PW].

Potentilla anserina

Silverweed

DISTRIBUTION Up to 845m. Widespread throughout British Isles, except higher-altitude areas such as in Scotland, northwest Highlands and Islands and Grampian Mountains; in Ireland, Wicklow, Donegal and Clare.

HABITAT Upper parts of salt marshes, shores and sand dunes, arable field edges, places that flood periodically, and grassy areas.

DESCRIPTION Prostrate perennial, spreading by runners; named after the felty underside of its leaves, which flash silver if turned over. These grow in tufts and have 15–25 sharply toothed, oblong leaflets. In summer, yellow flowers appear on single stalks.

NOTES Silverweed is a wild food with an international history of use, eaten by indigenous peoples in North America, Alaska, Canada and Europe. In the British Isles, it has kept people alive during times of food scarcity, particularly in the Highlands of Scotland and the Hebrides, where it was known as Brisgein or Brisgean. However, it was no mere famine food. As a wild crop it was systematically harvested using a plough to turn up the roots; areas of

silverweed were claimed and jealously guarded. It is tenacious, growing in poor soil where little else thrives and cropping in years when other crops fail.

USES/RECIPES Roots need a good scrubbing to remove any earth. Boil for 20 minutes and serve with butter and perhaps a dash of soy sauce. Alternatively, roast or sweat in butter or oil for 30–40 minutes. To make flour for baking and thickening: leave cleaned roots in a sunny spot for a few days until dry. Chop them finely then reduce to powder in a blender, coffee grinder or kitchen mill. Leaves are reputed to be edible, but I find the texture unpalatable. Chopped finely, they impart some flavour.

BENEFITS The roots are high in magnesium and phosphorus.

HARVESTING NOTES My friends Lesley and Tom Kilbride (see Wild Food Directory, p.387) have silverweed growing in the sand at the edge of a beach near their house at Applecross in the Scottish Highlands. This makes the roots easy to harvest, but in most places they take quite a bit of digging. Other than sandy sea shores, the easiest place from which to harvest them is at the edges of cultivated fields.

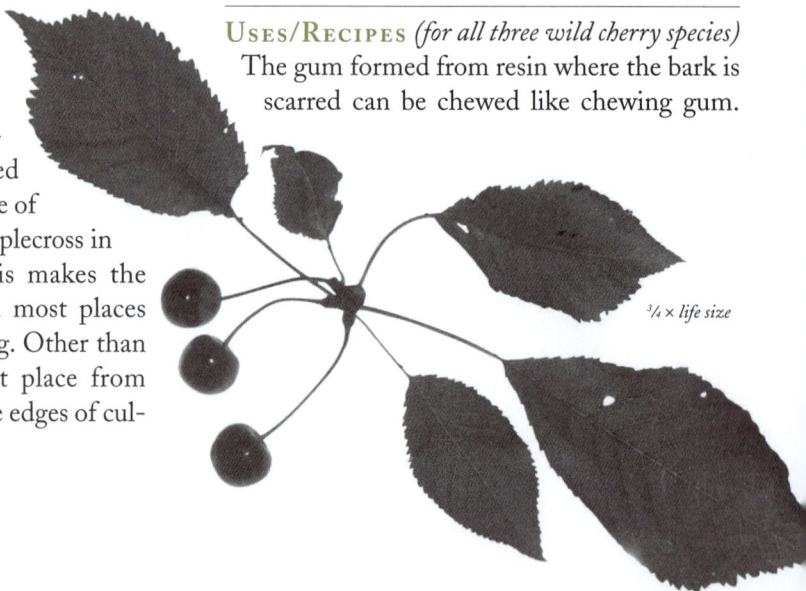

Prunus avium

Wild Cherry

DISTRIBUTION Up to 400m. In England and Wales, widespread throughout; in Scotland, found in most areas, but absent much of the Highlands, Grampians, Western Isles and Northern Isles; in Ireland, widespread in southeast and northeast but scattered areas only west and central.

HABITAT Deciduous woodlands and hedges, usually on gravel soils, but also widely planted in parks and gardens.

DESCRIPTION Native tree, up to 25m high and rather wide. Bark is reddish brown with horizontal lines on younger trees. Flowers are white with long stalks, in clusters of 2–6. Ripe in June, the cherries are red or black and can be sweet or sour.

SIMILAR SPECIES Height distinguishes mature plants from dwarf cherry, which grows up to only 5m high, while bird cherry has much smaller, darker fruit and flowers arranged in dangling spikes. Distribution details can help confirm which species you have found, as many areas only have one or the other.

USES/RECIPES *(for all three wild cherry species)* The gum formed from resin where the bark is scarred can be chewed like chewing gum.

¾ × life size

Infuse flowers in milk for making custard, especially good with **Japanese knotweed**. Like flowers of other *Prunus*, they taste of almonds. In Japan, the leaves are salted and used to wrap *sakuri mochi*, a sweet made with rice, bean paste, agar-agar and sugar. The cherries are plentiful but much overlooked. Wild cherry is sometimes sweet, sometimes sour; bird cherry is always bitter and dwarf cherry always a little sour. Once cooked and sweetened the flavour of all three is richer than that of any cultivated variety. Sweeter fruit can be eaten raw, for example with goats' cheese on walnut and raisin bread; bitter or sour fruit should be cooked and passed through a sieve or else stoned beforehand using a cherry-pitter. Cooked cherries can be used to make game sauce, especially good with wild duck, or as jams, jellies or syrup for ice creams and cakes.

HUNGARIAN SOUR CHERRY SOUP: 150g sugar, zest ½ lemon, a pinch of salt, a pinch of ground cinnamon, 500g wild cherries (stoned), 1 table-spoon plain flour, 100ml soured cream. Add the sugar, lemon zest, salt and cinnamon to 1 litre boiling water. Boil for 5 minutes. Add the cherries; simmer for a further 5 minutes. In a small bowl, mix the flour into the soured cream. Slowly add a cup of cooked cherries then add this mixture to the rest of the cooked cherries. Simmer until thick and leave to cool. Keep covered in the fridge to prevent a skin forming. Serve chilled with a blob of soured cream in each bowl.

Prunus cerasifera

Cherry Plum

DISTRIBUTION Up to 300m. In England and Wales, found throughout but more widespread south of line Severn Estuary–the Wash, except Cornwall, west Devon and Wiltshire; in Scotland, found at a few locations in south,

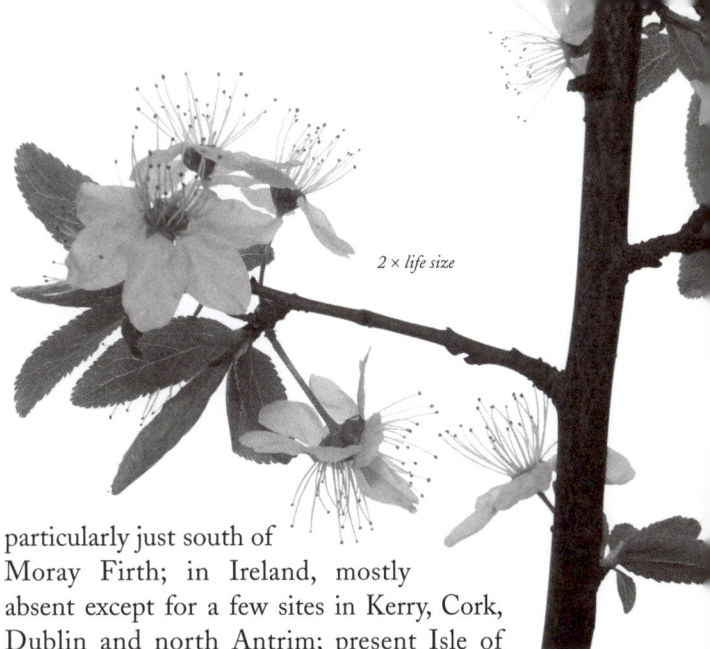

2 × life size

particularly just south of Moray Firth; in Ireland, mostly absent except for a few sites in Kerry, Cork, Dublin and north Antrim; present Isle of Man and Channel Islands.

HABITAT Not strictly a wild plum, this plant has been widely planted in gardens, hedgerows and public spaces and is naturalized in some places.

DESCRIPTION Naturalized small tree or shrub, up to 8m high. The first *Prunus* to flower, February onwards, with newly emerging leaves accompanying the flowers. Cherry plums are 20–30mm wide, round and either red or yellow or a combination of the two.

SIMILAR SPECIES There are two other round plums: bullace are smaller, green or yellow, and sour. Greengages are green and usually, but not always, larger. You could mistake unripe cherry plums for small greengages.

USES/RECIPES Many people consider the fruit ornamental – but I'm not one of them! They are exquisitely juicy and sweet if you catch them at their best. Cook them if you like, but it's a shame to do so; save that for harder, sourer specimens that need a bit of cooking and sugar to soften and sweeten them up.

HARVESTING NOTES Lay a large sheet on the ground below the tree to catch the fruit, give the branches above a good shake, then pick up the corners of the sheet and carry your harvest home.

Wild damson

Prunus cerasus

Dwarf Cherry

DISTRIBUTION Up to 300m. Found in scattered areas throughout the British Isles: in England, mostly Norfolk and Cornwall; in Wales, mostly southwest; in Scotland, a few places in southern border counties, in east and below Moray Firth; in Ireland, few central, more common north and parts of south and southeast; present Isle of Man and Channel Islands.

HABITAT Woodland edges and hedges. Plants usually originate from deliberate planting but are also spread by suckers and seed from fallen fruit, occasionally forming dense thickets.

DESCRIPTION Naturalized shrub or small tree, up to 5m high. Bark redder than wild cherry, flowers white or pinkish, in small clusters. Cherries ripe in July, generally quite sour, red, with streaks of yellow, though occasionally black.

NOTES This species is a parent of the cultivated morello cherry; it is high in malic acid and used to make various alcoholic drinks, including cherry brandy.

USES/RECIPES See **wild cherry**.

Prunus domestica

Wild Plum

DISTRIBUTION Up to 300m. In England, widespread, except parts Yorkshire, Durham, Cumbria and Northumberland; in Wales,

widespread; in Scotland, scattered southern areas but only few sites in central and northern parts, absent Western and Northern isles; in Ireland, throughout but more widespread in Cork and in east, especially northeast.

HABITAT Old hedgerows, woodland and field edges.

DESCRIPTION Shrubs or small trees, very like blackthorn, but without thorns, and the larger flowers appear at the same time as the leaves. Some plums look like cultivated plums; bullace plums are green or yellow and always round; damsons are purplish black, either plum shaped or round.

NOTES Wild plums grow from seed of cultivated plums, which are thought to be the product of cross breeding between sloes and cherry plums. The wild plants gradually revert to type, with each successive bird or human or other mammal-sown seed producing trees with slightly smaller, sourer fruit. There are several subspecies of *P. domestica*, including cultivated greengage subsp. *italica*, introduced from France and first grown in Suffolk by the Gage family, who gave it its name. You may find them in old hedgerows but they are not strictly wild. The wild varieties damson and bullace are both forms of subsp. *insititia*.

USES/RECIPES The flowers also give an almond flavour to ice cream and syrups; they can be added to salads.

SWEET PICKLED DAMSONS: Use enough malt or even balsamic vinegar to cover the damsons, with a weight ratio of 2:1 sugar:damson. Add spices, such as cloves or ginger, and lemon zest and cinnamon to taste. Heat everything together for 15 minutes or until damsons are soft. Place in sterilized jars, cover with boiling sweet vinegar and seal immediately. The longer they are left, the better the flavour. The almond flavour of the kernels gradually infuses into the pickling liquor, which becomes a fantastic ingredient in itself and is good for dressings or meat sauces. Damsons mix well with blackberries, for example in crumbles. For a cold soup use a fruity red wine, add brown sugar, reduce wine then add damsons and lemon zest while it's hot, leave for an hour then pass through a sieve and chill. Use sweetened as a dessert with ice cream or unsweetened as a sauce with cold meats [EC]. With their high pectin content damsons make good jellies and jams; damson compote can be used to make fantastic ice cream and yogurt, but my personal favourite is to eat it with porridge.

Bird cherry

BENEFITS Plums contain very little vitamin C but are a good source of minerals, especially iron and potassium.

½ × life size

Bird cherry in flower

Prunus padus

Bird Cherry

DISTRIBUTION Up to 650m. In England, widespread north of Peak District and widely planted in the south, except Norfolk and parts of West Midlands, where native; in Wales, widespread and mainly native except Anglesey and parts of southwest; in Scotland, widespread but less common in Highlands, naturalized on Isle of Lewis; in Ireland, found Fermanagh, Monaghan and other northern counties, mostly absent Down and west Donegal, with scattered areas in south, where mostly native; naturalized on Isle of Man and Channel Islands.

HABITAT Damp woodland, stream banks and wooded fen areas, usually on alkaline soil.

DESCRIPTION Native or naturalized shrub or small tree, up to 15m high. Flowers blossom in long dangling spikes, in contrast to clusters of other wild cherries. Bird cherries ripe in July. They are small, black and quite bitter.

USES/RECIPES See **wild cherry**.

HARVESTING NOTES *(for all three cherry species)*
Record cherry-tree locations through the year ready for the cherry season in July. They are easy to recognize by their bark and easy to spot when in blossom. Taller trees keep their fruit out of reach of all human foragers except those who own a fruit-picking ladder or know a tree surgeon with a cherry picker. Fortunately, they usually sucker and produce smaller trees near by, so it should be easy to reach fruit somewhere near the biggest tree. You need to move quickly once the fruit is ripe as birds, especially jays, quickly strip the trees once the fruit starts to ripen.

Prunus spinosa

Blackthorn/Sloe

DISTRIBUTION Up to 500m. Widespread throughout the British Isles except: in Scotland, higher-altitude areas, such as North West Highlands and Grampian Mountains; in Ireland, western part of Mayo.

HABITAT Hedges, open woodland and woodland edges, waste ground, cliff slopes and the prostrate form on shingle beaches.

DESCRIPTION This widespread native hedgerow shrub is familiar to most people by sight if not by name. As a small tree it reaches up to 4m high and is usually as broad as it is tall. At the end of winter, the black, thorny branches (hence blackthorn)

3 × life size

produce white flowers singly or in pairs along the branch tips before there are any leaves; the blackthorn is the second herald of spring, coming into blossom just after the cherry plum. In late autumn, the branches are leafless again but laden with sloes: little black, round fruits, with a bluish bloom.

USES/RECIPES Flowers make almond-flavoured syrup, using sugar and water and plenty of flowers: the more flowers, the stronger the almond flavour. Pour over ice cream, poach tart fruits or **Japanese knotweed** in it or make into dessert jelly. Sloe gin, for which the berries are used, has become quite trendy and is now being mass produced. Unless someone planted sloes in anticipation of the trend some 20 years ago, a serious foraging operation is afoot somewhere! Sloe jelly (for how to make, see **crab apple**) accompanies pork like apple sauce but with more edge. Use it or the stoned berries to make meat sauces. Combine chocolate and sloes in desserts and cakes. Cowell wrote in *A Floral Guide for East Kent* (1839) that the French (in the nineteenth century) pickled unripe sloes as a substitute for olives. Pushing raw sloes through a sieve (with the back of a ladle) changes the flavour of the fruit, perhaps by activating an enzyme; the resultant purée is slightly sweet, much less astringent and makes a pleasant accompaniment to cheese.

HARVESTING NOTES The tough thorns are an obstacle and a hazard (see p.22); you may want to wear a pair of thick gardening gloves.

Crosses with *P. domestica* are not uncommon. They are worth looking for: the fruit is larger and easier to harvest as the bushes are not so spiny.

PEARS

Like feral apple trees, feral pears don't really need describing: if it has pears on it, it's a pear tree! Both trees often grow where someone has dropped a core, usually some distance from the tree on which it grew.

Two species benefit from this unintended act: the plant gets its seed dispersed and we are provided with more free apples and pears. This is an echo of our more unconscious reciprocal relations with other species, before we tethered ourselves to plants through domestication. Someone has not worked hard to put that tree there; we should eat the fruit of their effortlessness and not allow them to rot on the ground.

There are two truly wild pear species, both extremely rare. Neither has particularly palatable fruit, which perhaps serves to show the unpromising raw material from which the wonderful cultivated pear came. On the other hand, perhaps someone will find a way of using wild pears that reveals the potential our ancestors saw in them.

½ × life size

life size

Pyrus pyraster
Wild Pear

DISTRIBUTION Botanical recorders tend not to distinguish between feral and wild pears, so there is no precise data available.

HABITAT Open woods, hedgerows, scrub and thickets.

DESCRIPTION Native, deciduous shrub or tree, up to 20m high. Distinguished from cultivated pear by thorny branches and smaller, usually round (but sometimes pear-shaped) fruit, which are never sweet.

SIMILAR SPECIES Plymouth pear *P. cordata* is much smaller, no higher than 4m, with tiny, round fruits, no more than 18mm wide, with no end sepals. It is restricted to a few locations in Cornwall and Devon.

Rosa canina
Dog-rose

DISTRIBUTION Up to 550m. In England, widespread, but less common in east above the Wash and northwards into Yorkshire; in Wales, widespread; in Scotland, sporadic throughout but absent Western and Northern isles; in Ireland, sporadic but more common in Cork and the northeast.

HABITAT Hedgerows, woodland edges, waste ground, cliffs, river banks, railway embankments, roadsides.

DESCRIPTION Native deciduous shrub forming clumps 1–3m high with long, arching stems bearing solid, hooked thorns. Leaves have 2–3 pairs of leaflets. Flowers delicate pink, in clusters of 2–5. Red berries or hips can be anything from round to elongated-egg shape. Flowers June–July; hips ripe from September.

SIMILAR SPECIES Field-rose *R. arvensis* has white, not pink, flowers, which generally outlast dog-rose; due to rather weak stems, it grows by climbing over other plants and sometimes colonizes large areas.

NOTES Dog-rose is our commonest wild rose, well known for its pretty pink flowers in summer and its red berries in an otherwise quite colourless winter landscape. The flowers have a subtle flavour and are slightly sweet, with a soft texture like thin slivers of velvet gelatine.

3 × life size

USES/RECIPES Add flower petals to salads or use to decorate desserts; chefs at the London restaurant Le Caprice made a show of them by suspending them in a clear jelly.

ROSE-PETAL SYRUP: Heat 1 litre water with 200g sugar, a piece of cinnamon stick and a little lemon zest. Allow to cool, then add 50g rose petals; use the resulting syrup for poaching peaches [EC]. In Lebanon the whole flowers are boiled to make a summer drink. Rose hips were collected from hedgerows by children for industrial-scale production of rose-hip syrup during the Second World War, a then much-needed vitamin-C supplement (for recipe, see **Burnet rose**). However, the only diet that needs supplementing is a poor one. In our post-war land of plenty why not simply have a good diet and enjoy the syrup as food? It makes a lovely, if subtle, flavouring and accompaniment to apples and ice cream, among other things.

SWEDISH ROSE-HIP SOUP: 1 litre water, 250g sugar, 1 star anise, $\frac{1}{8}$ cinnamon stick, $1\frac{1}{2}$ cloves, freshly grated zest 1 lemon, 500g rose hips. Boil water, sugar, spices and lemon. Drop 500g rose hips in for 5 minutes. Blitz, then pass through muslin. Sip with almond cookies and ice cream [EC]. In Italy, rose hips are cooked whole with white wine and sugar then passed through a jelly bag to make jam. For water mint and dog-rose chermoula, a sort of fragrant and spicy Middle Eastern pesto, see **water mint.**

HARVESTING NOTES Instead of collecting whole flowers, take just the petals, so that fruit can still form. Keep cool in a sealed container immediately after picking or they will shrivel. Hips are best after a few frosts (or a night in the freezer), when the flavour is richer and the flesh is soft and sticky; at this point you can squeeze out the pulp through the end of the berries. Birds and other animals seem to avoid them in Kent, perhaps because the seeds are too hard to crack, so they can remain on the bushes as late as February.

USES/RECIPES Flowers, use as for **dog-rose**. The black hips have a rich smoky flavour reminiscent of chocolate and blackcurrants. **BASIC ROSE HIP SYRUP** (same method for all varieties): Dissolve 2kg sugar in 1 litre water, whilst bringing to boil, then add ½kg rose hips, spice with orange zest and/or star anise, if you like, simmer for 10 minutes, then blitz and pass through a jelly bag/piece of muslin placed over a sieve [PW]. Use burnet rose hip syrup to make long summer drinks, pour on ice cream or chocolate pudding, or use in dressing for a Moroccan-style salad with couscous, mint and coriander [JT]. Picked before frost, when the texture is still firm, they make an interesting addition to breads and cakes; you will need to halve them and clean out the seeds.

Rosa pimpinellifolia

Burnet Rose

DISTRIBUTION Up to 610m. Mostly scattered over British Isles, but more common in coastal areas except in England, Devon and southeast coast; in Scotland, absent Western and Northern isles; in Ireland, in Donegal. Native but often planted in public places: introduced to several areas in England, in Midlands and south; also in Wales.

HABITAT Usually sand dunes and sea cliffs; also sandy heaths, chalky scrub and hedgerows.

DESCRIPTION A short shrub, usually less than 1m high with upright stems covered with straight prickles and bristles. Leaves have round-toothed leaflets like salad burnet. Flowers are white, the hip round and purplish black. Burnet rose has the Latin name *R. pimpinellifolia*, which means 'with leaves like burnet' (salad burnet used to be known as pimpinella) and so is named twice after this plant.

2 × life size

Rosa rugosa

Japanese Rose

DISTRIBUTION Up to 400m. Naturalized from gardens. In England and Wales, widespread; in Scotland found in most areas, but mostly absent Highlands, Grampians and Western Isles and not found in Northern Isles; in Ireland, in southeast and northeast, sporadic west and central.

HABITAT Increasingly common as stand-alone thickets on beaches and sea cliffs but also found in hedgerows, waste ground and roadside verges.

DESCRIPTION This shrub has dark brown woody stems covered with hairlike prickles, some thick and some thin. The flowers are

deep pink and the hips big, orange and pumpkin shaped, ripe from July onwards.

USES/RECIPES Flowers are larger and have a much stronger scent and flavour than dog-rose. Use to make jelly and jam (see **dog rose**), for yogurt, cakes and pastries. Rose petals of other fragrant species are the familiar flavour of Turkish delight. **ROSE-WATER**: Place petals in freshly boiled water, leave for 24 hours then strain. Rose-water flavours fruit and other desserts, makes a delicate sorbet and is sprinkled over rice in Iran. North African spice

Jesse Dunford-Wood's Rose Hip Jelly with Orange Panna Cotta

SERVES 6

FOR THE JELLY
300g rose hips
1 litre water
peel of 1 small orange
2 cardamom pods
a knob of fresh root ginger, peeled and finely
    sliced
1 small lemon, thinly sliced, plus a little extra
    fresh lemon juice to taste

100g caster sugar, plus extra to taste
7 leaves gelatine per 1 litre stock

FOR THE PANNA COTTA
1½ gelatine leaves
150ml milk
50g caster sugar
zest of 1 small orange
150ml double cream

FIRST PREPARE THE JELLY: Make a stock with the rose hips, water, orange peel, cardamom pods, ginger, sliced lemon and sugar as suggested or to taste, plus maybe a little extra lemon juice to taste: it will be fragrant, unusual, complex and delicious. Bring to the boil and cook for 5 minutes. Leave overnight to infuse. Strain off the stock, taste and add more sugar as required. Add a little stock syrup (equal quantities of sugar and water boiled) and add gelatine, at 7 soaked leaves per litre of stock. Allow the jelly to set in a mould.

TO MAKE THE PANNA COTTA: Soak the leaf gelatine in cold water so that it can 'bloom'. Heat half of the milk and all the sugar in a pan with the orange zest. Bring to the boil, which will melt the sugar and infuse the orange. Take off the heat, stir in the gelatine until fully dissolved and pass into the cold cream and add the other half of the milk.

Once the jelly has set in the mould, add the panna cotta on top, and leave to set.

blend, *ras el-hanout*, is made from dried rose buds and spices such as cinnamon, mace, galingal, aniseed and nutmeg. It is used to flavour game, lamb and couscous. The dried petals can be used alone to flavour desserts. The hips are larger, with more substantial flesh, and easier to harvest than those of our native species.

Rubus caesius

Dewberry

DISTRIBUTION Up to 320m. In England, found most counties, apart from Devon, Cornwall, Staffordshire and Derbyshire, and less-common in the North; in Wales, mostly coastal, although only a few places in Powys; in Scotland, very rare; in Ireland, scattered areas Galway–Wexford, a few places in Fermanagh and coastal Kerry.

HABITAT Hedges and woodland edges, heaths and scrub, usually on alkaline soil and often among brambles.

DESCRIPTION Low-lying shrub with long trailing stems and leaves like bramble but always with only three leaflets. The stems are round and have fewer prickles than brambles. White flowers appear May–September. Dewberries have a blue waxy bloom, making them

4 × life size

appear dusty, and fewer but larger segments than blackberries; ripe from late July.

NOTES The dewberry looks a lot like blackberry. In many areas it is quite common: lots of people have probably picked dewberries thinking them blackberries. It is seldom so abundant as the blackberry; often one or two plants, alone or among brambles, though it does sometimes form larger patches.

USES/RECIPES Perhaps scarcity leads me to exaggerate their qualities, but I much prefer dewberries to blackberries: they are juicier and have a brighter flavour. Eat them fresh with cream, or allow them to stand alone in a one-fruit summer pudding or ice cream.

RUSSIAN DEWBERRY SAUCE: Press 2 tablespoons fresh uncooked dewberries through a sieve using the back of a ladle. Mix the fruit pulp with a teaspoon of freshly grated horseradish root, a tablespoon of fresh lemon juice, a little finely grated fresh root ginger and 2 rounded tablespoons soured cream. Serve cold, with poultry or rabbit.

Rubus chamaemorus

Cloudberry

DISTRIBUTION Up to 1160m. In England, found only in one 10 sq km in Shropshire and North York Moors and in higher regions of Pennines and Cheviot Hills; in Wales, only Powys; in Scotland, in Southern Uplands, west of Argyle and Bute, through most of Grampian and Monadhliath mountains and northwest Highlands; in Ireland, only Sperrin Mountains.

HABITAT Highland areas, moors and bogs, mostly on acid peat on hill tops. Elsewhere in Europe, they grow in similar habitats at much lower altitudes.

DESCRIPTION Cloudberry grows in quite large patches, with palmate leaves like mallow or lady's mantle but more wrinkled and hairy. The stems have no prickles, each bearing one large white flower in June–August, then a single fruit with a few large segments. Cloudberries can be found August–October, but mostly in August. They are first red, then deep orange and finally a pale yellow orange.

NOTES I first encountered cloudberries thanks to retired forester Stan Firth, who spent the day walking with me high up in the hills of the Scottish Borders to show me where they grow. They really do crown the hills – you might say they are the icing on the cake – growing on the flat boggy areas of hill tops. Like their high-altitude neighbours, crowberries, these berries are a reward for committed walkers; their most obvious use is as much needed immediate sustenance, having hiked to the kind of altitude where they are generally found! Oddly, in Scandinavia, where they are hugely popular, they grow at much lower altitudes, often in boggy woods. In Finland and Sweden there are enough to support a small industry making jams, yogurt and vinegars. In Norway there are strict customary rights over cloudberry patches, which override the Everyman rule that otherwise entitles everyone to forage pretty much at will. Great wrath is incurred by anyone found picking on someone else's cloudberry patch.

USES/RECIPES They are at their absolute best when the colour changes from deep to yellow orange. Cloudberries taste like something between peach and orange, but not as sweet. In Finland they are baked in milk and cinnamon; another Finnish speciality is to serve them on top of slices of melted Leipäjuusto, a Lappish mozzarella-like cheese, the name of which means 'bread cheese'. Apparently, the Laplanders used to bury them in snow to preserve them through the winter. Alaskan Inuit eat them fresh with milk and sugar. In Norway they are enjoyed as a special dessert at Christmas, served with cream.

Rubus fruticosus agg.

Brambles/Blackberries

Brambles, like dandelions in the daisy family, are not a species but a grouping of many similar ones.

DISTRIBUTION Up to 490m. Widespread throughout British Isles, but a few places have almost none: in Scotland, north of Isle of Lewis, likewise much of northern Highlands and border areas, where Moray, Aberdeenshire, Perth and Kinross meet.

HABITAT Woodland, waste ground, hedgerows, banks.

DESCRIPTION A scrambling shrub with arched, angled green or red stems, bearing many sharp thorns. Leaves have 3–5 oval-oblong leaflets. White/pink flowers May–September; berries June–October, red at first, turning black when ripe.

NOTES My memories of childhood family blackberrying expeditions are as vivid as the stains the berries left on my trousers. In good years there was enough fruit for each happy Irving to return with several full containers despite constant gorging on the job. Blackberrying or brambling is the major unbroken British foraging tradition. Lots of people express amazement at what I do for a living,

⁷/₁₀ × life size

but a few questions usually reveal that I am talking to another forager: pretty much everyone has picked and eaten wild blackberries. For some reason they still register as an immediately available food source; why this should be is not clear, because more often than not plums and apples fall to the ground in public places and rot.

USES/RECIPES Softer blackberries are good raw, on their own, with cream, to make sorbet or fools. Firmer fruit is less sweet and better for cooking (try adding a little wild mint). Preserve the flavour of blackberries for winter months, with jams and jellies or fruit vinegar – a delicious ingredient for salad dressings, puddings and sauces (see pp.16–17). Use leaves as tea, either fresh or dried. Their flavour improves with slow drying, which promotes a kind of fermentation.

HAZARDS The presence of maggots is more a source of revulsion than a hazard. I see them as a bonus source of protein, although my wife does not! Check the end of each blackberry for holes if you are especially bothered, or leave your blackberries in a bowl of slightly salted water for a few hours when you get home. Any maggots present should soon wriggle out. Rinse the fruit afterwards and leave it to dry. Getting thorns embedded in my skin is an inevitable downside of foraging for a living – not only when picking blackberries but also when collecting fungi or woodland plants such as wood sorrel. For damage limitation, use one hand to pick and the other to push back troublesome branches with a thick glove or a crooked stick, which you can also use to pull heavily laden branches within reach. Heavy metals from car-exhaust fumes accumulate in soil or settles as dust on plants. A Joint Food Safety and Standards Group study published by the Ministry of Agriculture and Fisheries (MAFF) in 2000 looked at heavy-metal contents of blackberries picked from a variety of locations, including urban roadsides. The authors concluded that levels of heavy metals consumed even by people eating above average levels of fruit from beside urban roads do not constitute a health risk; this is based on a recommended maximum daily or weekly intake of heavy metals agreed by, among others, the World Health Organization. We inevitably consume a minute quantity of heavy metals in our food, and eating blackberries from the side of the road does not significantly increase this amount. I am still wary of eating berries from beside a really busy road, though I will collect them from beside quieter roads.

2 × life size

HARVESTING NOTES Avoid picking too many blackberries into one container because the fruit at the bottom will get squashed. And don't use a bag as the sides will also press into the fruit and pulp it. Softer fruit is sweeter, more squashable and less durable; better to eat it fresh. It's worth picking soft and firm fruit into separate containers. Or else gorge on the soft ones while collecting the others!

Rubus idaeus

Raspberry

DISTRIBUTION Up to 745m. Native – but often growing from bird-sown seed, which could be from wild or cultivated fruit. In British Isles, very widespread, but absent or infrequent: in England, in Cambridgeshire; in Scotland, in much of northernmost Highlands and Western Isles; in Ireland, to west of Cork, Kerry and Mayo, parts of Tipperary, Meath and Donegal.

HABITAT Open woods, railway embankments, heaths and waste places.

DESCRIPTION A tall perennial that grows upright, in contrast to other *Rubus* species. Canes are round with weak prickles. Leaves have 5–7 oval leaflets with a distinctly white underside. Plants produce white flowers May–August; raspberries ripen June–September.

NOTES There are few greater treats than stumbling across a patch of

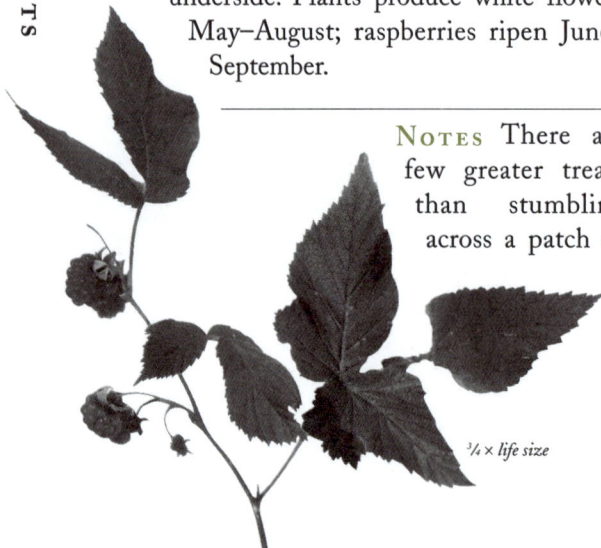

¾ × life size

raspberries on a hot summer's day when you are thirsty. If you are really lucky, you might discover a patch with enough fruit to take some home. I haven't collected great quantities of raspberries in my area of Kent, where most plants grow in woods with fairly dense canopy and tend not to fruit, but elsewhere (in Wales, for example) they can be quite abundant. In much of continental Europe, they replace the blackberry as the most common hedgerow berry.

USES/RECIPES Raspberries are too good to cook. Apart from eating them just as they are, they make a lovely fool, or a purée, made with icing sugar and the berry pulp (passed through a sieve), which can be folded into whipped cream (and served with Summer Pudding) or ice cream for home-made raspberry ripple.

HARVESTING NOTES In contrast to blackberries and dewberries, the fruit comes away from its core when picked, making it even more delicate and in need of especially careful transportation.

Rubus saxatilis

Stone Bramble

DISTRIBUTION Up to 970m. In England, found in much of Pennines, North York Moors, Cumbrian Mountains, parts of Southern Uplands but almost entirely absent south; in Wales, in hilly and mountainous areas, such as Brecon Beacons, Black Mountains and Snowdon; in Scotland, in much of Argyll and Bute, Sterling, Perth and Kinross, west Aberdeenshire, widespread on Skye and Reay Forest/Ben Hope, and other scattered higher-altitude areas of Highlands; in Ireland, in parts of Clare, Antrim, Fermanagh and Londonderry.

2 × life size

HABITAT Rocky and woody areas, usually on damp, alkaline soil.

DESCRIPTION Perennial shrub with flowering stems that grow afresh and die back every year. Leaves have only 3 leaflets (brambles may have 5). The creamy-white flowers grow in small clusters June–August. The berries are ripe August–September: red with 2–6 red segments (drupes), larger than those of blackberries.

NOTES Grazed by roe deer and once known as roebuck-berry, in Britain this a scarce plant, despite a fairly wide distribution. Elsewhere in Europe it is common, particularly in Sweden and in Finland, where the berries are called Lillukka.

USES/RECIPES Stone bramble berries have a sharp but pleasant taste, although to our sugar-hungry palates they are probably best sweetened, either raw or cooked, if you are lucky enough to find them in any quantity. They have larger pips than the other *Rubus* species, so should be passed through a sieve. Use to make a tart fruit jelly, of the pudding or jam variety, or to flavour meat sauces.

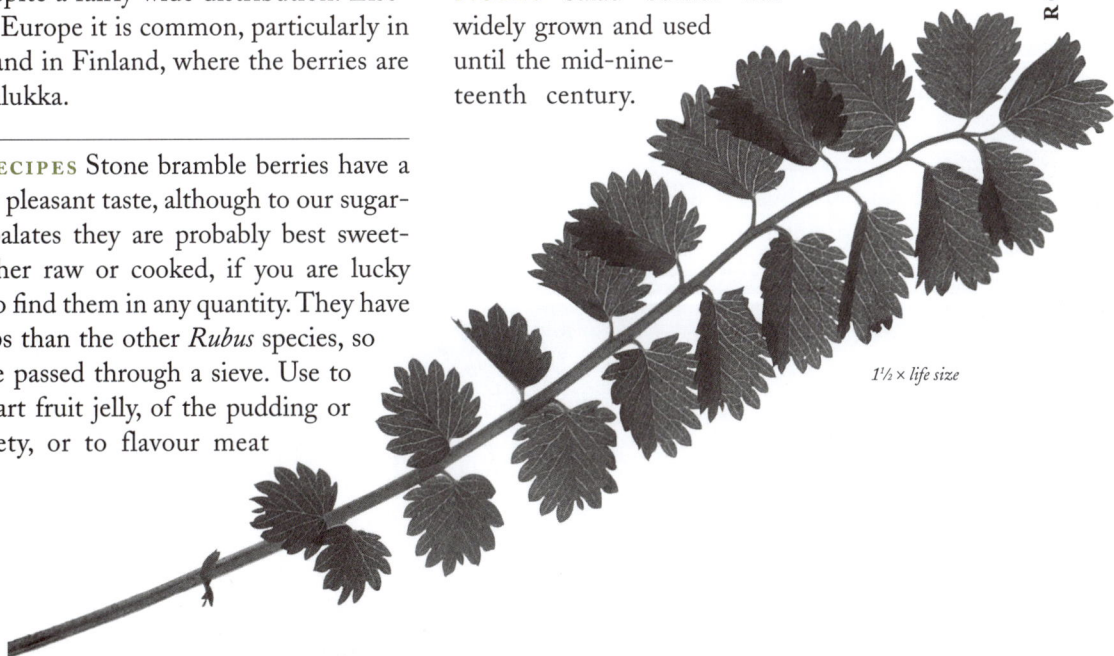

Sanguisorba minor

Salad Burnet

DISTRIBUTION Native. Up to 500m. In England, occurs throughout; in Wales, mostly polarized towards north and south; in Scotland, in Kirkcudbrightshire and eastern Coastal Lowlands, Fife–Berwickshire; in Ireland, sparse, mostly central, Galway and Clare in west–Leinster in east.

HABITAT Grassland and roadside verges on poor, dry soils, nearly always on chalk and limestone but occasionally on clay; occasionally in quarries and rock crevices.

DESCRIPTION Leaves have 3–12 pairs of rounded, toothed leaflets. Ball-shaped flower heads are first green then purplish red on stalks 15–40cm high.

SIMILAR SPECIES Great burnet *S. officinalis* has fewer leaflets per leaf, larger, egg-shaped flowers and is taller. It is also good to eat. Fodder burnet *S. minor* subsp. *muricata* has larger leaves and is bushier. Once grown for fodder, it is now naturalized.

NOTES Salad burnet was widely grown and used until the mid-nineteenth century.

1½ × life size

The word burnet probably derives from the French *brunette*, referring to the red-mahogany colour of the flowers.

USES/RECIPES Leaves have a delicate, cucumber-like flavour: use to enhance salads, summer drinks, such as Pimm's, marinades or cooked food, especially soups, added just at the last minute. In central Italy they are cooked with beans. The eighteenth-century American cookery writer Maria Eliza Ketelby Rundell recommended it as herb for stewing beef. Can also be pickled or used to make herb butter or herb vinegar. I often graze on them while out walking.

HARVESTING NOTES The winter plants tend to cleave to the earth, so you have to bend down and trace with your fingers the pairs of round fine-toothed leaflets, and tease them from the grass; in summer the leaves are larger and more upright so they are easier to harvest, even among long grass. Salad burnet is intolerant of grazing so, unlike with daisy and cabbage family species, the whole rosette should not be collected. Take no more than one-third of the leaves from each plant.

Sorbus

The *Sorbus* genus contains many species with only the most subtle variations among them; some of our native species are found nowhere else on Earth. They are too numerous to describe here, but I have yet to find one with an unpalatable berry. Historic texts refer to the use of Sorbus berries in brewing or ground and mixed with grain flours for making bread.

GENERAL HAZARDS The seeds, especially those of

rowan, contain cyanogenic glucosides, not in quantities likely to result in poisoning, but a staple diet of rowanberry bread might cause problems. All berries of this group contain sorbitol, which was first extracted from rowan-berries. Sorbitol is very sweet but since the body cannot convert it to sugar it has no calorific value; it is manufactured as an artificial sweetener. Eating large amounts causes gastrointestinal problems for some people. The irritant parascorbic acid is also present but breaks down once the fruits have either been cooked or allowed to blett. Blett is a polite term that essentially means the fruit has started to rot. Several other fruits are deliberately eaten in this state, including medlars and rose hips.

Sorbus aria

Whitebeam

DISTRIBUTION: Up to 455m. Native and most common in England, in Hampshire, Dorset, Wiltshire, Berkshire, Hertfordshire, Gloucestershire and Kent; in Wales, also native along Wyre valley; otherwise elsewhere in England and Wales, scattered as a naturalized tree; in Scotland, naturalized and frequent in north Aberdeenshire and Fife but scarce elsewhere; in Ireland, very scarce.

HABITAT Open woodland, scrub and hedgerows, especially on calcareous soils; also planted on streets, in parks and gardens.

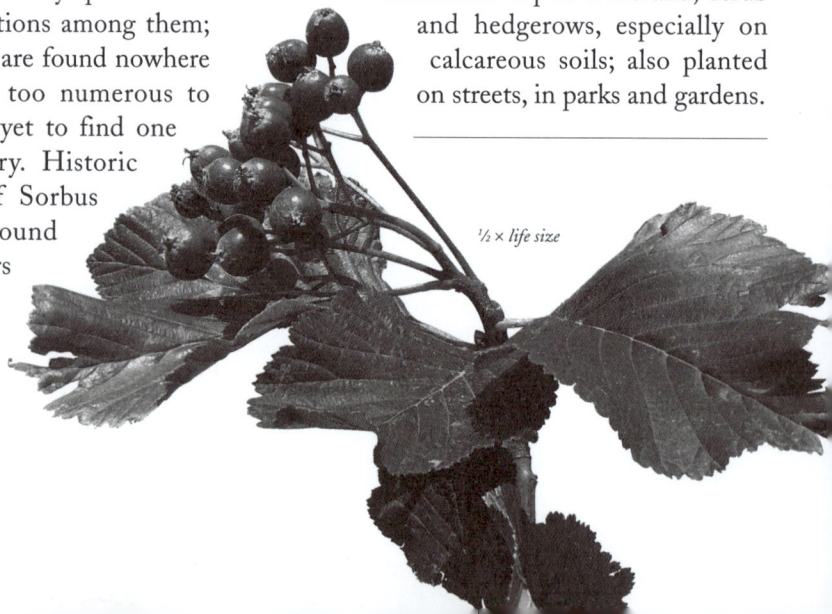

½ × life size

DESCRIPTION Deciduous tree of medium height, usually up to 15m high but can reach 20m. Leaves variable, usually rounded, sometimes lobed, with toothed edges and downy white undersides. These are very eye-catching from a distance, as are the scarlet berries.

SIMILAR SPECIES Swedish whitebeam *S. intermedia* has deeply toothed, almost lobed leaves and much larger berries.

USES/RECIPES When soft and ripe, the berries become sticky with a subtle apple flavour that is gradually overtaken by the marzipan taste of the seeds. Add whole berries to breads and cakes or blitz in stock syrup to make an appley, almondy pouring syrup.

Sorbus aucuparia

Rowan

DISTRIBUTION Up to 870m. Widespread throughout British Isles; only less so in parts of central Ireland.

HABITAT Woods, especially in mountainous areas; rocky places. In lowlands, on dry, gravelly, acid soils.

DESCRIPTION A small, native deciduous tree, up to 20m high. Leaves have 5–7 pairs of long, thin-toothed leaflets; cream flowers in large umbels, a bit like elderflower. The bright orange berries that hang in bunches are eye catching, abundant and about the size of a pea.

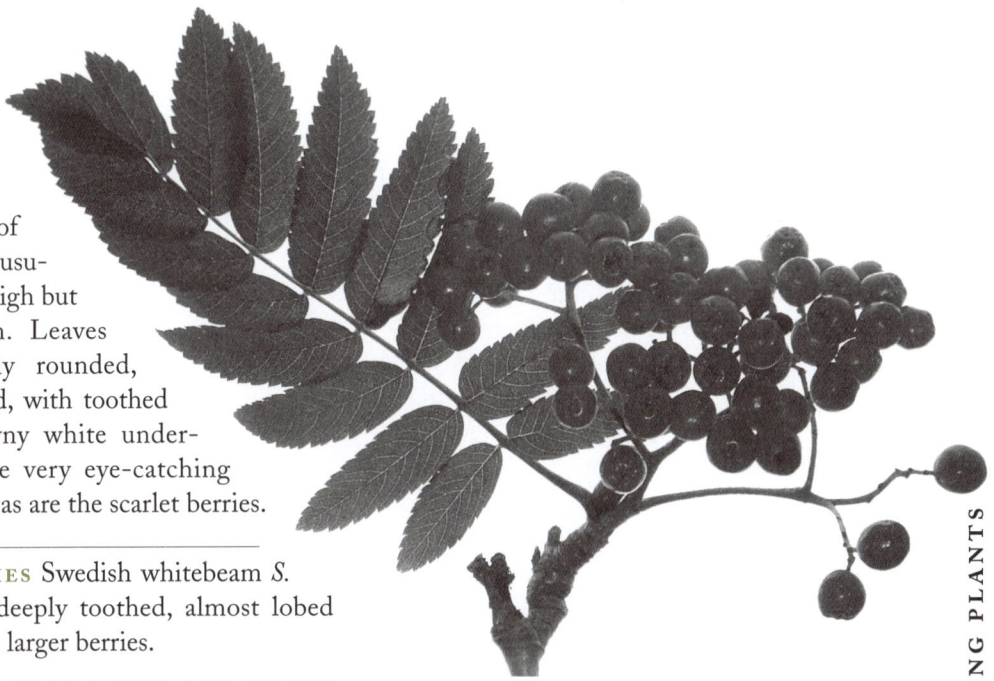

SIMILAR SPECIES In leaf or flower you might confuse true service-tree for rowan, but its berries resemble small pears or apples. In fruit some other *Sorbus*, such as whitebeams, have orange berries, but their leaves are not divided.

USES/RECIPES Make jelly from the berries. Early rowan has more pectin; later rowan is better for flavour and colour, the lack of pectin can be made up using crab apples; use one-quarter rowan, three-quarter apples (see p.269). Especially good with mutton, either a blob on the plate or in sauce; also good with cured meats, cold roasted meats and cheese. The berries give tartness and bite to sweet and savoury dishes such as soups and sorbets. An old way of preserving the berries was to steep them for several weeks in water or vinegar, then boil briefly before straining. The high malic-acid content makes them unquestionably bitter, but no more than, say, Seville oranges. Recently a cultivar with sweet berries has been produced.

HAZARDS Raw berries contain parasorbic acid, an irritant that can cause vomiting and gastroenteritis. It is destroyed by heat; cooked berries are perfectly safe.

Sorbus domestica

True Service-tree/ Whitty Pear Tree

DISTRIBUTION Up to 300m. In England, only eight trees in Wyre Forest area of Worcestershire and along Severn Estuary, with a few naturalized from cultivated trees in scattered locations, including one on Isle of Man; in Wales, 22 trees known from cliffs on Glamorgan coast and Severn Estuary.

HABITAT Cliff ledges and gorges, parks and gardens.

DESCRIPTION Deciduous tree, up to 20m high, with orangey-brown bark and leaves with long, thin toothed leaflets. At 20–30mm long the fruits or whitty pears are quite large for a *Sorbus*; they are green with reddish-brown blotches and, as the name suggests, pear shaped.

NOTES A tree in Wyre Forest mentioned in records from 1678, was thought to have been planted from continental stock, but, in 1973, trees were found on coastal cliffs, where any planting is doubtful. Nennius, a ninth-century Welsh monk, recorded that apples grew on an ash tree at the mouth of the River Wye. Patrick Roper, author of *Chequer: Wild Service Tree*, thinks this tree may have been an ancestor of the modern true service-trees in that area.

USES/RECIPES On the Continent, a cider-like drink is made from the fruits; in Italy bletted fruits are eaten whole or made into jam.

BENEFITS A 2008 study found several beneficial phytochemicals in true service-tree fruit and concluded that eating it may improve the health of diabetes sufferers.

Sorbus torminalis

Wild Service-tree/ Chequer Tree

DISTRIBUTION Up to 300m. In England, mostly widespread south of Humber, but only few scattered areas north; in Wales, widespread but more sparse; in Scotland, only one location, in Moray, where introduced.

HABITAT A rather scarce tree of ancient woodland, also occurring in hedgerows and on scrub. It has also been planted in parks and gardens, especially in the last 15 years or so.

DESCRIPTION Native, deciduous tree, up to 25m high. Leaves have 3–4 pairs of toothed, pointed lobes; all except the lowest pair point upwards. The berries are like tiny russet apples or pears, hard and greenish brown. Once they have been bletted by the first frost they become soft and reddish brown.

NOTES From Henry Phillips, *Pomarium Brittanicum* (1820):

The fruit of the tree partakes of the quality of the Medlar, both in green and in ripe state. It is gathered in branches and put into or hung on a cleft stick of about a yard long which becomes a mass of berries. In this state the fruit is sold by the country people and then hung up in a garden to receive the damp air of night which causes it to undergo a kind of putrefactive fermentation and in this soft state it is eaten and has a more agreeable acid than Medlar.

The wild service-tree originated in ancient woodland; its berries have probably been eaten as long as we have been here, although its distribution is quite localized. Variously called sarvies, sorbus, service or chequer berries, the practice of collecting the berries and allowing them to blett continued until fairly recently; they were still available in shops and London markets in the nineteenth century. Once collected and bletted wild service-tree berries can last through the winter if stored correctly; children at one time ate them as enthusiastically as they now eat sweets.

UsES/RECIPES Bletted berries are sweet and sticky with the taste (and almost the texture) of tamarind combined with raisins. The tamarind flavour is due to the combined presence of malic and citric acids. The seed is also pleasant to eat; it is soft and quite nutty, with a subtle almondy flavour. Just munching them raw is pleasant but a major authority on this tree, Patrick Roper, writes in *Chequer: Wild Service Tree* that the cooked berries were formerly eaten with bread and potatoes, in brain and wild-service berry omelette, and in stews. They can also be turned into jam or steeped in sugar and spirits to become the liqueur or cordial known as ratafia.

HARVESTING NOTES Berry harvests vary greatly from year to year, but good yields follow a hot, dry summer in the previous year. On a big tree, much of the fruit will be out of reach to you, but not to birds, which seem to know exactly when they are ready. This is why the berries should not be left on the tree to blett, as I did the first year I gathered them. I had just started to pick when a large flock of starlings joined me. I spent as much time waving things to scare off the birds as I did picking. A passer-by was fascinated to see my day's bounty and clearly wanted to try them; the 'bounty' was rather sparse but I felt obliged to offer a handful. No doubt by unconscious association, I mentioned my avian rivals. 'Oh,' she replied, 'my surname is Starling.'

SAXIFRAGE FAMILY
Saxifragaceae

Chrysosplenium oppositifolium

Opposite-leaved Golden-saxifrage

DISTRIBUTION Up to 1100m. In England, widespread north of line Flamborough Head–Severn estuary and south of line Severn–Thames estuaries except parts Somerset, Wiltshire, Hampshire and area north of North Downs, otherwise sporadic; in Wales, absent only few places in Anglesey and Glamorgan; in Scotland, widespread throughout, except higher-altitude areas of Grampian Mountains, North West Highlands and much North Highland, and found Orkney but not Shetland; in Ireland, widespread north of line Dundalk Bay–Killala Bay and in coastal counties of east and south, sporadic in all remaining counties; present on Channel Islands and Isle of Man.

HABITAT Shady stream edges and mountain ledges; boggy ground in woods and by springs, often on quite acidic soil.

DESCRIPTION Native perennial. Slightly hairy; square stems creep along the ground and frequently put down roots forming dense mats. Leaves opposite, rounded with tapering bases and rounded teeth. Flowers, March–May, with yellow–green bracts and no petals, on top of dense clusters of leaves.

SIMILAR SPECIES Alternate-leaved golden-saxifrage *C. alternifolium* has alternate, kidney-shaped leaves and does not form mats. It also prefers more alkaline soil, but the two plants are often found together.

USES/RECIPES Leaves of both of these plants can be used as salad. They have a good, succulent texture; the flavour is mild with a slight bitterness, which is less evident after the plants have flowered. They can also be cooked and used as greens.

SEA-BUCKTHORN FAMILY
Elaeagnaceae

½ × *life size*

Hippophae rhamnoides

Sea-buckthorn

DISTRIBUTION Up to 300m. Native only on east coast of England. In British Isles, common along much of coastline except less so: in Wales, on west coast; in Scotland, where few sites only on coast of West and North Highland, and east coast of Grampian, and absent Western and Northern Isles; in Ireland, few locations on west and south coasts. Scattered inland sites: far fewer in Wales, Scotland and Ireland than England; present Channel Islands and Isle of Man.

HABITAT Native on sand dunes and cliffs; widely planted to stabilize banks and as an ornamental for its bright orange berries, in gardens and on roadsides. In China it is used extensively to reclaim deserts.

DESCRIPTION Small, deciduous shrub, up to 3m high, with many long, thin, silvery leaves and hard, sharp thorns. Tiny green flowers appear March–April; berries are bright orange in dense clusters, ripening September.

USES/RECIPES Berries make jams and jellies for serving with game, cold meats and cheeses. Use to make simple meat sauces with just-reduced stock, berries/jelly and seasoning, especially for venison.

SEA-BUCKTHORN DRESSING: (a great mayonnaise-style salad dressing without eggs) Put frozen berries straight into a blender, blitz with a teaspoon of Dijon mustard and a splash of sherry vinegar, then drizzle pomace olive oil on to it – this greatly mellows the sourness of the berries; pass through a fine sieve. Serve with rabbit terrine, cold venison or other game [SW]. Serve sea-buckthorn jelly with any desserts involving white chocolate, such as soufflé, mousse, bavaroise; alternatively, use jelly made from fresh berry juice as a glaze.

BENEFITS Very high in vitamin C (more than in oranges); also beta-carotene (more than in carrots); and vitamin B2; the seeds are high in vitamin E. Also high in potassium and quercetin, a flavonoid with anti-inflammatory, antioxidant and anti-tumour properties. Regular consumption of quercetin-containing foods may also reduce the risk of pancreatic cancer.

HAZARDS None to humans, but the berries contain an acid that corrodes metal; if you need to keep a sauce or syrup for any length of

289

Sami Tellberg's White Chocolate Mousse with Sea-buckthorn Caramel & Sorbet

SERVES 10

FOR THE WHITE CHOCOLATE MOUSSE:
100g caster sugar
500ml fresh orange juice
8 egg yolks
1 vanilla pod, seeds only
300g white chocolate, melted
1 leaf gelatine
a drop of sea-buckthorn berry juice
500ml whipping cream
You will also need 150ml silicon moulds

FOR THE SEA-BUCKTHORN CARAMEL:
240g sea-buckthorn berries
240g caster sugar
350ml water

FOR THE SEA-BUCKTHORN SORBET:
1 litre sea-buckthorn berry juice
800g caster sugar
2 vanilla pods, seeds only
100g glucose, warmed
4 leaf gelatine (soaked and melted with a
    drop of sea-buckthorn berry juice)

FOR THE MOUSSE: Cook the sugar, orange juice, egg yolks and vanilla seeds in a bain-marie until they thicken (82°C), then pass through a fine sieve. Mix in the melted white chocolate and leaf gelatine, soaked and melted with a drop of juice. Whip the cream until soft-peak stage and fold into the chocolate mix, first one-third then the rest. Pour mixture into silicon moulds, freeze overnight, pop out of moulds and place on a wire rack above a baking sheet. This will allow excess glaze to fall off and therefore keeps it tidy.

FOR THE CARAMEL: Bring the berries and sugar to the boil until they form a light caramel; add the water, boil again then mix in a blender and pass through a fine sieve. Cool, then pour most of the caramel over the frozen chocolate mousses as they sit on the wire rack, setting the rest aside. Leave to set in the fridge until served. Leave some caramel aside in room temperature to drizzle around the mousse to serve. (This caramel works equally well with other desserts such as crème caramel or pear tarte Tatin, as the acidity of the fruit makes a refreshing contrast to the caramel.)

FOR THE SORBET: Mix all ingredients together until dissolved then pass through a fine sieve. Churn in ice-cream machine. Serve next to the caramel-glazed mousse.

Serve with a crispy tuille or similar for texture contrast.

time, store it in a glass rather than a metal container.

HARVESTING NOTES It is virtually impossible to pick the berries without squashing them. In Finland a special device is used to squeeze out the juice while they are still on the trees. Without this device, the best method is to cut off the branch ends or the smaller side branches, berries and all, and put them in a freezer. The frozen berries are easily removed by bashing the branches. Cut branches will not produce fruit the following year.

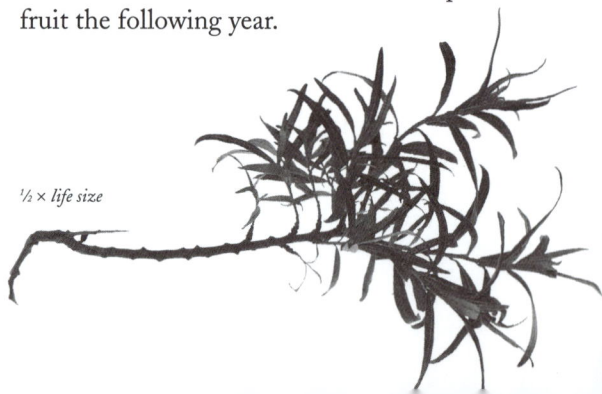

½ × life size

SEDUM FAMILY
Crassulaceae

'Crassula' derives from the Latin *Crassus*, meaning 'thick': the plants grow in thick patches; most species also have thick, succulent leaves, enabling them to withstand intense heat. Both characteristics are put to an interesting use in urban building design: roofs are covered with sedums as a way of minimizing the heat absorption of buildings. This is not a new use; house leeks have been grown on roofs for centuries, but with global warming it may become increasingly necessary.

Several sedum species have been and can be used for their succulent and crunchy leaves. Biting stonecrop gets its alternative name wall-pepper as well as its Latin name *acre* from its acrid, peppery flavour and is also quite tart. Taking a bite in isolation, the pepperiness is overpowering; mixing it with other salad ingredients tempers this effect, although I find it quite unpleasant even so. Both white stonecrop and reflexed stonecrop are much milder. Stonecrops have been used by various indigenous peoples, such as the first peoples of British Columbia who eat the leaves and stalks of *Sedum divergens* (not a British species) with animal grease, before and after the flowering stage. The traditional use in this country was to pickle the leaves for use in salad. The leaves of biting stonecrop have also been dried and used as a peppery seasoning. Reflexed stonecrop was introduced by Dutch settlers as a salad crop and named by seventeenth-century diarist John Evelyn as a plant for the kitchen garden.

Sedum album

White Stonecrop

DISTRIBUTION Up to 570m. In England, widespread but absent parts of Northumberland, Durham, Yorkshire, Lincolnshire, Cambridgeshire, Huntingtonshire, Kent, Sussex, Hampshire, Devon and Cornwall; in Wales, widespread most counties but absent parts of Merioneth, Radnorshire, Brecknockshire, Glamorgan and Pembrokeshire; in Scotland, although present in east Sutherland, east Ross, the North and Mid Ebudes and Orkney,

2 × life size

mostly found south of Glen Mor and predominately in Central Lowlands and eastern Coastal Lowlands; in Ireland, present all counties but more abundant in north and southeast; present Channel Islands, Isle of Man and Isles of Scilly.

HABITAT Dry areas with little or no soil, such as rocks, walls, shingle beaches and paths.

DESCRIPTION Mat-forming perennial, with alternate green leaves, sometimes tinged with red, cylindrical, up to 12mm long, almost at right angles to the stalks. Flowers white, up to 9mm wide, in flat-topped clusters resembling umbels, on red stems, up to 15cm high. Flavour mild, slightly tart.

SIMILAR SPECIES English stonecrop *S. anglicum* has smaller (up to 5mm long) oval bluish-green leaves, and white flowers in small-er clusters, not umbel like, on much shorter stems, up to 5cm high. Biting stonecrop/wall-pepper *S. acre* has leaves no more than 6mm long, pressed up against the stem. Taste very peppery. It also has larger (up to 15mm wide), yellow flowers.

USES/RECIPES As well as looking quite unique, the leaves are tart and succulent; chef James Lowe describes them as being like tiny, lemony pea pods. They should either be used raw or after brief cooking; cooking turns them a brighter green. Serve raw with pâté, pork pies, potted meat; the succulence, sharp tang and slight bitterness balances the richness, sweetness and fattiness of the meat. Serve as a garnish with fried fish such as halibut, brill or plaice.

DIVER-CAUGHT PLAICE WITH WHITE STONE-CROP: Once the fish has finished cooking, drain off the juices and leave it to rest. Get a pan really hot, throw in a knob of butter, splash of water and the cooking juices from the fish – throw in the stonecrop and stir fast for about 30 seconds. Serve with the fish [JL].

HAZARDS Mildly toxic, due to the alkaloid sedine, which causes gastric upset if large amounts of the raw plant are consumed; it also contains the alkaloid sedamine that is used as a sleep aid. Not surprisingly, excessive consumption has also been reported to cause drowsiness. Both alkaloids are destroyed by heating; so cooked leaves can be eaten in quantity without risk of either symptom, they also contain oxalic acid, so should still be used in moderation.

Sedum rosea

Roseroot

DISTRIBUTION Up to 1160m. In England, only commonly found mid-west Yorkshire and Cumbria; in Wales, scarce, locally common

2 × life size

2 × life size

Caernarvonshire, Merioneth, Pembrokeshire, Carmarthenshire, Brecknockshire and Glamorgan, Anglesey and Monmouthshire; in Scotland, widespread in west, north of Central Lowlands, also common in Western and Northern Isles, and in east scattered locations in Grampian Mountains, North Highland, Grampian coast and Southern Uplands; in Ireland, scarce, recorded mainly in west coastal counties of Donegal, Leitrim, Mayo, Galway, Clare and Kerry; introduced onto Isle of Man.

HABITAT Rock crevices and ledges on coastal cliffs and mountains.

DESCRIPTION Hairless, upright perennial. Leaves fleshy, spatula shaped with rounded teeth, pointing upwards and overlapping. The thick woody-looking rhizome is clearly visible above ground and smells of roses if cut or broken, hence the name. Flowers are yellow–greenish yellow, in dense clusters.

USES/RECIPES Stems and leaves are used by Canadian Inuit as vegetables. Native American Indians preserved the leaves by lacto fermentation. Their succulent texture makes them a good addition to a stir fry. Roots were eaten by Inupiaq and St Lawrence Island Eskimos, after harvesting them in the early spring.

BENEFITS The plant is used in herbal medicine as an adaptogen, aphrodisiac and general tonic to enhance mood and physical stamina.

Sedum rupestre

Reflexed Stonecrop

DISTRIBUTION Mostly lowland. In England, widespread south of line Morecambe Bay–Kingston-upon-Hull, sporadic north of line, absent Cheviot; in Wales, widespread except parts Pembrokeshire, Glamorgan, Radnorshire and Merioneth; in Scotland, scarce, present only south of Glen Mor, Central Lowlands and eastern Coastal Lowlands; in Ireland, sporadic in Cork, Waterford, north Tipperary, Sligo and counties of Ulster; present Channel Islands, Isle of Man and Isles of Scilly.

HABITAT Walls, stony paths and rocky ground.

DESCRIPTION Mat-forming perennial, leaves cylindrical with pointed ends, 8–20mm long, much longer than biting stonecrop *S. acre* or white stonecrop *S. album*. Yellow flowers grow in dense clusters on upright stems.

USES/RECIPES Pickle in the same pickling mixture as for **rock samphire**. Use the pickled stonecrop mixed with some of the fresh stuff, some of the yellow flowers perhaps and serve it as a pickled/textural foil for chicken liver pâté – smooth version – and hot toast [JDW].

HAZARDS As for **white stonecrop**.

2 × life size

Sedum telephium

Orpine/Midsummer Men

DISTRIBUTION Up to 455m. In England, sporadic throughout but more abundant Cumbria, East Anglia, Home Counties and counties along south coast; in Wales, common, except areas of Flintshire, Denbighshire, Merioneth, Brecknockshire and Glamorgan; in Scotland, sporadic in eastern Coastal Lowlands south of Glen Mor and lower-altitude areas of Grampian Mountains and Southern Uplands, more widespread in Central Lowlands and Dumfries and Galloway; in Ireland, scarce, mostly in Ulster, but also Galway, Clare and a few counties in Leinster; present Isle of Man.

HABITAT Woods, hedgebanks, rocky ground, cliffs.

DESCRIPTION Perennial, up to 80cm high: thick, fleshy bluish-green leaves, bluntly toothed, alternate or in whorls of 3. Pink flowers 6mm wide, in umbel-like clusters.

SIMILAR SPECIES Ice-plant *S. spectabile*, a popular garden plant has larger, paler leaves.

USES/RECIPES Leaves are an excellent wild-salad ingredient, used as such in England in the Middle Ages, with a slightly tart flavour and a marvellous succulent texture. Use young leaves in salads; young and old leaves boiled briefly or fried.

Umbilicus rupestris

Wall-pennywort/Navelwort

DISTRIBUTION Up to 550m. In England, widespread throughout southwest, but less so Wiltshire and east Gloucestershire, also found in Lake District, south Hampshire, West Sussex, Surrey and Welsh border counties; in Wales, widespread throughout; in Scotland, only in Argyll and Sterling, Strathclyde and Ayrshire and Dumfries and Galloway; in Ireland, widespread but sporadic in central and east Central Lowlands, Antrim and Mayo; present Channel Islands, Isle of Man and Isles of Scilly.

HABITAT Walls, rock crevices and rocky banks, mostly areas with acid soil.

DESCRIPTION Fleshy, hairless perennial. Leaves circular, up to 7cm wide, dark green, with rounded teeth and a navel-like central dip, where they join the stalk. Flowers, June–August on an upright spike, are bell shaped, greenish white–cream.

NOTES Pennywort is a prolific plant in certain areas, most notably Cornwall, Eire and Wales. Like ivy-leaved toadflax and trailing bellflower it grows all over garden walls. It looks so attractive that its presence seems deliberate, and you wonder at first whether it really is a wild plant. In summer, once the dramatic flower spikes appear, the leaves die back for a few months, reappearing in winter.

USES/RECIPES Among the most interesting-looking leaves you are likely to put on your plate. They start small, about the size of a modern new penny piece, but grow to the size of an old penny – 40mm wide or more. Quite thick but with a succulent texture; the only comparable wild leaves are **spring beauty** and fellow

René Redzepi's Turbot with Herbs

SERVES 4

FOR THE TURBOT
1 small turbot, about 1kg
2 tbsp unsalted butter
4 fresh thyme sprigs

FOR THE SALT-BAKED CELERIAC:
1 litre water
600g salt
1kg plain flour
1 large organic celeriac, peeled

FOR THE CELERIAC PUREÉ:
1kg peeled and diced celeriac
groundnut oil, to sauté
240g double cream
40g brown butter, made by melting butter
    over a medium heat until golden brown

60ml water
salt, to season

FOR THE WATERCRESS EMULSION:
140g watercress leaves, picked from stems
20ml water
30g cider vinegar, plus extra or fresh lemon
juice to taste
6g Dijon mustard
220g grapeseed oil

FOR THE GARNISH:
8 large ramsons leaves
20 tiny ramsons leaves
lots of orpine leaves
60ml water
50g butter

Fillet the fish, cut off the skin and divide into 50g portions. Sauté each portion on one side in a warm pan, finish off with a knob of butter and the thyme, baste it for a few seconds. Be careful not to over cook.

Mix the water, salt and flour to make a dough, spread out and cover the celeriac completely. Bake for 10 minutes at 220°C and 35 minutes at 160°C. Cool down and cut out long, round sticks with an apple corer.

Sauté the celeriac in groundnut oil until slightly golden on the one side, drain the excess fat, cool down and place in a vacuum bag. Put in a pot with boiling water and cook for 35 minutes or until completely tender.

Meanwhile, reduce the cream to one-third. Blend the cooked celeriac pieces with the rest of the ingredients until smooth, season with salt and pass through a piece of muslin.

Put the watercress, water, vinegar and Dijon mustard in a Thermomix or blender and blitz, then pour in the oil while mixing as quickly as possible. Strain the mixture through a piece of muslin and keep on ice until ready to serve. Add extra acidity with either more vinegar or some fresh lemon juice just before serving, if necessary.

Cut the stalks off the big ramsons leaves. Heat the water and whisk in all the butter to form an emulsion.

TO SERVE: Drag half a spoonful of the celeriac purée across the plate, heat the salt-baked celeriac in the butter emulsion and add the ramsons stems for the last few seconds. Plate the turbot along with the salt-baked celeriac, ramsons stalks and leaves and sauce, and the slightly warm watercress emulsion. Finally, sprinkle lots of orpine leaves over the dish and serve.

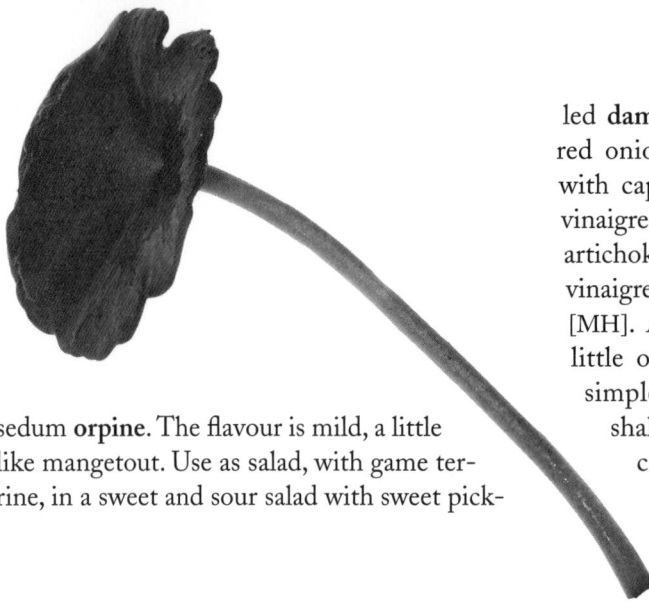

led **damsons**, wild damson jelly and pickled red onion. Or with smoked salmon, mixed with capers and shallots, dressed with light vinaigrette [PW]. With raw, shaved Jerusalem artichokes (just one other earthy flavour) and vinaigrette of cider vinegar and rapeseed oil [MH]. As a green vegetable, dressed with a little oil and seasoned; an interesting and simple garnish. Or lightly pan fry with shallots, garlic and almonds, served with crevettes or langoustines and dill soured cream [BW].

sedum **orpine**. The flavour is mild, a little like mangetout. Use as salad, with game terrine, in a sweet and sour salad with sweet pick-

VALERIAN FAMILY
Valerianaceae

Plants of this family are characterized by opposite leaves without stipules and flowers arranged in cymes with small calyxes and funnel-shaped corollas. Three plants of particular economic importance belong to this family: lamb's lettuce, which is also a common wild plant; common valerian, harvested for its sedative roots, and *Nardostachys jatamansi*, also known as spikenard, the perfume with which Mary Magdalene anointed the feet of Christ.

Centranthus ruber

Red Valerian

DISTRIBUTION Up to 300m. In England, widespread south of line Bootle–Skegness, only less so parts of Cheshire, Staffordshire, Shropshire, Suffolk, Essex and north Hampshire, north of line much less common; in Wales, widespread except high-altitude areas; in Scotland, scarce, only found south of Glen Mor, mostly Central Lowlands and eastern Coastal Lowlands; in Ireland, all counties but more abundant in southeast and east; present Channel Islands, Isle of Man, Isles of Scilly and Lundy.

HABITAT Walls, cliffs, roadsides, gardens, rocky ground.

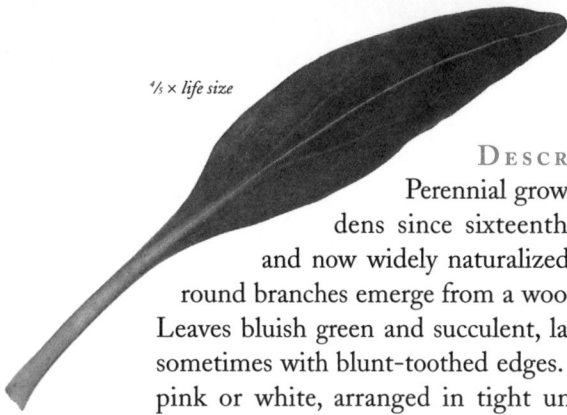

DESCRIPTION

Perennial grown in gardens since sixteenth century and now widely naturalized. Several round branches emerge from a woody stock. Leaves bluish green and succulent, lanceolate, sometimes with blunt-toothed edges. Flowers, pink or white, arranged in tight umbel-like clusters, forming a sort of blunt cone at the top of the plants.

USES/RECIPES The thick fleshy leaves make quite a substantial salad ingredient or green vegetable. They are mildly bitter. If you find this unpleasant, mix with milder, acidic or stronger flavours or mask the bitterness with sweetness, fat or grease.

Valeriana officinalis

Common Valerian

DISTRIBUTION Up to 805m. Pretty much throughout British Isles, except in England, absent much of Kent, the Fens, East Midlands; in Scotland, absent much of the Outer Hebrides.

HABITAT River banks, fens, wet woodland.

DESCRIPTION Upright perennial, up to 1.2m high. Lower stem hairy, leaves opposite, pinnate, stalked below, stalkless above. Leaflets lanceolate with blunt teeth. At first glance the plant could be mistaken for an umbellifer, with its compound leaves and flowers arranged in an umbel-like formation, up to 12cm wide; pink flowers with a distinct medicinal aroma, a bit like Germoline.

SIMILAR SPECIES Marsh valerian *V. dioica* has simple basal leaves, pinnately lobed stem leaves and paler flowers in a smaller, less umbel-like formation.

USES/RECIPES Flowers are used as flavouring for sauces and desserts. For example, French chef Marc Veyrat flavours semolina with them. Marc also makes a delicate sauce with a few flowers, crème fraîche and a little white wine and fish stock; the sauce is served with fried sea bass and garnished with a few more flowers (François Couplan and Marc Veyrat, *Herbier gourmand*). Leaves have a very unique, slightly medicinal flavour and a touch of bitterness.

Valerianella locusta

Lamb's Lettuce/ Common Cornsalad

DISTRIBUTION Up to 364m. In England, widespread south of line Liverpool–Skegness, sporadic north of line; in Wales, found lower-altitude areas and common in all coastal counties; in Scotland, scarce, scattered locations Central Lowlands and eastern Coastal Low-

lands to south of Grampian Mountains, also coastal areas and islands to west, south of Isle of Skye, Aberdeen, Easterness, east Ross and west Sutherland; in Ireland, coastal counties, more common in east and south, sporadic elsewhere; present Channel Islands, Isle of Man and Isles of Scilly.

HABITAT Walls and at wall bases, gardens, on paths, scree and rocky areas; sand and shingle beaches.

DESCRIPTION Basal leaves are spatula shaped, bright green, in a rosette that becomes increasingly bushy before putting up flowering stems, which have much smaller and thinner leaves with a few irregular teeth and small clusters of greyish-white flowers at the top. Overall appearance of the mature plant is similar to blue-flowered forget-me-nots *Myosotis* (various species).

SIMILAR SPECIES Keel-fruited cornsalad *V. carinata* and narrow-fruited cornsalad *V. dentata* (as well as other less common species of cornsalad) can only be distinguished from common cornsalad by close examination of their fruit, but are equally good to eat. The young rosettes could be confused with those of **broad-leaved willowherb**, which has darker (edible) leaves.

NOTES I once spent a week in Cornwall looking for lamb's lettuce. We went for numerous walks and found plenty of foragables but no lamb's lettuce. On the morning we were due to leave, I took one last stroll up the lane of Ali's parents' house and found several lamb's lettuce plants at the base of their neighbour's garden wall. The lesson in how the things you are looking for are often close to home wasn't over yet. As is often the way, having found something for the first time, we spotted masses more lamb's lettuce as we wended our way out of Cornwall. Much of it had gone to seed, and I gathered some to scatter in my neighbourhood in Kent. I set out to do this the following day, only to discover lamb's lettuce growing profusely in a neighbour's garden. When I asked her if I could pick it, she led me to the back garden, which was like a lawn of lamb's lettuce. The garden had been rotavated then left; lamb's lettuce is an early colonizer of bare soil but soon crowded out by other plants: I had a ready supply of lamb's lettuce throughout the following two winters, but after that buttercup took over, leaving little space for much else. The well-weeded gardens of other neighbours, however, continue to produce a regular crop.

USES/RECIPES In France, lamb's lettuce is called *mâche*. Leaves from the winter rosettes are best; those from older plants are tiny and fiddly. Use in a mixed salad, but the flavour is delicate, so be careful not to drown it with more strongly flavoured ingredients. It also has a pleasant texture, which is somehow crisp but soft at the same time; this also is delicate and soon collapses in the presence of acidity or heat. Use dressings that are only slightly acidic and cold, for example serve with green sauce and cold lamb [JL], or as an accompaniment to poached carp, with finely sliced fennel bulb, chopped fennel fronds, capers, olive oil and just a drop or two of fresh lemon juice [JL]. If you have plenty of it, and you tire of eating it as a salad, it can also be lightly steamed and eaten as a vegetable or made into a simple soup, with potato, onions and cream.

BENEFITS High calcium and folic-acid content; also high in iron, vitamin C and beta-carotene.

VIOLET FAMILY
Violaceae

Viola odorata

Sweet Violet

DISTRIBUTION In England, throughout, except parts of Somerset, Cheshire, Greater Manchester and Merseyside and the Pennines; in Wales, found mostly in Anglesey, Clwyd and Gwynedd, Gwent, Glamorgan and south Dyfed; in Scotland, scarce but quite frequent in Fife, Lothian and south Galloway; in Ireland, common in the east, as far west as Cork, and in Ulster, mainly in Tyrone; present Isle of Man, Isles of Scilly and Channel Islands.

HABITAT Hedgebanks, open woodland, churchyards; usually on chalk or other alkaline soils.

DESCRIPTION Native perennial, with creeping runners. Leaves with long stalks, cordate with bluntly toothed edges; leaves get bigger after flowering. Flowers usually dark violet/white but also pink/yellow; they consist of 2 opposite pairs of petals and a single larger petal or spur that points downwards and backwards.

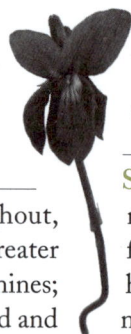

SIMILAR SPECIES Dog violet *V. canina* has no runners and leaves do not enlarge after flowering; hairy violet *V. hirta* is – of course – hairier. Marsh violet *V. palustris* is found in much wetter habitats.

NOTES This is our only especially fragrant violet – leaves of other species are just as good but their flowers are only useful as decoration.

USES/RECIPES Flowers are used in Turkey to make violet sugar, which is dissolved in water to make sorbet.
VIOLET SUGAR: Put flowers in a jar, then a layer of sugar, another layer of flowers and so on. Leave for a week or more, then sieve out flowers.
VIOLET JELLY: Pour 1.5 cups boiling water over 1 cup flowers and leave to infuse for 12 hours. Add juice of 1 lemon, reheat and dissolve in $2\frac{1}{2}$ cups sugar, add 110g pectin and jar. The flowers are also good to use untreated, especially just after opening, when they are most aromatic and flavoursome. Leaves can be used in salads (see **meadowsweet**): they are attractive with a mild flavour and can also be cooked, producing mucilage that acts as a thickener.

WALNUT FAMILY
Juglandaceae

Juglans regia

Walnut

DISTRIBUTION In England, scarce in the southwest, west of Somerset, north of Humber, West Midlands, Sussex and much of Norfolk, elsewhere widespread; in Wales, mostly absent, found only in a few 10 sq km in north of Powys and Clwyd in north and in Dyfed and Gwent in south; in Scotland and Ireland, almost entirely absent.

HABITAT Hedges, roadsides, woods, parks and gardens.

DESCRIPTION Up to 30m high. Leaves with 3–9 leaflets, oval and pleasantly aromatic, due to a substance on leaves that washes off and inhibits growth of plants beneath. Green walnuts are egg shaped, greyish green and strongly aromatic; as they mature, the outer casing darkens and shrivels, revealing the crinkly brown shell of the ripe nut.

NOTES Most walnut trees are planted, although they do occasionally set seed. Many of the planted trees are in public spaces, but the plentiful nuts are often left for the rooks and squirrels. Walnut oil has been used to make oil paints.

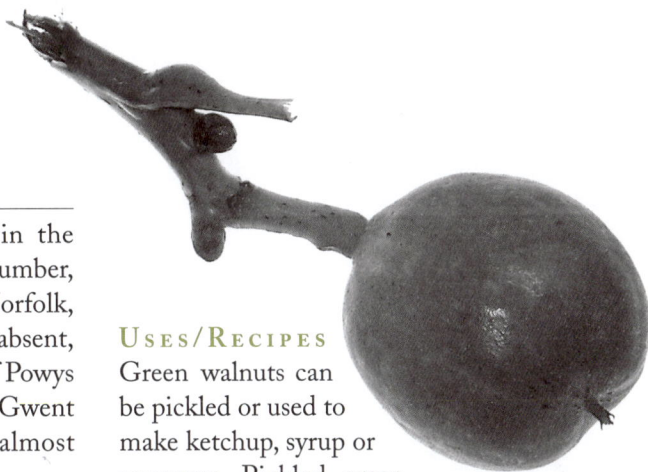

USES/RECIPES
Green walnuts can be pickled or used to make ketchup, syrup or conserve. Pickled green walnuts work well with cheese, beef dishes and tomato dishes, but remember not to use too much salt in the dish as they are very salty. Brown/black walnuts can be eaten alone, or, for example, used in salad and sauces, to make an oil or vinegar and to flavour ice cream.

PICKLED GREEN WALNUTS: Check each walnut to ensure that the shells are soft: use a knitting needle or similar implement; if it doesn't penetrate, they are no good for pickling; if it does, soak the nuts in brine (100g salt/1 litre water) for 14 days. Stir once a day and change the brine halfway through. Allow them to dry for a day (by this point they will be quite black). Then heat them to near boiling in malt vinegar, plain or, if you prefer, flavoured with cloves, white pepper and mace; jar and store for 3 months before using.

WALNUT KETCHUP: (Tastes very similar to Worcestershire sauce and improves with age.) Follow brining procedure for pickled green walnuts, then blend the dried walnuts with malt vinegar and spices. For each 12 walnuts: 1 litre vinegar, 4 garlic cloves, 1 large onion, 1 teaspoon each of ground mace and ground cloves. Leave to infuse for a week, then strain through muslin; when liquid stops dripping, squeeze out what remains with your hands; boil in a large pan for a few minutes then bottle while still hot.

HARVESTING NOTES Walnut trees can be harvested twice a year: once when the walnuts are green and the inner shell is still soft; once when the rest of the nuts are brown.

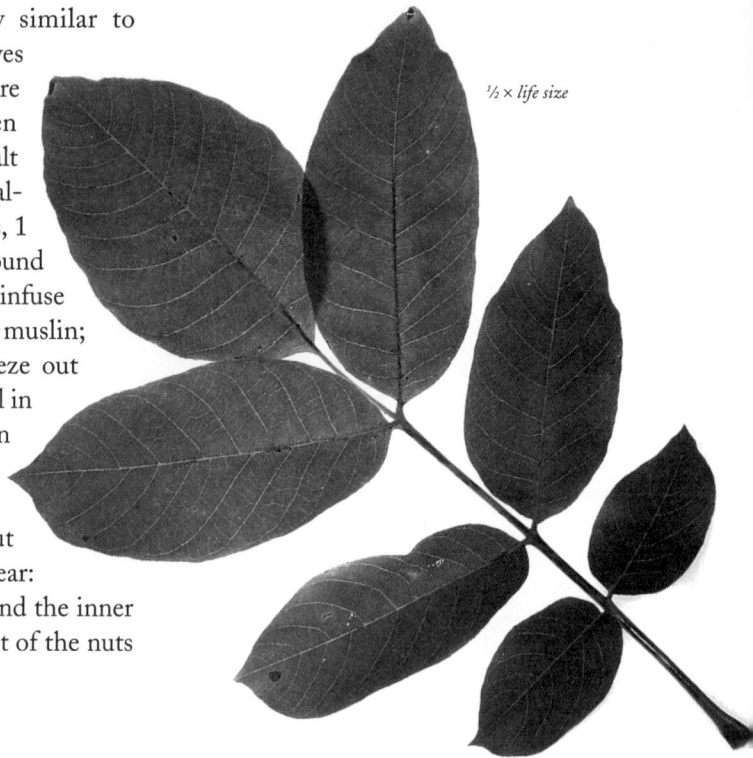

½ × life size

WILLOWHERB FAMILY
Onagraceae

Most willowherbs, with the notable exception of rosebay willowherb, have notched petals. Willowherbs produce passable salad leaves and greens and abundant edible flowers, but their main attraction is their health benefits; it would be worth developing ways of using them for food on these grounds alone.

The plants, hoary willowherb in particular, have a reputation for benefiting the prostate gland. Although no extensive clinical studies have yet been carried out, some laboratory studies have produced results suggesting anti-prostate cancer properties for this plant and also for rosebay willowherb. I find the idea of including certain plants in my diet for health reasons much more appealing than paying high prices for nutritional supplements. Another species, evening primrose, is best known as the source of a popular supplement, evening primrose oil. The family includes one fruit-bearing group of plants: the fuchsias. They produce small sausage-shaped fruits with a delicate, sweet flavour; I have been known to nibble them from my neighbour's garden.

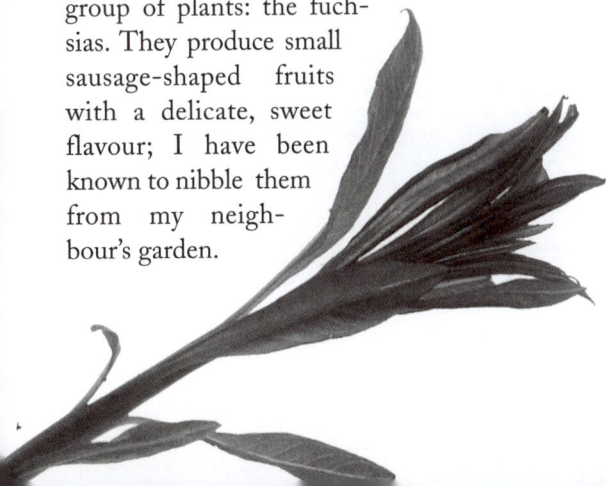

Chamerion angustifolium

Rosebay Willowherb

DISTRIBUTION Up to 975m. In England and Wales, widespread throughout; in Scotland, widespread, only less so north of Glen Mor; in Ireland, widespread to east, decreasing westward to become widely scattered on west coast; present Isle of Man, Isles of Scilly and Channel Islands.

HABITAT Disturbed and burnt ground (hence North-American name 'fireweed') on roadsides, open woods, sand dunes, railway embankments and waste ground. Has increased in lowland areas in recent years whilst in traditional habitats of upland rocky areas and scree frequency is unchanged.

DESCRIPTION Clump forming, practically hairless perennial, up to 1.2m high. Young

1½ × life size

shoots look like asparagus shoots with a punk hairstyle! Most other willowherbs produce basal rosettes at their early growth stage. Leaves are arranged in a spiral; they are long and thin, untoothed, resembling willow leaves. Stems are often reddish purple; flowers bright pink, up to 30mm wide, with 4 petals on long racemes, which taper to a point.

USES/RECIPES Young shoots and tops of older, pre-flowering plants can be used like asparagus, which they also resemble slightly in flavour. Serve with English asparagus and sauce mousseline or hollandaise [SW].

ROSEBAY WILLOWHERB HORTA-STYLE: Set aside a bowl of cold water with ice cubes in it. Drop 5 or 6 willowherb shoots or tops briefly into boiling water then transfer to the cold water with ice. Heat up a frying pan and add 1 tablespoon each of butter and olive oil. When the butter gets some colour, add the willowherb, fry each side for about 1 minute or until coloured. Pour in juice from half a lemon, stir gently and lift to a warm plate. Pour the butter and juice from the pan on top of the willowherbs. Season then serve immediately with rustic bread and fresh lemon slices [AH]. Flowers can be added to summer salads as they are, but the flavour is really brought out by drying them or by steeping in warm syrup. Cool, then leave in the fridge for a week or so. Use as a cordial, adding a touch of fresh lemon juice as a foil for the sweetness – a lovely fragrant, honeyed, herbal-tea taste and quite delicious. Can be made into jelly or sorbet, or granita, using just syrup, with perhaps a little fresh lemon juice, frozen in a container, stirring often, bringing the frozen crystals into the middle until a delicious icy mess is formed [JDW].

Epilobium montanum

Broad-leaved Willowherb

DISTRIBUTION Up to 845m. Widespread throughout British Isles, only less so in Scotland, north of Glen Mor; in Ireland, in Galway.

HABITAT Woods, gardens, old walls, waste ground, hedgebanks, rocky ledges.

DESCRIPTION Perennial, 30–60cm high. Leaves broader than other willowherbs, ranging oval–broad lanceolate; short stalked with rounded bases, in opposite pairs or sometimes whorls of 3. Flowers, June–August, rosy pink, 6–9mm wide.

SIMILAR SPECIES From a distance it can be mistaken for lamb's lettuce, but it has much firmer, darker and glossier leaves.

⅓ × life size

NOTES This common willowherb is familiar to most gardeners as a persistent weed. Diligent weeders will only know it at its earliest stages, when it consists of little clusters of glossy, quite dark green leaves.

USES/RECIPES Very young leaves are an excellent bulking salad ingredient with a mild flavour and good texture. They soon become bitter, however, even before the main stem emerges.

Epilobium parviflorum
Hoary Willowherb

DISTRIBUTION Up to 365m. In England and Wales, widespread throughout; in Scotland, widespread from Central Lowlands south to border except at higher altitudes in Southern Uplands, absent Lewis, present other Western Isles and Orkney; in Ireland, widespread throughout; present Isle of Man and Channel Islands.

HABITAT Mostly wet places, such as marshes, fens and stream edges, often growing with marsh willowherb *E. palustre*; also waste ground and in urban settings.

DESCRIPTION Perennial, 30–90cm. Stem hairy and rounded. Leaves also hairy, mostly opposite, lanceolate and stemless, with

rounded base. Flowers pale pink and very small, up to 9mm wide.

SIMILAR SPECIES American willowherb *E. ciliatum* is taller, with longer hairs, much larger and darker flowers and leaf bases lobed, partially surrounding main stem.

USES/RECIPES Young leaves in salads, cooked or as a tea.

Epilobium tetragonum
Square-stalked Willowherb

DISTRIBUTION Up to 300m. In England and Wales, widespread south of line Humber estuary–St David's Head except West Midlands and Radnorshire, Cardiganshire and Brecknockshire, absent Cumbria and west Lancashire; in Ireland, in a few southern coastal counties and around Dublin and Belfast; present Isles of Scilly and Channel Islands.

HABITAT Hedgerows, gardens, cultivated fields, stream banks, edges of woods, waste ground.

DESCRIPTION Perennial, up to 75cm high. Distinguished by square stem, which has many flattened, fine white hairs. Leaves alternate, strap shaped, tapering at ends to a blunt point. Flowers are pale pink and small, with petals 7–9mm long; seed capsules large, up to 10cm long.

USES/RECIPES According to *Sturtevant's Edible Plants of the World* (1972), this plant was used as a vegetable in Iceland and northern Asia.

Oenothera biennis

Common Evening Primrose

DISTRIBUTION Up to 300m. Native of North America. In England, common south of line Lancashire's River Ribble–Humber Estuary fairly common, but scarce Devon, Cornwall, Kent, and Sussex, north of line mostly absent; in Wales, only a few places – Anglesey, Pembrokeshire and border counties to east; in Scotland, only very few locations Ayrshire, Roxburghshire, Berwickshire, Fife, Angus and east Perth; in Ireland, only Kilkenny and Waterford; present Isle of Man and Isles of Scilly.

HABITAT Open ground on sandy soils, particularly as short-lived early colonizer of disturbed ground, becoming less dominant as other plants gain a foothold. Otherwise roadsides, railway embankments, formerly cultivated fields, waste ground, sand dunes and river banks.

DESCRIPTION Tall biennial, commonly up to 1m high. Leaves lanceolate, short stemmed, dull green and slightly crinkled, forming a basal rosette at first. Stems are hairy and green; flowers, June–September, yellow, with petals up to 30mm long. Seed pods woody, with 4 sections that fold back at the top.

SIMILAR SPECIES Large-flowered evening primrose *Oe. glazioviana* has much larger

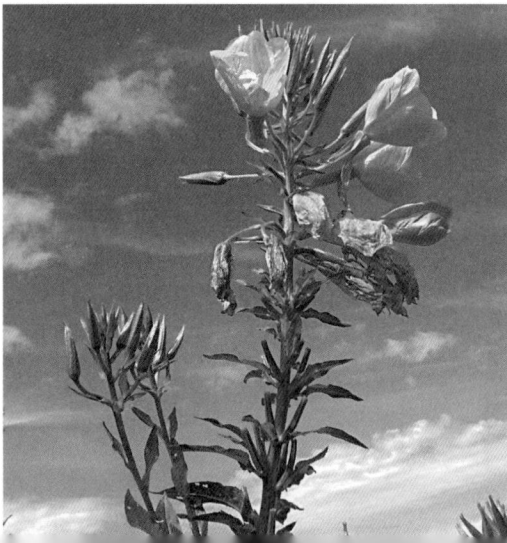

petals, up to 50mm long, reddish upper stem and hairs with swollen red bases; also generally taller and can reach 1.8m high and is found in areas where *Oe. biennis* is absent.

NOTES Fairly common wild plants, recognizable in late summer by their bright yellow flowers, held high enough to notice from a considerable distance. Evening primrose is so called because its flowers open 6–7 pm; the rest of the day they are tightly closed.

USES/RECIPES Roots are said to have been cultivated for food in both Europe and North America; however, they caused unpleasant irritation in the back of my throat when I ate them, and this seems to be a common experience. They may perhaps need much longer cooking than I have given them. Leaves are also described by many authors as edible, but in my experience they have the same irritant effect as the roots. Flowers are sweet and substantial, with very large petals. Use in salads, or chiffonade for a dramatic garnish for desserts. Toast seeds and add to salads or use in soups, breads and cakes.

BENEFITS Seeds contain gamma-linolenic acid (GLA), from which its oil is extracted; the similar starflower oil is extracted from borage seed. GLA is an omega-6 fatty acid that has been known to alleviate symptoms of eczema, pre-menstrual syndrome, some allergies and rheumatoid arthritis.

HARVESTING NOTES Cut the dead stems and turn them upside down into a bag and shake; then crush the individual seed pods to remove any remaining seeds.

½ × life size

WINTERGREEN FAMILY
Pyrolaceae

Leaves of related *Gaultheria* species flavour root-beer; they contain oil of wintergreen, which is also found in birch and meadowsweet. Oil of wintergreen is toxic in large amounts, especially to children with an allergy to the chemically similar aspirin. Chef Scott Wade uses leaves of cultivated varieties of *Gaultheria* sparingly as flavouring for veal cheeks. The sweet juicy berries of *Gaultheria shallon* were once eaten by indigenous peoples in Canada, either fresh or cooked and pressed into cakes for winter storage.

Pyrola minor
Common Wintergreen

DISTRIBUTION Mostly found in Scotland, particularly in Grampian, Tayside, the Borders, Argyle, Fife and Central; in England, sporadic in Yorkshire and West Midlands, only slightly more common in West Sussex, Gloucestershire, Northumberland, Cumbria and Durham; in Wales, almost entirely absent, a few records in Pendine, Neath and Newport areas; in Ireland, very rare, with most records in Ulster.

HABITAT Acid soil on sand dunes, moors, pinewoods.

DESCRIPTION Leaves evergreen, in rosettes, pale green, alternate, oval with leaf blades longer (up to 4cm) than stalks. Inflorescence an erect raceme with small (6mm wide) spherical pale pink flowers. The styles do not protrude.

SIMILAR SPECIES Intermediate wintergreen *P. media* has larger, more rounded dark green leaves, larger flowers (up to 10mm wide) and protruding styles.

USES/RECIPES Leaves do not taste strongly of wintergreen and are rather bitter. Use sparingly in salads.

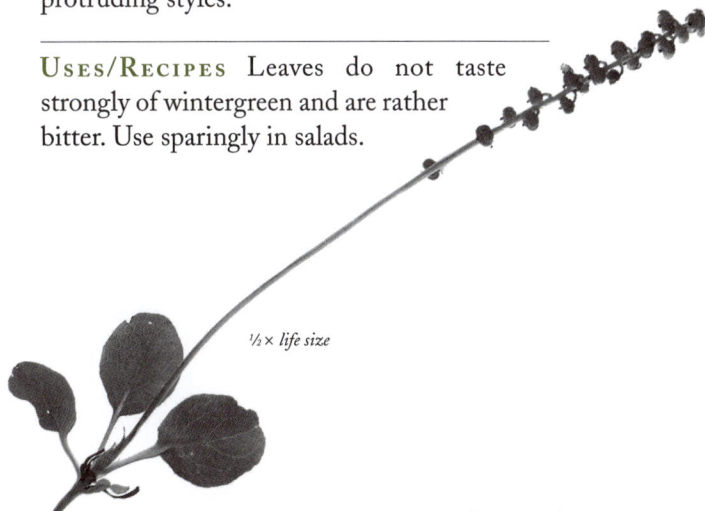

½ × *life size*

WOOD SORREL FAMILY
Oxalidaceae

Oxalis species occur on every continent – I once found the delicious leaves of one growing up from the cracks in the pavement in Sydney – and have been eaten by many indigenous peoples. One South American species, oca *Oxalis tuberosa*, has an edible tuber and has been hailed as a possible future food crop. Unfortunately, of the species that grow wild in the British Isles, only pink-sorrel and the very rare Bermuda buttercup *Oxalis pes-caprae* have underground parts large enough to be worth considering.

Several of the species that follow are naturalized garden plants. Although planted as ornamentals they are excellent food plants; many of them are rampant and become invasive, in which case developing a place for them at the dinner table is a win–win situation.

Oxalis acetosella

Wood Sorrel

DISTRIBUTION Up to 1160m. Widespread, except: in England, absent southeast Yorkshire, Lincolnshire, Essex, Bedfordshire, Buckinghamshire, Oxfordshire and much of Fens; in Scotland, absent Caithness and Western and Northern Isles; in Ireland, areas in north Munster, northwest Leinster and Connaught; present Jersey in Channel Islands and Isle of Man.

HABITAT Moist, shady places in woods, typically deciduous woods, but often confer plantations on site of former deciduous woodland; also moors with few or no trees, finding shade under small shrubs or bracken. Even in woods with dense canopy it thrives best under bracken, bramble or other vegetation.

DESCRIPTION Native perennial. Creeping plant that spreads both by rhizome and seed. Trifoliate with cordate leaflets, purplish below with red stems. At night or just before rain the leaflets droop. Flowers, April–May, reveal presence of the plant in less noticeable places – beneath other plants or ground cover such as fallen branches. They are pale lilac with darker

lilac veins, with 5 rounded petals, each flower on a separate stalk. An Old English name for the plant, *alleluia*, refers to the fact that it flowers at Easter, the time of Christ's resurrection.

SIMILAR SPECIES White clover has oval leaflets and grows in grassy areas. Non-native *Oxalis* are either pink or yellow flowered and mostly grow in more open spots near human habitation. All have cordate leaflets and are good to eat.

NOTES Wood sorrel may well be the original shamrock of the Irish, used by St Patrick to explain the doctrine of the trinity to a sceptical Celtic audience. References to shamrock in James Farewell's satire on the Irish, *The Irish Hudibras, or Fingallian Prince* (1689), refer to it as a woodland plant used for both food and drink. Clover, the plant now thought of as the shamrock, is neither a woodland plant nor used for any kind of drink, though it has been for food. Oxalic acid is the source of its flavour and has the effect of making your mouth water. It has been used to produce what William Woodville, the eighteenth-century English physician and botanist, referred to in his *Medical Botany* as 'pleasant whey' by boiling the leaves in milk.

USES/RECIPES Leaves are good in salads, both fruit and savoury; as a garnish for savoury dishes and desserts. Crushed with sugar and mixed in water they make a kind of lemonade substitute; blend with crème anglaise, a little water and extra sugar for a sweet sorrel sauce [RR]. Excellent as a salad with sautéd wild mushrooms, or in a butter sauce to accompany fish [AN]. Flowers make a pretty addition to salads.

BENEFITS Leaves are a good source of vitamin C and beta-carotene.

HARVESTING NOTES Bright green carpets of wood sorrel leaves are easy to spot where there is little or no ground cover but are often concealed where there is. Grasp the stalks just under the leaves and tug sharply to snap off at the base; this way you get a longer stalk, which is actually the tastiest part. In loose earth hold down the soil with one hand so as not to pull up the rhizomes – if you do uproot any, replant them near by and start a new colony. Wood sorrel is tenacious and seems to grow back with no ill effects; it is probably adapted to repeated grazing.

Oxalis corniculata

Procumbent Yellow-sorrel

DISTRIBUTION Up to 300m. Grown in the British Isles since seventeenth century. In England, south of line Bootle–Skegness widespread except areas of Devon, Wiltshire, Hampshire, Gloucestershire, Huntingdonshire, Cambridgeshire, Derbyshire and Lincolnshire, north of line sparse; in Wales, scarce and sporadic, absent hilly and mountainous areas; in Scotland, scarce, sparse in Forth and Borders and Renfrewshire, Wigtownshire, North and Mid-Ebudes, Moray and south

Aberdeen; in Ireland, sparse, isolated localities in Ulster, Dublin, Kilkenny, Waterford, Cork and Kerry; present Channel Islands, Isle of Man and Isles of Scilly.

HABITAT Cultivated fields and gardens (especially greenhouses), paths and waste ground, preferring open, sunny position.

DESCRIPTION Creeping perennial, with stems that put down roots. Leaves bronze green, with several yellow flowers, June–September growing from one main stem.

SIMILAR SPECIES Least yellow-sorrel *O. exilis* has smaller leaves and flowers that grow singly and appear earlier; it grows in both sunny positions and shade, found in cracks in pavements, at base of walls and on path edges. Upright yellow-sorrel *O. stricta* has upright, non-rooting stems and green leaves in whorls; it is found in shady places in cultivated fields and gardens, especially on sandy soils.

USES/RECIPES Leaves are used in Lebanon either fresh in salads or dried as an acidic spice. Use seed pods in salads.

Oxalis incarnata

Pale Pink-sorrel

DISTRIBUTION Up to 300m. In England, scarce, sparsely present in Cheshire, Lancashire and southeast Yorkshire and most common along south coast in Sussex, Hampshire and the southwest, sporadic in Home Counties, Norfolk, Oxfordshire, Herefordshire, Worcestershire and Warwickshire; in Wales, sparsely present Cardiganshire and Carmarthenshire; in Scotland,

rare, only found in Lanarkshire, Renfrewshire, Wigtownshire, North Ebudes and Shetland; in Ireland, recorded in one 10sq km each in Antrim, Dublin, Wexford and Cork; present Channel Islands and Isle of Man.

HABITAT Hedgerows, old walls, cracks in pavements; preferring shady positions.

DESCRIPTION Perennial, spreading by bulblets, with upright stems from which grows a crown of both leaves (which are hairless) and flowers, each on a single stalk, all stalks growing from the same point.

Pink-sorrel flowers

Pink-sorrel leaf

SIMILAR SPECIES Pink-sorrel *O. articulata* also has flowers growing from the same point on an upright stem, but the leaves are hairy and emerge from the base of the plant.

USES/RECIPES These leaves are the most delicate and finely textured of all the *Oxalis* species and are the most suited as a garnish for food with soft textures, such as ice cream, sorbet and soft cheese. Pink-sorrel has thick, juicy stems which can be chopped and used in salads or as a vegetable.

YAM FAMILY
Dioscoreaceae

Tamus communis

Black Bryony

DISTRIBUTION In England, absent north of line Sunderland–Seascale and south of this line in the Pennines, elsewhere widespread throughout; in Wales, absent Powys and North Dyfed, widespread elsewhere; in Scotland and Ireland, absent.

HABITAT Woodland, hedgebanks, scrub, mostly on calcareous soils.

DESCRIPTION Climbing vine, without tendrils; dark green glossy, cordate leaves. Flowers, yellowish green and bell shaped; berries bright red.

USES/RECIPES The young shoots are very popular in the Bodrum area of Turkey; also in Spain, where they are eaten after boiling, often with hard-boiled eggs, in omelettes, with ham or chorizo, sautéd or tossed in oil, and in stews with potato. The tubers are massive and full of starch, a potentially excellent food source. However, they are also full of calcium-oxalate crystals. Like **lords-and-ladies**, there are several historical accounts of methods of making them safe to eat, but these methods as described simply don't work.

HAZARDS The aforementioned problems with the tubers. The berries are also poisonous.

¼ × life size

Flowering plants

Monocotyledons

ARUM FAMILY
Araceae

Most members of this family are armed to the teeth with raphides, bundles of calcium oxalate needle-shaped crystals, which fire themselves into the soft tissues of mouth and throat when plant material is bitten into. In many species they are coated with the irritant protease that causes swelling; swallowing them could cause the throat to swell enough to prevent breathing.

Raphides are also found in various species of yam, which are rendered edible by elaborate processing. Several Arum species that contain calcium oxalate have either been selectively bred or are processed in such a way as to remove the crystals. In both India and Oman, *Remusatia vivipara* tubers are eaten but only after long, slow cooking to destroy the oxalates. *Calocasia esculenta* is widely used as its proliferation of names illustrates: taro in the Pacific Islands, eddo in West Africa, Japanese potatoes in Japan and old cocoyam in the West Indies.

With all this in mind, you can perhaps understand how hopeful I was of obtaining something palatable from our native Arum, lords-and-ladies (also known as cuckoo pint) *Arum maculatum*; particularly as so many references are made to its use as food in historical and ethnobotanical literature. However, for me it remains firmly in the category of poisonous plants. I have a certain respect for it as the only plant (or mushroom, for that matter) by which I have ever been poisoned, albeit under deliberate and controlled conditions. I have tried eating *Arum maculatum* after boiling, baking, even baking and boiling, and finally baking, drying and grinding into powder, which is then left for several months before being used, as some authors suggest. None of these methods produces an end product that does not burn my mouth. The effect is less than it would be raw, since the irritant protease that coats the raphides is destroyed by heat, but even this is pretty unpleasant. It is frustrating, as the roasted tubers are delicious, like a combination of roast chestnut and banana. Just when I thought I had carried out the last of these experiments, I read an account of the leaves being used, stuffed like vine leaves in Turkey. A glutton for punishment, I went out, found some leaves and boiled them for at least 20 minutes. Cautiously, but full of hope and anticipation, I put a little

piece in my mouth. Like the cooked root, it was delicious, and I had a strong urge to swallow it and eat some more. Like the cooked root, it took a few moments but soon produced a burning sensation that didn't stop for several hours, despite spitting out the leaf and rinsing my mouth repeatedly. I swear, this time, I really am through with this plant.

Acorus calamus

Sweet Flag

DISTRIBUTION Native of Asia and North America. Up to 300m. It is most common in England, especially Home Counties, Worcestershire, Staffordshire, Leicestershire, parts of Derbyshire and Nottinghamshire, Cheshire, north Lancashire and mid- and southwest Yorkshire, sparse elsewhere; in Wales, rare, isolated localties in Anglesey, Denbighshire, Montgomeryshire, Carmarthenshire and Pembrokeshire; in Scotland, scarce, sporadic in Central Lowlands and eastern Coastal Lowlands north to Moray Firth, Dumfries and Galloway and Main Argyll; in Ireland, rare, mostly east Ulster, also in Dublin, Carlow and west Cork; present Channel Islands.

HABITAT Shallow water: edges of ponds, lakes, rivers and canals.

DESCRIPTION Upright perennial, up to 1m high, with bright green, sword-shaped leaves, 10–20mm wide, growing in bunches. A distinct rib runs up the middle of the leaf and usually one or both edges are crinkled: these crinkles and the smell of tangerines released if the leaves are crushed identify the plant when not in flower. The tiny yellowy-green flowers are on a curved spadix, up to 80mm long, which ends in a point and grows at an angle of 45 degrees two-thirds up the stem. The lower two-thirds of the stem are flattened and winged; the top one-third resembles the leaves.

SIMILAR SPECIES Leaves resemble the leaves of iris species, which are poisonous, of which some but not all leaves may be slightly crinkled, and reed sweet-grass *Glyceria maxima*, which are sometimes crinkled at their tips; neither plant smells of tangerines.

NOTES In his *Outlines of Botany* (1835), Gilbert Thomas Burnett complains that sweet flag was 'consumed in great quantities by perfumers and makers of hair powder, and that in the area of London it has been almost wholly destroyed by their continual maraudings' – a cautionary tale for over zealous foragers.

USES/RECIPES Leaves and stalks have a delicate tangerine tang and can be used to flavour milk puddings; the whole roots are rather overpowering but can also be used in moderation for flavouring, in particular in place of orange zest, for example in potato mousseline (mashed potato with lots of flavoured cream, in this case infused with sweet flag) served with scallops and light garlic butter [SW]. Infusing it in cream takes the edge off the slight bitterness. The tender core of young roots can be used in salad; the lower (underground) part of the stem is best for candying.

HAZARDS Contains essential oil of calamus, similar to safrole in sassafras, which has been found to cause tumorous growths in lab rats. However, there is no evidence of any harmful effects in humans as a result of eating the plant. (See p.21 for general remarks about the relevance of animal poisonings and poisonings from essential oils to the use of the plants as food.)

HARVESTING NOTES Younger stalks, 30cm or less high, are easily separated from rhizomes by grasping them firmly at the base and giving them a brisk tug.

Arum maculatum

Lords-and-Ladies/ Cuckoo Pint

DISTRIBUTION Up to 425m. In England, widespread, only less so south Lancashire, Cumbria, south Northumberland and Cheviot Hills; also in Wales, only less so Merioneth; in Scotland, found mainly Central Lowlands and eastern Coastal Lowlands north to east coast of Caithness, also Kirkcudbrightshire, Wigtownshire, Main Argyll, Mid Ebudes and Orkney; in Ireland, abundant except Tyrone, Donegal, west Mayo, west Galway and much of Kerry; present Isle of Man, Channel Islands and Lundy.

HABITAT Woods and woodland edges, hedgebanks.

DESCRIPTION Distinctive, dark green arrow-shaped leaves, up to 20cm long, often with dark purple blotches, emerging January, when surrounding ground has little else growing; consequently easy to notice and identify, as they are throughout their growth cycle. In April their highly distinctive flowers emerge, consisting of two unusual structures, the spathe and the spadix: the spathe is a green leaflike structure that looks like a monk's hood; it surrounds the spadix, which looks like a long electrode and bears many tiny male and female flowers. They are fertilized by flies, attracted by the smell of rotten flesh that they emit. Once fertilized, they produce a stalk full of bright orange berries.

SIMILAR SPECIES Italian lords-and-ladies *Arum italicum* is larger, with a yellow spadix. It is grown in gardens but naturalized in some areas.

USES/RECIPES Tubers were once grown on the Isle of Portland, in Dorset, for the manufacture of a form of starch known as Portland sago. Making the starch, similar to arrowroot or cornstarch, is quite a simple process that leaves behind the noxious calcium oxalate, making the end product safe to eat. Chop the tuber finely, place with some water in a jar then shake the jar vigorously (with the lid on) and leave to settle. Pour off the liquid and the floating pieces of tuber, then transfer the remaining paste to a dish and place in the sun to dry. The berries are said to be sweet, which has led to several cases of poisoning, as they also contain high concentrations of calcium oxalate.

²/₃ × life size

BULRUSH FAMILY
Typhaceae

Typha latifolia

Reedmace/Bulrush

DISTRIBUTION Up to 500m. In England and Wales, found in most lowland areas; in Scotland, widespread in the Borders and north of Southern Uplands, absent higher-altitude areas of Grampians and Southern Uplands and most areas north of Glen Mor, although present in a few localities in Easterness, East Ross and east Sutherland; in Ireland, widespread but more sparsely distributed in and around higher-altitude areas; present on Channel Islands and Isles of Scilly; introduced to the Isle of Man.

HABITAT Often in large clumps, adorning the edges of ponds, lakes or slow-moving rivers; also in dykes and streams.

DESCRIPTION Leaves fleshy, greyish green and flat, resembling giant leeks at first, later sheathing or surrounding the flowering stem. Flower spikes, consisting of many tiny, petal-less flowers, are in two distinct sections, the thinner male section

above, both initially green. In June, the male part swells and produces a mass of yellow pollen that drops on to and fertilizes the female part, which then turns a rich chocolate brown, with the golden male section withering above. These are the flower heads in their post-coital stage! The chocolate-brown cigar-shaped seed heads are a familiar sight for many people, being commonly known as bulrushes and used as decoration.

SIMILAR SPECIES The poisonous yellow iris *Iris pseudacorus* and stinking iris *I. foetidissima* have flat leaves for their entire length so that the bases of the leaf bundles are oval in cross section; those of reedmace leaves are round. Remains of last year's seed heads are a good sign, but still check the shape of the leaf bases, as irises often grow alongside reedmace. Lesser reedmace *T. angustifolia* has narrower leaves with curved backs and thinner flower spikes, with a gap between male and female parts; it is just as good to eat as reedmace.

NOTES Reedmace has been

Pollen-laden flower spike

⅓ × life size

eaten by many cultures, including those in New Zealand, Jamaica, China, Pakistan, India and Africa. Australian Aborigines still roast the roots, and in the nineteenth century the young shoots were used in Germany for salads. Reedmace provide one kind of food or another throughout the year and is prolific, producing as much as 142 metric tonnes of rhizome per 0.4 ha. Many tonnes of the rhizomes are dredged out of ponds and lakes every year and discarded; given that 1 ton of rhizomes yields 0.23 tonnes of flour, that's a lot of good food going to waste.

USES/RECIPES Hearts: carefully remove any tough parts of the leaves. Boil or steam the tender, white inner section and serve with butter or a light sauce, or use in salads. Slicing the base of the heart thinly shows off the exquisite structure of the leaves in cross section; the little chambers are air pockets, which conduct air down into the submerged roots. The flavour is delicate, reminiscent of palm heart. The whole flower and a portion of the stem beneath can be eaten when very young and tender. Blanch and use in warm salads. Pollen can be used in place of flour for baking, thickening and so on: it is highly nutritious with the same sweet and slightly soapy taste as the hearts. To obtain a starch extract similar to cornflour, pound the rhizomes in water in order to dissolve all the starch, strain the liquid and allow the starch to settle, then pour off the water and allow the residue to dry.

BENEFITS Reedmace flour has higher mineral content than any flour except potato and has more protein than rice or maize.

HAZARDS Take care that contaminants are not present in the water. Your local Environment Agency office should be able to advise you. As a precaution, don't eat the rhizomes raw and take care not to expose the flesh to any bacteria present in mud by breaking them.

HARVESTING NOTES Hearts: when the leaf bundles are about 1m high, feel the bases to check whether the flower stem has started to develop, in which case the core will be woody and inedible. Good ones will give a little when squeezed. Cut or break them off as near to the roots as you can. Flower spikes: harvest when still fully sheathed, they should be tender enough to be cut through quite easily; if not, move further up until you reach a tender part and cut there. Rhizomes: gather in autumn–early spring. It is a messy job and often quite smelly, but bear in mind that the rotting vegetation that causes this is highly nutritious for the living plants. Follow the dying growth from the reedmace down to its base to be sure you are not pulling up an iris rhizome, then get a grip beneath it and push it up out of the mud. Clean and dry the rhizomes before use. Collect pollen from early June. Test flowers that are showing a bit of yellow on the male part by flicking them – if this produces a cloud of dust, they are ready! A bag will suffice to catch the pollen, but the best receptacle is an inverted 4-litre plastic milk container with an extra hole in the side for inserting the flower (this method was devised by Californian wild-food educator John Goude). When you've inserted the flower, shake or tap it to release the pollen, then unscrew the cap to release the pollen when you get home.

CAPE PONDWEED FAMILY
Aponogetonaceae

Aponogeton distachyos

Cape Pondweed

DISTRIBUTION Naturalized pond plant, native of South Africa. Although capable of producing seed in the British Isles, it hasn't spread much, with only scattered localities in England, mostly Sussex, Norfolk, Kent, Surrey, Dorset and Cornwall, as well as three in Wales and Scotland combined.

HABITAT Ponds and lakes.

DESCRIPTION Strap-shaped leaves, up to 7cm long, float on the water surface; flowers have fleshy white petals and black anthers, and are arranged in a spike of up to 10 flowers that smell distinctly of vanilla.

USES/RECIPES In South Africa (where they are available tinned) the flowers are known as 'water-blommetjies' or water blossoms. The flowers themselves, if used, cook away completely. They are used to greater effect in a simple salad with chickweed or another mild salad leaf, or as a garnish with vanilla ice cream. For cooking, they should be used when they have

Water-blommetjie Bredie/Pondweed Stew

Joan Swart, Hermanus, Cape Town. Rep. of SA
SERVES 6

1 basket water-blommetjies (approx. 1kg)
  and sufficient water to cover them (approx.
  2 litres)
100ml unsalted butter
50ml sunflower/rapeseed oil
1.5kg lamb or mutton (rib, neck or tail),
  diced into 3cm chunks
600g Roscoff onions, diced
2 garlic heads, peeled, heart removed

1kg potatoes (Maris Piper or Desirée), peeled
  and sliced
20g Maldon sea salt
10g cracked white pepper
2 cloves
2 large lemons, juiced
250ml mineral water
250ml Chenin Blanc or Sauvignon Blanc
50ml Worcestershire sauce (optional)
30ml sweet chilli sauce (prepared) or sweet
  chilli chutney (both optional)
6 portions cooked savoury rice, to serve

Break the pedicel off the water-blommetjies and remove any hard leaves. Rinse well. Boil for 10 minutes and drain. Put to one side.

FOR THE BREDIE: Heat the butter and oil in a pan. Fry the meat until brown on both sides – though not cooked yet. Remove and put in a deep cooking pot (*potjie*/three-legged cauldron) or an Irish self-basting pot. Sweat the diced onion and garlic slowly in the pan – do not brown. Disperse this over the meat. Scatter the water-blommetjies on top and lastly layer the sliced potatoes. Season with the salt, pepper and cloves. Squeeze over the juice of the two lemons and add the water and wine. (At this point you can add the chilli and Worcestershire sauce, if you choose.) Put the lid on and let it slowly simmer until the meat is tender and the potatoes, cooked (approximately 2–3 hours). Serve with fragrant and savoury rice.

started to form seed or already have seed. Use leaves and shoots as greens. Eat rhizomes roasted or raw: they have a fresh, nutty flavour but are rather small so you would need to find a lot to make harvesting worthwhile; they are eaten by the Khoi and San peoples, the first-known inhabitants of the southern tip of Africa.

BENEFITS Flowers contain folic acid.

HARVESTING NOTES Flowers should be soaked in salt water to remove grit before use. The tuber is harvested in the autumn and winter.

FLOWERING RUSH FAMILY
Butomaceae

Butomus umbellatus

Flowering Rush

DISTRIBUTION Up to 300m; mostly lowland areas. Found mostly in England south of the Humber, more sparse to the north, absent Cornwall and much of Derbyshire and Hampshire; in Wales, found only on Anglesey, on or near the Gower peninsula and in Cardiff and Newport districts; in Scotland, very scarce, but found along Tweed and Ayr rivers; in Ireland, along rivers Erne and Bann, Liffey and Shannon and on Lough Neagh and Strangford Lough; present Isle of Man and Jersey.

HABITAT Nutrient-rich water in chalk and limestone regions, in ponds, lakes, canals, reservoirs and slow-flowing streams and rivers, also well-managed ditches on grazed marshes; occurs either at the water's edge or submerged/emerging from deeper water. Submerged forms are often found alongside arrowhead *Sagittaria sagittifolia*, mostly in slow-flowing water.

DESCRIPTION Hairless perennial reaching up to 1.5m high. Leaves are strap shaped with a distinct angle on the back; all grow from the base of the plant. Most easily recognized and distinguished by its umbels of bright pink flowers, each about 2.5cm wide, with 3 pink petals and 3 smaller pink sepals; the only rush species that produces a coloured flower.

USES/RECIPES Tubers can be eaten either raw or roasted and whole, or ground into flour. They are nutty, sweet and delicious.

ECOLOGICAL CONSIDERATIONS This is quite a scarce plant in the wild, so unless you are able to replenish the population it is best to stick to eating ones from your own pond – flowering rush is easily obtained from garden centres.

½ × life size

GRASS FAMILY
Poaceae

Grasses provide daily food for most of the world's population in the form of edible seeds, such as wheat, rye, maize, barley, oats, millet and rice, which are rich in carbohydrates and proteins. Nowadays most of these grains come from cultivated varieties, but for much of human (pre)history, wild grasses, including the ancestors of the aforementioned cultivars, proved more than adequate. Wild-grass grains are small, but contain more protein than cultivated grains. In spite of their size, the majority can be harvested in large quantities.

Considering that no ploughing, sowing or weeding is involved to produce the crop in the first place, wild grass grains are an easy source of food. Small-grained grasses have often been preferred to larger-grained wheat, barley and oats because of their superior flavour. The honey-flavoured grains of manna or floating sweet-grass *Glyceria fluitans* was once in great demand in Europe and Russia in the courts of nobles. The minute cultivated grain tef *Eragrostis tef* has a similar status as a luxury food in Eritrea and Ethiopia; it is made into a fermented flat bread, known as '*injera*', which is pliable and slightly sour tasting. I have been fortunate enough to try it, cooked by members of the Eritrean refugee community in Canterbury and served with meat sauce; it is the nicest bread I have ever tasted, although quite unlike any other.

African wild grasses can be harvested at rates of up to 2kg per hour; some are still harvested commercially, for example wild millets *Panicum turgidum* and *Cenchrus biflorus* and African wild rice *Oryza barthii*. Many of these species are more drought resistant than cultivated grains, and capable of reclaiming desert by binding together the sand with their roots. Wild grasses were also used to stabilize the dust bowls of North America, the consequence of years of industrial wheat production. While working on this project, Professor Jack Harlan, a specialist in crop domestication and evolution, harvested tall fescue *Festuca arundinacea* (which is also found in the British Isles) at a rate of 4.5kg per hour. Yields of up to 800kg per hectare have been obtained from other North American wild grasses (Harlan in Harris & Hillman, *Foraging and Farming*), and wild rice *Zizania aquatica* is harvested commercially on a fairly large scale. In Asia, cockspur *Echinochloa crus-galli* is a weed of paddy fields; it is eaten by the rural poor of a number of Asian countries (R. A. Ragu, ed., *Ethnobotany of Rice Weeds in South Asia*, 1999). The grains of a cultivar of this grass are used in Japan to make dumplings and macaroni. Polish ethnobotanist and forager Wojtek Szymanski finds the wild plant quick and easy to harvest but quite difficult to dehusk. A similar species, *E. macrocarpa*, was used in Russia to make flour for flat cakes in the twentieth century (R. Yu. Roshevits, *Grasses*, 1980).

Comparatively little is known about historic European uses of wild grasses but the use of floating sweet-grass is well documented. Grains have been found at mesolithic sites in Denmark, and it is likely to have been part of the mesolithic diet throughout Europe. Until at least the nineteenth century, it was eaten in Denmark, Sweden, Holland, Germany, Russia, Poland and even in the British Isles, and was known as 'manna-croup'. This is a term also applied to a kind of wheat semolina, which became a substitute for the real thing. Floating sweet-grass was commercially harvested in Poland as recently as 1925. A few other grasses are known to have been used. *Bromus* species were used by neolithic peoples in Poland; *Bromus secalinus* was harvested there during the Second World War. Grains of *Bromus* species were also used by indigenous North Americans, and a now extinct species, *B. mango,* was once the main cereal grain used in Chile. Quaking grass *Briza media* is said to have been used in twentieth-century Bosnia, although I have found the minute and flimsy seeds impossible to process by hand, and hairy finger-grass or common crabgrass *Digitaria sanguinalis* was harvested in great quantities in central Europe and sold in the markets. It was considered a luxury food, and by the nineteenth century it was also taken into cultivation in former Czechoslovakia, north Germany and the Italian island of Ponza, as well as parts of southern Russia. The grains have traditionally been cooked by frying – this is called '*frike*' in the Middle East – or by boiling in milk. Hairy finger-grass is found in the British Isles, but only as a rather scarce alien.

The grains are not the only useful parts of grasses: the leaves are also perfectly edible to ruminants, although not to us, since they contain cellulose, which our digestive system is not able to digest. Grass leaves nevertheless form the basis for much of our food, since we consume the carcasses of grazing mammals such as cattle, sheep and rabbits, as well as milk and milk-based products. Non-meat eaters may be less struck by this as a lesson in providence, but populations of wild species cause serious ecological disruption when carnivores don't keep them in check. For this reason, the present deer, squirrel, rabbit and wild goat populations are problematic for our native flora; eating more wild meat would be good both for us and for it. Wild herbivores eat a diversity of wild plants resulting in meat of a quality and nutrient content superior even to the best organic meat.

Grass leaves themselves can be consumed by people in one form: the nutritious juice can be extracted using a good juicer. As well as this, among our native grasses is one that is used as a vanilla-like spice: the coumarin-rich sweet vernal-grass. Another (rare) British species, holy grass *Hierochloe odorata*, also contains coumarin. In Poland, where it is known as zubrowka, it is used to flavour vodka (but then again, in Poland, pretty much everything is used to flavour vodka ...). Sugar, itself originally considered a spice, was first produced from the thick stems of sugar cane *Arundinaria gigantea*, which Sanjida O'Connell describes as 'the grass that changed the world' in her eponymous book. The sweetness of sugar conceals a bitter past: sugar plantations were the driving force behind the African slave trade and introduced us to the modern afflictions of diabetes and tooth decay. Bamboo shoots are also edible grass stems, with a sting in the tail, or should I say, nail. They were used as an instrument of torture by the Japanese who inserted them beneath their victim's fingernails and left them there to grow.

___

GENERAL HAZARDS Most wild grasses are susceptible to infection by the fungus ergot *Claviceps purpurea*, which causes severe poisoning if eaten. Symptoms include stomach cramps, vomiting, dizziness and pupil dilation. Eaten over long periods more serious symptoms occur, including hallucinations and gangrene. Harvesting in dry periods in early summer is safest, as the fungus develops in wetter conditions, usually later in the season. The infestation is also quite easy to detect, as the grass seed heads are blackened with the sooty spores of the fungus, and the black, drumstick-like fruiting bodies can be seen poking out from the grains. In dry conditions, any attempt to harvest grains from infected grass will release clouds of black sooty dust. Grasses that are wilted or have dark, smutty moulds on them should also be avoided.

___

HARVESTING NOTES There are many possible methods of collecting the grains, including cutting down the whole grass stem as you would when harvesting wheat or barley, but the most efficient are those where the grains are shaken loose and caught from where they stand. In Germany and Poland, a method was employed which is similar to traditional methods for harvesting juniperberries. A sheet was placed beneath the panicles, which were then shaken

or beaten with a stick so that the grains fell on to the sheet. Another method, used in both Poland and Germany (Prussia), was to beat the grains into a fine horsehair sieve, whereas in Russia, peasants used to harvest the grains of floating sweet-grass by wading in the water and running a felt hat through the stands of grass so that the ripe grains dropped into it. A similar result is achieved using a sweep net, a stronger version of a butterfly net, normally used to sample insects within grassland. To make your own sweep net, buy a landing net from a fishing tackle shop, remove the net from the frame and in its place attach a piece of linen or similar material, sown into a sock-like shape. Leave the handle off the net, grip it firmly and sweep it violently from side to side through the thickest stands of grass you can find. The sweeping motion keeps the net open like a windsock; a cloud of seeds is bashed loose, and most of them settle into the base of the net. This method collects quite a few insects as well! You could also simply bunch together several stems, bend them over into a large bag and shake vigorously, but this method is far less productive.

___

PROCESSING THE GRAINS After harvesting, some grasses need to be parched over a low heat in a large pan or frying pan, shaking or stirring continually to avoid burning. This makes it easier to separate the husks from the grains; other species can be easily dehusked (hulled) after thorough drying in the sun. After this the husks must be either rubbed or pounded until they shatter and come loose from the grains.

POUNDING METHOD: Put them in a deep (to prevent grain escaping), robust (to withstand pounding) vessel such as a wooden barrel or metal bath, then pound repeatedly with something heavy. I use a ground working tool with a heavy flat base called an elephant's foot, pounding about thirty times, taking a

Grass infected with ergot

breather, then again until the husks have been removed. Ojibwa people in North America used the rubbing method to dehusk wild rice: they would lay the grain on a rough surface such as hide or wood, and tread it repeatedly (see Thayer, 2006) with clean moccasins. The next stage is to winnow away the chaff – the loosened husks and any other debris. On a day with a gentle wind, empty the grain on to a large sheet, then with a person on each corner of the sheet, toss it repeatedly. The chaff will gradually blow away as the grain falls back on to the sheet. For smaller amounts, drop handfuls into the sweep net; in the absence of wind you can just blow across it as it falls.

THE GRASSES

Grasses are something of a specialist subject. Thorough treatment of them is beyond the scope of this book, not least because it is in theory possible to use the grains of all our native species and those of many alien species. Detailed coverage is therefore limited to the small number of grass species of which I currently have first-hand knowledge. However, I would recommend experimenting with the various wild relatives of oats and barley, which have quite large grains, as well as with the various bromes, the seeds of which resemble wild rice.

Anthony North's Gooseberry Soufflé & Hay Ice Cream

SERVES 8

FOR THE ICE CREAM: Put 350ml milk, 150ml double cream and 300g sweet vernal grass hay into a pan and warm through so hay infuses. Pass through a fine sieve and discard the hay. Whisk 50g pasteurized egg yolk and 120g sugar together. Add to infused-milk mixture. Churn in an ice-cream maker or put into freezer and stir occasionally.

FOR THE SOUFFLÉ BASE: Whisk 2 eggs and 2 egg yolks with 50g sugar until light and fluffy. Add 100g sifted flour. Put 250g milk and 1 vanilla pod and its seeds (cut open and seeds scraped loose so all the flavour infuses) into a pan and warm through. Remove pod. Slowly add warm milk to egg mixture and mix until smooth. Put into a thick-bottomed pan. Cook on stove on a high heat until it forms a thick paste, using a wooden spoon to beat. Cool the paste down and add a further 6 egg yolks, one at a time.

FOR THE GOOSEBERRIES: Dissolve 300g sugar in 300ml water to make stock syrup, in which poach 1 punnet gooseberries, topped and tailed. Strain to remove excess syrup.

TO MAKE THE SOUFFLÉS: Preheat the oven to 220°C. Put the soufflé base into a large bowl, add 60ml vodka and 3 tablespoons of the gooseberry pulp and mix together. Whisk 8 egg whites with 1 heaped tablespoon of sugar (best to use a machine to avoid tired arms) until you can turn bowl upside down and the mixture won't fall out. Add a quarter of the egg white–sugar mixture to soufflé base mix, mix roughly then gently fold in the rest of egg white–sugar mixture. Grease 8 ramekin dishes with butter and dust with caster sugar: it is imperative ramekins are well buttered and sugared so soufflés rise nice and straight. Carefully divide soufflé mix among ramekins. With a spoon, make an incision in middle of each soufflé and put a spoonful of gooseberries in each. Cook in the oven for 10–14 minutes. Serve immediately: each soufflé with a scoop of hay ice cream. The tart soufflé perfectly balances the richness of the hay ice cream.

Anthoxanthum odoratum

Sweet Vernal-grass

DISTRIBUTION Up to 1030m. Widespread throughout the British Isles, only less so in England, in parts of the Fens.

HABITAT Moors, open woodland and all types of grassland.

DESCRIPTION Tufted perennial grass of medium height, 10–50cm high. Panicles 1–12cm long, 6–15mm wide, oval–oblong, quite loose when in flower but more compact once grain has formed. Distinguished by vanilla-like scent.

USES/RECIPES The scent and flavour of this grass are due to coumarin, also found in **melilot, bastard balm** and **sweet woodruff**. Use fresh green leaves and, later, hay in similar ways to these plants, infusing the flavour into sauces, braising liquid, cooked fruit and so on. The juiced green leaves have an intense flavour almost like liquorice, the result of the combined flavours of coumarin and chlorophyll. Sweet vernal-grass juice makes a spectacular grass-green jelly, with a little fresh lemon juice added to temper the richness of the flavours. The hay has little or no chlorophyll and hence has a more pure coumarin flavour.

HAZARDS The highly toxic parasitic fungus ergot may be present (for description of ergot poisoning, see p.324). Do not harvest seeds after damp weather, particularly if black sooty deposits or dark protrusions are present on the seed head.

²⁄₃ × life size

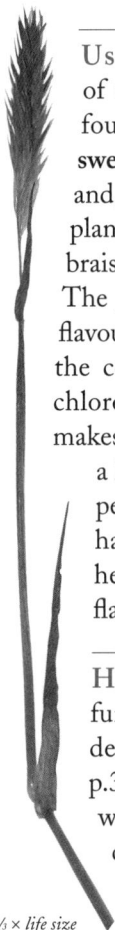

HARVESTING & PROCESSING NOTES If you want to use the green grass, you will need to find plants that are at least flowering in the first instance, in order to be sure you have the right grass. Use a wheat grass juicer for juicing – other kinds will not be able to cope with grass fibres.

Bromopsis erecta

Upright Brome

DISTRIBUTION In England, common in much of south and east but less so in Kent, Norfolk, Essex and the Fens and almost entirely absent south and west of Bridgwater, Somerset, quite widespread in the Midlands and northeast up to Newcastle, scarce elsewhere; in Wales, found only a few places on north and south coasts; in Scotland, almost entirely absent; in Ireland, sporadic in central area, except in Dublin area, where quite common.

HABITAT Dry, infertile ground on calcareous soil on sand dunes, waste ground, roadsides and lightly grazed pasture.

DESCRIPTION Perennial, up to 1m high. Lower leaves flat, with inrolled margins, upper leaves up to 6mm wide and bristly. Pannicles up to 15cm long, upright, with rough stalks and spikelets up to 35mm long.

USES/RECIPES Cook grains slowly with carrots, onions, celery, chicken stock, bouquet garni and plenty of salt and pepper for at least an hour. Add to broths and soups, such as fish, lamb or chicken, or add to salads, such as with some orzo pasta (shaped like rice), chopped chorizo, fresh

parsley, lemon zest and grated raw courgette, in a nice lemony dressing [JDW].

HABITAT Damp soils, in woods, marshes and rough grassland.

HAZARDS The highly toxic parasitic fungus ergot may be present (see p.324 for description of ergot poisoning) Do not harvest seeds after damp weather, particularly if black sooty deposits or dark protrusions are present on the seed head.

DESCRIPTION Tall, perennial grass, up to 1.2m high. Leaves furrowed and ridged, rough to the touch especially if rubbed downwards. Inflorescences in a loose panicle with whorled branches, roughly cone shaped. Spikelets 4–6mm long, lanceolate. This grass often sets seed in pasture where other species will not, as its leaves are unpalatable to livestock.

Deschampsia cespitosa

Tufted Hair-grass

DISTRIBUTION Found throughout the British Isles, with the exception of the Channel Islands.

HAZARDS The highly toxic parasitic fungus ergot may be present (for description of ergot poisoning, see p.324). Do not harvest seeds after damp weather, particularly if black sooty deposits or dark protrusions are present on the seed head.

René Redzepi's Biodynamic Milk Cheese & Grass Seeds

SERVES 4

FOR THE GRASS SEEDS
130g brown sugar and a little water
200g tufted hair-grass seeds

FOR THE BIODYNAMIC MILK CHEESE
1 litre milk (we use fresh biodynamic milk from an old Danish breed of dairy cow)

48g double cream
20g buttermilk
8g rennet

FOR THE GREEN STRAWBERRIES:
150g green strawberries, rinsed and green pit removed

Lightly toast the seeds in a pan with no oil. In another pan caramelize the sugar with the water. Add the seeds and cool down the mixture. Crush the caramel so that it forms smaller crunchy pieces, about the size of poppy seeds.

Heat the milk and cream to 33°C, add the buttermilk and rennet. Put the mixture in a 1-litre plastic container, cover with lid. Steam the container at 33°C for 1¼ hours. After this cool the container down in the fridge. Then cut the cheese into six pieces and put the pieces on kitchen towel to absorb excess liquid. Keep cool until serving time. Be careful – they are fragile.

Juice the strawberries. Add sugar until it holds 12 brix on a refractometer (a way of measuring sugar content in a given liquid). Keep cool.

TO SERVE: Roll the fresh cheese in the grass/caramel crumble. Put in a deep bowl. Pour over the green strawberry juice.

Elytrigia repens

Couch Grass

DISTRIBUTION Up to 845m. In England and Wales, widespread throughout; in Scotland, found throughout, except high-altitude areas of Southern Uplands, Grampian Mountains, North West Highlands, Caithness and the isles of Skye and Lewis; in Ireland, found throughout, but less abundant west Donegal, Leitrim, west Mayo, northeast and southeast Galway, Clare and Kerry; on Channel Islands, Isle of Man and Isles of Scilly.

HABITAT Cultivated ground, rough grassland, waste ground, field edges and roadsides.

DESCRIPTION Mostly distinguished by its long, creeping underground rhizomes, which make it so hard to eradicate and consequently a great pest to gardeners. Above ground it forms tufts up to 1.2m tall. Leaves are quite soft, flat and with a few hairs on their upper face. Inflorescences are long (5–20cm) and thin, with stalkless spikelets that overlap.

USES/RECIPES Roots have a slight liquorice flavour; they are also good source of various nutrients. They can be ground down and used as flour, but the resulting bread is very coarse. The young tips of the rhizomes are much less fibrous and can be eaten raw or cooked. *E. arenarius* has good edible seeds; in Iceland as well as North America bread was once made from them, and they were were much used by the Vikings in Iceland and Greenland. *E. giganteus* seeds have also been used to make bread.

HAZARDS The highly toxic parasitic fungus ergot may be present (see p.324 for description of ergot poisoning). Do not harvest seeds after damp weather, particularly if black sooty deposits or dark protrusions are present on the seed head.

Festuca arundinacea

Tall Fescue

DISTRIBUTION Up to 430m. In England, throughout, except Dartmoor and Exmoor; in Wales, absent only Cambrian Mountains and parts of Snowdonia; in Scotland, absent most of Highlands, Outer Hebrides and Grampian Mountains but widespread elsewhere; in Ireland, widespread in most lowland areas.

HABITAT Rough grassland, in meadows, on river banks and cliffs.

DESCRIPTION Tall perennial, up to 2m high, forming dense tufts. Rough-edged leaves up to 10mm wide, at base of which are hairy auricles. The lower stem is surrounded by a whitish sheath. Panicles usually consist of pairs of branches, each with several elliptical–oblong spikelets, 10–18mm long.

¾ × life size

HARVESTING/PROCESSING NOTES This grass is produced on a huge scale for seed for pasture and is harvested by combine. It also often grows in abundance as a wild plant and is quite easy to harvest by hand. However, it is extremely difficult to dehusk, since after

removing the main outer coating, there remains a tight inner husk that has to be scraped off in some way. If modern techniques for polishing seeds such as rice were applied to this problem it could become worthwhile to gather it, but for now I find it too much trouble.

Glyceria fluitans

Manna Grass/ Floating Sweet-grass

DISTRIBUTION Up to 720m. Widespread throughout the British Isles, only less so in Scotland, in Easterness; in Ireland, in Cavan and west Mayo.

HABITAT In still or slow-moving water or muddy places.

DESCRIPTION Hairless perennial grass with creeping underwater stems and wavy upright inflorescences. Branches are mostly in pairs (with some solitary); each pair consists of one branch with 2–4 panicles and another with only one.

USES/RECIPES Grains are best soaked in water for a few hours, then, once swollen, can be baked or boiled; they were traditionally boiled in milk or wine but are also pleasant, with a mild sweet flavour, cooked until tender in well-seasoned water with a bouquet garni. Serve mixed with vinaigrette, freshly grated carrot and lots of herbs, or hot, with chopped duck confit and fresh thyme, served with pink roasted duck breast and wild cabbage leaves [JDW]. The following is a variation on a Belarusian recipe for manna croup, which these days is made using the semolina-like wheat product, but probably originated when manna croup still referred to grains of this grass.

BELARUSIAN VEGETABLE PORRIDGE: Grate 3 carrots then sweat in a little butter and some sugar. Add 500ml milk and more butter, and bring to the boil. Add 200g soaked manna grass seeds then simmer until it thickens. Stir in plenty of chopped parsley, tarragon and a bit of marjoram. Finish in the oven [JDW]. Manna grass seeds have been compared to both quinoa and poppy seeds; following the latter comparison, they can be used in place of poppy seeds for Joe Tyrrell's Polish poppy seeds bread, see **common poppy**.

BENEFITS Grains contain 75 per cent starch and sugar, 10 per cent protein, 0.5 per cent fat.

HARVESTING/PROCESSING NOTES This is one of the easiest grasses to de-husk; there is no need to toast the grains first.

Phragmites australis

Common Reed

DISTRIBUTION Up to 470m. In England, widespread except high-altitude areas; in Wales, all coastal counties with scattered localities inland; in Scotland, on much of west coast and Central Lowlands, sporadic elsewhere but absent Southern Uplands, Grampian Mountains, North West Highlands, Caithness and the Isle of Lewis; in Ireland, only absent high-altitude areas; on Channel Islands, Isle of Man and Isles of Scilly.

HABITAT In water, in dykes (including brackish), lakes, swamps, fens, riversides.

DESCRIPTION Tallest grass in the British Isles, reaching heights of up to 3.5m; forms dense beds often covering considerable areas.

Leaves lanceolate, greyish green, very broad (up to 5cm). Panicles like feather dusters.

USES/RECIPES Remove outer leaves from young shoots, leaving the soft inner core, which is only 2.5–3cm long. These are excellent blanched, then served with cream, fresh lemon juice and salt. Rhizome tips are tender and can be used like bamboo shoots.

HARVESTING NOTES Harvest young shoots in spring; the tips of rhizomes summer–autumn.

⅓ × life size

LILY FAMILY
Liliaceae

This family is best known for those staple flavouring ingredients of the Allium genus – onions, garlics and leeks. The many wild allium species present these familiar flavours in surprising new ways, including garlic-flavoured leeks, edible garlic-flavoured flowers, as well as oniony and garlicky leaves, seeds and bulbils. Asparagus is another familiar edible *Liliaceae* species, which has grown wild in the British Isles for millennia. The spikes are generally smaller than cultivated varieties, but are in no way inferior. One other species, the day lily, provides a plentiful supply of delicious edible flowers.

ALLIUMS

There are an extraordinary number of wild Allium species growing in the British Isles, almost spanning the whole year in terms of their availability as food. They can be eaten at pretty much every growth stage, with flowers, seeds and bulbils providing unusual but excellent forms of garlic flavouring. Ramsons occupies a particular place in my affections, as it brought about my accidental beginnings as a professional forager. Ali and I had dropped into the Goods Shed in Canterbury for lunch and asked what the soup of the day was. We must have looked unimpressed when they said

it was wild garlic, as the waiter protested, 'But it's absolutely delicious!' When we explained that we had eaten wild garlic in some form every day of the previous week and just fancied a change, he got very excited. It turned out that they were having trouble obtaining a regular supply. Later, the then head chef, Blaise Vasseur, would not let us leave until we promised to bring him several kilos the following day. When we subsequently came up with the goods, he pressed us for more and more wild edibles, and went on to put us in touch with several other like-minded chefs in the area, including Ben Walton, whose recipes are featured throughout the book.

Allium ampeloprasum

Wild Leek

DISTRIBUTION Up to 300m. In England, found only Lancashire in north, remaining sites south of Severn Estuary, mostly Cornwall; in Wales, sites in Anglesey and Denbighshire; in Ireland principally coastal Down, Leitrim, Sligo, Galloway, Clare and Cork, also Waterford and Wexford; also Sark, while subsp. *bulbiferum* only occurs on the Channel Islands.

HABITAT Hedgebanks and roadside verges, path edges, cliff slopes, often among dense and lush vegetation; also waste ground.

DESCRIPTION The tallest of the wild garlics by far, with stems reaching 2m high. The greyish-green leaves are flat and hollow, rough edged with an angle or keel running down their back. Prior to flowering they really look like cultivated leeks. Subsp. *ampeloprasum* has a massive ball of flowers, 7–10cm wide, many pale purple bell-shaped flowers and few-to-no bulbils; subsp. *babingtoni* or Babington's leek has few flowers and many large bulbils; subsp. *bulbiferum* has many flowers and bulbils.

NOTES Three varieties grow in the British Isles, but subsp. *babingtoni* is most frequent and endemic; that is, it doesn't grow anywhere else. It somehow manages to grow with its bulbs at surprising depths, so that the leaf bundles are self-blanched, sometimes for 25cm or so. Cultivated leeks have to be earthed up in order to create the same effect. Subsp. *ampeloprasum* is scarce and declining and should not be harvested. A cultivated variety known as elephant garlic is grown for its huge cloves; yet another variety used to be cultivated for pickling in Denmark.

USES/RECIPES Leaves are used for flavouring in Spain. The pre-flowering leaf

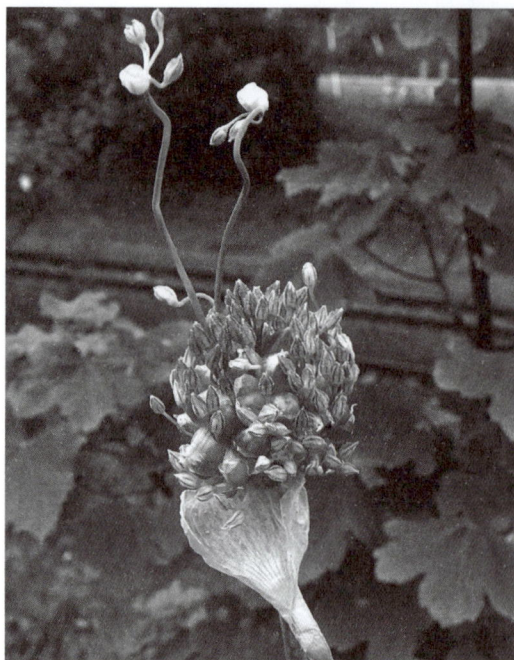

growth can be prepared as leeks, to which they are similar, although with a slight garlic flavour. Bulbils can be used in place of garlic cloves.

BABINGTON'S LEEK WITH STEAMED SKATE: Put the whole leeks in a sauté pan with 100ml water, 100g butter, some salt, pepper and thyme. Place a cartouche (a circle of greaseproof paper, slightly larger than the diameter of the pan) on top, and allow to cook for 5–10 minutes or until liquid evaporates. Remove from heat, allow to cool, then cut into small pieces. Skin the skate wing, steam, then remove from cartilage. Warm the leeks in a sauce made with reduced fish stock, white wine and butter, serve with braised baby onions, a little three-cornered garlic and ratte (charlotte or other) potatoes [JDW].

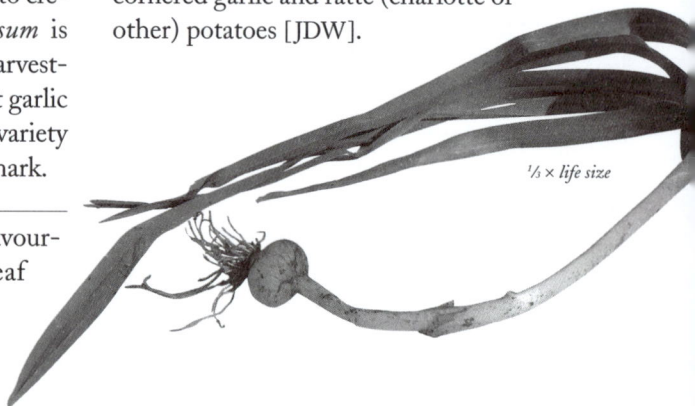

⅓ × life size

Allium oleraceum

Field Garlic

DISTRIBUTION Up to 365m. In England, in scattered areas on steeply sloping ground, more frequent some areas in north above the Wash and West Midlands but absent Cornwall and Sussex; in Wales, native to Flintshire and Denbighshire; in Scotland, native to Aberdeenshire, Moray and Perth and Kinross; in Ireland, naturalized populations Antrim, Wexford, Cork, Clare and Limerick.

HABITAT Dry field edges and grassy areas, especially on banks or slopes.

DESCRIPTION Quite tall, up to 80cm, with 3–4 long, thin, half-round solid leaves (ribbed at the back and grooved at the front), which surround the lower part of flower stem. Flower heads nearly always have flowers as well as bulbils, with two long, pointed papery bracts. Flowers June–August: brownish pink or greenish white, arranged loosely with long stalks. Bulbils also brownish.

SIMILAR SPECIES Keeled garlic *A. carinatum*, which has similar papery bracts, has deep pink

flowers and thin, flat leaves, maximum height 60cm.

USES/RECIPES Use the leaves like chives; the bulbils as for sand leek or crow garlic.

HARVESTING NOTES Unless you find an especially good area for this plant, don't collect it in any quantity. Its populations are declining, although this is probably due more to the loss of the nutrient-poor calcareous grasslands that it prefers than to popularity with foragers.

Allium roseum

Rosy Garlic

DISTRIBUTION Up to 300m. In England, found in most counties south of the Wash, also sporadic in Lancashire, Cheshire and

Yorkshire; in Wales, handful of locations, in Dyfed and Gwent and Anglesey in north; in Scotland, only found Renfrewshire; present Channel Islands, Isle of Man and Isles of Scilly.

HABITAT Rocky slopes, roadsides, waste ground, often in coastal areas or areas with mild climate, with little frost and dry summers.

DESCRIPTION Quite tall, up to 75cm high. Has 2–4 straplike leaves with smooth edges and slight grooves; the leaves surround only the bottom quarter of the stem. Quite large flowers, 10–12mm long, rose pink–white, either many with a few purple bulbils (subsp. *roseum*), or fewer with many bulbils (subsp. *bulbiferum*).

USES/RECIPES Bulbils can be used as for **sand leek**. Leaves are a bit tough and not really worthwhile, although better when they emerge in spring. Flowers are the prettiest of all the garlic flowers, with a delicate flavour.

CORNISH LAMB SADDLE SKEWERS ON ROSY GARLIC STEMS WITH ROAST GARLIC POTATOES, ROSEMARY CARROTS, ROAST SHALLOTS AND ROSY GARLIC BULBILS: (serves 4) *For the lamb saddle*: Take 1 short saddle of lamb, taken off the bone and trimmed of all fat and sinew; dice into 16 cubes. Skewer cubes and 12 small shallots alternately on to 4 rosy garlic stems (4 pieces of meat and 3 shallots on each). Place kebabs into a hot pan with a little oil and colour on both sides. Place in a roasting tin, season with salt and put into preheated oven (200°C) for 3 minutes. Remove and allow to rest for 10 minutes. *For the garlic potatoes*: Bake 3 large jacket potatoes for 1¼ hours at 200°C. After 35 minutes, add 1 garlic bulb to the oven wrapped in aluminium foil (or **kelp**). Just before the potato is cooked, heat 150ml double cream. Halve the cooked potatoes, scoop out flesh and force through a fine sieve with the garlic, then mix in the warm cream. Season with salt and serve. *For the carrots*: Cut 4 large

carrots into 3 equal pieces each, cover with water and simmer until cooked then add 2 fresh rosemary sprigs and a touch of salt. Allow to cool with the rosemary in the water. To reheat, add to the lamb sauce. *For the shallots and garlic bulbils*: Preheat the oven to 200°C. Lay out some aluminium foil and place 12 large, peeled shallots, 20 rosy garlic bulbils, sugar, salt and oil. Lay another sheet of foil over the top and seal up to form a pouch. Place in the oven on a baking sheet for 25 minutes. Remove from the oven and remove from the foil and place back in the oven on the same baking sheet for 5 minutes. Remove from the oven and baking sheet, and allow to cool. To reheat, add to the lamb sauce. *For the sauce*: In a heavy-bottomed pan, reduce 50g sugar and 50ml vinegar to syrup, then add 300ml red wine and do the same. Finally, add 300ml lamb or chicken stock and reduce to sauce consistency. *To serve*: Heat 4 plates. Place the potato in the centre followed by the carrots, shallots, bulbils and some steamed wild cabbage or sea beet. Place the lamb on top and then finish with the sauce and a few rosy garlic flowers [NO].

HARVESTING NOTES Easily spotted in summer, with its bright pink flowers held aloft above surrounding vegetation. Flowers keep

longer if the whole stem is harvested with them still attached.

Allium schoenoprasum

Chives

DISTRIBUTION Up to 300m. Native: in England, in Cornwall and border counties of England and Scotland; in Wales, in a few sites in south; in Ireland, in east Mayo. Naturalized or alien occurrences sparsely distributed throughout England, with greatest occurrence in parts of southeast, southern Scotland, Wales and Ireland.

HABITAT Usually native near rivers or on rocky grasslands; also found as a garden escape on waste ground.

DESCRIPTION Up to 50cm high. Leaves long, thin, round and hollow. June–August purple balls of flowers appear on a leafless stem.

SIMILAR SPECIES Thrift *Armeria maritima* looks somewhat similar but has no odour or flavour of onions. Crow garlic *Allium vineale* has similar-looking leaves but they are only half round.

USES/RECIPES Leaves and flowers can be used as herbs, chopped finely and added to salads or to cooked dishes just before serving.

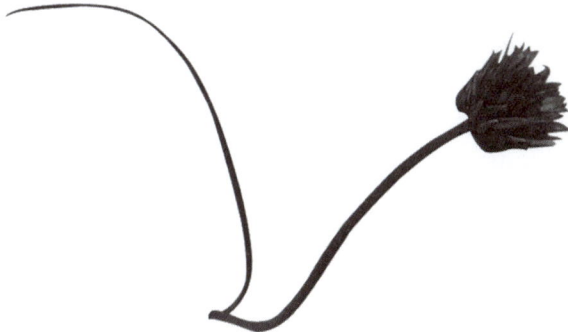

Allium scorodoprasum

Sand Leek/Rocambole

DISTRIBUTION Up to 300m. In England, locally abundant Cumbria southeast–Humber; in Scotland, found eastern areas Aberdeen–Forth and Borders, and west in Dumfries and Galloway; in Ireland, found in Cork, Kerry and Waterford; in Wales, found in Carmarthenshire.

HABITAT Rough grassland, path edges, sand dunes, roadside verges, disused railway banks.

DESCRIPTION Up to 1m high. Shiny leaves up to 20mm wide with rough edges and angled backs. Sometimes no flowers, only a ball of purple bulbils; flowers, if present, are few and purple. The British sand leek has more bulbils than continental varieties. Forms isolated clumps, not extensive colonies like three-cornered and few-flowered garlics.

NOTES This form of garlic was certainly in use at the time of seventeenth-century writer and diarist John Evelyn, who preferred it to the bulbs of the cultivated variety – in salads at least. The bulbils rather than the bulbs were still in use in the eighteenth century, for sauces, salads and generally in place of cultivated garlic or shallots.

USES/RECIPES Bulbils can be chopped finely or crushed (smaller ones used whole) and added to salads, dressings and cooked dishes. Leaves can be used in place of three-cornered garlic, few-flowered garlic or chives.

WILD GARLIC SOUP: (Which can also be made using the leaves of ramsons, three-cornered garlic or few-flowered garlic.) Make a soup base with sweated shallots, diced potato and chicken or vegetable stock then add the finely chopped leaves just before serving.

HARVESTING NOTES The leaves taste more strongly of garlic in summer.

Allium triquetrum

Three-cornered Garlic

DISTRIBUTION Up to 300m. In England, found mostly southwest and near south coast (but scarce Kent) as well as in and around London; in Wales, only northwest and southwest tips; in Scotland, almost entirely absent; in Ireland, most common coastal counties in south but also eastern coastal counties; present Channel Islands, Isle of Man and Isles of Scilly.

HABITAT Roadside verges, field edges, hedgebanks, open woodland and waste ground; thrives in areas with little frost, where summers are rarely wet.

DESCRIPTION Distinguished first by its long, triangular-shaped leaves and then by green striped, white bell-shaped flowers. Each plant has 3–4 leaves, which do not surround the flower stalk.

SIMILAR SPECIES As you would expect, few-flowered garlic *A. paradoxum* has fewer flowers. These have no green stripe and many green bulbils with a mild flavour (we call them garlic peas). It also has only one leaf per plant and this surrounds or sheathes the flower stalk. This plant is more tolerant of cold and is common in many parts of Scotland.

NOTES An invasive garden escape, three-cornered garlic has been cultivated in Britain since 1759 and has now extensively colonized many areas of southern England and Ireland. Many gardeners don't realize they have it, mistaking it for a white-flowered bluebell family species. I thought as much when I first saw it, but the strong smell of garlic in a lane with this plant growing in profusion on both banks gave the game away. Both this species and few-flowered garlic are sometimes referred to as wild leeks.

USES/RECIPES Leaves are milder than ramsons; they are juicy and sweet and the preferred choice for salads. To make the most of the garlic flavour, tear into pieces about 4cm long and add to dishes for the last few seconds of cooking or a

³⁄₄× life size

Few-flowered garlic *life size*

Peter Weeden's Brown Crab and Three-Cornered Garlic Tart with Eggs, Cream and Spiced Brown Crab

PASTRY 30cm savoury tart case, or lots of little ones, blind-baked at 160°C for about 15 minutes. Cut 250g of three-cornered garlic into 5cm lengths, blanch in salted water, refresh in salted, iced water and gently squeeze dry.

FILLING 600ml liquid (half milk, half double cream), 3 eggs, 2 extra yolks. Beat, season and taste, then add 250g fresh white crabmeat. Assemble by first putting the three-cornered garlic in the bottom, then pouring the white crabmeat mixture on top.

COOKING TIME 25–30 minutes at 150°C. Serve brown crabmeat on the side, seasoned with fresh lemon juice, Tabasco sauce, horseradish cream, Worcestershire sauce and cracked pepper, to taste, with more three-cornered garlic dressed with vinaigrette. Eat while still warm.

moment before serving so that it only wilts slightly. For example, pan fry for a few moments with lobster, fresh lime juice, soy sauce and fish sauce [EC]. Cooked for longer it is still worthwhile, you will need a bit more of it, as it cooks down, and the final flavour is more like onion than garlic.

POTATO AND THREE-CORNERED GARLIC BAKE: In an ovenproof dish, boil 300ml milk, 300ml double cream with thyme, rosemary, salt and pepper then add several layers each of sliced waxy potatoes (750g in all) and chopped three-cornered garlic (500g in all). Bring back to boil then place in preheated oven 140/150°C, for about 40 minutes or until potatoes are soft [PW]. Use instead of chives or spring onions, for example in mash. Grill oysters with tarragon, lemon, and three-cornered leek butter [BW].

Flowers are more suitable than ramsons flowers as a salad ingredient or as a garnish, being more substantial and with a softer texture. Leaves make lovely garlic butter (you can use any of the garlic leaves, but this one, ramsons and few-flowered garlic are best). Chop, blanch, refresh (cool with water) and squeeze the leaves then liquidize with a little white wine, salt and pepper. At this stage you can freeze the purée or you can beat into softened butter and then freeze in cling-filmed rolls for garlic butter all year round. Adding chopped seaweeds to this butter tastes remarkably good, giving lovely savoury flavours.

Allium ursinum

Ramsons/Wild Garlic

DISTRIBUTION Up to 450m. In England, widespread, but less so Thames Estuary, Fens and East Midlands; in Wales, widespread in most parts; in Scotland, widespread throughout; in Ireland, scattered localities, most common in north and southeast; present Isle of Man. Introduced in Northern Isles and Jersey.

HABITAT Open woodland or hedgebanks on woodland edges.

DESCRIPTION Quite unmistakable, if you take into account appearance, habitat and scent. Leaves are broader than all the other wild garlics, up to 25cm long and tapering at both ends; they emerge late February–early March as little shoots, later forming thick carpets that infuse the vicinity with the scent of garlic. Balls of white star-shaped flowers emerge early April, after which the leaves begin to wither, leaving the seed pods that swell at the flower bases as these die back.

²/₃ × life size

NOTES One of the best known of our British wild foods, it is now cultivated by a number of growers to supply demand from restaurants. Ramsons is an indicator of ancient woodland; it always gives me goose bumps to think of the continuity of a place where it grows. People have probably gathered it for as long as our islands has been populated; charred remains of a bulb were found at a mesolithic site in Halsskov, Denmark. More recently, bulbs were salted for year-round use in the Russian peninsula of Kamchatka. These days the leaf is the most popular part, perhaps because the bulbs of cultivated garlic are so widely available and the leaf provides a novel form in which to eat garlic.

USES/RECIPES Bulbs are milder than cultivated garlic, but tougher; use them like onions. For most uses, the stalks should be removed and cooked separately, for slightly longer than the green part – the blade – of the leaf. The volatile oil that gives the blade its flavour evaporates quickly on heating, so if you want a strong garlic flavour, cook briefly – this way the texture also remains. Use to finish off lamb stew; add them after blanching for just a couple of seconds. Use with pasta instead of garlic and parsley. If you do cook them for longer, the remaining flavour is more oniony and you will need to use a lot more leaves, which is fine as they are usually found in great abundance.

A PLATE OF ALLIUM FLAVOURS: Onion bouillon: put onions in oven in cling film, with a drop of water, on a rack above an oven tray. Cook at 90°C for 24 hours. The onions caramelize and lose their juices – the bouillon – into the tray. Serve with cooked and pickled onions, onion compote, steamed large ramsons leaves and wild thyme oil. Last of all, add a forest of small foraged leaves, very small ramsons leaves, found beneath the mature plants and the small (1–2 cm wide) leaves of young garlic mustard [RR].

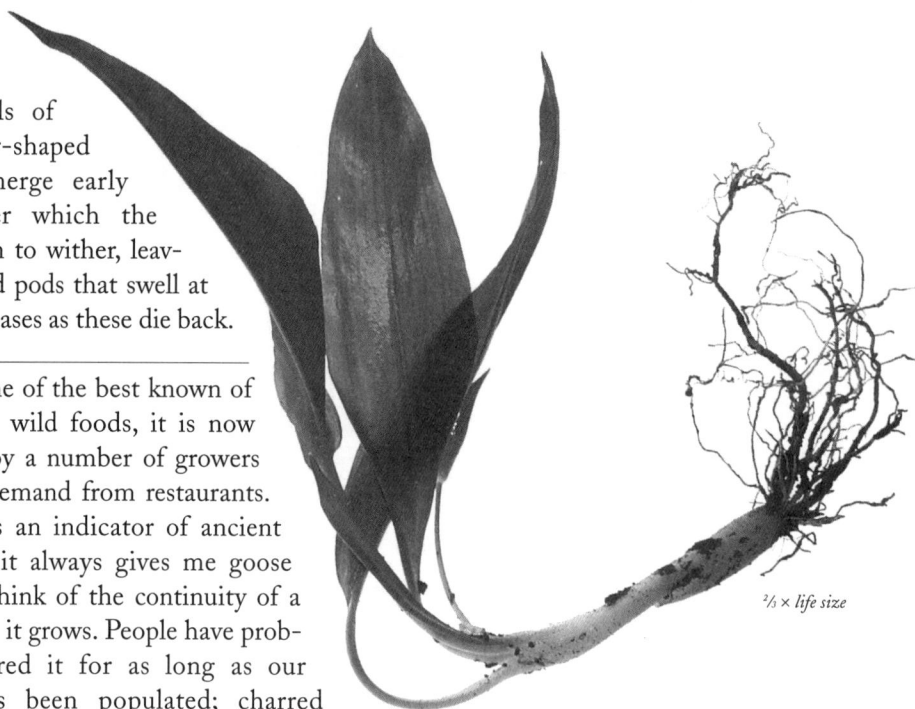

GARLIC OIL: Blend pomace olive oil with leaves or stalks and salt; the green-leaf oil looks amazing – use it for drizzling and dressings; stalk oil is less green, better for marinating [BW].

PESTO: Just garlic leaves, olive oil and walnuts.

AÏOLI: Simply add ramsons leaves to mayonnaise and blend.

CANAPÉ OF CHERRY TOMATOES: Stuff cherry tomatoes with wild garlic, Cheddar, a tiny amount of crème fraîche and finely chopped eggs and whelks [BW].

WILD GARLIC FRITTATA: Add chopped leaves to an open omelette, finished under the grill. Or simply add the leaves to sandwiches, for example cream cheese and smoked salmon. The flowers look delightful and pack quite a garlic kick – throw them into soups before serving for a stunning visual effect. The swollen ovaries make them a bit overpowering for salads – crush the whole flower head and use them like garlic cloves in sauces, with fried potatoes or rubbed into meat. This is a much easier source of garlic than peeling and chopping cultivated garlic cloves. Seed pods can be crushed like garlic cloves; the whole head of seed pods can be deep fried.

HARVESTING NOTES This is multi-sensory foraging: you can often smell ramsons before you see it. If you collect the bulbs, thin out rather than clear an area. Seeds will fall on to the bare ground and sprout; the bulbs you leave will soon divide, replacing those taken.

Allium vineale

Crow Garlic/Wild Onion

DISTRIBUTION Up to 455m. In England and Wales, found throughout; in Scotland, on west coast but absent north of Glen Mor, except isles of Raasay and Rona; in Ireland, native to lowland areas south of line Limerick–Dublin but naturalized in scattered areas to north.

HABITAT Sand dunes, roadsides, dry grassland and cultivated ground.

DESCRIPTION Up to 80cm high. Small chive-like, half-round leaves appear and die back prior to the emergence of flower stems, which produce a small ball of green or purple bulbils and varying amounts of greenish/pink flowers (often none), June–August.

1¹⁄₂ × life size

USES/RECIPES Leaves can be used like chives, best when they first emerge in spring, later they become tough. Bulbs are fiddly but worth the effort: they are like small, slightly garlicky onions. Bulbils can be used as seasoning, sprinkled into soups, or sprouted.

CROW GARLIC DRESSING: Juice and zest 1 lemon, 1 lime and 1 orange, boil with 2 tablespoons sugar, then blend with 2 tablespoons toasted crow garlic bulbils and 750ml pomace-olive oil [BW].

HARVESTING NOTES Crow garlic is often quite abundant and in some areas an invasive weed; you may be able to harvest it in bulk with the enthusiastic permission of whoever owns the land.

Asparagus officinalis

Garden Asparagus

DISTRIBUTION Lowland plant. In England, quite frequent from Midlands down via bird-sown seed of cultivated plants; in Wales, found in a few coastal localities in north and in south on Gower peninsula and about 40km west along coast; in Scotland, found East Lothian; in Ireland, found Dublin.

HABITAT Well-drained soils on sand dunes, grassy heaths, field edges and orchards.

DESCRIPTION Upright perennial, mature plants reach up to 1.5m high. Young stems or spears are thinner than those of cultivated plants, the rootstock of which is much deeper in the ground. Older stems branch and produce modified stems or cladodes, which have the appearance of feathery leaves; they are deep green, flexible and up to 32mm long. June–September, small bell-shaped yellow flowers emerge from the apexes of the branches.

Mature growth bears bright red berries that persist through the winter.

USES/RECIPES Young stems make perfectly good eating, despite being thinner than cultivated asparagus. Boil or steam for a few minutes and serve with wild chervil butter and perhaps a little fresh lemon juice or hollandaise sauce. Berries: during a naval blockade, the king of Prussia held a competition to find the best coffee substitute; ground asparagus berries won first prize. They have an interesting flavour, though I have yet to try cooking with them.

HARVESTING NOTES You will need a keen eye to notice the young spikes among vegetation; the best time to find the plants is at the later stages when quite noticeable, with either yellow flowers or bright red berries. Make a note of it and come back the following spring.

Asparagus prostratus

Wild Asparagus

DISTRIBUTION In England, found in Cornwall and one site in Dorset; in Wales, in a few places in south; in Ireland, in a few places in southeast.

HABITAT On coastal cliffs and sand dunes.

DESCRIPTION Usually prostrate perennial, but occasionally somewhat upright. Otherwise similar to garden asparagus, but cladodes stiff, blue-green and rarely more than 16mm long.

NOTES In late spring, produce going by the name of *asparagus sauvage* (wild asparagus) is sold at French markets and occasionally makes its way north across the Channel. It is not true asparagus, but spiked Star-of-Bethlehem *Ornithogalum pyrenaicum*, also known as bath asparagus: it is the flower stem and buds that are eaten, whereas asparagus spikes are young stems with undeveloped 'leaves' at their tip. There are two species of true asparagus found in the wild: garden asparagus *Asparagus officinalis* is an escape from cultivation, though it has been here since at least Roman times; wild asparagus *A. prostratus* is native and the real wild asparagus.

ECOLOGICAL CONSIDERATIONS Nationally scarce, listed as endangered on the *Vascular Plant Red Data List for Great Britain* (JNCC, 2005) and therefore should not be harvested. On Hœdic, an island off Brittany, it is plentiful and is harvested by the local people.

Hemerocallis fulva

Orange Day-lily

²/₃ × life size

DISTRIBUTION Up to 300m. In England, occurs in scattered areas northwest, Midlands and east, but most widespread southeast and, in particular, southwest; in Wales, only Caernarvonshire, Glamorgan and Monmouthshire; in Scotland, a few places in Grampian, east Highlands and west coastal areas, south of Isle of Mull; in Ireland, absent; present Isle of Man.

HABITAT Roadsides, banks, waste ground.

DESCRIPTION Garden escape; the rampant spread of its fleshy rhizomes often produces dense, persistent clumps. Stems reach up to 1m. Basal leaves form a distinctive fan shape; they are linear with parallel veins, tapering to a point, bending outwards from the middle. Flower stems emerge from the middle, becoming much taller than the leaves. Flowers are large, up to 8cm wide, horizontal–almost upright, not drooping, consisting of 6 orange petals that are rolled at the margin. The throats of the flowers are yellow with a red band; long stamens emerge from them.

NOTES A commonly grown garden plant that has also naturalized in many places, possibly from garden waste, since, due to its invasive nature, it is often purged to make room for other plants. Once it has a foothold it tends to persist. It is cultivated in China as a food plant.

USES/RECIPES Flowers are substantial as well as flavoursome and sweet, making them one of the best raw edible flowers. Eat straight off the plant or in salads, stuff them or make tempura with them; collect old and withered flowers and dry for later use: they give body and flavour to casseroles and soups. Buds can be chopped and used in salads, boiled/ steamed whole for a few minutes or chopped and fried. Tubers can be boiled and served with butter, instead of potatoes; raw in salads, they taste sweet and nutty.

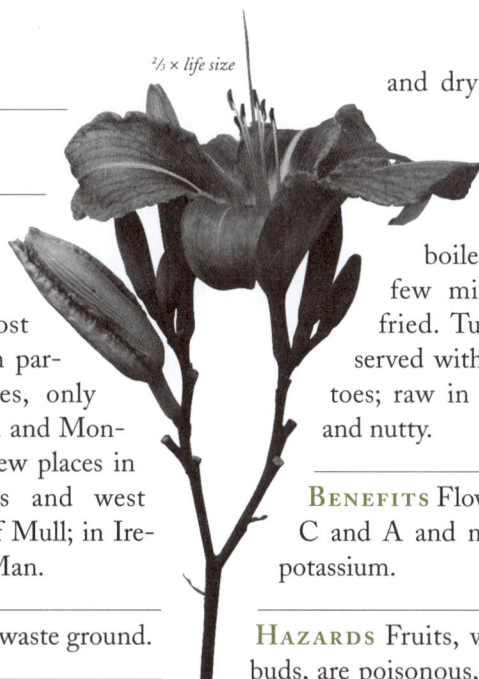

BENEFITS Flowers are high in vitamins C and A and minerals phosphorus and potassium.

HAZARDS Fruits, which are similar to the buds, are poisonous, but the buds very obviously have clear layers of petals when cut. Unfortunately, the flowers of certain genetic strains are also poisonous: symptoms include vomiting and diarrhoea. Be cautious when eating them from a particular stand for the first time.

HARVESTING NOTES Even on the plant the flowers wither after a day or so, hence the name day-lily, so they won't tolerate being transported or stored for any period, although chilling them will help. Buds last a bit longer and will even open up if you keep them.

Ornithogalum pyrenaicum

Bath Asparagus/ Spiked Star-of-Bethlehem

DISTRIBUTION A lowland plant. Nationally quite scarce (in Wales, Scotland and Ireland, absent); in England, locally abundant, in Bath/Bristol area, also found Cambridgeshire/ north Bedfordshire and scattered localities in Sussex and Wiltshire.

HABITAT Open woodland, especially with elm, ash and maple; meadows and banks, hedgerows. Both its stronghold in the Bath/Bristol area and the Cambridgeshire/north Bedfordshire sites are rather warm and continental, with drier winters and summer rainfall. In both areas it occurs on limestone.

DESCRIPTION Leaves appear in early spring and wither just before or after the flowers; they are long, thin (30–60cm x 3–6mm) and curved both at the back and the front; a slight whitish bloom makes them pale greyish green and not at all shiny. The flowering stems initially have the appearance of ears of corn, with a tight bundle of unopened flower buds at their ends. As they open, the top half of the stem becomes adorned with star-shaped flowers, which are greenish white–yellow, with green stripes.

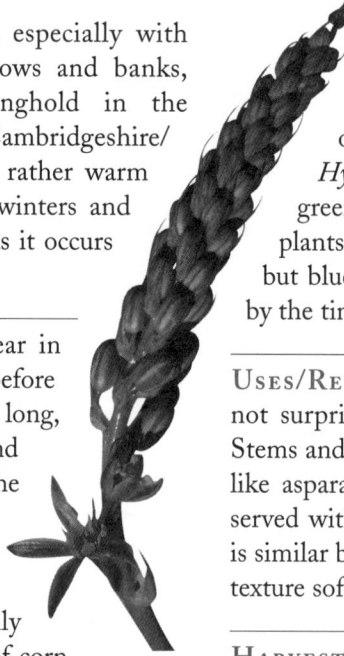

SIMILAR SPECIES Star-of-Bethlehem *O. umbellatum* has shorter, thinner leaves with a white stripe on the midrib. Leaves of bluebell *Hyacinthoides non-scripta* are darker green, glossy with a keeled back. The two plants are often found in the same area, but bluebells will have mostly gone to seed by the time bath asparagus buds emerge.

USES/RECIPES Leaves taste faintly of onion, not surprising given the family relationship. Stems and flower buds: use the top 13cm or so like asparagus, briefly steamed or boiled and served with butter or hollandaise. The flavour is similar but more delicate than asparagus, the texture softer.

HARVESTING NOTES Flower buds and stems appear from mid-May. Collecting them does no harm to the plants as they primarily reproduce by bulbs, which are nourished by the leaves, not the flower stems.

ORCHID FAMILY
Orchidaceae

All orchid flowers have the same, quite elaborate general form that consists of an outer whorl of three coloured sepals and an inner whorl of three petals, the upper two identical and symmetrical, the lower one much larger, like a swollen lip, which often extends backwards to form a spur. Other than the making of salep, a flour produced from the tubers of dried wild orchids, there is one well-known edible use of orchids: the seed pods of the orchid plant vanilla, which develop their familiar flavour through a fermentation process.

Orchis mascula

Early Purple Orchid

DISTRIBUTION Up to 880m. In England, widespread but scarce or absent Cheviot, south Lancashire, southwest Yorkshire, Cheshire, Staffordshire, Warwickshire, Leicestershire, Fens and Greater London; in Wales, in most counties but more widespread Pembrokeshire, Carmarthenshire, northern coastal counties and border areas; in Scotland, widespread on west coast, although scarce in Outer Hebrides, also found in Grampians and the Borders, Dundee area and around Moray Firth; in Ireland, all counties but more abundant Londonderry, Antrim, Down, Leitrim, Fermanagh and Cork; present Channel Islands and Isle of Man.

HABITAT Meadows, woodland, hedgebanks.

DESCRIPTION Basal leaves are long, oblong–lanceolate with dark purple blotches. Flowers form a cylindrical spike on a stout central stem that is sheathed by the leaves: usually purple, sometimes pink, often with an unpleasant smell. A hood is formed by upper sepal and petals; the side sepals arch upward like wings. The lower lip is 3-lobed with small black dots in its centre; it protrudes backwards into an upward-pointing spur.

NOTES The tubers of several orchid species are used for making salep, a highly nutritious beverage that has been made for centuries in Turkey and Iran. Salep was popular in Britain before coffee was widely available; served with

bread and butter, it was considered a good working-man's breakfast. To begin with, all salep was imported but once people cottoned on to what it was made from, it was produced in Britain as well, using tubers of early purple orchid. Oxfordshire was the most important centre for its production. Tubers were harvested as the plant started to die back, at which stage there are two tubers beneath each plant. One is rather withered, having sustained the plant during the growth period; the other is swollen with nutrients ready for the following year's growth. The latter was used for making salep. Other native orchids could just as well have been used for the same purpose and have been elsewhere. It is not clear whether our salep industry was destructive or the orchids were managed and harvested so as to ensure a future crop. What is certain is that present-day commercial collection of wild orchid tubers for salep is unsustainable and poses a serious threat to orchid populations. In Turkey, where ice cream made from salep has become increasingly popular, whole areas are stripped of orchids, destroying the bacteria with which they form a symbiotic relationship. The result is that the orchids would not able to re-colonize even if re-introduced.

USES/RECIPES Tubers are boiled briefly, and the skin is removed; then they are placed in an oven for a few minutes, until the flesh has turned from milky white to translucent. After this they are left in the sun to dry completely. Salep beverage is made by boiling the ground tubers in milk with cinnamon and sugar; a thick and comforting drink, without the sugar and cinnamon it is still slightly sweet and quite bland. This natural sweetness and the thick consistency are the qualities that recommend it.

ECOLOGICAL CONSIDERATIONS Several orchid species are protected under Schedule 8 of the Wildlife and Countryside Act 1981, which makes it an offence to harvest them at any stage. Early purple orchid is not one of these, but it is an offence to dig up tubers without the landowner's permission; even if you have this permission or are the landowner, they should not be harvested unless you are in a position to replenish the population in some way. In Turkey, the cultivation of orchids for salep production has begun in order to conserve the wild population.

SEDGE FAMILY
Cyperaceae

Bolboschoenus maritimus

Sea Club-rush/ Seaside Bulrush

DISTRIBUTION Up to 300m. Widespread in most coastal areas of the British Isles except: in England, some coastal areas of north Devon and Cornwall, east Norfolk, southeast and northeast Yorkshire and Cumbria; in Wales, the southern area of Cardigan Bay; in Scotland, most of Grampian, North Highland, West Highland, Western Isles, Fife and Berwickshire, Orkney; in Ireland, parts of May and Clare.

HABITAT Salt/brackish marshes and tidal river banks.

DESCRIPTION Native perennial, hairless, up to 1m high. Stem sharply triangular, upper parts rough; leaves 3–8mm wide, flat, with a keel at the back and rough edges. Flowers reddish brown, in fat grasslike spikes at the top of the stem, with two leaves either side, like dividers; the leaves are much taller than the spikes, some of which are stalked.

SIMILAR SPECIES None that grow in similar habitats.

USES/RECIPES In *A Floral Guide for East Kent*, the nineteenth-century botanist M. H. Cowell writes that the roots were ground and used for making bread, but only in times of scarcity. I have not tried this, but the young tubers are succulent and tasty, slightly sweet, a bit like pignuts.

½ × life size

Cyperus longus

Sweet Galingale

DISTRIBUTION Up to 300m. Mostly southern England: largely introduced but native in Hampshire, Cornwall and Devon; in Wales, Gwynedd, Dyfed and Glamorgan, elsewhere in England and Wales found in Home Counties, Essex, Dorset, Worcestershire and along both sides of Severn estuary, sporadic as far north as line Barrow-in-Furness–Tees Bay, absent north of the line. In Scotland, scarce, on Isle of Arran and Firth of Forth; not found in Ireland; present Channel Islands and introduced to Isle of Man.

HABITAT Marshes, wet pastures on coast; inland on pond margins and in ditches, usually planted.

¹/₇ × life size

DESCRIPTION Rapidly spreading, hairless perennial, forming thick clumps. Up to 1.2m high. Stems triangular and smooth; leaves like grass, arching and glossy with rough edges, up to 7mm wide. Umbels are twice compound with long, leafy bracts; spikelets brown, about 1cm long, in groups of 5 or 6.

SIMILAR SPECIES Leaves are similar to a number of *Carex* species, but the plant is distinguished by its aromatic rhizomes.

NOTES Galingale is closely related to tiger nut *Cyperus esculentus*; according to the Rev. C. A. Johns in his *Flowers of the Field* it was at one time 'much esteemed as a tonic'. Dried and powdered galingale rhizomes were formerly used as a substitute for the oriental spice galangal from the fourteenth century onwards. It was used to make a spicy sauce, called galantine, with bread, vinegar, ginger and cinnamon; the sauce was used in a stuffing for goose and as a marinade for pork and hastellettes (parts of the innards of wild boar). A related plant nutgrass *Cyperus rotundus* provides a fascinating example of how foraging can enhance the growth of a plant. Regular gathering of tubers prevents the build-up of bulky woody tubers that hinder the growth of new ones. Instead of the resource being depleted, the harvest increases in places where tubers are harvested (Hillman, 1989).

USES/RECIPES Roots can replace horseradish for a sweeter, more fragrant and less pungent flavour, with beef, chicken, crème fraîche and cream, eggs, salmon and fish (especially smoked), sausages and yogurt. Use in place of galangal in oriental cuisine; it is milder and sweeter.

WATER PLANTAIN FAMILY
Lismataceae

Sagittaria sagittifolia

Arrowhead

DISTRIBUTION Up to 300m; mostly lowland areas. In England, mostly absent north of line Blackpool–Flamborough Head and also from most of Devon, Dorset, Cornwall and Hampshire, present in varying degrees in remaining counties; in Wales and Scotland, very scarce; in Ireland, found in river and lough basins in Central and east Central Lowlands, as well as in the south of Leinster and in Ulster.

HABITAT Lakes, ponds, canals and slow-flowing rivers and streams, often with yellow water lily *Nuphar lutea*.

DESCRIPTION Native. Freshwater perennial, named after its unmistakable arrowhead-shaped leaves. These are held upright on long stalks up to 20cm long. Flowers have 3 white petals and purple centres and grow July–August on tall, leafless stalks. May also have long, thin submerged leaves and floating oval leaves. Tubers are formed on the end of runners and become buried in mud.

NOTES The closely related *S. latifolia* is an important plant of both Chinese and Japanese cuisine and has been cultivated in North America to supply the demand of the Chinese population there. It has also been grown for food in south China, Malaysia, Korea, the Philippines and the Pacific Islands, and several

⅓ × life size

Native American peoples have used it, harvesting it from vast, dense colonies. Arrowhead can be used in similar ways. Extensive stands of arrowhead do not form in the British Isles because we lack the flood plain and swamp habitats where such colonies could develop. In Poland, arrowhead is common enough to be harvested from slow-flowing rivers and lakes. Oddly, in North America, it is invasive and considered a noxious weed. The following Uses/Recipes is based on written accounts of usage in China, Japan and North America.

USES/RECIPES Tubers look like big water chestnuts and are full of starch: *S. latifolia* tubers are known as Wapato potatoes by the Wapato Native Americans of Oregon for this reason. Soak for half an hour to remove bitterness, then boil or roast; peel afterwards. Alternatively, fry in pieces like chips. In Japan they are known as Kuwai and are served as part of New Year celebrations. Ground tubers are dried and used as flour in baking and as a thickening agent. Young leaves and shoots are used as vegetables and added to rice dishes.

HARVESTING NOTES To harvest these tubers, you have to get right into the water and stomp your feet for several minutes until they begin to float to the surface. I did make one impromptu attempt when I came across a few plants in a Kentish river. Being unprepared, I jumped in wearing just my underpants, but my stomping and groping brought to the surface only one small tuber, still attached to its stem, which I replaced and left to grow. Native American Potawatomi had a less labour-intensive method of gathering the tubers: they used to steal the caches collected by beavers and musk rats. The only *Sagittaria* tubers I have eaten were tiny *S. japonica* ones, purchased from an aquatic-plants dealer, which didn't allow for much experimentation.

ECOLOGICAL CONSIDERATIONS A plant not only insufficiently plentiful to harvest but also in decline in recent years due to the eutrophication of rivers (an excessive build-up of nutrients, usually fertilizer run-off from arable fields, that can change the aquatic ecosystem, so that some plants die off and others newly colonize).

Ferns

Ferns are a primitive form of plant that reproduce by means of spores. They cannot be considered as a major source of food: bracken is almost certainly dangerous if eaten too often and too little is known about the edibility or toxicity of most other species of fern.

Ethnobotanist James Duke relates how the deer in his neighbourhood refrain from eating the ostrich fern *Matteuccia struthiopteris* in his garden. Ostrich fern fiddleheads (the young shoots, so called because they are shaped like the end of a violin) are harvested in great quantities in Canada and North America but are a seasonal product eaten in small quantities. Duke interprets the deers' avoidance of them as an indication that occasional, moderate use is probably the right approach.

Adiantum capillus-veneris

Maidenhair Fern

DISTRIBUTION Very sparse throughout the British Isles, although locally common in areas. Native at a few sites: in England, on coast of Cumbria, Cornwall, Dorset and Devon; in Wales, on south coast; in Ireland, on west coast; on Isle of Man. Present as an introduction in a few additional places, mostly in England, in the south; in Scotland, entirely absent.

HABITAT Warm, damp shady places, on calcareous substrate such as alkaline rocks in damp crevices or lime-mortared walls.

DESCRIPTION Fronds consist of many drooping, delicate, roughly fan-shaped leaflets, on black, wiry stalks. At their base is a thick rhizome covered with brown scales.

USES/RECIPES This fern is not plentiful enough to justify harvesting, the following is given for information purposes only. Used to make a simple tea by infusing the leaves and also to make *Sirop de capillaire* ('capillaire' being an alternative name for this fern), which was formerly used in a variety of drinks recipes in Europe and North America. The recipe that follows is taken from William B. Dick's *Encyclopedia of Practical Receipts and Processes* (New York: Dick and Fitzgerald, 1872):

Sirop de capillaire (maidenhair syrup) Take 1 pound maidenhair herb, and 5½ gallons boiling water. Macerate till cold; strain without pressing, so as to get 5 gallons; take the whites of 3 eggs beaten to froth, and mix them with the infusion; keep back a quart of the liquid; then dissolve and boil in the above 80 pounds sugar by a good heat; when the scum rises, put in a little from the quart of cold liquid, and this will make the scum settle; let it raise and settle 3 times; then skim, and when perfectly clear add ½ pint orange-flower water; then boil once up again and strain.

HAZARDS Said to be abortifacient, it should therefore be avoided during pregnancy.

ECOLOGICAL CONSIDERATIONS Ferns have suffered terribly from the ravages of fern collectors in the past; it would be tragic to see populations of this scarce fern damaged again by over collection. That said, this species will probably benefit from global warming; with the decline of cold winters, the northwest coast and shady, urban localities should see increased populations.

½ × life size

Athyrium filix-femina

Lady Fern

DISTRIBUTION Up to 1005m. Widespread throughout British Isles, only less so in England, Fens and east Suffolk; in Ireland, central and east Central Lowlands.

HABITAT Woodland and well-shaded hedge-banks, especially on damp, acid soils.

DESCRIPTION Fiddleheads are thin and delicate, without scales. Pale green fronds are up to 1m long stalks with few scales, growing in graceful formations, with middle one/s upright, the others arching outwards slightly. They are lanceolate, divided 2–3 times, with many pinnae or leaflets arranged closely, almost overlapping, and pinnules or smaller leaflets often also subdivided; the final subdivisions are finely toothed.

SIMILAR SPECIES Male-fern *Dryopteris filix-mas* has darker green fronds with slightly more scales; pinnules mostly lobed, not further subdivided, but lower ones may be. Male-fern has been used medicinally but cannot be considered safe to eat: some people are allergic to it, and large doses cause coma, blindness and even death. Broad buckler fern *D. dilatata* has fronds finely divided, like lady fern but triangular and with distinctive lower leaflets: the downward-pointing subdivisions are much longer (see photograph below).

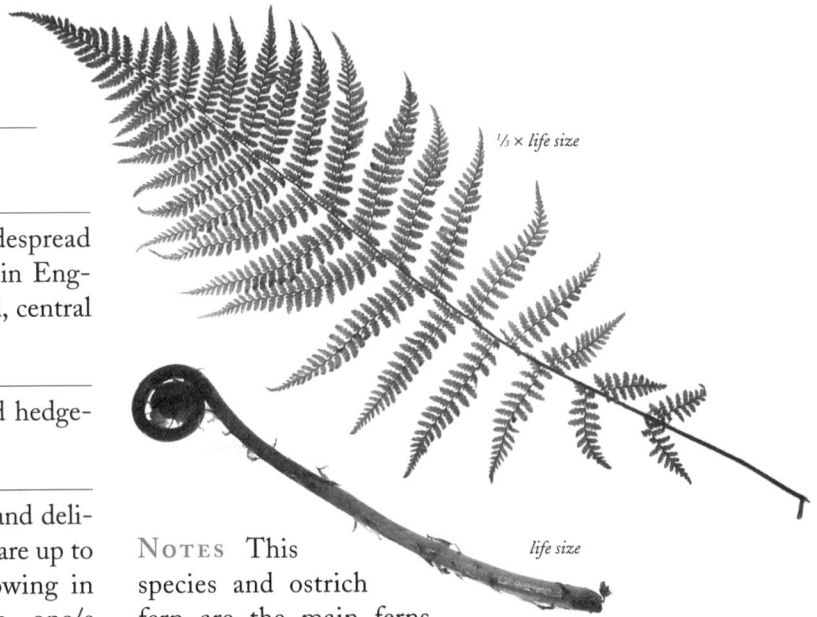

⅓ × life size

life size

⅓ × life size

NOTES This species and ostrich fern are the main ferns eaten in the United States and Canada; in Canada, in particular, their harvest and use is greatly celebrated. Both the fiddleheads and rhizomes were eaten by indigenous Canadians.

USES/RECIPES Fiddleheads should be blanched briefly in salted water. Serve with butter or a light dressing. Add to wild leaf salads. Warm through in chicken stock with salt and pepper and serve with leeks and asparagus, all scattered over and around slices of poached and roasted organic chicken breast, finished with a lovely chicken gravy [JDW]. Or as a garnish, with a little ragout of red signal crayfish and diced stewed vegetables warmed in a little of the 'bisque' made from the crayfish shells, carrot, celeriac, parsnip and button onions, all of which sits under a nice crisp fillet of zander, another British river fish [JDW].

HAZARDS Poisoning as a result of eating partially cooked fiddleheads of the related ostrich fern, which is common elsewhere in Europe, have been reported. Symptoms include diarrhoea, vomiting, stomach cramp and headache, with some people being more susceptible than others. Some wild-food authorities question the identity of the ferns eaten in these cases, but there is no doubt that some people are sensitive to partially cooked ostrich fern. There are no records of poisoning with lady fern; in addition, extracts from the plants have been used as medicine with no records of adverse side-effects. Nevertheless, it makes sense to see how you react to them before eating too many (see also SIMILAR SPECIES).

HARVESTING NOTES Snap off fiddleheads at the base; only collect those where fronds are still tightly curled.

Polypodium vulgare
Common Polypody

DISTRIBUTION In England, widespread in southwest and Norfolk, slightly less so in rest of south and east and Home Counties, fairly widespread in West Midlands but largely absent East Midlands, present Cumbria, Lancashire and north Northumberland, absent much of rest of north; in Wales, widespread throughout, except north Clwyd; in Scotland, widespread throughout, except Grampian Mountains, Glasgow area, Skye and Caithness.

HABITAT Walls, trees, rocks.

DESCRIPTION Rhizomes fleshy, running along the surface of whatever the fern is attached to. Fronds oblong, up to 50cm long, slender, leaflets all of roughly equal length, starting several centimetres up from the base, with smooth edges and blunt tips.

SIMILAR SPECIES Western polypody *P. Interjectum* has oval–lanceolate fronds and is found on limestone and lime-mortar walls. The rare southern polypody *P. cambricum* has much shorter fronds (up to 15cm long), which are triangular–ovate, and is found in similar habitats to western polypody. Hard fern *Blechnum spicant* has lanceolate fronds with leaflets starting at the base.

NOTES The rhizomes are chewed as an appetite stimulant by northwest coast Canadian indigenous peoples. In Sweden, children also chew them for their flavour; they contain polypodoside, which is sweet and tastes like liquorice. Swedish chef Gustav Otterberg has developed several uses for them, all of which hark back his childhood experiences chewing polypody rhizomes while out wandering in the woods.

USES/RECIPES Scrape off bark, dry and grind to powder; use as a spice, for example with duck liver. Mix with sugar, for dusting confectionery or sweet pickling vegetables such as carrots and parsnips. Season ice cream with tiny pieces of fresh root and serve with rhubarb [all the preceding: GO].

HAZARDS Should be avoided by people suffering from gastric problems, diabetes or hypoglycemia.

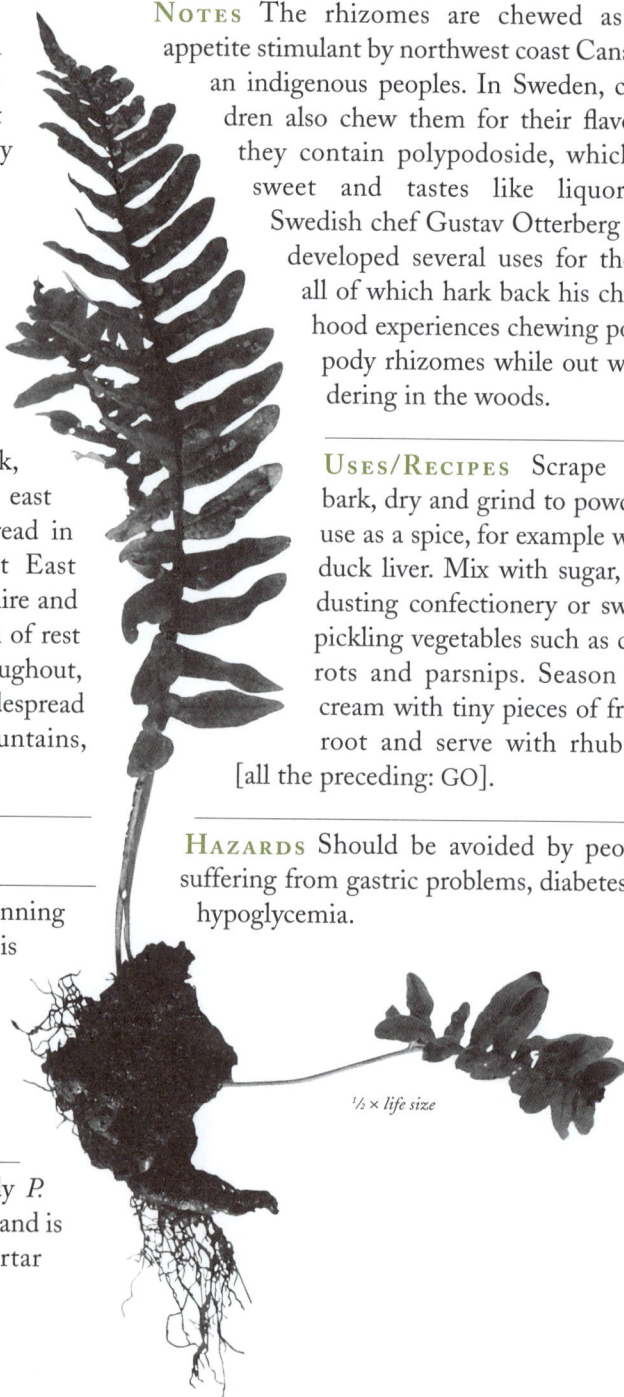

½ × life size

Pteridium aquilinum

Bracken

DISTRIBUTION Up to 585m. Widespread throughout British Isles, only less so: in England, in the Fens; in Scotland, in Caithness and Isle of Lewis.

HABITAT Woodland, moor, heath and ungrazed pasture, with a preference for acid soil.

DESCRIPTION Single fronds grow up at intervals from creeping rhizomes. They can reach up to 4m long but are usually no more than 1.2m, though they can be as wide as they are long. They are 2/3 times pinnate; unlike the lady fern ferns described here, the pinnae are not all in one plane, forming a single, flat surface, but turned at right angles to the main stem and thereby arranged in layers. Bracken forms extensive colonies whereas individual plants of ferns, such as lady fern, are clearly separated one from the other.

NOTES Bracken fiddleheads appear in the spring, and there is a huge market for them among Japanese people, who have eaten them for centuries and call them Warabi. They are also part of the traditional Korean diet. Elsewhere, the plant or its close relatives have been used by various peoples for their starchy rhizomes. Bracken roots were gathered by first peoples of Vancouver Island, who considered them a luxury food, eating them boiled. Many other Canadian first peoples ate them roasted. In Siberia a kind of beer was made by fermenting the roots with barley. Bracken root is a traditional food of both Maoris in New Zealand and Aboriginal Australians. However, European bracken rhizomes contain very little starch.

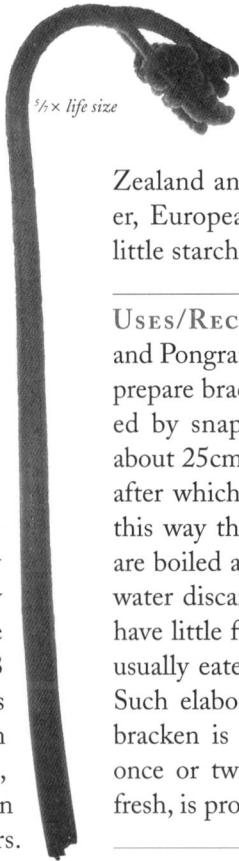

USES/RECIPES My Korean friends Jonghwan and Pongran Son use an elaborate procedure to prepare bracken. The young shoots are collected by snapping them off at the base when about 25cm tall, then boiled for about 2 hours, after which they are left in the sun to dry. In this way they can be stored indefinitely. They are boiled again for 1 hour before use, and the water discarded. After all this processing they have little flavour but a good texture. They are usually eaten cold after frying with soy sauce. Such elaborate processing is probably wise if bracken is to be eaten regularly, but if eaten once or twice at the time of year when it is fresh, is probably not necessary.

HAZARDS Has been shown to be harmful to cattle embryos, so do not eat during pregnancy. Bracken fronds contain the cyanide-producing glycoside prunasin, the enzyme thiaminase, which causes vitamin B1 deficiency, and ptaquiloside, which is known to cause cancers in cattle after prolonged, large-scale consumption. Stomach and oesophageal cancer incidence is high in Japan, where people eat them all year round, in both fresh and preserved forms. Although this could be due to other factors, I certainly would not risk eating bracken so frequently. Small-scale seasonal consumption is a different matter and is unlikely to pose a risk.

⁵/₇ × life size

Conifers

No conifer other than juniper and yew is native to England, Wales or Ireland; only the Scots pine, juniper and yew are native to Scotland. Non-native conifers have long been popular as ornamentals, though; extensive non-native conifer plantations have replaced native and in some cases ancient woodland in much of the British Isles.

Few new conifer plantations are now being planted, partly because logging the timber is not presently profitable and partly due to a backlash against planting of non-native trees. However, while there are still plenty of them around, we may as well make use of them. If you live near a pinetum (a collection of pine trees, many of which were planted in the nineteenth century), you may be lucky enough to find the cones of the stone pine *Pinus pinea*, which contain pine-nuts. The seeds of Scots Pine are also edible, just much smaller. The only other conifer you are likely to encounter that produces large nuts is the monkey puzzle or Chile pine *Araucaria araucana*, but it only produces viable fruit where both male and female trees are present. Edible conifer needles on the other hand are easy to find and are used as herbs or to make infusions in oil, syrup or water for a refreshing tea.

GENERAL HAZARDS The young growth tips of conifers are close at hand for just about everyone, but be sure not to collect needles from the deadly yew *Taxus baccata* by mistake. Also avoid the western red cedar *Thuja plicata* and Leyland cypress *Cupressocyparis leylandii*, both of which have fernlike, scaly foliage, not needles – these trees contain toxic levels of the volatile oil thujone.

NOTES In Canada, the inner bark of many conifer species have been harvested and eaten by indigenous peoples; the inner bark of Scots pine *Pinus sylvestris* can be made into flour for baking and is said to have been used in this way in Norway, Sweden and Lapland. This may have been more of a survival food than something eaten by choice. The same could not be said of 'tree breast milk', the name given by the Native American Nlaka'pamux peoples to the mysterious sugary substance that used to be found like a sweet frost on Douglas fir trees in Canada. It appeared at the tips of branches on the hottest days of summer, but only on trees enjoying plentiful supplies of both moisture and sunshine, almost like a squeal of delight from a tree that knew it had it good. In recent years it has not been found; no one knows for sure why that is.

POISONOUS SPECIES

Taxus baccata

Yew

DISTRIBUTION Up to 470m. In England, found most areas, but absent much Northumberland, parts East Riding of Yorkshire; in Wales, found most areas but absent parts Gwynedd and Carmarthenshire; in Scotland, mostly in Southern Uplands, though not west coast; in Ireland, mostly in Ulster but also scattered localities elsewhere.

HABITAT In deciduous woods but also sometimes in woods exclusively of yew; commonly found in churchyards, parks and gardens. It prefers well-drained soil on chalk or limestone.

DESCRIPTION

Short, up to 25m high, stout evergreen with broadly spreading branches, at least one thick, fluted trunk and short needles arranged like a double-sided comb. The needles end in a hard point and are dark green above and yellowish-green below. This is the only conifer that produces true berries; these often occur on female trees in great profusion: they are waxy in appearance and a pinkish red, shaped like a cup, with a brown seed clearly visible inside.

SIMILAR SPECIES

Douglas fir *Pseudotsuga menziesii* needles lack the hard point at the end and are very aromatic, and generally longer, less glossy and thinner. Douglas fir has large cones, not berries, is generally much taller and does not have a fluted trunk.

HAZARDS

The mucilaginous flesh of the globular red berries that adorn the tree in the autumn is sweet and harmless, but the seeds have caused fatal poisonings when chewed. The seed toxins are also found in the leaves, twigs and bark, and include various alkaloids, an irritating volatile oil and a glycoside that breaks down to form cyanide. Poisoning produces symptoms such as vomiting, abdominal pain, drowsiness, dizziness, coma and, in extreme cases, death by respiratory and heart failure.

EDIBLE SPECIES

Juniperus communis

Juniper

DISTRIBUTION

Up to 975m. In England, mostly upland areas of Yorkshire, Cumbria, Durham and Northumberland, and in south, small concentrations in southeast, Greater London, Hertfordshire, Wiltshire and Gloucestershire, sporadic elsewhere; in Wales, mostly Gwynedd and north of Clwyd, sporadic elsewhere; absent Montgomeryshire and Cardiganshire; in Scotland, absent much of Strathclyde and Ayrshire, widespread Argyll and Stirling and north of Central Lowlands except east coast; in Ireland, scarce, mostly found northwest Clare–Antrim; few locations Kerry, Tipperary, Offaly, Westmeath, Fermanagh and Down.

HABITAT

Chalk downs, heaths, moors, pine and birch woods.

DESCRIPTION

Small tree or shrub, upright or prostrate, up to 4m high. Leaves short, spiky needles, up to 1.5cm long, in successive whorls of 3. Flowers small and yellow, May–June; later

½ × life size

forming small, green cones that in their second year become dark blue: these are known as juniper berries, although strictly speaking they are not berries at all.

NOTES There is a legitimate concern that too many people gathering a particular wild plant will impact adversely on it, yet juniper has suffered the reverse: wild juniper plants were once actively tended, but this stopped as their use petered out; by 2008 the UK Biodiversity Action Plan for juniper cited 'low economic and cultural value' as a factor in its decline. Native juniper berries were formerly harvested for gin manufacture and cooking (the English 'gin' derives from the French *genévrier* meaning 'juniper'); berries are now imported from Tuscany. Prior to the civil war in former Yugoslavia, a substantial amount also came from there. All berries were or are harvested from wild trees: there are no juniper plantations anywhere.

USE/RECIPES Berries can be used dried, fresh or roasted as a seasoning; these are often used in game dishes but can also be ground or finely chopped and used in place of black pepper or nutmeg, in salads (especially with fool's watercress) or with mashed potatoes, for example. Wood can be used for smoking salmon and pork. Needles can be used as a seasoning, in a spice bag, though, or you will be spitting them out as you eat. The flavour is similar to that of the berries.

HAZARDS Oil from the related *Juniperus sabina* is said to be abortifacient; there is no evidence that eating berries of our native species is harmful, but out of caution they should be avoided during pregnancy.

HARVESTING NOTES Harvest blue berries by spreading out a cloth beneath the bush and whacking the branches with a stick or other implement. The berries should drop off on to the cloth; unfortunately, so will the dead needles. To sort one from the other, place the mixture in one end of a tray or box, tip slightly and gently tap the sides so that the berries roll down to the other end. Repeat two or three times, until the berries are free of debris.

Picea abies

Norway Spruce

DISTRIBUTION In England, widespread, yet sparse in Cheviot Hills, Northumberland, Cumbria, the northeast, Yorkshire, Cheshire, Herefordshire, Greater London, Kent, Sussex

NOTES This tree is known to most people as the Christmas tree.

USES/RECIPES Needles of both spruces make delicious syrup. Young shoots produced in early–mid May are best and may also be added to bread and savoury pies or used in marinades to flavour meat. The syrup can be used diluted as a drink or served with cold meat or cheese, or as a base for game *jus*.

and Cornwall; in Wales, widespread but less so Merioneth and Brecknockshire; in Scotland, widespread but sporadic north of Glen Mor, Grampian Mountains, Ayrshire, Wigtownshire, Kirkcudbrightshire and Western Isles; absent Northern Isles; in Ireland, sporadic throughout, occurs all counties except Armagh, Leitrim, Westmeath, Dublin, Wexford, Waterford, East Cork, Limerick and Clare; present Isle of Man and Alderney.

HABITAT Woodland, plantations, gardens, often planted but also naturalized.

DESCRIPTION Tall conifer, up to 60m high, with reddish-brown bark. Young trees conical, the familiar Christmas-tree shape; older trees slightly less so, the tops thickening out. Needles 10–25mm long, 4-sided, ending in a sharp point. Cones hang down from the branches: cylindrical and about 7cm long.

SIMILAR SPECIES Sitka spruce *Picea sitchensis* is smaller, up to only 40m high, with purplish-brown bark and slightly smaller, flat bluish-green needles, also ending in a sharp point. Older trees have a broader base than Norway spruce.

Pinus sylvestris

Scots Pine

DISTRIBUTION Up to 675m. In England and Wales, widespread; in Scotland, widespread, only less so Grampian Mountains, North West Highlands, North Highlands and Northern and Western isles, yet only native a few areas in Grampian Mountains and North West Highlands; in Ireland, common but only sporadic Dublin, Clare, Limerick, north Kerry, Donegal and many small areas where not found; present on Channel Islands and Isle of Man.

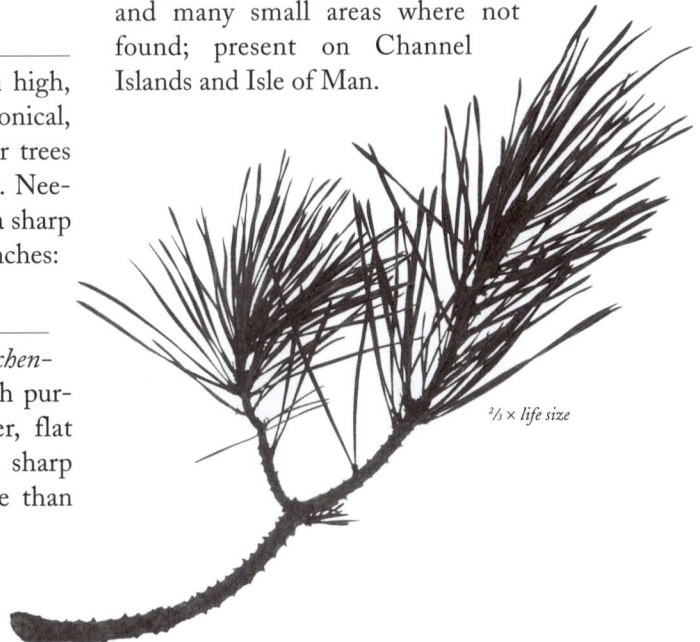

²⁄₃ × life size

HABITAT As a wild and native tree, on stony or sandy acid soils; waterlogged peat, or in with other Scots pines or in mixed woodland. Elsewhere planted in a variety of soil types and places; it can become invasive of heaths.

DESCRIPTION Tall, flat or dome-topped evergreen, up to 30m high. Reddish-brown bark with flaky scales; needles bluey green, 3–8cm long, in several twisted pairs on side shoots.

USES/RECIPES

PINE SYRUP (also use spruce and Douglas fir): dissolve 80g citric acid and 1.2kg sugar in 1 litre hot but not boiling water, then add 250g needles and leave to steep for 24 hours. The citric acid helps to draw out the aromatic oil from the needles. Use the syrup diluted as a drink, to make jelly, sorbet or to glaze roasted meat, especially game.

Pseudotsuga menziesii

Douglas Fir

DISTRIBUTION In England, widespread in south and east, less so Essex and the Fens, sporadic Midlands and the North; in Wales, widespread; in Scotland, mostly Glen Mor, Main Argyll and **Central and eastern Coastal Lowlands north to east Sutherland**; scattered localities elsewhere; **present Isle of Man.**

HABITAT Plantations and parks.

DESCRIPTION Very tall conifer, up to 100m high. Reddish-brown bark; on older trees deeply fissured. Needles are arranged in the same plane, so branches are roughly flat; the needles themselves flat and quite soft, with two white lines underneath, either side of the midrib. Cones, 10–20cm long, hang down from the branches; distinctive, long, 3-pronged bracts protrude between the scales. Leaves have a strong resinous aroma, especially when crushed.

SIMILAR SPECIES The deadly **yew** *Taxus baccata* is smaller and stouter with red berries, a fluted trunk and darker, glossier foliage, which is not aromatic. Do not harvest Douglas fir unless you are sure of the difference between the two trees.

USES/RECIPES Needles have a sharper flavour than **Norway spruce**. Use young and old needles to make flavoured oil: add a little garlic, mustard, salt and pepper to some fir needles and combine in a blender (one with very sharp blades); pass through a fine sieve. Drizzle on baked monkfish [EC]. Use syrup (for method, see **Scots pine**) for granita; serve with venison. Flavoured onion sauce: infuse bay leaves, cloves and fir needles and onion in milk. Use this infusion to make bread sauce or thicken it and serve with roast pork [ST]. Mix in needles among potatoes or root vegetables when roasting [BW]. Calvados and Douglas fir sauce: infuse a few grams of needles in some reduced veal stock, then strain. Pan fry some apple pieces until golden, finely chop some parsley and a few more fir needles then add all three to the sauce, along with a good slug of Calvados. Serve with roast pheasant and braised red cabbage [PB].

Seaweeds /
Marine Algae

Seaweeds are an abundant wild resource, with remarkable proven health benefits. Yet not only do we leave this edible coastal bounty unharvested, but some even buy seaweed imported from Brittany, the USA or that other island nation, Japan. The Japanese on the other hand have developed a huge aquaculture to supply the seaweeds that constitute 10 per cent of their national diet.

Edible seaweeds are some of the larger examples of marine algaes, many of which are microscopic. Marine algaes comprise 93.85 per cent of all marine flora, perform 60 per cent of global photosynthesis and are responsible for 33 per cent of all the carbon dioxide fixed by living things.

The three main groupings of seaweeds – brown, green and red – are classified according to their pigmentation, which determines which kinds of light they are able to use to create food. The colour of particular seaweed indicates in reverse which kinds of light it is able to harvest: every one, except the colour it is. Green and red algae are both classified as plants and share a common ancestor with the flowering plants, whereas brown algae are considered a separate group. Different groups of seaweeds are usually found in particular zones on the shore, a fact unrelated to their pigment.

GENERAL USES/RECIPES Seaweeds should be unwashed until just prior to use, to retain the preservative coating of salt-water. Washing with warm water loosens sand particles; for some species such as sea lettuce and laver, washing in several changes of water may be necessary. All seaweeds can be used in some fairly simple ways. Although gutweed, sea lettuce and the outer parts of dabberlocks fronds are quite tender, most seaweeds have quite a robust texture and are quite chewy, especially when raw. The toughest of them – kelp and laver – can be softened by hours of boiling, as when making laver bread, or by toasting. The texture becomes much less daunting when fresh seaweeds are chopped into small pieces or fine slivers or when dried seaweed is broken into small pieces. Pieces or slivers can be added to all manner of dishes (tartar sauce, for example), for flavour, colour, texture and nutrition. Add the slivers to soups or salads, either purely of seaweeds or with coastal leaves such as sea-purslane, sea sandwort, rock samphire or marsh samphire (blanched). Dress with sesame seeds, miso paste, sake or rice wine vinegar, a little sugar and olive oil and perhaps a pinch of chilli [AN]. Serve as a bed for deep-fried oysters [MH]. Miso is a traditional Japanese seaweed soup (see dabberlocks), but Kentish chef Anthony North, who is classically trained but with distinct oriental influences, first made me aware of other possibilities when he made a wild fennel and tomato consommé and finished it with very fine slivers of laver, dulse and sea lettuce (Anthony also makes excellent gutweed bread).

SEAWEED TAPENADE: All seaweeds, raw, not too much kelp, chopped fine: 500g seaweed, 200g shallots, 4 garlic cloves finely chopped, a little grated bitter vetch, 200g chopped green olives, olive oil, English mustard and dittander, lady's smock or black mustard leaf (julienned), instead of wasabi. Goes well with mackerel [EC].

BROWN SEAWEEDS
Phaeophyta

Once used on a large scale for potash and later for iodine, brown seaweeds are now harvested on an even greater scale for alginic-acid production. Alginic acid is used to make alginates, which not only have various medical and industrial uses but also a role in processed foods, such as sauces, dressings and ice creams. There is also a massive aquaculture of various types of kelp in China and Japan, both for alginate production and for use as food in its own right. Wakame is also cultivated on a large scale.

GENERAL BENEFITS Iodine is an essential element of human diet; it is essential to the healthy functioning of the thyroid gland. 'Kelp' tablets are a big hit in the supplements market; the blurb on the bottle of one brand states that each tablet contains iodine derived from 30mg kelp *Ascophyllum nodosum* (which is in fact a kind of wrack). The daily requirement for iodine is easily met by eating small amounts of either kelp or wrack. Alginic acid is also beneficial, as it limits the amount of fat absorbed by the human gut; it also binds with heavy metals, enabling them to be removed from the body. Brown seaweeds are also rich in vitamin C, beta-carotene and vitamin B12, which is a scarce nutrient in the plant kingdom.

Fucus serratus

Toothed Wrack

DISTRIBUTION Along entire coastline of the British Isles.

HABITAT On rocks, from the lower tidemark to about halfway up to the upper tidemark.

DESCRIPTION Many forked fronds, 60–180cm long, roughly 2cm wide, with serrated edges, a distinct midrib and pointed, jelly-filled sacks (receptacles) at the tips of some of the branches.

SIMILAR SPECIES There are many similar *Fucus* species, all of which are edible, but this is by far the most common.

USES/RECIPES *(for wracks)* The texture of this seaweed raw is a bit challenging, although the midrib was at one time eaten as a snack in

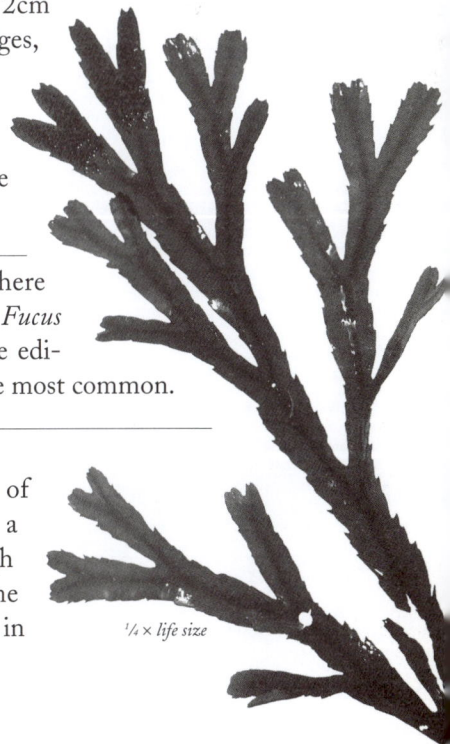

¹/₄ × life size

Scotland. As with other seaweeds, the texture is less noticeable when it is chopped finely. It comes into its own when cooked for long periods, however, especially with beans, which also require long cooking. Much of each frond will disintegrate altogether, adding flavour and thickening the dish but what remains is soft, almost like terrestrial greens in appearance, and very tasty. Fronds can also be dried and toasted, then used as a condiment or added to bread. Dry them in the sun or on a radiator, then toast for 20 minutes in a hot oven, crush or else blend to very small pieces and store in an airtight container.

Fucus vesiculosus

Bladder Wrack

DISTRIBUTION Along entire coastline of the British Isles.

HABITAT On rocky shores, between the high and low tidemarks, usually around the midpoint and higher up than toothed wrack.

DESCRIPTION Fronds forked, with a pronounced midrib; edges are smooth, and they have round air bladders, usually in pairs.

BENEFITS With its high iodine content and anti-inflammatory mucilage, bladder wrack is used to treat underactive thyroid and goitre.

¹/₂ × life size

Boiled up as a hot poultice, it is applied to swollen joints and given internally to relieve symptoms of rheumatoid arthritis. Laboratory studies suggest that bladder wrack may be antibacterial, antiviral, anticoagulant, antilipidaemic (lowers blood cholesterol) and hypoglycaemic (lowers blood sugar), and, traditionally, in the West and in China it has been included in many remedies. Its rich nutritional value means that it is a useful herb in convalescence and for building up reserves when one is weak.

USES/RECIPES As for toothed wrack.

Himanthalia elongata

Thongweed/Sea Spaghetti

DISTRIBUTION Found on coasts everywhere in the British Isles except southeast England.

HABITAT Rocky shores, close to the low tidemark, usually below toothed wrack.

DESCRIPTION The fronds are shaped like a concave mushroom, but the more noticeable and useful parts of this seaweed are the straplike reproductive fronds or receptacles. During the main growth period, February–May, they reach 5–25cm long, branching in two several times.

USES/RECIPES Dried or pickled in France. I fry it on a high heat until browned and crispy, then serve with fish.

¹/₃ × life size

KELP

These large, leathery brown seaweeds grow in great colonies known as kelp forests, which are whole ecosystems in themselves. Kelp has a long history of economic use: it has been harvested for compost, burnt as a source of alkaline ash, used for making glass, soap and alum (a dye fixative), and iodine. It is still harvested in vast quantities for alginates, which have many commercial applications, including cosmetics, toothpaste and ice cream. Kelp and other seaweeds are a natural source of glutamic acid, from which monosodium glutamate (MSG) derives. Given the appetite-enhancing properties of MSG, including kelp in your cooking will ensure people stay hungry after each course. Just don't put it in your dessert unless you intend your dinner guests to leave wanting more!

Laminaria digitata

Tangle/Oarweed

DISTRIBUTION On suitably rocky habitats on most coasts of the British Isles.

HABITAT Mostly extreme lower part of rocky shores, only exposed during neap-tides, in many places only exposed once every 2 weeks; sometimes in rock pools; attached to solid, stable rocks.

DESCRIPTION Deep brown, with a thick, oval rubbery stipe, up to 15mm wide and 30cm long. The lamina or blade is split by wave action into finger-like segments (hence *digitata*); the whole algae may be several metres long.

SIMILAR SPECIES The cuvie *L. hyperborea* is distinguished by its rigid, circular stipe, which holds the blade up even at the lowest tides. As a result it can only grow where it is never fully

⅙ × life size

exposed, otherwise the blades would dehydrate, and it would die. Blades can be up to 3.5m long. The stipe is rough, allowing various red seaweeds to grow on it, and brittle, snapping when bent.

USES/RECIPES The Japanese name for kelp is '*kombu*'. In Japanese cuisine it is used to make a kind of gloopy stock known as '*dashi*', which forms the basis for soups such as miso (see **dabberlocks**), noodle broths, dipping sauces and simmered dishes known as '*nimono*'.

DASHI: Soak 20g dried/ 100g fresh *kombu* in 1 litre water for 1 hour then boil water; once boiling take out the *kombu*, and add 20g bonito (dried fermented smoked skipjack tuna) fish flakes. Take off the heat and leave to infuse for 20 minutes, stirring occasionally. Pass mixture through a fine sieve. The softened *kombu* can be eaten after making the stock [AN].

There is a fish and chip shop in Dorset that offers kelp deep fried with fish. I cook it with carrots, lots of butter and just enough water to cover, and a little Chardonnay vinegar, cooked until most of the liquid is absorbed or the carrots are al dente. This makes a fresh-tasting vegetable side dish and looks terrific – once cooked kelp turns a deep green. Wrap whole fish in kelp before placing it on a barbecue so it can steam in its own moisture. It is like using tin foil only more organic, keeping the fish nice and moist and infusing a delicate seaweed flavour. The Maori use a form of kelp that can be opened up to form a bag in which to cook fish over an open fire.

¹⁄₆ × life size

Laminaria saccharina

Sugar Kelp

DISTRIBUTION Suitable habitats throughout the British Isles.

HABITAT In my experience, found closer to land than oarweed, though generally said to grow at around the low tidemark and below, on rocky shores.

DESCRIPTION Similar to oarweed, but the blade is narrower, its centre thickened and its edges wavy, the effect something like a frilled or pleated piece of cloth. Its main growth period is winter–April.

USES/RECIPES As for **oarweed**.

Alaria esculenta

Dabberlocks/ Atlantic Wakame

DISTRIBUTION In England, only in Cornwall, Somerset, Northumberland and south to Flamborough Head; in Wales, absent easterly parts of north and south coasts; in Scotland, throughout; in Ireland, throughout, except Dublin and parts of east Cork.

HABITAT On rocks near low tidemark, always below the water.

DESCRIPTION Stipe 10–30cm long and 0.6–1.25cm wide, round or oval in cross-section. The blades can be yellow, brown or olive green and up to 4m long, though usually smaller, wavy and ribbon like, with a solid midrib that is almost as wide as the stipe for its entire length. On older plants, flat, leaf-like reproductive growths called sporophylls grow out of the sides of the stipe below the blade, roughly 10cm long. With several on each side, they resemble fingers.

NOTES This species is similar to the Japanese wakame *Undaria pinnatifida* and can be used in place of it in Japanese recipes. Japanese wakame is considered an invasive species in places where it has begun to get a foothold, such as Ramsgate Marina in Kent. It is distinguished by the wavy edges of its blades and lower stipe.

USES/RECIPES

MISO SOUP: Take 400ml dashi stock, 1½ tablespoons miso paste (typically made from lacto-fermented soy beans – rice and/or barley are sometimes used too), 20g Atlantic wakame (or other fresh seaweed), cut into slivers, 120g fresh tofu, diced, 2 spring onions, finely sliced. Warm the dashi, add some to the miso to dissolve it; return dissolved miso to the pot and add the wakame, tofu and spring onions. Season with soya sauce [AN]. Atlantic wakame can also be used in any Japanese recipe that calls for wakame, in particular in seaweed salads, as described in the seaweed introduction (p.362).

¹⁄₆ × life size

GREEN SEAWEEDS
Chlorophyceae

Green algae occur on land, in fresh water and salt water, and are thought to be the antecedents of all terrestrial plants. They contain beta-carotene as a pigment to supplement the activity of chlorophyll.

The main edible green seaweed genus is *Ulva*, which includes thin sheets known as sea lettuce, species with thinner strands and the swollen tubes of gutweed *U. intestinalis* (formerly classified as *Enteromorpha*, now an obsolete classification). Gutweed is one of several *Ulva* species tolerant of low salt levels; one species, *U. cylindracea,* is found exclusively in freshwater rivers.

GENERAL BENEFITS Green seaweeds are rich in protein as well as oleic and alpha-linoleic acid.

Codium fragile
Dead Men's Fingers

DISTRIBUTION Found on coasts of south and southwest of England, Wales, west and southeast Scotland and Orkney.

HABITAT Grows below the low tidemark on rocky coasts.

DESCRIPTION Fronds are dark green, upright and branched dichotomously; the branches soft and velvety.

USES/RECIPES Deep-fry in tempura batter or shallow fry briefly and serve with dulse and chicken skin crisps (see p.372).

ECOLOGICAL CONSIDERATIONS This is an invasive, non-native species. Finding large scale uses for it would greatly benefit our coastal eco systems.

⅓ × life size

Ulva intestinalis

Gutweed

DISTRIBUTION Found pretty much on all coasts of the British Isles.

HABITAT At all shore levels, also in brackish dykes, sometimes with quite low salt concentrations; even freshwater rivers, where tidal water occasionally backwashes. Attached to rocks or shells or detached, swollen and floating, often forming large masses.

DESCRIPTION Thin green tubes, 10–30cm long, 6–18mm wide, resembling intestines when inflated with oxygen, which enables it to float. Otherwise, the tubes are flat and resemble a narrower version of sea lettuce. Summer annual, found April–August.

USES/RECIPES Similar to **sea lettuce**, the deep-fried version being like the 'crispy seaweed' sold in Chinese restaurants (which is in fact finely shredded cabbage). Sprinkle with a little icing sugar to sweeten it for the full effect and use as a side dish or a spectacular garnish. Use in bread.
TOFU SANDWICH: Tofu dipped in cornflour and sesame seeds deep fried: take two pieces and place crispy seaweed, Japanese mayonnaise and wild mushrooms in between [AN].

Ulva lactuca

Sea Lettuce/Green Laver/ Oyster-green

DISTRIBUTION Found pretty much on all coasts of the British Isles.

HABITAT Very abundant throughout the inter-tidal areas of rocky shores; on salt marshes and estuaries.

DESCRIPTION Light–deep green, thin, wavy margined sheets (fronds) that vary in size but can reach 1m long and 30cm wide. Attached to rocks by a round holdfast.

NOTES Sea lettuce is actually a generic term for *Ulva* species with wide, thin fronds, of which this species is by far the most common. *Ulva* are eaten in the West Indies, Japan, Iceland, Chile and several regions of China.

USES/RECIPES The most tender of all our seaweeds: the large fronds can be used roughly chopped as a main or supplementary ingredient for pasta dishes, risottos and salads. They also make delicious and beautiful translucent crisps when deep fried.
SEA LETTUCE WITH STEAMED MUSSELS: Sweat shallots in butter, throw in mussels, sea lettuce, a splash of cider, salt and pepper [JL].
SEA LETTUCE RISOTTO: (serves 4) Put 3 tablespoons olive oil in a thick-bottomed pan on a moderate heat. Sweat 1 medium onion, chopped, then a minute later 3 garlic cloves, finely chopped, until translucent; add a sprig each of thyme and rosemary. Add rice and a knob of butter. Cook rice until translucent. Slowly add stock, letting the rice absorb it until cooked (approx. 10 minutes). Roughly chop up sea lettuce and stir into risotto. Cook for a further 2 minutes until sea lettuce is warmed through. Season with salt and pepper. Add Parmesan and a knob of butter to finish it off. Garnish with sprinkling of dried sea lettuce (put on baking sheet in the oven for 20 minutes at 200°C) to give a stronger flavour to the dish [AN].

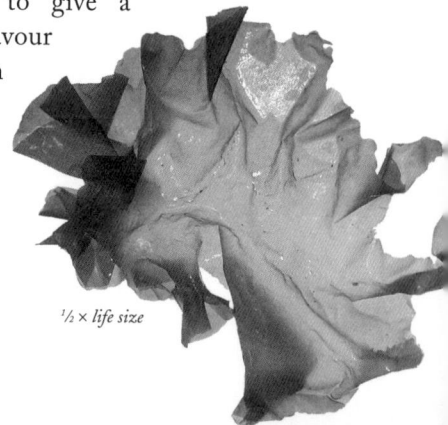

¹⁄₂ × life size

RED SEAWEEDS
Rhodophyceae

Despite their name, some of these red seaweeds are purple or, in certain conditions, green. Among them are several economically important species, used for the production of the gelatinous carageenen, named after Carrageen moss *Chrondrus crispus*. It has a host of uses, for example in toothpaste, ice cream, milkshakes and processed foods; it functions as a stabilizer, thickener and setting agent.

Several other *Rhodophyceae* species are used to manufacture agar jelly, which is available for culinary uses under the name agar agar. Two of our native red seaweeds, *Gracilaria confervoides* and *Ahnfeltia plicata*, could be used for this purpose. Laver or nori is the most widely consumed of red seaweeds, with an unbroken tradition of use in Wales and a huge aquaculture devoted to it in Japan. *Sargassum muticum*, a non-native species occasionally found on our shores, is eaten in China and Japan.

GENERAL BENEFITS
Red seaweeds contain very high levels of protein, up to 40 per cent of dry matter in some species.

Chondrus crispus

Irish/Carrageen Moss

DISTRIBUTION Pretty much throughout the British Isles, with the exception of Lincolnshire and parts of the East Riding of Yorkshire, Suffolk and Norfolk coasts.

HABITAT Rocky shores, usually, but not always, under water, either in rock pools or below the tidemark.

DESCRIPTION Purple, red or even green after prolonged exposure to sunlight, with branched fronds widening to rounded tips. These tips are iridescent underwater,

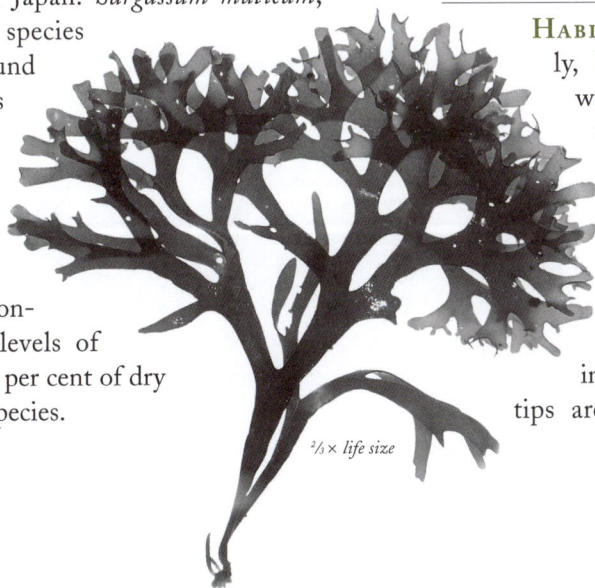

²/₃ × life size

Michael Bremner's Brown Crab & Seaweed Panna Cotta with Lettuce Gazpacho

SERVES 4

FOR THE PANNA COTTA:
300ml whole milk
brown crab meat, from 1 small crab
1 tsp stock syrup
30g fresh Irish moss, chopped
salt and pepper
½ small garlic clove

FOR THE GAZPACHO:
½ head Little Gem lettuce
½ green pepper
½ green chilli
½ celery stick
½ fennel bulb
a few leaves wild chervil

a few leaves fresh parsley
½ garlic clove
50ml white wine vinegar, to taste
¼ cucumber
½ finely diced shallot
olive oil
seasoning

TO SERVE:
Extra-virgin olive oil
½ head Little Gem lettuce
white crab meat, from 1 small crab
a few radishes, thinly sliced
wild pea shoots and baby small wild leaves,
    such as wood sorrel and garlic mustard
    seedlings

FOR THE PANNA COTTA: Put all ingredients except the brown crabmeat into a pan; simmer for 20 minutes. Add the crabmeat and simmer for a further 5 minutes. Pass through a sieve and pour into four individual ramekins. Chill until set and ready to serve.

FOR THE GAZPACHO: Put all ingredients in a food processor; blend, then pass through a sieve.

TO SERVE: Put some chiffonaded lettuce on the plate and place the panna cotta on top, then 'dress' with the gazpacho. Drizzle the olive oil around it and top the panna cotta with the white crab meat. Finish with some baby wild leaves, pea shoots and thin radish slices.

emitting a bluish-pink glow. The whole sea-weed is slippery to touch.

SIMILAR SPECIES False Irish moss *Mastocar-pus stellatus* fronds have thickened edges, pro-ducing a groove in the middle and a U-shaped cross-section that is especially pronounced at the frond base. It is covered in small nipple-like reproductive bodies, which make it rough to the touch.

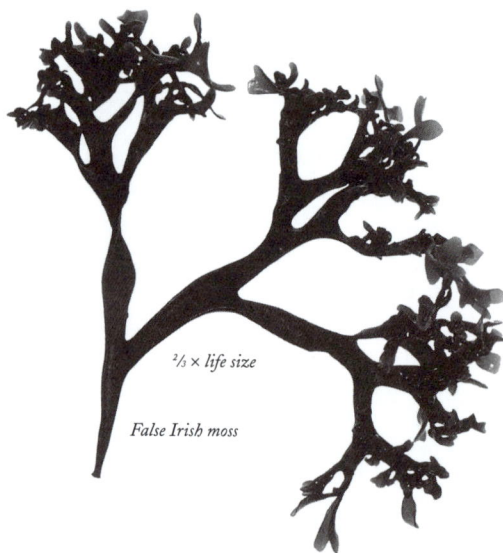

⅔ × life size

False Irish moss

USES/RECIPES Both Irish moss and false Irish moss can be used as a source of vegetable gelatine. Traditionally used for milk puddings, they have a slightly fishy after-taste, which can be masked serving with acidic fruit. Richard Corrigan makes an Irish moss pudding – a set custard made with cream, condensed milk and buttermilk, flavoured with vanilla – which he serves on top of layers of rosehip syrup, apple jelly and apple purée. These are served with oatcakes flavoured with almonds and dulse. Irish moss jellies made with acid fruit will not set well as acids interfere with the setting properties of carageenan. These seaweeds can also be used as thickeners or for making set savoury dishes.

IRISH MOSS DRINK is made in the West Indies – experiment with quantities until you get a flavour you prefer: simmer the fronds in water with cinnamon and linseed until the water thickens then add condensed milk, nutmeg and vanilla essence. Drink after you have left it to cool, whisking occasionally to prevent setting.

BENEFITS Contains large amounts of polysaccharides, up to 10 per cent protein plus iodine and bromine. Taken for coughs and bronchitis, it encourages the coughing up of phlegm and soothes dry and irritated mucus membranes. It can also be used as a demulcent in gastric ulcers, to relieve both constipation and diarrhoea, and to soothe inflammation in cystitis and other urinary infections.

Osmundea pinnatifida

Pepper Dulse

DISTRIBUTION Throughout the British Isles, except in England, Lincolnshire and parts of East Anglia; in Ireland, the east coast.

HABITAT Very abundant on moderately wave-exposed rocky shores, forming a broad zone at most shore heights, covering the rock surface in many places.

DESCRIPTION Fronds are flat and rather tough and branched alternately. Plants found higher up the shore are smaller and yellowish green, whereas lower down the shore they can reach 8cm long and are reddish brown.

USES/RECIPES As the name suggests, this seaweed has a peppery flavour. Use fronds in small amounts to add spice to seaweed salads or miso soup.

Palmaria palmate

Dulse/Dillisk

DISTRIBUTION Most of the British Isles, but absent some less rocky coasts of eastern England.

HABITAT Above and below the low tidemark, on rocks but also on the stipes of the cuvie *Laminaria hyperborea*.

½ × life size

DESCRIPTION Dark reddish brown, leathery, thin, flat fronds much divided into lobes about 30mm wide, up to 1m long but usually no longer than 40cm.

NOTES In Ireland, dulse is still eaten as it has been for centuries: Irish chef Chris McGowan tells me that as a child he ate it as you would crisps, carrying a bundle of the dried fronds in his pocket. Celtic St Cuthbert is said to have collected dulse, known to him as 'duileasg', from the rocks for food.

USES/RECIPES Boiled for a few minutes, chopped finely and added to garlic mashed potato (see **rosy garlic**).
DULSE AND CHICKEN SKIN CRISPS: (Adapted from a recipe by Danish chef René Redzepi in the *Noma* cookbook.) In a roasting tin or other ovenproof dish, place a layer of dulse fronds on top of a layer of raw chicken skin. Season with salt, pepper and herbs, if you like, then cover with kitchen foil and weight down so that the chicken skin and dulse won't curl up. A tin of the same size with heavy (ovenproof) objects in it will do, or a good quantity of dried beans. Place in a hot oven for 30 minutes.

LAVER

Known as 'nori' by the Japanese and used in many forms in Japanese cuisine, laver is probably the best-known edible seaweed in the British Isles. The texture is robust, especially for something so thin, enabling the fronds to withstand the heat of summer sun on exposed rocks: they dry out until crisp and appear dead, but once the tide comes in are revived as if nothing had happened. In a culinary context this means laver can withstand aggressive heat treatment.

Porphyra linearis

DISTRIBUTION Along most of the coast of the British Isles in appropriate places.

HABITAT Mostly the upper shore, particularly common on rocks near sand, so the narrow blades fan out over the sand at low tide; near man-made structures such as harbour walls and sea defences.

DESCRIPTION Red or brown fronds that taper towards the base. Grows mostly in winter, October–April.

Porphyra purpurea

Purple Laver

DISTRIBUTION Along coast of the British Isles in appropriate habitats.

HABITAT More sheltered sites than the other two laver species given here, sometimes extending into estuaries.

DESCRIPTION Difficult to identify accurately; usually shaped like a large beech leaf, dark purplish–yellowish, thin and slippery. Found all year round but much more abundant in summer.

Porphyra umbilicalis

Laver

DISTRIBUTION Around most of coast of British Isles but restricted to rocky beaches.

HABITAT Mostly just below *Porphyra linearis* on rocky shores but also attached to stones in sandy areas or much further down the beach.

DESCRIPTION Very thin sheetlike fronds, green–purplish brown, longer than they are wide, with wavy margins; often attached by a point within the frond, hence the name *umbilicilis*. Found year round but mostly in summer.

GENERAL USES/RECIPES (all laver) Traditionally used to make laver bread, by boiling the fronds for several hours. The finished product is fried in butter with oats or oatmeal (and cream if you like) and served with bacon – strangely similar to the method of making and serving Dock Pudding in Cumbria and Yorkshire (see p.173) – or simply spread on toast. Dorothy Hartley wrote in *Food in England* that

⅔ × life size

laver or 'sloke' was eaten cold with cold mutton and hot with hot boiled bacon. In keeping with this tradition, award-winning chef Mark Hix serves laver bread with a bacon chop and cockles; he also makes 'sea biscuits' using sun-dried laver. This is the seaweed used for wrapping sushi rice. In Japan, it is dried in sheets of many layers pressed together, which are often toasted, resulting in a richer flavour. Dried, flaked nori and sesame seeds can also be added to tempura batter, perhaps for a tempura of 'sensai' (the Japanese for wild herbs), see p.12.

Joe Tyrrell's Laver and Ricotta Cakes

200g cooked laver or sea lettuce	salt and pepper, to taste
200g ricotta	flour, beaten egg and crushed oat cakes, to
juice and zest of ½ lemon	coat
50g Parmesan	horseradish sauce, to serve

The recipe is easy: once you have cooked and squeezed dry the seaweed, simply blend with the ricotta, lemon zest and juice and Parmesan; taste for seasoning. Chill for about an hour then roll into smallish balls, pat into a disc and coat in flour, dip in egg and then roll in the crushed oatcakes; pan fry until golden. Serve with a little horseradish sauce.

My favourite way of using laver is to toast the fresh fronds by dry frying them in a hot pan. It is amazing how long they withstand intense heat without burning. The toasted pieces can be used straight away or stored in a dry, airtight container. When reconstituted they are much more tender than the fresh fronds, with a delicious rich smoky flavour. Use with other rich flavours such as roasted vegetables, tomatoes or bacon.

BENEFITS Rich in protein and lots of vitamins B and C.

Mark Hix's Fried Oysters and Laverbread

SERVES 4

12 rock oysters, shucked
120g laverbread
100g butter

Gently heat the laverbread in a saucepan with about half of the butter. Heat the rest of the butter in a frying pan until it's foaming and, quite literally, toss the oysters for 10–15 seconds in the butter. Remove from the heat.

Spoon the laverbread onto warmed plates and scatter the oysters and butter over.

3
Resources

FURTHER READING

Books and Journals

Akeroyd, John, *The Encyclopedia of Wild Flowers* (Paragon, Bath, 2003)

Blamey, Marjorie, and Grey-Wilson, Christopher, *Cassell's Wildflowers of Great Britain & Northern Europe* (Cassell, London, 2003)

Booth, Michael, *Sacré Cordon Bleu: What the French Know about Cooking* (Jonathan Cape, London, 2008)

Bryant, Charles, *Flora Diaetica: Or, History of Esculent Plants, Both Domestic and Foreign* (B. White, London, 1783)

Burnett, Gilbert T., *Outlines of Botany* (John Churchill, London, 1835)

Couplan, François, *La Cuisine Sauvage: Encyclopedie des Plants Comestibles de l'Europe Vol 2* (Equilibres, Conde-sur-Noireau, 1989)

Couplan, François, and Veyrat, Marc, *Herbier Gourmand* (Hachette, Paris, 1997)

Cowell, Matthew Henry, *A Floral Guide for East Kent* (W. Ratcliffe, Faversham, 1839)

Duke, James, with Ayensu, E., *Medicinal Plants of China* (Reference Publications, Algonac, Michigan, 1985)

Edmonds, Jennifer M., and Chweya, James A., *Black Nightshades: Solanum Nigrum L. and Related Species* (International Plant Genetic Resources Institute, 1997)

Eidlitz, Kirstin, 'Food and emergency food in the circumpolar area', *Stud Ethnog Upsaliensia*, vol. 32, 1969, pp. 1–75

Eley, Dr Geoffrey, *Wild Fruits and Nuts* (EP Publishing, Wakefield, 1976)

Ertug, F., 'Wild edible plants of the Bodrum area', *Turkish Journal of Botany*, vol. 28, 2004, pp. 161–174

Farley, John, *The London Art of Cookery* (Price, Dublin, 1783)

Farewell, James, *The Irish Hudibras* (London, Baldwin, 1698)

Fern, Ken, *Plants for a Future: Edible & Useful Plants for a Healthier World* (Permanent Publications, Clanfield, 1997)

Forsythe, Albert Alexander, *British Poisonous Plants* (HMSO, London, 1968)

Frohne, Dietrich, and Pfänder, Jürgen Garrard, *Poisonous Plants: a handbook for doctors, pharmacists, toxicologists, biologists and veterinarians* (Manson, London, 2005)

Garrard, I. and Streeter, D., *The Wildflowers of the British Isles* (Midsummer Books, London 1998)

Gott, B., 'The ecology of root use by the aborigines of southern Australia', *Archeology in Oceania*, vol. 17, 1982, pp. 59–67

Gray, Patience, *Honey from a Weed: Fasting and Feasting in Tuscany, Catalonia, the Cyclades and Apulia* (Prospect Books, London, 1986)

Grey, Elizabeth, Countess of Kent, *A True Gentlewoman's Delight* (W.G. Gent, London,

1682; repr. Falconwood Press, New York, 1991)

Guarrera, P. M., 'Food medicine and minor nourishment in the folk traditions of central Italy (Marche, Abruzzo and Latium)', *Fitoterapia*, vol. 74, 2003, pp. 515–44

Harlan, Jack, 'Wild grass-seed harvesting in the Sahara and sub-Sahara of Africa', in Harris, D. R., and Hillman, G. C. (eds), *Foraging and Farming*, pp. 79–98 (Unwin Hyman, London, 1989)

Harlan, Jack, *Crops and Man* (American Society of Agronomy: Crop Science Society of America, Madison, Wis., 1992)

Hartley, Dorothy, *Food in England* (Macdonald & Jane, London, 1954)

Hillman, G. C., 'Late Palaeolithic plant foods from Wadi Kubbaniya in Upper Egypt: dietary diversity, infant weaning and seasonality in a riverine environment', in Harris, D. R., and Hillman, G. C. (eds), *Foraging and Farming*, pp. 207–39 (Unwin & Hyman, London, 1989)

Hix, M., *British Regional Food* (Quadrille, London, 2006)

Hogg, Robert, and Johnson, George G., *Wild Flowers of Great Britain: Botanically and popularly described, with copious notices of their history and uses* (11 vols; London Horticultural Press, London, 1863–80)

Johns, Rev. C. A., *Flowers of the Field* (SPCK, London, 1890)

Kubiak-Martens, L., 'New evidence for the use of root foods in pre-agrarian subsistence recovered from the late Mesolithic site at Halsskov, Denmark', *Vegetation History and Archaeobotany*, vol. 11, 2002, pp. 23–32

Kuhnlein, Harriet V., and Turner, Nancy. J., *Traditional Plant Foods of Canadian Indigenous Peoples* (Gordon and Breach, New York, 1991)

Lightfoot, John, *Flora Scotica: or, a Systematic Arrangement, in the Linnæan method, of the native plants of Scotland and the Hebrides* (2 vols; B. White, London, 1777)

Mabey, Richard, *Food for Free* (Harper Collins, London, 2001)

McGee, Harold, *On Food and Cooking: The Science and Lore of the Kitchen* (Scribner, New Jersey, 1984)

Nott, J., *The Cook's and Confectioner's Dictionary: Or, the Accomplish'd Housewife's Companion* by cook John Nott, cook to his grace the Duke of Bolton (Charles Rivington, London, 1723)

O'Connell, Sanjida, *Sugar: The Grass that Changed the World* (Virgin Books, London, 2004)

Parkinson, John, *Theatrum botanicum: The theatre of plants; or, An herball of a large extent* (printed by T. Cotes, London, 1640)

Philips, Roger, *Wild Food* (Orbis, London, 1983)

Phillips, Henry, *Pomarium Brittanicum* (Henry Colburn, London, 1820)

Philp, Eric G., *Atlas of the Kent Flora*, (Kent Field Club, Maidstone, 1982)

Pieroni, Andrea, 'Gathered wild food plants of the Upper Valley of the Serchio River', *Economic Botany*, vol. 53, 1999, pp. 327–41

Pieroni, Andrea, and Leimar Price, Lisa (eds), *Eating and Healing: Traditional Food as Medicine* (Food Products Press, New York, 2006)

Poland, John, and Clement, Eric, *The Vegetative Key to the British Flora*, (BSBI, London, 2009)

Preston, C. D., Pearman, D. A., and Dines, T. D. (eds), *New Atlas of the British & Irish Flora* (Oxford University Press, Oxford, 2002)

Rackham, Oliver, *The History of the Countryside* (J. M. Dent, London, 1986)

Ragu, R. A. (ed.), *Ethnobotany of Rice Weeds in South Asia* (Andhra Pradesh Agricultural University, India, 1999)

Redzepi, René, with a foreword by Claus

Meyer, *Noma: Nordic Cuisine* (Politikens Forlag, Denmark, 2006)

Redzic, Sule, J., 'Wild Plants and their traditional use in human nutrition in Boznia-Herzegovina', *Ecology of Food and Nutrition*, vol. 45, 2006, pp.189–232

Rich, Tim, *Crucifers of Great Britain and Ireland BSBI Handbook 6* (Botanical Society of the British Isles, London 1991)

Rivera, D., Obon, C., Heinrich, M., Inocencio, C., Verde, A., Fajardo, J., 'Gathered Mediterranean Food Plants – Ethnobotanical Investigations and Historical Development' *Forum Nutr.*, vol. 59, pp. 18–74

Roper, Patrick, *Chequer: Wild Service Tree* (Sage Press, Rye, 2004)

Rose, Francis, *Grasses, Sedges, Rushes and Ferns* (Viking, London, 1989)

Rose, Francis, revised and updated by Claire O'Reilly, *The Wildflower Key* (Frederick Warne, London, 2006)

Roshevits, R. Yu., *Grasses: An introduction to the study of fodder and cereal grasses* (Indian National Scientific Documentation Centre, New Delhi, 1980)

Salisbury, William, *The Botanist's Companion* (London, 1816)

Spencer, Colin, *British Food: An Extraordinary Thousand Years of History* (Grub Street, London, 2002)

Sturtevant, E. Lewis, *Sturtevant's Edible Plants of the World* (ed. U. P. Hedrick; Dover Publications, New York, 1972)

Szafer, Wladyslaw (ed.), *The Vegetation of Poland* (Pergamon, Oxford, 1966)

Tardio, J., Pascual, H., and Morales, R., *Alimentos Silvestres de Madrid* (Ediciones La Libreria, Madrid, 2002)

Thayer, S., *The Forager's Harvest* (Forager's Harvest, Ogema, 2006)

Weeks, C. A.; Croasdale, M.; Osborne, M. A.; Hewitt, L.; Miller, P. F.; Robb, P.; Baxter, M. J.; Warriss, P. D.; Knowles, T.G. 'Multi-Element Survey of Wild Edible Fungi and Blackberries', *Food Additives and Contaminants*, vol. 23, 2006, pp. 140–147(8). Also available online: www.archive.food.gov.uk/maff/archive/food/infsheet/2000/no199/199multi.htm

Woodville, William, *Medical Botany* (4 vols; J. Phillips, London, 1790–93)

GLOSSARIES

Botanical

Alien: a non-native plant, usually introduced deliberately or otherwise, by human activity.

Alternate leaves: leaves arranged, usually on either side of the stem, at differing heights, that is, not in opposite pairs.

Ancient woodland: a woodland that has been continuously managed at least as far back as AD1700.

Annual: a plant that completes its life cycle within one year, often leaving no trace but seeds for some part of the year.

Aromatic: a plant with a strong scent produced by aromatic essential oils.

Auricles: pairs of lobes at the base of grass leaf-blades.

Axil: the point at which a leaf joins the stem.

Basal leaves: leaves at the base of a plant.

Biennial: a plant that completes its life cycle over two years and does not flower in the first year.

Blade: the main part of a leaf, either side of the midrib and above the stalk.

Blanched: deprived of light, so that leaves and stems become pale and less bitter.

Bract: *1.* small leaf-like growth forming whorl where the rays join the stem of umbellifers.
2. e.g. lesser burdock, henbit, leaf-like growth at the point where flower stalks join the stem.

Bracteole: *1.* small leaf-like growths forming whorls at the base of umbellules.
2. small leaf-like growth at the point where flowers or fruits/ seeds join the flower stalk, e.g. sea purslane.

Bulbil: small bulb-like growth in leaf axils or at the base of flower stalks; a means of asexual reproduction.

Bulb: underground growth consisting of layers of swollen leaves, both a storage organ and a means of asexual reproduction.

Calyx: a whorl of sepals, sometimes fused into a tube.

Calyx teeth: angular protrusions at the end of a calyx tube.

Casual: a plant that grows from non-wild seed sources, such as garden plants, contaminated grain seed or birdseed; such plants generally do not persist.

Catkin: a spike of minute, usually single-sex flowers, on trees and shrubs.

Clasping: a stalkless leaf with a lobed base that surrounds the stem of the plant, e.g. wild turnip, common sorrel, perennial sow-thistle.

Compound leaf: leaf with clearly defined sub-divisions or leaflets.

Corolla: tube formed by fused petals.

Cordate: heart shaped.

Corymb: flat-topped inflorescence, with inner

flower stalks much shorter than the outer, e.g. greater burdock, yarrow, tansy.

Cotyledon: the first leaf or leaves produced by a plant following germination. They differ in shape from the leaves at later growth stages.

Deciduous: woody plants that shed then re-grow their leaves annually.

Dicotyledon: plants that have two cotyledons at the seedling stage.

Drupe: fleshy, single-seeded fruit, e.g. sloes, the individual segments of blackberries.

Elliptical: leaf widest in the middle and taper-ing to each end, length up to three times width, e.g. strawberry tree, sea purslane.

Escape: plant forming casual populations and arising from seed or discarded plant material of cultivated plants.

Entire: leaf with untoothed and unlobed edges.

Erect: upright.

Fruit: the ripe seeds and what surrounds them, which may be either fleshy or dry.

Herb: plant without woody stems.

Inflorescence: an arrangement of flowers on a stem, often branched, which begins above the last leaf or leaves.

Introduced: non-native, or alien plant.

Keel: keel-like ridge down the back of a leaf, e.g. keeled garlic, sea club-rush.

Lanceolate: spearhead-shaped leaf, narrow, tapered at each end, with a pointed tip, widest towards the base.

Leaflet: small, sub-unit of a compound leaf, like a small leaf.

Linear: flat leaf or leaflet with parallel sides, e.g. grasses, orange day lily, bitter vetch leaflet.

Midrib: the thick central vein of a leaf.

Monocotyledon: plants with single-leaved seedlings.

Native: a plant with well established populations that got here without human intervention.

Naturalized: an alien plant that has formed an established population.

Node: the part of the stem from which leaves emerge.

Oblong: a leaf two or three times as long as it is broad.

Opposite: leaves growing from the stem in opposite pairs.

Obovate: leaf with a blunt tip, and a more pointed base, widest above the middle.

Oval: leaf broadest in the middle, tapering to each end, length up to two times width.

Palmately lobed: leaf with several (at least three) lobes fanning out in a hand-like shape, e.g. mallow, cloudberry, lady's mantle.

Panicle: branched inflorescence.

Pappus: collection of fine hair-like structures attached to a seed to enable wind dispersal.

Peduncle: the stalk of an inflorescence.

Perennial: plant that completes its life cycle over a number of years, usually flowering every year.

Perianth segments: the leaf-like structures of flowers.

Petals: the inner perianth segments or floral leaves, arranged in a whorl and often, but not always, brightly coloured.

Pinnae: leaflet of a fern.

Pinnate: compound leaf with more than three leaflets arranged along the leaf stalk, usually in opposite pairs, e.g. wild chervil, rowan, hairy bitter-cress.

Pinnately lobed: leaf with variably deep lobes (not leaflets), sometimes cutting nearly to the midrib, e.g. black mustard, ragwort, lousewort.

Prostrate: plants growing more or less horizon-tally along the ground.

Raceme: inflorescence with stalked flowers arranged on a single peduncle, e.g. lesser burdock, wild mignonette, tuberous pea.

Rays: the stalks of an umbel, supporting the umbellules.

Rhizome: swollen underground stem that per-sists for more than one season of growth.

Rosette: basal arrangement of leaves protruding

like spokes of a wheel from a central hub – the taproot of the plant.

Scrub: land, such as neglected pasture or arable land, which is beginning to transform into woodland, with numerous young trees and/or shrubs present.

Sepal: floral leaf; one of the outer whorl of perianth segments, usually, but not always, green.

Sessile: stalkless.

Shrub: woody perennial, often lacking a main trunk, smaller than a tree.

Simple: leaf not subdivided into leaflets.

Spadix: a cigar shaped inflorescence, e.g. cuckoo pint.

Spathe: hood like structure surrounding a spadix, e.g. cuckoo pint.

Spike: inflorescence on a single stem with unstalked flowers.

Stalk: a non-scientific term describing the rigid structure attaching a leaf or flower to a stem.

Stem: the main axis of a plant, from which leaves and flowers arise.

Stipe: stem of marine algae.

Stipule: small leaf-like or scale-like structure at the base of a leaf stalk, in some cases fused with it.

Strap-shaped: long, thin leaf with roughly parallel edges, e.g. sea aster, cape pondweed.

Subspecies: a variety of a species clearly identifiable by variations in colour, structure or ecology.

Tendril: wire-like protrusion, usually from the tips of leaves by which plants, especially in the pea family, attach themselves to nearby objects in order to gain support and climb.

Ternate: compound leaf divided into three roughly equal parts; these may in turn be similarly divided (two- or three-ternate).

Tree: a tall, woody plant with a main trunk.

Trifoliate: compound leaf having three leaflets, i.e. once ternate.

Tuber: swollen root.

Umbel: branched inflorescence in an umbrella shape, with the rays all growing from the end point of a stem.

Umbellule: sub-unit of a compound umbel, a cluster of small flowers supported by a ray.

Vein: thin strands that visually divide leaves into sections, made up of tissues that conduct water and nutrients.

Whorled: arrangement of leaves or flowers in a circular fashion around a stem.

Winged: referring to a leaf stalk or stem of a plant, with thin wing-like protrusions, which, for a leaf, are an extension of the leaf blade.

Culinary

Blanched: boiled for only a few seconds.

Chiffonade: chopped into fine strips.

Chitterlings: pigs' intestines.

Confit: cooked slowly in fat.

Deglaze: to use liquid, usually wine or stock, to remove the brownings from a pan after frying or roasting meat, vegetables or even fruit.

Julienne: to chop into fine, matchstick-like pieces

Mandolin: hand device for making very thin slices, for example of potatoes.

Refresh: to cool down a cooked item of food, to prevent further cooking.

Roux: a mixture of butter and flour used for thickening.

Siphon: injects CO_2 into liquids to make foams or just a more frothy liquid.

Stock syrup: basic syrup made using one part water to one part sugar.

Velouté: originally a sauce made from a stock base, now often served alone like a miniature portion of soup.

Vinaigrette: mixture of oil and vinegar, usually in a ratio of 5:2.

CHEF DIRECTORY

This book would not have been possible without the hard work and ideas of the following chefs, many of whom have worked with me from the outset, finding uses and developing recipes for the plants.

Michael Bremner pursued a pastry apprenticeship at the Michelin-starred Orrery restaurant, and later became head pastry chef at Marco Pierre White's Quo Vadis. He is now head chef at Due South in Brighton, where he continues to impress with his innovative seasonal recipes.

Paul Brown is one of two gifted and enthusiastic northerners I got to know through supplying Le Caprice in London. The other is **Kevin Gratton**, head chef there until 2006, who now runs the kitchen at Scott's of Mayfair, where his menu won the Catey's Menu of the Year award in 2008. Paul took over as head chef in 2006. Both worked many of our ingredients into the recipes at Le Caprice, producing food that somehow manages to be simple and sophisticated at the same time. Paul in his own words, 'Working at the Walnut Tree Inn [Abergavenny] gave me my first experience of foraging. After service we would all jump in Franco's [Taruschio, the Italian head chef and owner] car and race down to the forest, where there would be an abundance of wild mush-

rooms. At other times there would be carpets of wild garlic and loads of berries to pick. These things are hidden to people with untrained eyes who just walk past them, but you soon become familiar with them and they start to make cooking more interesting.'

Andrew Clarke was head chef at the Swan at West Malling until 2007 and is currently gaining further experience in London with a view to setting up his own restaurant. Whilst at the Swan he used lots of our wild produce, as well as finding time to get out and forage himself, to the point that he was offering to sell wild mushrooms to us!

Eoin Corcoran Ever since I first called him at Lindsay House in 2005, Irish chef Eoin has enthused, encouraged, inspired and generally made me feel what we are doing is worthwhile. Eoin's enthusiasm reminds me of punk gigs I went to as a teenager; his approach to food is all raw energy and delight. Just mention a new wild ingredient and his mind fires up, which has led to some interesting hours of culinary experimentation with him in the kitchen. In the past, Eoin has worked with Max Fischer and Tom Aikens, but now works for Richard Corrigan, running the oyster bar downstairs at the revamped Bentley's seafood restaurant.

Eion's former colleague at Lindsay House, **Chris McGowan**, produced the gorgeous recipe for wild celery soup on p.116.

Richard Corrigan's restaurants Bentleys and Lindsay House have been customers of ours since 2004. In 2006 and 2007, Richard was a winner of BBC2's *Great British Menu* competition; on both occasions wild ingredients (supplied by us) were key components in his winning dishes.

François Couplan, PhD, is an ethnobotanist, who has been researching and teaching the uses of plants since 1975. In addition to his scientific training he has had personal experience of living with nature. He is a successful author whose fifty or so books have been published in several languages; he also writes regular columns for various nature, health and cookery magazines. He has researched the diet of our paleolithic forefathers at the National Museum of Natural History in Paris. He also works with several top chefs in Europe and in the US, including Marc Veyrat in Annecy (France) and Jean-Georges Vongerichten in New York, helping them incorporate wild plants into their menus. (See Wild Food Directory.)

Jesse Dunford-Wood cooks food firmly based in the British tradition, although his experiences working in Sydney with Mark Best, in Chicago with Charlie Trotter, and at New York's Nori Sugie have also been strong influences. He worked for two years with Oliver Peyton in the National Gallery's Dining Rooms, winning *Time Out*'s award for Best British Restaurant in 2007. In 2008 Jesse took time out to plan his own restaurant but he also found time to attend to the many little packages of wild ingredients I posted to him from Kent. The results of this collaboration are peppered throughout the book. We often say that chefs working with wild ingredients are like

artists discovering a new colour; Jesse's parents are artists who were always keen to experiment with new kinds of food so he understands this better than most!

Mark Hix is a champion of British food who has also very much championed wild food in general and Forager in particular in the past few years, both as a chef and a food writer – Mark writes a weekly food column for the Saturday *Independent* and has authored several books, including *Fish etc* and *British Regional Food*. Mark was executive chef of Caprice holdings until 2007, and as such was responsible for the Ivy, Le Caprice and J Sheekey's, as well as for setting up the Rivington Grill and overseeing the reopening of Scott's of Mayfair. In 2008 he opened two restaurants of his own, Hix Oyster Bar and Chop House in London and Hix Oyster Bar and Fish House in Dorset. Mark also appeared on *Great British Menu* TV series in 2007 and two of his courses, both of which were made primarily from wild ingredients, were served at the final banquet.

Rafael Lopez Soriano currently works at the Goods Shed in Canterbury, which is where our story began (see **ramsons**, p.337). Raf initially worked under **Blaise Vasseur**, who established the Goods Shed before handing the reins to Raf in 2004. Both Blaise's and Raf's provenance-based approach to food has been pivotal to our development. As a child, Rafael had a little foraging business of his own: he used to sell wild asparagus, figs, prickly pears, rabbit and blackberries to customers in the bars in his neighbourhood in Spain.

James Lowe got in touch shortly before the completion of this book and jumped into the project with both feet, producing several excellent recipes and flavour combinations. James learnt to cook at La Trompette and Heston Blumenthal's Fat Duck and is currently head chef at St John Bread and Wine. In his own words, 'A trip to Noma in Copenhagen introduced me to foraged items that I was sure must have English equivalents. When I contacted Miles it was like starting all over again – I discovered a diversity of new ingredients, each week receiving something new to experiment with. The ingredients are ultra seasonal, often only available for a few weeks so you have to think fast and work out what you're going to do with them.'

Issaac McHale currently works at the Michelin-starred Ledbury in Ladbroke Grove, London. He got in touch in 2007 to ask us about supplying burdock to the restaurant and went on to give me some helpful insights into Japanese uses of wild foods.

Anthony North had a classical French training at the Connault Hotel in London, under Michel Bourdin, but also has Asian leanings, at one time working as sous chef at Nobu in London. As head chef at the George Vaults in Rochester he won Kent Restaurant of the Year 2004. As head chef at the Dining Room at the Railway Hotel in Faversham Anthony's unique fusion style flourished, receiving enthusiastic reviews in all the broadsheet newspapers. By the time you read this, Anthony will be on the other side of the planet: he plans to open his own restaurant in New Zealand.

Gustav Otterberg is head chef at Swedish restaurant Leegontornet (which means 'lion tower'). He is very much of the same culinary philosophy as Rene Redzipe, in fact I got to know him through Swedish forager Roland Ritman, who supplies both Rene and Gustav with wild produce.

Nathan Outlaw was inspired to become a chef by watching his chef father at work in the kitchen from an early age. As a small boy he

went out with his father foraging. They returned from long spring and summer walks laden with wild garlic, mint, pennywort and fennel; in the autumn they gathered brambles and sloes. He has worked for chefs Peter Kromburg, Eric Chavot, Gary Rhodes and Rick Stein. He currently heads up the Michelin-starred Nathan Outlaw within the Marina Villa Hotel in Fowey, Cornwall. He works closely with Cornish forager Anne Misselbrook (see Wild Food Directory), who is a great inspiration with her insatiable enthusiasm for wild food.

Derek Quelch has worked at Claridges and the Savoy but at the time of writing is head chef at the Goring Hotel. As far as I'm aware, Derek was the first person to put hogweed on the menu as a side vegetable; it was so popular customers repeatedly requested it when it was out of season. In his own words, 'I love the forager concept because it is taking food back to its natural roots; it is not new: people were cooking with these ingredients centuries ago. The challenge for me is to educate myself and to learn what to do with them. In an age of supermarkets, it is very exciting to be using edible plants that we walk past every day without realising it.'

René Redzepi is head chef of 2-star Michelin sensation Noma in Copenhagen and has been both supportive and inspiring to work and converse with during the writing of this book. René previously worked at the 3-star Le Jardin Des Sens in Montpellier, France, Ferran Adrià's el Bulli in Roses, Spain, and Thomas Keller's 3-star Michelin restaurant The French Laundry. René has pioneered Nordic Cuisine, eschewing the use of Mediterranean ingredients such as tomatoes, lemons and wine, instead using Nordic ingredients such as barley, musk ox, shellfish and of course, wild plants and mushrooms. He has nurtured a small army of foragers, who now supply a swelling number of Nordic restaurants. René's dishes reflect his commitment to principles of quality, seasonality and regionality but they are also run through with originality, feeling and imagination.

Jimmy Shave sounds like an urban legend, but he's a rural phenomenon. As a child he envied all his mates who ate frozen and prepackaged foods, while his mother served up fresh veg, wild meats, fish, fungi and berries, which were grown, caught or gathered by his father. Only when he started working as a chef did he realize that he had spent his childhood eating like a king. Jimmy trained under Marco Pierre White and now runs the Granville, sister pub to Steve Harris's Sportsman in Tankerton.

Sami Tallberg was Simon Wadham's predecessor at the Rivington Grill, where he helped develop a modern British menu built around seasonal British ingredients. Sami is now back in his native Finland where he oversees Carelia and three other restaurants in Helsinki. Sami has been a pleasure to work with, developing recipe ideas for several of the ingredients described in this book. For a Finnish chef, this is a natural progression, as Finnish food is already firmly based on wild produce, with its strong emphasis on wild meat, fish, wild berries and wild mushrooms. **Antti Ahokas** is another Finnish chef who has been exploring wild produce in a bit more depth, I met him as part of a group of Finnish head chefs for whom Sami had organized a wild food seminar.

Joe Tyrrell was head chef at the Gate in Hammersmith (one of the best vegetarian restaurants in the country) when I met him. At the Gate, Joe used to put on a wild food festival in spring, with a balanced six-course vegetarian menu. He is currently a full-time father. In his own words, 'For me as a chef it all started when I was a kid. I baked at home with my mum and on scout camping holidays we made basic breads over the open fire. Later a teacher made us pick nettles and dandelions from our school garden to make nettle soup and dandelion tea. I forget the taste of them but will always remember the exciting notion that I could run away and live off the land.'

Scott Wade worked with Marco Pierre White at Mirabelle, White's (where he became head chef) and Drones. In 2005 he earned the Gun *Time Out*'s London Gastropub of the Year award. We first met him at Oliver Peyton's Inn the Park but it was at Daniel Clifford's Hedley in Brentwood that Scott really made his mark using wild ingredients, earning accolades from several restaurant reviewers, including Jay Rayner and Terry Durack. In his own words, 'Foraging fits perfectly with my ethos on cooking. I'm all for country sports, fishing, hunting, foraging. Nothing beats catching your fish for supper, or shooting a bird then treating it with respect by cooking it properly, garnishing whatever you cook with some foraged plants or mushrooms.' (All initials [SW] refer to Scott Wade's recipes.)

Simon Wadham is head chef at the Rivington Grill in Shoreditch, London, a position he took over after working for Oliver Peyton for a number of years. Simon's recipe for sea sandwort was, as far as I know, the first dish featuring that ingredient ever to appear on a British menu.

Ben Walton was our second ever customer, and has always seemed to share our view that wild food is not just a novelty but a different approach to food. In his own words, 'Foraged goods provide flavours and textures not experienced before, but to get unfamiliar (both to you and the customer) produce on to the menu, you have to think harder, outside what you have been trained to do. What will it go with? How do you keep it? How long will it be available?

Cooked or raw? Better known ingredients have hundreds of well-known uses; here you are starting with a clean slate. But to come up with new flavour combinations using simple, local ingredients like these is incredibly satisfying. I'm just not interested in creating amazing flavours at the expense of the planet or by turning it into something which has little or nothing to do with the original ingredient. It's great to know that you can surprise people without having to fly something in from Rwanda.'

Peter Weeden is the most enthusiastic and committed of all our customers – no British restaurant has ever had a menu so solidly built around wild ingredients as the Paternoster Chophouse in London, where Peter (at the time of writing) works as head chef. He doesn't use wild ingredients for the sake of it, but he puts in time and effort trying out different cooking methods, different flavour and texture combinations, before deciding whether something goes on the menu or not. In his own words, 'My interest in foraging stems from my time as a child when I was exposed to fresh air. With three young children, my parents had the good sense to take us out of the hourse for long country walks in a vain attempt to exhaust us. We were instrumental in the collection of elderberries for

wine, chestnuts to roast on the open fire and blackberries to add to crumbles. Some ten or fifteen years later whilst working in Norwich I realized that I had perhaps been given a bit of a head start on the foraging front – I was well informed compared to some of my chef peers who had gone to catering college to get out of school, many of whom didn't really seem to even enjoy real food. We were paying real money for stuff which guys collected for a living: chanterelles, puffballs, parasol mushrooms, elderflower and samphire. I knew where some of these things grew and went on expeditions to the forest with my girlfriend … on our days off. On the drive to Thetford I would be on the lookout for things which could end up in the pot, counting pheasants and rabbits, dreaming about the numerous berries and mushrooms we passed. There is more diversity of textures and flavours in wild food than you could ever find in a grocer's or supermarket. We used to have a kitchen list which didn't change. But once you let go of the idea that you can only use certain ingredients, you open yourself up to other possibilities and you can do anything at all …Without recipes to fall back on, trusting someone else's judgement, you have to form an opinion.'

WILD FOOD DIRECTORY

Courses

The British Phycological Society
Offers seaweed identification courses.
www.brphycsoc.org

François Couplan
François is the author of the *Encyclopedia of Edible Plants of North America*, which covers the 4,000 plants known to have been used on this continent for food. When not travelling in Africa, Central America or South-east Asia looking for new plants and new people to learn from, François lives in Switzerland and the south of France. He regularly organizes edible plant seminars, where participants are not only shown plants in the field but get to cook outstanding meals with them. He has also established a school to give students an in-depth understanding of the ageless relationship between people and plants.
CH-1692 Massonnens, Switzerland
tel : ++41.26.653.19.78
fax : ++41.26.653.27.47
email : fc@couplan.com
website : www.couplan.com

Martin Denny
Martin is a real Norfolk man of the land who offers wild food teaching days for small parties by prior arrangement.
2 Silfield Terrace, Kings Lynn
Norfolk PE30 5NQ
tel: 01553 769340
mob: 07909 928644

Forager
We offer a range of courses on different aspects of finding and using edible plants, including basic plant identification, how to cook with wild plants, and edible plants in particular habitats.
www.forager.org.uk

Neal Hone
Offers wild food foraging courses in the Warwickshire countryside. Neal is another of our suppliers, who sends things to us which we have trouble finding in Kent. He also teaches course on mushroom cultivation. See our Forager website for details.
tel: 07986 031989
email: wildfood@live.co.uk

Lesley Kilbride
Lesley and husband Tom raised ten children on a smallholding on a diet heavily supplemented by wild food! Lesley takes parties out to discover the wild foods, as well the medicinal and dye plants available in the Scottish Highlands.
tel: 01520 755260
email: lesleykilbride@yahoo.com

Anne Misselbrooke
Anne runs one-day courses covering coastal and inland edible wild plants. Her sheer enthusiasm for wild food is second to none and she has several times expanded the boundaries of my knowledge both by sending me new plants that have turned out to be good edibles, and by tracking down species, such as wild pear and burnet rose, which I had previously had trouble

finding. Anne has been sending Cornish for-agables to us since 2004 and always has a story to tell about her latest find or foraging escapade. Anne also supplies a number of restaurants in Cornwall, including 15 Cornwall and Restaurant Nathan Outlaw. Also check our Forager website for updates regarding Anne's courses.
29 Harmony Close,
Redruth
Cornwall TR15 1ET
tel: 01209 217194
mob: 07973831420

Equipment

Brow Farm
Brow farm sell hand-operated grain mills that can be clamped to a kitchen table, like a mincer or coffee grinder. They do a good job for larger grains, such as upright brome or black bindweed as well as nuts and roots that have been previously dried and chopped. They also sell juicers that can handle grass leaves.
www.browfarmwheatproducts.co.uk

Thermomix
A very useful piece of kit for your wild food kitchen. With it you can blend, weigh, mix and cook for precise times at precise temperatures without changing vessels.
www.UKThermomix.com

Websites

Botanical Society of the British Isles
The Botanical Society of the British Isles is the leading society promoting the study and enjoyment of British and Irish wild plants.
www.bsbi.org.uk

Steve Brill
Another American forager, Steve Brill leapt to fame after being arrested for eating a dandelion in New York's Central Park. The park subsequently employed him to teach the public about wild food!
www.wildmanstevebrill.com

Eatweeds
Excellent resources for foragers including instructional videos and a regular newsletter.
www.eatweeds.co.uk

Marcus Harrison
Marcus Harrison is the author of the Johnny Jumbalaya series of wild food books. The website is packed with useful information and photographs.
www.countrylovers.co.uk/wfs/index.htm

Mark Hix
This archive of Mark Hix's food column in *The Independent* often contains recipes for wild plants.
www.independent.co.uk

John Kallas
John's *Wild Food Adventures* magazine is an invaluable information source, full of practical tips that go beyond the depth of coverage found in most wild food books. The website is also an excellent resource, albeit focused mostly on North American species.
www.wildfoodadventures.com

Henriette Kress
Mainly deals with medicinal properties of plants but also contains some useful information about edible uses and nutrition.
www.henriettesherbal.com

Lukasz Lukzaj
Lucasz is one of Europe's leading authorities on edible wild plants and also has a very interesting sideline in edible insects.
www.luczaj.com/ang_index.htm

Plants for a Future
Over the course of ten years, whilst working as a bus driver, Ken Fern collated an exhaustive database of edible (and otherwise useful) plants. Although his work is published in more depth in book form (see Further Reading) the main database is published for free on the internet.
www.pfaf.org/index.php

Reforesting Scotland
A community woodland organisation that for a number of years has championed the development of non-timber forest products (NTFPs), including foraged food. Forest Harvest is the branch of their project devoted to NTFPs; the website includes a directory of wild food and other businesses.
www.forestharvest.org.uk
www.reforestingscotland.org

Sam Thayer
Sam has written one of the most in-depth and practical books ever published on foraging, based on years of personal experience. His website is also a mine of information.
www.foragersharvest.com

Wild Food as Medicine

Alex Laird BSc DipPhyt MNIMH Medical Herbalist
Alex is co-founder of Living Medicine, a world herbal and food medicine centre with community medicinal gardens nationwide. It aims to revive the world's herbal and food medicine heritage and link medicinal gardens worldwide. People of all cultures are encouraged to exchange knowledge and reclaim responsibility for their everyday healthcare.
Living Medicine
68 Hurlingham Rd
London SW6 3RQ

tel: 0207 736 8975
fax: 020 7371 8450
email: info@livingmedicine.org
website: www.livingmedicine.org

Mandy Oliver DipAroma DipPhyt MNIMH
A practicing member of the National Institute of Medical Herbalists and an aromatherapist, Mandy Oliver produces her own tinctures and remedies, many of them from wild crafted plants.
Gatefield Clinic, 9 Gatefield Lane
Faversham, Kent ME13 8NX
tel: 07833 798229

Wild Food Suppliers

Martin Denny
Martin supplies a wide variety of wild plants and fungi through the seasons.
2 Silfield Terrace, Kings Lynn
Norfolk PE30 5NQ
tel: 01553 769340
mob: 07909 928644

Forager
www.forager.org.uk

Neal Hone
Wild herbs, salad leaves and fruit to the restaurant trade. Also cultivated exotic and wild seasonal mushrooms.
Tel: 07986 031989
email: wildfood@live.co.uk

Anne Misselbrooke
Anne forages for an increasingly wide range of edible plants, which she delivers in person in Cornwall, or by courier for places further afield.
29 Harmony Close, Redruth
Cornwall TR15 1ET
tel: 01209 217194
mob: 07973831420

INDEX

ACKNOWLEDGEMENTS

In the course of writing this book I have been helped a great many people with expertise in their various fields, all of whom gave generously of their time in various ways. Thanks are due to the many botanists who have contributed invaluable advice regarding the main body of the text: John Akeroyd, Tim Rich at the Museum of Wales, Martin Samford of the Suffolk Biological Records Centre, Mark Watson from Kew, Edinburgh, Sabina Knees, Charles Nelson, Chris Preston of the Centre for Ecology and Hydrology, David Pearman and Paul Green. Christine Maggs of Queen's University Belfast and Juliet Brodie from the Natural History Museum advised on, read and corrected the seaweed section and also sent me samples of seaweeds not found in Kent. The following people sent me plants or parts of plants, or helped me to locate plants that I had difficulty finding: Fay McKenzie of the Agronomy Institute at Orkney College, Paul Green, Richard Brown at Emorsgate Seeds, Sandy Millar, Eric Philp, Stan Firth, Les Bates, Neal Hone, Anne Misselbrooke, John and Isobel Collier, Lliam Rooney. Thanks also to Martin Griffiths of the Durrell Institute of Conservation and Ecology for spending time in the field helping me identify grasses. Thanks to Dr J. Howard Bradbury at the Australian National University for advice regarding the toxicity of arum species. Thanks to consultant ecologist Patrick Roper for advice on Sorbus species. To Fay Robinson for information on dock pudding, and all the people in Cumbria who responded to my newspaper advertisement regarding Easter ledge pudding. I am also indebted to several ethnobotanists and foragers who gave invaluable advice regarding the uses of the plants and/or commented on early drafts of the manuscript: Lukasz Luczaj, Frank Cook, James Duke, François Couplan, Wojtek Szymanski, Andrea Pieroni, Mark Nesbitt of Kew gardens, London, Alison Dyke of Reforesting Scotland, Marcus Harrison of the Wild Food School in Cornwall. Thanks to Chris Gibson and Ian Taylor of Natural England, as well as Deborah Long and Dominique Price from Plantlife International, all of whom gave invaluable information about the ecology and conservation of plants covered in this book. Thanks to Keith Hunt of DEFRA's Veterinary Laboratories Agency for advice regarding liver fluke. Alex Laird, herbal medicine practitioner, contributed her depth of knowledge to many of the Benefits entries. Henriette Kress also advised on the medicinal benefits of hawthorn. Thanks also to the following people who offered comments and suggestions on the manuscript: my parents Liz and Edward Irving, James Thwaites (he of the Hebrew world view!), food writer Jill Dupleix, and friends Nick Winter, Rob Allen and Chris Erskine. Thanks also to Blaise Vasseur for drafting me into the foraging business back in 2003; to Fergus Drennan for hard work and good company in 2004–5. Also many thanks to Ross Evans, Carl Daniel Smith, Anthony Tunstall and all the other foragers who covered for me while I was writing the book. Thanks also to Slow Food London and Sustain for all the support and interest which they have shown over the years. Finally, thanks to Ben and Leo, 'the Smoothers' who inspired me with their knowledge of wild plants in Switzerland all those years ago.

PICTURE CREDITS

(t = top, b = bottom, l = left, r = right)

All photographs by Miles Irving with the exception of the following:

Nick Bonnet 6, 25, 43, 49, 78t, 259t, 357b

John Crellin 214t

Paul Hackney 315t&b

Ali Irving 2, 5, 29 (plus 'Forager' typographical design)

Rimantas Pankeviãius 333t&b

Lliam Rooney 47, 137, 148l, 168b, 215b, 218t

John Somerville 171b, 217, 332t, 335t

Universitat de les Illes Balears 346 (http://herbarivirtual.uib.es)